GOLF DIGEST'S
GOLF
WEEKENDS

THE BEST PLACES TO PLAY AND STAY
NEAR THE NATION'S BIGGEST CITIES

WITH **Golf** Digest COURSE REVIEWS

Fodor's Travel Publications
New York · Toronto · London · Sydney · Auckland
www.fodors.com

GOLF DIGEST'S GOLF WEEKENDS

EDITOR: John D. Rambow
EDITORIAL PRODUCTION: Tom Holton
EDITORIAL CONTRIBUTORS: Shelley Arenas, Diane Bair, Brian Boese, Laura Knowles Callanan, Hollis Gillespie, Ron Kaspriske, Steve Knopper, Jessica E. Lee, Gary McKechnie, Emmanuelle Morgen, Pete Nelson, Jennifer Paull, Matthew Rudy, Sarah Sper, Judy Sutton, Greg Tasker, John Vlahides, CiCi Williamson, Kay Winzenried, Pamela Wright, Bobbi Zane
MAPS: David Lindroth, Inc.; Mapping Specialists, cartographers; Rebecca Baer and Bob Blake, map editors
DESIGN: Tigist Getachew, art director; Melanie Marin, senior picture editor
PRODUCTION/MANUFACTURING: Robert B. Shields

Copyright
Copyright © 2004 by Fodors LLC and The Golf Digest Companies

Fodor's is a registered trademark of Random House, Inc.

First Edition

ISBN 1-4000-1368-2
ISSN 1551-6415

Photo Credits
Cover Photo (Burnt Pine Golf Club): © 2004 Sandestin Golf and Beach Resort; p. 1, The Creek at Hard Labor/Georgia Department of Natural Resources; p. 25, Sugarloaf USA; p. 59, Szurlej/Golf Digest; p. 87, Szurlej/Golf Digest; p. 110, The Broadmoor; p. 134, Dave Richards; p. 162, Szurlej/Golf Digest; p. 184, La Quinta Resort; p. 218, www.peterwongphotography.com; p. 248, Szurlej/Golf Digest; p. 281, © 2004 Sandestin Golf and Beach Resort; p. 315, Szurlej/Golf Digest; p. 339, Szurlej/Golf Digest; p. 369, Joel Reiner/Quicksilver Photography; p. 402, Hawk Lake Golf Club.

Special Sales
This book is available for special discounts for bulk purchases for sales promotions or premiums. Special editions, including personalized covers, excerpts of existing books, and corporate imprints, can be created in large quantities for special needs. For more information, write to Special Markets/Premium Sales, 1745 Broadway, MD 6-2, New York, New York 10019, or e-mail specialmarkets@randomhouse.com.

PRINTED IN THE UNITED STATES OF AMERICA

10 9 8 7 6 5 4 3 2 1

CONTENTS

GOLF DIGEST'S GOLF WEEKENDS

Two things are certain: there aren't enough good weekends for a golf trip, and the ones that do happen are always too short. You can make them longer, however, by really going away, taking in a new course or two, and leaving the concerns of home life behind. And, surprise, planning a getaway doesn't have to be stressful, regardless of whether you're deciding where to go next month or next weekend. That's where this book comes in.

Each chapter, using a different major U.S. city as its base, covers up to seven different destinations that make for rewarding multiday trips. We've rounded up the most challenging and striking courses, and we've also provided a sampling of good hotels and restaurants in the area, for when your game is through. Some of the destinations are well known, but many will probably be new to you. Either way, *Golf Weekends* makes sure you know your options. You don't want to miss a course that was right around the next bend, just because you didn't know it was there.

The golf listings, taken from the current edition of *Golf Digest's Places to Play,* include ratings from the magazine's readers as well as complete stats and contact information. Course comments, written by seasoned *Golf Digest* staff writers Matthew Rudy and Ron Kaspriske, highlight the courses that are especially worthwhile and extraordinary. Once you've decided on your courses and tee times, consult the Where to Stay and Where to Eat sections for ideas on rounding out your weekend.

With the practical information in this book, you can easily call to confirm the details that matter and study up on where you'll want to play and where you'll want to eat and sleep. Then toss *Golf Weekends* in your bag for the journey.

The hotel and restaurant recommendations come from magazine and newspaper staff writers and freelancers who live and play in the area they cover for us—they're the kind of people you'd poll for ideas if you knew them.

MATTHEW RUDY, who wrote introductions and selected courses for half of our weekend destinations, has been a travel and instruction editor at *Golf Digest* since 1999. He is a former golf reporter for *Sports Illustrated* and has authored three books: *Golf Digest's The Swing: Secrets of the Game's Greatest Golfers, Breaking 90 with Johnny Miller,* and, with

Michelle McGann, *The Complete Idiot's Guide to Golf.* He lives in Easton, Connecticut, with his wife, Fernanda.

RON KASPRISKE, a sports writer since 1991, has covered golf since 1997. An associate editor at *Golf Digest,* he edits the Digest section and is one of the lead instruction writers. He also writes the occasional travel feature. His favorite course is Augusta National, and his handicap is 12; he has yet to hit a hole in one. He lives with his wife in Connecticut.

HOW TO USE THIS BOOK

For every weekend destination we include, our goal is to provide you with good options for golf courses, hotels, and restaurants. Alphabetical organization makes it easy to navigate through these pages. Still, we've made certain decisions and used certain terms that you need to know about. For starters, everything you read about in this book is recommended by our writers and editors, and no property mentioned has paid to be included.

Organization

The destinations covered in each chapter are all centered around a major city. With the exception of the Dallas & Fort Worth chapter, we don't include places in the major cities themselves. This is a book for getaways, after all.

After some words of introduction come the golf courses, listed in alphabetical order. The Where to Stay and Where to Eat sections follow, with suggestions for places for all budgets, also arranged alphabetically. The Essentials section provides information about how to get there and other logistical details.

Courses

Yardage is given from the back and from the front tees, as is the par, USGA course rating, and slope.

Green fee: The fees listed represent the lowest and the highest fee for 18 holes of golf.

Cart fee: Cart fees are charged on either a per-cart or a per-person basis. If cart fees are included in the green fee, this is noted as well.

Walking policy: "Walking at certain times" means that cart use is sometimes mandatory—usually when the course gets busy.

Season: A course's "season" is made up of the months it's open.

High: During these months, the high season, the course is most likely to be busy, and its fees tend to be at their highest.

Tee times: The number of days prior to play that reservations can be made.

Notes: This section includes additional information that's good to know, including any *Golf Digest* rankings the course may have received.

Credit cards: AE, D, DC, MC, and V indicate whether American Express, Discover, Diners Club, MasterCard, or Visa are accepted.

Comments: Quick takes on the courses from *Golf Digest* editors Matthew Rudy and Ron Kaspriske.

Ratings: Star ratings, taken from the 2005 edition of *Golf Digest's Places to Play*, are derived from ballots filled in by 20,000 avid golfers. Those voting rated the courses they played over the previous year and were judging five criteria: the overall golf experience, the value for the money, the standard of service, the overall conditioning, and the normal pace of play for 18 holes. This is what the ratings mean:

UR. An unrated course. Note that these courses are not necessarily ones that would have earned fewer than three stars. Courses that may have received fewer than 10 ballots or have only recently opened are also unrated.

★★★ Very good. Tell a friend it's worth getting off the highway to play it.

★★★★ Outstanding. Plan your next vacation around it.

★★★★★ Golf at its absolute best. Pay any price to play at least once in your life.

Where to Stay

The places we list—whether homey bed-and-breakfasts, mom-and-pop motels, grand inns, chain hotels, or luxury resorts—are the cream of the crop in each price and lodging category.

Baths: You'll find private bathrooms unless noted otherwise.

Credit cards: AE, D, DC, MC, and V following lodging listings indicate whether American Express, Discover, Diners Club, MasterCard, or Visa are accepted.

Facilities: We list what's available but we don't specify what costs extra. When pricing accommodations, always ask what's included. The term *hot tub* denotes hot tubs, whirlpools, and Jacuzzis. Assume that lodgings have phones, TVs, and air-conditioning and that they permit smoking, unless we note otherwise.

Closings: Assume that lodgings are open all year unless otherwise noted.

Meal plans: Hostelries operate on the European Plan (EP, with no meals) unless we specify that they use the Continental Plan (CP, with a Continental breakfast), Breakfast Plan (BP, with a full breakfast), or Modified American Plan (MAP, with breakfast and dinner).

Prices: Price categories are based on the price range for a standard double room during high season, excluding service charges and tax. Price categories for all-suites properties are based on prices for standard suites.

WHAT IT COSTS

$$$$	over $215
$$$	$165–$215
$$	$115–$165
$	$65–$115
¢	under $65

Where to Eat

We make a point of including local food-lovers' hot spots as well as neighborhood options, with cheaper as well as more expensive options.

Credit cards: AE, D, DC, MC, and V following restaurant listings indicate whether American Express, Discover, Diners Club, MasterCard, or Visa are accepted.

Dress: Assume that no jackets or ties are required for men unless otherwise noted.

Meals and hours: Assume that restaurants are open for lunch and dinner unless otherwise noted. We always specify days closed and meals not available. When traveling in the off-season, be sure to call ahead.

Reservations: They're always a good idea, but we don't mention them unless they're essential or are not accepted.

Prices: The price categories listed are based on the cost per person for a main course at dinner or, when dinner isn't available, the next most expensive meal.

WHAT IT COSTS

$$$$	over $21
$$$	$16–$21
$$	$11–$16
$	$6–$11
¢	under $6

Essentials

Details about transportation and other logistical information end each chapter. Be sure to check Web sites or call for particulars.

An Important Tip

All prices, opening times, and other details in this book are based on information supplied to us at press time, but changes occur all the time in the travel world, especially in seasonal destinations, and Fodor's cannot accept responsibility for facts that become outdated or for inadvertent errors or omissions. So always confirm information when it matters, especially if you're making a detour to visit a specific place.

Let Us Hear from You

Keeping a travel guide fresh and up-to-date is a big job, and we welcome any and all comments. We'd love to have your thoughts on places we've listed, and we're interested in hearing about your own special finds. Our guides are thoroughly updated for each new edition, and we're always adding new information, so your feedback is vital. Contact us via e-mail in care of editors@fodors.com (specifying *Golf Digest's Golf Weekends* on the subject line) or via snail mail in care of *Golf Digest's Golf Weekends* at Fodor's, 1745 Broadway, New York, New York 10019. We look forward to hearing from you. And in the meantime, have a great weekend.

—The Editors

AROUND ATLANTA

Hard Labor Creek State Park Golf Course

By Matthew Rudy and Hollis Gillespie

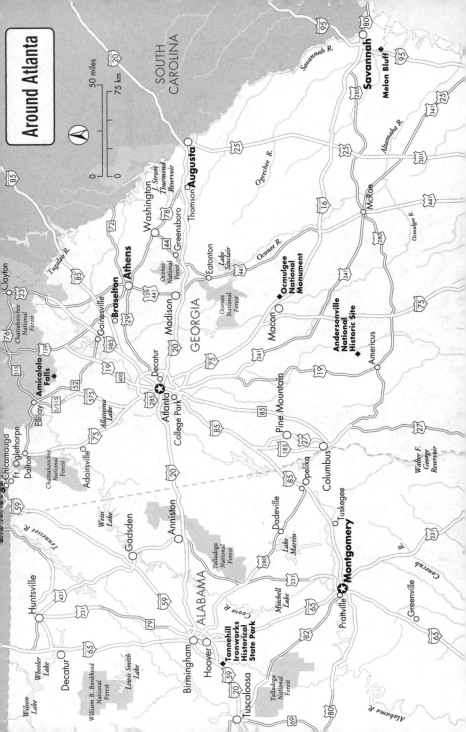

Atlanta natives aren't quite sure how they feel about the perception, at least in golf circles, that their city is mostly just a place to fly into and pick up the rental car on the way to the Masters in Augusta. It certainly doesn't help that those more interested in playing golf than watching it have so many great weekend getaway options within easy driving distance.

Atlantans have a right to feel put out about slights to their golf scene, real or perceived. Greater Atlanta has more than enough to keep any golf traveler occupied for at least a month, both on the course and off. The city is surrounded by wonderful daily-fee and resort courses, and a 30-minute drive in any direction puts you in rolling Georgia pine forests and in the vicinity of golf. In the city itself is a collection of well-loved daily-fee courses, including the Bobby Jones Golf Club, named after the most famous of Atlanta's native golfers. The best is the North Fulton Golf Course, designed by tour player Chandler Egan in the 1930s. Its collection of private courses is first-rate as well. Atlanta Athletic Club's Highlands course has been the site of two PGA Championships (1981 and 2001) and a U.S. Open (1976).

East Lake Golf Club have the most inspirational story attached to it. Designed by Donald Ross, what was Bobby Jones's childhood course fell into disrepair in the 1970s. Restored to its former excellence, it is now in the regular host-club rotation for the PGA Tour Championship, and serves as both a training ground for disadvantaged kids from Atlanta's inner city and as a monument to Jones's unparalleled amateur career.

Atlanta's centralized location makes it a popular commercial center and airline connection hub. It also makes for many possible weekend getaways. Drive a few hours east and you can reach the historic architecture of Savannah and the charm of St. Simons Island. Trek north and Montgomery, Alabama, and Chattanooga, Tennessee, are within easy reach. Both are mature, full-size cities in their own right, complete with bustling nightlife and first-class dining. For those who want to spend a little less time in the car, Augusta (yes, the Masters is here, but so are some fabulous resort and daily fee courses) is 1½ hours away, and you can get from downtown Atlanta to the spa and golf courses at Braselton's Château Élan in about the same amount of time. As you try to decide, keep in mind how varied the weather can be. Thanks to the jet stream, you can be boiling in downtown Atlanta in July and still feel wonderfully cool on the coast in St. Simons Island.

Hard Labor Creek State Park Golf Course (18)	6,444/4,854	72/75	71.5/68.6	129/123	$23/$28
Highland Walk (18)	6,045/4,657	72/72	71.4/67.7	131/120	$16/$21
Lane Creek Golf Club (18)	6,725/5,195	72/72	72.6/68.4	134/115	$33/$43
University of Georgia Golf Course (18)	6,828/5,669	72/73	73.8/68.2	133/120	$18/$35

ATHENS

Atlanta might get a youth transfusion from its universities downtown, but Athens is the quintessential college town. It's hard to identify where the University of Georgia ends and Athens begins, and the locals wouldn't have it any other way. This is a laid-back, easy-going kind of place, filled with casual restaurants, bars, and coffee shops. Rock bands R.E.M. and the B-52's got their start in the thriving Athens club scene, and both have been known to return to play unannounced sets in local bars.

Finding the best golf in the area takes a little bit of effort, but is worth the hunt. Aside from having perhaps the most unique name of any golf course in the country, Hard Labor Creek State Park Golf Course is the class act of this group—and about a 20-minute drive from town. The University of Georgia Golf Course, a mid-1960s Robert Trent Jones design, is right in town and has some potential, but it's clear where UGA's loyalties lie. The football stadium looms just down the street, and that's where the real action is.

Courses
Golf Digest REVIEWS

HARD LABOR CREEK STATE PARK GOLF COURSE. Facility Holes: 18. Opened: 1967. Architect: James B. McCloud. Yards: 6,444/4,854. Par: 72/75. Course Rating: 71.5/68.6. Slope: 129/123. Green Fee: $23/$28. Cart Fee: $12 per person. Discounts: Weekdays, twilight, seniors, juniors. Walking: Walking at certain times. Season: Year-round. Tee Times: Call 14 days in advance. Notes: Range (grass), lodging (20). ✉ 1400 Knox Chapel Rd., Rutledge 30663, 45 mi from Atlanta ☎ 706/557-3006 or 888/353-4592 ⊕ www.golfgeorgia.org ▤ AE, D, MC, V. *Comments: Hard Labor Creek turns into a waterfall on the par-3 5th.* ★ ★ ★ ¹/₂

HIGHLAND WALK. Facility Holes: 18. Opened: 2002. Architect: Dennis Griffith. Yards: 6,045/4,657 Par: 72/72. Course Rating: 71.4/67.7. Slope: 131/120. Green Fee: $16/$21. Cart Fee: $12 per person. Tee Times: Call golf shop. ✉ Victoria Bryant State Park, 1415 Bryant Park Rd., Royston 30662 ☎ 706/245-6770 or 800/434-0982 ⊕ www. gastateparks.org ▤ AE, D, MC, V. UR

If ever a golfer represented the heart and soul of a city, it is Bobby Jones and Atlanta. This bustling, modern city with roots in the Old South pays tribute to their favorite son at the Atlanta History Center (404/814-4000, www. atlantahistorycenter.com), home to a permanent Bobby Jones exhibit. Memorabilia from Jones's legendary career, including his historic Grand Slam year, 1930, are on display.

LANE CREEK GOLF CLUB. Facility Holes: 18. Opened: 1992. Architect: Mike Young. Yards: 6,725/5,195. Par: 72/72. Course Rating: 72.6/68.4. Slope: 134/115. Green Fee: $33/$43. Cart Fee: Included in green fee. Discounts: Twilight. Walking: Walking at certain times. Season: Year-round. Tee Times: Call golf shop. Notes: Range (grass, mat). ⊠ 1201 Club Dr., Bishop 30621, 8 mi from Athens ☎ 706/769-6699 or 800/842-6699 ▤ MC, V. *Comments: The par-4 4th is a virtual island—334 yards surrounded by water.* ★★★

UNIVERSITY OF GEORGIA GOLF COURSE. Facility Holes: 18. Opened: 1968. Architect: Robert Trent Jones/John LaFoy. Yards: 6,828/5,669. Par: 72/73. Course Rating: 73.8/68.2. Slope: 133/120. Green Fee: $18/$35. Cart Fee: $13 per person. Walking: Unrestricted walking. Season: Year-round. Tee Times: Call golf shop. ⊠ 2600 Riverbend Rd., 30605 ☎ 706/369-5739 ⊕ www.golfcourse.uga.edu ▤ MC, V. *Comments: Proximity to both town and Georgia football is its biggest advantage.* ★★½

Where to Stay

🏨 **ASHFORD MANOR.** This 1893 Victorian mansion sits amid 5 secluded, forested acres brimming with magnolias and rosebushes. The estate has been in the same family for over a century, which is evident in the care taken here, where there are landscaped gardens that terrace to a pool and, beyond that, nature trails leading to a creek. All rooms have private baths and vistas overlooking the wooded panorama. There's an inventiveness in the rooms' furnishings, which are more creative than those in most bed-and-breakfasts. For example, some rooms include bearskin rugs and mounted animal heads. ⊠ 5 Harden Hill Rd., Watkinsville 30629 ☎ 706/769-2633 ⊕ www. ambedandbreakfast.com ➘ 6 rooms, 1 suite ♨ Pool ▤ AE, MC, V ⦿ BP $-$$.

🏨 **BEST WESTERN COLONIAL INN.** Just a half mile from the UGA campus, this inn's a favorite among relatives who come to attend graduation. Don't expect to be blown away by the architectural design, as the hotel building itself, like the rooms it offers, is basic. Rooms, however, are still quite comfortable, with thick flowery bedspreads; each room comes equipped with a coffeemaker. Excellent freshly baked cookies are offered every afternoon. Directly across the street is the Varsity Drive-In, where hungry students feast on smothered hot dogs and heaps of fries. ⊠ 170 N. Milledge Ave., 30607 ☎ 706/546-7311 or 800/528-1234 🖶 706/546-7959 ⊕ www.bestwestern.com ➘ 69 rooms ♨ Some microwaves, some refrigerators, pool ▤ AE, D, DC, MC, V ¢-$.

☎ **MAGNOLIA TERRACE.** In the middle of the historic district, this B&B is in a mansion from 1912. Each room is decorated with a mishmash of antiques. The rooms are warmly designed with rich, stately colors, such as burnt orange and velvet red. Some rooms are carpeted with intricate Persian rugs, and many have working fireplaces. Several of the bathrooms have large claw-foot tubs. ⊠ 288 Hill St., 30601 ☎ 706/548-3860 🖷 706/369-3439 ⊕ www.bbonline.com/ga/magnoliaterrace ⇆ 8 rooms, 1 suite ♿ In-room data ports, cable TV ▤ AE, D, MC, V ⑩ BP $-$$.

☎ **NICHOLSON HOUSE.** This 19th-century house, on 6 acres of an 18th-century land grant originally deeded to William Few, one of Georgia's two signers of the U.S. Constitution, literally is a two-over-two log house. Its original structure is now hidden beneath a 1947 colonial revival exterior. The inn has a wide front veranda with rocking chairs. The richly colored rooms are furnished with a mix of antiques and good reproductions. ⊠ 6295 Jefferson Rd., 30607 ☎ 706/353-2200 🖷 706/353-7799 ⊕ www.bbonline.com/ga/nicholson ⇆ 7 rooms, 2 suites ▤ AE, D, MC, V ⑩ BP $-$$.

Where to Eat

✕ **HARRY BISSETT'S.** At one of the best restaurants in Athens, you can expect Cajun recipes straight from New Orleans. Nosh on oysters on the half shell at the raw bar while waiting for a table (if it's the weekend, expect to wait a while). Popular main dishes include amberjack Thibodaux (a broiled fish fillet smothered in crawfish étouffée) and chicken Rochambeau (a terrine of chicken breast, béarnaise, ham, and a wine sauce). ⊠ 279 E. Broad St. ☎ 706/353-7065 ▤ AE, D, MC, V ☺ No lunch Mon. $$-$$$$.

✕ **LAST RESORT GRILL.** This is a pleasant place to unwind—especially with the restaurant's cheery sidewalk café section. The menu, a cross between Tex-Mex and California, includes such items as salmon and black-bean quesadillas, and grilled shiitake mushrooms and feta cheese tossed with pasta. ⊠ 174 W. Clayton St. ☎ 706/549-0810 ▤ AE, D, MC, V $-$$$$.

✕ **WEAVER D'S FINE FOODS.** Besides serving some of the best soul food around, Weaver D's is also a piece of musical history: R.E.M. was so inspired by the restaurant's motto, "Automatic for the People," that it named an album after it. The cooks specialize in hearty, homey food—fish and chicken, barbecued pork, meat loaf, and steak with gravy. All entrées come with vegetables fresh from the garden. ⊠ 1016 E. Broad St. ☎ 706/353-7797 ▤ No credit cards $.

Essentials

Getting Here
Athens is 70 mi east of Atlanta. To get here take I–85 north to Route 316 U.S. 29 east.

Visitor Information
🛈 **Athens Welcome Center** ⊠ 280 E. Dougherty St. ☎ 706/353-1820 ⊕ www.visitathensga.com.

Forest Hills Golf Club (18)	6,875/4,875	72/72	72.2/68.3	126/116	$15/$22
Golf Club at Cuscowilla (18)	6,847/5,348	70/72	72.3/69.6	130/123	$85/$125
Jones Creek Golf Club (18)	7,008/5,430	72/72	73.8/72.4	137/130	$22/$37
Reynolds Plantation (54)					
Great Waters (18)	7,048/5,082	72/72	73.8/69.2	135/114	$105/$115
National (18)	7,015/5,292	72/72	72.7/69.5	127/116	$90/$158
Plantation (18)	6,698/5,121	72/72	71.7/68.9	128/115	$90/$158

AUGUSTA

No town has earned more name recognition and less nationwide exposure from a single event within its borders than Augusta, Georgia. We all know it as the home of the Masters, the most-watched golf tournament on television and arguably the most prestigious tournament to win on any schedule. But the coverage of the Masters on CBS is carefully controlled by the Augusta National Golf Club—you certainly don't get much of a look at the town in which the tournament is played. If your only visit to the city is during Masters week, you won't get a true feel for all the interesting golf, dining, and cultural options available—the place is more or less crammed to the rafters.

The 51 other weeks of the year, Augusta is quite a bit more accessible. Take a tour down the Riverwalk Augusta boardwalk on the Savannah River, which cuts through town. The walk is lined with shops, restaurants, and markers commemorating Augusta's past. Unless you're extremely well connected, a round of golf at Augusta National probably won't be on your schedule, but the Augusta area has a handful of courses that can serve as worthy substitutes.

The best is the Jones Creek Golf Club. Designed by Rees Jones in 1987, Jones Creek has the feel of a private club, and the manicured fairways of one, too. The most interesting, though, is Forest Hills Golf Club, which was built in 1927 by Donald Ross. It's fun to think of Ross and Augusta National designer Alister Mackenzie knocking around Augusta at roughly the same time, designing two courses that would get such dramatically different amounts of exposure.

If you're interested in just *watching* the Masters, your best option is for one of the practice rounds earlier in the week (the actual tournament play is not open to the general public). Tickets are awarded on a lottery basis; write to the Masters Tournament Practice Rounds office (Box 2047, Augusta, GA

30903) by July 15 of the year preceding the tournament. For more information, visit the Masters' Web site at www.masters.org.

Courses

Golf Digest REVIEWS

FOREST HILLS GOLF CLUB. Facility Holes: 18. Opened: 1926. Architect: Donald Ross. Yards: 6,875/4,875. Par: 72/72. Course Rating: 72.2/68.3. Slope: 126/116. Green Fee: $15/$22. Cart Fee: $14 per person. Discounts: Juniors. Walking: Unrestricted walking. Season: Year-round. Tee Times: Call 7 days in advance. Notes: Metal spikes, range (grass). ✉ 1500 Comfort Rd., 30909, 140 mi from Atlanta ☎ 706/733-0001 ▤ AE, D, MC, V. *Comments: At nearly 7,000 yards, this place must have been something back in the days of hickory shafts.* ★ ★ ★

GOLF CLUB AT CUSCOWILLA. Facility Holes: 18. Opened: 1998. Architect: Bill Coore/ Ben Crenshaw. Yards: 6,847/5,348. Par: 70/72. Course Rating: 72.3/69.6. Slope: 130/123. Green Fee: $85/$125. Cart Fee: $16 per person. Discounts: Juniors. Walking: Walking with caddie. Season: Year-round. Tee Times: Call 14 days in advance. Notes: Range (grass), lodging (30). ✉ 355 Cuscowilla Dr., Eatonton 31024, 75 mi from Atlanta ☎ 706/485-0094 or 800/458-5351 ▤ AE, D, MC, V. *Comments: A Crenshaw-Coore masterpiece.* ★ ★ ★ ★ ½

If your only visit to Augusta is Masters week, you won't get a true feel for all the options available.

JONES CREEK GOLF CLUB. Facility Holes: 18. Opened: 1986. Architect: Rees Jones. Yards: 7,008/5,430. Par: 72/72. Course Rating: 73.8/72.4. Slope: 137/130. Green Fee: $22/$37. Cart Fee: $11 per person. Discounts: Seniors, juniors. Walking: Walking at certain times. Season: Year-round. Tee Times: Call 7 days in advance. Notes: Range (grass). ✉ 777 Jones Creek Dr., Evans 30809, 5 mi from Augusta ☎ 706/860-4228 ▤ AE, MC, V. *Comments: Plenty of water and out-of-bounds markers to snare off-line shots.* ★ ★ ★ ★

REYNOLDS PLANTATION. Facility Holes: 54. Cart Fee: $20 per person. Walking: Walking at certain times. Season: Year-round. Notes: Range (grass), lodging (99). ✉ 100 Linger Longer Rd., Greensboro 30642, 75 mi from Atlanta ☎ 706/467-3159 or 800/852-5885 ⊕ www.reynoldsplantation.com ▤ AE, MC, V.

Great Waters. Holes: 18. Opened: 1992. Architect: Jack Nicklaus. Yards: 7,048/5,082. Par: 72/72. Course Rating: 73.8/69.2. Slope: 135/114. Green Fee: $105/$115. *Comments: Nicklaus doesn't want you to feel cheated. You just might use every ball in your bag.* ★ ★ ★ ★ ½

National. Holes: 18. Opened: 1997. Architect: Tom Fazio. Yards: 7,015/5,292. Par: 72/72. Course Rating: 72.7/69.5. Slope: 127/116. Green Fee: $90/$158. *Comments: Tom Fazio's design is a great (and equally brutal) companion to the Great Waters 18.* ★ ★ ★ ★

Plantation. Holes: 18. Opened: 1987. Architect: Bob Cupp/Fuzzy Zoeller/Hubert Green. Yards: 6,698/5,121. Par: 72/72. Course Rating: 71.7/68.9. Slope: 128/115. Green Fee: $90/$158. *Comments: The first to be built here, and the most fun to play for the average player.* ★ ★ ★ ★ ½

Where to Stay

🏨 **AZALEA INN.** This restored Victorian mansion provides uncluttered rooms decorated with rich colors. They're a good showcase for fine furnishings and architectural accents, such as lace-canopied beds, brass-framed mirrors, and stately fireplace mantles. The inn is in an upscale residential neighborhood, and you're encouraged to enjoy your Continental breakfast in bed or in the dining room that overlooks the pathway to the Savannah River and the city's celebrated Riverwalk, which leads to Augusta's bustling old-town district. ✉ 312-334 Greene St. ☎ 706/724-3454 🖷 706/724-1033 🛏 21 rooms ♿ Some kitchenettes, cable TV, meeting rooms, free parking ☰ AE, MC, V $-$$.

🏨 **PARTRIDGE INN.** This National Trust Historic hotel is at the gateway to Summerville, a hilltop neighborhood of summer homes from 1800. From the roof there's a good view of downtown Augusta. For over a century this hotel has been a bastion of Augusta society, hosting presidents, dignitaries, and sports, rock, and movie stars alike. In keeping with this demanding clientele, the business facilities are state-of-the-art, while the hotel itself manages to maintain its individuality. None of the 159 rooms are decorated the same. Many open directly onto a sweeping common veranda, and some have their own patio. Everything is tastefully understated, with monochromatic colors accented by occasional period pieces and artful draperies. ✉ 2110 Walton Way, 30904 ☎ 706/737-8888 or 800/476-6888 🖷 706/731-0826 ⊕ www.partridgeinn.com 🛏 133 rooms, 26 suites ♿ Restaurant, in-room data ports, some kitchens, pool, bar, lobby lounge, concierge floor, Internet, business services, meeting rooms ☰ AE, D, DC, MC, V ℐℐ BP $-$$.

🏨 **PERRIN GUEST HOUSE INN.** In this 1863 house on three acres, the large guest rooms come with fireplaces. Afternoon wine and tea are included. ✉ 208 LaFayette Dr. ☎ 706/731-0920 or 800/668-8930 🛏 10 rooms ♿ In-room hot tubs, microwaves, meeting rooms ☰ AE, MC, V ℐℐ CP $-$$.

🏨 **RADISSON RIVERFRONT HOTEL.** This chain hotel aims to provide rooms that are elegant but still comfortable, and it succeeds. The carpets, coverings, and pillows are all plush. One big plus is the location: right on the river. Not only does this ensure beautiful views from many of the rooms, but the hotel is within easy walking distance of coffeehouses, art galleries, and museums. ✉ 2 10th St. ☎ 706/722-8900 or 800/333-3333 🖷 706/823-6513 🛏 189 rooms, 19 suites ♿ Restaurant, in-room data ports, cable TV, gym, sauna, hiking, lobby lounge, meeting rooms, free parking ☰ AE, D, MC, V $$$-$$$$.

Where to Eat

✕ **LA MAISON ON TELFAIR.** Operated by chef-owner Heinz Sowinski, La Maison presents a classic French menu of game, sweetbreads, and, with a nod to the chef's heritage, Wiener schnitzel. One standout is the maple-leaf duck breast over a couscous salad and fennel-orange slaw. The experience is enhanced by the dining room's elegant chandeliers and rich wood paneling. ✉ 404 Telfair St. ☎ 706/722-4805 ☰ AE, D, DC, MC, V ⊘ Closed Sun. No lunch $$$-$$$$.

✕ **LUIGI'S.** This traditional, thick-tomato-sauce, old-time Italian restaurant has been operated by the same proud family for decades. The menu also includes Greek dishes such as moussaka and baklava, served with the same confidence that has made this place a favorite among locals for over 50 years. The food is so delicious and the surroundings so welcoming that you may want to stick around like a visiting relative. ⊠ 590 Broad St. ☎ 706/722-4056 ☰ AE, MC, V $$-$$$$.

Essentials

Getting Here

The trip east along I-20 from Atlanta to Augusta is 150 mi.

Visitor Information

🚹 **Augusta Metropolitan Conventions and Visitors Bureau** ⊠ 1450 Greene St., 30901 ☎ 706/823-6600 or 800/726-0243. **Georgia Welcome Center** ⓓ Box 211090, Martinez 30917 ☎ 706/737-1446.

BRASELTON

Before the emergence of the Château Élan winery and resort, Braselton's main claim to fame was its role in a messy Kim Basinger bankruptcy filing. The prominent actress bought the entire town when she was at the height of her popularity, then was forced to sell when movie roles weren't coming so quickly. With all that hoopla behind it, the town is now working on retaining its charm as a turn-of-the-20th-century farming community while also emphasizing its accessibility to the ever-increasing sprawl of metro Atlanta.

The centerpiece of the area, Château Élan, is an ambitious resort with a stylized hotel accompanied by a spa, winery, equestrian complex, and two highly rated golf courses. It's magnificent enough to deserve its own exit off of I-85. In addition to the two public courses, the resort also has a private 18-hole course designed by Gene Sarazen, who was a friend of the Château's founder.

Courses   Golf Digest REVIEWS

BRIDGEMILL ATHLETIC CLUB. Facility Holes: 18. Opened: 1998. Architect: Desmond Muirhead/Larry Mize. Yards: 7,085/4,828. Par: 72/72. Course Rating: 74.0/69.0. Slope: 140/119. Green Fee: $59/$79. Cart Fee: Included in green fee. Discounts: Twilight. Walking: Unrestricted walking. Season: Year-round. High: Apr.–Oct. Tee Times: Call golf shop. Notes: Range (grass). ⊠ 1190 BridgeMill Ave., Canton 30114, 32 mi from Atlanta ☎ 770/345-5500 ☰ AE, D, MC, V. *Comments: The 16th is a 200-yard, island green par-3.* ★ ★ ★ ½

BridgeMill Athletic Club (18)	7,085/4,828	72/72	74.0/69.0	140/119	$59/$79
Château Élan Resort (36)					$32/$77
Château Élan (18)	7,030/5,092	71/71	73.5/70.8	136/124	
Woodlands (18)	6,738/4,850	72/72	72.6/68.5	131/123	
Chicopee Woods Golf Course (27)					$34/$41
Mill/School (18)	6,926/5,013	72/72	73.0/68.0	130/116	
School/Village (18)	7,040/5,001	72/72	74.0/69.0	135/117	
Village/Mill (18)	7,008/4,988	72/72	73.4/67.6	133/118	
Emerald Pointe Golf Resort & Conference Center (18)	6,341/4,935	72/72	70.1/68.3	124/117	$20/$55
Renaissance Pineisle Resort (18)	6,527/5,297	72/72	71.6/70.6	132/127	$39/$74
Reunion Golf Club (18)	6,882/5,006	72/72	73.8/69.7	142/126	$40/$75
Royal Lakes Golf & Country Club (18)	6,980/4,820	71/73	73.6/69.3	139/122	$40/$55

CHÂTEAU ÉLAN RESORT. Facility Holes: 36. Architect: Denis Griffiths. Green Fee: $32/$77. Cart Fee: Included in green fee. Discounts: Weekdays, twilight, seniors, juniors. Walking: Walking at certain times. Season: Year-round. High: Apr.–Oct. Tee Times: Call 7 days in advance. Notes: Range (grass), lodging (380). ⊠ 6060 Golf Club Dr., 30517, 45 mi from Atlanta ☎ 678/425-6050 or 800/233-9463 ⊕ www.chateauelan.com ▤ AE, D, DC, MC, V.

Château Élan. Holes: 18. Opened: 1989. Yards: 7,030/5,092. Par: 71/71. Course Rating: 73.5/70.8. Slope: 136/124. *Comments: The more muscle-bound of the two. A stout test.* ★★★★

Woodlands. Holes: 18. Opened: 1996. Yards: 6,738/4,850. Par: 72/72. Course Rating: 72.6/68.5. Slope: 131/123. *Comments: Shorter and more reasonable, with well-done changes of scenery.* ★★★★ ½

CHICOPEE WOODS GOLF COURSE. Facility Holes: 27. Opened: 1991. Architect: Denis Griffiths. Green Fee: $34/$41. Cart Fee: $13 per person. Discounts: Twilight, seniors, juniors. Walking: Unrestricted walking. Season: Year-round. Tee Times: Call 5 days in advance. Notes: Range (grass). ⊠ 2515 Atlanta Hwy., Gainesville 30504, 30 mi from Atlanta ☎ 770/534-7322 ⊕ www.chicopeewoodsgolfcourse.com ▤ AE, MC, V.

Mill/School. Holes: 18. Yards: 6,926/5,013. Par: 72/72. Course Rating: 73.0/68.0. Slope: 130/116.

School/Village. Holes: 18. Yards: 7,040/5,001. Par: 72/72. Course Rating: 74.0/69.0. Slope: 135/117.

Village/Mill. Holes: 18. Yards: 7,008/4,988. Par: 72/72. Course Rating: 73.4/67.6. Slope: 133/118.

Comments: Local knowledge is crucial for all the blind shots. ★★★

RENAISSANCE PINEISLE RESORT. Facility Holes: 18. Opened: 1973. Architect: Gary Player. Yards: 6,527/5,297. Par: 72/72. Course Rating: 71.6/70.6. Slope: 132/127. Green

Fee: $39/$74. Cart Fee: Included in green fee. Discounts: Weekdays, twilight, seniors, juniors. Walking: Walking at certain times. Season: Year-round. High: May–Oct. Tee Times: Call 14 days in advance. Notes: Range (grass), lodging (254). ⊠ 9000 Holiday Rd., Lake Lanier Islands 30518, 45 mi from Atlanta ☎ 770/945-8921 ⊟ AE, D, DC, MC, V. *Comments: Spectacular surroundings on Lake Lanier.* ★ ★ ★ ¹/₂

REUNION GOLF CLUB. Facility Holes: 18. Opened: 2001. Architect: Michael Riley. Yards: 6,882/5,006. Par: 72/72. Course Rating: 73.8/69.7. Slope: 142/126. Green Fee: $40/$75. Cart Fee: Included in green fee. Discounts: Weekdays, twilight, seniors, juniors. Walking: Mandatory cart. Season: Year-round. High: Apr.–Oct. Tee Times: Call 7 days in advance. Notes: Range (grass). ⊠ 5615 Grand Reunion Dr., Hoschton 30548, 35 mi from Atlanta ☎ 770/967-8300 ⊕ www.reuniongolfclub.com ⊟ AE, D, MC, V. *Comments: The par-5 7th has alternate greens and a nasty set of bunkers.* ★ ★ ★ ¹/₂

ROYAL LAKES GOLF & COUNTRY CLUB. Facility Holes: 18. Opened: 1989. Architect: Hogan/Rochlin. Yards: 6,980/4,820. Par: 71/73. Course Rating: 73.6/69.3. Slope: 139/122. Green Fee: $40/$55. Cart Fee: Included in green fee. Discounts: Weekdays, twilight, seniors, juniors. Walking: Walking at certain times. Season: Year-round. Tee Times: Call 4 days in advance. Notes: Range (grass). ⊠ 4700 Royal Lakes Dr., Flowery Branch 30542, 35 mi from Atlanta ☎ 770/535-8800 ⊟ AE, MC, V. *Comments: The handsome layout is obscured by all the houses.* ★ ★ ★ ¹/₂

Where to Stay

🏨 **CHÂTEAU ÉLAN.** On this 16th-century-style French château is Georgia's best-known winery, all of it part of 2,400 rolling acres about an hour north of downtown Atlanta. Château Élan is also a complete resort: European luxury blends with Southern hospitality at the inn and spa, which has private villas, golf courses, and an equestrian center. The large guest rooms are done in a style in keeping with the inn's elegant exterior, which has pitched roofs and towering bay windows. ⊠ 100 Rue Charlemagne, 30517 ☎ 770/932-0900 or 800/233-9463 🖷 770/271-6005 ⊕ www.chateauelanatlanta.com ⤶ 297 rooms, 20 suites ♿ 8 restaurants, in-room data ports, cable TV, 18-hole golf course, 7 tennis courts, pool, gym, hair salon, massage, sauna, spa, steam room, bicycles, horseback riding ⊟ AE, D, MC, V $$$-$$$$.

🏨 **GLEN-ELLA SPRINGS.** This restored old hotel is 5 mi down a gravel road—it was once an Indian trail leading to the narrowest part of Lake Rabun and is therefore a shortcut to the other side. Today, the retreat remains almost as isolated as it was then, peaceful and welcoming. The rooms are fine examples of bucolic grace and comfort, and their French doors let out onto a common veranda furnished with rocking chairs. Outside is a panorama of meadowlands, complete with feeding deer and other wildlife. The beds are big and comfortable, with hand-stitched quilts and frames that look like they were built by pioneers (and just may have been). The floors are the original heart of pine from more than a century ago, smoothed to a handsome polish by time and upkeep. The bathrooms are more modern, though, with jetted tubs and upscale amenities. ⊠ 1789 Bear Gap Rd., Clarkesville 30523 ☎ 706/754-7295 or 877/456-7527 🖷 706/754-1560 ⊕ www.glenella. com ⤶ 12 rooms, 4 suites ♿ Restaurant, picnic area, in-room data ports, pool, outdoor hot tub, hiking, recreation room, shop, meeting rooms, free parking, shop; no room TVs ⊟ AE, MC, V ⅋ BP $$-$$$.

HOLIDAY INN EXPRESS CHÂTEAU ÉLAN LODGE. This hotel offers one of the few economy options available in Braselton. The rooms are sizable, with the pleasant, soothing color scheme the chain is known for. In-room amenities such as coffeemakers and ironing boards add to the comfort level, and standard business facilities, such as Internet access and fax service, are available in the lobby. ⊠ 2069 Hwy. 211, 30517 ☎ 770/867-8100 🖶 770/867-3236 ⊕ www.ichotelsgroup.com ↩ 80 rooms ⚕ Restaurant, cable TV, 2 tennis courts, pool, gym, shop, laundry service, concierge, Internet, free parking, some pets allowed ⊟ AE, D, MC, V $-$$.

Where to Eat

✗ **DADO'S.** This drive-through restaurant has been a mainstay in rural Braselton since the days before the tiny town became a ritzy spa destination. Here they serve fast food good and greasy, soft-serve ice cream, and fried chicken. Breakfast, hearty fried fare meant to stick to your ribs, is also available six days a week. ⊠ 5051 Hwy. 53 ☎ 706/654-2490 ⊟ No credit cards ⊙ Closed Sun. $.

✗ **GLEN-ELLA SPRINGS.** The Glen-Ella Springs restaurant draws a loyal crowd from far and wide. The dinner menu is as sophisticated as the surroundings are rustic: entrées might include chicken encrusted with macadamia nuts, or Low-Country shrimp atop stone-ground grits. Breakfasts are just as mouthwatering, featuring dishes such as French toast stuffed with peach compote, and an assortment of vegetable and meat frittatas. ⊠ 1789 Bear Gap Rd., Clarksville ☎ 706/754-7295 or 877/456-7527 ⊟ AE, MC, V ⊙ No lunch $$$$.

✗ **VERSAILLES RESTAURANT.** You could definitely do worse in the tiny town of Braselton than this exquisite brasserie, which has an intricate glass atrium above it. Bathed in either daylight or starlight, diners help themselves to a lush buffet for breakfast or dinner, while the dinner's à la carte menu includes grilled pork tenderloin with spaetzle, corn-crusted sea scallops with fingerling potatoes, and seared foie gras with apple chutney. The wine list concentrates on bottles from the nearby Château Élan Winery, and the sommelier has many ideas on which grapes best complement the entrées. On Friday and Saturday evenings a buffet is also available. ⊠ Château Élan, 100 Rue Charlemagne ☎ 678/425-0900 ⊟ AE, D, MC, V $$$$.

Essentials

Getting Here
Braselton is in Jackson county along I-85, 45 minutes northeast from downtown Atlanta. Interstate exits 126 and 129 both lead into Braselton. Principal roads also include Routes 211, 53, 60, and 124.

Visitor Information
🔊 www.braselton.net**Braselton Library** ⊠ 65 Frances St. ☎ 706/654-1992. **Town of Braselton** ⊕ www.braselton.net.

Barnsley Gardens (18)	7,200/6,200	72/72	74.5/76.2	141/138	$75/$105
Bear Trace at Harrison Bay (18)	7,140/5,290	72/72	73.8/71.2	132/123	$35/$59
Nob North Golf Course (18)	6,573/5,448	72/72	71.7/71.7	128/126	$21/$25

CHATTANOOGA, TN

Sitting on the Tennessee River and at the foothills of the Smoky Mountains, Chattanooga is a peaceful, cosmopolitan city of 200,000. Not only is it one of the most naturally beautiful places in the United States, but it's fabulous for those interested in the outdoors—bass fishing, boating, and yes, golf. Try the Jack Nicklaus–designed Bear Trace at Harrison Bay just outside town, or drive a few miles across the nearby Georgia state line and visit Barnsley Gardens, the former estate of a Southern shipping magnate. The Barnsley grounds have been transformed into a golf course, luxury hotel, and spa. Its course, the General, is rated one of the best in Georgia and the region.

Courses

GolfDigest REVIEWS

BARNSLEY GARDENS. Facility Holes: 18. Opened: 1999. Architect: Jim Fazio. Yards: 7,200/6,200. Par: 72/72. Course Rating: 74.5/76.2. Slope: 141/138. Green Fee: $75/$105. Cart Fee: Included in green fee. Discounts: Guest, seniors, juniors. Walking: Unrestricted walking. Season: Year-round. High: Apr.–June. Tee Times: Call 7 days in advance. Notes: Range (grass), lodging (72). ✉597 Barnsley Garden Rd., Adairsville, GA 30103, 60 mi from Atlanta ☎770/773-2555 or 877/773-2447 ⊕www.barnsleyinn.com ☰AE, D, DC, MC, V. *Comments: The General course feels as if it's been here for centuries.* ★ ★ ★ ★ ¹/₂

BEAR TRACE AT HARRISON BAY. Facility Holes: 18. Opened: 1999. Architect: Jack Nicklaus. Yards: 7,140/5,290. Par: 72/72. Course Rating: 73.8/71.2. Slope: 132/123. Green Fee: $35/$59. Cart Fee: Included in green fee. Discounts: Weekdays, twilight, seniors, juniors. Walking: Unrestricted walking. Season: Year-round. Tee Times: Call 30 days in advance. Notes: Range (grass). ✉8919 Harrison Bay Rd., Harrison 37341, 20 mi from Chattanooga ☎423/326-0885 or 877/611-2327 ⊕www.beartrace.com ☰AE, D, MC, V. *Comments: Upholds the Nicklaus tradition of spectacular views and difficult, difficult holes.* ★ ★ ★ ★

NOB NORTH GOLF COURSE. Facility Holes: 18. Opened: 1978. Architect: Ron Kirby/Gary Player. Yards: 6,573/5,448. Par: 72/72. Course Rating: 71.7/71.7. Slope: 128/126. Green Fee: $21/$25. Cart Fee: $12 per person. Discounts: Seniors, juniors. Walking: Unrestricted walking. Season: Year-round. Tee Times: Call 5 days in advance. Notes: Range (grass). ✉298 Nob N. Dr., Cohutta 30710, 25 mi from Chattanooga, TN ☎706/694-8505 ☰MC, V. *Comments: Just across the border in Georgia. Very playable.* ★ ★ ★ ★

Where to Stay

CHATTANOOGA CHOO-CHOO HOLIDAY INN. This hotel incorporates the land-mark 1905 Southern Railway terminal. It's been renewed with restaurants, lounges, shops, exhibits, well-groomed gardens, and an operating trolley on 30 acres. Trains are parked on the tracks. Besides standard rooms in three buildings, the hotel has Victorian parlor cars, replete with the brocade and red upholstery of the period, that have been converted to overnight berths. ⊠ 1400 Market St., 37402 ☎ 423/266-5000 or 800/872-2529 🖷 423/265-4635 ⊕ www.choochoo.com ⤵ 303 rooms, 10 suites, 48 rail-cars ⚐ 5 restaurants, 3 tennis courts, 3 pools (1 indoor), hot tub, lounge ⊟ AE, D, DC, MC, V $$.

CHATTANOOGA CLARION HOTEL. Perhaps the best thing about this hotel is its location; about two blocks from the Riverwalk, which allows for a waterside stroll to the city's Bluff View Arts District of galleries, restaurants, bookstores, and a coffee shop. The rooms are done in a basic sort of bank-lobby aesthetic. Some rooms, geared to attract business travelers, have fully stocked desks and speakerphones along with the requisite in-room coffeemakers, irons, and ironing boards. Everyone staying here can can use the Internet access, fax machine, and other basic office services available in the lobby around the clock. ⊠ 407 Chestnut St., 37402 ☎ 423/756-5150 or 800/252-7466 🖷 423/265-8708 ⊕ www.chattanoogaclarion.com ⤵ 203 rooms, 2 suites ⚐ 2 restau-rants, in-room data ports, pool, gym ⊟ AE, D, DC, MC, V $-$$.

MARRIOTT AT THE CONVENTION CENTER. This 16-floor downtown convention hotel is the town's largest. Rooms are spacious, and those on the higher floors have a great view of either the Tennessee River or Lookout Mountain. Adjacent to the city's convention center, this hotel is the choice of many business travelers: the desks are have large work surfaces, and the king-size beds have pillow-top mattresses and plush duvets. ⊠ 2 Carter Plaza, 37402 ☎ 423/756-0002 or 800/841-1674 🖷 423/266-2254 ⊕ www.marriotthotels.com ⤵ 342 rooms, 2 suites ⚐ 2 restaurants, 2 pools (1 indoor), health club, lounge, laundry service ⊟ AE, D, DC, MC, V $-$$.

READ HOUSE HOTEL & SUITES. The Georgian-style Read House dates from the 1920s and has been restored to the original grandeur that drew heads of state in its heyday. The lobby has a large archway, stately columns, and polished walnut panels. Mailboxes from the days when guests stayed for months still neatly line one passage-way. Guest rooms in the main hotel continue the Georgian motif; rooms in the annex are more contemporary. ⊠ 827 Broad St., 37402 ☎ 423/266-4121 or 800/333-3333 🖷 423/267-6447 ⊕ www.readhouse.com ⤵ 140 rooms, 100 suites ⚐ Restaurant, coffee shop, dining room, pool, hot tub, sauna, lounge ⊟ AE, DC, MC, V $.

Where to Eat

✕ **BIG RIVER GRILLE & BREWING WORKS.** You can watch the brewing process through a soaring glass wall beside the bar of this restored trolley warehouse, hand-somely designed with high ceilings, exposed brick walls, and hardwood floors. Order the sampler for a taste of this microbrewery's four different concoctions. The sandwiches and salads are generous and tasty. ✉ 222 Broad St. ☎ 423/267-2739 ⚒ Reservations not accepted ⊟ AE, D, DC, MC, V $-$$$.

✕ **SOUTHSIDE GRILL.** This handsome downtown restaurant in a former meatpacking plant reinterprets the food of the region with a lighter touch. Hardwood floors offset the dark paneled walls, which are hung with fine art. Smoked salmon on a crispy grits cake and grilled rib eye with crawfish cakes and chilled leek soup are just two possible choices on the seasonally changing menu. ✉ 1400 Cowart St. ☎ 423/266-9211 ⊕ - www.southsidegrill.com ⊟ AE, D, MC, V $$$-$$$$.

✕ **TOWN & COUNTRY.** A casual Chattanooga fixture with great food and service, Town & Country combines Southern cuisine with beef, chicken, prime rib, and seafood entrées. Prices are reasonable. ✉ 110 N. Market St. ☎ 423/267-8544 ⊟ AE, D, DC, MC, V $-$$$.

✕ **212 MARKET.** This restaurant near the Tennessee Aquarium serves New American cuisine, with an emphasis on healthy fare. Try the grilled salmon, or the Taylor River enchilada with fresh spinach, black beans, cheeses, and salsa. The cavernous, contemporary dining room is bright and unpretentious. ✉ 212 Market St. ☎ 423/265-1212 ⊕ - www.212market.com ⊟ AE, D, DC, MC, V $$-$$$.

Essentials

Getting Here
To get to Chattanooga, take I-75 north to its intersection with I-24. The distance is 120 mi.

Visitor Information
🛈 **Chattanooga Area Convention and Visitors Bureau** ✉ 2 Broad St., 37402 ☎ 423/756-8687 or 800/322-3344 ⊕ www.chattanooga.net/cvb/.

MONTGOMERY, AL

Begun in the late 1980s, Alabama's Robert Trent Jones Golf Trail was one of the most ambitious golf projects ever undertaken. Built as an investment for Retirement Systems of Alabama, a huge pension fund, this collection of 18 courses—and 378 holes—is over a 100-mi stretch running from Huntsville to Mobile. The eight facilities, including the Montgomery-area Cambrian Ridge, Capitol Hill, and Grand National, have won nearly universal acclaim for their Jones designs.

Grand National's Lake and Links courses and Cambrian Ridge's Canyon/Sherling course all made *Golf Digest*'s Top 10 list for Alabama in 2003. All

Resort at Callaway Gardens (54)					
Lake View (18)	6,031/5,285	70/70	68.6/71.1	123/121	$55/$75
Mountain View (18)	7,057/4,883	72/72	73.7/69.4	139/120	$95/$110
Robert Trent Jones Golf Trail at Cambrian Ridge Golf Club (27)					$35/$57
Canyon/Loblolly (18)	7,297/4,772	71/71	74.6/67.8	140/126	
Canyon/Sherling (18)	7,424/4,857	72/72	75.4/68.1	142/127	
Loblolly/Sherling (18)	7,130/4,785	71/71	73.9/67.0	133/119	
Robert Trent Jones Golf Trail at Capitol Hill (54)					
Judge (18)	7,794/4,955	72/72	77.8/68.3	144/121	$45/$67
Legislator (18)	7,323/5,414	72/72	74.1/71.5	126/119	$35/$57
Senator (18)	7,697/5,122	72/72	76.6/69.6	131/121	$35/$57
Robert Trent Jones Golf Trail at Grand National Golf Club (54)					
Lake (18)	7,149/4,910	72/72	74.9/68.7	138/117	$35/$57
Links (18)	7,311/4,843	72/72	74.9/69.6	141/113	$35/$57
Short (18)	3,328/1,715	54/54			$18
Still Waters Resort (36)					$53/$58
Legend (18)	6,407/5,287	72/72	70.8/71.1	129/126	
Tradition (18)	6,906/5,048	72/72	73.5/69.5	139/126	

that golf under one banner is almost enough to make you forget that there are other places to play, but don't. A short drive away, roughly equidistant between Montgomery and Atlanta, is the Resort at Callaway Gardens. It has three courses every bit as good as the ones on the Trail, and luxurious rooms as well.

Courses

Golf Digest REVIEWS

RESORT AT CALLAWAY GARDENS. Facility Holes: 54. Cart Fee: Included in green fee. Discounts: Twilight. Season: Year-round. High: Mar.–Nov. Tee Times: Call 3 days in advance. Notes: Metal spikes, range (grass), lodging (810). ✉ GA Hwy. 18 at intersection GA Hwy. 354, Pine Mountain 31822, 30 mi from Columbus ☎ 706/663–2281 or 800/ 225–5292 ⊕ www.callawayonline.com ▤ AE, D, DC, MC, V.

Lake View. Holes: 18. Opened: 1950. Architect: J. B. McGovern/Joe Lee/Dick Wilson. Yards: 6,031/5,285. Par: 70/70. Course Rating: 68.6/71.1. Slope: 123/121. Green Fee: $55/$75. Walking: Walking at certain times. *Comments: Easiest of the three, and best for beginning players.* ★★★ ½

Mountain View. Holes: 18. Opened: 1964. Architect: Dick Wilson/Joe Lee. Yards: 7,057/ 4,883. Par: 72/72. Course Rating: 73.7/69.4. Slope: 139/120. Green Fee: $95/$110. Walking: Mandatory cart. *Comments: Site of the PGA Tour's Buick Challenge. Fall scenery is unbelievable.* ★★★★

ROBERT TRENT JONES GOLF TRAIL AT CAMBRIAN RIDGE GOLF CLUB. Facility Holes: 27. Opened: 1993. Architect: Robert Trent Jones. Green Fee: $35/$57. Cart Fee: $15 per person. Discounts: Juniors. Walking: Unrestricted walking. Season: Year-round. High: Feb.–May. Tee Times: Call 7 days in advance. Notes: Metal spikes, range (grass). ✉ 101 Sunbelt Pkwy., Greenville 36037, 40 mi from Montgomery ☎ 334/382–9787 or 800/949–4444 ⊕ www.rtjgolf.com ▤ AE, D, MC, V.

Canyon/Loblolly. Holes: 18. Yards: 7,297/4,772. Par: 71/71. Course Rating: 74.6/67.8. Slope: 140/126.

Canyon/Sherling. Holes: 18. Yards: 7,424/4,857. Par: 72/72. Course Rating: 75.4/68.1. Slope: 142/127.

Loblolly/Sherling. Holes: 18. Yards: 7,130/4,785. Par: 71/71. Course Rating: 73.9/67.0. Slope: 133/119.

Comments: The three 9s that make up this club are all immaculate. ★ ★ ★ ★ ¹/₂

ROBERT TRENT JONES GOLF TRAIL AT CAPITOL HILL. Facility Holes: 54. Opened: 1999. Discounts: Juniors. Walking: Unrestricted walking. Season: Year-round. High: Feb.–May. Tee Times: Call 120 days in advance. Notes: Range (grass), lodging (90). ✉ 2600 Constitution Ave., Prattville 36066, 10 mi from Montgomery ☎ 334/285–1114 or 800/949–4444 ⊕ www.rtjgolf.com ▤ AE, D, MC, V.

Judge. Holes: 18. Architect: Robert Trent Jones Jr. Yards: 7,794/4,955. Par: 72/72. Course Rating: 77.8/68.3. Slope: 144/121. Green Fee: $45/$67. Cart Fee: $14 per person. UR

Legislator. Holes: 18. Architect: Robert Trent Jones. Yards: 7,323/5,414. Par: 72/72. Course Rating: 74.1/71.5. Slope: 126/119. Green Fee: $35/$57. Cart Fee: $15 per person. *Comments: Ranked 9th in* Golf Digest's *Best New Affordable Courses in 2000. Big greens will give you some interesting putts.* ★ ★ ★ ★ ¹/₂

Senator. Holes: 18. Architect: Robert Trent Jones. Yards: 7,697/5,122. Par: 72/72. Course Rating: 76.6/69.6. Slope: 131/121. Green Fee: $35/$57. Cart Fee: $15 per person. *Comments: A little bit of Scotland 10 mi outside Montgomery.* ★ ★ ★ ★ ¹/₂

ROBERT TRENT JONES GOLF TRAIL AT GRAND NATIONAL GOLF CLUB. Facility Holes: 54. Opened: 1992. Architect: Robert Trent Jones. Discounts: Juniors. Walking: Unrestricted walking. Season: Year-round. Tee Times: Call golf shop. Notes: Range (grass), lodging (129). ✉ 3000 Sunbelt Pkwy., Opelika 36801, 55 mi from Montgomery ☎ 334/749–9042 or 800/949–4444 ⊕ www.rtjgolf.com ▤ AE, D, MC, V.

Lake. Holes: 18. Yards: 7,149/4,910. Par: 72/72. Course Rating: 74.9/68.7. Slope: 138/117. Green Fee: $35/$57. Cart Fee: $15 per person. *Comments: Which course is the class of the Trail? It's a toss-up between the Lake and the Links courses.* ★ ★ ★ ★ ¹/₂

Links. Holes: 18. Yards: 7,311/4,843. Par: 72/72. Course Rating: 74.9/69.6. Slope: 141/113. Green Fee: $35/$57. Cart Fee: $15 per person. *Comments: Ranked 9th in 2001 Best in State.* ★ ★ ★ ★ ¹/₂

Short. Holes: 18. Yards: 3,328/1,715. Par: 54/54. Green Fee: $18. Cart Fee: $10 per person. *Comments: Might be the best 18-hole par-3 course in the country.* ★ ★ ★ ★ ¹/₂

STILL WATERS RESORT. Facility Holes: 36. Green Fee: $53/$58. Cart Fee: Included in green fee. Walking: Unrestricted walking. Season: Year-round. Tee Times: Call 7 days in advance. Notes: Metal spikes, range (grass), lodging (71). ✉ 161 Harbor Dr., Dadeville 36853, 55 mi from Montgomery ☎ 256/825-7021 or 888/797-3767 ⊕ www. stillwaters.com ▤ AE, D, MC, V.

Legend. Holes: 18. Opened: 1972. Architect: George Cobb. Yards: 6,407/5,287. Par: 72/ 72. Course Rating: 70.8/71.1. Slope: 129/126. *Comments: A nice test, but it's tough to compete with the Trail.* ★ ★ ★ ½

Tradition. Holes: 18. Opened: 1997. Architect: Kurt Sandness. Yards: 6,906/5,048. Par: 72/72. Course Rating: 73.5/69.5. Slope: 139/126. *Comments: Despite the name, this one is the newer of the two here.* ★ ★ ★

Where to Stay

🏨 **EMBASSY SUITES HOTEL.** This all-suites high-rise hotel between the city's Civic Center and the old railroad station has some good perks: sprawling rooms that include TVs and phones in the bedrooms as well as the den area, plus kitchenettes. A spectacular atrium lobby filled with plants resembles a tropical rain forest. Glass elevators give you a bird's-eye view. ✉ 300 Tallapoosa St., 36104 ☎ 334/269-5055 ⊟ 334/269-0360 ⊕ www.jqhhotels.com ⇨ 237 suites ⟂ Restaurant, in-room data ports, kitchenettes, microwaves, refrigerators, cable TV, indoor pool, health club, hot tub, sauna, steam room, lounge, laundry service, concierge, business services, meeting rooms, airport shuttle ▤ AE, D, DC, MC, V ❑ BP $-$$.

🏨 **GUESTHOUSE INTERNATIONAL HOTELS AND SUITES.** Elvis Presley once slept here, but you're more likely to run into legislators and businesspeople than rock stars. The Civic Center is two blocks away. The hotel's atrium lobby has a waterfall, palm trees, and wrought-iron sofa sets that help establish a New Orleans theme. ✉ 120 Madison Ave., 36104 ☎ 334/264-2231 or 800/214-8378 ⊟ 334/263-3179 ⊕ www. guesthouseintl.com ⇨ 153 rooms, 19 suites ⟂ Restaurant, in-room data ports, some microwaves, some refrigerators, cable TV, pool, gym, lounge, laundry facilities, business services, meeting rooms, some pets allowed, no-smoking rooms ▤ AE, D, DC, MC, V $.

🏨 **LA QUINTA INN.** This affordable, two-story, adobe-style inn is just off I-85. Decorated in a standard but comfortable way, rooms are done in light earth tones and are outfitted with heavy drapes. ✉ 1280 East Blvd., 36117 ☎ 334/271-1620 ⊟ 334/ 244-7919 ⊕ www.laquinta.com ⇨ 130 rooms ⟂ In-room data ports, cable TV, pool, laundry facilities, some pets allowed ▤ AE, D, DC, MC, V ❑ CP ¢.

🏨 **RED BLUFF COTTAGE.** This bright, cheerful home in the heart of downtown overlooks the Alabama River plain. There's a raised porch that lets you survey the view, and a gazebo on the grounds. Each of the guest rooms—all on the ground floor—is decorated with antique furniture and wall hangings. One has an adjacent children's room. The library has a common TV, movies, and lots of books. ✉ 551 Clay St., Box 1026, 36101 ☎ 334/264-0056 or 800/551-2529 ⊟ 334/263-3054 ⊕ www.redbluffcottage.com ⇨ 4 rooms ⟂ In-room data ports, library, recreation room; no room TVs, no smoking ▤ AE, D, MC, V ❑ BP $.

Where to Eat

✕ **CHRIS' HOT DOGS.** A Montgomery tradition since it began as a simple hot dog stand in 1917, this eatery has booths and an old-fashioned lunch counter with stools. The famous sauce combines chili peppers, onions, and herbs to give the hot dogs a one-of-a-kind flavor. Try the hot dog with "kitchen chili," a thick, hot chili of beans and onions that you eat with a knife and fork. ⊠ 138 Dexter Ave. ☎ 334/265–6850 ⌲ Reservations not accepted ▤ No credit cards ⊘ Closed Sun. ¢.

✕ **CORSINO'S.** Serving Montgomery since 1954, this family-run restaurant is one of the city's most popular. The noontime crowd gathers daily from state government offices and downtown businesses to enjoy the pasta dishes here. You can also choose a savory, foot-long Italian sandwich served on hot, homemade Italian bread, or a hand-tossed New York-style pizza. The restaurant isn't fancy, just comfortable and friendly. ⊠ 911 S. Court St. ☎ 334/263–9752 ⌲ Reservations not accepted ▤ No credit cards ⊘ Closed weekends $–$$.

MARTIN'S RESTAURANT. Martin's—a Montgomery institution since 1940—is plain but comfortable, with friendly servers dishing out generous helpings of home-cooked fresh vegetables, Southern-fried chicken, and delicious panfried catfish. The corn-bread muffins seem to melt in your mouth. ⊠ 1796 Carter Hill Rd. ☎ 334/265–1767 ▤ No credit cards ⊘ Closed Sat. $–$$.

✕ **SAHARA RESTAURANT.** Joe and Mike Deep's Sahara has been one of Montgomery's favorite traditional Southern restaurants since 1952. Linen tablecloths and uniformed servers add to the charm. Fresh snapper, grouper, and scampi are often served broiled, and succulent steaks are grilled over coals. The seafood gumbo is a specialty. ⊠ 511 E. Edgemont Ave. ☎ 334/262–1215 ▤ AE, D, DC, MC, V ⊘ Closed Sun. $$$–$$$$.

✕ **VINTAGE YEAR.** Owner-chef Judy Martin's innovative menu makes this restaurant in the Cloverdale district one of Montgomery's best. She insists on only the freshest snapper, tuna, shrimp, salmon, and other fish, as well as lamb and duck, and prepares them with an assortment of fresh herbs. A couple of standouts include sautéed grouper in a mushroom-dill sauce and beef tenderloin with Portobello mushrooms stuffed with Maytag blue cheese. ⊠ 405 Cloverdale Rd. ☎ 334/264–8463 ⌲ Reservations essential ▤ AE, MC, V ⊘ Closed Sun. and Mon. No lunch $$–$$$$.

Essentials

Getting Here

Birmingham is 150 mi southwest of Atlanta via I–85.

Visitor Information

🛈 **Montgomery Visitors Center** ⊠ 300 Water St., 36104 ☎ 334/262–0013 or 800/240–9452 ⊕ www.visitingmontgomery.com.

Bacon Park Golf Course (27)					$20/$30
Cypress/Live Oak (18)	6,679/5,160	72/72	72.3/69.3	132/113	
Cypress/Magnolia (18)	6,573/4,943	72/72	71.6/68.4	126/109	
Magnolia/Live Oak (18)	6,740/5,309	72/72	72.1/70.5	129/118	
The Club at Savannah Harbor (18)	7,288/5,261	72/72	74.6/70.4	134/117	$85/$115
Henderson Golf Club (18)	6,650/4,788	71/71	72.8/68.3	138/117	$33/$44
Mary Calder Golf Club (9)	2,900/2,502	35/35	69.2/68.0	122/114	$21/$23
Southbridge Golf Club (18)	6,990/5,181	72/72	73.4/69.2	136/118	$26/$49
Wilmington Island Club (18)	6,715/5,191	71/71	72.5/70.7	133/129	$56

SAVANNAH

As cities and towns of all sizes labor to revive and revitalize their historic cores, one has already emerged from that transformation. Savannah's began in 1955, when a group of seven ladies formed the Historic Savannah Foundation to raise enough money to save one of the most impressive of the city's houses. The group persevered and continued on to other buildings, in the end preserving and restoring more than 1,000 buildings within the 2½-square-mile Historic District, the nation's largest.

Once you've done the obligatory tours, pack your clubs into the trunk and try some of Savannah's finest golf courses. A museum piece worthy of its location on the Savannah waterfront is the Wilmington Island Club, a 1920s Donald Ross design that is open for limited public play. Ross also designed (or helped design) the Bacon Park and Mary Calder public courses in town. The best new course is the Club at Savannah Harbor, one of the last projects that Sam Snead consulted on before his death in 2002.

Courses

Golf Digest REVIEWS

BACON PARK GOLF COURSE. Facility Holes: 27. Opened: 1926. Architect: Donald Ross/Ron Kirby/Denis Griffiths. Green Fee: $20/$30. Cart Fee: Included in green fee. Walking: Walking at certain times. Season: Year-round. Tee Times: Call golf shop. ⊠ Shorty Cooper Dr., 31406 ☎ 912/354-2625 ⊕ www.baconparkgolf.com ▭ AE, MC, V.

Cypress/Live Oak. Holes: 18. Yards: 6,679/5,160. Par: 72/72. Course Rating: 72.3/69.3. Slope: 132/113.

Cypress/Magnolia. Holes: 18. Yards: 6,573/4,943. Par: 72/72. Course Rating: 71.6/68.4. Slope: 126/109.

Magnolia/Live Oak. Holes: 18. Yards: 6,740/5,309. Par: 72/72. Course Rating: 72.1/70.5. Slope: 129/118.

Comments: Twenty-seven-holer codesigned by Donald Ross. Mediocre conditioning. ★★

THE CLUB AT SAVANNAH HARBOR. Facility Holes: 18. Opened: 2000. Architect: Bob Cupp/Sam Snead. Yards: 7,288/5,261. Par: 72/72. Course Rating: 74.6/70.4. Slope: 134/117. Green Fee: $85/$115. Cart Fee: Included in green fee. Discounts: Twilight, juniors. Walking: Walking at certain times. Season: Year-round. High: Sept.–May. Tee Times: Call 5 days in advance. Notes: Range (grass), lodging (400). ⊠2 Resort Dr., 31421 ☎912/201-2007 ▤AE, D, DC, MC, V. *Comments: Very playable.* ★★★★

HENDERSON GOLF CLUB. Facility Holes: 18. Opened: 1985. Architect: Mike Young. Yards: 6,650/4,788. Par: 71/71. Course Rating: 72.8/68.3. Slope: 138/117. Green Fee: $33/$44. Cart Fee: Included in green fee. Walking: Walking at certain times. Season: Year-round. Tee Times: Call golf shop. ⊠1 Al Henderson Dr., 31419 ☎912/920-4653 ⊕www.hendersongolfclub.com ▤AE, MC, V. *Comments: Lots of local play.* ★★½

MOVIE GOLF

The Legend of Bagger Vance, about a World War I war hero's mythical match against Bobby Jones and Walter Hagen, was filmed in Savannah.

MARY CALDER GOLF CLUB. Facility Holes: 9. Opened: 1946. Yards: 2,900/2,502. Par: 35/35. Course Rating: 69.2/64.8. Slope: 122/114. Green Fee: $21/$23. Cart Fee: Included in green fee. Walking: Unrestricted walking. Season: Year-round. Tee Times: Call golf shop. ⊠W. Lathrop Ave., West Chatham ☎912/238-7100. *Comments: Semiprivate, but you can get on. UR*

SOUTHBRIDGE GOLF CLUB. Facility Holes: 18. Opened: 1988. Architect: Rees Jones. Yards: 6,990/5,181. Par: 72/72. Course Rating: 73.4/69.2. Slope: 136/118. Green Fee: $26/$49. Cart Fee: Included in green fee. Walking: Mandatory carts. Season: Year-round. Tee Times: Call up to 7 days in advance. ⊠415 Southbridge Blvd., 31405 ☎912/651-5455 ⊕www.southbridgegc.com ▤AE, D, MC, V. *Comments: Good value. UR*

WILMINGTON ISLAND CLUB. Facility Holes: 18. Opened: 1927. Architect: Donald Ross. Yards: 6,715/5,191. Par: 71/71. Course Rating: 72.5/70.7 Slope: 133/129. Green Fee: $56. Cart Fee: Included in green fee. Year-round. Tee Times: Call golf shop. ⊠612 Wilmington Island Rd., 31410 ☎912/897-1615 ▤D, MC, V. *Comments: Recent renovations have made a big difference. UR*

Where to Stay

⌨ **ELIZA THOMPSON HOUSE.** Built by a socially prominent widow around 1847, this lovely Victorian town house is now a long-established B&B. The rooms are lavishly decorated with marble baths and antiques. The walls, painted in deep colors such as forest green or pencil yellow, are a stunning backdrop for the plush bedding and other touches. Complimentary afternoon wine and cheese are served in the parlor or on the patio. The garden courtyard is a good place for reading or just taking time to smell the flowers. ⊠5 W. Jones St., 31401 ☎912/236-3620 or 800/348-9378 ⊟912/238-1920

⊕ www.elizathompsonhouse.com ⤴ 25 rooms ⌂ In-room data ports, cable TV ⊟ MC, V ⦿ BP $$$-$$$$.

⊞ **HYATT REGENCY SAVANNAH.** At this seven-story modern riverfront hotel, the main architectural features are a towering atrium and glass elevators. Rooms have modern furnishings, marble baths, and balconies overlooking either the atrium or the Savannah River. MD's Lounge is ideal for having a drink while you watch the river traffic drift by. Windows, the hotel's restaurant, serves a great Sunday buffet. ⊠ 2 W. Bay St., 31401 ☎ 912/238-1234 or 800/233-1234 ⊟ 912/944-3673 ⊕ www.savannah-online.com/hyatt ⤴ 325 rooms, 22 suites ⌂ Restaurant, indoor pool, health club, bar, lounge, business services, meeting rooms ⊟ AE, D, MC, V $$$$.

⊞ **KEHOE HOUSE.** A Victorian from the 1890s, the Kehoe has brass-and-marble chandeliers, a courtyard garden, and a music room. On the main floor a double parlor holds two fireplaces and has 14-foot ceilings that sweep the eye upward. Staying here is like visiting a rich relative: heirlooms grace common areas and every guest room. Rates include access to the Downtown Athletic Club. ⊠ 123 Habersham St., 31401 ☎ 912/232-1020 or 800/820-1020 ⊟ 912/231-0208 ⊕ www.kehoehouse.com ⤴ 13 rooms, 2 suites ⌂ Internet, meeting rooms ⊟ AE, D, DC, MC, V ⦿ BP $$$-$$$$.

⊞ **MAGNOLIA PLACE INN.** Looking out directly across the large Forsyth Park, this 1878 inn commands an impressive view. Inside are regal antiques, prints, and porcelain from around the world. You could imagine that one of Savannah's wealthy old cotton merchants occupied such a mansion, with its expansive verandas, lush terraces, and soaring ceilings. Many rooms have Jacuzzis and fireplaces. ⊠ 503 Whitaker St., 31401 ☎ 912/236-7674 or 800/238-7674 ⊟ 912/231-1218 ⊕ www.magnoliaplaceinn.com ⤴ 13 rooms, 3 suites, 2 town houses ⌂ Some in-room hot tubs, in-room VCRs, Internet ⊟ AE, MC, V ⦿ BP $$$-$$$$.

Where to Eat

✕ **BELFORD'S STEAK AND SEAFOOD.** In the heart of the City Market district of restaurants and shops, Belford's is great for Sunday brunch, when so many downtown places are closed. A complimentary glass of sparkling wine arrives at your table when you place your order. Brunch entrées include egg dishes, such as smoked salmon Florentine and crab frittatas. The lunch and dinner menus also focus on seafood, including grouper with Georgia pecans and Low-Country shrimp and grits. ⊠ 315 W. St. Julian St. ☎ 912/233-2626 ⊟ AE, D, DC, MC, V $$-$$$$.

✕ **ELIZABETH ON 37TH.** Regional specialties are the hallmark at this acclaimed restaurant, inside a turn-of-the-20th-century mansion with hardwood floors and spacious rooms. Chef Elizabeth Terry's dishes include Maryland crab cakes and a plate of roasted shiitake and oyster mushrooms as well as fried grits with country ham and red-eye gravy. End your meal with a piece of the Savannah cream cake, which is similar to a trifle. ⊠ 105 E. 37th St. ☎ 912/236-5547 ⊕ www.elizabethon37th.com ⌕ Reservations essential ⊟ AE, D, DC, MC, V ⦸ No lunch $$$$.

✕ **JOHNNY HARRIS.** What started as a small roadside stand in 1924 has grown into one of the city's mainstays, with a menu that includes steaks, fried chicken, seafood, and meats spiced with the restaurant's famous tomato-and-mustard sauce. The lamb barbecue is a treat, and the sauces here are so famous that they're available for purchase. There's live music Friday and Saturday night, and dancing on the first Saturday of the month. ⊠1651 E. Victory Dr. ☎912/354-7810 ▤AE, D, DC, MC, V ⊗Closed Sun. $$-$$$.

✗ **THE LADY & SONS.** Proprietor Paula Deen makes sure that no one leaves hungry after attacking her famous buffet. It's stocked for both lunch and dinner with such specials as crispy but moist fried chicken; the best baked spaghetti in the South; green beans cooked with ham and potatoes; tender, sweet creamed corn; and lemonade. ⊠ 102 W. Congress St. ☎912/233-2600 ▤AE, D, MC, V ⊗ No dinner Sun. $$-$$$$.

✗ **NITA'S PLACE.** Juanita Dixon has a reputation for perfectly preparing down-home Southern cooking at this renowned steam-table operation. People flock here for salmon patties, baked chicken, perfectly cooked okra, outstanding squash casserole, and homemade desserts. The fresh vegetables and other side dishes alone are worth the trip, if only for the sheer number (11) to choose from: rutabagas, fried corn, string beans, potato salad, collard greens, sautéed spinach, black-eyed peas, macaroni and cheese, fried sweet potatoes, baked sweet potatoes, and Nita's famous squash casserole. ⊠ 129 E. Broughton St. ☎912/238-8233 ⌦ Reservations not accepted ▤MC, V ⊗ Closed Sun. No dinner Mon.-Thurs. $-$$.

✗ **OLDE PINK HOUSE.** This brick Georgian mansion was built in 1771 for James Habersham, one of the wealthiest Americans of his time. Inside are the original pine floors, Venetian chandeliers, and 18th-century English antiques. The she-crab soup is a light but flavorful version of this Low-Country specialty. Regional ingredients find their way into many of the dishes, including the black grouper, stuffed with blue crab and served with a sauce of Vidalia onions. ⊠23 Abercorn St. ☎912/232-4286 ▤AE, MC, V ⊗ No lunch $$-$$$$.

✗ **17 HUNDRED AND 90.** Chef Deborah Noelk keeps things creative in her kitchen. The restaurant, part of Savannah's oldest inn, is in a rustic structure surrounded by ancient oaks covered with Spanish moss. Entrées include pan-seared veal medallions with artichoke hearts and capers in a lemon butter; roasted half duckling with a port wine-lingonberry sauce; and local shrimp stuffed with scallops and crabmeat. The building has a ghost story to go with dinner, so make sure the waiter fills you in. ⊠307 E. Presidents St. ☎912/231-8888 ▤AE, D, DC, MC, V ⊗ No lunch weekends $$$-$$$$.

Essentials

Getting Here

To get here by car take I-75 south to I-16 east into downtown Savannah, a trip of 250 mi.

Visitor Information

🛈 **Savannah Area Convention & Visitors Bureau** ⊠101 E. Bay St., 31401 ☎912/644-6401 or 877/728-2662 🖷912/944-0468 ⊕ www.savcvb.com.

AROUND
BOSTON

Sugarloaf Golf Club

By Ron Kaspriske, Pam Wright, and Diane Bair

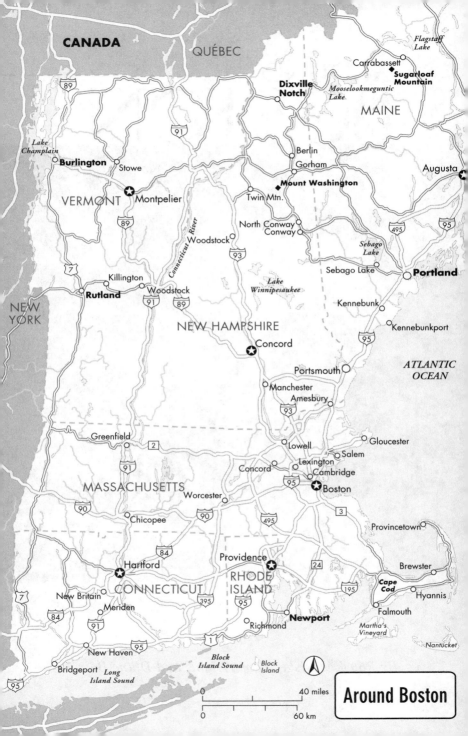

America's founding fathers didn't give much thought to golf when they were planning Boston, so it's understandable that most of the top-quality courses are in the suburbs. If you don't wish to stray far from city center, there's always the adequate William J. Devine Golf Course, built in 1896 and the second-oldest public golf course in the United States. But few other major cities have as much good golf within a four-hour drive of their city center. Whether it's a links-style, seaside, or a mountainous course you want, getting some good golf is almost as easy as pointing your car in any direction and heading out.

To the west and north of Boston are the ski-resort towns of Burlington and Rutland, Vermont, as well the Mount Washington and Dixville Notch areas of New Hampshire. Golf at these destinations is typified by scenic hills and valleys. Fall brings crowds as well as steep room prices, but this time of year is still the best to visit. The fall foliage is unrivaled, making golf courses as well as the roadside part of a vivid spectacle. Summer is also an option—the crisp, cool evenings can be a nice break from Beantown's humidity.

Dixville Notch, the most remote of the golf destinations in this chapter, is 215 mi from Boston's city center, but well worth the drive to reach the Balsams resort, one of the best-kept golf secrets. Rutland, Mount Washington, Dixville Notch, and Sugarloaf can all provide you with as much solitude as you want, but consider Burlington if you want some nightlife to keep you up well past sunset.

If you head to Cape Cod or to Coastal Maine in summer, you'll be driving along with the large crowds heading for the beach and for lobster restaurants. Think about waiting until after Labor Day to make a long weekend to either place. You may get some chilly weather, but green fees and hotel rates typically drop. For Maine, our pick is the Samoset Resort and Golf Club in Rockport, some 190 mi north of Boston. Known by some as the "Pebble Beach of the East," it's a real gem. In Cape Cod, the 36-hole Pinehills Golf Club doesn't have ocean views but is a terrific facility, with courses that are in great shape.

Although the variety is great in Maine and in Cape Cod, the weather isn't. You can expect to be able to play from May to October, but hearty players have been known to don ski caps and take to the links in April and November.

Basin Harbor Club (18)	6,511/5,700	72/72	70.7/67.1	120/113	$37/$47
Cedar Knoll Country Club (27)					$27
North/South (18)	5,863/4,646	71/70	68.5/68.0	119/108	
North/West (18)	6,541/5,360	72/72	70.8/69.5	124/112	
South/West (18)	6,072/4,924	71/70	67.7/67.1	117/109	
Kwiniaska Golf Club (18)	6,848/5,246	72/72	72.7/70.6	129/115	$20/$35
Stowe Country Club (18)	6,206/5,346	72/74	70.4/66.5	122/115	$30/$75
Sugarbush Golf Club (18)	6,524/5,187	72/72	71.7/70.4	128/119	$54
Vermont National Country Club (18)	7,035/4,966	72/72	73.6/69.2	133/116	$120
Williston Golf Club (18)	5,725/4,753	69/72	68.0/64.1	118/106	$23

BURLINGTON, VT

Burlington's combination of good golf and other diversions around town has fueled its popularity as a golf destination. Granted, the golf season here is far too short. The locals will tell you that golfers can tee it up from April to the end of October and that's not a lie. However, if you want to play in April or October, be prepared to grip the club with your warmest mittens. If you come here from June to September, though, you'll have some outstanding weather, not to mention great views of gorgeous Lake Champlain and the Adirondack and Green mountains.

Vermont National Country Club should be at the top of your list of courses to play. The five-year-old course was built on rolling farmland and designed by Jack Nicklaus and son Jackie, who was on the bag when a then-46-year-old Jack won the Masters in 1986.

Lodging options are plentiful for golfers, especially if you want to take advantage of the nearby ski resorts like Stowe and Sugarbush or stay at Lake Champlain in Burlington.

Courses

Golf Digest REVIEWS

BASIN HARBOR CLUB. Facility Holes: 18. Opened: 1927. Architect: Alex Campbell/ William F. Mitchell/Geoffrey S. Cornish. Yards: 6,511/5,700. Par: 72/72. Course Rating: 70.7/67.1. Slope: 120/113. Green Fee: $37/$47. Cart Fee: $35 per cart. Discounts: Twilight, juniors. Walking: Unrestricted walking. Season: May–Oct. Tee Times: Call 3 days in advance. Notes: Range (grass), lodging (136). ✉ 4800 Basin Harbor Rd., Vergennes 05491, 30 mi from Burlington ☎ 802/475-2309 ⊕ www.basinharbor.com ▤ MC, V.

TEE TOTALING

African-American golfers were not allowed to compete on the PGA Tour until 1961. Nowadays, with Tiger Woods leading the charge, the sport has become far more inclusive than ever before. Early golf history does show that another black golfer, Dr. George F. Grant of Boston, played an integral role in the development of the sport: in 1899 he invented the wooden golf tee. Until that time, pinching small piles of dirt into a peaked platform was the common method of teeing off. The basic model of Dr. Grant's golf tee is still used today.

Comments: One of the few courses to take advantage of Lake Champlain. The lakeside views are great, but be ready to play in the wind. ★ ★ ★

CEDAR KNOLL COUNTRY CLUB. Facility Holes: 27. Opened: 1994. Architect: Raymond Ayer. Green Fee: $27. Cart Fee: $27/cart. Walking: Unrestricted walking. Season: Apr.–Oct. High: July and Aug. ✉ Hwy. 116, Hinesburg 05461 ☎ 802/482-3186.

North/South. Holes: 18. Yards: 5,863/4,646. Par: 71/70. Course Rating: 68.5/68.0. Slope: 119/108.

North/West. Holes: 18. Yards: 6,541/5,360. Par: 72/72. Course Rating: 70.8/69.5. Slope: 124/112.

South/West. Holes: 18. Yards: 6,072/4,924. Par: 71/70. Course Rating: 67.7/67.1. Slope: 117/109.

Comments: This 27-hole course is short and a pushover for accomplished golfers, but perfect for high handicappers. A fun round. UR

KWINIASKA GOLF CLUB. Facility Holes: 18. Opened: 1964. Architect: Bradford Caldwell. Yards: 6,848/5,246. Par: 72/72. Course Rating: 72.7/70.6. Slope: 129/115. Green Fee: $20/$35. Cart Fee: $24 per cart. Discounts: Twilight. Walking: Unrestricted walking. Season: Apr.–Nov. High: May–Sept. Tee Times: Call 1 day in advance. Notes: Range (grass). ✉ 5531 Spear St., Shelburne 05482, 7 mi from Burlington ☎ 802/985-3672 ⊕ www.kwiniaska.com ☰ MC, V. *Comments: The front 9 is fairly flat, but the back 9 play through hills.* ★ ★ ★

STOWE COUNTRY CLUB. Facility Holes: 18. Opened: 1950. Architect: Walter Barcomb. Yards: 6,206/5,346. Par: 72/74. Course Rating: 70.4/66.5. Slope: 122/115. Green Fee: $30/$75. Cart Fee: $17 per person. Discounts: Weekdays, twilight. Walking: Unrestricted walking. Season: May–Oct. High: July–Sept. Tee Times: Call 30 days in advance. Notes: Range (grass). ✉ 744 Cape Cod Rd., Stowe 05672, 37 mi from Burlington ☎ 802/253-4893 or 800/253-4754 ⊕ www.stowe.com ☰ AE, D, DC, MC, V. *Comments: Area is known for skiing, but the mountains are perfect for the short but scenic layout. Although the course opened over 50 years ago, the layout is still challenging for mid-to-high handicappers.* ★ ★ ★ ¹/₂

SUGARBUSH GOLF CLUB. Facility Holes: 18. Opened: 1962. Architect: Robert Trent Jones. Yards: 6,524/5,187. Par: 72/72. Course Rating: 71.7/70.4. Slope: 128/119. Green Fee: $54. Cart Fee: $15 per person. Discounts: Twilight, juniors. Walking: Unrestricted walking. Season: May–Oct. High: July–Sept. Tee Times: Call 3 days in advance. Notes: Range (grass), lodging (150). ⊠ Golf Course Rd., Warren 05674, 45 mi from Burlington ☎ 802/583-6725 or 800/537-8427 ⊕ www.sugarbush.com ▤ AE, D, MC, V. *Comments: Another ski area that needed to find a way to make money in summer. The layout is fun and very challenging.* ★ ★ ★

VERMONT NATIONAL COUNTRY CLUB. Facility Holes: 18. Opened: 1999. Architect: Jack Nicklaus/Jack Nicklaus Jr. Yards: 7,035/4,966. Par: 72/72. Course Rating: 73.6/69.2. Slope: 133/116. Green Fee: $120. Cart Fee: Included in green fee. Walking: Unrestricted walking. Tee Times: Call up to 3 days in advance. ⊠ 1227 Dorset St., South Burlington 05403 ☎ 802/864-7770 ⊕ www.vnccgolf.com ▤ AE, D, DC, MC, V. *Comments: Great mountain views. Many forced carries. Pricey, but the club has great service and is always well maintained.* ★ ★ ★ ★

WILLISTON GOLF CLUB. Facility Holes: 18. Opened: 1926. Architect: Ben Murray. Yards: 5,725/4,753. Par: 69/72. Course Rating: 68.0/64.1. Slope: 118/106. Green Fee: $23. Cart Fee: $25 per cart. Discounts: Twilight. Walking: Unrestricted walking. Season: May–Nov. Tee Times: Call 4 days in advance. ⊠ 424 Golf Course Rd., Williston 05495, 7 mi from Burlington ☎ 802/878-3747 ▤ MC, V. *Comments: Tight but very short course. Older design is interesting to play, but there's no need for a driver.* ★ ★ ★

Where to Stay

⊡ INN AT THE ROUND BARN FARM. A Shaker-style round barn (one of only eight in the state) dominates the farm's 215 acres. The inn's guest rooms, inside an 1806 farmhouse, are sumptuous, with eyelet-trimmed sheets, elaborate four-poster beds, rich-color wallpapers, and brass wall lamps for easy bedtime reading. Seven have fireplaces, four have whirlpool tubs, and five have steam showers. ⊠ 1661 E. Warren Rd., Waitsfield 05673 ☎ 802/496-2276 🖶 802/496-8832 ⊕ www.innatroundbarn.com ↪ 10 rooms, 2 suites ♿ Some in-room hot tubs, indoor pool, bicycles, billiards, hiking, horseback riding, cross-country skiing, library, recreation room; no room phones; no room TVs, no kids under 15, no smoking ▤ AE, D, MC, V ❚◯❙ BP $$–$$$$.

⊡ INN AT SHELBURNE FARMS. The turn-of-the-20th-century Tudor-style inn overlooks Lake Champlain, the distant Adirondacks, and the sea of pastures that make up this 1,400-acre working farm. Rooms are individually styled with early-1900s reproduction wallpapers and antique furnishings. Some rooms come with fireplaces, and all have pretty views of meadows, gardens, or Lake Champlain. ⊠ 1611 Harbor Rd., Shelburne 05482 ☎ 802/985-8498 🖶 802/985-8123 ⊕ www.shelburnefarms.org ↪ 24 rooms, 17 with bath; 2 cottages ♿ Restaurant, tennis court, lake, boating, fishing, billiards, croquet, hiking, shop; no room phones, no room TVs, no smoking ▤ AE, D, DC, MC, V ☺ Closed mid-Oct.–mid-May $–$$$$.

⊡ STOWEFLAKE MOUNTAIN RESORT AND SPA. Accommodations start at comfortable country-inn rooms and go up to luxurious spots with fireplaces, wet bars, refrigerators, and balconies at this resort with scenic mountain views. One- to three-bedroom fully equipped town houses are also available. The on-site boutique spa is an added bonus. ⊠ 1746 Mountain Rd., Stowe 05672 ☎ 802/253-7355 🖶 802/253-6858

⊕ www.stoweflake.com ⇌ 94 rooms, 30 town houses ⑤ 2 restaurants, some in-room data ports, some in-room hot tubs, some kitchenettes, some microwaves, cable TV, driving range, putting green, 2 tennis courts, pool, sauna, spa, bicycles, sleigh rides, recreation room, business services, meeting rooms, no-smoking rooms ⊟ AE, D, DC, MC, V ⑩ BP $$$–$$$$.

⊡ **SUGARBUSH INN.** If you plan to golf the Robert Trent Jones golf course at Sugarbush, this casual country inn is on-property. Rooms are cozily furnished in country prints and reproduction antiques. The dark-paneled library or the sitting room with a fireplace are good places to relax. Golf packages are available. ⊠ 2405 Sugarbush Access Rd., Warren 05674 ☎ 802/583–6100 or 800/537–8427 ⊕ www.sugarbush.com ⇌ 44 rooms ⑤ 2 restaurants, cable TV, health club, library, concierge; no-smoking rooms ⊟ AE, MC, V ⑩ CP $$.

⊡ **TOPNOTCH AT STOWE RESORT AND SPA.** One of the state's poshest resorts occupies 120 acres overlooking Mt. Mansfield. Floor-to-ceiling windows, a freestanding circular stone fireplace, and cathedral ceilings distinguish the lobby. Country-decorated rooms have thick carpeting and accents such as painted barn-board walls or Italian prints. The large European spa provides 20 massage-treatment rooms and fitness programs. ⊠ 4000 Mountain Rd., Stowe 05672 ☎ 802/253–8585 or 800/451–8686 ⌨ 802/253–9263 ⊕ www.topnotch-resort.com ⇌ 77 rooms, 13 suites, 30 town houses ⑤ 2 restaurants, room service, cable TV, 13 tennis courts (4 indoor), 2 pools (1 indoor), fitness classes, health club, massage, sauna, spa, horseback riding, cross-country skiing, sleigh rides, bar, recreation room, some pets allowed, no-smoking rooms ⊟ AE, D, DC, MC, V ⑩ BP $$$–$$$$.

⊡ **VILLAGE GREEN AT STOWE.** Hills, greens, and fairways surround this 40-acre site, the singular place to stay at the Stowe Country Club. Two- and three-bedroom, fully equipped condo units are perfect for families, groups, or those who want space and amenities that include gas fireplaces, full kitchens, living rooms, and two full baths. ⊠ 1003 Cape Cod Rd., Stowe 05672 ☎ 802/253–9705 or 800/451–3297 ⊕ www.vgasstowe.com ⇌ 16 3-bedroom units, 45 2-bedroom units ⑤ Kitchens, cable TV, tennis courts, indoor pool, sauna, spa, recreation room ⊟ AE, D, DC, MC, V $$$–$$$$.

Where to Eat

✗ **COMMON MAN.** Twin fillets of rainbow trout and grilled salmon share the menu with French classics such as braised rabbit, *entrecôte maison* (sirloin steak with an herb-and-garlic butter sauce), rack of lamb, and roast duck. The restaurant, a local institution since 1972, is housed in a mid-1800s barn with hand-hewn rafters and crystal chandeliers. Dinner is served by candlelight. ⊠ 3209 German Flats Rd., Warren ☎ 802/583–2800 ⊟ AE, D, MC, V ⊗ Closed Mon. mid-Apr.–mid-Dec. No lunch $$–$$$.

✗ **FIVE SPICE CAFE.** Choose from specialities like the Vietnamese steak, spicy northern Burmese chicken, or the house deep-fried, brandy-flamed red snapper at this inventive Asian eatery. The dim sum Sunday brunch has more than 50 dishes. Make reservations, or expect to wait for a table; this small and casual eatery is nearly always packed. ⊠ 175 Church St. ☎ 802/864–4045 ⊟ MC, V $–$$$.

✗ **MIGUEL'S STOWE AWAY.** Miguel's has all the Tex-Mex standards along with tasty surprises such as snow crab enchiladas, braised pork, and sirloin marinated in lime, garlic, cilantro, and adobo. The cozy front room has a pool table (no quarters required) and a bar stocked with frosty Corona beer. Dine alfresco on a garden patio surrounded by flowering yucca plants and summer perennials. ⊠ 3148 Mountain Rd., Stowe ☎ 802/ 253-8900 or 800/245-1240 ☰ AE, D, MC, V ⊗ No lunch $$-$$$$.

Essentials

Getting Here

To get to Burlington, take I-93 north from Boston 65 mi to I-89 north. Continue on I-89 north for 150 mi to Burlington exits 13 and 14. It's about a 4-hour drive from Boston.

To get to the Sugarbush area, take I-93 north from Boston 65 mi to I-89, then 120 mi north to Vermont exit 9 (Middlesex). Down the ramp, make a left onto Route 2 east. Follow Route 2 east about 2 mi to Route 100B. Turn right on Route 100B; follow it south for 15 mi to Waitsfield and 18 mi to Warren. It's about a 3-hour drive from Boston.

To get to Stowe, take I-93 north from Boston 65 mi to I-89 north. Follow I-89 north for 125 mi to Vermont exit 10. Turn right off the exit onto Route 100 north for 10 mi to Stowe. It's about a 3½-hour drive from Boston.

Visitor Information

🛈 **Lake Champlain Regional Chamber of Commerce** ⊠ 60 Main St., 05401 ☎ 802/863-3489 ⊕ www.vermont.org. **Stowe Visitor Information** ⊠ 51 Main St. ⌂ Box 1320, Stowe 05672 ☎ 802/253-7321 or 877/467-8693 ⊕ www.gostowe.com. **Sugarbush Chamber of Commerce** ⊠ General Wait House, 4061 Main St., Rte. 100 ⌂ Box 173, Waitsfield 05673 ☎ 802/496-3409 or 800/828-4748 ⊕ www.sugarbushchamber.org.

CAPE COD

The stereotypical Cape Cod visit is one made up of whale-watching and ice cream, summer league baseball games, and all the seafood you'd care to eat. It would seem that golf doesn't fit into the equation, but that's simply not the case. Golf has become an established member of this peninsula region that lies one hour southeast of Boston. The 70-mi-long arm stretches into the Atlantic Ocean and is overrun with beachgoers in the summer—making for lots of traffic jams and crowded restaurants. We suggest traveling to the Cape after the last beach chair has been repacked into the back of the station wagon. Fall is the perfect time to play here—not just for the solitude but also for a peek at New England's famous fall foliage.

Course	Yards	Par	Course Rating	Slope	Green Fee
Blue Rock Golf Course (18)	3,000/2,200	54/54	56.4/55.8	83/80	$25/$42
Cape Cod National Golf Course (18)	6,954/5,047	72/72	73.6/70.8	129/123	$105
Captains Golf Course (36)					$35/$60
Port (18)	6,724/5,282	72/72	72.1/70.5	131/119	
Starboard (18)	6,776/5,359	72/72	71.5/70.6	122/118	
Farm Neck Golf Club (18)	6,815/4,987	72/72	72.8/64.3	135/118	$50/$135
Highland Golf Links (9)	5,299/4,782	70/74	65.0/67.4	103/107	$32/$40
New Seabury Country Club (36)					
Ocean (18)	7,140/5,731	72/72	75.8/74.0	133/129	$56/$150
Dunes (18)	6,340/4,748	70/70	71.0/67.8	120/114	$71
Olde Barnstable Fairgrounds Golf Course (18)	6,503/5,162	71/71	70.7/69.2	123/118	$40/$60
Pinehills Golf Club (36)					$75/$95
Jones (18)	7,175/5,380	72/72	73.8/71.2	135/125	
Nicklaus (18)	7,243/5,185	72/72			

Be sure to see all of the Cape by traveling U.S. Hwy. 6 to the tip in Provincetown. And, while you're out there, stop at nearby Highland Golf Links, in the town of North Truro. The linksy, 9-hole relic is the Cape's oldest golf course, dating back to 1892. While it's basic golf at best, it's still charming.

On the way down from Boston, Pinehills Golf Club, just before the Cape, should be your first stop. The 36-hole facility has full-fledged, tournament-caliber courses by Rees Jones and Jack Nicklaus Jr.

Courses

Golf Digest REVIEWS

BLUE ROCK GOLF COURSE. Facility Holes: 18. Opened: 1962. Architect: Geoffrey S. Cornish. Yards: 3,000/2,200. Par: 54/54. Course Rating: 56.4/55.8. Slope: 83/80. Green Fee: $25/$42. Cart Fee: $5 per cart. Discounts: Twilight, juniors. Walking: Unrestricted walking. Season: Year-round. High: June–Oct. Tee Times: Call golf shop. Notes: Range (grass), lodging (49). ⊠ 48 Todd Rd., South Yarmouth 02664, 70 mi from Boston ☎ 508/ 398-9295 or 800/237-8887 ▤ MC, V. *Comments: Par-3 course lined with pines and oaks. There is one 255-yard hole, but this is basically a very well-groomed irons-only course.* ★ ★ ★ ★

CAPE COD NATIONAL GOLF COURSE. Facility Holes: 18. Architect: Brian Silva. Yards: 6,954/5,047. Par: 72/72. Course Rating: 73.6/70.8. Slope: 129/123. Green Fee: $105. Cart Fee: $20 per person. ⊠ 173 Orleans Rd., Rte. 28, Pleasant Bay, Chatham 02633 ☎ 508/ 432-5400 ⊕ www.wequassett.com ▤ AE, D, DC, MC, V. *Comments: The neighboring Wequassett Inn vies with New Seabury Country Club as the best place for golfers to stay* *while visiting. Glacially formed mounds, ridges, and hollows mark Cape Cod National. There are a lot of blind shots and punch-bowl greens. Open to resort guests only.* UR

CAPTAINS GOLF COURSE. Facility Holes: 36. Opened: 1999. Architect: Geoffrey S. Cornish/Brian Silva. Green Fee: $35/$60. Cart Fee: $30 per cart. Discounts: Weekdays, twilight, juniors. Walking: Unrestricted walking. Season: Year-round. High: June–Oct. Tee Times: Call 5 days in advance. Notes: Range (grass). ⊠ 1000 Freeman's Way, Brewster 02631, 100 mi from Boston ☎ 508/896-1716 or 877/843-9081 ⊕ www.captainsgolfcourse.com ⊟ MC, V.

Port. Holes: 18. Yards: 6,724/5,282. Par: 72/72. Course Rating: 72.1/70.5. Slope: 131/119. *Comments: Don't expect many waterside holes. Some hills. Architect Brian Silva broke up the original 18 at Captains and added 18 more holes in 1999.* ★ ★ ★ ★

Starboard. Holes: 18. Yards: 6,776/5,359. Par: 72/72. Course Rating: 71.5/70.6. Slope: 122/118. *Comments: Tougher than the Port, but no water. Most of the holes were part of the original 18.* ★ ★ ★ ★

FARM NECK GOLF CLUB. Facility Holes: 18. Opened: 1979. Architect: Geoffrey S. Cornish/William G. Robinson. Yards: 6,815/4,987. Par: 72/72. Course Rating: 72.8/64.3. Slope: 135/118. Green Fee: $50/$135. Cart Fee: $13 per person. Discounts: Twilight. Walking: Walking at certain times. Season: Apr.–Dec. Tee Times: Call 2 days in advance. Notes: Range (grass, mat). ⊠ Farm Neck Way, Oak Bluffs 02557, 10 mi from Falmouth ☎ 508/693-3057 ⊟ AE, MC, V. *Comments: If you venture off the Cape to nearby Martha's Vineyard, this course is where you want to play. Framed by scrub oaks and sea pines. New back 9 have a lot of water for you to contend with.* ★ ★ ★ ★ ¹/₂

HIGHLAND GOLF LINKS. Facility Holes: 9. Opened: 1892. Architect: Isiah Small. Yards: 5,299/4,782. Par: 70/74. Course Rating: 65.0/67.4. Slope: 103/107. Green Fee: $32/$40. Cart Fee: $24 per cart. Walking: Unrestricted walking. Season: Apr.–Dec. High: July–Oct. Tee Times: Call golf shop. ⊠ 10 Lighthouse Rd., North Truro 02652, 45 mi from Hyannis ☎ 508/487-9201 ⊟ MC, V. *Comments: Views of the Atlantic and the Highland Lighthouse are outstanding, but don't come here expecting much from the golf course.* ★ ★ ★ ¹/₂

NEW SEABURY COUNTRY CLUB. Facility Holes: 36. Opened: 1962. Architect: William F. Mitchell. Cart Fee: Included in green fee. Season: Year-round. Tee Times: Call golf shop. Notes: Range (grass, mat), lodging (100). ⊠ Shore Dr. W, Mashpee 02649, 15 mi from Hyannis ☎ 508/539-8322 ⊕ www.newseabury.com ⊟ AE, MC, V.

Ocean. Holes: 18. Yards: 7,140/5,731. Par: 72/72. Course Rating: 75.8/74.0. Slope: 133/129. Green Fee: $56/$150. *Comments: Holes along the water on the back 9, like the 12th, are memorable. Linksy feel with marshland and high fescue guarding the fairways.* ★ ★ ★ ★ ¹/₂

Dunes. Holes: 18. Yards: 6,340/4,748. Par: 70/70. Course Rating: 71.0/67.8. Slope: 120/114. Green Fee: $71. *Comments: Renovations added 300 yards to the course, extending it beyond 6,000 yards. It's target golf, but it's fun.* ★ ★ ★ ★

OLDE BARNSTABLE FAIRGROUNDS GOLF COURSE. Facility Holes: 18. Opened: 1992. Architect: Geoffrey S. Cornish/Brian Silva/Mark Mungeam. Yards: 6,503/5,162. Par: 71/71. Course Rating: 70.7/69.2. Slope: 123/118. Green Fee: $40/$60. Cart Fee: $30 per cart. Discounts: Weekdays, twilight. Walking: Unrestricted walking. Season: Year-round. Tee Times: Call 7 days in advance. Notes: Range (mat). ⊠ Rte. 149, Marstons Mills

02648, 5 mi from Hyannis ☎508/420–1141 ▤MC, V. *Comments: A good value for the price. Parkland-style course in decent shape.* ★★★★

PINEHILLS GOLF CLUB. Facility Holes: 36. Green Fee: $75/$95. Cart Fee: Included in green fee. Discounts: Weekdays, twilight. Walking: Unrestricted walking. Season: Apr.–Dec. Tee Times: Call 7 days in advance. Notes: Range (grass). ✉54 Clubhouse Rd., Plymouth 02360, 45 mi from Boston ☎508/209-3000 ⊕ www.pinehillsgolf.com ▤AE, MC, V.

Jones. Holes: 18. Opened: 2001. Architect: Rees Jones. Yards: 7,175/5,380. Par: 72/72. Course Rating: 73.8/71.2. Slope: 135/125. *Comments: Built on rolling terrain. The best hole is the 15th, a par-5 with an elevated view of the entire course.* UR

Nicklaus. Holes: 18. Opened: 2002. Architect: Jack Nicklaus. Yards: 7,243/5,185. Par: 72/72. *Comments: The longest course in the Cape Cod area.* UR

Where to Stay

▥ CAPTAIN FREEMAN INN. The opulent details at this splendid 1866 Victorian include a marble fireplace, herringbone-inlay flooring, ornate Italian ceiling medallions, and 12-foot ceilings. Guest rooms have hardwood floors, antiques, and eyelet spreads. The eight "luxury rooms" truly deserve the name. ✉ 15 Breakwater Rd., Brewster 02631 ☎508/896-7481 or 800/843-4664 ᠁508/896-5618 ⊕ www.captainfreemaninn.com ⇩ 12 rooms ⚇ Dining room, cable TV, in-room VCRs, pool, beach, bicycles, badminton, croquet; no kids under 10, no smoking ▤MC, V ⓄⒾBP $$–$$$$.

▥ COUNTRY LAKE. This family-oriented lakefront lodge is on 3 acres of landscaped grounds and about 3 mi from downtown Hyannis. A private dock has rowboats. Some efficiencies are available. Kids under 13 stay free. ✉1545 Iyanough Rd., Rte. 132, Hyannis 02601 ☎508/362-6455 ⊕ www.sunsol.com/countrylake ⇩ 20 rooms ⚇ Picnic area, some kitchenettes, cable TV, pool, dock, boating, fishing library, no-smoking rooms ▤AE, D, MC, V ⓄClosed Dec.–Mar. ¢–$.

▥ HYANNIS INN MOTEL. The second-oldest motel in Hyannis was built by the current owner's grandfather and retains a casual, family-friendly atmosphere. The motel is set back from the road with a manicured lawn in front and pink roses growing along the white rail fence. The main building served as press headquarters during John F. Kennedy's presidential campaign; there's also a 1981 wing. ✉473 Main St., Hyannis 02601 ☎508/775-0255 or 800/922-8993 ᠁508/771-0456 ⊕ www.hyannisinn.com ⇩77 rooms ⚇ Restaurant, in-room data ports, some in-room hot tubs, some refrigerators, cable TV, indoor pool, 2 saunas, lounge, no-smoking rooms ▤AE, D, MC, V ⓄClosed Dec. and Jan. ¢–$$.

▥ NEW SEABURY RESORT AND CONFERENCE CENTER. This self-contained resort community on a 2,000-acre point surrounded by Nantucket Sound has one- and two-bedroom furnished apartments in 13 clustered villages. The resort's golf courses are open to the public from September to May. From late June through August a three-night stay is required, and a two-night stay is mandatory throughout the rest of the year. ✉Rock Landing Rd. ⓓBox 549, New Seabury 02649 ☎508/477-9400 or 800/999-

9033 🚗 508/477-9790 🌐 www.newseabury.com 🛏 140 1- and 2-bedroom units ♿ 2 restaurants, kitchens, 2 18-hole golf courses, 16 tennis courts, 2 pools, health club, beach, boating, bicycles, shops, no-smoking rooms ➟ AE, DC, MC, V $$$$.

🌊 OCEAN EDGE RESORT AND GOLF CLUB. Sweeping water views, extensive grounds, and top-notch amenities including tennis and golf draw vacationers to this 400-acre Cape Cod resort. The spacious rooms are furnished with light woods, glossy white trim work, and designer quilts. Rent a villa for extra space. ✉ 2907 Rte. 6A, Brewster 02631 ☎ 508/896-9000 or 800/343-6074 🚗 508/896-9123 🌐 www. oceanedge.com 🛏 90 rooms, 2 suites, 177 suites ♿ 3 restaurants, room service, in-room data ports, some microwaves, cable TV, driving range, 18-hole golf course, putting green, 9 tennis courts, pro shop, 6 pools (2 indoor), gym, hot tub, beach, bicycles, bar, children's programs (ages 4–12), playground, business services, airport shuttle, no-smoking rooms ➟ AE, D, DC, MC, V 🍴 MAP $$$$.

🌊 WEQUASSETT INN RESORT & GOLF CLUB. Rooms here are in 20 Cape-style cottages and an attractive hotel complex. The properly as a whole lies on 22 acres of woods and hugs Pleasant Bay and the Atlantic Ocean. Gracious service, sweeping water-front views, luxurious dining, and plenty of sunning and sports are among the draws. Spacious rooms have country pine furniture and such homey touches as handmade quilts and duck decoys. The golf privileges are at the Cape Cod National Golf Course. ✉ 173 Orleans Rd., Rte. 28, Pleasant Bay, Chatham 02633 ☎ 508/432-5400 or 800/ 225-7125 🚗 508/432-5032 🌐 www.wequassett.com 🛏 102 rooms, 2 suites ♿ 2 restaurants, grill, room service, cable TV, golf privileges, 4 tennis courts, pool, gym, wind-surfing, boating, piano bar, baby-sitting, business services, no-smoking rooms ➟ AE, D, DC, MC, V ⊗ Closed Nov.–Apr. $$–$$$$.

Where to Eat

✗ BAXTER'S FISH N' CHIPS. The delicious fried clams here are served with home-made tartar sauce. Picnic tables let you soak up the sun while you dine on lobster, burg-ers, or delicacies from the excellent raw bar. ✉ 177 Pleasant St., Hyannis ☎ 508/775-4490 ⚓ Reservations not accepted ➟ AE, MC, V ⊗ Closed mid-Oct.–Apr. and weekdays Labor Day–mid-Oct. $–$$.

✗ ROOBAR. A bit of Manhattan on Main Street, RooBar has a dark, sophisticated feel, with good music and a trendy bar scene at night. From the wood-fired oven come piz-zas like scallop and prosciutto with asparagus and goat cheese. Other dishes include the Big-Ass Grilled Shrimp in a red curry-coconut sauce and the fire-roasted chicken rubbed with toasted fennel and cumin seeds. ✉ 586 Main St., Hyannis ☎ 508/778-6515 ✉ 285 Main St., Falmouth ☎ 508/548-8600 ⚓ Reservations essential ➟ AE, MC, V $–$$$$.

✗ SPARK FISH. "Spark" refers to a wood-fire grill, which the kitchen uses often. The menu emphasizes simple ingredients—fresh herbs, garlic, and fruit salsas—and lets you taste the flavors of local seafood, quality meats, and good vegetables. The understated interior is as unfussy as the menu. In the off-season, there's comfortable fireside dining. ✉ 2671 Rte. 6A, Brewster ☎ 508/896-1067 ➟ MC, V $$–$$$$.

✗**VINING'S BISTRO.** Chatham's restaurants tend to serve conservative fare, but the cuisine at this bistro is among the most inventive in the area. The wood grill, where the chef employs zesty spices from all over the globe, is the center of attention. The exotic Bangkok fishermen's stew, the spit-roasted Jamaican chicken, and the Portobello mushroom sandwich are among the best dishes. ✉ 595 Main St., Chatham ☎ 508/945-5033 ♨ Reservations not accepted ▭ AE, D, MC, V ⊘ Closed mid-Jan.–Apr. $$$–$$$$.

Essentials

Getting Here

The Cape is 60 mi from Boston. Take I-93 south from Boston to Route 3 south, across the Sagamore Bridge, which becomes U.S. 6, the Cape's main artery. From the Bourne Bridge, you can take Route 28 south to Falmouth and Woods Hole (about 15 mi), or go around the rotary, following the signs to U.S. 6; this will take you to the Lower Cape and central towns more quickly. Summer weekends, avoid arriving in the late afternoon. U.S. 6, Route 6A, and Route 28 are heavily congested eastbound on Friday evening, westbound on Sunday afternoon, and in both directions on summer Saturdays.

Visitor Information

🖪 **Cape Cod Chamber of Commerce** ✉ U.S. 6 and Rte. 132, Hyannis ☎ 508/862-0700 or 888/332-2732 ⊕ www.capecodchamber.org.

COASTAL MAINE (WITH PORTLAND)

More than 20 courses have been built in Maine since the late 1990s. This may not sound all that impressive compared to golf boomtowns like Scottsdale, Arizona, and Myrtle Beach, South Carolina, but let's not forget, we're talking about Maine. Golf is an afterthought here, ranking well behind things like having heat in wintertime and harvesting lobster in summer.

Still, if you hug the coast from the New Hampshire border town of Kittery all the way to Bar Harbor and Arcadia National Park, you can find some high-quality golf. The state's motto is "The Way Life Should Be," and that includes green fees—those under $50 are alive and well in Maine.

Coastal Maine's courses come in many designs, including the sand-and-pines feel at Dunegrass and the hills at the Ledges Golf Club. But don't come here looking for a true links golf experience. Despite the proximity to the Atlantic Ocean, most courses are parkland. That said, if you're looking for windswept

COASTAL MAINE (WITH PORTLAND) COURSES	YARDAGE	PAR	COURSE	SLOPE	GREEN FEE
Cape Arundel Golf Club (18)	5,869/5,134	69/70	67.0/68.6	117/106	$50
Dunegrass Golf Club (18)	6,644/4,920	71/71	71.6/68.0	134/113	$65/$90
Ledges Golf Club (18)	6,981/4,988	72/72	74.0/70.9	137/126	$50/$65
Links at Outlook (18)	6,524/5,025	71/71	70.2/66.0	125/111	$41/$48
Point Sebago Golf & Beach Resort (18)	7,002/4,866	72/72	73.7/68.4	135/117	$37/$57
Sable Oaks Golf Club (18)	6,359/4,786	70/70	71.9/68.0	134/118	$25/$45
Samoset Resort and Golf Club (18)	6,591/5,034	70/72	70.7/71.2	130/125	$68/$125

fairways, Kennebunkport's Cape Arundel Golf Club, more than a century old, might give you a taste of what to expect on a course in Scotland.

As far as where to stay, your best option might be to drive 185 mi from Boston to the Samoset Resort and Golf Club in Rockport, stay and play there, then work your way back down to the coast toward home. With each stop, it becomes more and more strange that so few golfers come to this part of the country.

Courses

Golf Digest REVIEWS

CAPE ARUNDEL GOLF CLUB. Facility Holes: 18. Opened: 1896. Architect: Walter Travis. Yards: 5,869/5,134. Par: 69/70. Course Rating: 67.0/68.6. Slope: 117/106. Green Fee: $50. Cart Fee: $24 per cart. Discounts: Twilight. Walking: Unrestricted walking. Season: Apr.–Nov. High: June–Sept. Tee Times: Call 1 day in advance. ⊠ 19 River Rd., Kennebunkport 04046, 20 mi from Portland ☎ 207/967-3494 ▤ AE, MC, V. *Comments: Framed by the Kennebunk River and intersected by the tidal Bass Creek. Blind shots and small greens make it a tough test, even if it's less than 6,000 yards long.* ★ ★ ★ ½

DUNEGRASS GOLF CLUB. Facility Holes: 18. Opened: 1998. Architect: Dan Maples. Yards: 6,644/4,920. Par: 71/71. Course Rating: 71.6/68.0. Slope: 134/113. Green Fee: $65/$90. Cart Fee: Included in green fee. Discounts: Weekdays. Walking: Mandatory cart. ⊠ 200 Wild Dunes Way, Old Orchard Beach 04064, 12 mi from Portland ☎ 207/934-4513 or 800/521-1029 ⊕ www.dunegrass.com ▤ AE, MC, V. *Comments: Pinehurst in Maine. Huge sand areas and tall pines guard the fairways. Great greens and always in good condition.* ★ ★ ★ ★

LEDGES GOLF CLUB. Facility Holes: 18. Opened: 1998. Architect: William Bradley Booth. Yards: 6,981/4,988. Par: 72/72. Course Rating: 74.0/70.9. Slope: 137/126. Green Fee: $50/$65. Cart Fee: $15 per person. Discounts: Twilight. Walking: Unrestricted walking. Season: Apr.–Dec. Tee Times: Call 7 days in advance. Notes: Range (grass). ⊠ 1 Ledges Dr., York 03909, 15 mi from Portsmouth ☎ 207/351-3000 ⊕ www.ledgesgolf.

com ▤ MC, V. *Comments: One of the state's newest courses. Massive rock outcroppings and huge elevation changes make it very scenic. Several forced carries.* ★ ★ ★ ★

LINKS AT OUTLOOK. Facility Holes: 18. Opened: 2000. Architect: Brian Silva. Yards: 6,524/5,025. Par: 71/71. Course Rating: 70.2/66.0. Slope: 125/111. Green Fee: $41/$48. Cart Fee: $14 per person. Walking: Unrestricted walking. Season: Apr.–Nov. Tee Times: Call up to 7 days in advance. ✉ Rte. 4, South Berwick, ME 03908 ☎ 207/384–4653 ⊕ - www.outlookgolf.com ▤ D, MC, V. *Comments: Built on former farmland, this course has a heathland; look for 11 holes and a tree-lined look on the other 7. The 18th plays toward a New England red barn.* ★ ★ ★

POINT SEBAGO GOLF & BEACH RESORT. Facility Holes: 18. Opened: 1996. Architect: Phil Wogan/George Sargent. Yards: 7,002/4,866. Par: 72/72. Course Rating: 73.7/68.4. Slope: 135/117. Green Fee: $37/$57. Cart Fee: Included in green fee. Discounts: Weekdays, twilight, juniors. Walking: Walking at certain times. Season: May–Nov. High: Aug.–Sept. Tee Times: Call golf shop. Notes: Range (grass, mat), lodging (350). ✉ 261 Point Sebago Rd., Casco 04015, 20 mi from Portland ☎ 207/655–2747 or 800/655–1232 ⊕ www.pointsebago.com ▤ D, MC, V. *Comments: Routed along the shore of Lake Sebago just north of Portland. Built on 300 acres so there's plenty of room to air out the driver. Great diversity in design of holes.* ★ ★ ★ ★

SABLE OAKS GOLF CLUB. Facility Holes: 18. Opened: 1988. Architect: Geoffrey S. Cornish/Brian Silva. Yards: 6,359/4,786. Par: 70/70. Course Rating: 71.9/68.0. Slope: 134/118. Green Fee: $25/$45. Cart Fee: $15 per person. Discounts: Weekdays, guest, twilight. Walking: Unrestricted walking. Season: Apr.–Dec. High: June–Sept. Tee Times: Call 7 days in advance. ✉ 505 Country Club Dr., South Portland 04106, 3 mi from Portland ☎ 207/775–6257 ⊕ www.sableoaks.com ▤ AE, D, DC, MC, V. *Comments: A high handicapper might struggle with the blind shots, but well-groomed fairways and fast greens are a joy for players of all abilities. On this well-thought-out course, players can expect to use every club in their bag.* ★ ★ ★ ★

SAMOSET RESORT AND GOLF CLUB. Facility Holes: 18. Opened: 1978. Architect: Robert Elder. Yards: 6,591/5,034. Par: 70/72. Course Rating: 70.7/71.2. Slope: 130/125. Green Fee: $68/$125. Cart Fee: Included in green fee. Discounts: Twilight, juniors. Walking: Unrestricted walking. Season: Apr.–Nov. High: June–Oct. Tee Times: Call golf shop. Notes: Range (grass, mat), lodging (178). ✉ 220 Warrenton St., Rockport 04856, 80 mi from Portland ☎ 207/594–1431 or 800/341–1650 ⊕ www.samoset.com ▤ AE, D, DC, MC, V. *Comments: Well north of Portland, but worth the trip up the coast. Stay here first and then work your way back down to courses closer to Boston. Set on a spectacular promontory overlooking Penobscot Bay, the course has 7 holes bordering the ocean and 6 others with water views.* ★ ★ ★ ★

Where to Stay

🏨 **BLACK POINT INN.** Toward the tip of the peninsula that juts into the ocean at Prouts Neck stands this stylish, tastefully updated resort, where there are spectacular views of the Maine coast. Rooms, most with ocean views, are available in the main inn and four guest houses; rates include a five-course dinner and breakfast daily. The extensive grounds contain beaches, trails, and gardens. ⊠510 Black Point Rd., Scarborough 04074 ☎207/883-2500 or 800/258-0003 🖷207/883-9976 ⊕www.blackpointinn. com 🖅73 rooms, 12 suites ⚴Restaurant, in-room data ports, cable TV, golf and tennis privileges, 2 pools (1 indoor), gym, hair salon, hot tub, massage, sauna, boating, bicycles, croquet, volleyball, bar, library, Internet, business services; no-smoking rooms ☴AE, D, MC, V †⊙IMAP $$$$.

CAPTAIN LORD MANSION. Of all the mansions in Kennebunkport's historic district that have been converted to inns, this 1812 contender is the most stately and sumptuously appointed. Distinctive architecture, including a suspended elliptical staircase, gas fireplaces in all rooms, and near-museum-quality accoutrements, make the hotel formal but not stuffy. Six rooms have whirlpool tubs. The extravagant suite has two fireplaces, a double whirlpool, a hydro-massage body spa, a TV/VCR and stereo system, and a king-size canopy bed. ⊠Pleasant and Green Sts. ⌂Box 800, Kennebunkport 04046 ☎207/967-3141 🖷207/967-3172 ⊕www.captainlord.com 🖅15 rooms, 1 suite ⚴In-room data ports, in-room hot tubs, Internet, meeting rooms; no room TVs, no kids under 12, no smoking ☴D, MC, V †⊙IBP $$$$.

INN AT ST. JOHN. This gem of a small hotel was built by railroad tycoon John Deering in 1897. Victorian accents flavor the rooms, which have a mix of traditional and antique furnishings—no two are alike. It's an uphill walk to downtown attractions from here. ⊠939 Congress St., Portland 04102 ☎207/773-6481 or 800/636-9127 🖷207/756-7629 ⊕www.innatstjohn.com 🖅37 rooms, 22 with bath ⚴In-room data ports, some microwaves, some refrigerators, cable TV with movies, some pets allowed, no-smoking rooms ☴D, DC, MC, V †⊙ICP ¢–$$$.

INN BY THE SEA. This all-suites inn welcomes dogs as well as families. All the spacious suites include kitchens and overlook the Atlantic, and it's just a short walk down a private boardwalk to sandy Crescent Beach, a popular family spot. Its shingle-style design includes a varied roofline punctuated by turretlike features and gables, balconies, a covered porch supported by columns, an open deck, and big windows. ⊠40 Bowery Beach Rd., Cape Elizabeth 04107, 7 mi south of Portland ☎207/799-3134 or 800/888-4287 🖷207/799-4779 ⊕www.innbythesea.com 🖅25 suites, 18 cottages ⚴Restaurant, in-room data ports, kitchens, microwaves, refrigerators, cable TV, in-room VCRs, tennis court, pool, croquet, lobby lounge, baby-sitting, dry cleaning, Internet, meeting rooms, some pets allowed; no smoking ☴AE, D, MC, V $$$–$$$$.

POINT SEBAGO GOLF & BEACH RESORT. This very casual, bustling, mega-resort on the shores of Sebago Lake is jam-packed with vacationing families throughout summer. There's plenty to do, from boating and fishing, golf, entertainment, and group activities planned from dusk to dawn. Accommodation, which include one- and two-bedroom cottages, two-bedroom homes, mobile park units, and travel trailers, must be rented by the week. ⊠261 Point Sebago Rd., Rte. 302, Casco 04015 ☎207/655-3821 or 800/530-1555 🖷207/655-3371 ⊕www.pointsebago.com 🖅200 units ⚴2 restaurants, snack bar, kitchens, microwaves, refrigerators, cable TV, 18-hole golf course, pro shop, pool, lake, hot tub, beach, dock, boating, marina, waterskiing, fishing, badminton, basketball, boccie, croquet, horseshoes, shuffleboard, softball, volleyball, lounge, nightclub, recreation room, video game room, shops, children's programs (ages 3–20), some pets allowed, no-smoking rooms ☴AE, D, MC, V $$–$$$$.

⊞ RHUMB LINE. Although the rooms are standard motel fare, the facilities set this family-friendly motor lodge apart. It's on the trolley line, making it easy to get around the Kennebunk area. Lobster bakes (extra charge) are held nightly weekends late May through June and daily July and August. ⊠ 41 Turbats Creek Rd. ⌖ Box 3067, Kennebunkport 04046 ☎ 207/967–5457 or 800/337–4862 ⊟ 207/967–4418 ⊕ www. rhumblinemaine.com ⤙ 56 rooms, 3 suites ⟁ Snack bar, refrigerators, cable TV, 3 pools (1 indoor), health club, hot tub, sauna, meeting rooms, no-smoking rooms ⊟ AE, D, MC, V ⥝⊙⥝ CP $–$$$.

⊞ SAMOSET RESORT AND GOLF CLUB. Sweeping views of Penobscot Bay and lush accommodations make this 230-acre resort a favorite retreat for mid-coast Maine travelers. You enter a soaring wood-and-timber lobby, with large chandeliers and fine ocean views. Rooms are furnished with jewel-color fabrics, set against neutral-color walls, with decks or terraces overlooking the ocean or fairways. ⊠ 220 Warrenton St., Rockport 04856 ☎ 207/594–2511 or 800/341–1650 ⊟ 207/594–0048 ⊕ www.samoset.com ⤙ 178 rooms ⟁ Restaurant, café, grill, room service, in-room data ports, cable TV, 18-hole golf course, 4 tennis courts, pro shop, 2 pools (1 indoor), health club, hot tub, massage, sauna, basketball, croquet, shuffleboard, volleyball, children's programs (ages 5–12); no smoking ⊟ AE, D, MC, V $$$$.

Where to Eat

✕ CAPE ARUNDEL INN. In the candlelit dining room, every table has ocean views. The menu changes seasonally, but you can expect dishes like Maine stew with truffle oil and grilled duck breast, marinated in Grand Marnier. ⊠ 208 Ocean Ave., Kennebunkport ☎ 207/967–2125 ⊟ AE, D, MC, V $$$$.

✕ FORE STREET. Two of Maine's best chefs, Sam Hayward and Dana Street, opened this restaurant in a cavernous warehouse on the edge of the Old Port. Every table in the two-level main dining room has a view of the enormous brick oven and hearth and the open kitchen, where creative entrées such as roasted Maine lobster, apple-wood-grilled Atlantic swordfish loin, and cassoulet are prepared. ⊠ 288 Fore St., Portland ☎ 207/775–2717 ⊟ AE, MC, V ⊘ No lunch $$–$$$$.

✕ HUGOS. Chef-owner Rob Evans has turned Hugos, always a popular eatery, into one of the city's best restaurants. The subdued yet elegant dining room is a perfect background for Evans's masterful, creative cuisine. The prix-fixe menu, which may include pistachio-crusted lobster or panfried Deer Isle scallops, changes weekly. ⊠ 88 Middle St., Portland ☎ 207/774–8538 ⊟ AE, MC, V ⊘ Closed Sun. and Mon. No lunch $$$$.

✕ JOSEPH'S BY THE SEA. Big windows frame the ocean beyond the dunes at this fine restaurant, which offers outdoor dining in season. Appetizers might include goat cheese terrine and a lobster-and-potato pancake; try the grilled Tuscan swordfish or seared sea scallops for your main course. ⊠ 55 W. Grand Ave., Old Orchard Beach ☎ 207/934–5044 ⊟ MC, V ⊘ Closed late Dec.–Mar. No lunch $$$–$$$$.

✕ STREET AND CO. Fish and seafood are the specialties here, and you won't find any better or fresher. You enter through the kitchen, with all its wonderful aromas, and dine amid dried herbs and shelves of staples at one of a dozen tables. Their surfaces are copper, so that a skillet of steaming seafood can be placed directly in front of you. Some good choices are lobster diavolo for two, scallops in Pernod and cream, and sole française. A vegetarian dish is the only nonseafood option. ⊠ 33 Wharf St., Portland ☎ 207/775-0887 ⊟ AE, MC, V ⊗ No lunch $$$.

Essentials

Getting Here

Getting to Portland is a straight shot up I-95 north to I-295. Congress Street leads from I-295 into the heart of Portland; the Gateway Garage on High Street, off Congress, is a convenient place to leave your car downtown. North of Portland, U.S. 1 brings you to Freeport's Main Street, which continues on to Brunswick and Bath.

To get to the Cape Arundel and Kennebunk area, take I-95 north to the New Hampshire–Maine border, where the road turns into the Maine Turnpike. Take exit 3, then follow Route 35. To reach southern coastal towns, travel I-95 north to exit 1, then follow Route 1 north. To Old Orchard Beach, travel north I-95 to Maine exit 5. To reach Sebago Lake, take I-95 to the Maine Turnpike, exit 8, then Route 302 west. To the Belgrade Lakes region, take I-95 to the Maine Turnpike, exit 31, then follow Route 27 north.

Visitor Information

⚘ Convention and Visitors Bureau of Greater Portland ⊠ 245 Commercial St., Portland 04101 ☎ 207/772-5800 or 877/833-1374 ⊕ www.visitportland.com. **Old Orchard Beach Chamber of Commerce** ⊠ U.S. 302 ⊘ Box 600, Old Orchard Beach 04064 ☎ 207/934-2500 ⊕ www.oldorchardbeachmaine.com. **Kennebunk and Kennebunkport Chamber of Commerce** ⊠ Box 740, Kennebunk 04043 ☎ 207/967-0857 ⊕ www.oldorchardbeachmaine.com.

DIXVILLE NOTCH, NH & SUGARLOAF RESORT, ME

First, let's make something perfectly clear. The reason you're driving all the way up I-93 and then even farther north up U.S. 3 through New Hampshire is to reach the Balsams, one of the classiest, most satisfying golf resorts in the world. The fact that there are no other golf courses within 40 mi should not sway your decision. The 15,000-acre estate was built in the shadows of "The Notch," a 1,000-foot-tall sheer granite wall. Legendary architect Donald Ross built the course before World War I, but the design still holds up.

The Balsams Grand Resort Hotel (18)	6,804/5,069	72/72	72.8/67.8	130/115	$50/$60
Belgrade Lakes Golf Club (18)	6,653/4,881	71/71	71.6/67.1	142/117	$50/$75
Sugarloaf Golf Club (18)	6,910/5,376	72/72	74.3/73.7	151/136	$53/$110

If you don't mind doing a little more driving, head northeast across the state line for a doubleheader at Maine's Sugarloaf Resort, approximately 80 mi from the Balsams. Although Sugarloaf is a ski resort in winter, don't think that means golf takes a backseat. The course, planned by Robert Trent Jones Jr., perennially grabs *Golf Digest*'s number-one slot for the top course in Maine and is every bit as fulfilling as the Balsams. Sugarloaf Mountain and four more nearby towering peaks provide a backdrop for grueling play on severely undulated greens that have striking changes in elevation.

The best time to visit both courses is between late September and early October, when the autumn colors in this region would make Italian ices look bland.

Although there aren't many other golf options nearby, Belgrade Lakes Golf Club, approximately 40 mi south of Sugarloaf, is the type of course that could make your all-time favorites list. It's ranked No. 2 in the state by *Golf Digest*.

Courses   **Golf** Digest REVIEWS

THE BALSAMS GRAND RESORT HOTEL. Facility Holes: 18. Opened: 1912. Architect: Donald Ross. Yards: 6,804/5,069. Par: 72/72. Course Rating: 72.8/67.8. Slope: 130/115. Green Fee: $50/$60. Cart Fee: $18 per person. Discounts: Twilight. Walking: Unrestricted walking. Season: May–Oct. High: July–Aug. Tee Times: Call 3 days in advance. Notes: Metal spikes, range (grass, mat), lodging (200). ⊠ Rte. 26, Dixville Notch 03576, 110 mi from Manchester ☎ 603/255-4961 ⊕ www.thebalsams.com ⊟ AE, D, MC, V. *Comments: Classic Donald Ross course. The 18th hole climbs 145 feet from tee to green. Don't bother walking this course unless you are a triathlete.* ★ ★ ★ ★

BELGRADE LAKES GOLF CLUB. Facility Holes: 18. Opened: 1998. Architect: Clive Clark. Yards: 6,653/4,881. Par: 71/71. Course Rating: 71.6/67.1. Slope: 142/117. Green Fee: $50/$75. Cart Fee: $32 per cart. Discounts: Twilight, juniors. Walking: Unrestricted walking. Season: May–Nov. Tee Times: Call 7 days in advance. ⊠ West Rd., Belgrade Lakes 04918, 13 mi from Augusta ☎ 207/495-4653 ⊕ www.belgradelakesgolf.com ⊟ AE, MC, V. *Comments: If you're looking for a third course to round out your trip, travel 40 mi south of Sugarloaf and play here. One gorgeous hole after another, built on the side of a small mountain. Massive boulders line many fairways. A strong second to Sugarloaf as Maine's top course.* UR

SUGARLOAF GOLF CLUB. Facility Holes: 18. Opened: 1986. Architect: Robert Trent Jones Jr. Yards: 6,910/5,376. Par: 72/72. Course Rating: 74.3/73.7. Slope: 151/136. Green Fee: $53/$110. Cart Fee: $18 per person. Discounts: Guest, twilight, juniors. Walking: Unrestricted walking. Season: May–Oct. Tee Times: Call golf shop. Notes: Metal spikes, range (grass, mat), lodging (100). ✉ R.R. 1, Box 5000, Carrabassett Valley 04947, 100 mi from Portland ☎ 207/237–2000 or 800/843–5623 🌐 www.sugarloaf.com 💳 AE, D, MC, V. *Comments: Deep in the mountains in Western Maine. Par-3 11th hole has a tee that sits 130 feet above the green. Back 9 cross water five times, and all four par-5s are triple dogleg holes. Slope of 151 makes it a brutal test of golf.* ★★★★½

Where to Stay

THE BALSAMS WILDERNESS. Inside the pine groves of the north woods, this lavish hotel has been rolling out the red carpet since 1866 for families, golf enthusiasts, and skiers. The historic property is on a grand scale, with ballrooms, a massive lobby area, an ornate dining room, sunrooms, a billiards room, and wraparound porches. The individually decorated rooms vary in size but are generally spacious and comfortably furnished; all have mountain views. Inside the resort's 15,000 acres, hiking, biking, golf, and guided nature programs are all at your doorstep. ✉ Rte. 26, Dixville Notch 03576 ☎ 603/255–3400 or 800/255–0600, 800/255–0800 in NH 📠 603/255–4221 🌐 www.thebalsams.com 204 rooms 3 restaurants, some in-room hot tubs, driving range, 18-hole golf course, 6 tennis courts, pool, gym, bicycles, billiards, hiking, bar, library, shops, children's programs (ages 1–12), dry cleaning, laundry service, business services; no smoking 💳 AE, D, MC, V ⊗ Closed late Mar.–mid-May and mid-Oct.–mid-Dec. FAP $$$$.

BETHEL INN AND COUNTRY CLUB. This premier resort is made up of a cluster of four colonial buildings set on 200 acres in the middle of historic Bethel's town square. Accommodations include standard and deluxe rooms, suites, and one- and two-bedroom town houses on the resort's golf course. ✉ 1 Broad St., Bethel 04217 ☎ 207/824–2175 or 800/654–0125 📠 207/824–2233 🌐 www.bethelinn.com 60 rooms in 5 bldgs., 40 suites/town houses Dining room, 2 restaurants, cable TV, some in-room VCRs, driving range, 18-hole golf course, putting green, tennis courts, pool, gym, health club, boating, cross-country skiing, children's programs (ages 4–12; June–Labor Day), bar, business services, some pets allowed, no-smoking rooms; no a/c in some rooms 💳 AE, D, DC, MC, V MAP $$$$.

COLEBROOK COUNTRY CLUB. This family-owned, year-round motel's ground level, outside-entry rooms come with basic amenities. The on-site 18-hole golf course is a plus for duffers. ✉ Rte. 26, R.R. 1, Box 2, Colebrook, NH 03576 ☎ 603/237–5566 🌐 - www.northcountrychamber.org 18 rooms Cable TV, 18-hole golf course, lounge; no-smoking rooms 💳 AE, MC, V ¢–$.

GRAND SUMMIT HOTEL AT SUGARLOAF. Sweeping mountain views await you at the casual hotel, which is actually on the mountain. The spacious rooms are done in soft, warm tones. ✉ 5092 Access Rd., Carrabassett Valley 04947 ☎ 207/237–2000 or 800/843–5623 📠 207/237–2874 🌐 www.sugarloaf.com 120 rooms Restaurant, room service, some minibars, some refrigerators, cable TV, in-room VCRs, 18-hole golf course, pro shop, indoor pool, health club, hot tub, massage, sauna, mountain bikes, hiking, lounge, recreation room, concierge, meeting rooms; no-smoking rooms ▭ AE, D, MC, V $$.

⊞ INNS AT POLAND SPRING. If you're looking for value, you won't find much better than the accommodation/meal packages at this casual, 800-acre resort. There are five lodging options, including rooms in the Maine Inn, a turreted Victorian Inn, the 1902 Roosevelt House, and the motel-style motor court. Cottages are also available. Bring your own soap and towels, and don't forget your swimsuit, tennis racket, and golf clubs. No one-night stays; rooms are available for two-nights (weekends) with three meals; three nights (holiday weekends) with five meals; and five nights (midweek, Sunday-Friday) with 10 meals. ⊠ Rte. 26, Poland Spring 04274 ☎ 207/998-4351 ⊕ www. polandspringinns.com ⇆ 200 rooms ⚿ Restaurant, dining room, some kitchens, some microwaves, some refrigerators, 18-hole golf course, putting green, 2 outdoor tennis courts, pro shop, pool, hiking; no a/c in some rooms, no room phones, no room TVs, no kids under 16 ▭ AE, D, MC, V ⊙ Closed mid-Oct.–late May ¶◎¶ MAP ¢–$.

⊞ PRESSEY HOUSE BED AND BREAKFAST. The all-suites, octagonal 1850s Greek Revival inn on the shores of Messalonskee Lake is on the National Register of Historic Places. Rooms are fully furnished with country antiques and have full kitchens; some are large and suitable for families. Some have fireplaces or private decks overlooking the water. ⊠ 32 Belgrade Rd., Oakland 04963 ☎ 207/465-3500 or 877/773-7738 ⊕ www. presseyhouse.com ⇆ 5 suites ⚿ Dining room, kitchens, cable TV, lake, dock, boating, fishing, ice-skating; no a/c in some rooms, no room phones, no smoking ▭ No credit cards ¶◎¶ BP $–$$.

Where to Eat

✗ THE BALSAMS WILDERNESS. The grand dining room at this resort includes chandeliers, white linens, and uniformed waitstaff. Despite the lavish surroundings, the service is unpretentious and friendly. The menu, which changes daily, employs classic dishes that use fresh ingredients creatively: veal medallions and seared scallops with sun-dried-tomato cream are a couple of examples. A grand buffet is available Saturday evenings. ⊠ Rte. 26, Dixville Notch ☎ 800/255-0600, 800/255-0800 in NH ▭ AE, D, MC, V $$$$.

✗ COLEBROOK HOUSE. This casual, come-as-you-are mainstay eatery dishes up platefuls of favorites, like prime rib, chops, steaks, and chicken dishes. There are surprises, too, like the blackened scallops with fresh pineapple salsa. ⊠ 132 Main St., Colebrook, NH ☎ 603/237-5521 ▭ MC, V $–$$.

✗ INNS AT POLAND SPRING. Bring your appetite to this come-as-you-are, all-you-can-eat breakfast and dinner buffets. Every Tuesday and some weekends, you can add a lobster or two ($6.95 per lobster extra) to the dinner buffet. Comfort food at its best. Melee's Delee restaurant, located at the resort's golf course, serves lunch fare like sandwiches, burgers, and salads. ⊠ Rte. 26, Poland Spring ☎ 207/998-4351 ▭ AE, D, MC, V ⊙ Closed mid-Oct.–late May $.

Essentials

Getting Here

To reach Dixville Notch, take I-93 north to exit 35, then Route 3 north to Colebrook. Route 3 winds through forests and small towns along the way. Then, go east on Route 26 for 11 mi to Dixville Notch. Route 26 slices east-west to and from Colebrook and Errol. It's a winding, dramatic drive through Dixville Notch—worth the trip. It's about 220 mi, about a 4½- to 5-hour drive from Boston to the Balsams Resort in Dixville Notch.

To reach Sugarloaf, take I-95 north into Maine, then I-95 (Maine Turnpike) north to Augusta, exit 31B. Follow Route 27 north through Farmington and Kingfield, straight to Sugarloaf. It's about a 4½-hour drive from Boston.

To travel from the Balsams in Dixville Notch to Sugarloaf, take Route 26 east to Route 16 north into Maine. Route 16 turns into Route 4; follow this to Route 142 north into Kingfield. From Kingfield, follow Route 27 north to Sugarloaf. It's about 80 mi.

Visitor Information

North Country Chamber of Commerce ᗰ Box 1, Colebrook, NH 03576 ☎ 603/237-8939, 800/698-8939 in NH ⊕ www.northcountrychamber.org. **Sugarloaf Area Chamber of Commerce** ✉ 1001 Carriage Rd., Carrabassett Valley 04947 ☎ 207/235-2645 ⊕ www.sugarloafareachamber.org.

MOUNT WASHINGTON, NH

The tallest mountain in New Hampshire serves as a beacon for golf courses and resorts dotted around small towns like North Conway, Woodstock, and Berlin. Golfers heading up I-93 from Boston can get to this region in less than two hours, although it will take nearly three to reach Mount Washington itself. The Mount Washington Hotel & Resort is the perfect home base. The 27-hole facility includes the Mount Washington Golf Course, which was designed by Donald Ross in 1915. If Mount Washington is full, there are still many other hotel options, since most of the golf courses in the area are connected to a hotel.

The prevailing geological features of the area include rolling fairways, gentle streams, and great views of the White Mountains. Many courses are in valleys below the mountains, and these lowland courses, like Jack O'Lantern and Ragged Mountain, tend to play longer than their yardage suggests due to soft, moist conditions. Other courses, like Owl's Nest, are mountainous—walking is more difficult, but it's tough to beat the scenery. If you want to get away from the fast-paced Boston city life, this is the best destination.

Jack O'Lantern Resort (18)	6,003/4,917	70/71	68.6/67.5	117/113	$38/$42
Mount Washington Hotel & Resort (27)					$60/$75
Mount Pleasant (9)	3,215/2,475	35/35	71	122	
Mount Washington (18)	6,638/5,336	71/71	70.1/70.1	123/118	
North Conway Country Club (18)	6,659/5,394	71/71	71.9/70.1	126/118	$35/$55
Owl's Nest Golf Club (18)	6,818/5,296	72/72	74.0/69.8	133/115	$19/$59
Ragged Mountain Golf Club (18)	7,059/4,963	72/72	74.9/71.0	149/125	$39/$59
Wentworth Golf Club (18)	5,5,81/5,087	70/70	66.0/66.2	122/114	$15/$45
White Mountain Country Club (18)	6,428/5,350	71/72	68.9/69.6	115/114	$31/$39

The area doesn't have much in terms of nightlife, but it does have all the peace and quiet you can handle. It's easy to forget life's troubles while standing in a fairway in the middle of the White Mountain National Forest.

Courses

JACK O'LANTERN RESORT. Facility Holes: 18. Opened: 1947. Architect: Robert Keating. Yards: 6,003/4,917. Par: 70/71. Course Rating: 68.6/67.5. Slope: 117/113. Green Fee: $38/$42. Cart Fee: $28 per cart. Discounts: Weekdays, twilight. Walking: Walking at certain times. Season: May–Oct. Tee Times: Call golf shop. Notes: Lodging (65). ⊠ Rte. 3, Box A, Woodstock 03292, 60 mi from Manchester ☎ 603/745-3636 ⊕ www. jackolanternresort.com ⊟ AE, D, MC, V. *Comments: Plays along railroad tracks and the Pemigewasset River. A valley course, with lodging available.* ★ ★ ★ ★

MOUNT WASHINGTON HOTEL & RESORT. Facility Holes: 27. Green Fee: $60/$75. Discounts: Weekdays, twilight. Walking: Unrestricted walking. Season: May–Nov. Tee Times: Call 7 days in advance. Notes: Range (grass), lodging (284). ⊠ Rte. 302, Bretton Woods 03575, 90 mi from Concord ☎ 603/278-4653 or 800/258-0330 ⊕ www. mtwashington.com ⊟ AE, D, MC, V.

Mount Pleasant. Holes: 9. Opened: 1895. Architect: Alex Findlay/Geoffrey S. Cornish/ Brian Silva. Yards: 3,215/2,475. Par: 35/35. Course Rating: 71.0. Slope: 122. Cart Fee: Included in green fee.

Mount Washington. Holes: 18. Opened: 1915. Architect: Donald Ross. Yards: 6,638/ 5,336. Par: 71/71. Course Rating: 70.1/70.1. Slope: 123/118. Cart Fee: $30 per cart.

Comments: Although the resort has 27 holes, focus your attention on Mount Washington, a combination of scenery and legendary architecture. ★ ★ ★ ¹/₂

NORTH CONWAY COUNTRY CLUB. Facility Holes: 18. Opened: 1895. Architect: Alex Findlay/Phil Wogan. Yards: 6,659/5,394. Par: 71/71. Course Rating: 71.9/70.1. Slope: 126/ 118. Green Fee: $35/$55. Cart Fee: $24 per cart. Discounts: Twilight, seniors. Walking:

Walking at certain times. Season: Apr.–Nov. Tee Times: Call golf shop. Notes: Range (grass). ✉Norcross Circle, North Conway 03860, 46 mi from Woodstock ☎603/356–9391 ☰MC, V. *Comments: Great views of the White Mountains on this very old course.* ★ ★ ★ ¹/₂

OWL'S NEST GOLF CLUB. Facility Holes: 18. Opened: 1998. Architect: Geoffrey S. Cornish/Brian Silva/Mungeam. Yards: 6,818/5,296. Par: 72/72. Course Rating: 74.0/69.8. Slope: 133/115. Green Fee: $19/$59. Cart Fee: $16 per person. Discounts: Weekdays, twilight, seniors, juniors. Walking: Walking at certain times. Season: Apr.–Nov. High: July–Sept. Tee Times: Call 7 days in advance. Notes: Range (grass). ✉40 Club House La., Campton 03223, 60 mi from Concord ☎603/726–3076 or 888/695–6378 ⊕www.owlsnestgolf.com ☰AE, MC, V. *Comments: Spectacular course with a front 9 in a valley and a mountainous back 9. Great elevation changes and views.* ★ ★ ★ ★

RAGGED MOUNTAIN GOLF CLUB. Facility Holes: 18. Opened: 1999. Architect: Jeff Julian. Yards: 7,059/4,963. Par: 72/72. Course Rating: 74.9/71.0. Slope: 149/125. Green Fee: $39/$59. Cart Fee: Included in green fee. Walking: Walking at certain times. Tee Times: Call up to 14 days in advance. ✉Ragged Mountain Rd., Danbury 03230, 66 mi from North Conway ☎603/768–3300 ⊕www.ragged-mt.com ☰AE, D, MC, V. *Comments: Relatively new course built at the base of a ski resort. Some elevation changes and great views of the White Mountains.* ★ ★ ¹/₂

WENTWORTH GOLF CLUB. Facility Holes: 18. Opened: 1895. Yards: 5,5,81/5,087. Par: 70/70. Course Rating: 66.0/66.2. Slope: 122/114. Green Fee: $15/$45. Cart Fee: $12.50 per person. Walking: Walking at certain times. Season: May–Oct. High: July–Sept. Tee Times: Call golf shop. ✉Rte. 16A, Jackson 03846, 10 mi north of North Conway ☎603/383–9641 ⊕www.wentworthgolf.com ☰AE, D, MC, V. *Comments: This very old course is for history buffs and beginners only. Very short.* ★ ★ ¹/₂

WHITE MOUNTAIN COUNTRY CLUB. Facility Holes: 18. Opened: 1974. Architect: Geoffrey S. Cornish. Yards: 6,428/5,350. Par: 71/72. Course Rating: 68.9/69.6. Slope: 115/114. Green Fee: $31/$39. Cart Fee: $13 per person. Discounts: Weekdays, twilight. Walking: Unrestricted walking. Season: May–Oct. Tee Times: Call 7 days in advance. Notes: Range (grass), lodging (4). ✉1 Country Club Dr., Ashland 03217, 25 mi from Concord ☎603/536–2227 ⊕www.playgolfnh.com ☰AE, D, MC, V. *Comments: This has some hilly fairways and uneven lies.* ★ ★ ★

Where to Stay

🖸JACK O'LANTERN. Modern, airy cottages dot the resort's fairways, which hug the Pemigewasset River. Homes may be partitioned off into single rooms or suites, or you can opt for a full, three-bedroom rental. All cottages have either a sundeck or a screened porch, some overlooking the fairways and many with full kitchens. Golf packages are available. ✉Rte. 3, Woodstock 03293, Near Exit 30, I-93 ☎603/745-8121, 800/227-4454 outside NH 🖶 603/745-8197 ⊕www.jackolanternresort.com ⇥50 rooms, 50 suites ⚹Restaurant, some kitchens, some microwaves, some refrigerators, cable TV, 18-hole golf course, 2 outdoor tennis courts, 2 pools (1 indoor), wading pool, hot tub, sauna, lounge, recreation room, no-smoking rooms ☰AE, D, MC, V ⊙Closed late Oct.–mid-May $$.

MOUNT WASHINGTON HOTEL & RESORT. This lavish, 1902 historic resort sits in the shadows of Mount Washington, New Hampshire's highest peak. Rooms are decked out with bright white woodwork, porcelain bath fixtures, and country prints. Amenities include golf courses and tennis courts, as well as guided hiking, horseback riding, and nature programs. There are lots of public rooms, with elegant woodwork, roaring fireplaces, and cozy chairs and couches, and a large wraparound porch. ⊠ Rte. 302, Bretton Woods 03575 ☎ 800/314-1752 🖷 603/278-8858 ⊕ www.mtwashington.com 🛏 200 rooms ♨ 8 restaurants, barbecues, room service, some in-room hot tubs, cable TV, some in-room VCRs, 1 18-hole golf course, 1 9-hole golf course, 12 tennis courts, pro shop, 2 pools (1 indoors), gym, mountain bikes, billiards, croquet, hiking, horseback riding, 5 lounges, pub, library, recreation room, video game room, shops, baby-sitting, children's programs (ages 5-16), meeting rooms; no a/c in some rooms, no smoking ⊟AE, D, DC, MC, V ⦿ MAP $$-$$$$.

RAGGED MOUNTAIN. Two-bedroom condominium units, with kitchenettes and large living rooms, provide space for up to six people. Because they're in Danbury Village, a five-minute drive from the Ragged Mountain resort, the units have home-away-from-home convenience. The resort also has available for rent a 2,000-square-foot log cabin on top of Ragged Mountain's Northeast Peak as well as a four-bedroom "golf house," which overlooks the 9th hole. ⊠ 620 Ragged Mountain Rd., Danbury 03230 ☎ 603/768-3600 or 800/400-3911 🖷 603/768-3929 ⊕ www.ragged-mt.com 🛏 8 units ♨ Kitchens, microwaves, refrigerators, cable TV, in-room VCRs; no smoking ⊟AE, MC, V $$$.

Where to Eat

✕ **PETER CHRISTIAN'S TAVERN.** Exposed beams, wooden tables, a smattering of antiques, and half shutters on the windows make Peter Christian's a restful haven. The fare tends toward the traditional and the hearty, from beef stew to mustard-chicken cordon bleu. ⊠ 186 Main St., New London ☎ 603/526-4042 ♨ Reservations not accepted ⊟AE, D, MC, V $.

✕ **WOODSTOCK INN.** The inn has two restaurants: the elegant Clement Room Grill, which has a popular Mediterranean seafood sauté, and the more casual Woodstock Station, whose menu ranges from meat loaf to fajitas. The on-site Woodstock Inn Brewery focuses on its six year-round brews, like the popular malty Red Rack Ale and the unfiltered Old Man Oatmeal Stout, and four seasonal brews. ⊠ U.S. 3, North Woodstock ☎ 603/745-3951 or 800/321-3985 ⊟AE, D, MC, V $$-$$$$.

Essentials

Getting Here

The main (and fastest) route from Boston to Portsmouth and the New Hampshire coast is I-95 to exit 7 (Portsmouth). If you're heading to the west side of the state, take I-93, which passes through Manchester and Concord before cutting a path through the White Mountains (the Lincoln-Woodstock area).

To reach the Ragged Mountain area, take I-93 north to exit 17. Take Route 4 west for about 30 minutes into Danbury.

To reach the Mount Washington area, take I-93 north through Franconia Notch Parkway to exit 35, Route 3 north. Take Route 3 north to Twin Mountain. Follow Route 302 east to Mount Washington Hotel and Resort.

I-89 originates from Concord, in the Merrimack Valley, and will take you to the New London area. Route 101 connects Keene and Manchester, then continues to the seacoast.

Visitor Information

🄵 **Mt. Washington Valley Chamber of Commerce** 🖃 Box 2300, North Conway 03860 ☎ 800/367-3364 ⊕ www.mtwashingtonvalley.org.

NEWPORT, RI

Let's face it, you're probably making a trip up to Newport to appease a nongolfing person in your life. This waterfront city's boutique stores, turn-of-the-20th-century mansions, and tall sailing ships are all draws for a weekend getaway. Although your real motives may be thinly disguised, it's a perfect spot to slip out and play. The Newport area lacks the large variety of courses that some other destinations might have, but all the area courses are solid and will keep you as happy as other members of your party might be when shopping in the local candle stores.

The trip from New York City can go surprisingly fast if there's no traffic along I-95, but don't plan on a quick drive on a Friday afternoon in summer. Choose off-peak summer days or even a period in late spring or early fall to make sure you have a satisfying golf trip in one of America's most beautiful cities.

At the top of the course list is the Newport National Golf Club and its Vineyards course—a gorgeous farmland track with views of the Sakkonet River. Built in 2003, Newport National is the best addition to the public golf scene in Rhode Island in over a decade.

On your way to or from Newport, make a stop at either Richmond Country Club or Foxwoods Golf & Country Club, off exit 3 on I-95. Both are less than 45 minutes from Newport. Richmond Country Club is the only Rhode Island course to receive four stars in *Golf Digest's Places to Play*. Foxwoods is linked to the massive Connecticut casino with the same name, which is another 30 minutes away across the border.

Foxwoods Golf & Country Club (18)	6,004/4,881	70/70	69.1/67.7	131/126	$38/$53
Green Valley Country Club (18)	6,830/5,459	71/71	72.0/69.5	126/120	$42/$45
Jamestown Golf Club (9)	6,096/5,502	72/72	69.7/69.7	110/110	$24/$26
Montaup Country Club (18)	6,513/5,417	71/73	71.3/71.4	130/118	$40/$44
Richmond Country Club (18)	6,826/4,974	71/71	72.1/70.4	121/113	$30/$35

Courses

Golf Digest REVIEWS

FOXWOODS GOLF & COUNTRY CLUB. Facility Holes: 18. Opened: 1995. Architect: Tripp Davis III. Yards: 6,004/4,881. Par: 70/70. Course Rating: 69.1/67.7. Slope: 131/126. Green Fee: $38/$53. Cart Fee: Included in green fee. Discounts: Seniors. Walking: Mandatory cart. Season: Apr.–Dec. High: June–Oct. Tee Times: Call 7 days in advance. Notes: Range (grass, mat). ✉87 Kingstown Rd., Richmond 02898 ☎401/539-4653 ⊕www.foxwoodsgolf.com ▭AE, D, DC, MC, V. *Comments: Truth be told, the casino should put more money into the design. Less than a decade old, it's one of the newest courses in Rhode Island but very short.* ★ ★ ★

GREEN VALLEY COUNTRY CLUB. Facility Holes: 18. Opened: 1957. Architect: Manuel Raposa. Yards: 6,830/5,459. Par: 71/71. Course Rating: 72.0/69.5. Slope: 126/120. Green Fee: $42/$45. Cart Fee: $28 per person. Discounts: Weekdays, twilight. Walking: Walking at certain times. Season: Apr.–Dec. High: May–Oct. Tee Times: Call 3 days in advance. Notes: Metal spikes, range (grass, mat). ✉371 Union St., Portsmouth 02871, 5 mi from Newport ☎401/849-2162 ▭AE, D, MC, V. *Comments: A pleasant surprise. Scenic views of Narragansett Bay. Tough course when the wind blows. Typical country club in design.* ★ ★ ★ ¹/₂

JAMESTOWN GOLF CLUB. Facility Holes: 9. Opened: 1895. Yards: 6,096/5,502. Par: 72/72. Course Rating: 69.7/69.7. Slope: 110/110. Green Fee: $24/$26. Cart Fee: $22 per cart. Walking: Unrestricted walking. Season: Apr.–Dec. Tee Times: Call golf shop. ✉245 Conanicus Rd., Jamestown 02835 ☎401/423-9930 ▭No credit cards. *Comments: Charming 9-hole course just south of the Newport Bridge on Conanicut Island. The staff claims it's the oldest public golf course in the United States.* UR

MONTAUP COUNTRY CLUB. Facility Holes: 18. Opened: 1923. Yards: 6,513/5,417. Par: 71/73. Course Rating: 71.3/71.4. Slope: 130/118. Green Fee: $40/$44. Cart Fee: $32 per cart. Walking: Unrestricted walking. Season: Year-round. High: Apr.–Nov. Tee Times: Call 1 day in advance. ✉500 Anthony Rd., Portsmouth 01871, 15 mi from Newport ☎401/683-0955 ▭MC, V. *Comments: The best course in the area before Newport National came along.* ★ ★ ★ ★

RICHMOND COUNTRY CLUB. Facility Holes: 18. Opened: 1993. Architect: Geoffrey Cornish/Brian Silva. Yards: 6,826/4,974. Par: 71/71. Course Rating: 72.1/70.4. Slope: 121/113. Green Fee: $30/$35. Cart Fee: $24 per cart. Discounts: Weekdays, twilight. Walking: Unrestricted walking. Season: Apr.–Nov. Tee Times: Call golf shop. ✉74 Sandy Pond Rd.,

Richmond 02832, 30 mi from Providence ☎ 401/364–9200 ▤ MC, V. *Comments: Off I–95 on your way from New York. Tall pines and sand scrub.* ★ ★ ★ ★

Where to Stay

Virtually all Newport B&Bs and some other hotels have two-night minimums on summer weekends. Three-night minimums often apply on holiday and festival weekends.

▦ **CASTLE HILL INN & RESORT.** On a 40-acre peninsula overlooking Narragansett Bay and the Atlantic, this turreted Victorian inn from 1874, adjacent to beach houses, harbor houses, and a separate chalet, contains rooms with luxurious linens, fine furnishings, and period antiques. Most have marble showers and fireplaces, and some have panoramic ocean views. The rooms in the beach house and harbor house are more modern. In summer, there is a Sunday brunch that's popular, and a full English tea is served each afternoon. There are hiking trails to the Castle Hill Lighthouse and a private beach. ✉ 590 Ocean Ave., 02840 ☎ 401/849–3800 or 888/466–1355 🖷 401/849–3838 ⊕ - www.castlehillinn.com ↩ 25 rooms ⬧ Restaurant, in-room data ports, some in-room hot tubs, some kitchenettes, some refrigerators, some in-room VCRs, spa, beach, hiking, bar, laundry service; no smoking ▤ AE, D, DC, MC, V ⑩ BP $$$$.

▦ **FRANCIS MALBONE HOUSE.** The design of this stately painted-brick house is attributed to the architect Peter Harrison. A lavish inn with period reproduction furnishings, the 1760 structure was tastefully doubled in size in the mid-1990s. The rooms in the main house are all in corners (with at least two windows) and look out either over the courtyard, which has a fountain, or across the street to the harbor. Most rooms have working fireplaces. ✉ 392 Thames St., 02840 ☎ 401/846–0392 or 800/846–0392 🖷 401/848–5956 ⊕ www.malbone.com ↩ 18 rooms, 2 suites ⬧ In-room data ports, some in-room hot tubs, some refrigerators, cable TV, business services; no kids under 13, no smoking ▤ AE, MC, V ⑩ BP $$$–$$$$.

▦ **IVY LODGE.** The only B&B in the mansion district, this Victorian, grand but still small by Newport standards, has gables and a Gothic turret. Designed by Stanford White, the home has 11 fireplaces, large and lovely rooms, a spacious dining room, window seats, and two common rooms. The defining feature is a Gothic-style oak entryway with a three-story turned-baluster staircase and a dangling wrought-iron chandelier. In summer, you can relax in wicker chairs on the wraparound porch. ✉ 12 Clay St., 02840 ☎ 401/849–6865 🖷 401/849–2919 ⊕ www.ivylodge.com ↩ 7 rooms, 1 suite ⬧ Some in-room data ports, some in-room hot tubs, some refrigerators, cable TV, some in-room VCRs ▤ AE, D, MC, V ⑩ BP $$$–$$$$.

▦ **JAILHOUSE INN.** Built in 1772, this former colonial jail, minutes from downtown Newport, has simple, updated rooms with fresh white walls, contemporary furnishings, and lots of skylights and windows. There's a small front porch for lingering and it's a short stroll to the harbor. Free parking on-site is an added bonus. ✉ 13 Marlborough St., 02840 ☎ 401/847–4638 or 800/427–9444 🖷 401/849–0605 ⊕ www.jailhouse.com ↩ 16 rooms, 8 suites ⬧ Dining room, in-room data ports, refrigerators, cable TV ▤ AE, D, MC, V ⑩ CP $$$$.

HAVEN'T OUIMET?

Francis Ouimet (1893–1967) is one of the most important figures of early American golf. His stunning David-beats-Goliath victory at the 1913 U.S. Open in Brookline, Massachusetts, over two British champions showed that play in the United States had matured. Finally American golfers were ready to take on the world. A room at the William F. Connell Golf House & Museum is devoted to Ouimet's accomplishments. The museum is in Norton, Massachusetts, 28 mi northeast of Providence. For more information, visit www.ouimet.org.

☷ **SANFORD-COVELL VILLA MARINA.** This impressive waterfront Victorian home with a majestic, 35-foot entrance hall was built in 1869 by architect William Ralph Emerson. A saltwater lap pool, dock with seating, and wraparound porch add to the inn's charm, as do original details like parquet floors, walnut wainscoting, and frescoes. Children are welcome here. ✉72 Washington St., 02840 ☎401/847-0206 ᐧ401/ 848-5599 ⊕ www.sanford-covell.com ⇆5 rooms ⚴ Pool, laundry facilities, some pets allowed (fee); no a/c, no room phones, no smoking ⊟No credit cards ❤⃝CP $$$–$$$$.

Where to Eat

✕**ASTERIX & OBELIX.** Danish chef John Bach-Sorensen makes eating as fun and colorful as the madcap French cartoon characters his eatery was named after. An auto repair garage before Sorensen took it over, the restaurant has a concrete floor painted to look like it's been covered with expensive tiling. Asian twists enliven the French-influenced Mediterranean fare, accompanied by a carefully selected menu of wines, brandies, and aperitifs. Sunday brunch is served year-round. There's outside dining in the open front of the building, and entertainment some evenings. ✉599 Thames St. ☎401/841-8833 ⊟AE, D, DC, MC, V ⊘No lunch $$$–$$$$.

✕**FLO'S CLAM SHACK.** Fried seafood, steamed clams, cold beer, and the best raw bar in town keep the lines long here in summer. The rest of the year, Flo's, established in 1936, is a favorite with locals. An upstairs bar serves baked, chilled lobster, and outside seating is available. Flo's is across the street from First Beach. ✉4 Wave Ave. ☎401/ 847-8141 ⚴Reservations not accepted ⊟MC, V ⊘Closed Jan. $–$$.

✕**THE MOORING.** The quintessential Newport dining experience—great seafood, prepared either traditionally or inventively—plus a great view of the Newport scene—boats, boats, and more boats. The seafood chowder at this family-oriented restaurant has won the local cook-off so many times that it was removed from further competition. Popular choices include the lobster and the seafood scampi. In fine weather you can dine on the enclosed patio overlooking the harbor; on chilly winter evenings, take advantage of the open fire in the sunken interior room. ✉Sayer's Wharf ☎401/846-2260 ⊘Closed Mon. and Tues. Nov.–Mar. ⊟AE, D, DC, MC, V $$–$$$$.

✕**OCEAN BREEZE CAFE.** Tables and booths surround an espresso bar and take-out counter at this small, very popular breakfast and lunch spot in downtown Newport.

Don't miss the freshly baked muffins and famous home fries, served with overstuffed omelets or eggs Benedict. Sandwiches like the turkey with melted Havarti cheese, bacon, tomato, and cranberry dressing on grilled sourdough bread; salads; and clam chowder are lunch favorites. ⊠ 580 Thames St. ☎ 401/849–1750 ⌦ Reservations not accepted ▤ AE, MC, V ⊗ No dinner ¢–$$.

Essentials

Getting Here

Newport is about a three-hour drive north from New York City. From the city, follow Route 95 north to exit 3A in Rhode Island. Bear right onto Route 138 east, then follow Route 1 north to the Jamestown/Newport Bridges exit. The Jamestown Bridge leads to the Newport Bridge ($2 toll). Take the first exit off the Newport Bridge (Scenic Newport).

Visitor Information

🛈 **Newport County Convention and Visitors Bureau** ⊠ Gateway Information Center, 23 America's Cup Ave. ☎ 401/849–8048 or 800/326–6030 ⊕ www.gonewport.com.

RUTLAND, VT

Like the area around Burlington, skiing is still king here. But in Rutland, just as in Colorado, Northern Michigan, or seemingly anywhere else that you can buy lift tickets, resort owners have made golf courses the perfect off-season enticement. The courses vary in quality, and are mostly mountainous in design. Branching out from Rutland, there are a number of great courses within an hour's drive east, and south of town heading back toward Boston.

The first stop on your tour should be Rutland Country Club. The club's history dates back to 1901, and its 6,100-yard design gives you a taste of golf at the turn of the 20th century. Woodstock, a quintessential New England town with white churches, memorable stores, and fall foliage, is a 30-mi drive east of Rutland. It makes a perfect one-day, stay-and-play town on your journey through central Vermont. Woodstock Country Club and the accompanying Woodstock Inn and Resort have often been regarded as one of the best golf destinations in New England.

Just down the road from Woodstock is the Killington Golf Resort and nearby Green Mountain National. If you have limited time, make sure you play Green Mountain National, *Golf Digest*'s second-ranked course in Vermont.

Course	Yards	Par	Course Rating	Slope	Green Fee
Green Mountain National (18)	6,589/4,740	71/71	72.1/68.9	138/126	$36/$68
Killington Golf Resort (18)	6,326/5,108	72/72	70.6/71.2	126/123	$51
Neshobe Golf Club (18)	6,362/5,042	72/71	71.6/64.9	125/115	$34/$36
Okemo Valley Golf Club (18)	6,400/5,105	70/70	71.1/70.1	130/125	$85
Rutland Country Club (18)	6,134/5,368	70/71	69.7/71.6	125/125	$84
Stratton Mountain Country Club (27)					$69/$99
Lake/Forest (18)	6,526/5,153	72/74	71.2/69.8	125/123	
Lake/Mountain (18)	6,602/5,410	72/74	72.0/71.1	125/124	
Mountain/Forest (18)	6,478/5,163	72/74	71.2/69.9	126/123	
Woodstock Country Club (18)	6,053/4,924	70/71	69.7/69.0	123/113	$62/$82

Courses

GREEN MOUNTAIN NATIONAL GOLF COURSE. Facility Holes: 18. Opened: 1996. Architect: Gene Bates. Yards: 6,589/4,740. Par: 71/71. Course Rating: 72.1/68.9. Slope: 138/126. Green Fee: $36/$68. Cart Fee: $19 per person. Discounts: Weekdays, twilight, juniors. Walking: Walking at certain times. Season: May–Nov. High: July–Oct. Tee Times: Call 7 days in advance. Notes: Range (grass, mat). ⊠ Rte. 100, Barrows-Towne Rd., Killington 05751, 15 mi from Rutland ☎ 802/422–4653 ⊕ www.greenmountainnational. com ⊟ AE, D, MC, V. *Comments: Carved through the Green Mountain National Forest. Be ready for tight, tree-lined fairways and slick greens. It's the best of the Rutland-area courses and easily the best public course in Vermont.* ★★★★

KILLINGTON GOLF RESORT. Facility Holes: 18. Opened: 1984. Architect: Geoffrey S. Cornish. Yards: 6,326/5,108. Par: 72/72. Course Rating: 70.6/71.2. Slope: 126/123. Green Fee: $51. Cart Fee: $16 per person. Discounts: Twilight, juniors. Walking: Unrestricted walking. Season: May–Oct. High: July–Oct. Tee Times: Call 14 days in advance. Notes: Metal spikes, range (mat), lodging (900). ⊠ 4763 Killington Rd., Killington 05751, 16 mi from Rutland ☎ 802/422–6700 ⊕ www.killingtongolf.com ⊟ AE, D, MC, V. *Comments: Nestled in the Green Mountains at a height of 2,000 feet. Elevation changes in the fairways can leave golfers with some testy uphill and downhill lies.* ★★★

NESHOBE GOLF CLUB. Facility Holes: 18. Opened: 1959. Architect: Steve Durkee. Yards: 6,362/5,042. Par: 72/71. Course Rating: 71.6/64.9. Slope: 125/115. Green Fee: $34/$36. Cart Fee: $28 per cart. Discounts: Twilight, juniors. Walking: Unrestricted walking. Season: Apr.–Oct. High: June–Sept. Tee Times: Call 3 days in advance. Notes: Range (grass). ⊠ Town Farm Rd., Brandon 05733, 15 mi from Rutland ☎ 802/247–3611 ⊕- www.neshobe.com ⊟ MC, V. *Comments: A pleasant surprise. A 1996 refurbishment gave the course 12 new holes. Some play is through trees but the course feels roomy off the tee. Low green fee makes it a good budget option.* ★★★ ½

OKEMO VALLEY GOLF CLUB. Facility Holes: 18. Opened: 2000. Architect: Steve Durkee. Yards: 6,400/5,105. Par: 70/70. Course Rating: 71.1/70.1. Slope: 130/125. Green

Fee: $85. Cart Fee: Included in green fee. Discounts: Juniors. Walking: Unrestricted walking. Notes: Range (grass). ✉ 89 Fox La., Ludlow 05149, 45 mi from Brattleboro ☎ 802/228-1396 ⊕ www.okemo.com ▤ AE, MC, V. *Comments: Course is attached to a resort. Built in Black River valley, the course is relatively flat compared to nearby courses. Feels like heathland. UR.*

RUTLAND COUNTRY CLUB. Facility Holes: 18. Opened: 1902. Architect: Wayne E. Stiles/John Van Kleek. Yards: 6,134/5,368. Par: 70/71. Course Rating: 69.7/71.6. Slope: 125/125. Green Fee: $84. Cart Fee: Included in green fee. Walking: Mandatory cart. Season: May–Oct. Tee Times: Call 2 days in advance. ✉ N. Grove St., 05701 ☎ 802/773-3254 ▤ D, MC, V. *Comments: One of the oldest public courses in the country. Classic country-club design.* ★ ★ ★ ★ ¹/₂

STRATTON MOUNTAIN COUNTRY CLUB. Facility Holes: 27. Opened: 1965. Architect: Geoffrey S. Cornish. Green Fee: $69/$99. Cart Fee: $17 per cart. Discounts: Weekdays, twilight, juniors. Walking: Walking at certain times. Season: May–Oct. High: June–Sept. Tee Times: Call golf shop. Notes: Range (grass, mat), lodging (400). ✉ R.R. 1, Box 145, Stratton Mountain 05155, 40 mi from Rutland ☎ 802/297-4114 or 800/787-2886 ⊕ www.stratton.com ▤ AE, D, MC, V.

Lake/Forest. Holes: 18. Yards: 6,526/5,153. Par: 72/74. Course Rating: 71.2/69.8. Slope: 125/123.

Lake/Mountain. Holes: 18. Yards: 6,602/5,410. Par: 72/74. Course Rating: 72.0/71.1. Slope: 125/124.

Mountain/Forest. Holes: 18. Yards: 6,478/5,163. Par: 72/74. Course Rating: 71.2/69.9. Slope: 126/123.

Comments: The 27 holes here are at the base of the Stratton Mountain ski slopes. Courses are solid but not spectacular. ★ ★ ★ ★

WOODSTOCK COUNTRY CLUB. Facility Holes: 18. Opened: 1895. Architect: Robert Trent Jones. Yards: 6,053/4,924. Par: 70/71. Course Rating: 69.7/69.0. Slope: 123/113. Green Fee: $62/$82. Cart Fee: $18 per person. Discounts: Weekdays, twilight. Walking: Unrestricted walking. Season: May–Nov. High: June–Sept. Tee Times: Call golf shop. Notes: Range (grass), lodging (145). ✉ 14 The Green, Woodstock 05091, 30 mi from Rutland ☎ 802/457-6674 ⊕ www.woodstockinn.com ▤ AE, MC, V. *Comments: Classic layout has been updated with a new fairway and greenside bunkers. The parkland course is set in the valley.* ★ ★ ★ ★

Where to Stay

▣ **BIRCH RIDGE INN.** A slate-covered carriageway leads to this former executive retreat, now a country getaway. Rooms are in styles that include colonial, Shaker, and mission, and all have a sitting area. Six rooms have gas fireplaces, four with whirlpool baths. ✉ Butler Rd. at Killington Rd., Killington 05751 ☎ 802/422-4293 or 800/435-8566 🖶 802/422-3406 ⊕ www.birchridge.com ➷ 10 rooms ⚑ Restaurant, some in-room hot tubs, cable TV, lounge; no a/c in some rooms, no kids under 12, no smoking ▤ AE, MC, V ⧀ BP $–$$$.

⚏ **CASCADES LODGE.** Value and convenience sets this property above most in the area. It's steps away from Killington Ski Resort lifts and within walking distance to golf, hiking, biking, fishing, and area restaurants. The family-run lodge has modest, cookie-cutter furnishings, but the rooms are spacious. ⊠ 58 Old Mill Rd., Killington 05751 ☎ 802/422-3731 or 800/345-0113 ⊟ 802/422-3351 ⊕ www.killingtonresorts.com ↩ 46 rooms ⚫ Restaurant, cable TV, indoor pool, gym, hot tub, lounge, some pets allowed; no-smoking rooms ⊟ AE, MC, V ⦿ BP $-$$.

⚏ **INN AT RUTLAND.** One alternative to Rutland's chain motel accommodations is this Victorian mansion. The ornate oak staircase lined with heavy embossed gold and leather wainscoting leads to rooms that blend modern bathrooms with late-19th-century touches such as elaborate ceiling moldings and frosted glass. The two large common rooms, one with a fireplace, have views of surrounding mountains and valleys. ⊠ 70 N. Main St., 05701 ☎ 802/773-0575 or 800/808-0575 ⊟ 802/775-3506 ⊕ www.innatrutland.com ↩ 11 rooms ⚫ Dining room, cable TV, library, no-smoking rooms ⊟ AE, D, MC, V $-$$$.

⚏ **MOUNTAIN TOP INN AND RESORT.** On 500 acres overlooking Chittenden Reservoir and the Green Mountain National Forest, this is a year-round outdoor enthusiast's inn. There's an equestrian center and a golf school, and activities include swimming and canoeing. A tip: opt for the more expensive deluxe rooms, which are larger and have spectacular views. ⊠ 195 Mountaintop Rd., Chittenden 05737 ☎ 802/483-2311 or 800/445-2100 ⊟ 802/483-6373 ⊕ www.mountaintopinn.com ↩ 35 rooms, 6 cottages, 6 chalets ⚫ Restaurant, cable TV, tennis court, driving range, pool, spa, beach, boating, fishing, hiking, horseback riding, lounge, recreation room, some pets allowed (fee), no-smoking rooms ⊟ AE, MC, V ⊗ Closed late Oct.–late Dec. and mid-Mar.–mid-May ⦿ BP, MAP $$$-$$$$.

✗⚏ **WOODSTOCK INN AND RESORT.** Resort entrepreneur Laurance Rockefeller, a longtime Woodstock resident, made this elegant country inn a flagship property of his Rockresorts chain. Rooms are spacious and serene, with neutral colors, handmade quilts, and hardwood furniture. Most of the lodgings are set well back from Woodstock's often noisy main street. ⊠ 14 The Green, Rte. 4, Woodstock 05091 ☎ 802/457-1100 or 800/448-7900 ⊟ 802/457-6699 ⊕ www.woodstockinn.com ↩ 144 rooms, 7 suites ⚫ 2 restaurants, cable TV, 2 18-hole golf courses, 12 tennis courts, 2 pools (1 indoor), health club, sauna, spa, croquet, racquetball, squash, cross-country skiing, meeting room, no-smoking rooms ⊟ AE, MC, V ⦿ MAP $$$-$$$$.

Where to Eat

✗ **GRIST MILL.** Locals fill this cozy Killington eatery that sits on Summit Pond overlooking the mountains. Tables clustered around the massive fireplace are popular in winter. The large menu includes sandwiches, burgers, ribs, steaks, and popular country-style turkey dinners; the rack of baby back ribs and large cuts of prime rib are top choices. Portions are hefty, and prices are reasonable. ⊠ Killington Rd. on Summit Pond, Killington ☎ 802/422-3970 ⊟ AE, MC, V $$-$$$.

✗ **HEMINGWAY'S.** Hemingway's is as good as dining gets in central Vermont. The restaurant has built a national reputation with house specialties like cream of garlic soup and seasonal dishes based on native game, fresh seafood, and prime meats. You can opt for the prix-fixe, three- to six-course menu, or the four-course wine-tasting menu on weekends. An à la carte menu is available during the week. Request seating in either the formal, vaulted dining room or the intimate wine cellar. ⊠ 4988 U.S. 4, Killington ☎ 802/422-3886 ⊕ www.hemingwaysrestaurant.com ⊟ AE, D, DC, MC, V ⊘ Closed early Nov., mid-Apr.–mid-May, and Mon. No lunch $$$$.

✗ **PIZZA JERKS.** This casual, cozy eatery is a local hot spot, serving up dishes of hefty platters of pizza pies. Pizzas come in red or white bases, with nearly 25 toppings available. The Tree Hugger pie, with fresh spinach, basil, tomatoes, garlic, and red onions and smothered with mozzarella, is one of the top sellers. ⊠ 1307 Killington Rd., Killington ☎ 802/422-4111 ⊟ AE, MC, V $-$$$.

Essentials

Take I-93 north from Boston 65 mi to I-89 north, then travel another 65 mi to Vermont exit 11 (Route 4/Rutland). Follow Route 4 west about 12 mi to Woodstock, 25 mi to Killington, and 40 mi to Rutland. Woodstock is about a 2½-hour drive from Boston; Woodstock is about 3 hours; Rutland about 3½ hours.

Visitor Information

🛈 **Rutland Region Chamber of Commerce** ⊠ 256 N. Main St., Rutland 05701 ☎ 802/773-2747 or 800/756-8880 ⊕ www.rutlandvermont.com.

AROUND
CHICAGO

Cog Hill Golf Club

By Matthew Rudy and Judy Sutton

Around Chicago

Because of its wide-open, car-friendly design, Chicago has always embraced golf to a greater degree than most other big American cities. The Chicago Golf Club was the only "western" club to be among the founding members of the USGA in 1895, and USGA and PGA national championships have been held in Chicago virtually nonstop ever since. The city's public golf tradition is equally well established, with more than 200 public-access courses in the city or the surrounding suburbs. Cog Hill Golf Club, 40 mi outside the city in Lemont, rivals Bethpage State Park's collection of courses as the finest public golf facility in the country. If you want to find a game, it's easier to do it here than in any other big American city.

Summer is the best time to be in the area, and not just because of the PGA Tour's Western Open, played at Cog Hill in June. Warm breezes, temperatures in the high 80s, and easy access to the irrigation powers of both Lake Michigan and the Ohio River turn most Chicago-area courses a lush emerald green. It makes you want to get out and play.

You might even see the PGA Tour's Jeff Sluman, the 1985 PGA Champion, out practicing near his Hinsdale home, or Luke Donald and Jess Daley hitting balls at their alma mater, Northwestern University. Abundant national and international flights into Chicago O'Hare (it's a hub for both United and American) make it an easy big city to reach. Midway Airport, which is closer to downtown, is an underrated option—it's easy to get to and quick to get in and out of. Even better, there's a golf course right down the street.

Chicago's status as "America's Golf City" has only stoked its residents' hunger for more and varied golf within easy driving distance. Get outside the city's traffic-stacked beltway, and it's easy to see why the game has flourished north, west, and south. Take I-94 north, up through Milwaukee, and farmland cascades away from the Lake Michigan shore. You think to yourself, "this is a perfect place for a golf course," and all of a sudden, you're in Kohler, where Blackwolf Run and Whistling Straits are ready to be part of a perfect golf weekend. To the west, the Mississippi River plain makes for flatter terrain—and more of a challenge for course designers— but the Tournament Players Club, at Rockford's Deere Run, and Gateway National, outside St. Louis, are both worth the drives by themselves. As you proceed south toward St. Louis, the weather stays mild longer into the winter. October is still prime golf season there.

			COURSE	SLOPE	
Bonnie Brook Golf Club (18)	6,701/5,559	72/73	72.4/72.2	126/124	$21/$38
Chalet Hills Golf Club (18)	6,877/4,934	73/73	73.4/68.1	131/114	$68/$78
Hawthorn Suites at Midlane (27)					$51/$65
Back/Front (18)	7,015/5,367	72/72	74.5/71.4	135/125	
Front/Middle (18)	7,073/5,635	72/73	74.4/72.7	132/124	
Middle/Back (18)	6,932/5,160	72/72	73.8/70.5	134/123	
Marengo Ridge Golf Club (18)	6,636/5,659	72/73	71.9/71.5	128/125	$20/$40
Orchard Valley Golf Club (18)	6,745/5,162	72/72	72.8/70.3	134/123	$50/$57
Pine Meadow Golf Club (18)	7,141/5,203	72/71	74.6/70.9	138/125	$72/$77
Steeple Chase Golf Club (18)	6,827/4,831	72/72	73.1/68.1	129/113	$28/$54
Stonewall Orchard Golf Club (18)	7,074/5,375	72/72	74.1/71.2	140/126	$39/$72
ThunderHawk Golf Club (18)	7,031/5,046	72/72	73.8/69.2	136/122	$25/$78

CHICAGOLAND NORTH

Lake County is where Chicago—and Illinois—ends and Wisconsin begins. Ask Chicagoans and they'll tell you that it's also where cars with Wisconsin plates start clogging the highway at 5 mph below the speed limit. But maybe those Wisconsin folks have the right idea slowing down here. Lake County is on Lake Michigan and midway between Chicago and Milwaukee. Not only is the main town, Waukegan, the freshwater salmon capital of the world, but neighboring Mundelein has more good golf courses for a town its size than just about any place in the country. Even if you only played the county's town courses, you'd still have a fine weekend of golf. Waukegan's municipal course, Bonnie Brook, has been around since the 1920s and is meticulously maintained. Mundelein has eight golf courses— not bad for a village of 5,000. Two are must plays—the municipal Steeple Chase Golf Club and the Jemsek-run Pine Meadow Golf Club. The best of the lot might be Orchard Valley Golf Club in Aurora, designed by Ken Kavanaugh and opened in 1993. It has a stimulating layout through wetlands and forest, and is groomed to country-club conditions. If that isn't enough excitement, you could always schedule an afternoon trip to the massive Six Flags Great America amusement park in Gurnee.

Courses

BONNIE BROOK GOLF CLUB. Facility Holes: 18. Opened: 1927. Architect: Jim Foulis. Yards: 6,701/5,559. Par: 72/73. Course Rating: 72.4/72.2. Slope: 126/124. Green Fee: $21/$38. Cart Fee: $28 per cart. Discounts: Twilight, seniors, juniors. Walking: Unrestricted walking. Season: Apr.–Nov. Tee Times: Call 7 days in advance. Notes: Range (grass, mat). ✉ 2800 N. Lewis Ave., Waukegan 60087, 25 mi from Chicago ☎ 847/360–4730 ⊕ www.waukeganparks.org ✉ MC, V. *Comments: Great value for town residents. An old-style test.* ★ ★ ★ ½

CHALET HILLS GOLF CLUB. Facility Holes: 18. Opened: 1995. Architect: Ken Killian. Yards: 6,877/4,934. Par: 73/73. Course Rating: 73.4/68.1. Slope: 131/114. Green Fee: $68/$78. Cart Fee: $15 per person. Discounts: Weekdays, twilight, seniors, juniors. Walking: Walking at certain times. Season: Mar.–Dec. Tee Times: Call 7 days in advance. Notes: Range (mat). ✉ 943 Rawson Bridge Rd., Cary 60013, 40 mi from Chicago ☎ 847/639–0666 ⊕ www.chaletgolf.com ✉ AE, D, MC, V. *Comments: Numbers 17 and 18 skirt a small lake, offering plenty of challenge.* ★ ★ ★ ★

HAWTHORN SUITES AT MIDLANE GOLF RESORT. Facility Holes: 27. Opened: 1964. Architect: Robert Bruce Harris. Green Fee: $51/$65. Cart Fee: Included in green fee. Discounts: Weekdays, twilight, seniors, juniors. Walking: Unrestricted walking. Season: Mar.–Nov. Tee Times: Call 7 days in advance. Notes: Metal spikes, range (grass). ✉ 4555 W. Yorkhouse Rd., Wadsworth 60083, 39 mi from Chicago ☎ 847/623–4653 ⊕ www.midlaneresort.com ✉ AE, D, MC, V.

If you want to find a game, it's easier to do it here than in any other big American city.

Back/Front. Holes: 18. Yards: 7,015/5,367. Par: 72/72. Course Rating: 74.5/71.4. Slope: 135/125.

Front/Middle. Holes: 18. Yards: 7,073/5,635. Par: 72/73. Course Rating: 74.4/72.7. Slope: 132/124.

Middle/Back. Holes: 18. Yards: 6,932/5,160. Par: 72/72. Course Rating: 73.8/70.5. Slope: 134/123.

Comments: Terrific course, but watch for the outings. ★ ★ ★ ½

MARENGO RIDGE GOLF CLUB. Facility Holes: 18. Opened: 1965. Architect: William James Spear. Yards: 6,636/5,659. Par: 72/73. Course Rating: 71.9/71.5. Slope: 128/125. Green Fee: $20/$40. Cart Fee: $15 per person. Discounts: Weekdays, twilight, seniors, juniors. Walking: Unrestricted walking. Season: Year-round. High: Apr.–Sept. Tee Times: Call golf shop. Notes: Range (grass). ✉ 9508 Harmony Hill Rd., Marengo 60152, 35 mi from Chicago ☎ 815/923–2332 ⊕ www.marengoridgegolfclub.com ✉ D, MC, V. *Comments: Wildly different 9s. The front is wide open, while the back is tucked into the trees.* ★ ★ ★ ★

ORCHARD VALLEY GOLF CLUB. Facility Holes: 18. Opened: 1993. Architect: Ken Kavanaugh. Yards: 6,745/5,162. Par: 72/72. Course Rating: 72.8/70.3. Slope: 134/123. Green Fee: $50/$57. Cart Fee: $14 per person. Discounts: Twilight, seniors, juniors. Walking: Unrestricted walking. Season: Apr.–Nov. Tee Times: Call 10 days in advance.

Notes: Range (grass, mat). ✉ 2411 W. Illinois Ave., Aurora 60506, 35 mi from Chicago ☎ 630/907-0500 ▤ AE, D, MC, V. *Comments: Wow. This is one of the best in Chicagoland. Marshes and other wetlands are challenging.* ★ ★ ★

PINE MEADOW GOLF CLUB. Facility Holes: 18. Opened: 1985. Architect: Joe Lee/ Rocky Roquemore. Yards: 7,141/5,203. Par: 72/71. Course Rating: 74.6/70.9. Slope: 138/ 125. Green Fee: $72/$77. Cart Fee: $16 per person. Discounts: Twilight, juniors. Walking: Unrestricted walking. Season: Mar.–Dec. Tee Times: Call 120 days in advance. Notes: Range (grass, mat). ✉ 1 Pine Meadow La., Mundelein 60060, 30 mi from Chicago ☎ 847/566-4653 ⊕ www.pinemeadowgc.com ▤ D, DC, MC, V. *Comments: Big, strong parkland layout developed by Cog Hill's owners, the Jemseks. Underrated.* ★ ★ ★

STEEPLE CHASE GOLF CLUB. Facility Holes: 18. Opened: 1993. Architect: Ken Killian. Yards: 6,827/4,831. Par: 72/72. Course Rating: 73.1/68.1. Slope: 129/113. Green Fee: $28/$54. Cart Fee: $15 per person. Discounts: Weekdays, twilight, seniors, juniors. Walking: Walking at certain times. Season: Mar.–Nov. High: May–Oct. Tee Times: Call 7 days in advance. ✉ 200 N. La Vista Dr., Mundelein 60060, 35 mi from Chicago ☎ 847/ 949-8900 ⊕ www.mundeleinparks.org ▤ AE, D, MC, V. *Comments: A slightly easier version of Pine Meadow. Operated by the town.* ★ ★ ★

STONEWALL ORCHARD GOLF CLUB. Facility Holes: 18. Opened: 1999. Architect: Arthur Hills/Steve Forrest. Yards: 7,074/5,375. Par: 72/72. Course Rating: 74.1/71.2. Slope: 140/126. Green Fee: $39/$72. Cart Fee: $8 per person. Discounts: Weekdays, twilight, seniors, juniors. Walking: Unrestricted walking. Season: Mar.–Dec. High: May–Oct. Tee Times: Call 7 days in advance. Notes: Range (grass). ✉ 25675 W. Hwy. 60, Grayslake 60030, 45 mi from Chicago ☎ 847/740-4890 ⊕ www.stonewallorchard.com ▤ AE, D, DC, MC, V. *Comments: Number 18 might be the hardest hole you'll ever play.* ★ ★ ★ ½

THUNDERHAWK GOLF CLUB. Facility Holes: 18. Opened: 1999. Architect: Robert Trent Jones Jr./Bruce Charlton. Yards: 7,031/5,046. Par: 72/72. Course Rating: 73.8/69.2. Slope: 136/122. Green Fee: $25/$78. Cart Fee: $28 per cart. Discounts: Weekdays, twilight, seniors, juniors. Walking: Walking at certain times. Season: Mar.–Nov. High: May–Oct. Tee Times: Call 30 days in advance. Notes: Range (grass, mat). ✉ 39700 N. Lewis Ave., Beach Park 60099, 50 mi from Chicago ☎ 847/872-4295 ⊕ www.lcppd.com ▤ AE, MC, V. *Comments: Massive boulders accent this Robert Trent Jones Jr. design.* ★ ★ ★

Where to Stay

🏨 **CANDLEWOOD SUITES.** These suites are either studios or one-bedroom accommodations. All have cooking facilities, so you can prepare meals in your room with ingredients from Candlewood Cupboard, which is on the premises, if you wish. Sophisticated rooms have dark-wood furniture, large desks, CD players, and comfortable recliner chairs. ✉ 1151 S. Waukegan Rd., Waukegan 60085 ☎ 847/578-5250 or 800/ 946-6200 🖨 847/578-5256 ⊕ www.candlewoodsuites.com 🛏 122 suites ♿ In-room data ports, kitchenettes, microwaves, refrigerators, in-room VCRs, laundry facilities, some pets allowed (fee), no-smoking rooms ▤ AE, D, DC, MC, V $.

CHARLES BLAIR MACDONALD

Among the legends of the game is Charles Blair Macdonald (1856–1939). Some claim he was born in Chicago, others in Niagara Falls, Ontario. Either way, his contribution to golf is unchallenged. He competed at the very highest levels and was instrumental in the formation of the USGA. But it is perhaps as an architect that he is best remembered. His Chicago Golf Club layout (1895) was the first 18-hole course in this country. Macdonald's other classics include those at National Golf Links (1911), St. Louis Country Club (1914), and the Yale Golf Course (1926).

▥ **COURTYARD BY MARRIOTT.** True to its name, this hotel 5 mi west of downtown has an interior courtyard with a pool. The hotel caters to the business crowd: rooms have high-speed Internet service and personal voice mail. The restaurant serves breakfast only. ⊠ 800 Lakehurst Rd., Waukegan 60085 ☎ 847/689-8000 or 800/321-2211 🖷 847/689-0135 ⊕ www.courtyard.com ☞ 137 rooms, 12 suites ♿ Restaurant, in-room data ports, some refrigerators, cable TV with movies, indoor pool, exercise equipment, hot tub, lobby lounge, laundry facilities, business services, free parking, no-smoking rooms ⊟ AE, D, DC, MC, V $.

▥ **HAWTHORN SUITES AT MIDLANE GOLF RESORT.** About 40 mi from Chicago, this property attached to the Midlane golf course offers all-suites accommodations, some with Jacuzzi tubs and fireplaces. Larger suites have full kitchens with dishwashers and dining tables. A complimentary shuttle serves area attractions, including Six Flags Great America and Gurnee Mills shopping mall. ⊠ 4555 W. York House Rd., Wadsworth 60083 ☎ 847/360-0550 🖷 847/625-8186 ⊕ www.midlaneresort.com ☞ 80 suites ♿ Restaurant, room service, in-room data ports, some in-room hot tubs, some kitchens, cable TV, 18-hole golf course, 9-hole golf course, pool, gym, hot tub, nightclub, business services, meeting rooms, no-smoking rooms ⊟ AE, D, DC, MC, V ⓘⓞⓘCP $$.

▥ **ILLINOIS BEACH RESORT AND CONFERENCE CENTER.** The three-story hostelry on the Lake Michigan shore is inside Illinois Beach State Park. Simple rooms are done in pastels with oak-color furniture. Suites and balcony rooms have a lakeside view. There's a private beach. ⊠ 1 Lake Front Dr., Zion 60099 ☎ 847/625-7300 🖷 847/625-0543 ⊕ www.ilresorts.com ☞ 92 rooms, 4 suites ♿ Restaurant, bar, picnic area, cable TV, indoor pool, gym, hot tub, beach, hiking, cross-country skiing, video game room, playground, business services, meeting rooms ⊟ AE, D, DC, MC, V $$.

Where to Eat

✕ **COUNTRY INN OF LAMBS FARM.** A hit with locals for its steak, fried chicken, and salad bar, this restaurant is on Lambs Farm, a nonprofit organization that caters to adults with developmental disabilities. It's also a popular spot for Sunday brunch for families who visit the adjacent farmyard and amusement park rides. Reservations are required weekends in summer, and there is a kids' menu. ⊠ Rte. 176 at I-94, Libertyville ☎ 847/362-4636 ⊟ AE, D, DC, MC, V ⓒ Closed Mon. No dinner $$-$$$.

✕**GALE STREET INN.** Barbecued baby-back ribs are the house specialty in this restaurant in Mundelein, 5 mi west of Libertyville, but the steaks and grilled seafood rank high among the menu favorites, too. Floor-to-ceiling windows in its maritime dining room and seating on its deck overlook Diamond Lake. There is karaoke on Wednesday and Thursday nights. ⊠906 Diamond Lake Rd., Mundelein ☎847/566–1090 ⊟AE, D, DC, MC, V ⊘Closed Mon. $$–$$$.

✕**MADISON AVENUE.** In this 1890s structure with a contemporary facade, you have broad views of the harbor through floor-to-ceiling windows. You can choose from chicken Kiev, barbecued ribs, and steak and seafood dishes, though the prime rib is a local favorite. ⊠34 N. Sheridan Rd., Waukegan ☎847/662–6090 ⊟AE, D, DC, MC, V ⊘No lunch weekends $$–$$$.

Essentials

Getting Here

Lake County is about 35 mi north of downtown Chicago. Its cities are accessible from I–94 north and U.S. 41 north. Mundelein is about 30 mi from downtown Chicago. Take I–94 to the IL–60/Town Line Road exit. To reach Waukegan, take I–94 north roughly 20 mi and merge onto U.S. 41 north, then travel 16 mi to exit 29. For Aurora, take I–290 west about 13 mi from downtown Chicago and merge onto I–88 west, then take the IL–31 exit toward Aurora/Batavia.

Visitor Information

🛈 **Green Oaks, Libertyville, Mundelein, Vernon Hills Chamber of Commerce** ⊠1123 S. Milwaukee Ave., Libertyville 60048 ☎847/680–0750 🖷847/680–0760 ⊕www. glmvchamber.org. **Lake County Illinois Convention and Visitors Bureau** ⊠5455 W. Grand Ave., Suite 302, Gurnee 60031 ☎847/662–2700 or 800/525–3669 🖷847/662–2702 ⊕www.lakecounty.org. **Marengo–Union Chamber of Commerce** ⊠116 S. State St., Marengo 60152 ☎815/568–6680 🖷815/568–6879 ⊕www.marengo-union.com.

COOK COUNTY

It's hard to say what sports the folks in Cook County care about more—golf, or minor league baseball. The golf here is a treat, with a delightful mix of old-style, turn-of-the-20th-century courses like those at Schaumburg Golf Club, and big, broad, tough modern tracks like the courses at Heritage Bluffs Golf Club. The best part is that you don't have to choose. Fill a four-day weekend with visits to all the courses listed here, then take in a Schaumburg Flyer or Kane County Cougar game. Both the Flyers, an independent league team, and the Cougars, a Class A affiliate of the Oakland As, have fanatical followings and sharp stadiums. The games are great for a relaxing night out

	Yards	Par	Course Rating	Slope	Green Fee
Heritage Bluffs Golf Club (18)	7,106/4,967	72/72	73.9/68.6	138/114	$33/$45
Schaumburg Golf Club (27)					
Player (9)	3,091/2,372	35/35	34.3/33.4	117/114	$18/$22
Tournament (18)	6,542/4,885	72/72	70.7/67.5	121/114	$36/$42
Silver Lake Country Club (36)					$33/$39
North (18)	6,826/5,659	72/77	72.1/71.9	119/117	
South (18)	6,290/5,011	70/72	69.4/68.0	116/112	

with your foursome or a family picnic behind the stands with the kids. If members of your group don't care much for baseball, that's okay, too— Schaumburg might be most famous for its Woodfield Mall, which feels like a small city made up of every retail establishment you can imagine.

Courses

Golf Digest REVIEWS

HERITAGE BLUFFS GOLF CLUB. Facility Holes: 18. Opened: 1993. Architect: Dick Nugent. Yards: 7,106/4,967. Par: 72/72. Course Rating: 73.9/68.6. Slope: 138/114. Green Fee: $33/$45. Cart Fee: $13 per person. Discounts: Weekdays, twilight, seniors, juniors. Walking: Unrestricted walking. Season: Apr.–Dec. High: May–Sept. Tee Times: Call 7 days in advance. Notes: Range (grass, mat). ✉ 24355 W. Bluff Rd., Channahon 60410, 45 mi from Chicago ☎ 815/467-7888 ⊕ www.channahonpark.org/golf.html ▭ D, MC, V. *Comments: Ten-minute tee intervals make this Dick Nugent parkland track a pleasure.* ★★★★

SCHAUMBURG GOLF CLUB. Facility Holes: 27. Opened: 1926. Architect: Bob Lohmann. Discounts: Weekdays, twilight, seniors, juniors. Walking: Unrestricted walking. Season: Apr.–Nov. Tee Times: Call golf shop. Notes: Range (grass, mat). ✉ 401 N. Roselle Rd., Schaumburg 60194, 30 mi from Chicago ☎ 847/885-9000 ⊕ www.parkfun.com ▭ AE, D, MC, V.

Player. Holes: 9. Yards: 3,091/2,372. Par: 35/35. Course Rating: 34.3/33.4. Slope: 117/114. Green Fee: $18/$22. Cart Fee: $9.50 per person. ★★★ ½

Tournament. Holes: 18. Yards: 6,542/4,885. Par: 72/72. Course Rating: 70.7/67.5. Slope: 121/114. Green Fee: $36/$42. Cart Fee: $15 per person. ★★★★

Comments: The clubhouse is, appropriately enough, built in a Frank Lloyd Wright style.

SILVER LAKE COUNTRY CLUB. Facility Holes: 36. Green Fee: $33/$39. Cart Fee: $14 per person. Discounts: Twilight, seniors, juniors. Walking: Unrestricted walking. Season: Mar.–Dec. Tee Times: Call 14 days in advance. ✉ 147th St. and 82nd Ave., Orland Park 60462, 22 mi from Chicago ☎ 708/349-6940 ⊕ www.silverlakecc.com ▭ AE, D, MC, V.

North. Holes: 18. Opened: 1927. Architect: Leonard Macomber. Yards: 6,826/5,659. Par: 72/77. Course Rating: 72.1/71.9. Slope: 119/117. *Comments: Hole number 10 is a 430-yard monster with waste areas and plenty of water.* ★★★ ½

South. Holes: 18. Opened: 1929. Architect: Raymond Didier. Yards: 6,290/5,011. Par: 70/72. Course Rating: 69.4/68.0. Slope: 116/112. *Comments: The 1st hole is a 570-yard par-5—the number one handicap hole. Welcome to Silver Lake.* ★ ★ ★ ★

Where to Stay

⊞ COUNTRY INNS & SUITES. The inviting lobby of this hotel, 2 mi west of the Woodfield Mall, has a fireplace, wood floors, and a beamed ceiling. Cozy rooms have feather bedding; you may want to splurge for a Jacuzzi suite with a fireplace. ✉ 1401 N. Roselle Rd., Schaumburg 60195 ☎ 847/839-1010 🖷 847/839-1212 ⊕ www.countryinns.com ➷ 49 rooms, 24 suites ♨ In-room data ports, some in-room hot tubs, microwaves, refrigerators, cable TV, indoor pool, gym, hot tub, laundry facilities, business services, no-smoking rooms ▤ AE, D, DC, MC, V ⍥ CP $$.

⊞ HYATT REGENCY WOODFIELD. This five-story hotel is across the street from the Woodfield Mall. Rooms are furnished with contemporary bedding and artwork, and perks include extra pillows and nightly turndown service. The on-site Tre Cena restaurant overlooks the pool. Try the breakfast buffet, which has made-to-order omelets. ✉ 1800 E. Golf Rd., Schaumburg 60173 ☎ 847/605-1234 or 800/233-1234 🖷 847/605-0328 ⊕ www.hyatt.com ➷ 470 rooms ♨ Restaurant, in-room data ports, refrigerators, cable TV, in-room VCRs, 2 pools (1 indoor), gym, hair salon, hot tub, business services, no-smoking rooms ▤ AE, D, DC, MC, V $$-$$$.

⊞ LA QUINTA MOTOR INN. One block west of I-290, this convenient stucco motel in south Schaumburg is 2 mi from the Schaumburg golf course and three blocks north of downtown. Rooms are basic but comfortable, and include coffeemakers and hair dryers. ✉ 1730 E. Higgins Rd., Schaumburg 60173 ☎ 847/517-8484 or 800/687-6667 🖷 847/517-4477 ⊕ www.laquinta.com ➷ 127 rooms ♨ In-room data ports, cable TV, pool, gym, laundry service, meeting rooms, some pets allowed, no-smoking rooms ▤ AE, D, DC, MC, V ⍥ CP $.

⊞ WYNDHAM GARDEN HOTEL. Tech-savvy rooms at this hotel in the Schaumburg business district have Sony PlayStations and high-speed Internet service. Bathrooms are stocked with pampering products from California's Golden Door Spa. The hotel is a mile from Woodfield Mall. ✉ 800 National Pkwy., Schaumburg 60173 ☎ 847/605-9222 or 800/996-3426 🖷 847/605-9240 ⊕ www.wyndham.com ➷ 188 rooms, 1 suite ♨ Restaurant, room service, in-room data ports, refrigerators, cable TV with video games, indoor pool, exercise equipment, hot tub, bar, laundry service, business services, no-smoking rooms ▤ AE, D, DC, MC, V ⍥ CP $-$$.

Where to Eat

✕ MAGGIANO'S LITTLE ITALY. Share enormous portions of red-sauce Italian food at this boisterous, wide-open space. The hearty fare includes brick-size lasagna, chicken Vesuvio, and veal scallopini. The key here is to go family-style: choose two plates for every three diners. If you dare to show up without a reservation, be prepared for a long wait. ⊠ 1901 E. Woodfield Rd., Schaumburg ☎ 847/240-5600 ⚓ Reservations essential ▭ AE, D, DC, MC, V $$-$$$$.

✕ **MORTON'S OF CHICAGO.** Generous cuts of steak draw suburbanites to this location of the national chain. You peruse a live menu here: Servers roll dinner selections out on carts and describe each dish in tantalizing, animated detail. Hearty eaters opt for the double filet mignon with béarnaise sauce or the tender prime rib. ⊠ 1470 McConnor Pkwy., Schaumburg ☎ 847/413-8771 ▭ AE, MC, V ⊘ No lunch $$-$$$$.

✕ **SHAW'S CRAB HOUSE.** Fresh crab and other seasonal seafood dishes pack them in at the sister location of the downtown Chicago original. A 1940s-style warehouse feel pervades both the upscale main dining room and Red Shell, a more casual area with a raw bar and live jazz. ⊠ 1900 E. Higgins Rd., Schaumburg ☎ 847/517-2722 ▭ AE, D, DC, MC, V ⊘ No lunch weekends $$$-$$$$.

Essentials

Getting Here

Schaumburg is about 30 mi west of downtown Chicago; Orland Park is approximately 30 mi south of the city. To get to Schaumburg, take I-90 west past O'Hare Airport, toward Rockford. Exit off Roselle Road toward Hoffman Estates/Schaumburg.

To get to Orland Park, take I-55 south toward St. Louis. Merge onto U.S. 45 south via exit 279A. U.S. 45 becomes La Grange Road/96th Avenue, which leads directly into the town's main shopping district.

Visitor Information

🔃 **Greater Woodfield Convention and Visitors Bureau** ⊠ 1430 Meacham Rd., Schaumburg 60173 ☎ 847/490-1010 or 800/848-4849 ⊕ www.chicagonorthwest. com. **Orland Park Chamber of Commerce** ⊠ 8799 W. 151st St., Orland Park 60462 ☎ 708/349-2972 🖷 708/349-7454 ⊕ www.orlandparkchamber.org.

GALENA & ROCKFORD

The Galena–Rockford area isn't exactly on a heavily traveled route anymore, as riverboats on the nearby Mississippi River lost their role as the primary means of transportation. But being off the beaten path adds a certain allure to this region. Well-preserved Civil War–era houses line Galena's streets, with around 85% of all the buildings in town on the National Historic Register. The East State Street Antique Malls in Rockford, the second-largest city in Illinois, has shops packed with finds like period furniture and hardware, collectible dolls, and estate jewelry. Beyond the charm of these cities, play here is outstanding. The Aldeen Golf Club, which hosted the 2001 Illinois Amateur, is a prime

Aldeen Golf Club (18)	7,131/5,075	72/72	74.2/69.1	134/117	$38/$44
Eagle Ridge Inn & Resort (54)					
General (18)	6,820/5,335	72/72	73.8/66.7	137/119	$80/$156
North (18)	6,875/5,578	72/72	73.2/72.1	132/125	$60/$116
South (18)	6,762/5,609	72/72	72.7/72.3	134/129	$60/$136
Meadows Golf Club (18)	6,667/5,199	72/72	72.6/68.7	132/114	$23/$40
Park Hills Golf Club (36)					$19/$22
East (18)	6,477/5,401	72/72	69.9/69.8	116/115	
West (18)	6,622/5,940	72/73	71.3/76.2	121/127	
PrairieView Golf Course (18)	7,117/5,269	72/72	72.3/71.6	123/117	$24/$36

example of Rockford's "Forest City" moniker. The Eagle Ridge Inn & Resort, a 6,800-acre collection of golf courses, luxury villas, and equestrian facilities, is Galena's golf centerpiece. The General course at Eagle Ridge is one of the five best courses in the state, with sweeping views of Thunder Bay and a mature forest. To finish off the weekend, head across the Mississippi to Dubuque, Iowa, and tee off at the four-star Meadows Golf Club.

Courses

GolfDigest REVIEWS

ALDEEN GOLF CLUB. Facility Holes: 18. Opened: 1991. Architect: Dick Nugent. Yards: 7,131/5,075. Par: 72/72. Course Rating: 74.2/69.1. Slope: 134/117. Green Fee: $38/$44. Cart Fee: $29 per cart. Discounts: Weekdays, twilight. Walking: Unrestricted walking. Season: Apr.–Nov. High: May–Sept. Tee Times: Call 7 days in advance. Notes: Range (grass). ⊠ 1900 Reid Farm Rd., Rockford 61114, 90 mi from Chicago ☎ 815/282-4653 or 888/425-3336 ⊕ www.aldeengolfclub.com ⊟ D, MC, V. *Comments: The 8th plays anywhere from 118 to 203 yards to an island green. Good luck pulling a club.* ★ ★ ★ ★ ½

EAGLE RIDGE INN & RESORT. Facility Holes: 54. Cart Fee: Included in green fee. Discounts: Weekdays, guest, twilight, juniors. Walking: Unrestricted walking. Season: Mar.–Oct. High: June–Sept. Tee Times: Call golf shop. Notes: Metal spikes, range (grass), lodging (400). ⊠ 444 Eagle Ridge Dr., Galena 61036, 20 mi from Dubuque, IA ☎ 815/777-2400 or 800/892-2269 ⊕ www.eagleridge.com/golf ⊟ AE, D, DC, MC, V.

General. Holes: 18. Opened: 1997. Architect: Roger Packard/Andy North. Yards: 6,820/5,335. Par: 72/72. Course Rating: 73.8/66.7. Slope: 137/119. Green Fee: $80/$156. *Comments: This course has appeared on plenty of Best Courses lists since it opened in 1997. The tee on number 14 is 180 feet above the fairway.* ★ ★ ★ ★

North. Holes: 18. Opened: 1977. Architect: Larry Packard/Roger Packard. Yards: 6,875/5,578. Par: 72/72. Course Rating: 73.2/72.1. Slope: 132/125. Green Fee: $60/$116. *Comments: This immaculately conditioned course has slightly more forgiving greens than the others at the resort.* ★ ★ ★ ★

South. Holes: 18. Opened: 1984. Architect: Roger Packard. Yards: 6,762/5,609. Par: 72/72. Course Rating: 72.7/72.3. Slope: 134/129. Green Fee: $60/$136. *Comments: The South course, the oldest of the three, meanders through a river valley.* ★ ★ ★ ★

MEADOWS GOLF CLUB. Facility Holes: 18. Opened: 1996. Architect: Bob Lohmann. Yards: 6,667/5,199. Par: 72/72. Course Rating: 72.6/68.7. Slope: 132/114. Green Fee: $23/$40. Cart Fee: $11 per person. Discounts: Weekdays, seniors, juniors. Walking: Unrestricted walking. Season: Mar.–Nov. Tee Times: Call 7 days in advance. ⊠ 15766 Clover La., Dubuque 52001, 190 mi from Chicago ☎ 563/583-7385 ⊕ www. meadowgolf.com ⊟ AE, D, MC, V. *Comments: Who knew Iowa had this many hills and valleys?* ★ ★ ★ ★

PARK HILLS GOLF CLUB. Facility Holes: 36. Architect: C. D. Wagstaff. Green Fee: $19/$22. Cart Fee: $12 per person. Discounts: Weekdays, juniors. Walking: Unrestricted walking. Season: Apr.–Nov. Tee Times: Call golf shop. Notes: Metal spikes, range (grass). ⊠ 3240 W. Stephenson Rd., Freeport 61032, 100 mi from Chicago ☎ 815/235-3611 ⊟ MC, V.

East. Holes: 18. Opened: 1955. Yards: 6,477/5,401. Par: 72/72. Course Rating: 69.9/69.8. Slope: 116/115. *Comments: With a green fee that's less than $30, this is the best course for your money in Illinois.* ★ ★ ★ ½

West. Holes: 18. Opened: 1966. Yards: 6,622/5,940. Par: 72/73. Course Rating: 71.3/76.2. Slope: 121/127. *Comments: Also a terrific value, this course plays longer than its yards imply.* ★ ★ ★ ½

PRAIRIEVIEW GOLF COURSE. Facility Holes: 18. Opened: 1992. Architect: William James Spear. Yards: 7,117/5,269. Par: 72/72. Course Rating: 72.3/71.6. Slope: 123/117. Green Fee: $24/$36. Cart Fee: $24 per cart. Discounts: Weekdays, twilight, seniors, juniors. Walking: Unrestricted walking. Season: Mar.–Nov. High: June–Sept. Tee Times: Call 7 days in advance. Notes: Range (grass, mat). ⊠ 7993 N. River Rd., Byron 61010, 12 mi from Rockford ☎ 815/234-4653 ⊕ www.prairieviewgolf.com ⊟ D, MC, V. *Comments: Prime design on the banks of the Rock River. Exceptionally well run.* ★ ★ ★ ★

Where to Stay

⚏ **EAGLE RIDGE INN AND RESORT.** At this resort you may stay in rooms at the inn, which overlook Lake Galena and have walkout balconies, or in a privately owned villa or spacious resort home. Up to eight bedrooms, fully equipped kitchens, fireplaces, washers and dryers, and daily maid service make the latter a good choice for large groups or families. Villas and homes have views of the lake and its smooth sand beach, the golf course, or the property's 6,800 wooded acres. You can rent a canoe or a pontoon boat at the on-site marina. Depending on the season, trail rides, hayrides, or sleigh rides tour the property. ⊠ Eagle Ridge Dr., Galena 61036 ☎ 815/777-2444 or 800/892-2269 🖷 815/777-4502 ⊕ www.eagleridge.com 🛏 80 rooms at inn; varying number of villas and homes ♿ 3 restaurants, room service, minibars, some refrigerators, cable TV, some in-room VCRs, driving range, 3 18-hole golf courses, 9-hole golf course, putting green, 4 tennis courts, indoor pool, gym, hot tub, massage, beach, boating, bicycles, cross-country skiing, downhill skiing, bar, children's programs (ages 2–16), playground, business services, airport shuttle, some pets allowed (fee), no-smoking rooms ☰AE, D, DC, MC, V $$$–$$$$.

⛺ **RIVERHOUSE BED & BREAKFAST INN & TEPEE.** You can rough it in a tepee with a chiminea firepot and portable toilets or enjoy a more pampered homestay at this riverside abode in Machesney, just 7 mi north of Rockford. The inn's suites have Old West, bordello, or log cabin themes as well as fireplaces and in-room whirlpool tubs. Common areas are full of frontier collectibles. Two resident cats roam the premises. ✉ 11052 Ventura Blvd., Machesney Park 61115 ☎ 815/636–1884 ⊕ www.riverhouse.ws 🛏 3 suites, 1 tepee ♿ Some in-room hot tubs, some refrigerators, cable TV, some in-room VCRs, pool, hot tub, volleyball, business services; no phones in some rooms; no smoking ☰MC, V ⊙ Tepee closed Nov.–Apr. ⎟⊙⎟ BP $–$$$.

Where to Eat

✗ **CAFÉ PATOU.** The diverse French and Italian menu at this bistro, which includes homemade pâtés, crepes, pasta, and seafood, has won over a loyal local following. The dessert sampler of the restaurant's six signature sweets, including chocolate mousse and crème brûlée, is not to be missed. Five dining rooms range in feel from Parisian café to French Quarter. A live band plays jazz Friday and Saturday. ✉ 3929 Broadway, Rockford ☎ 815/227–4100 ☰AE, D, DC, MC, V ⊙ Closed Sun. No lunch Sat. and Mon. and in spring and summer $$–$$$$.

✗ **FRIED GREEN TOMATOES.** The eponymous vegetables are picked green, then fried at this old brick farmstead. The rest of the menu doesn't stray too far from simplicity: Black Angus steak, for example, or hearty pasta dishes like spinach tortellini. The wine list is extensive in its by-the-glass, half-, or full-bottle selections. A pianist plays Friday and Saturday. ✉ 213 N. Main St., Galena ☎ 815/777–3938 ☰AE, MC, V ⊙ No lunch $$–$$$$.

✗ **PERRY STREET BRASSERIE.** Reproductions of medieval English brass and Celtic figures set the mood at this chic eatery. The menu changes monthly, but mixes simple, classic dishes and more adventurous preparations: Try the grilled quail on Israeli couscous. The chef's signature Chocolate Cup, a bowl of solid chocolate filled with dark and milk chocolate ganache, may satisfy even the most die-hard chocolate lover. ✉ 124 N. Commerce St., Galena ☎ 815/777–3773 ⟋ Reservations essential ☰MC, V ⊙ Closed Sun. and Mon. No lunch $$–$$$$.

Essentials

Getting Here

Rockford is about 85 mi west of downtown Chicago. Galena is still farther west, about 160 mi from the city.

To get to Rockford, take I-90 west for about 70 mi, heading toward O'Hare first, then following signs toward Rockford. Merge onto I-39 south/U.S. 51 south toward Rockford. After 3 mi, merge onto U.S. 20 west. In about 5 mi, take the IL-2 north/Main Street exit.

To reach Galena from Chicago, take I-90 west to I-39 south/U.S. 51 south toward Rockford, then merge onto U.S. 20 west. Stay on this road for about 80 mi.

Visitor Information

🛈 **Galena/Jo Daviess County Convention and Visitors Bureau** ✉ 101 Bouthillier St., Galena 61036 ☎ 877/464-2536 ⊕ www.galena.org. **Rockford Area Convention and Visitors Bureau** ✉ 211 N. Main St., Rockford 61101 ☎ 815/963-8111 or 800/521-0849 🖷 815/963-4298 ⊕ www.gorockford.com.

KOHLER, WI

How can a place be considered a great destination when it only has two places to go? Well, when those two places are Blackwolf Run and Whistling Straits . . . Pete Dye constructed a four-pack of the best high-end resort courses you can find anywhere. He crafted the Whistling Straits course, from a spectacularly perfect piece of lakefront land in Sheboygan, and it's universally regarded as a legitimate challenger to Pebble Beach as the best waterfront golf course in the country. If you can tear your eyes away from the golf course, you can see for miles from the ridge overlooking Lake Michigan. He unveiled the Irish course in 2000 with an equal amount of design pedigree.

Ten years earlier, Dye built the inland River and Meadow Valleys courses at Blackwolf Run in Kohler. Forget for a second the understated elegance of the American Club resort to which the courses are attached. The River and Meadow Valleys courses have stood up to major championship tests at the 1997 U.S. Women's Open (six-over was the winning score) and have claimed the handicaps of many a blissful resort visitor with their collection of herculean par-4s and par-5s. It might not take more than four days to play these four gems, but it may take you at least a month to recover from the punishment—and the excitement.

Courses   **Golf** Digest REVIEWS

BLACKWOLF RUN. Facility Holes: 36. Opened: 1988. Architect: Pete Dye. Cart Fee: Included in green fee. Discounts: Twilight. Walking: Unrestricted walking. Season: Apr.–Nov. High: June–Sept. Tee Times: Call golf shop. Notes: Range (grass), lodging (357). ✉ 1111 W. Riverside Dr., Kohler 53044, 55 mi from Milwaukee ☎ 920/457-4446 or 800/618-5535 ⊕ www.destinationkohler.com ▭ AE, D, DC,MC, V.

	Yards	Par	Course Rating	Slope	Green Fee
Blackwolf Run (36)					
Meadow Valleys (18)	7,142/5,065	72/72	74.7/69.5	143/125	$100/$141
River (18)	6,991/5,115	72/72	74.9/70.7	151/128	$123/$176
Whistling Straits Golf Club (36)					
Irish (18)	7,201/5,109	72/72	75.6/70.0	146/126	$100/$141
Straits (18)	7,343/5,381	72/72	76.7/72.2	151/132	$156/$272

Meadow Valleys. Holes: 18. Yards: 7,142/5,065. Par: 72/72. Course Rating: 74.7/69.5. Slope: 143/125. Green Fee: $100/$141. *Comments: The challenges here are the waste areas and heather, not the trees.* ★ ★ ★ ★ ★

River. Holes: 18. Yards: 6,991/5,115. Par: 72/72. Course Rating: 74.9/70.7. Slope: 151/128. Green Fee: $123/$176. *Comments: Carved out of mature forest, the River course is a scorer's pinnacle. Break 80 here and you can really play.* ★ ★ ★ ★ ★

Professionals were already complaining about the Straits course's difficulty more than two years before the 2004 PGA Championship.

WHISTLING STRAITS GOLF CLUB. Facility Holes: 36. Architect: Pete Dye. Cart Fee: Included in green fee. Discounts: Twilight. Walking: Walking with caddie. Season: Apr.–Oct. Tee Times: Call golf shop. Notes: Range (grass), lodging (357). ⌧ N8501 County Rd. LS, Sheboygan 53081 ☎ 920/565-6062 or 800/618-5535 ⊕ www.whistlingstraits. com ⊟ AE, D, DC, MC, V.

Irish. Holes: 18. Opened: 2000. Yards: 7,201/5,109. Par: 72/72. Course Rating: 75.6/70.0. Slope: 146/126. Green Fee: $100/$141. *Comments: At any other resort, the Irish course would be a marquee course. Here, it's "just" a warm-up for the Straits.* UR

Straits. Holes: 18. Opened: 1997. Yards: 7,343/5,381. Par: 72/72. Course Rating: 76.7/72.2. Green Fee: $156/$272. *Comments: The jaw-dropping beauty and scale are worth the huge green fee.* ★ ★ ★ ★ ★

Where to Stay

⊞ **AMERICAN CLUB.** Built in 1918 to house immigrant workers at the Kohler factory, this redbrick Tudor-style residence reopened as a luxury resort in 1981. Elegance emanates from the grand lobby and comfortable sitting areas, complete with plush furniture, handcrafted woodwork, and chandeliers. Guest rooms in the main building honor famous Americans throughout history with portraits and memorabilia. All have down comforters and Kohler whirlpool tubs. The adjacent carriage house, also built in 1918, has upgraded rooms—all with king beds and perks like private check-in and afternoon refreshments. It also houses the Kohler Waters Spa. The resort, about 5 mi west of Sheboygan in Kohler, is on 500 acres of gentle slopes and meadows, some of which is meticulously landscaped, and part of which acts as a wildlife preserve. ⌧ 444

KOHLER'S THREE-DOT ARCHITECT

Pete Dye was sitting in the grill room at Blackwolf Run. Having built four superior golf courses in the area, Dye is something of a celebrity here. Herb Kohler, who pretty much owns the town and commissioned Dye to build his treasured courses, walks into the busy grill room, sees Dye and announces for all to hear, "My friend Pete Dye is the best three-dot architect in the world!" Kohler holds up a cocktail napkin, and with his finger pointing at three imaginary spots on it, laughs, "He puts a dot here for the tee, here for the fairway, and here for the green! That's how he designs golf courses!"

Highland Dr., 53044 ☎ 920/457–8000 Ext. 700 or 800/344–2838 Ext. 700 🖷 920/457–0299 ⊕ www.destinationkohler.com ⟟ Main bldg.: 175 rooms, 10 suites. Carriage house: 46 rooms, 6 suites ♿ 10 restaurants, room service, in-room data ports, in-room hot tubs, minibars, some refrigerators, cable TV with movies, in-room VCRs, 3 18-hole golf courses, 6 tennis courts, 2 pro shops, 2 pools, gym, hair salon, hot tub, massage, sauna, spa, steam room, bicycles, hiking, horseback riding, cross-country skiing, wine bar, shops, laundry services, concierge, business services, no-smoking rooms ▭AE, D, DC, MC, V $$$–$$$$.

🏨 **BAYMONT INN.** Just west of town, this standard brick hotel, painted white with green shutters, is near restaurants and shopping malls. Pillow-top mattresses, down pillows, and ergonomic desk chairs add a luxe touch to some upgraded rooms. All rooms have coffeemakers and hair dryers. ✉ 2932 Kohler Memorial Dr., Sheboygan 53081 ☎ 920/457–2321 🖷 920/457–0827 ⊕ www.baymontinn.com ⟟ 96 rooms ♿ Cable TV with movies and video games, business services, some pets allowed, no-smoking rooms ▭AE, D, DC, MC, V ⦿CP $$.

🏨 **INN ON WOODLAKE.** Built in 1994, this Northside inn has turrets and looks over an 11-acre spring-fed lake with a private beach, a putting green, and a shopping complex. A circular drive leads you to the front entrance. Mission-style furniture fills the lobby, which is dominated by a large fireplace. The inn is 5 mi west of town. ✉ 705 Woodlake Rd., 53044 ☎ 920/452–7800 or 800/919–3600 🖷 920/452–6288 ⊕ www.innonwoodlake.com ⟟ 121 rooms ♿ Some in-room hot tubs, some microwaves, some refrigerators, cable TV with movies, in-room VCRs, pool ▭AE, D, DC, MC, V ⦿CP $$$–$$$$.

Where to Eat

✕**BLACKWOLF RUN.** This dining spot serving regional fare overlooks the Sheboygan River and has panoramic views of the finishing holes of the Pete Dye–designed Blackwolf Run golf course. Specialties include corn sausage chowder and beef tenderloin with seared jumbo scallops. Breakfast starts one hour before the first tee time of the day. There is a kids' menu. ✉ 1111 W. Riverside Dr. ☎ 920/457–4448 ▭AE, D, DC, MC, V $$$$.

✗**IMMIGRANT ROOM.** This restaurant is the premier dining spot at the American Club, and considered by many to be one of the best in the state. The six elegant dining rooms reflect the European ethnic mix of Wisconsin's early settlers—English, French, and German, for example. Game dishes like grilled elk chop and truffle honey-glazed quail are on the menu, along with more traditional meat and seafood selections. Friday and Saturday nights there is live entertainment. ⊠American Club, 444 Highland Dr. ☎920/457-8000 🎩Jacket required ☰AE, D, DC, MC, V ⊘Closed Sun. No lunch $$$$.

✗**RICHARD'S.** Linen tablecloths and fresh flowers add polish to this 1840s former stagecoach inn 5 mi west of Sheboygan in the small town of Sheboygan Falls. The kitchen turns out such dishes as prime rib, pasta primavera, and crab legs, as well as good oysters Rockefeller. ⊠501 Monroe St., Sheboygan Falls ☎920/467-6401 ☰MC, V ⊘Closed Mon. No lunch weekends $$-$$$.

Essentials

Getting Here

Kohler and Sheboygan are two hours north of Chicago in central Wisconsin. From downtown Chicago, take I-94 west toward Milwaukee about 87 mi. Merge onto I-43 north. After about 55 mi, merge onto WI-23 west via exit 126 toward Kohler and Sheboygan.

Visitor Information

🚹 **Kohler Visitor Information** ⊠444 Highland Dr., 53044 ☎800/344-2838 ⊕www.destinationkohler.com. **Sheboygan County Convention and Visitors Bureau** ⊠712 Riverfront Dr., Suite 101, Sheboygan 53081 ☎920/457-9495 or 800/457-9497 Ext. 700 🖨920/457-6269 ⊕www.sheboygan.org.

LEMONT

Cog Hill Golf Club has been such a dominant part of the golf scene both in the Lemont area and the West Chicagoland area overall, it's easy to overlook the other great courses that are spread over the vast western suburbs. To be sure, Cog Hill deserves the accolades it receives. Its Dubsdread course—one of four courses on the property—is one of the premier public courses in the country. You can play the same fairways PGA Tour players walk every year in the Western Open, and if the USGA had better taste, it would have picked Dubsdread to host the U.S. Open in 2006 instead of Torrey Pines in San Diego. Its number two course is a must-play as well.

But Cantigny Golf in Wheaton is nearly as good, albeit without the tournament history and Jemsek family legacy. The Prairie Bluff Golf Club merits a play on its challenging Roger Packard–Andy North design alone,

Big Run Golf Club (18)	7,025/5,420	72/72	74.4/71.9	142/130	$34/$51
Cantigny Golf (36)					$85
Lakeside/Hillside **(18)**	6,830/5,183	72/72	72.6/70.1	131/119	
Woodside/Hillside **(18)**	6,939/5,236	72/72	73.4/70.3	132/120	
Woodside/Lakeside **(18)**	6,981/5,425	72/72	73.8/71.9	138/127	
Youth Links **(9)**	6,981/5,425	72/72	73.8/71.9	138/127	
Cog Hill Golf Club	72				
No. 1 **(18)**	6,267/5,328	71/72	69.6/70.3	118/117	$19/$40
No. 2 (Ravines) **(18)**	6,268/5,564	72/72	69.8/70.5	120/115	$28/$51
No. 3 **(18)**	6,384/5,213	72/71	69.7/69.0	116/111	$35/$40
No. 4 (Dubsdread) **(18)**	6,940/5,590	72/72	75.4/71.6	142/130	$130
Gleneagles Golf Club (36)					$29/$35
Red **(18)**	6,090/6,090	70/74	67.6/71.3	112/111	
White **(18)**	6,250/6,080	70/75	70.1/72.3	120/114	
Prairie Bluff Golf Club (18)	6,832/5,314	72/72	72.1/70.1	122/115	$29/$41
Prairie Landing Golf Club (18)	6,950/4,859	72/72	73.2/68.3	136/124	$59/$94

and the fact that it was once the Joliet Prison exercise yard gives it some extra gawker appeal. Once you get to Lemont and away from the grind of Chicago's notoriously bad traffic, how can you not enjoy yourself?

Courses

Golf Digest REVIEWS

BIG RUN GOLF CLUB. Facility Holes: 18. Opened: 1930. Architect: Muhlenford/Sneed/Didier/Killian/Nugent. Yards: 7,025/5,420. Par: 72/72. Course Rating: 74.4/71.9. Slope: 142/130. Green Fee: $34/$51. Cart Fee: $16 per person. Discounts: Weekdays, twilight, juniors. Walking: Walking at certain times. Season: Year-round. Tee Times: Call 7 days in advance. Notes: Metal spikes. ✉ 17211 W. 135th St., Lockport 60441, 35 mi from Chicago ☎ 815/838-1057 ⊕ www.bigrungolf.com ▤ D, MC, V. *Comments: Built in 1930, this 7,025-yard monster was ahead of its time. The 18th must have been something with persimmon clubs.* ★ ★ ★ ★

CANTIGNY GOLF. Facility Holes: 36. Green Fee: $85. Cart Fee: $15 per person. Discounts: Seniors, juniors. Walking: Unrestricted walking. Season: Apr.–Oct. High: May–Sept. Tee Times: Call 14 days in advance. Notes: Range (grass). ✉ 27 W. 270 Mack Rd., Wheaton 60187, 30 mi from Chicago ☎ 630/668-3323 ⊕ www.cantignygolf.com ▤ AE, D, MC, V.

Lakeside/Hillside. Holes: 18. Opened: 1989. Architect: Roger Packard. Yards: 6,830/5,183. Par: 72/72. Course Rating: 72.6/70.1. Slope: 131/119.

Woodside/Hillside. Holes: 18. Opened: 1989. Architect: Roger Packard. Yards: 6,939/5,236. Par: 72/72. Course Rating: 73.4/70.3. Slope: 132/120.

Woodside/Lakeside. Holes: 18. Opened: 1989. Architect: Roger Packard. Yards: 6,981/5,425. Par: 72/72. Course Rating: 73.8/71.9. Slope: 138/127.

Youth Links. Holes: 9. Opened: 1997. Architect: Roger Packard/Andy North. Yards: 6,981/5,425. Par: 72/72. Course Rating: 73.8/71.9. Slope: 138/127.

Comments: A well-run caddie program makes all of Cantigny's 27 holes a viable option. ★★★★ ½

COG HILL GOLF CLUB. Facility Holes: 72. Discounts: Juniors. Walking: Unrestricted walking. Season: Apr.–Nov. High: Apr.–Oct. Tee Times: Call 90 days in advance. Notes: Range (grass, mat). ✉ 12294 Archer Ave., 60439, 28 mi from Chicago ☎ 630/257–5872 ⊕ www.coghillgolf.com ▤ D, DC, MC, V.

No. 1. Holes: 18. Opened: 1927. Architect: David McIntosh/Bert Coghill. Yards: 6,267/5,328. Par: 71/72. Course Rating: 69.6/70.3. Slope: 118/117. Green Fee: $19/$40. Cart Fee: $16 per person. *Comments: This is the original course built at the facility, and it still holds that 1920s charm. Short.* ★★★★

No. 2 (Ravines). Holes: 18. Opened: 1930. Architect: Bert Coghill/Rocky Roquemore. Yards: 6,268/5,564. Par: 72/72. Course Rating: 69.8/70.5. Slope: 120/115. Green Fee: $28/$51. Cart Fee: $16 per person. *Comments: It's overshadowed by Dubsdread, but this is the one to play if you can't get on the big course.* ★★★★

No. 3. Holes: 18. Opened: 1927. Architect: Dick Wilson/Joe Lee/David McIntosh. Yards: 6,384/5,213. Par: 72/71. Course Rating: 69.7/69.0. Slope: 116/111. Green Fee: $35/$40. Cart Fee: $16 per person. *Comments: Demands precision and shot shaping.* ★★★★

No. 4 (Dubsdread). Holes: 18. Opened: 1964. Architect: Dick Wilson/Joe Lee. Yards: 6,940/5,590. Par: 72/72. Course Rating: 75.4/71.6. Slope: 142/130. Green Fee: $130. Cart Fee: Included in green fee. *Comments: with all the doglegs and challenging approach shots, won't let you have the same shot twice. Very expensive for the area, but worth it.* ★★★★ ½

GLENEAGLES GOLF CLUB. Facility Holes: 36. Opened: 1924. Architect: Charles Maddox/Frank P. Macdonald. Green Fee: $29/$35. Cart Fee: $14 per person. Discounts: Twilight, seniors. Walking: Unrestricted walking. Season: Mar.–Dec. Tee Times: Call golf shop. Notes: Range (grass). ✉ 13070 McCarthy Rd., 60439, 25 mi from Chicago ☎ 630/257–5466 ⊕ www.golfgleneagles.com ▤ No credit cards.

Red. Holes: 18. Yards: 6,090/6,090. Par: 70/74. Course Rating: 67.6/71.3. Slope: 112/111. *Comments: More than just an overflow for the Cog Hill facility, it's an 80-year-old classic.* ★★★ ½

White. Holes: 18. Yards: 6,250/6,080. Par: 70/75. Course Rating: 70.1/72.3. Slope: 120/114. *Comments: Ordinary.* ★★★ ½

PRAIRIE BLUFF GOLF CLUB. Facility Holes: 18. Opened: 1998. Architect: Roger Packard/Andy North. Yards: 6,832/5,314. Par: 72/72. Course Rating: 72.1/70.1. Slope: 122/115. Green Fee: $29/$41. Cart Fee: $14 per person. Discounts: Weekdays, twilight, seniors, juniors. Walking: Unrestricted walking. Season: Mar.–Nov. High: May–Sept. Tee Times: Call 7 days in advance. Notes: Range (grass). ✉ 19433 Renwick Rd., Lockport 60441, 30 mi from Chicago ☎ 815/836–4653 ▤ AE, D, MC, V. *Comments: Wide open, so it all depends on the wind. Easy to score on a calm day.* ★★★★

PRAIRIE LANDING GOLF CLUB. Facility Holes: 18. Opened: 1994. Architect: Robert Trent Jones Jr. Yards: 6,950/4,859. Par: 72/72. Course Rating: 73.2/68.3. Slope: 136/124. Green Fee: $59/$94. Cart Fee: Included in green fee. Discounts: Twilight, seniors, juniors. Walking: Unrestricted walking. Season: Apr.–Nov. High: May–Oct. Tee Times: Call 14 days in advance. Notes: Metal spikes, range (grass). ⊠ 2325 Longest Dr., West Chicago 60185, 30 mi from Chicago ☎ 630/208-7600 ⊕ www.prairielanding.com ⊟ AE, D, DC, MC, V. *Comments: Try to visualize where the Joliet guard towers would have been.* ★ ★ ★ ★

Where to Stay

FAIRFIELD INN. Reasonably priced, modern, and convenient, this branch of the national Fairfield chain is within a 10-mi radius of more than 40 golf courses and near many local restaurants. Rooms have stereo systems and ample-size desks. ⊠ 820 W. 79th St., Willowbrook 60527 ☎ 630/789-6300 or 800/932-2198 ⊒ 630/789-5855 ⊕ - www.fairfieldinn.com ⌁ 129 rooms ⌂ In-room data ports, cable TV, pool, laundry service, free parking, no-smoking rooms ⊟ AE, D, DC, MC, V ⦿ CP $.

HOLIDAY INN. Guest rooms at this hotel, about 5 mi from Cog Hill, were remodeled in 2002 to include VCRs, two telephones with data ports in each room, and more modern bedding and furnishings. For advice on planning outings, the concierge service is helpful. A complimentary area shuttle takes you within a 10-mi radius of hotel. ⊠ 7800 Kingery Rd., Willowbrook 60527 ☎ 630/325-6400 or 800/465-4329 ⊒ 630/ 325-2362 ⊕ www.holiday-inn.com ⌁ 220 rooms ⌂ Restaurant, cable TV, pool, gym, sauna, bar, laundry service, business services, airport shuttle, no-smoking rooms ⊟ AE, D, DC, MC, V $$.

RADISSON HOTEL CHICAGO–ALSIP. You get what you'd expect from a Radisson here—clean rooms with adequate work space and all the basics, like coffeemakers and hair dryers. There's also a pool, fitness room, and game room. Locals come here to dine on generous-size steaks and chops at Allgauer's Grill. ⊠ 5000 W. 127th St., Alsip 60803 ☎ 708/371-7300 or 800/333-3333 ⊒ 708/371-9949 ⊕ www.radisson.com ⌁ 193 rooms ⌂ Restaurant, room service, in-room data ports, cable TV, indoor pool, gym, bar, video game room, laundry service, business services, some pets allowed (fee), no-smoking rooms ⊟ AE, D, DC, MC, V $$.

WHEATON INN. Four blocks from town and the train station, this redbrick inn serves a hearty breakfast on its back patio and offers afternoon wine-and-cheese receptions and pre-bedtime cookies and milk. Each room has its own Williamsburg color scheme and coordinated furnishings. ⊠ 301 W. Roosevelt Rd., Wheaton 60187 ☎ 630/ 690-2600 or 800/447-4667 ⊒ 630/690-2623 ⊕ www.wheatoninn.com ⌁ 16 rooms ⌂ Dining room, some in-room hot tubs, cable TV, meeting rooms, no-smoking rooms ⊟ AE, D, MC, V ⦿ BP $$-$$$$.

Where to Eat

✕ **EGG HARBOR CAFE.** In the back of Wheaton Town Square, this popular breakfast spot is part of a small suburban chain that serves substantial egg dishes, pancakes, and other breakfast extravagances. The fresh blended juices are a big hit. It opens at 6:30 AM daily. ⊠ 221 Town Sq., Wheaton ☎ 630/510-1344 ▭ AE, D, MC, V ⊗ No dinner $.

✕ **PUBLIC LANDING.** Fresh takes on traditional American classics are served in a land-mark building along the I&M Canal at this sister property of the elegant Tallgrass. Try the blackened-chicken spring rolls and regional trout dishes. The kids' menu has a pint-size serving of prime rib on weekends. ⊠ 200 W. 8th St., Lockport ☎ 815/838-6500 ▭ MC, V ⊗ Closed Mon. No lunch weekends $$–$$$$.

✕ **TALLGRASS.** Urbanites happily make the 60-mi trip from Chicago to this intimate French restaurant, in a restored 1895 commercial building with vintage wood paneling and original interior wood beams. Lobster dishes and rack of lamb with Gorgonzola are favorites, but the entire menu draws raves from those who flock here. You select from three-, four-, or five-course prix-fixe meals. The wine list is lengthy and full of reason-ably priced options. ⊠ 1006 S. State St., Lockport ☎ 815/838-5566 ⌒ Reservations essential ⏏ Jacket required ▭ MC, V ⊗ Closed Mon. and Tues. No lunch $$$$.

Essentials

Getting Here

Lemont is about 35 mi southwest of Chicago. To get here, take I-55 south from Chicago roughly 27 mi, to exit 271A, South Lemont Road. The town is right off the highway.

Visitor Information

🛈 **Lemont Chamber of Commerce** ⊠ 101 Main St., 60439 ☎ 630/257-5997 🖷 630/257-3238 ⊕ www.lemontchamber.com. **Lockport Chamber of Commerce** ⊠ 921 S. State St., Lockport 60441 ☎ 815/838-3357 🖷 815/838-2653 ⊕ www.lockportchamber.com. **Wheaton Chamber of Commerce** ⊠ 108 E. Wesley St., Wheaton 60187 ☎ 630/668-6464 🖷 630/668-2744 ⊕ www.wheatonchamber.org.

QUAD CITIES

The Mississippi River might dominate the Quad Cities (Rock Island and Moline, Illinois, and Bettendorf and Davenport, Iowa), but golf generates the most tourism here. The Quad Cities ranked number 2 on *Golf Digest*'s Best Golf Towns in America survey in 1998, and the golf landscape has only improved since then. The Tournament Players Club at Deere Run in Rock Island is one of the handful of public-access courses that hosts a PGA Tour event, the John Deere Classic, and both the Iowa and Illinois sides of the river are dotted with other four-star golf options. Weekend travelers from Chicago, as well as Des Moines and St. Louis, flock to the area to play golf during the day, then roll the dice on the riverboat casinos that line the

Emeis Golf Club (18)	6,463/5,549	72/72	71.9/74.0	120/115	$14
Glynns Creek Golf Course (18)	7,036/5,097	72/72	73.5/68.3	131/104	$18/$27
Palmer Hills Municipal (18)	6,535/5,923	71/71	71.5/74.0	124/130	$17/$19
Tournament Players Club (18)	7,183/5,179	71/71	75.1/70.1	134/119	$76/$123

Mississippi shores. And why not? Not only is it an easy drive from any of those cities, but green fees and hotel rooms rarely top $50, and events like the Bix Biederbecke jazz festival each July give the area a little extra flavor.

Courses

Golf Digest REVIEWS

EMEIS GOLF CLUB. Facility Holes: 18. Opened: 1961. Architect: C. D. Wagstaff. Yards: 6,463/5,549. Par: 72/72. Course Rating: 71.9/74.0. Slope: 120/115. Green Fee: $14. Cart Fee: $18 per person. Discounts: Seniors, juniors. Walking: Unrestricted walking. Season: Apr.–Nov. Tee Times: Call 3 days in advance. ✉ 4500 W. Central Park, Davenport, IA 52804 ☎ 319/326-7825 ▭ MC, V. *Comments: Reserve your opinion until after you play. The clubhouse isn't much to look at, but the course is terrific.* ★ ★ ★ ½

GLYNNS CREEK GOLF COURSE. Facility Holes: 18. Opened: 1992. Architect: Dick Watson. Yards: 7,036/5,097. Par: 72/72. Course Rating: 73.5/68.3. Slope: 131/104. Green Fee: $18/$27. Cart Fee: $12 per person. Discounts: Weekdays, twilight, seniors, juniors. Walking: Walking at certain times. Season: Apr.–Nov. High: June-Aug. Tee Times: Call 30 days in advance. Notes: Range (grass). ✉ 19251 290th St., Long Grove, IA 52756, 10 mi from Davenport ☎ 563/328-3284 ⊕ www.glynnscreek.com ▭ D, MC, V. *Comments: You can't beat the green fee for the wonderful setting inside a state park.* ★ ★ ★ ★

PALMER HILLS MUNICIPAL GOLF COURSE. Facility Holes: 18. Opened: 1975. Architect: William James Spear. Yards: 6,535/5,923. Par: 71/71. Course Rating: 71.5/74.0. Slope: 124/130. Green Fee: $17/$19. Cart Fee: $22 per cart. Discounts: Weekdays, twilight, seniors, juniors. Walking: Unrestricted walking. Season: Apr.–Nov. Tee Times: Call 7 days in advance. Notes: Range (mat). ✉ 2999 Middle Rd., Bettendorf 52722, 3 mi from Davenport ☎ 563/332-8296 ▭ D, MC, V. *Comments: No, not that Palmer. The town bought it from the Palmer family, who had used it privately for 50 years.* ★ ★ ★ ½

TOURNAMENT PLAYERS CLUB AT DEERE RUN. Facility Holes: 18. Opened: 2000. Architect: D. A. Weibring/Chris Gray. Yards: 7,183/5,179. Par: 71/71. Course Rating: 75.1/70.1. Slope: 134/119. Green Fee: $76/$123. Cart Fee: Included in green fee. Discounts: Twilight, seniors, juniors. Walking: Mandatory cart. Season: Mar.–Nov. Tee Times: Call 45 days in advance. Notes: Range (grass). ✉ 3100 Heather Knoll, Silvis 61282 ☎ 309/796-6000 or 877/872-3677 ⊕ www.tpc.com ▭ AE, DC, MC, V. *Comments: Even tour players at the John Deere Classic struggle with number 18, a par-5 with dangerous water around the green.* ★ ★ ★ ★ ½

Where to Stay

⚏ ABBEY HOTEL. Built in 1914 to house a cloistered Carmelite monastery, this formidable Romanesque structure on a bluff overlooking the Mississippi River is on the National Register of Historic Places. Fawn-and-beige guest rooms have Italian marble bathrooms, and tall arched windows overlook the river or the hotel's manicured grounds and sparkling swimming pool. Immediately outside Bettendorf proper, the hotel is ½ mi off I-74 at exit 4. ⊠ 1401 Central Ave., Bettendorf, IA 52722 ☎ 319/355–0291 or 800/438–7535 ⊟ 319/355–7647 ⊕ www.theabbeyhotel.com ➳ 19 rooms ⚐ Room service, in-room data ports, cable TV, some in-room VCRs, pool, exercise equipment, bar, business services, meeting rooms, airport shuttle; no smoking ⊟ AE, D, DC, MC, V ⏺ CP $.

⚏ FOUR POINTS SHERATON. Clubs, a casino, and a cluster of restaurants are nearby this hotel in the heart of the entertainment district. Rooms are technologically up-to-date, with Internet access via in-room TVs and convenient cordless phones. Some have views of the Mississippi River, which flows a block away. ⊠ 226 17th St., Rock Island 61201 ☎ 309/794–1212 or 888/625–5144 ⊟ 309/794–0852 ⊕ www.starwood.com/fourpoints ➳ 175 rooms ⚐ Restaurant, room service, in-room data ports, cable TV, indoor pool, gym, hair salon, massage, bar, laundry service, Internet, business services, meeting rooms, no-smoking rooms ⊟ AE, D, DC, MC, V $$.

⚏ HEARTLAND INN. The Iowa-and-Wisconsin-only chain ascribes to modest motel prices mixed with a few luxe touches. King- and queen-size beds have pillow-top mattresses, some rooms have hot tubs, and there's free access to a nearby health club. The motel is within walking distance of dining, shopping, movie theaters, and three large casinos. ⊠ 815 Golden Valley Dr., Bettendorf, IA 52722 ☎ 563/355–6336 or 800/334–3277 Ext. 14 ⊟ 563/355–0039 ⊕ www.heartlandinns.com ➳ 86 rooms ⚐ Some in-room hot tubs, some microwaves, pool, sauna, laundry facilities, business services, free parking, no-smoking rooms ⊟ AE, D, DC, MC, V ⏺ CP $–$$.

⚏ LODGE HOTEL AND CONFERENCE CENTER. The massive stone hotel with a nine-story tower section and sharply pitched roof looks like a European castle set down on the banks of the Mississippi. The opulent, medieval feel isn't just on the outside: guest rooms are finished in custom-made woodwork with deep marble fireplaces, one-of-a-kind tapestries, scores of rich oil paintings, and heavily draped four-poster oak beds. ⊠ 900 Spruce Hills Dr., Bettendorf, IA 52722 ☎ 563/359–7141 or 800/285–8637 ⊟ 563/359–5537 ⊕ www.lodgehotel.biz ➳ 210 rooms ⚐ Restaurant, in-room data ports, cable TV, 2 pools (1 indoor), gym, hot tub, sauna, 2 bars, business services, airport shuttle, some pets allowed (fee), no-smoking rooms ⊟ AE, D, DC, MC, V $.

Where to Eat

✕ THE DOCK. Almost every table has a panoramic view of the Mississippi through this riverfront restaurant's floor-to-ceiling windows. Surprising game dishes like emu and an indulgent pairing of steak and lobster are the menu's focus. The pecan-crusted snapper is a house favorite. ⊠ 125 S. Perry St., Davenport, IA ☎ 319/322–5331 ⊟ AE, D, DC, MC, V $$–$$$$.

✕**IOWA MACHINE SHED.** Old saw blades, miniature trucks, and other antique country bric-a-brac cover the interior of the oldest of six machine sheds. Plaid shirt-and denim-clad waitstaff deliver heaping, family-style portions of comfort food. Try the pot roast or the chicken-fried steak—and plan to share. If you want a lighter meal, graze on the salad bar. ✉7250 Northwest Blvd., Davenport, IA ☎319/391-2427 ▭AE, D, DC, MC, V $-$$$.

✕**ROCK ISLAND BREWING CO.** Local reggae, folk, or guitar-driven acts rock this restaurant and pub, so don't come here for a quiet tête-à-tête. The unfussy, standard bar fare includes burgers and quesadillas, but it also delves into seven variations on the chicken sandwich. ✉1815 2nd Ave., Rock Island, IL ☎309/793-1999 ▭AE, D, MC, V ◷Closed Sun. ¢-$.

Essentials

The Quad Cities are about 175 mi west of Chicago. As the name suggests, the area is made up of four distinct cities along the Mississippi River: Moline and Rock Island in Illinois, and Bettendorf and Davenport in Iowa. Although the Mississippi generally runs from north to south, in the Quad Cities the river runs from east to west, making Iowa north of Illinois.

Getting Here

To reach the Quad Cities from Chicago, take I-290 west for 13 mi to I-88 west for 140 mi. Continue onto I-80 west for 15 mi. The trip takes about three hours.

Visitor Information

🚩 **Bettendorf Chamber of Commerce** ✉2117 State St., Bettendorf, IA 52722 ☎563/355-4753 🖷563/355-7913 ⊕www.bettendorfchamber.com. **Davenport Chamber of Commerce** ✉130 W. 2nd St., Davenport, IA 52801 ☎563/322-1706 ⊕www.quadcities.com/davenport. **Quad Cities Convention and Visitors Bureau** ✉2021 River Dr., Moline, IL 61265 ☎563/322-3911 or 800/747-7800 🖷309/764-9443 ⊕www.visitquadcities.com.

WATERLOO & MADISON, IL

Luckily for visiting golfers, things have changed in Waterloo since Lewis & Clark camped here before their great trek west. The Waterloo–Madison area, in the corridor between Chicago and St. Louis and close to the Mississippi River, is stocked with a shocking number of four-star or better courses. Two of the best are Gateway National, across the river from St. Louis, and Eagle Creek Resort in Findlay, farther upstate. There's also the Spencer T. Olin Community Golf Course, which cuts through mature forest. The average green fee is very

Course	Yards	Par	Course Rating	Slope	Green Fee
Annbriar Golf Course (18)	6,841/4,792	72/72	72.3/66.4	141/110	$50/$60
Eagle Creek Resort (18)	6,908/4,978	72/72	73.5/69.1	132/115	$27/$55
Far Oaks Golf Club (18)	7,016/4,897	72/72	73.3/71.8	141/114	$48/$66
Fox Creek Golf Club (18)	7,027/5,185	72/72	74.9/72.1	144/132	$25/$45
Gateway National Golf Links (18)	7,178/5,187	71/71	75.0/69.4	138/114	$29/$57
Spencer T. Olin Community (27) Learning Center Course (9) Spencer T. Olin Course (18)	1,795/1,300 6,941/5,049	30/30 72/72	73.8/68.5	135/117	$20/$60

reasonable ($20 to $60); Eagle Creek Resort is the most expensive per round, but if you stay in one of the resort's villas, you receive a substantial price break. The less-expensive golf leaves you with plenty of cash to head into St. Louis for a ball game or a ride to the top of the Gateway Arch.

Courses

Golf Digest REVIEWS

ANNBRIAR GOLF COURSE. Facility Holes: 18. Opened: 1993. Architect: Michael Hurdzan. Yards: 6,841/4,792. Par: 72/72. Course Rating: 72.3/66.4. Slope: 141/110. Green Fee: $50/$60. Cart Fee: Included in green fee. Discounts: Twilight, seniors, juniors. Walking: Mandatory cart. Season: Year-round. High: May–Oct. Tee Times: Call 7 days in advance. Notes: Range (grass). ⊠ 1524 Birdie La., Waterloo 62298, 25 mi from St. Louis ☎ 618/939-4653 or 888/939-5191 ⊕ www.annbriar.com ⊟ AE, MC, V. *Comments: A creative treat from Hurdzan.* ★★★★ ½

EAGLE CREEK RESORT. Facility Holes: 18. Opened: 1989. Architect: Ken Killian. Yards: 6,908/4,978. Par: 72/72. Course Rating: 73.5/69.1. Slope: 132/115. Green Fee: $27/$55. Cart Fee: Included in green fee. Discounts: Weekdays, twilight, seniors, juniors. Walking: Mandatory cart. Season: Year-round. Tee Times: Call golf shop. Notes: Range (grass), lodging (138). ⊠ Eagle Creek State Park, Findlay 62534, 35 mi from Decatur ☎ 217/756-3456 or 800/876-3245 ⊕ www.eaglecreekresort.com ⊟ AE, D, DC, MC, V. *Comments: Built on the shores by the same designer who did Kemper Lakes, in Long Grove.* ★★★ ½

FAR OAKS GOLF CLUB. Facility Holes: 18. Opened: 1997. Architect: Bob Goalby/Kye Goalby. Yards: 7,016/4,897. Par: 72/72. Course Rating: 73.3/71.8. Slope: 141/114. Green Fee: $48/$66. Cart Fee: Included in green fee. Discounts: Twilight. Walking: Unrestricted walking. Season: Year-round. Tee Times: Call 7 days in advance. Notes: Range (grass). ⊠ 419 Old Collinsville Rd., Caseyville 62232 ☎ 618/628-2900 or 314/386-4653 ⊕ www.faroaksgolfclub.com ⊟ AE, MC, V. *Comments: This course is framed by prairie grass.* ★★★★

FOX CREEK GOLF CLUB. Facility Holes: 18. Opened: 1992. Architect: Gary Kern. Yards: 7,027/5,185. Par: 72/72. Course Rating: 74.9/72.1. Slope: 144/132. Green Fee: $25/$45.

Cart Fee: Included in green fee. Discounts: Weekdays, twilight, seniors. Walking: Mandatory cart. Season: Year-round. Tee Times: Call 7 days in advance. Notes: Metal spikes, range (grass). ✉6555 Fox Creek Dr., Edwardsville 62025, 20 mi from St. Louis, MO ☎618/692–9400 ⊕www.foxcreek.net ☰MC, V. *Comments: A demanding walk, and tough from the tee.* ★★★★

GATEWAY NATIONAL GOLF LINKS. Facility Holes: 18. Opened: 1998. Architect: Keith Foster. Yards: 7,178/5,187. Par: 71/71. Course Rating: 75.0/69.4. Slope: 138/114. Green Fee: $29/$57. Cart Fee: $8 per person. Discounts: Weekdays, twilight, seniors, juniors. Walking: Unrestricted walking. Season: Year-round. Tee Times: Call golf shop. Notes: Range (grass). ✉ 18 Golf Dr., Madison 62060, 4 mi from St. Louis, MO ☎618/482–4653 ⊕ www.gatewaynational.com ☰AE, MC, V. *Comments: You can see the Gateway Arch from the course. Terrific links-style course.* ★★★★

SPENCER T. OLIN COMMUNITY GOLF COURSE. Facility Holes: 27. Cart Fee: Included in green fee. Discounts: Seniors, juniors. Season: Year-round. Tee Times: Call golf shop. Notes: Range (grass). ✉ 4701 College Ave., Alton 62002, 25 mi from St. Louis ☎618/465–3111 ⊕ www.spencertolingolf.com ☰AE, MC, V.

Learning Center Course. Holes: 9. Opened: 2000. Architect: Arnold Palmer. Yards: 1,795/1,300. Par: 30/30. Walking: Unrestricted walking. UR

Spencer T. Olin Course. Holes: 18. Opened: 1989. Architect: Arnold Palmer/Ed Seay. Yards: 6,941/5,049. Par: 72/72. Course Rating: 73.8/68.5. Slope: 135/117. Green Fee: $20/$60. Walking: Walking at certain times. ★★★★

Comments: Arnold Palmer was old friends with Olin, an Alton resident, so when Alton built a muni, it went first-class.

Where to Stay

🏨 **COMFORT INN.** Take in views of St. Louis from this standard outpost of the national chain. The inn, perched on a bluff on the southeastern outskirts of Edwardsville, is 15 minutes from the famed arch and an easy drive to Fox Creek Golf Club. Three suites have microwaves, refrigerators, and hot tubs. ✉3080 S. Rte. 157, Edwardsville 62025 ☎618/656–4900 or 800/228–5150 🖷618/656–0998 ⊕www.comfortinn.com ⤶68 rooms, 3 suites ♿ In-room data ports, some in-room hot tubs, some microwaves, some refrigerators, cable TV, indoor pool, exercise equipment, hot tub, business services, meeting rooms, no-smoking rooms ☰AE, D, DC, MC, V ⏎CP $.

🏨 **EAGLE CREEK RESORT.** Vivid colors, structured sofas and wing chairs, and full floral arrangements throughout the resort create a seamless sophistication. Polished touches include sleek light fixtures and quartz or quarry tile floors, and sharp, understated room furniture, handmade by a nearby Amish community. Ten family suites have private patios. Beyond the full, on-site golf course, you can tee off at the minigolf course, sweat it out at the gym, or do laps in the indoor or outdoor pool, the latter with views of Eagle Creek State Park and Lake Shelbyville. ✑ Box 230, Findlay 62534 ☎800/ 876–3245 🖷217/756–3456 ⊕www.eaglecreekresort.com ⤶128 rooms, 10 suites ♿2 restaurants, room service, in-room data ports, some refrigerators, cable TV with movies, 18-hole golf course, miniature golf, 2 pools (1 indoor), gym, hot tub, sauna, bicycles, hiking, horseback riding, cross-country skiing, laundry services, business services, no-smoking rooms ▭AE, DC, MC, V $$$$.

HOMERIDGE BED & BREAKFAST. Period furnishings outfit this Civil War–era B&B in Jerseyville, 12 mi north of Alton. Patterned wallpaper and bold curtains offset the light wicker furniture in the inviting sitting room. The four guest rooms tend toward lots of flowers and lace, though Kathleen's room keeps the frills a bit more under wraps. All rooms have views of the hilly countryside. ✉1470 N. State St., Jerseyville 62052 ☎618/498–3442 ♼618/498–5662 ⊕ www.homeridge.com ⇆4 rooms ♨ Pool; no room phones, no room TVs, no smoking ▭AE, MC, V ⦿BP $.

INNKEEPER MOTEL. Though modest, this motel has clean, simple rooms, some with microwaves and refrigerators. An attached restaurant serves country breakfast all day. It's 7 mi north of Edwardsville on Route 157. ✉401 E. State St., Hamel 62046 ☎618/633–2111 ♼618/633–2117 ⇆28 rooms ♨ Some microwaves, some refrigerators, cable TV, some pets allowed (fee), no-smoking rooms ▭AE, D, MC, V ¢.

Where to Eat

✗**RUSTY'S RESTAURANT.** Dine beneath antique chandeliers in this restored 19th-century trading post, where veal saltimboca and steak à la Romano are favorites. Choose among daily fish specials, like rainbow trout dusted with almond flour or scallops seared with orange and ginger. There's a kids' menu, buffet lunch, and Sunday brunch, and live entertainment Friday and Saturday. ✉1201 N. Main St., Edwardsville ☎618/656–1113 ▭AE, D, DC, MC, V ⊘No lunch Sat. $$–$$$.

✗**TONY'S.** Family-owned and operated since 1954, this restaurant, made up of six dining rooms, serves pasta, steak, and seafood dishes. The signature dish is the Pepperloin steak, marinated in a secret sauce, rolled in cracked black pepper, and drizzled with garlic butter. ✉312 Piasa St., Alton ☎618/462–8384 ▭AE, D, DC, MC, V ⊘No lunch $–$$$$.

Essentials

Getting Here

Madison and Waterloo are about 300 mi south of Chicago. To get to either, take I–55 south toward St. Louis. Take IL–203 north via exit 48 to get to Madison, and IL–3 south via exit 6 to reach Waterloo. Madison is a four-hour drive; tack on an additional half hour for Waterloo.

Visitor Information

🛈 **Edwardsville/Glen Carbon Chamber of Commerce** ✉200 University Park Dr., Suite 260, Edwardsville 62025 ☎618/656–7600 ⊕ www.edglenchamber.com. **Greater Alton/Twin Rivers Convention and Visitors Bureau** ✉200 Piasa St., Alton 62002 ☎618/465–6676 or 800/258–6645 ⊕www.visitalton.com.

AROUND
DALLAS

Karsten Creek

By Matthew Rudy and Kay Winzenried

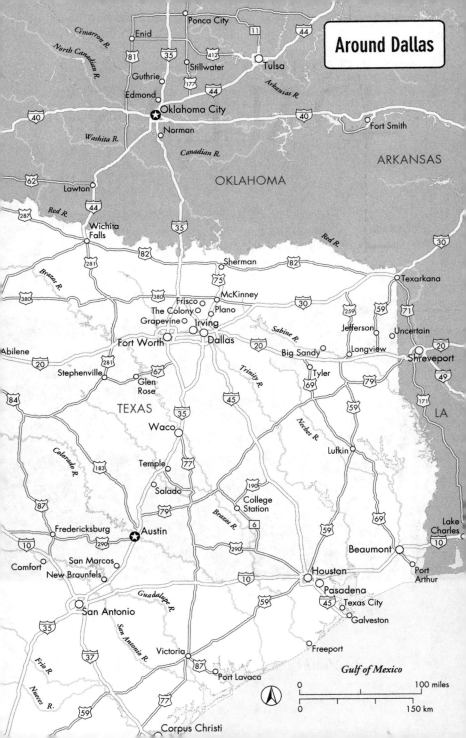

Around Dallas

One look at a map of Texas and it's easy to see how Dallas came to be the golf hub of the state. Not only is the city relatively central in Texas, but the Dallas–Fort Worth airport serves as the main way station for dozens of commuter flights around the state, as well as for a full slate of cross-country and regional flights from United and American.

Even if you never drove more than 30 mi outside of the Dallas city limits, you'd be able to find a wide variety of golf. From Tour 18 Golf Club, where you can play a reproduction of Augusta National's famously difficult 3-hole Amen Corner, to the conservative, all-male, and very exclusive Preston Trail Golf Club, which even Alex Rodriguez couldn't get in to, it shouldn't be too hard to find something that suits you. You can even play right off the plane—you can be on the first tee at Bear Creek Golf Club, on the grounds of DFW Airport, 20 minutes after picking up your luggage.

Dallas's city-run courses are justly acclaimed for their quality, more than carrying their weight in golf lore. Tenison Park was Lee Trevino's "office," where he learned how to play golf and how to hustle. Cedar Crest Golf Course might have the most impressive bloodlines of any city-owned course in the country. Designed by A. W. Tillinghast in 1917 as a private club, Cedar Crest was the site of the 1927 PGA Championship, which Walter Hagen won. After the city took it over in 1947, it became one of the jewels of the system.

Get outside the city limits and into the Metroplex, the local name given to the surrounding area that includes McKinney, Plano, Fort Worth, Irving, and Dallas suburbs, and you can be part of the perfect getaway. Fort Worth feels like Dallas did before it went big city, with honky-tonk bars, barbecue joints, and rodeo 50 weekends a year. McKinney used to be an isolated outpost too far north to live in and too boring to visit. Now, with the development of Hank Haney's Golf Ranch and the new Tournament Players Club design, it should be on everyone's map.

For those who don't mind spending a little more time in the car, Oklahoma City is well within one-day-drive striking distance. Most Dallas residents only make the drive to OKC when the University of Texas is playing Oklahoma or Oklahoma State, but a round at the Tom Fazio–designed Karsten Creek golf club is worth the trip all by itself. (The Woodlands, north of Houston, is another option. For information on this and other Houston-area courses, see Chapter 7.)

DALLAS

Bear Creek Golf Club (36)					$25/$69
East (18)	6,670/5,620	72/72	72.5/72.4	127/124	
West (18)	6,675/5,570	72/72	72.7/72.5	130/122	
Cedar Crest Golf Course (18)	6,550/5,594	71/75	71.0/76.0	121/116	$8/$21
Golf Club at Castle Hills (18)	7,152/5,481	72/72	74.3/71.4	139/119	$80/$100
Tangle Ridge Golf Club (18)	6,835/5,187	72/72	72.2/70.2	129/117	$28/$49
Tenison Park Golf Course (36)					$7/$21
Tenison Glen (18)	6,605/5,107	72/72	71.2/70.8	122/115	
Tenison Highlands (18)	7,078/5,905	72/72	73.9/68.2	129/119	$17/$42

FORT WORTH

Cliffs Resort (18)	6,808/4,876	71/71	73.9/68.4	143/124	$40/$90
Cross Timbers Golf Course (18)	6,734/5,051	72/72	71.5/68.2	128/113	$15/$35
Doral Tosero Golf Club (18)	7,005/5,097	72/72	75.6/64.5	143/110	$30/$55
Eagle Point Golf Club (18)	6,647/5,056	72/72	71.2/64.1	119/102	$20/$28
Golf Club at Fossil Creek (18)	6,865/5,066	72/72	73.6/68.5	131/111	$25/$75
Hidden Creek Golf Club (18)	6,753/4,968	71/71	73.8/66.7	139/110	$15/$38
Iron Horse Golf Course (18)	6,580/5,083	70/70	71.8/69.6	130/119	$29/$38
Links at WaterChase (18)	7,304/4,941	72/72	75.4/70.9	145/123	$30/$75
Sky Creek Ranch Golf Club (18)	6,953/5,390	72/72	73.4/72.8	136/132	$45/$75
Squaw Valley Golf Course (36)					$38/$48
Apache Links (18)	7,002/5,123	72/72	74.1/70.5	134/120	
Comanche Lakes (18)	7,000/5,016	72/72	73.9/70.3	132/119	$18/$40
Sugartree Golf Club (18)	6,775/5,254	71/71	72.8/71.0	138/126	$25/$45
Whitestone Golf Club (18)	7,117/5,201	72/72	74.4/71.2	135/125	$25/$52

IRVING

Cowboys Golf Club (18)	7,017/4,702	72/72	74.2/68.9	140/114	$45/$135
Four Seasons Resort and Club (18)	6,899/5,340	70/70	73.5/70.6	135/116	$150/$185
Tierra Verde Golf Club (18)	6,975/5,111	72/72	73.3/70.5	129/119	$47/$60
Tour 18 Golf Club (18)	7,033/5,493	72/72	74.3/66.3	138/119	$59/$95

	YARDAGE	PAR	COURSE	SLOPE	GREEN FEE
MCKINNEY & FRISCO					
Chase Oaks Golf Club (27)					
Black Jack (18)	6,762/5,105	72/72	74.4/70.0	139/128	$37/$57
Sawtooth (9)	3,250/2,746	36/36	70.1/72.0	130/124	$29
Hank Haney Golf Ranch					
Trails of Frisco Golf Club (18)	6,959/5,104	71/71	74.0/65.0	138/111	$59/$75
Tribute Golf Club (18)	7,002/5,302	72/72	73.2/65.6	128/111	$50/$105
Twin Creeks Golf Club (18)	6,924/4,790	72/72	73.2/66.5	131/107	$40/$60
Westin Stonebriar Resort (18)	7,021/5,208	72/72	73.8/71.0	133/121	$115

Even if you can't get out of Dallas for a golf break, you can still get a handle on your golf game in town. Some of the game's most respected instructors are based in the Dallas area and offer lessons to the public. Randy Smith is the head professional at Royal Oaks Country Club, where he has taught Dallas natives (and club members) Justin Leonard, Harrison Frazar, and D. A. Weibring. Haney's main facility is in McKinney (where you might see Mark O'Meara in the next hitting bay), but he also has three smaller outposts in Dallas itself, along with one in Austin.

THE METROPLEX

The great thing about playing golf in the Dallas–Fort Worth area is that each time you visit, there's likely to be at least one or two courses ready to play that didn't exist the last time you were there. In the past three years, more than 30 courses have opened, including a course that pays homage to the NFL's Dallas Cowboys, another with a Scottish links flair, and a resort course complex that is as tony as it gets in oil country. The Metroplex is quickly becoming a golf destination in its own right.

If Dallas is Texas with a sophisticated spin, Fort Worth is the real thing, where locals can spot a tourist just by the way his cowboy hat sits on his head. Since the 1850s, Fort Worth has been where the West begins. As the last stop on the Chisholm Trail, Forth Worth was the gathering point for the millions of head of cattle driven from the Great Plains of the American West. Here, that beef was loaded onto trains and shipped west and into the marketplace. The city's stockyards have since been rehabilitated into a rocking downtown entertainment district.

If you do manage to get some sleep, many terrific public courses await you in greater Fort Worth. The best of them might be the Links at WaterChase, a Steven D. Plumer design that's already mature enough to host a Texas State Open. Two other must-plays are Squaw Valley Golf Course and Whitestone Golf Club. Squaw Valley is a bit of a drive out of town, but you won't regret the time invested. Whitestone is a Jeff Brauer–Jay Morrish collaboration that, in time, will be one of the best courses in the state. But the Holy Grail is Shady Oaks, Ben Hogan's club. If a member invites you out for a round, drop everything and go.

Sandwiched between Dallas and Fort Worth, Irving gets lost in the shuffle every week of the year—except for the eight weeks that the Dallas Cowboys play at home. Even having the stadium in town is a mixed blessing. Thousands of fans visit, but most of them leave thinking Irving isn't much more than a collection of interstate exits. The quickest way to disabuse yourself of that notion is to take a room at the Four Seasons Resort and Club in, yes, Irving. Not only is the low-slung resort the quintessential luxury getaway from the bustle of Dallas, but its course is strong enough to host a PGA Tour event—the annual Byron Nelson Classic. And for the golfer, there's even more to see here. Next door, in Arlington (home of the Texas Rangers baseball team), Tierra Verde Golf Club is the only municipal course in the country to have earned Audubon Sanctuary status. And if you just can't get the Cowboys out of your head, there's always Cowboys Golf Club. The memorabilia in the clubhouse isn't the only place you can see past and present Cowboys, either. The course is close to the team's practice complex, so players regularly make the short drive over for some post-workout stress relief.

As it stands now, the McKinney area is a perfect Dallas compromise. It's far enough from the city center to keep its rural feel, but close enough to be convenient for dinner. Long term, the Fazio course at the Westin Stonebriar Resort should be the class of the area, but for pure fun, you owe it to yourself to visit the Tribute. It offers reproductions of famous British Open holes from Scotland, but without the long plane ride and bad food. Sure, the 1st and 18th here won't completely take you to St. Andrews and make you forget you're in desert scrubland, but they come close enough.

It's hard to knock the area for a quality golf trip, but the Metroplex has two flaws: The first is that it gives new meaning to the term "urban sprawl." You will have to spend some time in the car dealing with the area's infamous traffic and the 120-mi loop around the cities if you want to cover many of the area's best courses. The other is the land. Golf-course architects have to work extra hard to mold the flat terrain into a memorable golf experience. But most of them do.

THE TEXAS CONNECTION

Herbert Warren Wind, a highly respected writer for the *New Yorker* and other publications, once called Texas "the new Scotland" because of its habit of turning out so many championship golfers. "Lighthorse" Harry Cooper, Ben Hogan, Byron Nelson, Jimmy Demeret, Ben Crenshaw, Tom Kite, Justin Leonard, Babe Zaharias, Betsy Rawls, Kathy Whitworth—the list goes on and on. That illustrious group won scores of titles and more than 25 major championships among them. Cooper once bragged, "A team of Texans could beat a team from any country in the world." He may well have been right.

Courses

Golf Digest REVIEWS

Dallas

BEAR CREEK GOLF CLUB. Facility Holes: 36. Opened: 1981. Architect: Ted Robinson. Green Fee: $25/$69. Cart Fee: Included in green fee. Discounts: Weekdays, twilight, seniors, juniors. Walking: Walking at certain times. Season: Year-round. Tee Times: Call 7 days in advance. Notes: Range (grass). ⊠ 3500 Bear Creek Ct., 75261 ☎ 972/456–3200 ⊕ www.bearcreek-golf.com ☰ AE, MC, V.

East. Holes: 18. Yards: 6,670/5,620. Par: 72/72. Course Rating: 72.5/72.4. Slope: 127/124. ★★★★

West. Holes: 18. Yards: 6,675/5,570. Par: 72/72. Course Rating: 72.7/72.5. Slope: 130/122. ★★★ ½

Comments: A 36-hole course next to the Dallas–Fort Worth International Airport. It's the perfect place to begin (or end) a trip, as long as you don't mind hearing the engines of a Boeing 747 in your backswing. The West course is better than the East.

CEDAR CREST GOLF COURSE. Facility Holes: 18. Opened: 1923. Architect: A. W. Tillinghast. Yards: 6,550/5,594. Par: 71/75. Course Rating: 71.0/76.0. Slope: 121/116. Green Fee: $8/$21. Cart Fee: $20 per cart. Walking: Unrestricted walking. Season: Year-round Tee Times: Call up to 5 days in advance. ⊠ 1800 Southerland, 75223 ☎ 214/670–7615 ⊕ www.cedarcrestgolf.com ☰ AE, D, MC, V. ★★ ½

GOLF CLUB AT CASTLE HILLS. Facility Holes: 18. Opened: 1999. Architect: Jay Morrish/Carter Morrish. Yards: 7,152/5,481. Par: 72/72. Course Rating: 74.3/71.4. Slope: 139/119. Green Fee: $80/$100. Cart Fee: Included in green fee. Discounts: Weekdays, twilight, seniors, juniors. Walking: Walking at certain times. Season: Year-round. Tee Times: Call 7 days in advance. Notes: Range (grass). ⊠ 699 Lady of the Lake Blvd., Lewisville 75056 ☎ 972/899–7400 ⊕ www.thegolfclubch.com ☰ AE, MC, V. *Comments: Not for the squeamish, but certainly fun to look at.* ★★★★

TANGLE RIDGE GOLF CLUB. Facility Holes: 18. Opened: 1995. Architect: Jeff Brauer. Yards: 6,835/5,187. Par: 72/72. Course Rating: 72.2/70.2. Slope: 129/117. Green Fee: $28/$49. Cart Fee: $14 per person. Discounts: Twilight, seniors, juniors. Walking: Unrestricted walking. Season: Year-round. Tee Times: Call 7 days in advance. Notes: Range (grass). ⊠ 818 Tangle Ridge Dr., Grand Prairie 75052, 30 mi from Dallas ☎ 972/

299-6837 ⊕ www.tangleridge.com ⊟ AE, D, MC, V. *Comments: Lakeside course is fun to play and scenic but should not be at the top of your list.* ★ ★ ★ ★

TENISON PARK GOLF COURSE. Facility Holes: 36. Walking: Unrestricted walking. Season: Year-round. Tee Times: Call up to 4 days in advance. ⊠ 3501 Samuel Blvd., 75223 ☎ 214/670-1402 ⊕ www.tenisonpark.com ⊟ AE, MC, V.

Tenison Glen Holes: 18. Opened: 1927. Architect: Ralph Plummer. Yards: 6,605/5,107. Par: 72/72. Course Rating: 71.2/70.8. Slope: 122/115. Green Fee: $7/$21. Cart Fee: $12 per person. ★ ★ ★

Tenison Highlands. Holes: 18. Opened: 2000. Architect: D. A. Weibring/Steve Wolfard. Yards: 7,078/5,905. Par: 72/72. Course Rating: 73.9/68.2. Slope: 129/119. Green Fee: $17/$42. Cart Fee: $12 per person. ★ ★ ★ ★

Fort Worth

CLIFFS RESORT. Facility Holes: 18. Opened: 1988. Architect: Bruce Devlin/Robert von Hagge. Yards: 6,808/4,876. Par: 71/71. Course Rating: 73.9/68.4. Slope: 143/124. Green Fee: $40/$90. Cart Fee: Included in green fee. Discounts: Weekdays, twilight, juniors. Walking: Mandatory cart. Season: Year-round. High: Apr.–Oct. Tee Times: Call 7 days in advance. Notes: Range (grass), lodging (90). ⊠ 160 Cliffs Dr., Graford 76449, 75 mi from Fort Worth ☎ 940/779-4040 or 888/843-2543 ⊕ www.thecliffsresort.com ⊟ AE, D, MC, V. *Comments: A bit of a drive from Fort Worth. Be sure to ask for the yardage book.* ★ ★ ★ ★ ¹/₂

CROSS TIMBERS GOLF COURSE. Facility Holes: 18. Opened: 1995. Architect: Jeff Brauer. Yards: 6,734/5,051. Par: 72/72. Course Rating: 71.5/68.2. Slope: 128/113. Green Fee: $15/$35. Cart Fee: $10 per person. Discounts: Weekdays, guest, twilight, seniors, juniors. Walking: Walking at certain times. Season: Year-round. Tee Times: Call 7 days in advance. Notes: Range (grass). ⊠ 1181 S. Stewart, Azle 76020, 14 mi from Fort Worth ☎ 817/444-4940 ⊟ AE, D, MC, V. *Comments: Undulations will send good tee shots astray—and save some bad ones.* ★ ★ ★ ★

DORAL TOSERO GOLF CLUB. Facility Holes: 18. Opened: 2000. Architect: Greg Norman. Yards: 7,005/5,097. Par: 72/72. Course Rating: 75.6/64.5. Slope: 143/110. Green Fee: $30/$55. Cart Fee: Included in green fee. Walking: Unrestricted walking. Season: Year-round. Tee Times: Call up to 30 days in advance. ⊠ 15801 Championship Pkwy., 76177 ☎ 817/497-2582 ⊕ www.doraltesoro.com ⊟ AE, MC, V. *Comments: Giant greens and no rough. Learn to hit the bump-and-run shot before tackling this course.* UR

EAGLE POINT GOLF CLUB. Facility Holes: 18. Yards: 6,647/5,056. Par: 72/72. Course Rating: 71.2/64.1. Slope: 119/102. Green Fee: $20/$28. Cart Fee: $20 per cart. Discounts: Twilight, seniors, juniors. Walking: Unrestricted walking. Season: Year-round. Tee Times: Call golf shop. Notes: Range (grass), lodging (150). ⊠ 2211 I–35E North, Denton 76205, 35 mi from Dallas/Fort Worth ☎ 940/387-5180 ⊟ AE, D, DC, MC, V. *Comments: This good-value course is conveniently attached to a Radisson.* ★ ★ ★ ★

GOLF CLUB AT FOSSIL CREEK. Facility Holes: 18. Opened: 1987. Architect: Arnold Palmer/Ed Seay. Yards: 6,865/5,066. Par: 72/72. Course Rating: 73.6/68.5. Slope: 131/111. Green Fee: $25/$75. Cart Fee: Included in green fee. Discounts: Weekdays, twilight, sen-

IN THE ZONE

Native Texan Ben Hogan was well known for his icy stare and for being "in the zone" when playing. Once, paired with Claude Harmon at The Masters, he was so preoccupied that he apparently didn't notice that Harmon had scored a hole-in-one on the tough par-3 12th in the middle of "Amen Corner." After Hogan putted out for birdie, he said in all sincerity, "Claude, I can't remember the last time I made a two here. What did you have?"

iors, juniors. Walking: Mandatory cart. Season: Year-round. High: Apr.–Oct. Tee Times: Call 7 days in advance. Notes: Range (grass). ✉3401 Clubgate Dr., 76137 ☎817/498-5538 ⊕ www.fossil-creek.com ☰AE, MC, V. *Comments: Catch it at the right time—weekend fees get very high.* ★ ★ ★ ½

HIDDEN CREEK GOLF CLUB. Facility Holes: 18. Opened: 1997. Architect: Steven D. Plumer. Yards: 6,753/4,968. Par: 71/71. Course Rating: 73.8/66.7. Slope: 139/110. Green Fee: $15/$38. Cart Fee: Included in green fee. Discounts: Weekdays, twilight, seniors, juniors. Walking: Unrestricted walking. Season: Year-round. Tee Times: Call 7 days in advance. Notes: Range (grass). ✉700 S. Burleson Ave., Burleson 76028, 14 mi from Fort Worth ☎817/447-4444 ⊕ www.hiddencreekgolfcourse.com ☰AE, D, MC, V. *Comments: Save yourself for the 16th and 18th. They're brutal.* ★ ★ ★ ½

IRON HORSE GOLF COURSE. Facility Holes: 18. Opened: 1990. Architect: Dick Phelps. Yards: 6,580/5,083. Par: 70/70. Course Rating: 71.8/69.6. Slope: 130/119. Green Fee: $29/$38. Cart Fee: $12 per person. Discounts: Weekdays, twilight, seniors, juniors. Walking: Unrestricted walking. Season: Year-round. Tee Times: Call 5 days in advance. Notes: Range (grass). ✉6200 Skylark Circle, North Richland Hill 76180, 10 mi from Fort Worth ☎817/485-6666 or 888/522-9921 ⊕ www.ironhorsetx.com ☰AE, MC, V. *Comments: Tricky, hidden shots make pace of play slow.* ★ ★ ★ ½

LINKS AT WATERCHASE. Facility Holes: 18. Opened: 2000. Architect: Steven D. Plumer. Yards: 7,304/4,941. Par: 72/72. Course Rating: 75.4/70.9. Slope: 145/123. Green Fee: $30/$75. Cart Fee: Included in green fee. Discounts: Weekdays, twilight, seniors. Walking: Walking at certain times. Season: Year-round. High: Mar.–Oct. Tee Times: Call 7 days in advance. Notes: Range (grass). ✉8951 Creek Run Rd., 76120 ☎817/861-4653 ⊕ www.linksatwaterchase.com ☰AE, MC, V. *Comments: Water on 13 holes will make for a tough round, but there's a sports psychologist on call if you need one. Also has a 9-hole, par-3 course. Great practice facility with covered, heated hitting bays. UR*

SKY CREEK RANCH GOLF CLUB. Facility Holes: 18. Opened: 1999. Architect: Robert Trent Jones Jr./Gary Linn. Yards: 6,953/5,390. Par: 72/72. Course Rating: 73.4/72.8. Slope: 136/132. Green Fee: $45/$75. Cart Fee: Included in green fee. Discounts: Weekdays, twilight, seniors, juniors. Walking: Walking at certain times. Season: Year-round. High: Apr.–Oct. Tee Times: Call 7 days in advance. Notes: Range (grass). ✉600 Promontory Dr., Keller 76248, 10 mi from Fort Worth ☎817/498-1414 ⊕ www.skycreekranch.com ☰AE, D, DC, MC, V. *Comments: Plays through a housing development along Bear Creek. Had to be raised to avoid flooding problems. Fairly expensive.* ★ ★ ★ ★

SQUAW VALLEY GOLF COURSE. Facility Holes: 36. Opened: 2001. Architect: Jeff Brauer/John Colligan. Discounts: Weekdays, twilight, seniors, juniors. Season: Year-round. Tee Times: Call 5 days in advance. Notes: Range (grass, mat). ⊠ 2439 E. Hwy. 67, Glen Rose 76043, 60 mi from Fort Worth ☎ 254/897-7956 or 800/831-8259 ☰ AE, D, MC, V.

Apache Links. Holes: 18. Yards: 7,002/5,123. Par: 72/72. Course Rating: 74.1/70.5. Slope: 134/120. Green Fee: $38/$48. Cart Fee: Included in green fee. Walking: Unrestricted walking. UR

Comanche Lakes. Holes: 18. Yards: 7,000/5,016. Par: 72/72. Course Rating: 73.9/70.3. Slope: 132/119. Green Fee: $18/$40. Cart Fee: $12 per person. Walking: Unrestricted walking. ★ ★ ★ ★

Comments: Make the drive to Glen Rose for this one. It's special.

SUGARTREE GOLF CLUB. Facility Holes: 18. Opened: 1988. Architect: Phil Lumsden. Yards: 6,775/5,254. Par: 71/71. Course Rating: 72.8/71.0. Slope: 138/126. Green Fee: $25/$45. Cart Fee: $10 per person. Discounts: Weekdays, twilight, seniors, juniors. Walking: Unrestricted walking. Season: Year-round. Tee Times: Call 7 days in advance. Notes: Range (grass). ⊠ Hwy. 1189, Dennis 76439, 35 mi from Fort Worth ☎ 817/341-1111 ⊕ www.sugartreegolf.com ☰ AE, D, MC, V. *Comments: Close to the airport, and worth the trip.* ★ ★ ★ ★

WHITESTONE GOLF CLUB. Facility Holes: 18. Opened: 2000. Architect: Jeff Brauer/Jay Morrish. Yards: 7,117/5,201. Par: 72/72. Course Rating: 74.4/71.2. Slope: 135/125. Green Fee: $25/$52. Cart Fee: Included in green fee. Discounts: Weekdays, twilight, seniors, juniors. Walking: Mandatory cart. Season: Year-round. Tee Times: Call 7 days in advance. Notes: Range (grass, mat). ⊠ 10650 Hwy. 377 S, Benbrook 76126, 15 mi from Fort Worth ☎ 817/249-9996 ⊕ www.whitestonegolf.com ☰ AE, MC, V. *Comments: They've already got the greens running quick here.* ★ ★ ★ ★

Irving

COWBOYS GOLF CLUB. Facility Holes: 18. Opened: 2001. Architect: Jeff Brauer. Yards: 7,017/4,702. Par: 72/72. Course Rating: 74.2/68.9. Slope: 140/114. Green Fee: $45/$135. Cart Fee: Included in green fee. Discounts: Weekdays, twilight, seniors, juniors. Season: Year-round. High: Apr.-Oct. Tee Times: Call 30 days in advance. Notes: Range (grass). ⊠ 1600 Fairway Dr., Grapevine 76051, 20 mi from Dallas ☎ 817/481-7277 ⊕ www.cowboysgolfclub.com ☰ AE, MC, V. *Comments: America's Team now has its own golf course. May be the best offer in the country: all-inclusive fee covers all the golf you want to play for a day, plus food and (nonalcoholic) beverages.* ★ ★ ★ ★

FOUR SEASONS RESORT AND CLUB. Facility Holes: 18. Opened: 1986. Architect: Jay Morrish/Byron Nelson/Ben Crenshaw. Yards: 6,899/5,340. Par: 70/70. Course Rating: 73.5/70.6. Slope: 135/116. Green Fee: $150/$185. Cart Fee: $25 per person. Discounts: Twilight. Walking: Unrestricted walking. Season: Year-round. High: Apr.-June. Tee Times: Call golf shop. Notes: Range (grass). ⊠ 4150 N. MacArthur Blvd., 75038, 10 mi from Dallas ☎ 972/717-2530 or 800/332-3442 ☰ AE, D, DC, MC, V. *Comments: If you've got the cash, this is probably where you will want to stay and play. Room rates are generally $300 per night and up and the golf fees are closing in on $200 per round. The* *course is impeccably maintained and hosts the PGA Tour's Byron Nelson Championship.* ★ ★ ★ ★ ½

TIERRA VERDE GOLF CLUB. Facility Holes: 18. Opened: 2000. Architect: David Graham/Gary Panks. Yards: 6,975/5,111. Par: 72/72. Course Rating: 73.3/70.5. Slope: 129/119. Green Fee: $47/$60. Cart Fee: Included in green fee. Discounts: Weekdays, twilight, seniors, juniors. Season: Jan.–Nov. Tee Times: Call golf shop. Notes: Metal spikes. ⊠ 7005 Golf Club Dr., Arlington 76001 ☎ 817/572-1300 ⊕ www.arlingtongolf.com ▤ D, MC, V. *Comments: One of the best at this price anywhere.* ★ ★ ★ ★

TOUR 18 GOLF CLUB. Facility Holes: 18. Opened: 1995. Architect: Dave Edsall. Yards: 7,033/5,493. Par: 72/72. Course Rating: 74.3/66.3. Slope: 138/119. Green Fee: $59/$95. Cart Fee: Included in green fee. Discounts: Twilight. Walking: Mandatory cart. Season: Year-round. High: Apr.–Oct. Tee Times: Call 30 days in advance. Notes: Range (grass, mat). ⊠ 8718 Amen Corner, Flower Mound 75022, 10 mi from Dallas ☎ 817/430-2000 or 800/946-5310 ⊕ www.tour18golf.com ▤ AE, MC, V. *Comments: Play Amen Corner and the 17th at Sawgrass on this collection of reproductions.* ★ ★ ★ ★

McKinney & Frisco

CHASE OAKS GOLF CLUB. Facility Holes: 27. Architect: Robert von Hagge/Bruce Devlin. Cart Fee: $12 per person. Discounts: Weekdays, twilight, seniors, juniors. Walking: Walking at certain times. Season: Year-round. Tee Times: Call golf shop. Notes: Range (grass, mat). ⊠ 7201 Chase Oaks Blvd., Plano 75025, 14 mi from Dallas ☎ 972/517-7777 ⊕ www.chaseoaks.com ▤ AE, D, DC, MC, V.

Black Jack. Holes: 18. Opened: 1986. Yards: 6,762/5,105. Par: 72/72. Course Rating: 74.4/70.0. Slope: 139/128. Green Fee: $37/$57. *Comments: Lots of fun, but tough to get out here.* ★ ★ ★

Sawtooth. Holes: 9. Opened: 1981. Yards: 3,250/2,746. Par: 36/36. Course Rating: 70.1/72.0. Slope: 130/124. Green Fee: $29. *Comments: Very basic golf.* UR

HANK HANEY GOLF RANCH. ⊠ 4101 Custer Rd., McKinney 75070 ☎ 972/542-8800 or 972/529-2221 ⊕ www.hankhaney.com. *Comments: As you would expect, Haney's practice range is stellar, and the short 18-hole courses let you hit every shot in the bag.*

TRAILS OF FRISCO GOLF CLUB. Facility Holes: 18. Opened: 2000. Architect: Jeffery Bauer. Yards: 6,959/5,104. Par: 71/71. Course Rating: 74.0/65.0. Slope: 138/111. Green Fee: $59/$75. Cart Fee: Included in green fee. Discounts: Weekdays, twilight, seniors, juniors. Walking: Mandatory cart. Season: Year-round. High: Apr.–Sept. Tee Times: Call 7 days in advance. Notes: Range (grass, mat). ⊠ 10411 Teel Pkwy., Frisco 75034, 30 mi from Dallas ☎ 972/668-4653 ⊕ www.thetexasgolftrail.com ▤ AE, D, MC, V. *Comments: Jeff Brauer, who designs more courses than anyone in the Dallas area, did his best work here. Swampland was transformed into a striking golf course of big bunkers and wetland features.* UR

TRIBUTE GOLF CLUB. Facility Holes: 18. Opened: 2000. Architect: Tripp Davis. Yards: 7,002/5,302. Par: 72/72. Course Rating: 73.2/65.6. Slope: 128/111. Green Fee: $50/$105. Cart Fee: Included in green fee. Discounts: Weekdays, twilight, seniors, juniors. Walking: Unrestricted walking. Season: Year-round. Tee Times: Call 7 days in advance. Notes: Range (grass), lodging (7). ✉ 1000 Boyd Rd., The Colony 75056, 20 mi from Dallas ☎972/370–5465 ⊕ www.thetributegolflinks.com ⊟AE, D, DC, MC, V. *Comments: Ranked 14th in Texas. The 1st and 18th are reproductions of the same holes at St. Andrews. UR*

TWIN CREEKS GOLF CLUB. Facility Holes: 18. Opened: 1995. Architect: Palmer Course Design Co. Yards: 6,924/4,790. Par: 72/72. Course Rating: 73.2/66.5. Slope: 131/107. Green Fee: $40/$60. Cart Fee: $15 per person. Discounts: Weekdays, twilight, seniors, juniors. Walking: Unrestricted walking. Season: Year-round. Tee Times: Call 5 days in advance. Notes: Range (grass, mat). ✉ 501 Twin Creeks Dr., Allen 75013, 20 mi from Dallas ☎972/390-8888 ⊕ www.twincreeks.com ⊟AE, D, DC, MC, V. *Comments: Great design, but hampered by maintenance problems.* ★★★★

WESTIN STONEBRIAR RESORT. Facility Holes: 18. Opened: 2000. Architect: Tom Fazio. Yards: 7,021/5,208. Par: 72/72. Course Rating: 73.8/71.0. Slope: 133/121. Green Fee: $115. Cart Fee: Included in green fee. Walking: Mandatory cart. Season: Year-round. High: Apr.–Nov. Tee Times: Call golf shop. Notes: Range (grass, mat), lodging (301). ✉ 1549 Legacy Dr., Frisco 75007, 25 mi from Dallas ☎972/668-8748 ⊕ www.stonebriar.com ⊟AE, MC, V. *Comments: The first public Tom Fazio design in greater Dallas, this course has twisting, turning fairways; beautiful bunkering; and giant putting greens (6,000 square feet or larger). UR*

Where to Stay

Dallas

🏨 **ADOLPHUS.** Beer baron Adolphus Busch created this beaux-arts building, Dallas's finest old hotel, in 1912, sparing nothing in the way of rich ornamentation. The romantic European-style rooms have modern amenities. The celebrated French Room restaurant ($$$$) serves classics such as roast duck in port sauce. ✉ 1321 Commerce St., 75202 ☎214/742-8200 or 800/221-9083 🖶214/651-3561 ⊕ www.hoteladolphus.com ⟿407 rooms, 21 suites ♦3 restaurants, room service, in-room data ports, in-room safes, minibars, cable TV with movies, gym, bar, lobby lounge, concierge, parking (fee), no-smoking rooms ⊟AE, D, DC, MC, V $$$$.

🏨 **HOTEL INTER-CONTINENTAL.** The Tollway and Belt Line Road are lined with dining and nightlife options close to this hotel, which is in north Dallas, 10 minutes from the city center. Standard rooms may not be posh, but they're a good deal with lots of amenities, including coffeemakers, in-room Internet, and HBO. ✉ 15201 Dallas Pkwy., 75001 ☎972/386-6000 or 800/386-1592 🖶972/991-6937 ⊕ www.interconti.com ⟿494 rooms, 31 suites ♦Restaurant, room service, in-room data ports, some minibars, cable TV with movies, 4 tennis courts, pool, health club, hair salon, hot tub, basketball, racquetball, bar, baby-sitting, laundry services, concierge, concierge floor, Internet, business services, airport shuttle, free parking, no-smoking rooms ⊟AE, D, DC, MC, V $$-$$$.

🏨 **MELROSE.** Love Field airport is just 3 mi from this eight-story luxury hotel. Individually decorated rooms have marble baths, dark wood furniture, and deep rich colors; some rooms have four-poster beds. The Library Bar is a popular gathering place. ✉ 3015 Oak Lawn Ave., 75219 ☎214/521-5151 or 800/635-7673 🖶214/521-2470

CHANGES AROUND THE RANCH

When Hank Haney bought the land for his Golf Ranch from the estate of film star Audie Murphy, McKinney wasn't much more than a few paved streets, a diner, and (believe it or not) a brothel. As aerial pictures prove, the last 10 years have brought Dallas ever closer toward McKinney and nearby Frisco. Suddenly, the middle of nowhere is somewhere. A new, private TPC course is going in across the street from Haney's Golf Ranch, and, in Frisco, a Westin Resort with a Tom Fazio–designed course has opened.

⊕ www.melrosehotel.com ⇦ 158 rooms, 26 suites ⚹ Restaurant, room service, in-room data ports, in-room safes, cable TV with movies, bar, library, business services, free parking, no-smoking rooms ⊟ AE, D, DC, MC, V $$$$.

🏨 **WYNDHAM ANATOLE.** Politicians, including George W. Bush and Colin Powell, have made this huge glass-and-chrome complex their home away from home. There are standard, chain-hotel-style rooms here as well as deluxe suites, plus shops, a nightclub, and a croquet lawn to keep you entertained. Nana, one of the city's top-rated restaurants, has gorgeous skyline views. ✉ 2201 Stemmons Fwy., 75207 ☎ 214/748-1200 or 800/996-3426 🖷 214/761-7242 ⊕ www.wyndham.com ⇦ 1,491 rooms, 129 suites ⚹ 5 restaurants, room service, in-room data ports, in-room safes, cable TV with movies, 2 tennis courts, 2 pools (1 indoor), health club, hair salon, hot tub, spa, croquet, racquetball, squash, 5 bars, laundry services, concierge, business services, convention center, meeting rooms, airport shuttle, car rental, parking (fee), no-smoking rooms ⊟ AE, D, MC, V ⦿CP $$$.

Fort Worth

🏨 **COURTYARD BY MARRIOTT–BLACKSTONE.** Architectural elements of this historic downtown hotel have been preserved, but the guest rooms are completely up to date. Rooms, most with sitting areas and work space, are trimmed in dark woods and florals. The hotel does not have its own restaurant, but there is a Corner Bakery on the first floor and other dining options are within walking distance. ✉ 601 Main St., 76102 ☎ 817/885-8700 or 800/321-2211 🖷 817/885-8303 ⊕ www.marriott.com ⇦ 188 rooms, 15 suites ⚹ Restaurant, room service, in-room data ports, cable TV with movies, pool, hot tub, bar, laundry facilities, business services, parking (fee) ⊟ AE, D, DC, MC, V $-$$.

🏨 **DORAL TOSERO HOTEL & GOLF CLUB.** Formerly the Creeks at Beechwood, this resort has taken on new life under the Dorsal Tesoro flag. The sleek guest rooms in the 10-story tower have views of the golf course, designed by Jay Morrish. The resort is a mile from Texas Motor Speedway and less than 30 minutes from DFW Airport. ✉ 3300 Championship Pkwy., 76177 ☎ 817/961-0800 or 800/333-6725 🖷 817/961-0900 ⊕ www.doraltesoro.com ⇦ 273 rooms, 13 suites ⚹ Restaurant, in-room data ports, in-room safes, minibars, cable TV with movies, 18-hole golf course, pool, health club, hot tub, bar, laundry services, concierge, business services, free parking, no-smoking rooms ⊟ AE, D, DC, MC, V $$.

🏨 **ETTA'S PLACE.** The name of this bed-and-breakfast was inspired by Etta Place, a Fort Worth schoolteacher who may have been the sweetheart of the Sundance Kid. The inn was built in the 1990s to house artists and entertainers who performed at the now-closed Caravan of Dreams. Each room is individually decorated and each is named after a member of Butch Cassidy's gang. There's also a library and a music room with a Steinway baby grand. ⊠200 W. 3rd St., Sundance Sq. 76102 ☎817/654-0267 🖷817/878-2560 ⊕ www.ettas-place.com ➥9 rooms ⚄In-room data ports, some kitchenettes, cable TV, library, laundry services, business services; no smoking ⊟AE, D, DC, MC, V ⑪CP $$.

🏨 **RENAISSANCE WORTHINGTON.** This 12-story, white-concrete structure stretches across two city blocks and is a hub of activity, hosting business types as well as rodeo champions. It's within walking distance of many local attractions, restaurants, entertainment venues, and shops. Nationally known chef Grady Spears is at the helm of the clubby western-style restaurant, Chisholm Club. ⊠200 Main St., Sundance Sq., 76102 ☎817/870-1000 or 800/468-3571 🖷817/338-9176 ⊕ www.renaissancehotels.com ➥482 rooms, 25 suites ⚄2 restaurants, room service, in-room data ports, minibars, some refrigerators, cable TV with movies, pool, gym, hot tub, bar, concierge, business services, meeting rooms, parking (fee) ⊟AE, D, DC, MC, V $$$-$$$$.

🏨 **STOCKYARDS HOTEL.** A storybook place that's seen more than its share of cowboys, rustlers, gangsters, and oil barons, this hotel has been used in many a movie. There are four styles of rooms: Victorian, Native American, Mountain Man, and Old West. In the Booger Red Saloon, the bar stools are saddles. ⊠ 109 E. Exchange Ave., Stockyards, 76106 ☎817/625-6427 or 800/423-8471 🖷817/624-2571 ⊕ www.stockyardshotel. com ➥44 rooms, 8 suites ⚄Restaurant, in-room data ports, cable TV, bar, laundry facilities, business services, parking (fee) ⊟AE, D, DC, MC, V $$.

Irving

🏨 **COURTYARD LAS COLINAS.** This four-story hotel is off U.S. 114, about 4 mi from Bear Creek Golf Course and 3 mi from Texas Stadium. A blue, mustard, and orange color scheme make the rooms bright and cheerful. Nearby restaurants will deliver to the hotel. ⊠1151 W. Walnut Hill, 75038 ☎972/550-8100 🖷972/550-0764 ⊕ www.courtyard. com ➥147 rooms, 13 suites ⚄Grocery, in-room data ports, refrigerators, cable TV with movies, pool, gym, hot tub, laundry facilities, laundry services, business services, meeting rooms, free parking, some pets allowed ⊟AE, D, DC, MC, V $$.

🏨 **EMBASSY SUITES OUTDOOR WORLD.** This 12-story, all-suites hotel, built in 1999, is near Bass Pro Shops and Grapevine Mills outlet mall. Rooms have separate living rooms with pullout sofas. The corner suites on the 12th floor have cathedral ceilings and private, covered balconies. ⊠2401 Bass Pro Dr., 76051 ☎972/724-2600 or 800/ 362-2779 🖷972/724-2670 ⊕ www.embassysuitesoutdoorworld.com ➥329 suites ⚄Restaurant, room service, some in-room data ports, minibars, microwaves, refrigerators, cable TV with movies and video games, pool, gym, sauna, bar, laundry facilities, laundry service, business services, free parking, some pets allowed ⊟AE, D, DC, MC, V ⑪CP $-$$$$.

🏨 **FOUR SEASONS RESORT AND CLUB.** Looking like a country club designed by Frank Lloyd Wright, this sprawling resort has clean-line, contemporary interiors and wavelike fairways. Many rooms overlook the Tournament Players Course, site of the

PGA's Byron Nelson; others have a view of sunsets and the private Cottonwood golf course. All rooms have white duvets, chenille throws, and marble baths. Classic and specialty treatments are available at the full-service spa. Dining options include a rowdy sports bar and a refined Asian-style restaurant. ✉ 4150 N. MacArthur Blvd., 75038 ☎ 972/717-0700 or 800/332-3442 🖷 972/717-2550 ⊕ www.fourseasons.com ↪ 343 rooms, 14 suites ⑤ 3 restaurants, room service, in-room data ports, in-room safes, cable TV with movies, 18-hole golf course, 12 tennis courts, pro shop, 4 pools, health club, hair salon, spa, basketball, racquetball, squash, 3 bars, children's programs (ages 1–14), laundry services, concierge, business services, meeting rooms, free parking, no-smoking rooms ▤ AE, D, DC, MC, V $$$$.

☎ HILTON DFW LAKES EXECUTIVE CONFERENCE CENTER. This hotel complex is on 27 wooded, lakeside acres just 2½ mi north of DWF Airport. Designed for the business traveler, rooms have generous work spaces and conference options. Some rooms overlook the lake. ✉ 1800 Rte. 26 E, 76051 ☎ 817/481-8444 🖷 817/481-3160 ⊕ www. hilton.com ↪ 377 rooms, 18 suites ⑤ 2 restaurants, room service, in-room data ports, minibars, refrigerators, cable TV with movies and video games, 8 tennis courts, 2 pools, gym, hot tub, basketball, paddle tennis, racquetball, laundry service, concierge, business services, airport shuttle, free parking, no-smoking rooms ▤ AE, D, DC, MC, V $$$.

☎ OMNI DALLAS HOTEL PARK WEST. Rooms are spacious and modern in this hotel 4 mi from Texas Stadium and the Galleria mall. The landscaped grounds include a 12½-acre lake surrounded by a 10-km trail. ✉ 1590 LBJ Fwy., 75234 ☎ 972/869-4300 🖷 972/869-3295 ⊕ www.omnihotels.com ↪ 337 rooms ⑤ Restaurant, in-room data ports, cable TV with movies, in-room VCRs, pool, exercise equipment, hot tub, massage, bar, business services, free parking ▤ AE, D, DC, MC, V $$$.

McKinney & Frisco

☎ AMERIHOST INN. A convenient location on a busy north–south corridor and low rates are what make this standard hotel appealing. Next to the hotel are a sprawling ice-skating facility and a 14-screen multiplex theater. ✉ 951 S. Central Expressway, McKinney 75070 ☎ 972/547-4500 🖷 972/547-4340 ⊕ www.amerihostinn.com ↪ 61 rooms ⑤ Cable TV, pool, gym, hot tub, sauna, free parking, no-smoking rooms ▤ AE, D, DC, MC, V ¢.

☎ MARRIOTT AT LEGACY TOWN CENTER. Shops, restaurants, entertainment venues, and corporate offices surround this elegant, contemporary, Texas limestone hotel. Rooms have up-to-the-minute amenities for both business and leisure travelers, including coffeemakers and irons. Fluffy duvets in maroon and bronze top the beds. ✉ 7120 Dallas Pkwy., Plano 75024 ☎ 972/473-6444 or 888/222-8733 🖷 972/473-4225 ⊕ www.marriott.com ↪ 364 rooms, 40 suites ⑤ Restaurants, room service, in-room data ports, cable TV with movies, pool, health club, hot tub, massage, sauna, bar, laundry services, business services, parking (fee), no-smoking floors ▤ AE, D, DC, MC, V $–$$$.

☎ WESTIN STONEBRIAR RESORT. This tranquil golf resort, fronted by flower beds, a fountain, and a porte cochere, is a world away from the busy Legacy corridor nearby. Rooms and suites overlook the 160-acre golf course. The hotel's in-house restaurant, the Legacy Grill, is becoming a draw of its own. There are two shopping and entertainment centers on Legacy Drive. ✉ 1549 Legacy Dr., Frisco 75034 ☎ 972/668-8000 or 888/

627-8536 ☎972/668-8100 ⊕ www.westinstonebriar.com ⤶301 rooms, 12 suites ♨2 restaurants, room service, in-room data ports, in-room safes, minibars, refrigerators, cable TV with movies and video games, driving range, 18-hole golf course, pool, health club, hot tub, spa, bar, concierge, business services, free parking, no-smoking rooms ⊟AE, D, DC, MC, V $$-$$$$.

Where to Eat

Dallas

✗ **JEROBOAM.** An urban brasserie in a restored 1913 building, Jeroboam infuses French classics with a New American style. Soups are one highlight of the seasonal menu—think curried cauliflower or chilled lemon asparagus. Traditional favorites like braised lamb shanks are dressed up with dried figs. The raw bar includes Jonah crab claws, pickled rock shrimp, and oysters. The 56-page addendum of maps, regional descriptions, and tasting notes may make the all-French wine list daunting, but servers are ready and willing to help. ⊠ 1501 Main St. ☎214/748-7226 ⊟AE, D, MC, V ☉ No lunch weekends $$$-$$$$.

✗ **MATT'S RANCHO MARTINEZ.** Tex-Mex is served up for the masses in this Dallas institution. Specialties include chicken-fried steak, chiles rellenos, frogs' legs, and the signature Bob Armstrong dip—a decadent *chile con queso* dip loaded with beef, guacamole, and sour cream. The tree-covered patio is a pleasant spot for margarita sipping. ⊠ 6332 La Vista Dr. ☎214/823-5517 ⊟AE, D, DC, MC, V ☉ Closed Sun. $-$$.

✗ **NICK & SAM'S.** Cattle is king in Dallas, and you'd be hard-pressed to find a better slab of beef than Nick & Sam's 22-ounce, prime, aged Cowboy Cut. A side of Damn Good fries is the perfect accompaniment. Lighter appetites can opt for grilled swordfish with orange-butter sauce or a turn at the raw bar. The open kitchen and grand piano, not to mention the complimentary caviar and "negotiable" wine prices, make this upscale steak house more than a cut above. ⊠ 3008 Maple Ave. ☎214/871-7444 ⊟AE, D, DC, MC, V ☉ No lunch $$$-$$$$.

Fort Worth

✗ **ANGELO'S BARBECUE.** A Fort Worth institution since 1958, Angelo's is famous for succulent smoked ribs that are so tender that the meat falls off the bone, and for the stuffed bear that guards the front door. Arrive early: the place has been known to run out of ribs well before closing. ⊠ 2533 White Settlement Rd. ☎817/332-0357 ♨ Reservations not accepted ⊟No credit cards ☉ Closed Sun. $.

✗ **BISTRO LOUISE.** People drive 30 mi from Dallas to dine on pecan-fried chicken, macadamia-crusted shrimp, rosemary chicken, and the like. The Mediterranean-style dining room has ocher stucco walls, wood-beam ceilings, and floral tablecloths. ⊠ 2900 S. Hulen St. ☎817/922-9244 ⊕ www.bistrolouise.com ⊟AE, D, DC MC, V ☉ Closed Sun. $$$$.

✗ **JOE T. GARCIA'S.** This is the ultimate Tex-Mex joint, where cowboy-boot–clad customers drink Mexican beer and the bartenders mix potent margaritas. There's usually a wait for the tables, but with seating for more than 1,000 in the maze of dining rooms and patio areas, the line moves quickly. Dinner is limited to two choices: an enchilada-and-taco combo plate or fajitas. Lunch offers a more traditional menu, and on weekends there are Mexican breakfast specialties, including purported hangover-cure *menudo* (stew made with tripe, hominy, onions, and chili). ✉ 2201 N. Commerce St. ☎ 817/626–4356 ⚭ Reservations not accepted ▤ No credit cards $.

✕ **RANDALL'S GOURMET CHEESECAKE COMPANY.** A wine bar, café, and bakery all in one, Randall's serves many fine, Continental entrées, plus assuredly un-French but delicious cheesecake. You can start with a savory blend of smoked salmon and black lumpfish caviar, a fine prelude to an entrée of tuna Wellington or the Paris enchilada (a crepe stuffed with escargots, mushrooms, and goat cheese). Try to save room for the cheesecake—there are more than 60 varieties. ✉ 907 Houston St. ☎ 817/336–2253 ⚭ Reservations essential ▤ AE, D, MC, V ☾ Closed Sun. and Mon. No lunch $$$–$$$$.

✕ **REATA.** Cowhide seats, murals, and a digital view of the city set the scene in this Sundance Square hot spot. Try the excellent steaks, beer-batter quail, pan-seared pecan-crusted beef tenderloin, or the tamales. You may also want to sample something from the vodka and tequila bars. ✉ 310 Houston St. ☎ 817/336–1009 ⊕ www.reata.net ▤ AE, MC, V $$–$$$$.

Irving

✕ **BIG BUCK BREWERY AND STEAKHOUSE.** The ceilings soar high at this two-story microbrewery and chophouse, which resembles a north-woods hunting lodge. Ales and bitter and stout beers are served alongside huge cuts of meat, ribs, and sandwiches. Often-heard orders are for the Great White buffalo burger and the Grand Maytag steak fillet, served with a sauce of blue cheese and Grand Marnier. ✉ 2501 Bass Pro Dr., Grapevine ☎ 214/513–2337 ⊕ www.bigbuck.com ▤ AE, DC, MC, V $$–$$$$.

✕ **BRUNO'S ITALIAN RESTAURANT.** Picasso reproductions deck the walls of this upscale and romantic family-owned restaurant. The dishes are made from traditional recipes and the service is helpful and attentive. You might start with one of the delicious salads then move on to veal chops, rigatoni (famous for its robust tomato sauce), or capellini primavera, a good choice for vegetarians. Warm homemade bread accompanies all meals. ✉ 9462 N. MacArthur Blvd. ☎ 972/556–2465 ⚭ Reservations essential ▤ AE, D, DC, MC, V ☾ Closed Sun. No lunch Sat. $$–$$$$.

✕ **CAFE ON THE GREEN.** This minimalist restaurant within the Four Seasons Resort and Club is in a class of its own. Its windows overlook the resort's villas and pool. Seared salmon with black sesame seeds and wasabi-mashed potatoes, and juniper-rubbed duck breast with seared foie gras are representative of the chef's offerings. Breakfast is also available. ✉ 4150 N. MacArthur Blvd. ☎ 972/717–0700 ▤ AE, DC, MC, V $$$$.

✕ **COOL RIVER.** This restaurant is what you get when you cross a Rocky Mountain lodge with a West Texas ranch house. Shiner Bock–marinated rib eye and chicken-fried venison are popular menu items. A separate cigar lounge with leather chairs offers top-brand smokes and brandies, while an adjacent sports bar promises rowdy and packed game weekends. ✉ 1045 Hidden Ridge Rd., Las Colinas ☎ 972/871–8881 ▤ AE, DC, MC, V $$–$$$$.

McKinney & Frisco

✗ **BOB'S CHOP HOUSE.** This popular restaurant teams with businesspeople and locals drawn by the superbly grilled steaks and chops. The veal here is exceptional, too. Mahogany booths and white linen add to the clubby feeling. The wine list is top-notch. ⊠ 5760 Legacy Blvd., Plano ☎ 972/608-2627 ⌁ Reservations essential ▭ AE, DC, MC, V ⊘ Closed Sun. No lunch $$$$.

✗ **GOODHUE'S WOOD FIRED GRILL.** In a converted warehouse near McKinney's town square, the exposed brick walls and dark wood trim of this restaurant compliment the turn-of-the-20th-century feel of the restored neighborhood. Signature beef, lamb, and chicken dishes are grilled to perfection and accompanied by rich sauces and reductions. ⊠ 204 W. Virginia St., McKinney ☎ 972/562-7570 ▭ AE, DC, MC, V ⊘ Closed Sun. No lunch $$-$$$$.

✗ **JASPER'S.** Chef Kent Rathbun cooks juicy, perfect grill and barbecue specialties—what he calls "gourmet backyard cuisine"—at this casual restaurant. The homemade potato chips covered with melted blue cheese go great with the smoked baby back ribs and the peach barbecue pork tenderloin. ⊠ 7161 Bishop Rd., Plano ☎ 469/229-9111 ▭ AE, DC, MC, V ⊘ Closed Sun. $$$-$$$$.

Essentials

Getting Here

Main routes into the Dallas–Fort Worth area include I-35 from the north and south. The highway splits near Denton, so I-35 east heads to Dallas and I-35 west branches off toward Fort Worth. I-45 comes in from Houston, 240 mi to the southeast. The twin cities are linked by I-20, the southern route, and I-30, which covers the northern part of town. Dallas is circled by I-635, known as the LBJ Freeway, and Fort Worth is circled by I-820.

There are three tollways in the Metroplex: the Dallas North Tollway, running from I-35 east, north of downtown into Collin County to the north; George Bush Turnpike (Route 190), an east-west route in the area's northern suburbs; and Mountain Creek Bridge, in southwestern Dallas County.

McKinney is 30 mi north of downtown Dallas via U.S. 75 (the Central Expressway). Frisco is the same distance via the Dallas North Tollway. From Dallas, take U.S. 75 (the Central Expressway) north to McKinney. The Virginia Parkway and the Eldorado Parkway run east and west through McKinney. Route 121 cuts diagonally toward Frisco and, eventually, Fort Worth.

Visitor Information

🛈 **Dallas Convention & Visitors Bureau** ⊠ Old Red Courthouse, 100 S. Houston St. ☎ 214/571-1300 or 800/232-5527, 214/571-1301 recorded schedule of events ⊕ www.dallascvb.com. **Fort Worth Convention & Visitors Bureau** ⊠ 415 Throckmorton St., 76102 ☎ 817/336-8791 or 800/433-5747 ⊠ information centers: ⊠ Downtown, 4th St. at Throckmorton St. ⊠ Cultural District ⊠ 3401 W. Lancaster Ave. ⊠ The Stockyards, 130 E. Exchange Ave. ⊕ www.fortworth.com. **Irving Convention & Visitors**

Bureau ⊠ 1231 Greenway Dr., Suite 1060, 75038 ☎ 972/252-7476 or 800/247-8464 ⊕ www.irvingtexas.com. **McKinney Convention & Visitors Bureau** ⊠ 1650 W. Virginia St., 75069 ☎ 214/544-1407 or 888/649-8499 ⊕ www.mckinneycvb.org.

OKLAHOMA CITY, OK

Drive into Oklahoma City from the east and it's easy to see just how striking the land rush of 1889 must have been. More than 50,000 homesteaders set off from the Oklahoma border to stake their claim to open land. More than 10,000 of them set up around the Oklahoma rail station, on a beautiful plain and river basin. That town became Oklahoma City, and now, with a million people, it holds more than a third of the state's population. Add in two huge college campuses in neighboring towns—the University of Oklahoma in Norman and Oklahoma State in Stillwater—and you have a recipe for a vibrant, thriving capital. Formerly a major stop on the Chisholm Trail, Oklahoma City's stockyards still host the country's largest live cattle auction every Monday and Tuesday morning. The downtown Bricktown area, which used to be the center of railroad and manufacturing industries, has been restored into prime restaurant and shopping space. Western Avenue north of 50th Street is known as Restaurant Row, and there is a water taxi route along the canal that winds through the historic district.

The golf doesn't disappoint either. Karsten Creek gold course in Stillwater has no houses to disturb the view, and hole after hole of Tom Fazio masterpieces. A less-publicized treat is Silverhorn Golf Club, which is inside the city limits and offers one of the most remarkable golf experiences for the price around.

Courses   **Golf** Digest REVIEWS

CEDAR VALLEY GOLF CLUB. Facility Holes: 36. Opened: 1975. Architect: Duffy Martin/Floyd Farley. Green Fee: $15/$16. Cart Fee: $20 per person. Discounts: Weekdays, twilight, seniors, juniors. Walking: Unrestricted walking. Season: Year-round. Tee Times: Call 1 day in advance. Notes: Range (grass). ⊠ 210 Par Ave., Guthrie 73044, 25 mi from Oklahoma City ☎ 405/282-4800 or 877/230-7292 ▭ AE, D, DC, MC, V.

Augusta. Holes: 18. Yards: 6,602/5,170. Par: 70/72. Course Rating: 70.3/69.1. Slope: 108/114. *Comments: Sketchy conditions sabotage a terrific layout.* ★ ★ ★ ½

International. Holes: 18. Yards: 6,520/4,955. Par: 70/72. Course Rating: 71.1/68.4. Slope: 112/115. *Comments: Basic golf.* ★ ★ ½

CIMARRON NATIONAL GOLF CLUB. Facility Holes: 36. Architect: Floyd Farley. Cart Fee: $18 per cart. Discounts: Twilight, seniors. Season: Year-round. High: May–Sept. Tee

Course	Yards	Par	Course Rating	Slope	Green Fee
Cedar Valley Golf Club (36)					$15/$16
Augusta (18)	6,602/5,170	70/72	70.3/69.1	108/114	
International (18)	6,520/4,955	70/72	71.1/68.4	112/115	
Cimarron National Golf Club (36)					
Aqua Canyon (18)	6,415/5,339	70/71	69.6/68.2	114/110	$16/$18
Cimarron (18)	6,453/5,359	70/70	68.1/72.8	120/132	$14/$16
Coffee Creek Golf Course (18)	6,700/5,200	70/70	71.5/70.5	129/122	$17/$22
Earlywine Park Golf Course (36)					$17
North (18)	6,721/4,843	72/72	71.9/70.4	126/122	
South (18)	6,505/5,020	70/70	72.5/71.6	114/117	
Jimmie Austin University of Oklahoma Golf Course (18)	7,197/5,357	72/72	74.9/71.6	134/119	$33/$40
Karsten Creek (18)	7,095/4,906	72/72	74.8/70.1	142/127	$250
Kicking Bird Golf Club (18)	6,722/5,051	70/70	71.8/69.3	123/112	$18/$22
Lake Hefner Golf Club (36)					$11/$17
North (18)	6,970/5,169	72/72	74.2/69.6	128/117	
South (18)	6,305/5,393	70/73	68.9/71.2	111/115	
Lincoln Park Golf Course (36)					$11/$17
East (18)	6,535/5,276	70/71	70.0/70.8	120/117	
West (18)	6,576/5,343	71/72	70.1/72.4	122/125	
Silverhorn Golf Club (18)	6,768/4,943	71/71	73.4/71.0	128/113	$26/$31

Times: Call golf shop. Notes: Range (grass). ⊠ 500 Duffy's Way, Guthrie 73044, 20 mi from Oklahoma City ☎ 405/282-7888 ⊕ www.cimarronnational.com ▤ AE, D, MC, V.

Aqua Canyon. Holes: 18. Opened: 1994. Yards: 6,415/5,339. Par: 70/71. Course Rating: 69.6/68.2. Slope: 114/110. Green Fee: $16/$18. Walking: Unrestricted walking. *Comments: Maturing nicely. Right out in front of you.* ★ ★ ★

Cimarron. Holes: 18. Opened: 1992. Yards: 6,453/5,359. Par: 70/70. Course Rating: 68.1/72.8. Slope: 120/132. Green Fee: $14/$16. Walking: Walking at certain times. *Comments: Quirkier than Aqua Canyon. More blind shots and risk-reward.* ★ ★ ★

COFFEE CREEK GOLF COURSE. Facility Holes: 18. Opened: 1991. Yards: 6,700/5,200. Par: 70/70. Course Rating: 71.5/70.5. Slope: 129/122. Green Fee: $17/$22. Cart Fee: $13 per person. Discounts: Weekdays, twilight, seniors, juniors. Walking: Unrestricted walking. Season: Year-round. Tee Times: Call 7 days in advance. Notes: Range (grass). ⊠ 4000 N. Kelly, Edmond 73003, 8 mi from Oklahoma City ☎ 405/340-4653 or 866/650-4653 ⊕ www.coffeecreekgc.com ▤ AE, D, MC, V. *Comments: They'll get you around quickly.* ★ ★ ★ ½

EARLYWINE PARK GOLF COURSE. Facility Holes: 36. Green Fee: $17. Cart Fee: $20 per person. Discounts: Weekdays, twilight, seniors, juniors. Walking: Unrestricted walking. Season: Year-round. Tee Times: Call golf shop. Notes: Range (grass). ⊠ 11500 S. Portland Ave., 73170 ☎ 405/691-1727 ▭ MC, V.

North. Holes: 18. Opened: 1977. Architect: Randy Heckenkemper. Yards: 6,721/4,843. Par: 72/72. Course Rating: 71.9/70.4. Slope: 126/122. *Comments: Waist-high fescue makes missing dangerous.* ★ ★ ★ ½

South. Holes: 18. Opened: 1976. Architect: Floyd Farley. Yards: 6,505/5,020. Par: 70/70. Course Rating: 72.5/71.6. Slope: 114/117. *Comments: Basic golf.* ★ ★ ½

JIMMIE AUSTIN UNIVERSITY OF OKLAHOMA GOLF COURSE. Facility Holes: 18. Opened: 1951. Architect: Perry Maxwell/Robert Cupp. Yards: 7,197/5,357. Par: 72/72. Course Rating: 74.9/71.6. Slope: 134/119. Green Fee: $33/$40. Cart Fee: $11 per person. Discounts: Weekdays, twilight, seniors, juniors. Walking: Unrestricted walking. Season: Year-round. Tee Times: Call golf shop. Notes: Range (grass). ⊠ 1 Par Dr., Norman 73069, 15 mi from Oklahoma City ☎ 405/325-6716 ⊕ www.ou.edu/admin/jaougc ▭ AE, MC, V. *Comments: Back in the day it was the best around. Still very strong.* ★ ★ ★ ½

KARSTEN CREEK. Facility Holes: 18. Opened: 1994. Architect: Tom Fazio. Yards: 7,095/4,906. Par: 72/72. Course Rating: 74.8/70.1. Slope: 142/127. Green Fee: $250. Cart Fee: Included in green fee. Walking: Unrestricted walking. Season: Year-round. Tee Times: Call 7 days in advance. Notes: Range (grass), lodging (6). ⊠ 1800 S. Memorial Dr., Stillwater 74074 ☎ 405/743-1658 ⊕ www.karstencreek.net ▭ AE, MC, V. *Comments: Undisputed best public course in the state. Makes Stillwater worth the trip all by itself.* ★ ★ ★ ★ ½

KICKING BIRD GOLF CLUB. Facility Holes: 18. Opened: 1971. Architect: Floyd Farley/Mark Hayes. Yards: 6,722/5,051. Par: 70/70. Course Rating: 71.8/69.3. Slope: 123/112. Green Fee: $18/$22. Cart Fee: $10 per person. Discounts: Weekdays, twilight, seniors, juniors. Walking: Unrestricted walking. Season: Year-round. High: May–Sept. Tee Times: Call 7 days in advance. Notes: Range (grass, mat). ⊠ 1600 E. Danforth Rd., Edmond 73034, 10 mi from Oklahoma City ☎ 405/341-5350 ⊕ www.edmond.ok.com ▭ AE, D, MC, V. *Comments: You might wish for a cart or a caddie on the steep, uphill 18th.* ★ ★ ★

LAKE HEFNER GOLF CLUB. Facility Holes: 36. Green Fee: $11/$17. Cart Fee: $20 per cart. Discounts: Twilight, seniors, juniors. Walking: Unrestricted walking. Season: Year-round. Tee Times: Call golf shop. Notes: Range (grass). ⊠ 4491 S. Lake Hefner Dr., 73116 ☎ 405/843-1565 ▭ MC, V.

North. Holes: 18. Opened: 1995. Architect: Randy Heckenkemper. Yards: 6,970/5,169. Par: 72/72. Course Rating: 74.2/69.6. Slope: 128/117. *Comments: The newer of the two courses and far superior. Nice lake views.* ★ ★ ★ ½

South. Holes: 18. Opened: 1963. Architect: Floyd Farley. Yards: 6,305/5,393. Par: 70/73. Course Rating: 68.9/71.2. Slope: 111/115. *Comments: Doesn't have the luster of the North.* ★ ★ ★

LINCOLN PARK GOLF COURSE. Facility Holes: 36. Opened: 1925. Architect: Arthur Jackson. Green Fee: $11/$17. Cart Fee: $20 per cart. Discounts: Twilight, seniors, juniors. Walking: Unrestricted walking. Season: Year-round. Tee Times: Call 7 days in advance. Notes: Range (grass). ⊠ 4001 N.E. Grand Blvd., 73111 ☎ 405/424-1421 ▭ MC, V.

East. Holes: 18. Yards: 6,535/5,276. Par: 70/71. Course Rating: 70.0/70.8. Slope: 120/117. *Comments: Grand old 1920s classic.* ★★★

West. Holes: 18. Yards: 6,576/5,343. Par: 71/72. Course Rating: 70.1/72.4. Slope: 122/125. *Comments: Beautiful, but exceptionally hard to get a tee time.* ★★★★

SILVERHORN GOLF CLUB. Facility Holes: 18. Opened: 1991. Architect: Randy Heckenkemper. Yards: 6,768/4,943. Par: 71/71. Course Rating: 73.4/71.0. Slope: 128/113. Green Fee: $26/$31. Cart Fee: $11 per person. Discounts: Weekdays, twilight, seniors, juniors. Walking: Unrestricted walking. Season: Year-round. Tee Times: Call 7 days in advance. Notes: Range (grass). ⊠ 11411 N. Kelley Ave., 73131 ☎ 405/752-1181 ⊟ AE, D, DC, MC, V. *Comments: Makes great use of a tight property. Convenient to town.* ★★★★

Where to Stay

⊞ THE BILTMORE. Oklahoma's largest hotel, just minutes from the airport, the Biltmore is often filled with businesspeople in town to attend conferences and tourists here for rodeos and other events. The hotel interior is cowboy-casual with Western artifacts and memorabilia in hallway display cases. ⊠ 401 S. Meridian Ave., 73108 ☎ 405/947-7681 or 800/522-6620 🖶 405/947-4253 ⊕ www.biltmoreokc.com ⚊ 494 rooms, 15 suites ♨ 2 restaurants, cable TV with movies, 2 tennis courts, 4 pools, gym, 4 bars, laundry service, meeting rooms, airport shuttle, free parking, kennel, no-smoking rooms ⊟ AE, D, DC, MC, V ¢–$$.

⊞ WESTIN. This upscale downtown hotel is connected to the city's convention center and close to the Civic Center and the Bricktown entertainment district. Rooms are furnished with taupe fabrics, and blond-wood furniture. Serving Continental cuisine, the in-house restaurant is a more formal dining option than many of the nearby eateries. ⊠ 1 N. Broadway, 73102 ☎ 405/235-2780 or 800/285-2780 🖶 405/232-8752 ⊕ - www.westin.com ⚊ 395 rooms, 2 suites ♨ Restaurant, in-room data ports, cable TV with movies, pool, gym, hair salon, massage, bar, laundry service, concierge floor, business services, no-smoking rooms ⊟ AE, D, DC, MC, V $$–$$$.

Where to Eat

✗ ABUELO MEXICAN EMBASSY. Although there are plenty of Mexican restaurants in Oklahoma City, few have been around as long as Abuelo's. Serving mostly central-Mexican cuisine, Abuelo's offers 10 varieties of enchilada, which can be ordered in any combination. One house specialty is the enchiladas de Cozumel—avocado enchiladas with a seafood-and-mushroom white sauce. ⊠ 17 E. Sheridan Ave. ☎ 405/235-1422 ⊟ AE, D, MC, V $–$$.

✗ ANN'S CHICKEN FRY. Home-style cooking join nostalgic 1950s and '60s decorations at this Route 66 diner. The chicken-fried steak stands out. ⊠ 4106 N.W. 39th St. ☎ 405/943-8915 ⊟ No credit cards ⊘ Closed Sun. $.

✕ **BRICKTOWN RESTAURANT & BREWERY.** Even the shrimp are steamed in beer in this airy brewpub, where historical photographs are displayed against exposed brick. Land Run Lager and Copperhead Ale complement the chicken potpie, fish-and-chips, and hot links (spicy smoked sausages). ✉ 1 N. Oklahoma Ave. ☎ 405/232-2739 ▭ AE, D, DC, MC, V $$-$$$.

✕ **CATTLEMEN'S STEAKHOUSE.** Beef is the star attraction at this classic steak house in the heart of the Stockyards City district, but try not to miss the opportunity to order some authentic "lamb fries" (battered, fried testicles). Cowboys clad in spurs look right at home among the western murals, cattle-branding irons, and other western paraphernalia. ✉ 1309 S. Agnew Ave. ☎ 405/236-0416 ▭ AE, D, MC, V $$-$$$.

Essentials

Getting Here

To get to Oklahoma City from the Dallas–Fort Worth area, take I–35 north. I–35 takes you north and south through central Oklahoma; I–40 crosses east and west. I–44, which runs diagonally from the northeast to the southwest, intersects I–35 and I–40 in Oklahoma City.

Visitor Information

🛈 **Oklahoma City Convention & Visitors Bureau** ✉ 189 W. Sheridan St., 73102 ☎ 405/297-8912 or 800/225-5652 ⊕ www.visitokc.com. **Oklahoma City Welcome Center** ✉ State Capitol rotunda, N.E. 23rd St. and Lincoln Blvd. ✉ I–35 and N.E. 122nd St. ✉ I–40 at the Air Depot exit.

AROUND
DENVER

Broadmoor Golf Club

By Matthew Rudy and Steve Knopper

With more than 300 days of sun every year, mild

and dry summers, and (believe it or not) an 11-month golf season, is it any wonder that Denver's population has more than doubled since 1960? If the weather doesn't entice you here, then the scenery and location will. Set on rolling plains more than 5,000 feet above sea level, the mile-high city is surrounded by massive mountain ranges that frame the horizon. Thanks to being near the geographic center of the United States, Denver is a relatively short trip from just about anywhere in the continental United States.

Denver more than lives up to its reputation as a sports town, and the golf scene here is vibrant as well. The city's Cherry Hills Country Club has been the scene of two of the more dramatic U.S. Opens in history. Arnold Palmer beat a 20-year-old amateur named Jack Nicklaus by a shot in 1960, and in 1978 the unknown Andy North shocked the golf world when he won his first of two Opens, by a shot over Dave Stockton and J. C. Snead. The PGA Tour visits suburban Castle Rock every year for the International, and Mike McGetrick, one of the most prominent teachers on the LPGA Tour, is based in Denver.

When you play golf in Denver, you get a 10% distance bonus on all your shots, thanks to the city's altitude and the thinner air that accompanies it. Take the breathtaking (both literally and figuratively) drive to Steamboat Springs, another 1,000 feet up, and you may start to feel like John Daly.

The golf courses at Steamboat, Vail, and Aspen all make use of the same elevation changes that are so attractive to skiers. Red Sky Golf Club and the Club at Cordillera both look as if they were built by mountain climbers using rappelling gear. The ups and downs are disorienting enough without the calculus that goes into figuring out how far you can hit your 7-iron in the thin air. The courses in Castle Rock and Boulder are rolling rather than jagged, and use the Rockies as more of a backdrop than a design feature.

Denver is the only city of significant size within a 600-mi radius, which makes it a logical jumping-off point for weekend excursions—golf or otherwise. Vail and Aspen are less than two hours away by car, as are Boulder and Colorado Springs. Just about any drive out of the city is punctuated by breathtaking mountain scenery. In Rocky Mountain State Park, an hour outside the city, Trail Ridge Road crosses the Continental Divide more than 2 mi above sea level—and you don't even need an SUV to negotiate it. At Pikes Peak, 60 mi south of town, you can negotiate the mountainside curves made famous by the annual race of the same name. If you're in Vail, be sure to check out the Mount Evans Scenic Byway. The

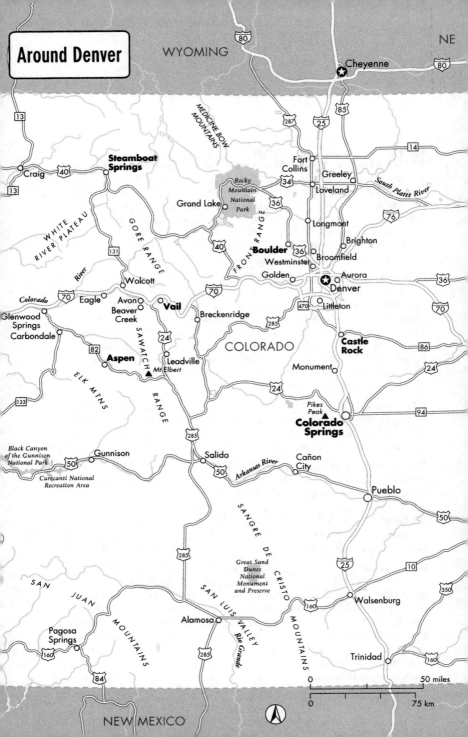

road, the highest paved surface in the United States, climbs more than 7,000 feet in 28 mi. At its apex, you can see the entire Front Range of the Rockies. Rocky Mountain High, indeed.

BOULDER

Just a half hour outside of Denver, Boulder is close enough to be convenient, but a world away from the traffic and congestion. Boulder Creek is filled with canoeists and kayakers, and the town's miles of public bike paths are more popular than the interstate. Rock climbers come to the area to be challenged.

Golf is well represented, too. The courses at the Omni Interlocken Resort and Mariana Butte take great advantage of their Flatiron Mountain backdrops, and the Olde Course at Loveland and Ute Creek make use of perfect, rolling terrain. The weather here is mild enough that you can play golf—or ride your bike—year-round.

To get the best feel of the city, take a walk around the Pearl Street pedestrian mall downtown. The four-block area is filled with shops, outdoor cafés, and coffeehouses, all with a laid-back Colorado charm.

Courses
Golf Digest REVIEWS

COAL CREEK GOLF COURSE. Facility Holes: 18. Opened: 1990. Architect: Dick Phelps. Yards: 6,957/5,185. Par: 72/72. Course Rating: 72.4/67.3. Slope: 136/118. Green Fee: $28/$42. Cart Fee: $15 per person. Discounts: Weekdays, twilight, seniors, juniors. Walking: Unrestricted walking. Season: Year-round. Tee Times: Call 6 days in advance. Notes: Range (grass, mat). ⊠ 585 W. Dillon Rd., Louisville 80027, 10 mi from Boulder ☎ 303/666-7888 ⊕ www.coalcreekgolf.com ☰ DC, MC, V. *Comments: Elevation changes make club selection a mystery.* ★ ★ ★ ½

INDIAN PEAKS GOLF CLUB. Facility Holes: 18. Opened: 1993. Architect: Hale Irwin/ Dick Phelps. Yards: 7,083/5,468. Par: 72/72. Course Rating: 72.5/69.9. Slope: 134/116. Green Fee: $35/$42. Cart Fee: $13 per person. Discounts: Weekdays. Walking: Unrestricted walking. Season: Year-round. Tee Times: Call 7 days in advance. Notes: Range (grass, mat). ⊠ 2300 Indian Peaks Trail, Lafayette 80026, 10 mi from Boulder ☎ 303/666-4706 ☰ D, MC, V. *Comments: Municipal course for the town of Lafayette. Designer Hale Irwin is a University of Colorado alum.* ★ ★ ★ ★

MARIANA BUTTE GOLF COURSE. Facility Holes: 18. Opened: 1992. Architect: Dick Phelps. Yards: 6,572/5,420. Par: 72/72. Course Rating: 70.8/67.5. Slope: 130/117. Green Fee: $26/$33. Cart Fee: $24 per cart. Discounts: Twilight. Walking: Unrestricted walking. Season: Year-round. High: Mar.–Nov. Tee Times: Call 5 days in advance. Notes: Range

Course	Yards	Par	Course Rating	Slope	Green Fee
Coal Creek Golf Course (18)	6,957/5,185	72/72	72.4/67.3	136/118	$28/$42
Indian Peaks Golf Club (18)	7,083/5,468	72/72	72.5/69.9	134/116	$35/$42
Mariana Butte Golf Course (18)	6,572/5,420	72/72	70.8/67.5	130/117	$26/$33
Olde Course at Loveland (18)	6,890/5,498	72/72	71.6/70.6	128/124	$20/$25
Omni Interlocken Resort Golf Club (27)					$55/$95
Eldorado/Vista (18)	6,957/5,161	72/72	72.3/68.2	136/130	
Sunshine/Eldorado (18)	6,955/5,200	72/72	72.2/69.4	133/132	
Vista/Sunshine (18)	7,040/5,655	72/72	72.5/71.8	136/142	
Ute Creek Golf Course (18)	7,167/5,509	72/72	73.3/69.6	133/127	$20/$36

(grass, mat). ✉ 701 Clubhouse Dr., Loveland 80537, 45 mi from Denver ☎ 970/667–8308 ▭ D, MC, V. *Comments: One of the most popular public courses in the area, it's the right mix of fun and hard.* ★ ★ ★ ★

OLDE COURSE AT LOVELAND. Facility Holes: 18. Opened: 1959. Architect: Dick Phelps/Henry Hughes. Yards: 6,890/5,498. Par: 72/72. Course Rating: 71.6/70.6. Slope: 128/124. Green Fee: $20/$25. Cart Fee: $24 per cart. Discounts: Twilight, juniors. Walking: Unrestricted walking. Season: Year-round. Tee Times: Call 5 days in advance. Notes: Range (grass, mat). ✉ 2115 W. 29th St., Loveland 80537, 45 mi from Denver ☎ 970/667–5256 ▭ MC, V. *Comments: Don't confuse this one with Scotland. Massive, mature trees protect most holes.* ★ ★ ★ ½

UTE CREEK GOLF COURSE. Facility Holes: 18. Opened: 1997. Architect: Robert Trent Jones Jr./Gary Linn. Yards: 7,167/5,509. Par: 72/72. Course Rating: 73.3/69.6. Slope: 133/127. Green Fee: $20/$36. Cart Fee: $24 per cart. Discounts: Twilight, seniors, juniors. Walking: Unrestricted walking. Season: Year-round. Tee Times: Call 7 days in advance. Notes: Range (grass, mat). ✉ 2000 Ute Creek Dr., Longmont 80501, 30 mi from Denver ☎ 303/774–4342 ▭ AE, D, MC, V. *Comments: Now coming into its own. Room to hit it.* ★ ★ ★ ★

Where to Stay

▣ **COLORADO CHAUTAUQUA ASSOCIATION.** Chautauqua, founded in 1898, remains a venue for recreation and cultural and educational enrichment. Lectures, concerts, and silent films accompanied by a pianist are part of the experience of staying here. (Some famous names, including Lyle Lovett, Randy Newman, David Byrne, and Shawn Colvin, have performed in the concert hall, which many have likened to the inside of an acoustic guitar.) The lodge rooms and cottages have been upgraded but retain their unique historic charm. Rooms and cottages are fully furnished, including linens and cooking utensils (in rooms with kitchens), but no daily housekeeping. The property also has some terrific spots for a picnic on a sunny afternoon. In summer there's a four-

CHERRY PICKING

Denver's Cherry Hills Country Club, site of the 2005 U.S. Women's Open, has hosted many USGA championships, including three U.S. Opens. Arnold Palmer captured the 1960 U.S. Open in dramatic fashion by coming from seven strokes back after three rounds to win by two strokes over Jack Nicklaus, then an amateur. In the final round of that tournament, Palmer drove the green of the 404-yard first hole—a commemorative plaque now marks the stop—and birdied six of the first seven holes. He shot a red-hot 30 on the front nine that day.

night minimum stay; in winter it's two nights. ⊠ 900 Baseline Rd., 80302 ☎ 303/442–3282 🖷 303/449–0790 ⊕ www.chautauqua.com ➷ 22 rooms, 60 cottages ⚲ Restaurant, 4 tennis courts, hiking, concert hall, playground, some pets allowed (fee); no TV in some rooms ▤ MC, V ¢–$$.

▥ HOTEL BOULDERADO. The gracious lobby of this elegant 1909 beauty has a soaring stained-glass ceiling, and the mezzanine beckons with many romantic nooks. When choosing a room, opt for the old building, where the spacious quarters are filled with period antiques and reproductions. The new wing is plush and comfortable but has less Victorian character. Mountain views and smoking rooms are available on request. The restaurant, Q's, serves stylish contemporary American cuisine. The Catacombs Blues Bar has live music three nights a week. Those staying here have access to the nearby health club, the Pulse. ⊠ 2115 13th St., 80302 ☎ 303/442-4344 or 800/433-4 344 🖷 303/442-4378 ⊕ www.boulderado.com ➷ 152 rooms, 8 suites ⚲ 3 restaurants, in-room data ports, business services, meeting rooms ▤ AE, D, DC, MC, V $$–$$$$.

▥ MILLENNIUM HOTEL BOULDER. This relatively large hotel has an unusual semi-circular design and is set amid immaculate gardens dotted with splashing fountains. The spacious rooms are done in light woods and pastel colors, and some have full baths with a mountain view. In keeping with Boulder's environmental concerns, all trash is recycled, and all water is treated and recirculated. ⊠ 1345 28th St., 80302 ☎ 303/443-3850 or 800/545-6285 🖷 303/443-1480 ⊕ www.millennium-hotels.com ➷ 249 rooms, 20 suites ⚲ Restaurant, 15 tennis courts, indoor-outdoor pool, gym, 2 hot tubs, basketball, bar, playground, laundry service, business services, meeting rooms, car rental, travel services ▤ AE, D, DC, MC, V $–$$$$.

▥ PEARL STREET INN. Fresh flowers, plush carpeting, watercolors of Colorado scenes, antiques, and the free use of light colors such as sage make this bed-and-breakfast reserved and refined. The guest rooms' four-poster beds are made of either brass or mahogany. The dining alcove and garden courtyard with a fountain are fine places to enjoy the full breakfasts of crispy waffles and homemade granola. Those staying here can enjoy an evening drink or a complimentary glass of wine at the mahogany, copper-top bar. ⊠ 1820 Pearl St., 80302 ☎ 303/444-5584 or 888/810-1302 🖷 303/444-6494 ⊕ www.pearlstreetinn.com ➷ 8 rooms ⚲ Bar ▤ AE, DC, MC, V ⦿ BP $$.

Where to Eat

✗**FLAGSTAFF HOUSE.** One of Colorado's finest, this restaurant is on the side of Flagstaff Mountain. You can sit on the enclosed patio and admire the views of Boulder while enjoying a selection from the remarkably comprehensive wine list. Chef Mark Monette has fresh fish flown in daily, grows some of the herbs for his cuisine, and is noted for the clever combinations of his ingredients and fanciful, playful presentations. The menu changes daily, but might include a ragout of porcini, royal trumpet, and shiitake mushrooms; buffalo filet mignon and foie gras Wellington, and Alaskan troll king salmon, grilled with shrimp on a skewer. ✉ 1138 Flagstaff Rd. ☎ 303/442–4640 🍴 Reservations essential ▤ AE, D, DC, MC, V ⊙ No lunch $$$$.

✗**MEDITERRANEAN CAFÉ.** After work, when it seems as if all of Boulder shows up for tapas, "The Med" becomes a real scene, and you may feel quite closed in, despite the restaurant's light and airy design. Abstract art, terra-cotta floors, and brightly colored tiles bring Santa Fe to mind. The open kitchen turns out daily specials such as barbecued mahimahi and horseradish-crusted tuna—dishes complemented by an extensive, well-priced wine list. Come here for a dose of local attitude and pretty people. During happy hour, weekdays from 3 to 6:30, some tapas are just $2. ✉ 1002 Walnut St. ☎ 303/444–5335 ▤ AE, D, DC, MC, V $–$$$.

✗**SUNFLOWER.** Storefront windows allow plenty of light into the colorfully painted dining room where chef-owner Jon Pell uses fresh, organic ingredients in savory dishes like tempeh scallopini or the "Bamboo Steamer," vegetables and udon noodles with a peanut sauce. Nonvegetarian entrées include New York steak, cioppino (a seafood stew made with tomatoes), and buffalo steak, and are all organic. You can end your lunch or dinner with the chocolate raspberry mousse, creamy but made without dairy, refined sugar, or eggs. Mr. Pell spent 16 years developing thedessert; he won't share the recipe. Brunch is served weekends 10 AM to 3 PM. ✉ 1701 Pearl St. ☎ 303/440-0220 ▤ AE, MC, V $$$–$$$$.

✗**ZOLO GRILL.** The superlative southwestern food here has Mexican and Native American touches—check out the barbecued red chili duck tacos and, for dessert, grilled banana cream pie. Huge picture windows overlook an active shopping center and the Flatirons beyond. Blond-wood furnishings, striking abstract art, and a high-tech open kitchen keep things urbane, and so do the bartenders, who have about 80 different tequilas on hand. There's also a good wine and beer list. ✉ 2525 Arapahoe Ave. ☎ 303/449-0444 ▤ AE, DC, MC, V $–$$$.

Essentials

Getting Here

To get here from downtown Denver, a 45-minute trip, take Federal Boulevard north to U.S. 36 and turn west, toward the mountains. Although traffic can be difficult on the relatively narrow highway during rush hour, it's usually a fast trip once you hit U.S. 36.

To get to downtown Boulder from the highway, take the Foothills Parkway to Pearl Street, then turn left and go straight to the pedestrian mall. Alternatively, you can continue on U.S. 36 until it turns into 28th Street, which gives you access to the University of Colorado campus in addition to downtown.

Visitor Information

🗓 **BOULDER CHAMBER OF COMMERCE** ✉ 2440 Pearl St. ☎ 303/442-1044 ⊕ - www.boulderchamber.com. **CITY OF BOULDER** ✉ 1777 Broadway ☎ 303/441-3090 ⊕ www.ci.boulder.co.us.

CASTLE ROCK

Until the 1970s, Castle Rock wasn't much more than small rhyolite-mining outpost 45 minutes south of Denver. Then, as Denver expanded and some of its residents starting looking for a way to get out of the urban bustle, Castle Rock, right on I-25, began to flourish. The massive Castle Pines gated community, built with two Jack Nicklaus-designed golf courses, became an anchor for the town.

CASTLE PINES

The International, the annual PGA Tour event held at the Country Club at Castle Pines, draws thousands each year.

Castle Pines' courses are open to members only, but you can get the same country club experience at two prominent daily-fee courses. The Ridge at Castle Pines North, developed by the same group that put together Castle Pines, benefits from the same attention to detail, and Red Hawk Ridge has some of the best golf for the price in the state.

Courses

Golf Digest REVIEWS

RED HAWK RIDGE GOLF CLUB. Facility Holes: 18. Opened: 1999. Architect: Jim Engh. Yards: 6,942/4,636. Par: 72/72. Course Rating: 71.6/67.5. Slope: 129/107. Green Fee: $36/$59. Cart Fee: $13 per person. Discounts: Weekdays, twilight, seniors, juniors. Walking: Unrestricted walking. Season: Year-round. Tee Times: Call 7 days in advance. Notes: Range (grass). ✉ 2156 Red Hawk Ridge Dr., 80104, 20 mi from Denver ☎ 720/733-3500 or 800/663-7150 ⊕ www.redhawkridge.com ☷ AE, MC, V. *Comments: Wide fairways and fun to play.* ★ ★ ★ ★

RIDGE AT CASTLE PINES NORTH. Facility Holes: 18. Opened: 1997. Architect: Tom Weiskopf. Yards: 7,013/5,001. Par: 71/71. Course Rating: 73.0/67.6. Slope: 134/123. Green Fee: $75/$120. Cart Fee: Included in green fee. Discounts: Twilight. Walking: Walking at certain times. Season: Mar.–Dec. High: May–Oct. Tee Times: Call 7 days in advance. Notes: Range (grass). ✉ 1414 Castle Pines Pkwy., 80104, 16 mi from Denver ☎ 303/688-0100 ⊕ www.theridgecpn.com ☷ AE, MC, V. *Comments: Imposing views of mountains.* ★ ★ ★ ★ ¹/₂

Red Hawk Ridge Golf Club (18)	6,942/4,636	72/72	71.6/67.5	129/107	$36/$59
Ridge at Castle Pines North (18)	7,013/5,001	71/71	73.0/67.6	134/123	$75/$12

Where to Stay

BEST WESTERN INN & SUITES OF CASTLE ROCK. This part of the national chain of hotels is a comfortable, centrally located place to stay that's a straight shot to the golf courses, mall, and hiking trails. ⊠595 Genoa Way, 80109 ☎303/814-8800 🖷303/814-6864 ⊕ www.bestwestern.com/castlerock ⇝37 rooms, 33 suites ⌂ Microwaves, refrigerators, indoor pool ⊟AE, D, DC, MC, V ⦿CP $-$$.

CASTLE ROCK COMFORT SUITES. The Castle Rock outlet of this national all-suites hotel chain is comfortable in a streamlined sort of way. It's within walking distance of the huge Factory Outlet mall, and fairly close to many other local attractions. ⊠4755 Castleton Way, 80109 ☎303/814-9999 or 303/433-9525 🖷303/814-0688 ⊕ www.comfortsuites.com/hotel/co154 ⇝68 suites ⌂ Microwaves, refrigerators, indoor pool, gym, Internet, business services, some pets allowed (fee) ⊟AE, D, DC, MC, V $.

Where to Eat

✕JARRE CREEK RANCH. Colorado loves its microbreweries, and this Castle Rock brewpub joined the crush in 1997. The generally lighter beers include signature Heffer Wizzen Golden Ale. The menu, a little fancier than your typical beer-and-burger joint, includes eggplant fries and jalapeño catfish. ⊠810 New Memphis Ct. ☎303/688-1945 or 303/688-8509 ⊕ www.jcrbrew.com ⊟AE, D, DC, MC, V $-$$$$.

Essentials

Getting Here

Castle Rock is 50 minutes from Denver. To get here, take I-25 south toward Colorado Springs to the Wolfensberger Road/Wilcox Street exit. Castle Rock isn't especially congested, but the sections of I-25 around Denver and the surrounding suburbs can be very busy during rush hour.

Visitor Information

CASTLE ROCK CHAMBER OF COMMERCE ⊠420 Jerry St., 80104 ☎303/688-4597 🖷303/688-2688 ⊕ www.castlerock.org.

Broadmoor Golf Club (45)					
East (18)	7,091/5,847	72/72	73.0/72.7	129/139	$95/$165
Mountain (9)	6,781/4,834	72/72	72.1/67.3		
West (18)	6,937/5,375	72/73	73.0/70.5	133/127	$90/$165
Country Club of Colorado (18)	7,028/5,357	71/71	72.4/69.3	138/124	$120
Eisenhower Golf Club (36)					$10/$55
Blue (18)	7,301/5,559	72/72	74.2/65.3	137/130	
Silver (18)	6,519/5,215	72/72	70.5/69.0	121/119	
King's Deer Golf Club (18)	6,945/5,138	71/71	72.0/68.7	136/124	$43/$55

COLORADO SPRINGS

It isn't hard to see why the U.S. Air Force Academy decided to set up shop in Colorado Springs. Aside from the obvious natural beauty of the surrounding lakes and mountain ranges, Colorado Springs is more than 1,000 feet higher above sea level than Denver. Those Air Force jets have that much less distance to climb to reach their altitude.

Colorado Springs started as a vacation getaway spot for visiting Europeans in the early 1870s. When gold was discovered nearby, so was Colorado Springs. The gold might be gone, but the things that drew tourists all the way from England are still in abundance.

The Broadmoor opened in 1891 as a casino serving those European guests, and it has only become more refined since then. Set on 3,000 acres in the Rocky Mountain foothills, the resort is famous for its pink stucco masonry and impressive golf courses and spa. Donald Ross designed the original resort course in 1918, and Robert Trent Jones and Arnold Palmer courses were added in 1965 and 1976.

Those staying at the Broadmoor—and in the rest of Colorado Springs—don't have to be content with the golf at the resort, good as it is. If you include the Air Force's Eisenhower Golf Club and King's Deer, then the golf options become almost as varied as the scenery.

Courses

Golf Digest REVIEWS

BROADMOOR GOLF CLUB. Facility Holes: 45. Cart Fee: Included in green fee. Discounts: Twilight, juniors. Season: Year-round. Notes: Range (grass), lodging (731). ✉ 1 Pourtales Rd., 80906 ☎ 719/577–5790 or 800/634–7711 ⊕ www.broadmoor.com ▭ AE, D, MC, V.

East. Holes: 18. Opened: 1918. Architect: Donald Ross/Robert Trent Jones. Yards: 7,091/ 5,847. Par: 72/72. Course Rating: 73.0/72.7. Slope: 129/139. Green Fee: $95/$165. Walking: Walking with caddie. *Comments: The original course is still the standard-bearer. Diabolical greens.* ★ ★ ★ ★ ½

Mountain. Holes: 9. Opened: 1975. Architect: Arnold Palmer. Yards: 6,781/4,834. Par: 72/72. Course Rating: 72.1/67.3. Slope: 133/117. *Comments: The toughest of the three, with the best view.* UR

West. Holes: 18. Opened: 1918. Architect: Donald Ross/Robert Trent Jones. Yards: 6,937/ 5,375. Par: 72/73. Course Rating: 73.0/70.5. Slope: 133/127. Green Fee: $90/$165. Walking: Walking with caddie. *Comments: Set on a ridge overlooking the city.* ★ ★ ★ ★ ½

COUNTRY CLUB OF COLORADO. Facility Holes: 18. Opened: 1973. Architect: Pete Dye. Yards: 7,028/5,357. Par: 71/71. Course Rating: 72.4/69.3. Slope: 138/124. Green Fee: $120. Cart Fee: Included in green fee. Discounts: Twilight, juniors. Walking: Unrestricted walking. Season: Year-round. High: May–Oct. Tee Times: Call 3 days in advance. Notes: Range (grass, mat), lodging (300). ✉ 125 E. Clubhouse Dr., 80906 ☎ 719/538–4095 ▤ AE, D, MC, V. *Comments: A Pete Dye design overshadowed by the Broadmoor. Worth a visit.* ★ ★ ★ ½

EISENHOWER GOLF CLUB. Facility Holes: 36. Green Fee: $10/$55. Cart Fee: $22 per person. Discounts: Twilight, juniors. Walking: Unrestricted walking. Season: Year-round. High: May–Oct. Tee Times: Call 6days in advance. Notes: Range (grass, mat). ✉ M-USAF Academy, Bldg. 3170, USAFA, 80840, 5 mi from Colorado Springs ☎ 719/333–4735 ⊕ - www.usafa.af.mil/eisenhower/course.html ▤ MC, V.

Blue. Holes: 18. Opened: 1963. Architect: Robert Trent Jones. Yards: 7,301/5,559. Par: 72/72. Course Rating: 74.2/65.3. Slope: 137/130. *Comments: As good as it gets. A must-play.* ★ ★ ★ ★ ½

Silver. Holes: 18. Opened: 1976. Architect: Frank Hummel. Yards: 6,519/5,215. Par: 72/ 72. Course Rating: 70.5/69.0. Slope: 121/119. *Comments: Short, especially at this altitude, but a blast to play.* ★ ★ ★ ★

KING'S DEER GOLF CLUB. Facility Holes: 18. Opened: 1999. Architect: Redstone Golf. Yards: 6,945/5,138. Par: 71/71. Course Rating: 72.0/68.7. Slope: 136/124. Green Fee: $43/$55. Cart Fee: Included in green fee. Discounts: Weekdays, twilight, juniors. Walking: Unrestricted walking. Season: Year-round. High: Apr.–Nov. Tee Times: Call 7 days in advance. Notes: Range (grass). ✉ 19255 Royal Troon Dr., Monument 80132, 20 mi from Colorado Springs ☎ 719/481–1518 ⊕ www.kingsdeergolfclub.com ▤ AE, D, MC, V. *Comments: The Divide course here is impeccably run by Troon Golf.* ★ ★ ★ ½

Where to Stay

🏨 **ANTLERS ADAM'S MARK.** General William Jackson Palmer, founder of Colorado Springs, donated his elk-hunting trophies for the hotel lobby—and coined its name in the process. Founded in 1883, the present building—wide, tall, and pink—dates from 1964. Some rooms have excellent views of nearby Pikes Peak. ✉ 4 S. Cascade Ave. (I-25, exit 142), 80903 ☎ 719/473–5600 or 800/444–2326 🖷 719/389–0259 ⊕ www.antlers.

com ⟿ 292 rooms, 9 suites ⚬ 2 restaurants, some microwaves, cable TV, some in-room VCRs, pool, gym, hot tub, bar, business services ▭ AE, D, DC, MC, V $$-$$$$.

THE BROADMOOR. The 3,500-acre Broadmoor, which includes a private lake, began as a gambling casino in 1891. The hotel is part of a massive complex that resembles a university campus; the main building is the most opulent, with regal rugs and chandeliers in the lobby and large rooms filled with pillows and bathrobes. Consider paying extra to book a room overlooking the huge pond at the rear of the building. ⊠ 1 Lake Ave., 80906, (I-25, exit 138) ☎ 719/634-7711 or 800/634-7711 🖷 719/577-5700 ⊕ www.broadmoor. com ⟿ 593 rooms, 107 suites ⚬ 9 restaurants, room service, in-room data ports, mini-bars, refrigerators, cable TV, some in-room VCRs, driving range, 3 18-hole golf courses, 12 tennis courts, 3 pools (1 indoor), lake, health club, hair salon, hot tub, massage, sauna, spa, steam room, boating, fishing, bicycles, horseback riding, shops, children's programs (ages 4-12), business services, airport shuttle ▭ AE, D, DC, MC, V $$$$.

CHEYENNE MOUNTAIN RESORT. A sprawling resort with a golf course and country club, along with tennis courts and a 35-acre lake for fishing and sailing, Cheyenne Mountain Resort aims for the active mountain-sports traveler. The Mountain View Dining Room, which specializes in buffets, is the better of two restaurants. The 146-acre Cheyenne Mountain Zoo is just down the road. ⊠ 3225 Broadmoor Valley Rd., 80906 ☎ 719/538-4000 or 800/428-8886 🖷 719/540-5779 ⊕ www.cheyennemountain.com ⟿ 316 rooms, 5 suites ⚬ 2 restaurants, room service, refrigerators, cable TV, 18-hole golf course, 20 tennis courts, lake, health club, boating, fishing, children's programs (ages 4-12), Internet, business services, airport shuttle ▭ AE, D, DC, MC, V ⦿ BP $-$$$.

SPURS N' LACE. Once a rancher's house, this three-story 1886 Victorian has beautiful upper-balcony views of Pikes Peak. Each of the rooms is uniquely furnished with Victorian and western antiques. ⊠ 2829 W. Pikes Peak Ave., 80904 ☎ 719/227-7662 or 800/378-9717 🖷 719/227-8701 ⊕ www.colorado-bnb.com/spursnlace ⟿ 5 rooms ⚬ Dining room, laundry facilities; no room TVs, no smoking ▭ AE, D, MC, V ⦿ BP ¢-$.

> The Broadmoor, opened in 1891 as a casino serving European guests, has only become more refined since then.

WYNDHAM COLORADO SPRINGS. This high-end chain hotel has a picture-perfect location, as if architects designed the rectangular building to line up exactly with Pikes Peak in the background. The suites are roomy, and the on-site Gratzi Restaurant has an excellent pasta bar for lunch. ⊠ 5580 Tech Center Dr., 80919 ☎ 719/260-1800 🖷 719/260-1492 ⊕ www.wyndham.com ⟿ 278 rooms, 33 suites ⚬ Restaurant, room service, some refrigerators, cable TV, 2 pools (1 indoor), health club, 2 hot tubs (1 outdoor), sauna, Internet ▭ AE, D, DC, MC, V ⦿ BP $-$$.

Where to Eat

✕ **LA PETITE MAISON.** In this romantic restaurant inside a restored late-1800s Victorian cottage, Parisian posters hang against the pale pink walls, and there are bouquets of fresh flowers on the tables. Try the curried shrimp with banana chutney, the grilled lamb loin with artichoke bottoms, or the pork chops with mashed potatoes. ✉1015 W. Colorado Ave. ☎719/632-4887 ▤AE, D, DC, MC, V ⊙Closed Sun. $$$-$$$$.

✗ **MAGGIE MAE'S.** This homey restaurant has a popular breakfast menu that's served all day long. The casual environment and varied menu, which includes omelets, pork chops, and fajitas, make it good for families. ✉2405 E. Pikes Peak Ave. ☎719/475-1623 ▤AE, D, MC, V ¢-$.

✗ **PENROSE ROOM.** One of the finest restaurants in the state, the Penrose Room is luxurious, with chandeliers, rich velvet draperies, and majestic views of the city and mountains. Try the chateaubriand, the grilled duck breast Bigarade, and the restaurant's signature dessert soufflées. There's entertainment nightly. ✉Broadmoor Hotel, 1 Lake Ave. ☎719/634-7711 ⌕ Reservations essential 🏛Jacket required ▤AE, D, DC, MC, V ⊙ No lunch $-$$.

✗ **PEPPER TREE.** On a hilltop, this restaurant has a great view of the city. Table-side preparations include pepper steak with Indian-mango chutney; one of the specials is calamari stuffed with crabmeat and bacon. ✉888 W. Moreno Ave. ☎719/471-4888 🖷719/471-0997 ▤AE, D, MC, V ⊙Closed Sun and Mon. No lunch $$$-$$$$.

Essentials

Getting Here
From Denver, take I-25 south towards Colorado Springs. The trip takes about 90 minutes.

Visitor Information
🛈 **COLORADO SPRINGS CONVENTION AND VISITORS BUREAU** ✉515 S. Cascade Ave. ☎800/888-4748 ⊕ www.coloradosprings-travel.com.

STEAMBOAT SPRINGS

One of the reasons Colorado is so popular with skiers is that you can leave Denver with its mere 20 inches of snow a year, drive 150 mi, and reach a place like Steamboat Springs, which gets almost 350 inches. Steamboat wears its badge as Ski Town USA proudly. The area is packed with downhill runs, cross-country trails, and ski jumping platforms—and the town's infrastructure is designed to handle the thousands of skiers who come to partake.

That's also good news for golfers, because summer weather is great here, with temperatures around 80° and almost no humidity, and there are plenty of places to eat and stay. The Sheraton Steamboat Resort, ski central when the snow falls, is transformed into a golf haven in summer thanks to its

STEAMBOAT SPRINGS COURSES	YARDAGE	PAR	COURSE	SLOPE	GREEN FEE
Grand Lake Golf Course (18)	6,542/5,685	72/74	70.5/70.9	131/123	$65
Haymaker Golf Course (18)	7,308/5,059	72/72	73.3/66.9	131/117	$54/$83
Sheraton Steamboat Resort & Golf Club (18)	6,902/5,462	72/72	72.0/72.2	138/125	$62/$110

Robert Trent Jones Jr. resort course. Better yet, rooms are generally $100 cheaper per night than in ski season. A little bit outside of town, Grand Lake Golf Course takes advantage of both the elevation changes and pine forests to make you feel as if you're playing alone.

Courses

Golf Digest REVIEWS

GRAND LAKE GOLF COURSE. Facility Holes: 18. Opened: 1964. Architect: Dick Phelps. Yards: 6,542/5,685. Par: 72/74. Course Rating: 70.5/70.9. Slope: 131/123. Green Fee: $65. Cart Fee: $25 per cart. Discounts: Juniors. Walking: Unrestricted walking. Season: May–Nov. High: July–Aug. Tee Times: Call 2 days in advance. Notes: Metal spikes, range (grass, mat). ⊠ 1415 County Rd. 48, Grand Lake 80447, 100 mi from Denver ☎970/627-8008 ⊕www.grandlakegolf.com ▤D, MC, V. *Comments: Deer, foxes, and bears live in the forest surrounding the course. Be careful if you miss.* ★ ★ ★ ★

HAYMAKER GOLF COURSE. Facility Holes: 18. Opened: 1997. Architect: Keith Foster. Yards: 7,308/5,059. Par: 72/72. Course Rating: 73.3/66.9. Slope: 131/117. Green Fee: $54/$83. Cart Fee: $16 per person. Discounts: Guest, twilight, juniors. Walking: Unrestricted walking. Season: May–Oct. High: June–Sept. Tee Times: Call 365 days in advance. Notes: Range (grass, mat). ⊠34855 U.S. Hwy. 40 E, 80477, 80 mi from Boulder ☎970/870-1846 or 888/282-2969 ⊕www.haymakergolf.com ▤AE, D, MC, V. *Comments: A links-style course in the mountains, believe it or not.* ★ ★ ★

SHERATON STEAMBOAT RESORT & GOLF CLUB. Facility Holes: 18. Opened: 1974. Architect: Robert Trent Jones Jr. Yards: 6,902/5,462. Par: 72/72. Course Rating: 72.0/72.2. Slope: 138/125. Green Fee: $62/$110. Cart Fee: $20 per person. Discounts: Guest, twilight, seniors, juniors. Walking: Walking at certain times. Season: May–Nov. Tee Times: Call golf shop. Notes: Range (grass, mat), lodging (317). ⊠2000 Clubhouse Dr., 80477, 157 mi from Denver ☎970/879-1391 or 800/848-8878 ▤AE, D, MC, V. *Comments: Quintessential mountain golf course. Relatively short.* ★ ★ ★ ★ ½

Where to Stay

🏨**RABBIT EARS MOTEL.** The playful pink neon bunny sign marking this place has been a local landmark since 1952. The Rabbit Ears stands across the street from hot springs and is near the downtown shops, bars, and restaurants. All rooms are equipped with coffeemakers; most have balconies and views of the Yampa River. ⊠201 Lincoln Ave., 80477 ☎970/879-1150 or 800/828-7702 🖷970/870-0483 ⊕www.rabbitearsmotel.com ⟋66 rooms ⓓ In-room data ports, some microwaves, refrigerators, cable TV, laundry facilities ⊟AE, D, DC, MC, V ⓞ CP $-$$$.

⚏ **SHERATON STEAMBOAT RESORT & CONFERENCE CENTER.** At this bustling high-rise, the amenities are classic resort-town—the four rooftop hot tubs have sweeping views of the surrounding ski slopes. The large rooms in the main building are standard issue, with muted color schemes and comforts like refrigerators. ⊠ 2200 Village End Ct., 80477 ☎ 970/879-2220 or 800/848-8877 🖷 970/879-7686 ⊕ www.sheraton.com/steamboat ⟋ 317 rooms ⓓ 2 restaurants, in-room data ports, in-room safes, refrigerators, cable TV, 18-hole golf course, pool, 4 hot tubs, sauna, steam room, ski shop, bar, meeting room ⊟AE, D, DC, MC, V $$-$$$$.

⚏ **STEAMBOAT BED AND BREAKFAST.** A former church, this blue-and-cream Victorian from 1891 still has a large arched doorway and stained-glass windows. Rooms have lace curtains and floral wallpaper and are filled with potted geraniums and period antiques. All rooms have mountain views. ⊠ 442 Pine St., 80477 ☎ 970/879-5724 🖷 970/870-8787 ⊕ www.steamboatb-b.com ⟋ 7 rooms ⓓ Hot tub; no room TVs ⊟AE, D, MC, V ⓞ BP $$-$$$.

⚏ **VISTA VERDE GUEST RANCH.** This all-inclusive, luxurious guest ranch sits on 540 acres. Each of the cabins has a woodstove and patio, and the three rooms in the main lodge all have balconies. Backpacking, gold-panning, and guided rock-climbing expeditions can be arranged, as can seasonal hot-air-balloon rides, hayrides, and cattle drives. ⊠ 31100 Seedhouse Rd., 80428 ☎ 970/879-3858 or 800/526-7433 🖷 970/879-1413 ⊕ www.vistaverde.com ⟋ 9 cabins, 3 rooms in lodge ⓓ Dining room, refrigerators, lake, gym, massage, fishing, bicycles, hiking, children's programs (ages 6–17), playground, laundry service, business services, airport shuttle; no a/c ⊟ No credit cards ⓧ Closed Apr., May, Oct., and Nov. ⓞ FAP $$$$.

Where to Eat

✗ **HARWIG'S GRILL.** The popular Harwig's, next door to L'Apogée, is run by the same team. The menu includes specialties from all over: home-cured salmon pastrami, raclette (melted cheese over boiled potatoes), jambalaya, and dim sum. The bar has 40 wines by the glass, including many lesser-known labels, and you can also order from L'Apogée's wine list. ⊠ 911 Lincoln Ave. ☎ 970/879-1980 ⊟AE, D, DC, MC, V ⓧ No lunch $$-$$$$.

✗ **L'APOGÉE.** At this former saddle-repair shop (from 1886), the rustic furnishings include a bar paneled with wine-crate ends, handmade chairs and tables, and an old-timey color scheme that brings to mind a saloon. The elegant dining room has stained glass, linen, and crystal tableware. Try oysters Rockefeller, wild mushrooms, or the filet mignon. There's open-air dining available on a sidewalk patio in season. ⊠ 911 Lincoln Ave. ☎ 970/879-1919 ⊟AE, D, DC, MC, V ⓧ No lunch $$-$$$$.

✗ **RIGGIO'S.** This local favorite looks industrial, but accents such as tapestries and murals soften the effect a bit. The menu includes such dishes as pollo piccata (strips of chicken sautéed in a white wine and lemon butter sauce with capers) and *melanzana* (grilled eggplant with spinach, roast peppers, fontina, and ricotta cheese). ⊠ 1106 Lincoln Ave. ☎ 970/879-9010 ⊟AE, D, DC, MC, V ⓧ No lunch $-$$$$.

✕**WINONA'S.** Wooden tables, with fresh flowers on every one, make a pleasant place for breakfast as well as good deli sandwiches and pastries. You choose the desserts from the deli cases. ✉617 Lincoln Ave. ☎970/879-2483 ▭MC, V ⊙No dinner $.

Essentials

Getting Here
To get here from Denver, take I-70 straight west, into the mountains. Take the Empire/ Granby exit, then U.S. 40, which turns into Lincoln Avenue and goes straight into Steamboat Springs.

Visitor Information
🛈**STEAMBOAT SPRINGS CHAMBER OF COMMERCE** ✉1255 Lincoln Ave., 80477 ☎970/879-0880 🖷970/879-2543 ⊕www.steamboat-chamber.com.

VAIL, ASPEN & BEAVER CREEK

Since the 1960s, Vail and Aspen have been the ski resorts of choice not just for Coloradoans, but also for serious, stylish skiers the world over, who come for the reliably dense snowfall and the spectacular slopes. But the fun doesn't stop when the snow melts. The terrain so prized for skiing is spectacular for golf once it's uncovered.

The many mountain golf courses built in the area since the mid-1980s are there to satisfy summer visitors and chalet owners who come to Vail and Aspen year-round. The best of these are part of high-end resorts. Vail Resort's brand new Red Sky Golf Club has courses by Tom Fazio and Greg Norman, each built on the slopes near Beaver Creek, 20 minutes from Vail. Similarly, the Club at Cordillera only recently got into the golf business, but its three courses have moved it to the forefront.

Courses   **Golf**Digest REVIEWS

ASPEN GOLF & TENNIS CLUB. Facility Holes: 18. Opened: 1962. Architect: Frank Hummel/Dick Phelps. Yards: 7,136/5,222. Par: 71/72. Course Rating: 73.7/69.1. Slope: 133/119. Green Fee: $35/$90. Cart Fee: $17.50 per person. Walking: Unrestricted walking. Season: Apr.–Oct. Tee Times: Call golf shop. ✉39551 Hwy. 82, Aspen 81611 ☎970/

VAIL, ASPEN & BEAVER CREEK COURSES	YARDAGE	PAR	COURSE	SLOPE	GREEN FEE
Aspen Golf & Tennis Club (18)	7,136/5,222	71/72	73.7/69.1	133/119	$35/$90
Beaver Creek Golf Club (18)	6,725/5,200	70/70	69.6/70.3	140/124	$45/$160
Breckenridge Golf Club (18)	7,276/5,063	72/72	73.3/67.6	149/129	$55/$95
Club at Cordillera (64)					
Mountain (18)	7,416/5,226	72/72	74.7/68.6	145/128	$237
Short (10)	1,252/592	27/27			$43
Summit (18)	7,441/5,425	72/72	74.0/69.5	135/130	$235
Valley (18)	7,413/5,087	71/71	72.2/68.1	130/121	$225
Cotton Ranch Club (18)	7,052/5,197	72/72	72.9/70.1	130/117	$50/$90
Eagle Vail Golf Club (18)	6,819/4,856	72/72	71.3/67.4	131/123	$55/$105
Red Sky Golf Club (36)					$175/$200
Greg Norman (18)	7,580/5,269	72/72	74.2/65.5	144/124	
Tom Fazio (18)	7,113/5,265	72/72	72.2/68.2	135/125	
River Valley Ranch Golf Club (18)	7,348/5,168	72/72	73.2/68.8	125/114	$40/$90
Sonnenalp Golf Club (18)	7,059/5,293	71/71	73.1/69.4	139/125	$52/$160
Vail Golf Club (18)	7,100/5,291	71/72	71.3/69.5	124/114	$50/$100

925-2145 ⊕ aspenrecreation.com ▤ AE, D, MC, V. *Comments: This muni is the value leader for the area.* ★ ★ ★

BEAVER CREEK GOLF CLUB. Facility Holes: 18. Opened: 1982. Architect: RobertTrent Jones Jr. Yards: 6,725/5,200. Par: 70/70. Course Rating: 69.6/70.3. Slope: 140/124. Green Fee: $45/$160. Cart Fee: Included in green fee. Walking: Mandatory carts. Season: May–Oct. Tee Times: Call golf shop. ⊠ 103 Offerson Rd., Avon 81620 ☎ 970/845-5775 ⊕ - www.beavercreek.snow.com ▤ AE, D, DC, MC, V. *Comments: You need to play a few times to get the feel. From mid-June through mid-September, you must stay at Beaver Creek Lodge to play.* ★ ★ ★

BRECKENRIDGE GOLF CLUB. Facility Holes: 18. Opened: 1985. Architect: Jack Nicklaus. Yards: 7,276/5,063. Par: 72/72. Course Rating: 73.3/67.6. Slope: 149/129. Green Fee: $55/$95. Cart Fee: $15 per person. Discounts: Twilight. Walking: Walking at certain times. Season: May–Oct. Tee Times: Call golf shop. Notes: Range (grass). ⊠ 200 Clubhouse Dr., Breckenridge 80424, 80 mi from Denver ☎ 970/453-9104 ⊕ www. breckenridgegolfclub.com ▤ AE, MC, V. *Comments: As hard as you'll find from the back tees.* ★ ★ ★ ★

CLUB AT CORDILLERA. Facility Holes: 64. Cart Fee: Included in green fee. Walking: Mandatory cart. Season: May–Nov. Tee Times: Call golf shop. Notes: Range (grass, mat), lodging (56). ⊠ 650 Clubhouse Dr., Edwards 81632, 100 mi from Denver ☎ 970/926-5100 or 800/877-3529 ⊕ www.cordillera-vail.com ▤ AE, D, MC, V.

BACK TO SCHOOL

If you're serious about improving your game, consider checking into the **Chuck Cook Golf Academy** (✉ Red Sky Golf Club, 376 Red Sky Rd., Wolcott ☎ 970/477–8350). Named one of the top-50 instructors by *Golf Digest*, Cook has coached U.S. Open champions Payne Stewart, Tom Kite, and Corey Pavin. Cook uses high-tech tools at the academy's intense two- and three-day sessions. For example, he employs four cameras to record your swing so that he can analyze everything from your stance to your grip.

Mountain. Holes: 18. Opened: 1994. Architect: Hale Irwin/Dick Phelps. Yards: 7,416/5,226. Par: 72/72. Course Rating: 74.7/68.6. Slope: 145/128. Green Fee: $237. *Comments: May not be worth the hefty fee, but it does have spectacular conditioning.* ★★★★

Short. Holes: 10. Opened: 1997. Architect: Dave Pelz. Yards: 1,252/592. Par: 27/27. Green Fee: $43. Cart fee: $12 per person. UR

Summit. Holes: 18. Opened: 2001. Architect: Jack Nicklaus. Yards: 7,441/5,425. Par: 72/72. Course Rating: 74.0/69.5. Slope: 135/130. Green Fee: $235. UR

Valley. Holes: 18. Opened: 1997. Architect: Tom Fazio/Dennis Wise. Yards: 7,413/5,087. Par: 71/71. Course Rating: 72.2/68.1. Slope: 130/121. Green Fee: $225. UR

COTTON RANCH CLUB. Facility Holes: 18. Opened: 1997. Architect: Pete Dye. Yards: 7,052/5,197. Par: 72/72. Course Rating: 72.9/70.1. Slope: 130/117. Green Fee: $50/$90. Cart Fee: Included in green fee. Discounts: Twilight, juniors. Walking: Walking at certain times. Season: Mar.–Nov. High: June–Sept. Tee Times: Call golf shop. Notes: Range (grass). ✉ 530 Cotton Ranch Dr., Gypsum 81637, 35 mi from Vail ☎ 970/524–6200 or 800/404–3542 ⊕ www.cottonranch.com ▭ AE, D, MC, V. *Comments: A half hour outside Vail, and worth the drive. There are plenty of blind holes and precipitous drop-offs, especially on the 8th hole.* ★★★ ½

EAGLE VAIL GOLF CLUB. Facility Holes: 18. Opened: 1975. Architect: Bruce Devlin/Bob von Hagge. Yards: 6,819/4,856. Par: 72/72. Course Rating: 71.3/67.4. Slope: 131/123. Green Fee: $55/$105. Cart Fee: Included in green fee. Discounts: Twilight. Walking: Mandatory cart. Season: May–Oct. Tee Times: Call golf shop. Notes: Range (grass, mat). ✉ 0431 Eagle Dr., Avon 81620, 107 mi from Denver ☎ 970/949–5267 or 800/341–8051 ▭ AE, MC, V. *Comments: Lots of strange carries and elevation changes* ★★★ ½

RED SKY GOLF CLUB. Facility Holes: 36. Green Fee: $175/$200. Cart Fee: Included in green fee. Walking: Walking at certain times. Season: May–Oct. Tee Times: Call 30 days in advance. ✉ 376 Red Sky Rd., Wolcott 81655 ☎ 866/873–3759 or 970/477–8400 ⊕ - www.redskygolfclub.com ▭ AE, D, DC, MC, V.

Greg Norman. Holes: 18. Opened: 2003. Architect: Greg Norman. Yards: 7,580/5,269. Par: 72/72. Course Rating: 74.2/65.5. Slope: 144/124.

Tom Fazio. Holes: 18. Opened: 2002. Architect: Tom Fazio. Yards: 7,113/5,265. Par: 72/72. Course Rating: 72.2/68.2. Slope: 135/125.

Comments: The Fazio has diverse views of forest, valley, and lake, while the Norman has great views of the Vail Valley. Only one course is open to the resort guest on any particular day (the other is open to country club members). To play at Red Sky, you must stay in the Lodge at Vail, the Pines Lodge in Beaver Creek, the Ritz-Carlton Bachelor Gulch, or other hotels owned by Vail Resorts. UR

RIVER VALLEY RANCH GOLF CLUB. Facility Holes: 18. Opened: 1998. Architect: Jay Morrish/Carter Morrish. Yards: 7,348/5,168. Par: 72/72. Course Rating: 73.2/68.8. Slope: 125/114. Green Fee: $40/$90. Cart Fee: Included in green fee. Discounts: Twilight, seniors. Walking: Unrestricted walking. Season: Mar.–Nov. High: June–Aug. Tee Times: Call 90 days in advance. Notes: Range (grass). ⊠ 303 River Valley Ranch Dr., Carbondale 81623, 15 mi from Glenwood Springs ☎ 970/963-3625 ⊕ www.rvrgolf.com ⊟ AE, MC, V. *Comments: Holes 12 through 15 make the round worth it.* ★ ★ ★ ★

SONNENALP GOLF CLUB. Facility Holes: 18. Opened: 1981. Architect: Bob Cupp/Jay Morrish. Yards: 7,059/5,293. Par: 71/71. Course Rating: 73.1/69.4. Slope: 139/125. Green Fee: $52/$160. Cart Fee: Included in green fee. Discounts: Weekdays, twilight, juniors. Walking: Unrestricted walking. Season: Apr.–Nov. Tee Times: Call 7 days in advance. Notes: Metal spikes, range (grass). ⊠ 1265 Berry Creek Rd., Edwards 81632, 110 mi from Denver ☎ 970/477-5370 or 800/654-8312 ⊕ www.sonnenalp.com ⊟ AE, D, MC, V. *Comments: Wonderful, but the houses intrude.* ★ ★ ★ ★ ¹/₂

> **RED SKY COURSES**
>
> Fazio's course heads through a pine forest and around a mountain lake, while Norman's 7,580-yard monster is protected by mountain outcroppings.

VAIL GOLF CLUB. Facility Holes: 18. Opened: 1966. Architect: Press Maxwell/Ben Krueger. Yards: 7,100/5,291. Par: 71/72. Course Rating: 71.3/69.5. Slope: 124/114. Green Fee: $50/$100. Cart Fee: $17 per person. Discounts: Guest, twilight. Walking: Walking at certain times. Season: May–Oct. High: June–Sept. Tee Times: Call 2 days in advance. Notes: Range (grass). ⊠ 1778 Vail Valley Dr., Vail 81657, 100 mi from Denver ☎ 970/479-2260 ⊟ AE, D, MC, V. *Comments: Watch the sun set at the base of the Gore Range.* ★ ★ ★ ¹/₂

Where to Stay

Aspen

🛏 **HOTEL ASPEN.** A few minutes from the mall and the mountain, this hotel on the town's main drag is a good find. The modern exterior is opened up with huge windows that take full advantage of the view; the lobby is done in a southwestern style. Rooms are comfortable, if not luxurious, with plenty of down pillows and comforters. Most have balconies or terraces. ⊠ 110 W. Main St., 81611 ☎ 970/925-3441 or 800/527-7369 📠 970/920-1379 ⊕ www.hotelaspen.com 📶 37 rooms, 8 suites ⟁ Some in-room hot tubs, microwaves, refrigerators, in-room VCRs, pool, 2 outdoor hot tubs, airport shuttle ⊟ AE, D, DC, MC, V 🍴 CP $-$$$$.

HALE IRWIN, NATIVE SON

PGA Tour and Champions Tour standout Hale Irwin, whose course designs include the highly acclaimed Mountain Course at Cordillera, has had a long love affair with Colorado. He grew up in the state and was one of the few students at the University of Colorado to participate in two sports—and even more rarely, to excel in both. In football, Irwin was a two-time All-Big Eight selection as a defensive back; as a golfer, his team captured the 1967 NCAA Championship.

ST. REGIS ASPEN. This hotel is memorable, even by Aspen standards. The grand reception area is comfortably furnished with overstuffed chairs with soft suede pillows, leather-topped tables, and rawhide lamp shades. The rooms follow suit with dark-wood furniture, muted colors, and such signature touches as bowls of fresh fruit. Luxurious baths are stocked with Bijan toiletries. The house restaurant is Olives, owned by celebrity chef Todd English; Whiskey Rocks is the chic place to drink. ⊠ 315 E. Dean St., 81611 ☎ 970/920-3300 or 888/454-9005 🖷 970/925-8998 ⊕ www.stregisaspen.com ➷ 257 rooms, 26 suites ♦ Restaurant, room service, in-room safes, minibars, in-room VCRs, pool, health club, hair salon, outdoor hot tub, sauna, steam room, bar, lobby lounge, business services, meeting room, airport shuttle ▤ AE, D, DC, MC, V $$$$.

SKY HOTEL. The Sky's sleek style and slope-side location make it ideal for those in search of something a little different. The lobby, with black walls and oversize white leather chairs—think *Alice in Wonderland*—leads to the 39 Degrees bar, which has a daily "altitude adjustment" happy hour with complimentary wine. The small guest rooms have yellow walls, white headboards, and black accents. Signature touches like Frette linens, Aveda bath products, and even your own bottle of oxygen make the Sky stand out. ⊠ 709 E. Durant Ave., 81611 ☎ 970/925-6760 or 800/882-2582 🖷 970/925-6778 ⊕ - www.theskyhotel.com ➷ 90 rooms ♦ Restaurant, room service, minibars, in-room VCRs, pool, health club, outdoor hot tub, ski shop, bar, concierge, business services, meeting rooms, airport shuttle, some pets allowed ▤ AE, D, DC, MC, V $$-$$$$.

Beaver Creek

BEAVER CREEK LODGE. A central atrium grabs all the attention at this European-style lodge. Rooms are generously proportioned—you'll probably get more space for your money here than at most other properties in the heart of the village. Rooms have kitchenettes (a few have full kitchens) and gas-burning fireplaces to keep out the chill. The Beaver Creek Chophouse is a convenient place to fuel up after a day outside. ⊠ 26 Avondale La., 81620 ☎ 970/845-9800 or 800/525-7280 🖷 970/845-8242 ⊕ www. beavercreeklodge.net ➷ 72 suites ♦ Restaurant, kitchenettes, in-room VCRs, indoor-outdoor pool, health club, hot tub, sauna, spa, bar, meeting room ▤ AE, MC, V $-$$$.

LODGE & SPA AT CORDILLERA. An aura of quiet luxury prevails at this mountaintop lodge, decorated to resemble the finest alpine hotels. The rooms vary quite a bit in size; those in the newer wing tend to be larger. There are wood-burning fireplaces in some of the older rooms, but the newer rooms have gas fireplaces. You can luxuriate in the spa after a morning spent hiking or cross-country skiing, or swim in the indoor pool with a view of the mountains through the wall of windows. Don't miss a meal at Picasso, which for years has been one of the region's top restaurants. The lodge is in the gated community of Cordillera, 15 minutes from Beaver Creek. ⊠ 2205 Cordillera Way, Box 1110, Edwards 81632 ☎ 970/926-2200 or 800/877-3529 ⊕ 970/926-2486 ⊕ www. cordillera-vail.com ⤴ 56 rooms ⚭ 4 restaurants, 10-hole golf course, 3 18-hole golf courses, 2 pools (1 indoor), health club, 2 hot tubs, spa, cross-country skiing, bar, business services, meeting rooms; no smoking ☰ AE, D, MC, V $$-$$$$.

PARK HYATT BEAVER CREEK RESORT & SPA. With a magnificent antler chandelier and towering windows opening out onto the mountain, the lobby of this hotel manages to be both cozy and grand. Rooms, designed with skiers in mind, include amenities such as heated towel racks. The Allegria Spa is on-site, and the Beaver Creek Golf Club (with preferred tee times for guests) is nearby. The newer and more luxurious restaurant here, Vue, serves French cuisine. ⊠ 136 E. Thomas Pl., 81620 ☎ 970/949-1234 or 800/233-1234 ⊕ 970/949-4164 ⊕ www.beavercreek.hyatt.com ⤴ 275 rooms, 5 suites ⚭ 2 restaurants, snack bar, in-room data ports, 5 tennis courts, pool, health club, 6 hot tubs, spa, 2 bars, lounge, children's programs (ages 3–13), business services, meeting rooms; no a/c ☰ AE, D, DC, MC, V $$-$$$$.

RITZ-CARLTON BACHELOR GULCH ON BEAVER CREEK. This log and timber building with elaborate stonework is, in a word, spectacular. The hotel's design is reminiscent of the grand old lodges in national parks like Yellowstone and Yosemite. The rooms—many with stone fireplaces—are distinctly western. For extra pampering stay on the club level, where there's concierge service and a never-ending supply of food and beverages in the private lounge. No matter where you stay, the level of service is extremely high. The excellent restaurant serves regional cuisine. For cocktails and cigars there's the intimate Fly Fishing Library, worth a look just to see the fishing lures on the walls. ⊠ 0130 Daybreak Ridge, Avon 81620 ☎ 970/748-6200 ⊕ 970/748-6300 ⊕ www.ritzcarlton.com ⤴ 208 rooms, 29 suites ⚭ 3 restaurants, room service, in-room data ports, in-room safes, minibars, 4 tennis courts, pool, health club, hot tub, spa, 3 bars, lounge, children's programs (ages 5–12), business services, meeting rooms ☰ AE, D, MC, V $$$-$$$$.

Vail

LODGE AT VAIL. The first facility to open in Vail, the Lodge has condos of many shapes and sizes. Some of the original rooms, decorated by their owners, are quite homey. The newer wing has some lovely suites with marble baths and more space. The signature restaurant, the Wildflower, serves creative American cuisine. Golfers can stoke up at the expansive breakfast and lunchtime buffets at Cucina Rustica, the hotel's other restaurant. It becomes a Tuscan grill at dinner. ⊠ 174 E. Gore Creek Dr., 81657 ☎ 970/476-5011 or 800/367-7625 ⊕ 970/476-7425 ⊕ www.lodgeatvail.com ⤴ 165 rooms, 8 suites, 46 1-, 2-, and 3-bedroom condos ⚭ 2 restaurants, cable TV, pool, gym, 4 hot tubs, sauna, spa, ski shop, bar ☰ AE, D, DC, MC, V $$-$$$$.

SITZMARK LODGE. This cozy lodge buzzes with a dozen languages, thanks to the international visitors who return year after year. Rooms, which range from moderate to large, have balconies that look out onto Vail Mountain or Gore Creek. Some have gas-burning fireplaces to keep things comfortable. Rooms use a blend of light woods and

---

VAIL RESORTS' BIRTH

The 1990s were an era of consolidation in the ski industry, and many of the major resorts were snapped up by companies that were, or shortly became, publicly traded. In 1996, in a move that surprised the ski industry, Vail purchased Breckenridge and Keystone resorts, then began selling stock as Vail Resorts. Since then, the company has purchased Heavenly in California, Snake River Lodge & Spa in Wyoming, and lodges at several other resorts.

---

cheerful floral fabrics for interiors. ⊠183 Gore Creek Dr., 81657 ☎970/476–5001 or 888/476–5001 🖷970/476–8702 ⊕www.sitzmarklodge.com 🗪35 rooms ♻Restaurant, room service, in-room data ports, in-room safes, refrigerators, pool, hot tub, sauna; no a/c ⊟D, MC, V $-$$$$.

🖭 VAIL CASCADE RESORT & SPA. Down-to-earth yet luxurious is the best way to describe this sprawling resort and spa. Despite its size, it manages to feel intimate. Rooms are eclectic, with rich plaid and floral fabrics, wicker furniture, and wrought-iron lamps. Those staying here have access to the adjoining Aria Spa & Club, a full-service health club. The best deals at any time of year are the packages, which might include sports massages in summer. ⊠1300 Westhaven Dr., 81657 ☎970/476–7111 or 800/282–4183 🖷970/479–7020 ⊕www.vailcascade.com 🗪292 rooms, 27 suites, 60 condominiums ♻Restaurant, cable TV, 8 tennis courts, pool, health club, hair salon, 4 hot tubs, spa, basketball, racquetball, squash, bar, cinema, shops, business services, meeting rooms; no a/c ⊟AE, DC, MC, V $$-$$$$.

Where to Eat

Aspen

✕**AJAX TAVERN.** The brains behind Mustards Grill and Tra Vigne, two of Napa Valley's finest eateries, have created this bright, pleasant restaurant, with mahogany paneling, diamond-pattern floors, leather banquettes, open kitchen, and an eager, unpretentious waitstaff. Try the grilled lamb chops with seasonal vegetables. The wine list, showcasing Napa's best, is almost matched by the selection of microbrews. Enjoy outstanding lunch offerings on the spacious, sunny patio, which abuts Aspen Mountain. ⊠685 E. Durant Ave. ☎970/920–9333 ⊕www.ajaxtavern.com ♻Reservations essential ⊟AE, D, DC, MC, V $$$$.

✕**LA COCINA.** For good and cheap eats, follow the locals. They'll lead you to this small Mexican restaurant (although no one can explain the garlic bread that comes with every dish). Order by the number: you'll get some combination of beans, rice, chicken, tortilla, and chili verde. Almost every night the house is packed full. If the wait is long, you might cop a free margarita or order of bean dip for your trouble. ⊠308 E. Hopkins Ave. ☎970/925–9714 ♻Reservations not accepted ⊟MC, V ⊗No lunch $-$$.

✕ **MAIN STREET BAKERY & CAFÉ.** Perfectly brewed coffee and hot breakfast buns and pastries are served at this café, which also has a full breakfast menu that includes homemade granola. On sunny days, head out back to the deck for the mountain views. This is also a good spot for lunch and dinner. Try the Yankee pot roast, chicken potpie, and homemade soups. ⊠ 201 E. Main St. ☎ 970/925-6446 ⊟ AE, MC, V ⊘ No dinner Apr.–June and Sept.–Nov. $–$$$.

Beaver Creek

✕ **FIESTA'S.** The Marquez sisters, Debbie and Susan, use old family recipes brought to Colorado by their great-grandparents to create great southwestern cuisine. Among the favorites are chicken enchiladas in a white jalapeño sauce and blue-corn enchiladas served Santa Fe–style, with an egg on top. Handmade corn tamales are stuffed with pork and smothered in a classic New Mexican–chili sauce. Brightly decorated with New Mexican folk art and paintings, Fiesta's has more than 20 tequilas available from the bar. ⊠ 57 Edwards Access Rd., Edwards ☎ 970/926-2121 ⊟ AE, D, MC, V $–$$.

✕ **REMINGTON'S.** In this stunning two-story space, hammered wrought-iron chandeliers cast a flattering light on the diners—a mix of casually dressed hikers and business executives. The innovative regional cuisine here is created by executive chef Stephan Schupbach, who's Swiss. Look for creatively prepared bison, salmon, steak, and Colorado trout on the frequently changing menu. ⊠ Ritz-Carlton Bachelor Gulch, 0130 Daybreak Ridge Rd., Avon ☎ 970/748-6200 ⌂ Reservations essential ⊟ AE, MC, V $$$$.

✕ **VUE.** This bistro got its name for its view of an outdoor ice rink. European-trained executive chef Pascal Coudouy shows off his range with constantly changing menus. Look for starters such as lobster consommé and caviar, followed by pan-seared black bass or gingerbread-crusted rack of lamb. For a sample of his skills, try the six-course tasting menu. ⊠ Park Hyatt Beaver Creek, 136 E. Thomas Pl. ☎ 970/949-1234 ⌂ Reservations essential ⊟ AE, MC, V ⊘ Closed Sun. and Mon. $$$$.

Vail

✕ **SWEET BASIL.** This restaurant may be understated, with blond-wood chairs and buff-color walls, but chef Bruce Yim's contemporary cuisine is anything but. He serves American favorites with unmistakable Mediterranean and Asian influences. The menu changes several times each season, but you might find grilled-crab dumplings, seared Hawaiian ahi, or grilled-beef tenderloin with foie-gras ravioli and wild mushroom and barley ragout. Pair these entrées with one of the hundreds of wines from the restaurant's cellar. Leave room for luscious desserts such as hot sticky toffee pudding cake or chocolate banana–cream tart. ⊠ 193 E. Gore Creek Dr. ☎ 970/476-0125 ⊟ AE, MC, V $$$$.

✕ **TERRA BISTRO.** With dark-wood furniture and walls hung with black-and-white photographs, this sleek space looks as if it belongs in a big city. Only the crackling fireplace reminds you that this is Vail. The menu focuses on contemporary American cuisine that throws in a few Asian, Mediterranean, and southwestern influences. White bean and squash sauté and peppered beef tenderloin in a cabernet reduction are headliners. The herbed Yukon Gold potatoes are a satisfying side. Organic produce and free-range meat and poultry are used whenever possible. ⊠Vail Mountain Lodge & Spa, 352 E. Meadow Dr. ☎970/476–6836 ▤AE, D, MC, V $$$$.

Essentials

Getting Here

From Denver to Vail, take I–70 west through the mountains to the Vail Road exit. Turn right on Vail, take an immediate right on any local road, turn right on Vail Valley Drive, and right again on Hanson Ranch Road. This will take you to the center of Vail. From Denver to Aspen, I–70 west takes you to the Colorado 91 exit; take that south towards Copper Mountain/Leadville. After about 22 mi, 91 becomes U.S. 24. Turn right on Colorado 82, which becomes East Cooper Avenue. Turn right onto South Spring Street, which becomes East Bleeker Street, then Rio Grande Place. This takes you to the heart of Aspen.

Visitor Information

Vail/Beaver Creek Reservations can provide you with information on golf courses, updates on events and activities, and get you booked at many of the hotels and condominium properties in the Vail Valley. Vail Valley Tourism and Convention Bureau operates a central reservations service. It also gives weather reports and information on events and activities.

🄵 **Aspen Chamber Resort Association** ⊠425 Rio Grande Pl., Aspen 81611 ☎970/925–1940 or 800/262–7736 ⊕www.aspenchamber.org.

Vail/Beaver Creek Reservations ☎800/525–2257. **Vail Resorts, Inc.** ⌂Box 7, Vail 81658 ☎970/476–5601 ⊕www.vail.com.

Vail Valley Tourism and Convention Bureau ⊠100 E. Meadow Dr., Vail 81658 ☎970/476–1000 or 800/824–5737 ⊕www.visitvailvalley.com.

AROUND
DETROIT

Boyne Highlands Resort

By Matthew Rudy and Greg Tasker

California might have the perfect golf

weather, but when it comes to top-rank public courses that are also easily accessible, Michigan stands alone. Take any of the interstates out of Detroit and you'll end up in exceptional golf territory.

Follow I–75 three hours north and you're in Gaylord, the golf epicenter of the Lower Peninsula, with a hundred first-class holes within 15 minutes of the highway. In fact, this entire stretch of coastline, from Traverse City on Lake Michigan to Oscoda on Lake Huron, makes up golf's "Fertile Crescent." Here there are at least a dozen public-access courses rated at least four stars in *Golf Digest's Places to Play,* from the $60 Gailes course at Lakewood Shores Resort to the $200+ Bay Harbor Golf Club. Great golf even thrives to the south, around Frankenmuth, one of the most popular tourist destinations in North America.

Detroit is the gateway to all of these places, but don't forget the Motor City in any conversation about public or private golf. It more than holds its own. The greatest architects have a wide body of work in Metro Detroit, starting with Donald Ross's private South course at Oakland Hills and the municipal Detroit Golf Club and the Rackham and Rogell golf courses. Oakland Hills might be the most difficult course in America, especially after some tweaks by Arthur Hills to get it ready for the 2004 Ryder Cup. Detroit's suburbs are also filled with classics new and old, from the Wilfried Reid–designed Old course at Indianwood Country Club to Shepherd's Hollow, a 27-hole complex Arthur Hills carved out of virgin timber on a Catholic priests' retreat.

One thing to keep in mind about any trip you take in the state is the Michigan Bonus. Because you're on the western edge of the Eastern time zone, the summer sun will still be shining when you finish that afternoon round at 8:45. From early May to late September, few places are more pleasant. You can also work on your game with nationally prominent teacher Rick Smith, who is based in Gaylord at Treetops Resort in summer.

FRANKENMUTH

Imagine miles of wood latticework, restaurant and store names ending in -hof, -brau, or -haus, and an annual parade that rivals the one in *Ferris Bueller's Day Off.* Frankenmuth's Bavarian obsession may seem impossibly

			RSE ►	SLOPE ►	
Bay County Golf Course (18)	6,557/5,706	72/74	71.3/72.4	113/114	$14/$20
Bay Valley Golf Club (18)	6,610/5,515	71/71	71.9/68.5	125/114	$44/$49
The Fortress (18)	6,813/4,837	72/72	73.6/68.8	138/124	$39/$59
Golf Club at Apple Mountain (18)	6,962/4,978	72/72	74.2/69.6	145/127	$45/$65
Sawmill Golf Club (18)	6,757/5,140	72/82	72.7/70.4	139/125	$28/$34
Timbers Golf Club (18)	6,674/4,886	72/72	72.7/69.1	133/113	$39/$49

hokey, but somehow it comes together, each year attracting over 3 million visitors intent on scoring handcrafted lederhosen or a sublime fried chicken dinner at Zehnder's. An influx of tourism traffic prompted the construction of a handful of challenging area courses beginning in the early 1990s. The most prominent course is the Fortress, set on a small parcel of land just outside of town, but the newer Timbers is just as good. Take a short drive to the neighboring cities of Saginaw and Bay City for the Golf Club at Apple Mountain or the Nicklaus-designed Bay Valley Golf Club. Although the flat Saginaw Valley throughout the area prevents the kind of dramatic elevation changes found at the best northern Michigan resorts, the courses here epitomize modern parkland golf.

Courses
Golf Digest REVIEWS

BAY COUNTY GOLF COURSE. Facility Holes: 18. Opened: 1966. Architect: Morenci. Yards: 6,557/5,706. Par: 72/74. Course Rating: 71.3/72.4. Slope: 113/114. Green Fee: $14/$20. Cart Fee: $20 per cart. Discounts: Weekdays, seniors, juniors. Walking: Unrestricted walking. Season: Apr.–Nov. Tee Times: Call golf shop. Notes: Range (grass). ✉ 584 Hampton Rd., Essexville 48732, 6 mi from Bay City ☎ 517/892-2161 ▬ MC, V. *Comments: While it's overshadowed by near-namesake Bay Valley, which is minutes away, it's still nearly as good, although not as well groomed.* ★★★

BAY VALLEY GOLF CLUB. Facility Holes: 18. Opened: 1973. Architect: Jack Nicklaus/ Desmond Muirhead. Yards: 6,610/5,515. Par: 71/71. Course Rating: 71.9/68.5. Slope: 125/ 114. Green Fee: $44/$49. Cart fee: Included in green fee. Discounts: Weekdays, twilight, seniors, juniors. Walking: Walking at certain times. Season: Apr.–Nov. High: May–Aug. Tee Times: Call golf shop. Notes: Range (grass), lodging (148). ✉ 2470 Old Bridge Rd., 48706, 5 mi from Bay City ☎ 989/686-5400 or 888/241-4653 ⊕ www.bayvalley.com ▬ AE, D, MC, V. *Comments: It only seems like Nicklaus and Muirhead had something evil planned for those who play from the tips (6,666 yards). Dozens of water hazards and ultrafast greens are the main challenges.* ★★★★

THE FORTRESS. Facility Holes: 18. Opened: 1992. Architect: Dick Nugent. Yards: 6,813/ 4,837. Par: 72/72. Course Rating: 73.6/68.8. Slope: 138/124. Green Fee: $39/$59. Cart Fee: Included in green fee. Discounts: Weekdays, twilight, seniors, juniors. Walking: Walking at certain times. Season: Apr.–Oct. High: June–Sept. Tee Times: Call golf shop. Notes: Range (grass). ⊠ 950 Flint St., 48734, 15 mi from Saginaw ☎ 989/652–0460 or 800/863–7999 ⊕ www.zehnders.com ☰ AE, D, MC, V. *Comments: Great fun, but wear a helmet. Crossing fairways and close holes turn some tight holes into shooting galleries.* ★ ★ ★ ★

GOLF CLUB AT APPLE MOUNTAIN. Facility Holes: 18. Opened: 1998. Architect: John Sanford. Yards: 6,962/4,978. Par: 72/72. Course Rating: 74.2/69.6. Slope: 145/127. Green Fee: $45/$65. Cart Fee: Included in green fee. Discounts: Twilight, seniors, juniors. Walking: Mandatory cart. Season: Apr.–Nov. Tee Times: Call golf shop. Notes: Range (grass). ⊠ 4519 N. River Rd., Freeland 48623, 9 mi from Saginaw ☎ 989/781–6789 or 888/781–6789 ⊕ www.applemountain.com ☰ AE, D, MC, V. *Comments: Built in the same tradition as some of the northern courses that use ski slopes as design features. The clubhouse ranks alongside other top resorts. UR*

ON THE UPSWING

From 1991 to 2000, an average of 22 new golf courses were built in Michigan each year, more than any other state in the union.

SAWMILL GOLF CLUB. Facility Holes: 18. Opened: 1997. Architect: John Sanford. Yards: 6,757/5,140. Par: 72/82. Course Rating: 72.7/70.4. Slope: 139/125. Green Fee: $28/$34. Cart Fee: $14 per person. Walking: Walking at certain times. Season: Apr.–Nov. Tee Times: Call golf shop. ⊠ 19 Sawmill Blvd., Saginaw 48603 ☎ 517/793–2692 ⊕ www.thesawmill.com ☰ D, MC, V. UR

TIMBERS GOLF CLUB. Facility Holes: 18. Opened: 1996. Architect: Lorrie Viola. Yards: 6,674/4,886. Par: 72/72. Course Rating: 72.7/69.1. Slope: 133/113. Green Fee: $39/$49. Cart Fee: Included in green fee. Discounts: Weekdays, twilight, seniors. Walking: Walking at certain times. Season: Apr.–Nov. High: June–Sept. Tee Times: Call golf shop. Notes: Range (grass, mat). ⊠ 7300 Bray Rd., Tuscola 48769, 4 mi from Frankenmuth ☎ 989/871–4884 or 888/617–1479 ⊕ www.timbersgolfclub.com ☰ MC, V. *Comments: Great use of rolling property and elevations, so take care to hit it straight. The club is convenient to town and the expressway.* ★ ★ ★ ½

Where to Stay

▥ **BAVARIAN INN LODGE.** Run by a third generation of the Zehnder family, this four-story, inn is ½ mi outside of town. A Bavarian theme runs throughout the inn with hand-carved woodwork and imported antique German furnishings. A family fun center with a game room is on the bottom floor. ⊠ 1 Covered Bridge La., 48734 ☎ 989/652–7200 or 888/775–6343 🖷 989/652–6711 ⊕ www.bavarianinn.com ⇙ 354 rooms ⚐ Restaurant, room service, cable TV, 4 tennis courts, 5 indoor pools, gym, 3 hot tubs, bar, business services; no smoking ☰ AE, D, MC, V $–$$.

▥ **DRURY INN.** Fitting in with the theme of Bavarian Frankenmuth, this four-story chain inn resembles an alpine chalet, but the interior is clearly contemporary. The main

GOLF-CRAZY MICHIGAN

With more than 850 open for play, Michigan is the state with the third largest number of golf courses, after California (912) and Florida (1,073). Many of its courses are also quite old, including more than 20 that opened before 1910. Respected designers such as Donald Ross, Tom Bendelow, and Willie Park Jr. were prolific in those early days, and Alister Mackenzie also has a couple well-respected designs. Today, the Michigan-based designers Tom Doak and Rick Smith carry on that tradition of excellence.

---

floor lobby is spacious with sofas and chairs clustered for family and business gatherings. The inn is in a commercial area within walking distance of downtown. ⊠ 260 S. Main St., 48734 ☎ 989/652-2800 🖷 989/652-2800 ⊕ www.druryinn.com ⇋ 78 rooms ₢ Cable TV, indoor pool, some pets allowed ⊟ AE, D, DC, MC, V ♥ CP $-$$.

🖸 **HAMPTON INN.** The branch of this chain hotel is about 2 mi west of Frankenmuth in a busy commercial area that has a Prime Outlets mall, restaurants, and a golf course. King deluxe rooms have a marble shower; double rooms have traditional-style furnishings. It's ½ mi off I-75 at the Birch Run exit. ⊠ 13120 Tiffany Blvd., Birch Run 48415 ☎ 989/624-2500 🖷 989/624-2501 ⊕ www.hampton-inn.com ⇋ 89 rooms ₢ In-room data ports, cable TV, pool, business services; no smoking ⊟ AE, D, DC, MC, V ♥ CP ¢-$.

🖸 **HOLIDAY INN EXPRESS.** You are four blocks from the factory outlets in Birch Run and 10 mi from Frankenmuth attractions when you stay in this motel that's ½ mi east of downtown Birch Run. Its three floors have modern furnishings. ⊠ 12150 Dixie Hwy., Birch Run 48415 ☎ 989/624-9300 or 888/624-9300 🖷 989/732-9640 ⊕ www. hiexpress.com ⇋ 95 rooms ₢ Cable TV, indoor pool, gym, hot tub, laundry facilities, business services, some pets allowed; no smoking ⊟ AE, D, DC, MC, V ♥ CP ¢-$$.

🖸 **ZEHNDER'S BAVARIAN HAUS.** Meticulously landscaped grounds and European architecture set off this two-story hotel ½ mi east of town. The hotel has chalet architecture and European furnishings. Owned by the Zehnder family since 1927, the hotel traces its history back to the mid-19th century. Four suites have wet bars, in-room hot tubs, and sitting areas. Many restaurants are within 1 mi. ⊠ 1365 S. Main, 48734 ☎ 989/652-6144 or 800/863-7999 🖷 989/652-9777 ⊕ www.zehnders.com ⇋ 137 rooms, 4 suites ₢ Restaurant, coffee shop, cable TV, indoor-outdoor pool, gym, hot tub, video game room, business services ⊟ D, MC, V $-$$$.

Where to Eat

✗ **BAVARIAN INN.** The Bavarian Inn, in the heart of Frankenmuth, is one of the state's largest and best-loved restaurants, with seven Bavarian-theme dining rooms and more than 1,000 (usually filled) seats. Waitstaff in lederhosen and dirndls serve up house specialties, including the famous all-you-can-eat family-style chicken dinners, Wiener schnitzel, and sauerbraten. Outside is a popular glockenspiel tower with Pied Piper figures. ⊠ 713 S. Main St. ☎ 989/652–9941 ⊕ www.bavarianinn.com ⊟ AE, D, MC, V ⊘ Closed early Jan. $–$$$.

✕ **ZEHNDER'S.** The Zehnder family's other restaurant (they own the Bavarian Inn across the street) is housed in a vintage downtown building dating from 1927. The menu has many of the same choices as the Bavarian Inn—all-you-can-eat family-style chicken dinners, Wiener schnitzel, and Bavarian sausages—but you can also select steak, seafood, or homemade pastries. ⊠ 730 S. Main St. ☎ 989/652–9925 ⊟ D, MC, V $$$–$$$$.

Essentials

Getting Here

Frankenmuth is an easy 90-minute drive from Detroit and its suburbs. Follow I–75 north toward Flint. Take exit 136 at Birch Run and then head east to Route 83. Follow Route 83 north to Frankenmuth.

Visitor Information

🖬 **Frankenmuth Convention and Visitors Bureau** ⊠ 635 S. Main St., 48734 ☎ 989/652–6106 or 800/386–8696 🖶 989/652–3841 ⊕ www.frankenmuth.org.

GAYLORD

An easy three-hour drive up I–75 from Detroit, Gaylord attracts four different kinds of enthusiasts. Snowmobilers whip around on some of the most extensive snowmobile trails in the state in winter. Then there are the fine ski areas, hunting grounds, and, oh yes, golf. Well-known instructor Rick Smith is part-owner of Treetops, making it the most prominent golf resort in the area. Each of the four courses on the property earned at least a four-star rating in *Golf Digest's Places to Play* and include Tom Fazio and Robert Trent Jones Jr. designs, but Smith's own Rick Smith Signature course might be the best of the group.

Players from the PGA Tour and the Champions Tour go head-to-head at Smith's Treetops par-3 course for the annual skins game, televised on ESPN. The four courses at Garland, 30 mi from Gaylord, might not have the same architectural pedigree as Treetops—the resort owners designed the courses—but the majestic log lodge, the biggest of its kind in the eastern United States dwarfs anything at Treetops in both scope and elegance.

Black Forest & Wilderness Valley Golf Resort (36)					
Black Forest (18)	7,044/5,282	73/74	75.3/71.8	145/131	$20/$47
Wilderness Valley (18)	6,485/4,889	71/71	70.6/67.8	126/115	
Elk Ridge Golf Club (18)	7,072/5,261	72/72	74.7/72.3	143/130	$50/$75
Garland (72)					
Fountains (18)	6,760/4,617	72/72	73.0/74.1	130/128	$95/$100
Monarch (18)	7,188/4,904	72/72	75.6/69.5	140/123	$70/$90
Reflections (18)	6,407/4,778	72/72	70.8/66.9	127/110	$30/$70
Swampfire (18)	6,854/4,791	72/72	73.9/68.4	138/121	$70/$90
Gaylord Country Club (18)	6,452/5,490	72/72	70.9/71.4	123/122	$30/$35
Otsego Club (36)					
Classic (18)	6,305/5,591	72/72	69.8/71.5	121/113	$29/$45
Tribute (18)	7,347/5,085	72/72	74.1/69.0	134/115	$95/$105
Treetops Resort (72)					
Rick Smith Signature (18)	6,653/4,604	70/70	72.8/67.0	140/123	$59/$99
Robert Trent Jones Masterpiece (18)	7,060/4,972	71/71	75.8/70.2	144/123	$59/$99
Tom Fazio Premier (18)	6,832/5,039	72/72	73.2/70.1	135/123	$59/$99
Tradition (18)	6,467/4,907	71/70	70.3/67.3	122/109	$35/$75

Courses

GolfDigest REVIEWS

BLACK FOREST & WILDERNESS VALLEY GOLF RESORT. Facility Holes: 36. Cart Fee: $18 per person. Discounts: Weekdays, guest, twilight, seniors, juniors. Season: Apr.–Nov. Tee Times: Call golf shop. Notes: Range (grass, mat). ✉ 7519 Mancelona Rd., 49735, 15 mi from Gaylord ☎ 231/585-7090 ⊕ www.blackforestgolf.com ⊟ AE, D, MC, V.

Black Forest. Holes: 18. Opened: 1992. Architect: Tom Doak. Yards: 7,044/5,282. Par: 73/74. Course Rating: 75.3/71.8. Slope: 145/131. Green Fee: $20/$47. Walking: Unrestricted walking. *Comments: The sophisticated design makes you think your way around. The forest? It really is black—so thick that if you visit, you won't come out. Bring two sand wedges. You may wear one out.* ★ ★ ★ ★

Wilderness Valley. Holes: 18. Opened: 1971. Architect: Al Watrous. Yards: 6,485/4,889. Par: 71/71. Course Rating: 70.6/67.8. Slope: 126/115. *Comments: Not in the same league as its sister course.* ★ ★ ★ ★

ELK RIDGE GOLF CLUB. Facility Holes: 18. Opened: 1991. Architect: Jerry Matthews. Yards: 7,072/5,261. Par: 72/72. Course Rating: 74.7/72.3. Slope: 143/130. Green Fee: $50/$75. Cart Fee: Included in green fee. Discounts: Weekdays, seniors, juniors. Walking: Walking at certain times. Season: May–Oct. High: June–Aug. Tee Times: Call golf shop. Notes: Range (grass). ✉ 9400 Rouse Rd., Atlanta 49709, 30 mi from Gaylord ☎ 989/785-2275 or 800/626-4355 ⊕ www.elkridgegolf.com ⊟ AE, D, MC, V. *Comments: It's not just a name: Elk do walk around the course. The play is peaceful and remote.* ★ ★ ★ ★ ¹/₂

GARLAND. Facility Holes: 72. Architect: Ron Otto. Cart Fee: Included in green fee. Discounts: Weekdays, twilight, juniors. Walking: Mandatory cart. Season: May–Oct. Tee Times: Call golf shop. Notes: Range (grass, mat), lodging (186). ⊠ 4700 N. Red Oak, Lewiston 49756, 30 mi from Gaylord ☎ 989/786-2211 or 800/968-0042 ⊕ www.garlandusa.com ▭ AE, D, MC, V.

Fountains. Holes: 18. Opened: 1995. Yards: 6,760/4,617. Par: 72/72. Course Rating: 73.0/74.1. Slope: 130/128. Green Fee: $95/$100. *Comments: Like all the courses here, it's designed to be scenic and fun. The water is more scenic than dangerous.* ★★★★

Monarch. Holes: 18. Opened: 1987. Yards: 7,188/4,904. Par: 72/72. Course Rating: 75.6/69.5. Slope: 140/123. Green Fee: $70/$90. *Comments: The longest and hardest of the four courses flows along rolling terrain and racks up almost 7,200 yards from the tips.* ★★★★ ¹/₂

Reflections. Holes: 18. Opened: 1990. Yards: 6,407/4,778. Par: 72/72. Course Rating: 70.8/66.9. Slope: 127/110. Green Fee: $30/$70. *Comments: The course is the easiest of the four, relatively flat, and good for beginners.* ★★★★

Swampfire. Holes: 18. Opened: 1988. Yards: 6,854/4,791. Par: 72/72. Course Rating: 73.9/68.4. Slope: 138/121. Green Fee: $70/$90. *Comments: A quirky course with some interesting water features. It demands accuracy off the tee.* ★★★★ ¹/₂

GAYLORD COUNTRY CLUB. Facility Holes: 18. Opened: 1924. Architect: Wilfried Reid. Yards: 6,452/5,490. Par: 72/72. Course Rating: 70.9/71.4. Slope: 123/122. Green Fee: $30/$35. Cart Fee: $15 per person. Discounts: Twilight. Walking: Unrestricted walking. Season: Year-round. High: June–Oct. Tee Times: Call golf shop. Notes: Range (grass). ⌂ Box 207, Gaylord 49735 ☎ 231/546-3376 ▭ MC, V. *Comments: The locals' favorite was designed by Wilfried Reid, who also designed the Olympic Club. It's $30 weekdays and worth three times that.* ★★★★

OTSEGO CLUB. Facility Holes: 36. Cart Fee: Included in green fee. Season: May–Oct. High: June–Aug. Tee Times: Call 120 days in advance. Notes: Range (grass), lodging (100). ⊠ 696 M-32, East Gaylord, 49735, 60 mi from Traverse City ☎ 989/732-5181 or 800/752-5510 ⊕ www.otsegoclub.com ▭ AE, D, MC, V.

Classic. Holes: 18. Opened: 1958. Architect: William H. Diddel. Yards: 6,305/5,591. Par: 72/72. Course Rating: 69.8/71.5. Slope: 121/113. Green Fee: $29/$45. Walking: Walking at certain times. *Comments: The Classic started the northern Michigan golf trend when in opened in 1958. It's still fun, and a good value at less than $50.* ★★★

Tribute. Holes: 18. Opened: 2001. Architect: Gary Koch. Yards: 7,347/5,085. Par: 72/72. Course Rating: 74.1/69.0. Slope: 134/115. Green Fee: $95/$105. Walking: Mandatory cart. *Comments: The design by Gary Koch should be the best of the lot.* UR

TREETOPS RESORT. Facility Holes: 72. Cart Fee: Included in green fee. Discounts: Twilight, juniors. Season: Apr.–Oct. Tee Times: Call golf shop. Notes: Range (grass), lodging (240). ⊠ 3962 Wilkinson Rd., 49735, 50 mi from Traverse City ☎ 989/732-6711 or 800/444-6711 ⊕ www.treetops.com ▭ AE, DC, MC, V.

Rick Smith Signature. Holes: 18. Opened: 1993. Architect: Rick Smith. Yards: 6,653/4,604. Par: 70/70. Course Rating: 72.8/67.0. Slope: 140/123. Green Fee: $59/$99. Walking:

Mandatory cart. *Comments: A big, sprawling course set on forested hillside is great for all handicaps.* ★ ★ ★ ★ ¹/₂

Robert Trent Jones Masterpiece. Holes: 18. Opened: 1987. Architect: Robert Trent Jones Jr. Yards: 7,060/4,972. Par: 71/71. Course Rating: 75.8/70.2. Slope: 144/123. Green Fee: $59/$99. Walking: Mandatory cart. *Comments: The most difficult course here is one of the hardest Robert Trent Jones Jr. has built. Views of the Pigeon River valley are spectacular.* ★ ★ ★ ★ ¹/₂

Tom Fazio Premier. Holes: 18. Opened: 1992. Architect: Tom Fazio. Yards: 6,832/5,039. Par: 72/72. Course Rating: 73.2/70.1. Slope: 135/123. Green Fee: $59/$99. Walking: Mandatory cart. *Comments: Difficulties come around the greens, not off the tee. Wildly undulating putting surfaces and penal greenside bunkers make this a deceptive 6,400-yarder.* ★ ★ ★ ★ ¹/₂

Tradition. Holes: 18. Opened: 1997. Architect: Rick Smith. Yards: 6,467/4,907. Par: 71/70. Course Rating: 70.3/67.3. Slope: 122/109. Green Fee: $35/$75. Walking: Unrestricted walking. *Comments: Designed to be a walking course complete with caddie program. You won't find water, but there are plenty of bunkers.* ★ ★ ★ ★

Where to Stay

🖬 **DAYS INN.** A fireplace in the lobby and larger-than-expected guest rooms add to the comfort at this two-story motel in an alpine village. All rooms have two vanities, refrigerators, and hair dryers, and some have in-room hot tubs. The inn is within walking distance of restaurants, theaters, and clubs, and 18 golf courses are within 20 mi. ⊠ 1201 W. Main St., 49735 ☎ 517/732-2200 or 800/388-7829 🖷 517/732-0300 ⊕ - www.daysinn.com ➥ 95 rooms ⚐ In-room data ports, some in-room hot tubs, refrigerators, cable TV, indoor pool, gym, hot tub, video game room, laundry facilities, business services, no-smoking rooms ☴ AE, D, DC, MC, V ⦿ CP $.

🖬 **GARLAND.** The beautiful resort on hundreds of hilly, wildlife-filled acres 3 mi outside of Gaylord is known for golf as well as other outdoor activities. The log lodge, the largest east of the Mississippi, has three floors of contemporary-style rooms. Rustic cottages on the Fountains course have gas log fireplaces and modern amenities like dishwashers, stoves, and gas grills. Garland is 3 mi outside of Gaylord. ⊠ 4700 N. Red Oak Rd., Lewiston 49756 ☎ 989/786-2211 or 800/968-0042 🖷 989/786-2254 ⊕ www. garlandusa.com ➥ 117 rooms, 60 cottages ⚐ Restaurant, picnic area, room service, refrigerators, cable TV, driving range, 4 18-hole golf courses, putting green, 2 tennis courts, 2 pools (1 indoor), gym, hot tub, massage, boating, fishing, bicycles, basketball, hiking, volleyball, cross-country skiing, downhill skiing, bar, business services, airport shuttle; no smoking ☴ AE, D, DC, MC, V ⦿ Closed mid-Mar. and Apr. $$$$.

🖬 **MARSH RIDGE.** Tucked away in a wilderness area 4 mi south of town, this year-round resort is popular with golfers in summer. Nongolfers come for spa weekends or murder mystery retreats, which unfold over several days. Three of the resort's seven buildings have rustic furnishings, and the others have a modern look. Standard Jacuzzi rooms have a refrigerator and microwave, and there are also town houses, theme suites, and a four-bedroom lodge. ⊠ 4815 Old U.S. 27 S, 49735 ☎ 989/732-6794, 800/743-

7529 in MI ☎989/732-2134 ⊕www.marshridge.com ⬅59 rooms ⟡ Restaurant, picnic area, some in-room hot tubs, some kitchenettes, refrigerators, cable TV, driving range, 18-hole golf course, putting green, pool, hot tub, sauna, cross-country skiing, business services; no smoking ⊟AE, DC, MC, V $-$$.

▦TREETOPS SYLVAN RESORT. Already a leading golf destination in northern Michigan, Treetops completed a $1.5 million renovation in summer 2003, with a new Spa & Fitness Center, paintball course, and lobby and room refurbishments. The expanded lobby is inviting and has a fireplace, cozy furniture, and a large-screen TV. Redesigned contemporary rooms are done in variations of burgundy, dark green, and mahogany, and have either a patio or balcony. Four championship courses and a par-3 course designed by Robert Trent Jones spread out across the resort's forests. ⊠3962 Wilkinson Rd., 49735 ☎989732-6711 or 800/444-6711 ☎989/732-6595 ⊕www.treetops.com ⬅228 rooms, 30 suites ⟡ Dining room, picnic area, room service, some kitchenettes, some refrigerators, cable TV, driving range, 5 18-hole golf courses, putting green, 2 tennis courts, 4 pools (2 indoor), gym, hair salon, hot tubs, spa, hiking, cross-country skiing, downhill skiing, bar, video game room, children's programs (ages 1–12), playground, business services, airport shuttle; no smoking ⊟AE, DC, MC, V $$-$$$$.

Where to Eat

✗SCHLANG'S BAVARIAN INN. Second-generation family members run this local institution 3 mi south of town, which opened in 1945. The warm fireplace in winter and a German-inspired menu, which includes kids' selections, make the eatery a family favorite. Opt for the ½-pound center-cut pork chops or the Wiener schnitzel. ⊠3917 Old U.S. 27 S ☎989/732-9288 ⊟MC, V ⊗Closed Sun. No lunch $$-$$$$.

✗SUGAR BOWL. The same Greek family has owned this downtown restaurant, opened in 1919, for three generations. There are two dining rooms; the Family Room serves moderately priced meals in a casual atmosphere—lots of wood trim and cushioned booths; the Open Hearth is slightly more upscale, with white tablecloths and cushioned chairs and a wine list. American and Greek entrées include chicken with lemon and feta, fresh Lake Superior whitefish, and roast prime rib. ⊠216 W. Main St. ☎989/732-5524 ⊟AE, D, MC, V ⊗Closed late Mar.–early Apr. ¢-$$.

Essentials

Getting Here
From Detroit, take I-75 north about 230 mi or 3½ hours. Take exit 282 and turn right onto Main Street, which leads to downtown Gaylord and nearby resorts.

Visitor Information
❼ Gaylord Area Convention and Tourism Bureau ⊠101 W. Main St., 49735 ☎989/732-4000 or 800/345-8621 ⊕www.gaylordmichigan.net.

The Dream (18)	7,000/5,118	72/72	73.7/68.6	135/117	$58/$69
Huron Breeze Golf & Country Club (18)	6,806/5,075	72/72	73.1/69.4	133/123	$20/$29
Lakewood Shores Resort (54)					
Blackshire (18)	6,898/4,936	72/72	71.9/66.8	125/105	$30/$62
Gailes (18)	6,954/5,246	72/73	75.0/72.2	138/122	$30/$62
Serradella (18)	6,806/5,295	72/74	72.3/70.1	124/116	$23/$35
Red Hawk Golf Club (18)	6,589/4,933	71/71	71.0/67.4	130/117	$39/$75
White Pine National Golf Course & Resort (18)	6,801/5,179	72/72	73.1/69.3	128/116	$38/$48

OSCODA

Low-key Oscoda, on the shores of Lake Huron, was once the home of the nation's largest Air Force base. When the base was decommissioned in the mid-1990s, the area promoted its less-developed, less-expensive, and more laid-back community as a Michigan getaway destination. While this does mean that mom-and-pop lakeside motels are the norm rather than luxury resorts with big-dollar golf course designs, it doesn't make the area's golf options any less attractive. The Gailes course at Lakewood Shores Resort seems like a piece of Scottish linksland transplanted into northeast Michigan. The wind tears at your clothes as it does at St. Andrews or Carnoustie. Round out a weekend playing some of the quality daily-fee courses that dot the U.S. 23 corridor, usually costing less than $50 a round. The major drawback to the area? Dining options here are limited to steaks, burgers, pizza, and fried fish.

Courses

Golf Digest REVIEWS

THE DREAM. Facility Holes: 18. Opened: 1997. Architect: Jeff Gorney. Yards: 7,000/5,118. Par: 72/72. Course Rating: 73.7/68.6. Slope: 135/117. Green Fee: $58/$69. Cart Fee: Included in green fee. Discounts: Weekdays, twilight. Walking: Mandatory cart. Season: Apr.–Nov. High: June–Sept. Tee Times: Call 30 days in advance. Notes: Range (grass). ✉ 5166 Old Hwy. 76, West Branch 48661 ☎ 989/345-6300 or 888/833-7326 🖃 AE, D, MC, V. *Comments: A beautiful course but a bit expensive for the area. Still, the pace and service are worth it.* ★ ★ ★ ★

HURON BREEZE GOLF & COUNTRY CLUB. Facility Holes: 18. Opened: 1988. Architect: William Newcomb. Yards: 6,806/5,075. Par: 72/72. Course Rating: 73.1/69.4. Slope: 133/123. Green Fee: $20/$29. Cart Fee: $10 per person. Discounts: Weekdays, twilight, seniors, juniors. Walking: Unrestricted walking. Season: Apr.–Oct. Tee Times: Call 90 days in advance. Notes: Range (grass). ✉ 5200 Huron Breeze Dr., Au Gres 48703, 50 mi from Bay City/Saginaw ☎ 989/876-6868 ⊕ www.huronbreeze.com ⊟ D, MC, V. *Comments: Four stars for $20. The open design is vulnerable to the lakeshore winds.* ★ ★ ★ ★

LAKEWOOD SHORES RESORT. Facility Holes: 54. Cart Fee: $13 per person. Discounts: Weekdays, twilight, seniors, juniors. Walking: Unrestricted walking. Season: Apr.–Nov. High: June–Aug. Tee Times: Call golf shop. Notes: Range (grass), lodging (80). ✉ 7751 Cedar Lake Rd., 48750, 80 mi from Saginaw ☎ 989/739-2075 or 800/882-2493 ⊕ www.lakewoodshores.com ⊟ MC, V.

Blackshire. Holes: 18. Opened: 2001. Architect: Kevin Aldridge. Yards: 6,898/4,936. Par: 72/72. Course Rating: 71.9/66.8. Slope: 125/105. Green Fee: $30/$62. *Comments: The course couldn't be more different than the Gailes, with its massive sand waste areas, à la Pine Valley. Play is challenging, but not nearly as good.* UR

Gailes. Holes: 18. Opened: 1992. Architect: Kevin Aldridge. Yards: 6,954/5,246. Par: 72/73. Course Rating: 75.0/72.2. Slope: 138/122. Green Fee: $30/$62. *Comments: Golf Digest's Best New Resort Course in 1993. Vintage Scottish golf, complete with sod-faced bunkers, mounding, and windswept moonscape. This is a must-play.* ★ ★ ★ ★ ¹/₂

Serradella. Holes: 18. Opened: 1969. Architect: Bruce Matthews/Jerry Matthews. Yards: 6,806/5,295. Par: 72/74. Course Rating: 72.3/70.1. Slope: 124/116. Green Fee: $23/$35. *Comments: An absolute steal in prime time.* ★ ★ ★ ¹/₂

RED HAWK GOLF CLUB. Facility Holes: 18. Opened: 1999. Architect: Arthur Hills/Chris Wilzynski. Yards: 6,589/4,933. Par: 71/71. Course Rating: 71.0/67.4. Slope: 130/117. Green Fee: $39/$75. Cart Fee: Included in green fee. Discounts: Weekdays, twilight. Walking: Unrestricted walking. Season: Apr.–Nov. Tee Times: Call 365 days in advance. Notes: Range (grass). ✉ 350 W. Davison Rd., East Tawas 48730, 65 mi from Bay City ☎ 517/362-0800 or 877/733-4259 ⊕ www.redhawkgolf.net ⊟ D, MC, V. *Comments: Golf Digest's No. 4 Public Course in Michigan in 1999. The 2nd and 3rd holes have incredible views and elevation changes.* ★ ★ ★ ★ ¹/₂

WHITE PINE NATIONAL GOLF COURSE & RESORT. Facility Holes: 18. Opened: 1992. Architect: Bruce Wolfrom/Clem Wolfrom. Yards: 6,801/5,179. Par: 72/72. Course Rating: 73.1/69.3. Slope: 128/116. Green Fee: $38/$48. Cart Fee: Included in green fee. Discounts: Weekdays, twilight, seniors, juniors. Walking: Walking at certain times. Season: Apr.–Nov. Tee Times: Call golf shop. Notes: Range (grass). ✉ 3450 N. Hubbard Lake Rd., Spruce 48762, 30 mi from Alpena ☎ 989/736-3279 ⊕ www. whitepinenational.com ⊟ AE, D, MC, V. *Comments: The ecologically sensitive course is built in a wildlife preserve. No water hazards to watch for.* ★ ★ ★ ¹/₂

Where to Stay

▥ **HURON HOUSE BED & BREAKFAST.** A secluded, sandy stretch of beach on Lake Huron provides a hideaway for this quiet B&B. The proprietors deliver breakfast to rooms each morning. Many rooms have lake views, and all have private hot tubs, either inside or outside on private decks. A perennial garden in the courtyard opens onto the beach. The inn is 2 mi south of Oscoda. ⊠ 3124 N. U.S. 23, 48750 ☎ 989/739-9255 ⊕ www. huronhouse.com ⇨ 14 rooms ⚖ Room service, some in-room hot tubs, some microwaves, refrigerators, cable TV, lake, beach; no room phones, no kids, no smoking ⊟ AE, D, MC, V ⍗ BP $$-$$$.

⌇⌇ **LAKE TRAIL RESORT.** Despite the obvious appeal of a Great Lake, sandy beach- es, and sunrises, there are very few resorts along Lake Huron's shoreline; the family- owned Lake Trail Resort happens to be one of them, with 300 feet of shorefront beach. Run by third-generation family members, this two-story motel is a throwback to the independent motels that catered to travelers before the chains. Even so, the motel has been modernized; rooms are painted in light colors—blue, white, and tan. The suites have in-room Jacuzzis. The grounds are well manicured and shaded, and you are free to use barbecue grills and picnic tables. Breakfast is served in the motel's breakfast bar. ⊠ 5400 U.S. 23 N, 48750 ☎ 989/739-2096 or 800/843-6007 ⊟ 989/739-2565 ⊕ - www.laketrailresort.com ⇨ 42 rooms, 20 suites, 2 cottages ⚖ Some refrigerators, cable TV, lake, tennis court, beach, boating, airport shuttle; no smoking ⊟ D, MC, V ⍗ CP ¢-$.

⌇⌇ **LAKEWOOD SHORES RESORT.** Though Lakewoods is not on Lake Huron, the resort does sit on its own private beach on small, inland Cedar Lake. That's probably just as well for water enthusiasts—Lake Huron never really gets warm, even during the dog days of summer. The golf resort community is family friendly with loads of out- door activities, including swimming, jet skiing, canoeing, and fishing. The Wee Links, an 18-hole pitch-and-putt course, is ideal for kids, families, and groups. All rooms overlook a golf course. ⊠ 7751 Cedar Lake Rd., 48750 ☎ 989/739-2073 or 800/882- 2493. ⊟ 989/739-1351 ⊕ www.lakewoodshores.com ⇨ 80 rooms ⚖ 2 restaurants, 3 18-hole golf courses, beach, jet skiing, fishing, business services; no smoking ⊟ AE, MC, V $.

Where to Eat

✕ **BIG BOY.** Although this restaurant chain got its start on the West Coast, Big Boy has long been a Michigan favorite for its all-you-can-eat soup, salad, and fruit bar. Popular sandwiches at this location, 20 mi south of Oscoda, include the Big Boy, the original double-decker burger, and the Slim Jim, which piles ham, Swiss cheese, lettuce, and tomato on a grilled Grecian roll. Save room for strawberry pie or hot fudge ice cream cake. ⊠ 1222 U.S. 23, East Tawas ☎ 989/362-4403 ⊟ MC, V $-$$.

✕ **WILTSE'S BREW PUB AND FAMILY RESTAURANT.** In naming its homemade ales and lagers, Wiltse's taps the region's rich lumbering history: its big malty brew, for example, is dubbed the Paul Bunyan Ale. Other beers reflect local landmarks, like the Au Sable River. The menu mixes American, Italian, and Mexican entrées. Try the Chicken Olé, marinated chicken breast grilled with fresh vegetables, or the country fried chicken and liver. Fresh Great Lakes fish favorites include planked whitefish, yellow perch, and wall- eye. ⊠ 5606 F-41 ☎ 989/739-2231 ⊟ D, MC, V $-$$$.

Essentials

Getting Here

Oscoda is 195 mi from Detroit. To get here, take I–75 north to exit 188. Follow the exit road east to Standish, then follow U.S. 23 north along Lake Huron to Oscoda. Plan around 3½ hours for the drive.

Visitor Information

🚩 **Oscoda Area Convention & Visitors Bureau** ✉ 4440 U.S. 23 N, 48750 ☎ 989/739–7322 or 800/235–4625 🌐 www.oscoda.com.

PETOSKEY

The Boyne company transformed Petoskey by turning an abandoned cement factory from a polluted Superfund site into Bay Harbor, a 27-hole wonder with 180-degree lake views, a thriving new marina, shops, an inn, and dozens of expensive houses. Petoskey's tax base mushroomed almost overnight, and the town became a weekend destination for Grand Rapids and Chicagoland boaters.

Bay Harbor is just the icing on the cake. Boyne also operates two other separate resorts just outside of town—Boyne Highlands and Boyne Mountain, which have a combined six additional golf courses and hundreds of guest rooms. There's enough golf here to satisfy even the most demanding weekender.

Courses   **Golf**Digest REVIEWS

BAY HARBOR GOLF CLUB. Facility Holes: 27. Architect: Arthur Hills. Green Fee: $59/$199. Cart Fee: Included in green fee. Discounts: Twilight. Walking: Mandatory cart. Season: Apr.–Oct. Tee Times: Call golf shop. Notes: Range (grass), lodging (735). ✉ 3600 Village Harbor Dr., Bay Harbor 49770, 5 mi from Petoskey ☎ 231/439–4028 🌐 www. bayharbor.com 🖃 AE, D, DC, MC, V. ★ ★ ★ ★

Links/Quarry. Holes: 18. Opened: 1996. Yards: 6,780/4,151. Par: 72/72. Course Rating: 72.2/69.3. Slope: 143/113.

Preserve/Links. Holes: 18. Opened: 1997. Yards: 6,810/4,087. Par: 72/72. Course Rating: 72.7/69.4. Slope: 142/113.

Quarry/Preserve. Holes: 18. Opened: 1997. Yards: 6,726/3,906. Par: 72/72. Course Rating: 72.5/69.1. Slope: 144/112.

Bay Harbor Golf Club (27)					$59/$199
Links/Quarry (18)	6,780/4,151	72/72	72.2/69.3	143/113	
Preserve/Links (18)	6,810/4,087	72/72	72.7/69.4	142/113	
Quarry/Preserve (18)	6,726/3,906	72/72	72.5/69.1	144/112	
Boyne Highlands Resort (72)					
Arthur Hills (18)	7,312/4,811	73/73	76.4/68.5	144/117	$70/$134
Heather (18)	6,890/4,794	72/72	74.0/67.8	136/111	$65/$129
Moor (18)	7,127/5,459	72/72	74.0/70.0	131/118	$40/$79
Ross (18)	6,814/4,929	72/72	75.5/68.5	136/119	$50/$99
Boyne Mountain Resort (36)					$29/$79
Alpine (18)	7,104/4,986	72/72	73.4/68.4	135/114	
Monument (18)	7,086/4,909	72/72	74.8/68.9	141/122	
Hidden River Golf & Casting Club (18)	7,101/4,787	72/72	74.3/67.4	140/117	$45/$85

Comments: The Arthur Hills–designed Links and Preserve 9s are more entertaining than the Quarry 9, which is brutal. Regardless, all three should be on any Michigan must-play list.

BOYNE HIGHLANDS RESORT. Facility Holes: 72. Cart Fee: Included in green fee. Discounts: Guest, twilight. Season: Apr.–Oct. Tee Times: Call golf shop. Notes: Range (grass), lodging (500). ✉ 600 Highland Dr., Harbor Springs 49740, 6 mi from Petoskey ☎ 231/526-3028 or 800/462-6963 ⊕ www.boynehighlands.com/summer/golf.html ▤ AE, D, DC, MC, V.

Arthur Hills. Holes: 18. Opened: 2000. Architect: Arthur Hills. Yards: 7,312/4,811. Par: 73/73. Course Rating: 76.4/68.5. Slope: 144/117. Green Fee: $70/$134. Walking: Mandatory cart. *Comments: The newest of the Highlands courses, it's very good, but not as good as Bay Harbor.* UR

Heather. Holes: 18. Opened: 1968. Architect: Robert Trent Jones. Yards: 6,890/4,794. Par: 72/72. Course Rating: 74.0/67.8. Slope: 136/111. Green Fee: $65/$129. Walking: Walking at certain times. *Comments: Almost as challenging as the Ross, with tight, tree-lined fairways and plenty of water.* ★★★★

Moor. Holes: 18. Opened: 1972. Architect: William Newcomb. Yards: 7,127/5,459. Par: 72/72. Course Rating: 74.0/70.0. Slope: 131/118. Green Fee: $40/$79. Walking: Mandatory cart. *Comments: The oldest and easiest of the courses here, it has a more mature look.* ★★★ ½

Ross. Holes: 18. Opened: 1985. Architect: William Newcomb/Everett Kircher/Jim Flick/ Stephen Kircher. Yards: 6,814/4,929. Par: 72/72. Course Rating: 75.5/68.5. Slope: 136/ 119. Green Fee: $50/$99. Walking: Mandatory cart. *Comments: The course is a creditable reproduction of Ross's style, with impeccable conditioning, dramatic forest views, and plenty of room to swing off the tee.* ★★★★

BOYNE MOUNTAIN RESORT. Facility Holes: 36. Architect: William Newcomb. Green Fee: $29/$79. Cart Fee: Included in green fee. Discounts: Guest, twilight, juniors. Walking: Mandatory cart. Season: May–Oct. High: June–Aug. Tee Times: Call 150 days in advance. Notes: Range (grass, mat), lodging (325). ✉ Deer Lake Rd., Boyne Falls 49713,

18 mi from Petoskey ☎231/549-6029 or 800/462-6963 ⊕www.boyne.com ▤AE, D, DC, MC, V.

Alpine. Holes: 18. Opened: 1974. Yards: 7,104/4,986. Par: 72/72. Course Rating: 73.4/ 68.4. Slope: 135/114. *Comments: The busy, carts-only course is nearly obsolete compared with Boyne's Monument course. If you can, play it during the week when the price is right ($29).* ★★★★

Monument. Holes: 18. Opened: 1986. Yards: 7,086/4,909. Par: 72/72. Course Rating: 74.8/68.9. Slope: 141/122. *Comments: Play here is like watching an episode of* Miami Vice *or another old show: You tackle 1980s railroad ties, split fairways, and big, obvious obstacles.* ★★★★

HIDDEN RIVER GOLF & CASTING CLUB. Facility Holes: 18. Opened: 1998. Architect: Bruce Matthews. Yards: 7,101/4,787. Par: 72/72. Course Rating: 74.3/67.4. Slope: 140/ 117. Green Fee: $45/$85. Cart Fee: Included in green fee. Discounts: Weekdays, twilight, seniors, juniors. Walking: Walking at certain times. Season: May–Oct. High: June–Aug. Tee Times: Call 200 days in advance. Notes: Range (grass). ⊠7688 Maple River Rd., Brutus 49716, 13 mi from Petoskey ☎231/529-4653 or 800/325-4653 ⊕www. hiddenriver.com ▤MC, V. *Comments: Resort-quality experience at a daily fee ($45) price make this course a local favorite, although a less-obvious choice.* ★★★★ ¹/₂

Where to Stay

▦**BAY HARBOR RESORT & MARINA.** The sprawling resort south of Petoskey stretches along 5 mi of Lake Michigan and was once the home of a cement plant and rock quarry. Upscale and self-contained, it includes a yacht club, equestrian club, swim club, and the Bay Harbor Lake Marina (the "Nautical Center of the Great Lakes"). Contemporary rooms have light wood or wicker furnishings, pastel colors, and plenty of windows. One-, two-, or three-bedroom condominiums or penthouse suites are available, and some have balconies which open up onto majestic Lake Michigan. Others overlook Bay Harbor Lake or the village, the only section of the resort open to the public. The resort has two museums: one highlights the region's history and the other has exhibits of classic cars. ⊠4000 Main St., Bay Harbor 49770 ☎231/439-2000 ⊕www. bayharbor.com ⇨92 rooms ♨3 restaurants, pool, gym, hot tub, marina, horseback riding, bar, shops, business services, some pets allowed (fee), no smoking rooms ▤AE, D, DC, MC, V $$$–$$$$.

▦**BAYWINDS INN.** The inviting lobby in this cozy, independently owned motel has a fireplace and is furnished with antiques. Attractive guest rooms have a Victorian flavor, with fresh flowers and floral prints, and the indoor pool is the area's largest. The inn is less than a mile from downtown Petoskey and within walking distance of boutiques, restaurants, and services. ⊠909 Spring St. (U.S. 131), 49770 ☎231/347-4193 or 800/ 204-1748 ⊜231/347-5927 ⊕www.baywindsinn.com ⇨52 rooms ♨Some in-room hot tubs, refrigerators, cable TV, indoor pool, exercise equipment, hot tub; no smoking ▤AE, D, MC, V ⊙CP $–$$.

▦**BOYNE HIGHLANDS.** Sister to the well-known, larger Boyne Mountain Resort, Boyne Highlands has 5,000 acres, two distinct hotels, town houses, and condos. The main lodge at the foot of the slopes resembles an old English manor house. The more intimate Bartley House, with fieldstone and wood accents, is a short walk from the lifts. In warm weather, the ski trails are used for hiking and mountain biking. ⊠ 600 Highland Dr., Harbor Springs 49740 ☎ 231/526-3001 ⎙ 231/526-3100 ⊕ www.boynehighlands. com ⇙ 176 rooms, 39 suites, 195 condos ⚿ Restaurant, 4 18-hole golf courses, tennis court, 3 pools, 2 gyms, hot tub, steam room, bicycles, hiking, cross-country skiing, down-hill skiing, ice-skating, bar, shops, baby-sitting, business services, convention center ⊟ AE, D, DC, MC, V $-$$$.

⊡ **BOYNE MOUNTAIN RESORT.** An institution among northern Michigan resorts, this full-service resort is surrounded by spectacular natural beauty. The popular desti-nation is in the midst of a quarter-billion dollar refurbishing project that includes the addition of Mountain Grand Lodge and Spa, a 222-room condominium/hotel and spa. Other improvements include specialty shops, a café, skating rink, and teen activity cen-ter. Two additional designer golf courses, expanded convention facilities, and enhanced Nordic, biking, and hiking trails are also in the works. ⊠ 1 Boyne Mountain Rd., Boyne Falls 49713 ☎ 231/549-6000 or 800/462-6963 ⎙ 231/549-6093 ⊕ www. boynemountain.com ⇙ 40 rooms, 5 suites, 138 condos, 12 cabins ⚿ Restaurant, din-ing room, some kitchenettes, cable TV, 9-hole golf course, 2 18-hole golf courses, ten-nis courts, 2 pools, gym, hot tub, beach, boating, bicycles, hiking, volleyball, ice-skating, cross-country skiing, downhill skiing, bar, shops, baby-sitting, business services ⊟ AE, D, DC, MC, V $.

⊡ **STAFFORD'S PERRY HOTEL.** The city's only remaining 19th-century hotel, Stafford's remains one of Petoskey's finest and occupies a vintage 1899 brick structure in the Gaslight District near restaurants and shopping. The individually appointed rooms have turn-of-the-20th-century wallpaper patterns; some rooms overlook Lake Michigan and others have views of the city's historic district. Be sure to spend time in a wicker chair on the long veranda and enjoy the sunset views. Ernest Hemingway (whose fami-ly summered on nearby Walloon Lake) and other luminaries once stayed here. ⊠ Bay and Lewis Sts., 49770 ☎ 231/347-4000 or 800/737-1899 ⎙ 231/347-0636 ⊕ http://theperryhotel.com ⇙ 80 rooms ⚿ 3 restaurants, cable TV, exercise equip-ment, hot tub, bar, business services; no smoking ⊟ AE, D, MC, V $-$$$$.

Where to Eat

✕ **ANDANTE.** A quiet, understated dining room in a former home at the edge of the city's Gaslight District is accented with impressionist-style art and classical music. The restaurant is considered to be among northern Michigan's best. The changing menu might have dishes like potato-crusted whitefish on a creamy sweet corn sauce or rioja-braised lamb shank with garlic mashed potatoes. ⊠ 321 Bay St. ☎ 231/348-3321 ⊟ AE, MC, V ⊗ Closed Sun. and Mon. Oct.–May. No lunch $$$$.

✕ **ARGONNE SUPPER CLUB.** Elegant in all white, this restaurant 4 mi north of downtown specializes in all-you-can eat shrimp, either batter-fried or steamed in the shell. Other popular entrées are the Alaskan king crab, hand-cut steaks, and fresh white-fish from Cross Fisheries in Charlevoix. ⊠ 11929 Boyne City Rd., Charlevoix ☎ 231/547-9331 ⊟ D, MC, V ⊗ Closed Sun.–Wed. Nov.–May. No lunch Nov.–May $$-$$$$.

✕**1891 WALLOON LAKE INN.** Ernest Hemingway's family vacationed at Walloon Lake during his youth. The family's cottage still exists and the writer's relatives can occasionally be found eating here. The dining room has views of the lake and a tree-lined coast 9 mi south of Petoskey. The menu is extensive—tuck into the filet mignon with morel mushrooms, braised lamb shanks, or, if you feel literary, ruby trout Hemingway, which is sautéed with shallots, garlic, cognac, and mushrooms. Finish with the crème caramel. ✉ Windsor St., Walloon Lake ☎ 231/535-2999 ⊕ www.walloonlakeinn.com ⊟ MC, V ⊘ No lunch $$$-$$$$.

✕**GARRETT'S ONE WATER STREET.** Enticing waterfront views and an airy design make this space inviting. Though the house specialty is prime rib, the menu generally capitalizes on fresh fish and seafood and local ingredients. Chef-owner Garrett Scanlan concocts a delightfully rich golden morel-stuffed shrimp from the regional abundance of morel mushrooms. Soups, appetizers, salads, and desserts round out the options. ✉ 1 Water St. ☎ 231/582-1111 ⊟ AE, MC, V $-$$.

✕**STAFFORD'S BAY VIEW INN.** The classic, white-clapboard Victorian inn has excellent views of Little Traverse Bay. Local whitefish, cold cherry soup, seared beef tenderloin medallions served with port and dried cherries, and fresh pastas are among the menu staples. The Sunday brunch s an area tradition, with four tables filled with hot and cold meats, breakfast items, salads, and sweets. Don't miss the signature cherry French toast at breakfast or the cherry pepper steak at dinner. ✉ 2011 Woodland Ave. ☎ 231/347-2771 Ⓨ BYOB ⊟ AE, MC, V $$$-$$$$.

✕**TANNERY SALOON.** People cram into this former town tannery for Sunday brunch, and with good reason. First, there's the thick French toast, and the sweet bread tray with a discriminating selection of chocolate, lemon, and orange breads and Danishes. Have a craving for something more substantial? Opt for roasted chicken or down-home biscuits and sausage gravy. The rustic eatery also has a reputation for mouthwatering baby back ribs and steaks at dinner. ✉ 220 S. Lake St. ☎ 231/582-2272 ⊟ AE, D, DC, MC, V $-$$.

Essentials

Getting Here

As you work your way around the northern tip of the lower peninsula, Petoskey sits near the apex, 40 minutes northeast around the coast from Traverse City and 260 mi from Detroit.

The best route to either Boyne or Petoskey is via I-75, which dissects the top of the Michigan's "mitten" as it veers north. From Detroit, follow I-75 north to exit 282. Follow Route 32 west to U.S. 131. Then take U.S. 131 north to Boyne and to Petoskey.

Visitor Information

🛈 **Boyne City Chamber of Commerce** ✉ 28 S. Lake St., Boyne City 49712 ☎ 231/582-6222 ⊕ www.boynecity.com. **Petoskey-Harbor Springs-Boyne County Visitors Bureau** ✉ 401 Mitchell St., 49770 ☎ 231/348-2755 or 800/845-2828 📠 231/348-1810 ⊕ www.boynecountry.com.

SANDUSKY, OH, COURSES	YARDAGE	PAR	COURSE	SLOPE	GREEN FEE
Sawmill Creek Golf & Racquet Club (18)	6,702/5,124	71/71	72.3/69.4	128/115	$27/$63
Sugar Creek Golf Course (18)	6,331/5,092	71/71	66.5/64.4	102/98	$12/$18
Thunderbird Hills Golf Club (36)					$21/$24
North (18)	6,464/5,993	72/74	70.3/74.0	109/121	
South (18)	6,235/4,660	72/72	68.9/65.6	114/103	

SANDUSKY, OH

Rarely are golf trips worth scheduling for the things you can do when you're off the course. Las Vegas is one—for obvious reasons—and Sandusky is another. To call the Sandusky-based Cedar Point an amusement park is sort of like calling Pebble Beach a course with a big water hazard down one side. It's not just a place to take the kids for a few roller-coaster rides. The park is like a Midwestern Disney World, a massive collection of thrill rides, water parks, five-star hotels, and high-end restaurants that could satisfy just about any kind of taste. Golf around Sandusky isn't as high-profile as in say, Orlando, but there are several attractive options. The area hugs the Lake Erie shore, and courses often have lake views and interesting terrain, along with a low-priced green fees.

Courses   **Golf** Digest REVIEWS

SAWMILL CREEK GOLF & RACQUET CLUB. Facility Holes: 18. Opened: 1974. Architect: George Fazio/Tom Fazio. Yards: 6,702/5,124. Par: 71/71. Course Rating: 72.3/ 69.4. Slope: 128/115. Green Fee: $27/$63. Cart Fee: $15 per person. Discounts: Weekdays. Walking: Walking at certain times. Season: Mar.–Nov. Tee Times: Call 7 days in advance. Notes: Lodging (245). ✉300 Sawmill Pkwy., Huron 44839, 60 mi from Cleveland ☎419/433-3789 or 800/729-6455 ⊕ www.sawmillcreek.com ⊟AE, D, DC, MC, V. *Comments: One of Tom Fazio's first courses has lake views and bizarre undulations on the greens.* ★ ★ ★ ½

SUGAR CREEK GOLF COURSE. Facility Holes: 18. Opened: 1963. Architect: Stan Neeb/Leon Neeb. Yards: 6,331/5,092. Par: 71/71. Course Rating: 66.5/64.4. Slope: 102/98. Green Fee: $12/$18. Cart Fee: $22/cart. Walking: Walking at certain times. Season: Mar.– Dec. High: June–Sept. Tee Times: Call golf shop. ✉950 Elmore East Rd., Elmore 43416, 20 mi from Toledo ☎419/862-2551 ⊟MC, V. *Comments: The greens make this pleasant daily-fee course worth a try. Immaculate conditioning and very true. UR*

THUNDERBIRD HILLS GOLF CLUB. Facility Holes: 36. Architect: Bruce Palmer. Green Fee: $21/$24. Cart Fee: $13 per person. Discounts: Weekdays, twilight, seniors, juniors. Season: Apr.–Oct. Tee Times: Call golf shop. Notes: Metal spikes, range (mat). ✉1316

Mudbrook Rd., SR 13, Huron 44839, 40 mi from Cleveland ☎419/433–4552 ⊕www. thunderbirdhills.com ☰D, MC, V.

North. Holes: 18. Opened: 1960. Yards: 6,464/5,993. Par: 72/74. Course Rating: 70.3/ 74.0. Slope: 109/121. Walking: Unrestricted walking. *Comments: The short, twisty test has water, blind shots—the works. Too bad there aren't any caddies.* ★ ★ ★ ¹/₂

South. Holes: 18. Opened: 1995. Yards: 6,235/4,660. Par: 72/72. Course Rating: 68.9/ 65.6. Slope: 114/103. Walking: Walking at certain times. *Comments: This newer, shorter sister course is more wide open.* ★ ★ ★ ¹/₂

Where to Stay

🎫 **BREAKERS EXPRESS.** Staying at one of Cedar Point's resorts has its advantages: It's less than 5 minutes' drive to the park and a 10- to 15- minute drive to the area's major golf courses. The least expensive of Cedar Point's resorts, Breakers Express does-n't have fancy amenities, but it does have a Snoopy-shape pool and access to Cedar Point Beach, making it popular with families. ⊠1201 Cedar Point Dr., 44870 ☎419/ 627–2106 ⊕www.cedarpoint.com 📇350 rooms ⚲Cable TV, pool, hot tub, video game room, laundry facilities; no smoking ☰D, MC, V ⊘Closed mid-Oct.–Apr. ¢–$$$.

🎫 **CLARION INN.** The Clarion Inn is a good compromise for a family weekend: it's near enough to both Cedar Point and the region's golf courses to be a convenient alternative to the amusement park hub. The Sandusky Mall, a decent selection of restaurants, and an eight-screen movie theater are nearby, and the inn's attractive garden area with fountains is a good spot to wind down. ⊠1119 Sandusky Mall Blvd., 44870 ☎419/ 625–6280 or 800/252–7466 📠419/625–9080 ⊕www.clarionsandusky.com 📇143 rooms ⚲Restaurant, room service, some in-room data ports, some microwaves, some refrigerators, cable TV with movies, indoor pool, exercise equipment, hot tub, dance club, video game room, laundry service, convention center, meeting rooms, some pets allowed; no smoking ☰AE, D, DC, MC, V ⅢCP $–$$.

🎫 **HOLIDAY INN HOLIDOME.** Though the Holiday Inn Holidome caters to business travelers and families visiting Cedar Point, the upside for golfers staying at this standard chain motel is that it's a quick drive along the lakeshore to area golf courses. The trop-ical indoor swimming pool has a poolside bar, and if you want to practice your putting, you can play on the hotel's indoor miniature golf course. If the family's along for the weekend, the Kidsuites (separate children's sleeping quarters designed to look like cas-tle) are a fun option. ⊠5513 Milan Rd. (Rte. 250), 44870 ☎419/626–6671 or 800/465– 4329 📠419/626–9780 ⊕www.holidayinn-sandusky.com 📇175 rooms, 15 suites ⚲Restaurant, room service, in-room data ports, some in-room hot tubs, microwaves, refrigerators, cable TV, miniature golf, 2 pools (1 indoor), gym, hot tub, badminton, bil-liards, Ping-Pong, bar, video game room, laundry facilities, laundry service, business serv-ices, meeting rooms; no smoking ☰AE, D, DC, MC, V ⅢCP $$.

🎫 **HOTEL BREAKERS.** When this hotel opened its doors in 1905, it claimed to be "the largest and greatest hotel on the Great Lakes." It's still impressive, with its Tiffany stained-glass windows and four-story rotunda with waterfall. Every room has a balcony—most have a view of Lake Erie. Kids like the Peanuts floor, where the rooms have Peanuts characters on the walls, as well as Beaches and Cream, a 1950s-style ice cream parlor. ⊠ 1 Cedar Point Dr., 44870 ☎ 419/627-2106 ⊕ www.cedarpoint.com ⇌ 650 rooms ♿ 2 restaurants, café, coffee shop, grocery, ice cream parlor, pizzeria, some in-room hot tubs, microwaves, refrigerators, cable TV, 3 pools (1 indoor), lake, outdoor hot tub, spa, beach, marina, video game room, shops, laundry facilities, concierge, meeting rooms, no-smoking rooms ⊟ D, MC, V ⊙ Closed mid-Oct.–Apr. $$–$$$.

▣ **SAWMILL CREEK RESORT.** Stroll the lakeside marina, play the challenging golf course, hike around the on-site nature preserve, or cool off in the outdoor pool at this sprawling nature-focused resort hotel, nestled on the shores of Lake Erie. A rustic Southwest style dominates the resort's interior: Rooms have Native American rugs and framed wildlife prints. Sandusky is about a 20-minute drive east. ⊠ 400 Saw Mill Creek, off Rte. 6, Huron 44839 ☎ 419/433-3800 or 800/729-6455 ⊕ www. sawmillcreek.com ⇌ 192 rooms, 48 suites ♿ 3 restaurants, some in-room data ports, some in-room hot tubs, some refrigerators, cable TV, 18-hole golf course, 2 pools (1 indoor), lake, gym, beach, dock, marina, bar, pub, sports bar, video game room, shops, laundry facilities, business services, convention center, meeting rooms, no-smoking rooms ⊟ AE, D, DC, MC, V $$$.

Where to Eat

✕ **BAY HARBOR INN.** The bay-side restaurant just outside Cedar Point amusement park is a favorite of park visitors: Its elegance is welcome after a hard day's play, and the dining room looks out on Sandusky Harbor and the marina. Seafood dominates the menu, but there's also pasta, filet mignon, and New York strip steak. ⊠ 1 Cedar Point Dr., Cedar Point Marina ☎ 419/625-6373 ⊟ AE, D, MC, V ⊙ No lunch $$$$.

✕ **DAMON'S GRILL AT BATTERY PARK.** The sports bar chain has wall-size big-screen televisions, local sports team memorabilia, and electronic trivia games. The menu is basic bar food: chicken, ribs, and steaks; the grilled chicken breast or the cold pork sandwich are good choices. Try the popular onion loaf appetizer, a tasty tangle of thin onion straws that are breaded and deep fried. ⊠ 701 E. Water St. ☎ 419/627-2424 ⊟ AE, D, MC, V $-$$$$.

✕ **DEMORE'S FISH DEN.** Known for Great Lakes fish and clam chowder, DeMore's catch comes fresh from its own wholesale distributorship, the largest for yellow perch in the Midwest. Fresh perch and walleye are specialties, as is the Giant Perch Sandwich. Dine casually indoors, or enjoy lakeshore breezes on the outdoor patio. ⊠ 302 W. Perkins Ave. ☎ 419/626-8861 ⊟ MC, V $.

✕ **SALMON RUN RESTAURANT.** It's not surprising that Salmon Run considers salmon their specialty—char-grilled Nova Scotia salmon to be precise. Other favorites from the restaurant's lengthy menu include Lake Erie walleye and perch and New York Strip glazed with Jamaican rum. The great food is complemented by fabulous views of Wilderness Creek. ⊠ 400 Sawmill Creek, in the Lodge at Sawmill Creek Resort, Huron ☎ 419/433-3800 ⊟ AE, D, DC, MC, V $$-$$$$.

Essentials

Getting Here

To get to Sandusky, 155 mi from Detroit, follow I-75 south to Toledo. Then take I-280 south to the Ohio Turnpike (I-80/90). Follow the turnpike east to exit 110(6A) and follow Route 4 north. Traffic moves quickly along the Ohio Turnpike.

If you're not in a hurry, you might consider the more scenic east-west Route 2 instead, taking in broad views of Lake Erie and its islands. Take I-75 south from Detroit to Toledo; at Oregon, take exit 7 and follow Route 2 east.

Try to arrive in Sandusky well before or after amusement park opening times, especially in July and August. Driving can be a nightmare along the major routes into the park, including Routes 2 and 6, but especially along Routes 4 and 250. Similarly, traffic along the same routes will be backed up at Cedar Point's closing time.

Visitor Information

⁊ Sandusky/Erie County Visitors and Convention Bureau ✉ 4424 Milan Rd., Suite A, 44870 ☎ 419/625-2984 or 800/255-3743 ⊕ www.sanduskyohiocedarpoint.com.

TRAVERSE CITY

Until the 1980s, Traverse City wasn't much more than an overgrown marina town with steady weekend tourist traffics. Since then, it has grown into a thriving city of 30,000, with new residents drawn to its spectacular lakeside scenery, good schools, and an efficient airport. The added population has its drawbacks (traffic jams are a way of life now), but the cultural benefits have been significant. Traverse City's collection of fine restaurants is as diverse as any city its size in the state, and an increased flight schedule into the Traverse City regional airport makes a trip to the area a quick, convenient hop from Detroit.

Many of the area's four-month-a-year ski resorts have transformed into year-round destinations. Shanty Creek resort used to close down when the ski season ended in March, but four golf courses built on and around its ski slopes fill its ski chalets year-round. The Tom Weiskopf-designed Cedar River course is a particularly heroic layout that requires long carries, binoculars, and an appreciation for the deep forest. Grand Traverse Resort and Spa is just down the street from the airport and has three 18-hole courses to play. And if you think the view from the picture window in Arcadia Bluffs' golf shop is spectacular, wait until you get to the holes that overlook Lake Michigan on this Rick Smith design.

TRAVERSE CITY COURSES	YARDAGE	PAR	COURSE	SLOPE	GREEN FEE
Antrim Dells Golf Course (18)	6,606/5,493	72/72	72.1/71.9	125/121	$33/$52
Arcadia Bluffs Golf Club (18)	7,404/5,529	72/72	75.1/69.2	143/121	$130/$160
Crystal Mountain Resort (36)					
Betsie Valley (18)	6,442/4,989	72/72	70.2/68.5	127/121	$20/$42
Mountain Ridge (18)	7,007/4,956	72/72	73.3/68.2	132/119	$50/$82
Grand Traverse Resort and Spa (54)					
The Bear (18)	7,083/5,424	72/72	76.8/73.1	146/137	$50/$140
Spruce Run (18)	6,304/4,726	70/70	70.8/68.2	130/125	$35/$100
The Wolverine (18)	7,038/5,029	72/72	73.9/68.1	144/121	$50/$140
Shanty Creek (54)					
Cedar River (18)	6,989/5,315	72/72	73.6/70.5	144/128	$65/$145
The Legend (18)	6,764/4,953	72/72	73.6/69.6	137/124	$59/$145
Schuss Mountain (18)	6,922/5,383	72/72	73.4/71.2	127/126	$45/$90
Summit (18)	6,260/4,679	72/72	71.7/70.7	120/113	$30/$60

Courses

Golf Digest REVIEWS

ANTRIM DELLS GOLF COURSE. Facility Holes: 18. Opened: 1973. Architect: Bruce Matthews/Jerry Matthews. Yards: 6,606/5,493. Par: 72/72. Course Rating: 72.1/71.9. Slope: 125/121. Green Fee: $33/$52. Cart Fee: Included in green fee. Discounts: Weekdays, twilight, juniors. Walking: Walking at certain times. Season: Apr.–Oct. High: June–Aug. Tee Times: Call 365 days in advance. Notes: Range (grass). ⊠ 12352 Antrim Dr., Atwood 49729, 35 mi from Traverse City ☎ 231/599-2679 or 800/872-8561 ⊕ - www.antrimdellsgolf.com ⊟ MC, V. *Comments: Handles heavy local traffic, and for good reason: It costs less than $60 to play and is always in great shape.* ★ ★ ★ ★

ARCADIA BLUFFS GOLF CLUB. Facility Holes: 18. Opened: 1999. Architect: Rick Smith/Warren Henderson. Yards: 7,404/5,529. Par: 72/72. Course Rating: 75.1/69.2. Slope: 143/121. Green Fee: $130/$160. Cart Fee: Included in green fee. Discounts: Twilight. Walking: Walking at certain times. Season: May–Nov. High: June–Aug. Tee Times: Call golf shop. Notes: Range (grass). ⊠ 14710 Northwood Hwy., Arcadia 49613, 40 mi from Traverse City ☎ 800/494-8666 or 800/494-8666 ⊕ www.arcadiabluffs.com ⊟ AE, D, MC, V. *Comments: Second in* Golf Digest's *Best New Upscale Courses survey in 2002. Routing takes great advantage of the lake frontage. Watch out for the long native grass.* UR

CRYSTAL MOUNTAIN RESORT. Facility Holes: 36. Discounts: Weekdays, twilight. Season: Apr.-Nov. Tee Times: Call golf shop. Notes: Range (grass, mat), lodging (230). ⊠ 12500 Crystal Mountain Dr., Thompsonville 49683, 30 mi from Traverse City ☎ 231/378-2000 or 800/968-7686 ⊕ www.crystalmountain.com ⊟ AE, D, DC, MC, V.

Betsie Valley. Holes: 18. Opened: 1977. Architect: Robert Meyer. Yards: 6,442/4,989. Par: 72/72. Course Rating: 70.2/68.5. Slope: 127/121. Green Fee: $20/$42. Cart Fee: $13 per person. Walking: Unrestricted walking. *Comments: Short, forgiving, and perfect for beginners taking lessons from Brad Dean's on-site golf academy—one of the best in the state.* ★ ★ ★ ★

Mountain Ridge. Holes: 18. Opened: 1992. Architect: William Newcomb. Yards: 7,007/ 4,956. Par: 72/72. Course Rating: 73.3/68.2. Slope: 132/119. Green Fee: $50/$82. Cart Fee: Included in green fee. Walking: Mandatory cart. *Comments: A great resort-course value and underappreciated area find.* ★★★★

GRAND TRAVERSE RESORT AND SPA. Facility Holes: 54. Cart Fee: Included in green fee. Discounts: Weekdays, guest, twilight. Season: Apr.–Nov. High: June–Aug. Tee Times: Call golf shop. Notes: Range (grass). ✉ 6300 U.S. 31 N, Acme, 49610, 6 mi from Traverse City ☎ 231/938-1620 or 800/748-0303 ⊕ www.grandtraverseresort.com ▤ AE, D, DC, MC, V.

The Bear. Holes: 18. Opened: 1985. Architect: Jack Nicklaus. Yards: 7,083/5,424. Par: 72/ 72. Course Rating: 76.8/73.1. Slope: 146/137. Green Fee: $50/$140. Walking: Mandatory cart. *Comments: Suspend any disbelief and take in Nicklaus' all-out effort to build the hardest course in Michigan. Home of the annual Michigan Open. Bring lots of balls—and a sweatband.* ★★★★

Spruce Run. Holes: 18. Opened: 1979. Architect: William Newcomb. Yards: 6,304/4,726. Par: 70/70. Course Rating: 70.8/68.2. Slope: 130/125. Green Fee: $35/$100. Walking: Walking at certain times. *Comments: Ease into the other two courses on the resort's original—and easiest—course.* ★★★★

The Wolverine. Holes: 18. Opened: 1999. Architect: Gary Player. Yards: 7,038/5,029. Par: 72/72. Course Rating: 73.9/68.1. Slope: 144/121. Green Fee: $50/$140. Walking: Mandatory cart. *Comments: Player designed this to be a sporty and more "resort-y" alternative to the Bear, and he succeeded. The course is great fun.* ★★★★

SHANTY CREEK. Facility Holes: 54. Cart Fee: Included in green fee. Discounts: Weekdays, twilight, juniors. Walking: Unrestricted walking. Season: Apr.–Oct. High: June–Sept. Tee Times: Call golf shop. Notes: Range (grass, mat), lodging (600). ✉ 1 Shanty Creek Rd., Bellaire 49615, 35 mi from Traverse City ☎ 231/533-8621 or 800/ 678-4111 ⊕ www.shantycreek.com ▤ AE, D, DC, MC, V.

Cedar River. Holes: 18. Opened: 1999. Architect: Tom Weiskopf. Yards: 6,989/5,315. Par: 72/72. Course Rating: 73.6/70.5. Slope: 144/128. Green Fee: $65/$145. *Comments: Long, tough, and protected by a lot of water. It's best for a low- to mid-handicapper.* ★★★★

The Legend. Holes: 18. Opened: 1985. Architect: Arnold Palmer/Ed Seay/Bob Walker. Yards: 6,764/4,953. Par: 72/72. Course Rating: 73.6/69.6. Slope: 137/124. Green Fee: $59/$145. *Comments: Elevated tee shots and greens galore, thanks to location on the side of a ski slope. Conditioning is excellent.* ★★★★ ½

Schuss Mountain. Holes: 18. Opened: 1972. Architect: Warner Bowen/William Newcomb. Yards: 6,922/5,383. Par: 72/72. Course Rating: 73.4/71.2. Slope: 127/126. Green Fee: $45/$90. *Comments: The course is solid but overshadowed by the two bigger-name courses.* ★★★★

Summit. Holes: 18. Opened: 1965. Architect: William H. Diddel. Yards: 6,260/4,679. Par: 72/72. Course Rating: 71.7/70.7. Slope: 120/113. Green Fee: $30/$60. *Comments: The resort's original course feels built rather than designed. Traffic isn't too heavy, which makes it a great option for kids and beginners.* ★★ ½

Where to Stay

BAYSHORE RESORT. On the sandy beaches of Lake Michigan's West Grand Traverse Bay sits this Victorian-theme hotel, 1 mi from downtown Traverse City. The resort opened in the early 1990s and instantly garnered media attention because of its "no smoking" policy. Despite the nod toward contemporary health concerns, the spacious lobby and antiques-laden rooms evoke another era. Rooms with a view of Lake Michigan's stunning blue waters cost more. ⌧ 833 E. Front St., 49686 ☎ 231/935-4400 or 800/634-4401 🖷 231/935-0262 ⊕ www.bayshore-resort.com ➲ 120 rooms ♿ Cable TV, indoor pool, gym, hot tub, beach, video game room, laundry facilities, business services, airport shuttle; no smoking ☰ AE, D, DC, MC, V ⌾ CP $$$-$$$$.

CRYSTAL MOUNTAIN. Tucked away on Michigan's northeast coast, this family-owned resort has already won over the public and the media despite the fact that it's still a destination in development. In 2003, the resort broke ground on a $23 million expansion project that includes cottages and a 1-acre water park with a 4,200-square-foot pool. Eleven ski trails, carved out of the hardwoods, opened in 2003, and make excellent hiking paths in warm months. Kayaking, canoeing, and mountain biking are also on-site. Lots of windows with views of the forested countryside, a soothing off-white and tan color scheme, and simple woodwork make the rooms and condos bright and airy. ⌧ 12500 Crystal Mountain Dr., Thompsonville 49683 ☎ 231/378-2000 or 800/968-7686 🖷 231/378-2998 ⊕ www.crystalmountain.com ➲ 68 rooms, 29 suites, 143 condo units ♿ 4 restaurants, 36-hole golf course, 2 pools (1 indoor), cross-country skiing, downhill skiing, 2 bars, business services, no smoking rooms ☰ AE, D, DC, MC, V $$-$$$$.

GRAINERY BED AND BREAKFAST. The 1892 gentleman's farm on 10 acres 3 mi south of downtown was converted into a bed-and-breakfast in 1990. Rooms in the house are uniquely appointed with antiques; all have private baths. Rooms in the carriage house have fireplaces, while the cottage has a private deck and sitting area. The breakfast room overlooks a pond. Any time of day you can snack on goodies from the dessert and fruit table, or relax on the two-person hammock or in the eight-person hot tub. You can practice your golf swing on two golf greens with provided clubs and balls. ⌧ 2951 Hartman Rd., 49684 ☎ 231/946-8325 ⊕ www.bbhost.com/thegrainery ➲ 4 rooms, 1 cottage ♿ Dining room, some in-room hot tubs, driving range, hot tub, no-smoking rooms; no room TVs ☰ AE, MC, V ⌾ BP $-$$.

⌕ **GRAND TRAVERSE RESORT.** One of northern Michigan's premier destinations is the 1,400-acre resort along the shores of Lake Michigan's East Grand Traverse Bay, acquired by the Grand Traverse Band of Ottawa and Chippewa Indians in early 2003. A $2.5 million renovation approved for 2004 includes new carpet, furniture, and flat-screen TVs for each room. The four-season resort hotel is well known for its 54 golf holes. For a little relaxation check out the resort's 7,000-square-foot spa complex. Within the complex you can take advantage of the state-of-the-art workout facilities and tennis center. Spacious rooms in the 17-story tower include wet bars, refrigerators, and hot tubs. ✉ 100 Grand Traverse Village Blvd., Acme 49610 ☏ 231/938-2100 or 800/748-0303 🖷 231/938-3859 ⊕ www.grandtraverseresort.com 🛏 424 rooms, 236 condominiums ♿ 3 restaurants, some in-room hot tubs, some kitchenettes, some refrigerators, cable TV, 3 18-hole golf courses, 9 tennis courts, 4 pools (2 indoor), gym, 5 hot tubs, beach, cross-country skiing, tobagganing, bar, children's programs (ages 6–12), laundry facilities, business services, airport shuttle ▭ AE, D, DC, MC, V $$$$.

⌕ **SHANTY CREEK.** A former Detroit steel worker built this expansive resort—popular with both golfers and skiers—in the early 1960s. Three villages have distinct accommodations and scenery. The newest, Cedar River Village, is set between hills. Summit Village has panoramic views of the northern Michigan countryside. The resort covers 4,500 acres in all and, besides golf and skiing, has activities which include mountain biking, horseshoes, and disc golf (a game in which a Frisbee is used instead of a golf ball). ✉ 1 Shanty Creek Rd., Bellaire 49615 ☏ 231/533-8621 🖷 231/533-7001 ⊕ www.shantycreek.com 🛏 600 rooms ♿ 4 restaurants, 4 18-hole golf courses, tennis courts, 5 pools (3 indoor), health club, spa, bicycles, mountain bikes, basketball, croquet, hiking, horseshoes, shuffleboard, volleyball, baby-sitting, meeting rooms, no smoking rooms ▭ AE, D, DC, MC, V $–$$.

Where to Eat

✕ **APACHE TROUT GRILL.** Look out over Lake Michigan from this grill, named for a fish rescued from the endangered species list. The dining room carries out the fish theme, with mounted fish and wood carvings on the walls and lamps carved in the shape of bears and fishing poles. The fresh fish specials are good either grilled or sautéed. There are also steaks, barbecued ribs, and several pasta dishes. ✉ 13671 S.W. Bay Shore Dr. ☏ 231/947-7079 ▭ AE, DC, MC, V $–$$$$.

✕ **BOAT HOUSE BLUE WATER BISTRO.** The cottagelike restaurant on the Old Mission Peninsula, 10 mi north of town, is right on Lake Michigan. Entrées include chicken, steak, fresh seafood, and vegetable specialties. Especially satisfying are the tender maple horseradish pork chops or almond-crusted walleye. Desserts are homemade. ✉ 14039 Peninsula Dr. ☏ 231/223-4030 ▭ AE, MC, V ☺ Closed Mon. No lunch Labor Day–Memorial Day $$$–$$$$.

✕ **LA SEÑORITA.** Bright, eye-catching fixtures complement the zesty fare. It's one of the few places in Traverse City to serve burritos, chimichangas, and fajitas as well as a fine selection of mesquite-grilled dishes. Other favorites include the linguine and any of the several signature burgers. ⊠ 1245 S. Garfield Ave. ☎ 231/947–8820 ⊕ www. lasenorita.net ▤ AE, D, MC, V $–$$$.

✕ **REFLECTIONS.** Stylish fare and an expansive view of East Grand Traverse Bay and Old Mission Peninsula make this fourth-floor restaurant in the Waterfront Inn a stand-out. In addition to the classic prime rib and Atlantic char-grilled salmon, you can try one of many sandwiches and entrée-size salads. Walleye and planked whitefish are favorite fish dishes. Choose from a number of homemade cheesecakes for dessert. ⊠ 2061 U.S. 31 N, North Traverse City ☎ 231/938–2321 ▤ AE, D, DC, MC, V $$$–$$$$.

✕ **WINDOWS.** Views of the bay from every table, an extensive wine list, and a menu that emphasizes both old favorites and artful, new cuisine are what often earns this establishment praise. Standouts on the seasonal menu include a gumbo made with duck and sausage, as well as the fresh seafood-and-veal Winn Dixie—veal sautéed with shrimp, artichokes, and mushrooms. The chocolate mousse Olivia, bittersweet chocolate mousse wrapped in a white chocolate lattice and drizzled with a refreshing raspberry sauce, is the best of the homemade desserts. ⊠ 7677 W. Bay Shore Dr. ☎ 231/941–0100 ▤ AE, DC, MC, V ☯ Closed Sun. and Mon. and Nov.–Apr. $$$$.

Essentials

Getting Here
Traverse City is about 253 mi from Detroit. From Detroit, take I-75 north about 200 mi to exit 254. Follow Route 72 west toward Kalkaska and then onto Traverse City. Turn left (south) on Route 31 and follow for about 10 mi into Traverse City.

Visitor Information
🔁 **Traverse City Convention and Visitors Bureau** ⊠ 101 W. Grandview Pkwy., 49684 ☎ 231/947–1120 or 800/872–8377 ⊕ www.mytraversecity.com.

AROUND
HOUSTON

La Cantera Golf Club

Ron Kapriske and Kay Winzenreid

It's a good thing that the Houston's sprawling Houston metroplex is loaded with over 100 golf courses. Like the rest of the major cities in this supersize state, traveling anywhere else in Texas takes time, and so area golfers can take solace in knowing they don't have to leave if they don't want to. But trust us, you'll want to.

It would be a shame for any golf aficionado to not visit great destinations like Austin and San Antonio. Don't forget Dallas either—at 240 mi from Houston, it's not too far out of reach. Many of its better golf stops, including Four Seasons Resort and Club, Cowboys Golf Club, and the Tribute at the Colony, are covered in Chapter 4.

The first stop on your list should be Austin. The hills around here give some real character to the area's courses. Thanks largely to its Barton Creek Resort & Country Club, Austin is on *Golf Digest*'s list of the top 50 golf destinations in the world. Leading the pack of quality golf locations here is the Westin La Cantera Resort, which plays host to a PGA Tour event each fall.

Considering the variety of fairways and greens in the Houston area, resident golfers never really had much incentive to travel to Louisiana. But all of that changed with the launch of the Audubon Golf Trail. Louisiana's version of the wildly successful Robert Trent Jones Golf Trail, which opened in Alabama a decade ago, the Audubon comprises nine very good—and reasonably priced—public golf courses. All are worth visiting, and three are a reasonable distance from Houston: Gray Plantation Golf Club near Lake Charles, the Cypress Bend Golf Resort & Conference Center on Lake Toledo, and Olde Oaks Golf Club near Shreveport.

If a long car ride to Bayou country isn't your thing, you may want to stay close to home and hit some of the courses along I–45 heading north out of Houston. Without traffic, you can be at the Tournament Players Club at the Woodlands in 45 minutes. The most famous of the public courses in the Houston area, it's well worth your time. The architects, Robert von Hagge and Bruce Devlin, did wonders with the flat terrain, adding water features to more than half the holes. The Pines course here is an often-ignored gem, with lots and lots of sand (more than 80 bunkers in all).

As in Houston, summer can be brutally hot and humid at any of these destinations. With luck, you're used to it. Don't let it sway you from traveling to one of these destinations between June and September. Typically, prices are lower and the courses are less crowded.

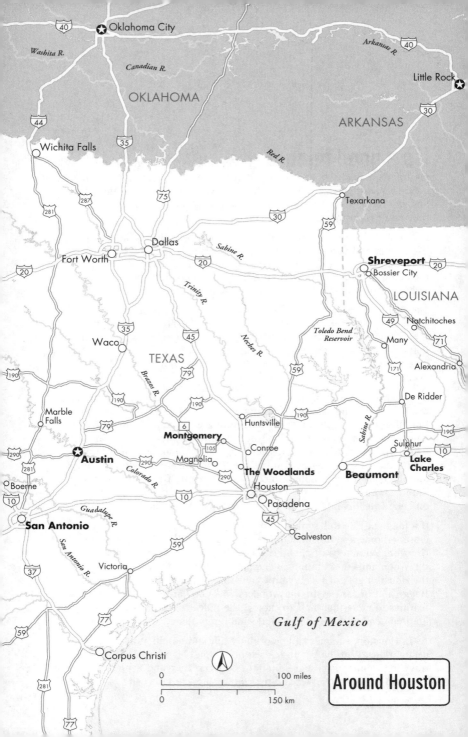

Around Houston

Barton Creek Resort & Country Club (72)					
Crenshaw Cliffside (18)	6,678/4,843	71/71	71.0/67.2	124/110	$95
Fazio Canyons (18)	7,161/5,078	72/72	74.0/70.6	135/121	$160
Fazio Foothills (18)	6,956/5,207	72/72	74.0/69.4	135/120	$135
Palmer-Lakeside (18)	6,657/5,067	71/71	71.0/71.0	124/124	$95
Forest Creek Golf Club (18)	7,147/5,394	72/72	73.8/71.9	136/124	$34/$59
Horseshoe Bay Resort (54)					$70/$121
Applerock (18)	6,999/5,509	72/72	73.9/71.6	134/117	
Ram Rock (18)	6,946/5,306	71/71	74.5/72.5	140/129	
Slick Rock (18)	6,834/5,832	72/72	72.6/70.2	125/115	
Lakeway Resort (36)					$40/$50
Live Oak (18)	6,623/5,403	72/72	71.6/71.5	123/117	
Yaupon (18)	6,590/5,032	72/72	71.1/69.6	131/115	
Roy Kizer Golf Course (18)	6,749/5,018	71/71	71.6/69.3	125/114	$18/$28

AUSTIN

Most of Texas may be as flat as a cornfield, but this isn't true of the Hill Country around Austin. The area near the state capital has some of the most interesting, not to mention prettiest, terrain in the Lone Star State. Golf-course architects look forward to the prospect of working here.

About 185 mi from Houston, Austin is the perfect getaway destination for Houstonites who need to see something different—and because of all the politicians at the Capitol as well as the students at the University of Texas, the nightlife here tends to be terrific.

The best golf destination in the Austin area is, by far, the Barton Creek Resort. In 2002 *Golf Digest* named it the 35th best golf resort in the nation. The four courses here are designed by Tom Fazio, Arnold Palmer, and Ben Crenshaw, who is an Austin native and two-time Masters winner. The appropriately named Fazio Foothills course is the must-play of the group.

If you're looking for some variety, head over to Horseshoe Bay Resort. The 54-hole Horseshoe Bay facility was designed by Robert Trent Jones, with the last of the three courses—Applerock—dating from 1986. Horseshoe Bay is on Lake LBJ, a 45-minute drive west of downtown Austin. If you're looking for something more affordable, check out the Roy Kizer Golf Course, a terrific municipal track.

Courses

BARTON CREEK RESORT & COUNTRY CLUB. Facility Holes: 72. Cart Fee: Included in green fee. Walking: Unrestricted walking. Season: Year-round. Tee Times: Call golf shop. Notes: Range (grass, mat). ⊠ 8212 Barton Club Dr., 78735 ☎ 512/329–4608 or 800/336–6158 ⊕ www.clubcorp.com ▭ AE, D, MC, V.

Crenshaw Cliffside. Holes: 18. Opened: 1991. Architect: Ben Crenshaw/Bill Coore. Yards: 6,678/4,843. Par: 71/71. Course Rating: 71.0/67.2. Slope: 124/110. Green Fee: $95. *Comments: This is a throwback to classic golf course designs. Many hills leave for interesting lies in the fairway, but it's all very scenic and playable.* ★ ★ ★ ★

Fazio Canyons. Holes: 18. Opened: 2000. Architect: Tom Fazio. Yards: 7,161/5,078. Par: 72/72. Course Rating: 74.0/70.6. Slope: 135/121. Green Fee: $160. *Comments: One of the best in Texas. Tall oaks outline the fairways and a creek winds through the middle.* ★ ★ ★ ★ ½

Fazio Foothills. Holes: 18. Opened: 1986. Architect: Tom Fazio. Yards: 6,956/5,207. Par: 72/72. Course Rating: 74.0/69.4. Slope: 135/120. Green Fee: $135. *Comments: Still the best at Barton Creek. Incredibly scenic.* ★ ★ ★ ★ ½

Palmer-Lakeside. Holes: 18. Opened: 1986. Architect: Arnold Palmer/Ed Seay/Tom Fazio/Crenshaw/Coore. Yards: 6,657/5,067. Par: 71/71. Course Rating: 71.0/71.0. Slope: 124/124. Green Fee: $95. *Comments: A pushover compared to the Fazio-designed courses, but it's still a lot of fun. Waterfall par-3 11th is one of the most memorable inland holes in the United States.* ★ ★ ★ ★

FOREST CREEK GOLF CLUB. Facility Holes: 18. Opened: 1989. Architect: Dick Phelps. Yards: 7,147/5,394. Par: 72/72. Course Rating: 73.8/71.9. Slope: 136/124. Green Fee: $45/$59. Cart Fee: Included in green fee. Discounts: Weekdays, twilight, seniors, juniors. Walking: Walking at certain times. Season: Year-round. Tee Times: Call 7 days in advance. Notes: Range (grass, mat). ⊠ 99 Twin Ridge Pkwy., Round Rock 78664, 10 mi from Austin ☎ 512/388–2874 ⊕ www.forestcreek.com ▭ AE, MC, V. *Comments: The low peak rate makes it a great value. Has classic Central Texas country-club design.* ★ ★ ★ ½

HORSESHOE BAY RESORT. Facility Holes: 54. Architect: Robert Trent Jones. Green Fee: $70/$121. Cart Fee: Included in green fee. Discounts: Weekdays, juniors. Walking: Mandatory cart. Season: Year-round. High: Mar.–Oct. Tee Times: Call 14 days in advance. Notes: Range (grass). ⊠ Bay W. Blvd., Horseshoe Bay 78657, 45 mi from Austin ☎ 830/598–6561 ⊕ www.horseshoebayresort.com ▭ AE, D, MC, V.

Applerock. Holes: 18. Opened: 1986. Yards: 6,999/5,509. Par: 72/72. Course Rating: 73.9/71.6. Slope: 134/117. *Comments: Golf Digest's choice for best new resort course in the nation in 1986. There's a good view of Lake LBJ from the 10th and 11th holes.* ★ ★ ★ ★ ½

Ram Rock. Holes: 18. Opened: 1981. Yards: 6,946/5,306. Par: 71/71. Course Rating: 74.5/72.5. Slope: 140/129. *Comments: Ranked among the best in Texas for years. Plays longer than its yardage suggests. Dry creek beds come into play on 6 holes.* ★ ★ ★ ★ ½

Slick Rock. Holes: 18. Opened: 1972. Yards: 6,834/5,832. Par: 72/72. Course Rating: 72.6/70.2. Slope: 125/115. *Comments: Very playable from the right tees. Robert Trent Jones knew how to build a resort course.* ★ ★ ★ ★ ½

LAKEWAY RESORT. Facility Holes: 36. Architect: Leon Howard. Green Fee: $40/$50. Cart Fee: $13 per person. Discounts: Weekdays, juniors. Walking: Unrestricted walking. Season: Year-round. Tee Times: Call golf shop. Notes: Range (grass, mat). ⊠ 510 Lakeway Dr., 78734 ☎ 512/261-7173 ⊕ www.lakewaygolfclub.com ☰ MC, V.

Live Oak. Holes: 18. Opened: 1966. Yards: 6,623/5,403. Par: 72/72. Course Rating: 71.6/71.5. Slope: 123/117. *Comments: Short course but very tight off the tees. Scenic.* ★ ★ ★

Yaupon. Holes: 18. Opened: 1971. Yards: 6,590/5,032. Par: 72/72. Course Rating: 71.1/69.6. Slope: 131/115. *Comments: If you can hit a 3-iron off the tee, you can play all day on this short but tight course.* ★ ★ ★

ROY KIZER GOLF COURSE. Facility Holes: 18. Opened: 1994. Architect: Randolph Russell. Yards: 6,749/5,018. Par: 71/71. Course Rating: 71.6/69.3. Slope: 125/114. Green Fee: $18/$28. Cart Fee: $10 per person. Discounts: Weekdays, twilight, seniors, juniors. Walking: Unrestricted walking. Season: Year-round. High: Apr.–Nov. Tee Times: Call up to 3 days in advance. Notes: Metal spikes, range (grass). ⊠ 5400 Jimmy Clay Dr., 78744 ☎ 512/444-0999 ⊕ www.ci.austin.tx.us/parks/kizer.htm ☰ D, MC, V. *Comments: Roy Kizer is a linksy municipal course that offers good value, with green fees less than $30.* ★ ★ ★ ½

Where to Stay

🏨 **BARTON CREEK RESORT.** This secluded 4,000-acre resort combines manicured grounds and natural spaces to show off the best of Texas Hill Country. With courses designed by the greats—Palmer, Crenshaw, and Fazio—there is no doubt which sport rules here. ⊠ 8212 Barton Club Dr., 78735 ☎ 512/329-4000 or 800/336-6158 📠 512/329-4597 ⊕ www.bartoncreek.com ⊷ 300 rooms, 16 suites ⚭ Restaurant, room service, in-room data ports, minibars, cable TV, 2 pools, driving range, 4 18-hole golf courses, putting green, tennis court, gym, hair salon, hot tub, massage, spa, bar, business services, airport shuttle, free parking ☰ AE, DC, MC, V $$$$.

🏨 **DRISKILL HOTEL.** This historic Renaissance Revival edifice fronting Congress Avenue was built in 1886 by cattle baron Jesse Driskill. Inside, its lobby is highlighted by vaulted ceilings, beautiful columns, and chandeliers. Each room is decorated with original art and rich fabrics. The chef at the elegant in-house restaurant is one of Texas's rising culinary stars. ⊠ 604 Brazos St., 78701 ☎ 512/474-5911 or 800/252-9367 📠 512/474-2214 ⊕ www.driskillhotel.com ⊷ 176 rooms, 12 suites ⚭ Restaurant, room service, cable TV, bar, business services, free parking ☰ AE, D, DC, MC, V $$$$.

🏨 **HORSESHOE BAY RESORT.** Texans have been known to brag a bit, but this megaresort is no stretch of the truth. Near the scenic Hill Country town of Marble Falls and on the shores of Lake LBJ, Horseshoe Bay covers every item on a vacationer's wish list. For the golfer there are three courses designed by Robert Trent Jones, and one by

Arnold Palmer on the way. There are also multiple swimming pools, including one with its own waterfall, plus paddleboats and Wave Runners for use on the lake. To top it all off the resort has a white-water adventure facility and private airport. ⊠ Box 7752, Horseshoe Bay 78657 ☎ 830/598-2511 or 800/252-9363 ⎙ 830/598-5525 ⊕ www. horseshoebaytexas.com ⤴ 100 rooms, 65 suites, 15 condos ⚫ 5 restaurants, room service, in-room data ports, minibars, cable TV, 3 pools, driving range, 3 18-hole golf courses, putting green, 18 tennis courts, health club, hot tub, massage, spa, marina, bar ⊟ AE, DC, MC, V $$$.

⭐ **LAKEWAY INN CONFERENCE RESORT.** This resort is on Lake Travis, about 20 mi from downtown Austin. Along with top-rated golf and tennis facilities, the resort offers myriad water activities, including boating. Some rooms have elegant chandeliers and fireplaces. ⊠ 101 Lakeway Dr., 78734 ☎ 512/261-6600 or 800/525-3929 ⎙ 512/261-7311 ⊕ www.lakewayinn.com ⤴ 239 rooms, 34 suites ⚫ Restaurant, room service, in-room data ports, some kitchenettes, cable TV, 2 pools, driving range, 5 18-hole golf courses, putting green, 26 tennis courts, hot tub, boating, marina, bar, playground, business services, airport shuttle ⊟ AE, D, DC, MC, V $$-$$$.

Where to Eat

✕ **BITTER END.** A polished, slightly industrial interior sets the stage for the cool crowd at this sleek brewpub. The semolina-fried calamari, wood-fired jerk-chicken pizza, and a revolving Mediterranean menu are all heightened by standout home-brewed ales. ⊠ 311 Colorado St., 78701 ☎ 512/478-2337 ⊟ AE, D, DC, MC, V ⊘ No lunch weekends $$-$$$$.

✕ **COUNTY LINE ON THE HILL.** This spot overlooks 20 mi of land belonging to the Barton Creek Resort & Country Club. You can dine outdoors on a semi-covered patio. Menu standouts include the barbecued meats, especially the baby back ribs, and the grilled salmon fillet. ⊠ 6500 W. Bee Cave Rd. ☎ 512/327-1742 ⊟ AE, D, DC, MC, V ⊘ No lunch $-$$$.

✕ **GÜEROS.** A former feed store, this restaurant has high ceilings, tall windows, a worn wood floor, and a rustic bar. After President Clinton ordered the Numero Dos (a Mexican plate including one tamale, one marinated chicken taco, one beef taco, guacamole, beans, and rice) during a visit to Austin, the dish was renamed El Presidente. The little *tacos al pastor* (marinated rotisserie-roasted pork with pineapple, cilantro, and onions) are stellar, and the fresh-lime margaritas justly famous. There's live music some nights. ⊠ 1412 S. Congress Ave., 78704 ☎ 512/447-7688 ⚖ Reservations not accepted ⊟ AE, D, DC, MC, V $-$$.

✕ **SHORELINE GRILL.** Right on the shoreline of Town Lake, this spot is popular for power lunches as well as romantic dinners. Floor-to-ceiling windows provide wonderful views of the lake, and candlelight and hardwood floors add to the elegant feel. It's known for prime rib, shark, and crème brûlée. Open-air dining is available on an enclosed patio with a view of the lake. ⊠ 98 San Jacinto Blvd. ☎ 512/477-3300 ⊟ AE, D, DC, MC, V ⊘ No lunch Sat. and Sun. $$$-$$$$.

Essentials

Getting Here

Houston is linked to the state capital by the hilly, four-lane blacktop of U.S. 290. It's a drive of 185 mi.

The major entryway into Austin is I-35, which links the city with Dallas/Fort Worth to the north, and San Antonio to the south. Loop 1 (also known to locals as MOPAC) joins with I-35 on the northern and southern outskirts of Austin, dispersing traffic to the west side of the city. U.S. 183 cuts through the city and provides access to the airport.

Visitor Information

🛈 **Austin Convention and Visitors Bureau** ✉ 201 E. 2nd St., 78701 ☏ 512/474–5171 or 800/926–2282 ⊕ www.austintexas.org. **Chamber of Commerce** ✉ 210 Barton Springs Rd., Suite 400, 78704 ☏ 512/478–9383 ⊕ www.austin-chamber.org.

BEAUMONT, TX & LAKE CHARLES, LA

The problem with residing in Texas is that you almost have to fly to go on vacation anywhere outside the Lone Star State. But Houston-area golfers are only 110 mi from Bayou Country and the Louisiana-Texas state line. Lake Charles, which is another 30 mi east of the border, may not be the first place that comes to mind when you think "golf trip," but when Lake Charles is combined with nearby Beaumont, it offers one of the best values for a golf foursome on the go. The area is easily accessible along I-10 and the terrain, though largely flat, has an Old South feel with tall oaks and water features aplenty. There is no resort to anchor the region, but there is plenty of golf within an hour's drive of wherever you decide to stay.

If you only visit one course, make it Gray Plantation. Opened in 1999, the course was immediately ranked among the top five in Louisiana and costs less than $50 to play. It's always in great condition and the level of service gives new meaning to the term "Southern hospitality."

Courses   **Golf** Digest REVIEWS

BAYOU DIN GOLF CLUB. Facility Holes: 27. Architect: Jimmy Witcher/Warren Howard. Green Fee: $13/$20. Cart Fee: $9 per person. Discounts: Weekdays, twilight, seniors, juniors. Walking: Unrestricted walking. Season: Year-round. Tee Times: Call 7 days in

Bayou Din Golf Club (27)					$13/$20
Bayou Back/Links Nine (18)	6,495/5,233	71/71	70.6/64.7	118/105	
Bayou Front/Bayou Back (18)	6,285/5,339	71/71	68.5/64.4	108/98	
Bayou Front/Links Nine (18)	7,020/5,672	72/72	72.1/66.1		
Belle Oaks Golf Club (18)	6,301/5,493	71/71	69.5/71.2	118/125	$20/$28
Gray Plantation Golf Club (18)	6,946/5,392	72/72	73.6/71.9	138/128	$24/$34
Mallard Cove Golf Course (18)	6,903/5,294	72/72	72.4/70.1	125/117	$10/$17
Pine Shadows Golf Center (18)	6,292/5,873	72/72	69.5/70.0	108/106	$10/$12

advance. Notes: Range (grass). ✉ 8537 LaBelle Rd., Beaumont 77705, 85 mi from Houston ☎ 409/796–1327 ▭ AE, D, MC, V.

Bayou Back/Links Nine. Holes: 18. Opened: 1959. Yards: 6,495/5,233. Par: 71/71. Course Rating: 70.6/64.7. Slope: 118/105.

Bayou Front/Bayou Back. Holes: 18. Opened: 1961. Yards: 6,285/5,339. Par: 71/71. Course Rating: 68.5/64.4. Slope: 108/98.

Bayou Front/Links Nine. Holes: 18. Opened: 1961. Yards: 7,020/5,672. Par: 72/72. Course Rating: 72.1/66.1. Slope: 116/103.

Comment: A great value. If you can only play 18 of the 27 holes, make sure Links Nine is on the docket. ★ ★ ★

BELLE OAKS GOLF CLUB. Facility Holes: 18. Opened: 1955. Architect: Ralph Plummer. Yards: 6,301/5,493. Par: 71/71. Course Rating: 69.5/71.2. Slope: 118/125. Green Fee: $20/$28. Cart Fee: Included in green fees. Discounts: Seniors. Walking: Unrestricted walking. Season: Year-round. Tee Times: Call golf shop. Notes: Range (grass). ✉ 15075 Country Club Rd., Beaumont 77705 ☎ 409/796–1311 ▭ MC, V. *Comments: Play here if you can't get on Bayou Din in Beaumont. Just basic golf. UR*

GRAY PLANTATION GOLF CLUB. Facility Holes: 18. Opened: 1999. Architect: Rocky Roquemore. Yards: 6,946/5,392. Par: 72/72. Course Rating: 73.6/71.9. Slope: 138/128. Green Fee: $24/$34. Cart Fee: $14 per person. Discounts: Twilight, seniors, juniors. Walking: Unrestricted walking. Season: Year-round. Tee Times: Call 2 days in advance. Notes: Range (grass). ✉ 6150 Graywood Pkwy., Lake Charles 70706, 125 mi from Houston ☎ 337/562–1663 ▭ AE, D, MC, V. *Comments: Worth building a golf vacation around. Part of the Audubon Golf Trail, Louisiana's answer to Alabama's Robert Trent Jones Golf Trail.* ★ ★ ★ ★ ½

MALLARD COVE GOLF COURSE. Facility Holes: 18. Opened: 1997. Architect: Kevin Tucker. Yards: 6,903/5,294. Par: 72/72. Course Rating: 72.4/70.1. Slope: 125/117. Green Fee: $10/$17. Cart Fee: $11 per person. Discounts: Weekdays, twilight, seniors, juniors. Walking: Unrestricted walking. Season: Year-round. High: Apr.–Oct. Tee Times: Call 2 days in advance. Notes: Range (grass). ✉ Chennault Air Base, Lake Charles 70602, 125 mi from Baton Rouge ☎ 318/491–1204 ▭ D, MC, V. *Comments: The city of Lake*

John James Audubon painted a number of his famous bird studies in the Bayou State. Fittingly, the nine courses that make up the Audubon Golf Trail are about more than golf: they are all members of the Audubon Cooperative Sanctuary for Golf Courses. This national program, offered by Audubon International, certifies courses that meet rigorous environmental criteria.

Charles's prize municipal golf course was renovated in 2001. A great complement to Gray Plantation. Golf in the shadows of a former Air Force base. ★ ★ ★

PINE SHADOWS GOLF CENTER. Facility Holes: 18. Opened: 1985. Yards: 6,292/5,873. Par: 72/72. Course Rating: 69.5/70.0. Slope: 108/106. Green Fee: $10/$12. Cart Fee: $9 per person. Discounts: Seniors. Walking: Unrestricted walking. Season: Year-round. High: May–July. Tee Times: Call golf shop. Notes: Metal spikes, range (grass). ⊠ 750 Goodman Rd., Lake Charles 70615. ☎ 337/433–8681 ⊕ www.swlaonline.com/pineshadows ⊟ AE, D, MC, V. *Comments: Golf on a budget. Nothing fancy but if you want to feel good about your golf game, you can go low on this shortish, flat course. UR*

Where to Stay

⛺ **HARRAH'S CASINO HOTEL.** An 8-acre tropical extravaganza set between the lake and I-10, this hotel/casino complex has waterfalls, rockscapes, Animatronic tropical birds perched hither and yon, and activity aplenty. Gambling is done on two paddle wheelers that cruise on Lake Charles. ⊠ 505 N. Lakeshore Dr., Lake Charles 70602 ☎ 337/437–1500 or 800/442–7724 ⧠ 337/437–6010 ⊕ www.casinocity.com ⇋ 264 rooms ♿ 5 restaurants, coffee shop, room service, pool, gym, 3 bars, lobby lounge, 2 casinos, video game room, airport shuttle, no-smoking rooms ⊟ AE, D, MC, V $–$$.

⛺ **ISLE OF CAPRI CASINO & HOTEL.** This complex has two floating gaming palaces, plus a grounded entertainment pavilion. Top-name performers appear in the Flamingo Bay Ballroom, which also hosts boxing matches. The modern, six-story, all-suites hotel has accommodations done in blond wood and pastels. ⊠ 101 Westlake Ave., Westlake 70669 ☎ 337/430–2400 or 888/475–3847 ⧠ 337/430–0963 ⊕ www.isleofcapricasino.com ⇋ 241 suites ♿ 3 restaurants, snack bar, room service, pool, 2 bars, lobby lounge, 2 casinos, nightclub, video game room, airport shuttle, no-smoking rooms ⊟ AE, D, MC, V $–$$.

Where to Eat

✕ **CAFÉ MARGAUX.** Think candlelight, soft pinks, white linens, tuxedoed waiters, and a 5,000-bottle mahogany wine cellar. Specialties include a marvelous lobster bisque, rack of lamb, good steaks, and roasted quail with raspberry demi-glace. ⊠ 765 Bayou

Pines E, Lake Charles ☎337/433-2902 🎩Jacket and tie 🖃AE, D, MC, V ⊘Closed Sun. $$$-$$$$.

✕STEAMBOAT BILL'S. In this busy, clattering country kitchen, you line up at the counter to place your order for fried, boiled, baked, or stuffed seafood platters. It couldn't be more casual. ⊠1004 Lakeshore Dr., Lake Charles ☎337/494-1070 🖃AE, D, MC, V $-$$.

Essentials

Getting Here
The drive to Lake Charles from Houston via I-10 takes about two hours.

Visitor Information
🛈 **Southwest Louisiana Convention and Visitors Bureau** ⊠1205 N. Lakeshore Dr., Lake Charles 70601 ☎337/436-9588 or 800/456-7952 ⊕ www.visitlakecharles.org.

SAN ANTONIO

Austin is often deemed the most scenic city in Texas, but San Antonio usually gets the nod for personality. From the Alamo to the River Walk to all the great Mexican restaurants, golfers often have the dilemma of trying to budget their time between playing some of the best public golf courses in the country and enjoying the city for its culture. Among the city's memorable courses are the 36 holes at the Westin La Cantera Resort (home of the PGA Tour's Valero Texas Open) and the quirky Brackenridge Park Municipal Golf Course, which was designed in 1916 by noted architect A. W. Tillinghast, of Winged Foot and Baltusrol fame. Brackenridge was once the site for the lowest tournament score in PGA Tour history due to Mike Souchak's 1955 score of 257 over 72 holes.

The terrain of the San Antonio area is varied: rugged in some spots, hilly in others, and parklike around town. And when Mother Nature didn't inspire, the architects did. Top-name designers were called in to convert once-rugged ranch lands into challenging courses of play that incorporate abandoned quarries, limestone landscapes, natural springs, and groves of oak and mesquite. For example, Keith Foster built the Quarry Golf Club inside and around an old limestone quarry.

Most of San Antonio's courses are north or west of the city center, taking advantage of the hilly terrain outside of town. Clubhouses and guest accommodations often incorporate mission-style architecture, echoing the

SAN ANTONIO COURSES	Yards	Par	Course Rating	Slope	Green Fee
Brackenridge Park (18)	6,185/5,216	72/72	70.1/69.2	122/112	$12/$21
Canyon Springs Golf Club (18)	7,077/5,234	72/72	72.8/70.0	130/115	$60/$99
Golf Club of Texas (18)	7,022/4,823	72/72	73.1/67.9	135/109	$35/$85
Hill Country Golf Club (18)	6,913/4,781	72/72	73.9/67.8	136/114	$125/$145
La Cantera Golf Club (36)					$55/$130
Palmer Course (18)	6,926/5,066	71/71	74.2/65.3	142/116	
Resort Course (18)	7,001/4,953	72/72	72.5/67.1	134/108	
Olympia Hills (18)	6,923/5,534	72/72	73.4/72.3	132/128	$40/$50
Pecan Valley Golf Club (18)	7,010/5,335	71/71	73.9/65.7	131/118	$75/$85
Quarry Golf Club (18)	6,740/4,897	71/71	72.4/67.4	128/115	$60/$79
Tapatio Springs Resort & Conference Center (27)					$80/$95
Lakes/Valley (18)	6,504/5,185	72/72	71.4/70.4	133/127	
Ridge/Lakes (18)	6,252/4,757	70/70	70.5/67.9	130/118	
Valley/Ridge (18)	6,500/5,122	72/72	71.7/70.2		

intense Spanish heritage of the region. Players love the climate, which seems to avoid the extremes of temperature found elsewhere in the state. One of the golfers who call San Antonio home is former British Open champ Bill Rogers, who teaches at the private Briggs Ranch Club.

Courses
Golf Digest REVIEWS

BRACKENRIDGE PARK MUNICIPAL GOLF COURSE. Facility Holes: 18. Opened: 1916. Architect: A. W. Tillinghast. Yards: 6,185/5,216. Par: 72/72. Course Rating: 70.1/69.2. Slope: 122/112. Green Fee: $12/$21. Cart Fee: $20 per cart. Discounts: Weekdays, twilight, seniors, juniors. Walking: Unrestricted walking. Season: Year-round. High: Mar.–Oct. Tee Times: Call golf shop. Notes: Metal spikes. ✉2315 Ave. B, 78215 ☎210/226-5612 ▭MC, V. *Comments: Some say Texas golf started at the Brack. It's easy and cheap—you gotta play it.* ★ ★ ★ ¹/₂

CANYON SPRINGS GOLF CLUB. Facility Holes: 18. Opened: 1998. Architect: Tom Walker. Yards: 7,077/5,234. Par: 72/72. Course Rating: 72.8/70.0. Slope: 130/115. Green Fee: $60/$99. Cart Fee: Included in green fee. Discounts: Weekdays, twilight, seniors, juniors. Walking: Mandatory cart. Season: Year-round. Tee Times: Call 7 days in advance. Notes: Range (grass). ✉24405 Wilderness Oak, 78258 ☎210/497-1770 or 888/800-1511 ▭AE, D, MC, V. *Comments: The 18th hole's waterfall is memorable. So are the roller-coaster greens.* ★ ★ ★ ★ ¹/₂

GOLF CLUB OF TEXAS. Facility Holes: 18. Opened: 1999. Architect: R. Bechtol/R. Russell/Lee Trevino. Yards: 7,022/4,823. Par: 72/72. Course Rating: 73.1/67.9. Slope: 135/

109. Green Fee: $35/$85. Cart Fee: Included in green fee. Discounts: Weekdays, twilight, seniors, juniors. Walking: Unrestricted walking. Season: Year-round. Tee Times: Call 30 days in advance. Notes: Range (grass), lodging (1). ⊠ 13600 Briggs Ranch, 78245 ☎ 210/677-0027 or 877/465-3839 ⊕ www.golfcluboftexas.com ▭ AE, D, DC, MC, V. *Comments: Lee Trevino's son Tony is director of instruction. Wind plays a key role in the course's difficulty, which is just the way Lee always liked it.* ★ ★ ★ ★

HILL COUNTRY GOLF CLUB. Facility Holes: 18. Opened: 1993. Architect: Arthur Hills. Yards: 6,913/4,781. Par: 72/72. Course Rating: 73.9/67.8. Slope: 136/114. Green Fee: $125/$145. Cart Fee: Included in green fee. Walking: Unrestricted walking. Season: Year-round. Tee Times: Call golf shop. ⊠ 9800 Hyatt Resort Dr., 78251 ☎ 210/520-4040 ⊕ - www.hillcountry.hyatt.com ▭ AE, D, DC, MC, V. *Comments: Decade-old Arthur Hills design. Because it's at the Hyatt Regency Hill Country Resort and Spa, you get great service along with pretty good golf.* ★ ★ ★ ★

LA CANTERA GOLF CLUB. Facility Holes: 36. Green Fee: $55/$130. Cart Fee: Included in green fee. Discounts: Weekdays, twilight, juniors. Walking: Unrestricted walking. Season: Year-round. Tee Times: Call 30 days in advance. Notes: Metal spikes, range (grass), lodging (508). ⊠ 16641 La Cantera Pkwy., 78256 ☎ 210/558-2365 or 800/446-5387 ⊕ www.lacanteragolfclub.com ▭ AE, D, DC, MC, V.

Palmer Course. Holes: 18. Opened: 2001. Architect: Arnold Palmer. Yards: 6,926/5,066. Par: 71/71. Course Rating: 74.2/65.3. Slope: 142/116. *Comments: Tons of blind shots, which is a downer. But you won't forget the striking 10th hole.* UR

Resort Course. Holes: 18. Opened: 1995. Architect: Tom Weiskopf/Jay Morrish. Yards: 7,001/4,953. Par: 72/72. Course Rating: 72.5/67.1. Slope: 134/108. *Comments: Overlooks the Six Flags Fiesta Texas theme park and plays host to the PGA Tour's Valero Texas Open. A lot of fun to play.* ★ ★ ★ ★ ½

OLYMPIA HILLS GOLF & CONFERENCE CENTER. Facility Holes: 18. Opened: 2000. Architect: Finger/Pete Dye/Spann. Yards: 6,923/5,534. Par: 72/72. Course Rating: 73.4/72.3. Slope: 132/128. Green Fee: $40/$50. Cart Fee: Included in green fee. Walking: Unrestricted. Season: Year-round. Tee Times: Call up to 7 days in advance. ⊠ 12900 Mount Olympus, Universal City 78148 ☎ 210/945-4653 ⊕ www.olympiahillsgolf.com ▭ AE, D, MC, V. *Comments: Not our first choice, but solid. In 2001 Golf Digest selected the course as one of the four best new affordable courses in the country.* UR

PECAN VALLEY GOLF CLUB. Facility Holes: 18. Opened: 1963. Architect: J. Press Maxwell. Yards: 7,010/5,335. Par: 71/71. Course Rating: 73.9/65.7. Slope: 131/118. Green Fee: $75/$85. Cart Fee: Included in green fee. Discounts: Weekdays, twilight, seniors, juniors. Walking: Unrestricted walking. Season: Year-round. Tee Times: Call 7 days in advance. Notes: Range (grass). ⊠ 4700 Pecan Valley Dr., 78223 ☎ 210/333-9018 ⊕ - www.thetexasgolftrail.com ▭ AE, D, DC, MC, V. *Comments: A classic, oak-lined, Texas golf course that's great for walkers.* ★ ★ ★ ★

QUARRY GOLF CLUB. Facility Holes: 18. Opened: 1993. Architect: Keith Foster. Yards: 6,740/4,897. Par: 71/71. Course Rating: 72.4/67.4. Slope: 128/115. Green Fee: $60/$79. Cart Fee: Included in green fee. Discounts: Twilight, juniors. Walking: Unrestricted walking. Season: Year-round. Tee Times: Call 30 days in advance. Notes: Metal spikes, range (grass). ✉444 E. Basse Rd., 78209 ☎210/824–4500 or 800/347–7759 ⊕www. quarrygolf.com ▤AE, D, DC, MC, V. *Comments: The front 9 is better than the back in terms of design, but the back gets all the attention because of the limestone quarry.* ★ ★ ★ ★

TAPATIO SPRINGS RESORT & CONFERENCE CENTER. Facility Holes: 27. Opened: 1980. Architect: Bill Johnston. Green Fee: $80/$95. Cart Fee: Included in green fee. Discounts: Weekdays, twilight, juniors. Walking: Mandatory cart. Season: Year-round. Tee Times: Call 7 days in advance. Notes: Range (grass, mat), lodging (123). ✉John's Rd. W, Boerne 78006, 25 mi from San Antonio ☎830/537–4611 or 800/999–3299 ⊕www. tapatio.com ▤AE, D, MC, V.

Lakes/Valley. Holes: 18. Yards: 6,504/5,185. Par: 72/72. Course Rating: 71.4/70.4. Slope: 133/127.

Ridge/Lakes. Holes: 18. Yards: 6,252/4,757. Par: 70/70. Course Rating: 70.5/67.9. Slope: 130/118.

Valley/Ridge. Holes: 18. Yards: 6,500/5,122. Par: 72/72. Course Rating: 71.7/70.2. Slope: 133/126.

Comments: The Ridge has plenty of blind shots and is not like any golf course you've ever played. Very strange. ★ ★ ★ ★

Where to Stay

🏨 **HYATT REGENCY HILL COUNTRY RESORT AND SPA.** On the western edge of the city, near Sea World, this sophisticated country resort occupies 200 acres on former ranch land. On the grounds is a 4-acre water park with a man-made river where you can go tubing. A restorative 21-room spa provides many services. ✉9800 Hyatt Dr., 78251 ☎210/647–1234 or 800/633–7313 🖷210/681–9681 ⊕ www.hillcountry.hyatt.com ⇥500 rooms, 57 suites ♿3 restaurants, 18-hole golf course, 3 tennis courts, 2 pools, health club, spa, bar ▤AE, D, DC, MC, V $$$$.

🏨 **MENGER HOTEL.** Since its 1859 opening, the Menger has lodged, among others, Robert E. Lee, Ulysses S. Grant, Theodore Roosevelt, Oscar Wilde, Sarah Bernhardt, and Roy Rogers and Dale Evans. There's a charming, three-story Victorian lobby, a sunny dining room, a flowered courtyard, and four-poster beds (in the oldest part of the hotel only). ✉204 Alamo Plaza, 78205 ☎210/223–4361 or 800/345–9285 🖷210/228–0022 ⊕ www.historicmenger.com ⇥291 rooms, 25 suites ♿Restaurant, bar, pool, gym, spa ▤AE, D, DC, MC, V $$$–$$$$.

🏨 **TAPATIO SPRINGS RESORT AND CONFERENCE CENTER.** This 1,800-acre spread 30 minutes' drive northwest of San Antonio captures the essence of the Hill Country with its limestone hills, sharp cliffs, and rocky streambeds. You're likely to see birds and wildlife on the 27-hole championship course, designed by Bobby Johnson. ✉Box 550, Boerne 78006 ☎830/537–4611 or 800/999–3299 🖷830/537–4611 ⊕-

www.tapatio.com 🛏 92 rooms, 20 suites, 40 condos ⚒ Restaurant, snack bar, cable TV, 3 9-hole golf courses, 2 tennis courts, pool, gym, hot tub, fishing, horseback riding 🚫 AE, D, DC, MC, V $$$–$$$$.

🏨 WESTIN LA CANTERA RESORT. The resort's name is derived from the Spanish word for rock or quarry, and indeed the area is rich in limestone. La Cantera's architecture is Spanish mission-style, with red-tile roofs, stone and stucco walls, and arched entryways, but the interior is more elegant, with slate floors, carved-wood furniture, and plush fabrics. Mark Miller of Santa Fe's notable Coyote Cafe helped conceive the resort's formal restaurant, Francesca's at Sunset. ✉ 16641 La Cantera Pkwy., 78256 ☎ 210/558-6500 or 800/937-8461 📠 210/558-2400 ⊕ www.westinlacantera.com 🛏 491 rooms, 17 suites ⚒ 3 restaurants, in-room data ports, refrigerators, cable TV, 2 18-hole golf courses, 6 pools, health club, 3 hot tubs, spa, 2 bars, some pets allowed (fee) 🚫 AE, D, DC, MC, V $$$$.

Where to Eat

✕ ANTLERS LODGE. Upscale dining with a rustic flair is what this restaurant does best. Its centerpiece is a huge chandelier with over 500 naturally shed pairs of antlers. The menu is known for rattlesnake fritters, buffalo shrimp, and 14-ounce New York strip steak. Try the chili-dusted ahi tuna steak. ✉ Hyatt Hill Country Resort, 9800 Hyatt Resort Dr. ☎ 210/520-4001 🚫 AE, D, DC, MC, V ⊗ Closed Mon. No lunch $$$–$$$$.

✕ BIGA. Chef-owner Bruce Auden's contemporary restaurant on the River Walk has a patio, a full bar, and a menu that will amaze you. Appetizers include Hudson Valley foie gras served with a maple waffle; and fried sweetbreads with bacon, spinach, sherry vinegar, goat cheese, and candied pecans. Entrées include phyllo-wrapped sea bass with creamy mustard leeks. ✉ 203 S. St. Mary's St. ☎ 210/225-0722 🚫 AE, D, DC, MC, V $$$–$$$$.

✕ COUNTY LINE BARBECUE. Texas is famous for its barbecued ribs, smoked brisket, and related fare, and this contender definitely holds its own among the competition. ✉ On the River Walk: 111 W. Crockett, Suite 104 ☎ 210/229-1941 ✉ 10101 I-10 W ☎ 210/641-1998 🚫 AE, D, DC, MC, V $–$$$.

✕ LA FONDA. This cheerful family-friendly restaurant, open since 1932, serves traditional Mexican fare, such as steak Tampiquena (grilled tenderloin strips with a green enchilada and charra beans), and a few Tex-Mex specialties as well. You'll get your money's worth with the Tex-Mex Deluxe: a 3-ounce tenderloin, oak-grilled and served with an enchilada, a beef taco, refried beans, and Spanish rice. ✉ 2415 N. Main Ave. ☎ 210/733-0621 🚫 AE, MC, V ⊗ No dinner Sun. $–$$.

✕ ZUNI GRILL. Given the choice between the warehouse-style interior and the patio with big shade umbrellas and a view of the river, pick the patio. The restaurant is known for its breakfast tacos, fajitas, and the Zuni Burger (served with white cheddar and onion bread). Try a cactus margarita—it's made with real prickly pear cactus juice. ✉ 511 River Walk St. ☎ 210/227-0864 ⊕ www.joesfood.com 🚫 AE, D, DC, MC, V $$$–$$$$.

Essentials

Getting Here

San Antonion is 200 mi from Houston and 275 mi from Dallas. Austin and Dallas are linked to San Antonio by I–35; Houston to the east by I–10. I–410 rings the city, with multiple access on major highways into Downtown.

Visitor Information

🔃 **San Antonio Convention & Visitors Bureau** ✉ 203 S. St. Mary's St., 78205 ✉ 317 Alamo Plaza, near the Alamo ☎ 210/207–6700 or 800/447–3372 ⊕ www. sanantoniocvb.com.

SHREVEPORT, LA

The drive from Houston to the military and industrial town of Shreveport is long and not particularly scenic, but for Houstonians who've been everywhere else, there are two golf courses in the Shreveport–Bossier City area worth a visit, plus a handful of others that can round out a long weekend.

Shreveport is home to major championship winners David Toms and Hal Sutton. The forests and hills of the area, in the northwest corner of Louisiana, are a pleasant change from the flat, almost sea-level courses around Houston. At night, the casinos along the Red River offer lively entertainment, and the adjacent hotels are the perfect headquarters for the trip.

The two must-play golf courses in the area are the Golf Club at StoneBridge, designed by Gene Bates and PGA Tour pro Fred Couples, and Olde Oaks Golf Club, which is part of Louisiana's Audubon Golf Trail. If you have an extra day on your schedule or want to play some golf on the way back to Houston, travel two hours south of Shreveport to Many, Louisiana, and play at Cypress Bend Golf Resort on massive Lake Toledo. It's also part of the Audubon Trail.

Courses   **Golf** Digest REVIEWS

BARKSDALE GOLF COURSE. Facility Holes: 18. Opened: 1999. Architect: Newgent. Yards: 5,904/5,075. Par: 70/71. Course Rating: 68.3/68.9. Slope: 118/113. Green Fee: $6/$18. Cart Fee: $13 per cart. Discounts: Twilight. Walking: Unrestricted walking. Season: Year-round. High: Apr.–Oct. Tee Times: Call golf shop. Notes: Range (grass). ✉ 185 Bossier Rd., Barksdale Air Force Base, 71110, 5 mi from Shreveport ☎318/456-2263 ▭MC, V. *Comments: This military course has regulations about who can play it. Call for details. UR*

Barksdale Golf Course (18)	5,904/5,075	70/71	68.3/68.9	118/113	$6/$18
Cypress Bend Golf Resort & Conference Center (18)	6,706/5,091	72/72	72.8/69.9	134/128	$55
Golf Club at StoneBridge (18)	6,954/5,456	72/72	74.0/65.3	148/108	$40/$50
Huntington Park Golf Course (18)	7,294/6,171	72/74	73.3/74.7	119/124	$10/$13
Olde Oaks Golf Club (27)					$40/$45
Cypress/Meadow (18)	7,200/5,100	72/72	74.8/69.2	130/107	
Oak/Cypress (18)	7,100/5,000	72/72	74.8/69.2	130/107	
Oak/Meadow (18)	7,200/5,100	72/72	74.3/69.3	134/111	
Querbes Park Golf Course (18)	6,207/5,360	71/71	69.0/70.0	118/110	$6/$13

CYPRESS BEND GOLF RESORT & CONFERENCE CENTER. Facility Holes: 18. Opened: 1999. Architect: Dave Bennett. Yards: 6,706/5,091. Par: 72/72. Course Rating: 72.8/69.9. Slope: 134/128. Green Fee: $55. Cart Fee: $15 per person. Discounts: Weekdays, seniors, juniors. Walking: Mandatory cart. Season: Year-round. High: Mar.–Nov. Tee Times: Call golf shop. Notes: Range (grass), lodging (98). ⊠2000 Cypress Bend Pkwy., Many 71449, 45 mi from Natchitoches ☎318/256–0346 or 888/256–4366 ⊟AE, D, DC, MC, V. *Comments: The course has 10 holes along Lake Toledo and is incredibly scenic. Take our word for it: go out of your way to play here on the way to or from Houston.* ★ ★ ★ ★

GOLF CLUB AT STONEBRIDGE. Facility Holes: 18. Opened: 1999. Architect: Gene Bates/Fred Couples. Yards: 6,954/5,456. Par: 72/72. Course Rating: 74.0/65.3. Slope: 148/108. Green Fee: $40/$50. Cart Fee: $11 per person. Discounts: Seniors, juniors. Walking: Unrestricted walking. Season: Year-round. Tee Times: Call 7 days in advance. Notes: Range (grass). ⊠301 StoneBridge Blvd., Bossier City 71111, 200 mi from Dallas ☎318/ 747–2004 ⊕www.stonebridgegolf.org ⊟AE, MC, V. *Comments: Bring a few sleeves of balls. There are tight, tree-lined fairways and lots of water, as though Fred Couples were designing the course for himself. Still, it's a great course. UR*

HUNTINGTON PARK GOLF COURSE. Facility Holes: 18. Opened: 1969. Architect: Tommy Moore. Yards: 7,294/6,171. Par: 72/74. Course Rating: 73.3/74.7. Slope: 119/124. Green Fee: $10/$13. Cart Fee: $8 per person. Discounts: Weekdays, twilight, seniors, juniors. Walking: Unrestricted walking. Season: Year-round. High: Apr.–Oct. Tee Times: Call up to 2 days in advance. Notes: Metal spikes, range (grass). ⊠8300 Pines Rd., 71129 ☎318/673–7765 ⊟MC, V. *Comments: Third-best area option (after StoneBridge and Olde Oaks), with some solid holes.* ★ ★ ¹/₂

OLDE OAKS GOLF CLUB. Facility Holes: 27. Opened: 1999. Architect: Kevin Tucker/Hal Sutton. Green Fee: $40/$45. Cart Fee: Included in green fee. Discounts: Twilight. Walking: Walking at certain times. Season: Year-round. Tee Times: Call 7 days in advance. Notes: Range (grass). ⊠60 Golf Club Dr., Haughton 71037, 3 mi from Bossier City ☎318/742–0333 ⊕www.oldeoaksgolf.com ⊟AE, D, MC, V.

Cypress/Meadow. Holes: 18. Yards: 7,200/5,100. Par: 72/72. Course Rating: 74.8/69.2. Slope: 130/107.

Oak/Cypress. Holes: 18. Yards: 7,100/5,000. Par: 72/72. Course Rating: 74.8/69.2. Slope: 130/107.

Oak/Meadow. Holes: 18. Yards: 7,200/5,100. Par: 72/72. Course Rating: 74.3/69.3. Slope: 134/111.

Comments: The 27-hole course is the first designed by Shreveport native Hal Sutton, with help from Kevin Tucker. Very pretty. UR

QUERBES PARK GOLF COURSE. Facility Holes: 18. Opened: 1922. Yards: 6,207/5,360. Par: 71/71. Course Rating: 69.0/70.0. Slope: 118/110. Green Fee: $6/$13. Cart Fee: $16 per cart. Discounts: Weekdays, twilight, juniors, seniors. Walking: Unrestricted walking. Season: Year-round. Tee Times: Call golf shop. Notes: Range (grass, mat). ⊠ 3500 Beverly Pl., 71104 ☏ 318/673-7773 ▤ MC, V. *Comments: Local municipal course. Not very memorable. David Toms grew up playing here.* ★ ½

Where to Stay

▓ **HORSESHOE HOTEL & CASINO.** With 26 stories and a $204 million investment, this all-suites hotel is just plain huge. Enormous crystal chandeliers hang over the sleek lobby. Suites have king-size beds, marble baths, and many small luxuries; there's even a TV in the bathroom. ⊠ 711 Horseshoe Blvd., Bossier City 71111 ☏ 318/742-0711 or 800/895-0711 ▤ 318/741-7870 ⊕ www.horseshoe.com ⇆ 606 suites ⟡ 5 restaurants, in-room data ports, cable TV, pool, health club, hair salon, lobby lounge, casino, nightclub, shop ▤ AE, D, DC, MC, V $$-$$$.

▓ **ISLE OF CAPRI HOTEL & CASINO.** Indoor waterfalls and palm trees in the casi-no area bring the tropics to mind. All accommodations are luxury suites with whirlpool baths. ⊠ 711 Isle of Capri Blvd., Bossier City 71111 ☏ 318/678-7777 or 800/843-4753 ▤ 318/262-6822 ⊕ www.isleofcapricasino.com ⇆ 310 suites ⟡ 3 restaurants, room service, in-room data ports, cable TV, pool, gym, lobby lounge, casino, nightclub, video game room, shop, baby-sitting ▤ AE, D, DC, MC, V $-$$$.

▓ **SHERATON SHREVEPORT HOTEL.** This hotel is near the convention center, so it caters to a mostly business clientele. Every room has a wet bar, a refrigerator, three phones, and a modem line. ⊠ 1419 E. 70th St., 71105 ☏ 318/797-9900 or 800/325-3535 ▤ 318/798-2923 ⊕ www.sheraton.com ⇆ 231 rooms ⟡ Restaurant, room serv-ice, in-room data ports, cable TV, pool, health club, laundry service, business services, car rental ▤ AE, D, DC, MC, V $-$$.

Where to Eat

✕ **JACK BINION'S STEAKHOUSE.** Two-fisted steaks are served at this handsome, always-busy restaurant in the Horseshoe Hotel. The Binion name is synonymous with Mississippi riverfront gaming. ⊠ 711 Horseshoe Blvd., Bossier City ☏ 318/742-0711 or 800/895-0711 ⟡ Reservations essential ▤ AE, D, DC, MC, V ✆ No lunch $$$-$$$$.

✕ **MONSIEUR PATOU.** Expect crystal and candlelight at this small, prix-fixe restau-rant. Classic French cuisine is represented by such dishes as roast duck, and lamb medal-

lions with *herbes de Provence* and sherry. ⊠855 Pierremont Rd. ☎318/868–9822
⌖ Reservations essential ▭AE, D, DC, MC, V $$$–$$$$.

✕ **SUPERIOR'S STEAKHOUSE.** Even with a reservation you may have to hang out in
the bar to wait for a table, but the fine mesquite-grilled steaks and the iced seafood
tower served here are worth the wait. ⊠6123 Line Ave. ☎318/869–3243 ▭AE, D, MC,
V $–$$$.

Essentials

Getting Here

Shreveport is a straight shot from Dallas on I–20. It takes about four hours to make the
trip by car. I–20 and U.S. 80 run east–west through the northern part of the state;
Route 1 cuts diagonally from the northwest corner to the Gulf of Mexico; I–49 connects Shreveport with southern Louisiana. Other north–south routes are U.S. 171, 71,
165, and 167.

You can also fly here from Dallas in about an hour.

🚹 AIRPORT INFORMATION **Shreveport Regional Airport** ☎318/673–5370.

Visitor Information

🚹 **Shreveport-Bossier Convention & Tourist Bureau** ⊠629 Spring St., 71166 ☎318/
222–9391 or 888/458–4748 🖷318/222–0056 ⊕ www.shreveport-bossier.org.

THE WOODLANDS &
MONTGOMERY COUNTY

If you want to get out of town but don't want to drive far, you can reach
most of the courses in this area in less than an hour from downtown Houston.
The area along I–45 north of Houston has enjoyed a golf boom in recent years
and has some outstanding places to stay as well. It's the quintessential white-
collar suburbia with shopping malls, tree-lined streets, and low crime—a nice
change from the flat, treeless confines of inner-city Houston.

The area's centerpiece is the Woodlands Resort in a town called the
Woodlands. The two courses there, TPC and the Pines course, are both
outstanding, and the TPC course is the site of the PGA Tour's annual Shell
Houston Open. Use the Woodlands as a starting point and continue north to
worthwhile courses like Wedgewood Golf Club in Conroe, Fish Creek Golf
Club and the Del Lago Golf Resort in Montgomery, and Texas National Golf

Augusta Pines Golf Club (18)	7,041/5,606	72/72	73.6/72.8	125/121	$45/$79
Del Lago Golf Resort (18)	6,794/5,180	72/72	72.6/71.7	131/122	$35/$45
Fish Creek Golf Club (18)	6,834/5,293	72/72	73.4/72.8	130/127	$30/$79
Lake Windcrest Golf Club (18)	6,574/5,030	72/72	71.0/69.6	128/117	$23/$59
Texas National Golf Club (18)	6,313/4,964	72/72	69.1/68.5	121/122	$20/$49
Wedgewood Golf Club (18)	6,817/5,071	72/72	73.7/69.6	134/128	$20/$45
Woodlands Resort (36)					
Pines (18)	7,004/5,614	72/72	72.2/72.1	126/120	$49/$69
TPC at the Woodlands (18)	7,018/5,326	72/72	73.7/72.1	136/128	$90/$130

Club in Willis. Near the Woodlands is another course with a familiar name: Augusta Pines Golf Club. Designed by the creators of Tour 18, this course has many holes inspired by the Augusta National Golf Club in Georgia. But legally, they can't tell you that.

Courses

GolfDigest REVIEWS

AUGUSTA PINES GOLF CLUB. Facility Holes: 18. Opened: 2001. Yards: 7,041/5,606. Par: 72/72. Course Rating: 73.6/72.8. Slope: 125/121. Green Fee: $45/$79. Cart Fee: Included in green fee. Discounts: Weekdays, twilight, juniors. Season: Year-round. Tee Times: Call 5 days in advance. Notes: Range (grass). ⊠ 18 Augusta Pines Dr., Spring 77389 ☎ 832/831-1000 ⊕ www.augustapinesgolf.com. *Comments: Right on the Montgomery County/Harris County line and near The Woodlands. Finishes with back-to-back island greens. UR*

DEL LAGO GOLF RESORT. Facility Holes: 18. Opened: 1985. Architect: Dave Marr/Jay Riviere. Yards: 6,794/5,180. Par: 72/72. Course Rating: 72.6/71.7. Slope: 131/122. Green Fee: $35/$45. Cart Fee: Included in green fee. Discounts: Weekdays, twilight, seniors, juniors. Walking: Walking at certain times. Season: Year-round. Tee Times: Call golf shop. Notes: Range (grass, mat). ⊠ 600 Del Lago Blvd., Montgomery 77356, 50 mi from Houston ☎ 936/582-7570 or 800/335-5246 ⊕ www.dellago.com ⊟ AE, D, MC, V. *Comments: The 6th hole gets attention because of its waterfall. A good solid course and another option for lodging if the Woodlands Resort is full.* ★ ★ ★ ½

FISH CREEK GOLF CLUB. Facility Holes: 18. Opened: 2001. Architect: Steve Elkington. Yards: 6,834/5,293. Par: 72/72. Course Rating: 73.4/72.8. Slope: 130/127. Green Fee: $30/$79. Cart Fee: Included in green fee. Discounts: Twilight, seniors, juniors. Walking: Unrestricted walking. Season: Year-round. Tee Times: Call golf shop. Notes: Metal spikes, range (grass). ⊠ 6201 Mulligan Dr., Montgomery 77316, 30 mi from Houston ☎ 936/588-8800 ⊟ AE, MC, V. *Comments: Great value and one of the area's best-kept secrets. PGA Tour pro Steve Elkington's design is fun to play. UR*

LAKE WINDCREST GOLF CLUB. Facility Holes: 18. Opened: 2001. Architect: Thomas E. Walker. Yards: 6,574/5,030. Par: 72/72. Course Rating: 71.0/69.6. Slope: 128/117. Green Fee: $23/$59. Cart Fee: Included in green fee. Discounts: Weekdays, twilight, seniors, juniors. Walking: Unrestricted walking. Season: Year-round. Tee Times: Call golf shop. Notes: Range (grass). ✉ 10941 Clubhouse Circle, Magnolia 77354 ☎ 281/259-2279 ⊕ www.lakewindcrestgolf.com ⊟ AE, MC, V. *Comments: Despite its name, not a traditional lakeside course. Still, a solid golf course and a good value under $60 per round. UR*

TEXAS NATIONAL GOLF CLUB. Facility Holes: 18. Opened: 1977. Architect: Jack Miller. Yards: 6,313/4,964. Par: 72/72. Course Rating: 69.1/68.5. Slope: 121/122. Green Fee: $20/$49. Cart Fee: Included in green fee. Discounts: Seniors. Walking: Walking at certain times. Season: Year-round. Tee Times: Call golf shop. Notes: Metal spikes, range (grass). ✉ 8720 Clubhouse Dr., Willis 77378 ☎ 936/856-4233 ⊟ AE, D, MC, V. *Comments: Remodeled in 1997. Solid, scenic course. UR*

WEDGEWOOD GOLF CLUB. Facility Holes: 18. Opened: 1988. Architect: Ron Prichard. Yards: 6,817/5,071. Par: 72/72. Course Rating: 73.7/69.6. Slope: 134/128. Green Fee: $20/$45. Cart Fee: Included in green fee. Discounts: Weekdays, twilight, seniors, juniors. Walking: Unrestricted walking. Season: Year-round. High: Mar.–Aug. Tee Times: Call golf shop. Notes: Range (grass, mat). ✉ 5454 Hwy. 105 W, Conroe 77304, 35 mi from Houston ☎ 936/441-4653 ⊕ www.wedgewoodgolfclub.com ⊟ AE, DC, MC, V. *Comments: Tall trees squeeze the fairways. The topography is somewhat hilly for the Houston area.* ★★★

WOODLANDS RESORT & COUNTRY CLUB. Facility Holes: 36. Discounts: Weekdays, twilight, juniors. Season: Year-round. High: Apr.–June. Tee Times: Call golf shop. Notes: Range (grass, mat), lodging (400). ✉ 2301 N. Millbend Dr., The Woodlands 77380, 25 mi from Houston ☎ 281/364-6440 ⊕ www.woodlandsresort.com ⊟ AE, D, DC, MC, V.

Pines. Holes: 18. Opened: 1976. Architect: Joe Lee/Ray Case. Yards: 7,004/5,614. Par: 72/72. Course Rating: 72.2/72.1. Slope: 126/120. Green Fee: $49/$69. Cart Fee: $14 per person. Walking: Walking at certain times. *Comments: If you like bunkers, you'll love this course. The designers also did courses at Walt Disney World.* ★★★★

TPC at the Woodlands. Holes: 18. Opened: 1985. Architect: Robert von Hagge/Bruce Devlin. Yards: 7,018/5,326. Par: 72/72. Course Rating: 73.7/72.1. Slope: 136/128. Green Fee: $90/$130. Cart Fee: Included in green fee. Walking: Unrestricted walking. *Comments: The 17th and 18th holes are two of the best finishing holes in Texas. Build your golf trip around this course. Watch out for the water!* ★★★★ ½

Where to Stay

🏨 **RESIDENCE INN–WOODLANDS I & II.** The Marriott chain has two properties in this popular business and resort area. All-suites accommodations come with ample work areas and fully equipped kitchens. The golf courses in Spring are 10 mi away. ✉ 1040 Lake Front Circle, The Woodlands 75380 ☎ 281/292-3252 or 800/331-3131 🖷 281/292-3252 ✉ 9333 Six Pines Dr., 75380 ☎ 281/419-1542 or 800/331-3131 🖷 281/

419–6824 ⊕ www.residenceinn.com ⟿ Woodlands I: 90 suites; Woodlands II: 96 suites
⟳ In-room data ports, cable TV, pool, gym, hot tub, some pets allowed (fee) ⊟ AE, D,
DC, MC, V $–$$.

⊡ **WOODLANDS RESORT & CONFERENCE CENTER.** This lakefront lodge is on
acres of manicured lawns, creating a quiet and lovely retreat with many amenities. The
Samsung World Championship is held here. ⊠ 2301 N. Millbend St., The Woodlands
77380 ☎ 281/367–1100 or 800/433–2624 ⊞ 281/364–6345 ⊕ www.woodlandsresort.
com ⟿ 402 rooms, 88 suites ⟳ 4 restaurants, room service, in-room data ports, cable
TV, 2 driving ranges, 36-hole golf course, 3 putting greens, 21 tennis courts, 5 pools,
health club, hair salon, hot tub, massage, spa, bicycles, billiards, hiking, bar, recreation
room, business services, airport shuttle, free parking ⊟ AE, D, DC, MC, V $$–$$$$.

Where to Eat

✕ **GLASS MENAGERIE.** Of the four dining options at the Woodlands Resort, this is
the finest. The view of Lake Harrison through oversize windows is complemented by the
natural tree line and golf course. Inside, the contemporary interior repeats the greens
and golds of the landscape. American favorites are grilled and baked with creative flair
here. Your appetizer might be a yellowfin tuna carpaccio or duck-and-foie-gras
dumplings. Entrées include grilled sturgeon with potato-fennel hash and roast loin of
lamb served on a tomato risotto. ⊠ 2301 N. Millbend St., The Woodlands 77380 ☎ 281/
364–6326 ⊟ AE, DC, MC, V $$$$.

✕ **LANDRY'S.** Look for the signature movie-marquee entrance and you'll probably find
folks lined up for a table at this Houston-based chain serving megaplatters of shrimp,
fish, and seafood. The menu is heavy on the fried side, but there are lots of grill and
broiler options, too. It's a casual, laid-back place where a pitcher of beer and a bucket of
peel-and-eat shrimp are the classic starters. ⊠ 1212 Lake Robbins Dr., The Woodlands
77380 ☎ 281/367–3773 ⊟ AE, DC, MC, V $–$$$.

Essentials

Getting Here
The Woodlands is 30 mi north of Houston via I-45.

Visitor Information
🚩 **Greater Houston Convention & Visitors Bureau** ⊠ 901 Bagby St., Houston 77002
☎ 713/437–5200 or 800/446–8786 ⊕ www.houston-guide.com.

AROUND
LOS ANGELES

La Quinta Resort & Club

Matthew Rudy and Bobbi Zane

The first 25 years of the 1900s were golden for

golf course design. While Pine Valley and the National Golf Links were capturing golfers' imaginations in the East, George Thomas was building in Los Angeles what many still consider three of the four best golf courses in California: the Los Angeles, Bel Air, and Riviera country clubs. That was just the start of the uninterrupted decades-long love affair Los Angeles has had for the game—in both its public and private incarnations.

The city has always been well represented in tournament golf—both with host courses and local professionals who made good. Ben Hogan won the 1948 U.S. Open—and the 1947 and 1948 L.A. Opens—at Riviera, which understandably became known as Hogan's Alley. Riviera also played host to the 1983 and 1995 PGA Championships, won by Hal Sutton and Steve Elkington, respectively. Riviera and the Los Angeles, Hillcrest, and Wilshire country clubs have all been L.A. Open tournament sites since the event began in 1926.

TIGER'S L.A. ROOTS

Tiger Woods grew up playing Navy Golf Course in Long Beach. His parents still own his childhood home in nearby Cypress and plan to turn it into a museum.

The courses in metro Los Angeles may be engrossing, but if you look farther afield you'll find plenty of other temptations. The city is the perfect jumping-off point for many weekend destinations. Just make sure you wait to leave after the traffic dies down. Those interested in pulsating nightlife and beating the odds can make the deceptively quick (but boring) drive across the desert to Las Vegas. After you spend the day playing on a Vegas course, you can head to a fine restaurant and then a Broadway-caliber show when night comes. On the other end of the adrenaline spectrum, Ojai and Santa Barbara cater to those who want some pampering—and peace and quiet—to go with the golf. Meanwhile, the Palm Springs area has drawn generations of celebrity golfers eastward, and is a must-visit for those determined to play holes they've seen on television. For the hard-core equipment junkie, the drive south to Carlsbad, headquarters of both Callaway and TaylorMade, is a must. The sun-splashed strip of oceanfront south of Los Angeles is famous for its incredible weather—all the way from Carlsbad down to the Mexican border. If it's beaches you crave, keep going down to the San Diego area, which has a dozen of the nation's best. At Torrey Pines, you can even see them from the course.

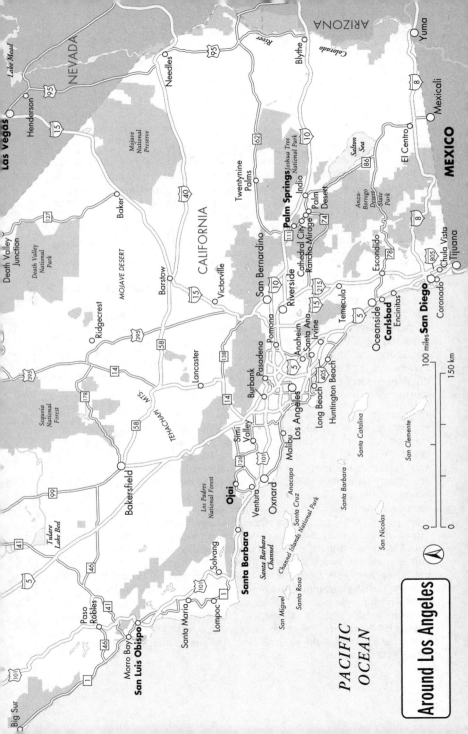

Around Los Angeles

CARLSBAD

Believe it or not, Carlsbad really is the center of golf universe, at least when it comes to equipment. The world headquarters of both Callaway and TaylorMade are just a long par-5 from each other in an office park near the Carlsbad airport, right up the road from a host of smaller golf-related companies, like Ashworth. It's only fitting that a place with so many golf-and-business visitors has some terrific places to play. The luxurious Four Seasons Resort Aviara is strategically located near Callaway and TaylorMade, and has an equally luxe Four Seasons hotel to go along with it. Also in the area is the venerable La Costa Resort & Spa, a longtime PGA Tour stop. Daily-fee courses complement the resorts, ranging from the posh Tom Fazio-designed Meadows Del Mar to the more egalitarian Encinitas Ranch Golf Club, which takes great advantage of its coastal hillside location. After your game is over, take a leisurely drive down the coast through Encinitas and Del Mar; the sunsets here are magnificent—and so are the fish tacos.

Courses   **Golf**Digest REVIEWS

ENCINITAS RANCH GOLF CLUB. Facility Holes: 18. Opened: 1998. Architect: Cary Bickler. Yards: 6,523/5,235. Par: 72/72. Course Rating: 71.2/70.3. Slope: 127/118. Green Fee: $50/$75. Cart Fee: $12 per person. Discounts: Twilight, juniors. Walking: Unrestricted walking. Season: Year-round. Tee Times: Call 7 days in advance. Notes: Range (grass, mat). ✉ 1275 Quail Gardens Dr., Encinitas 92024, 22 mi from San Diego ☎ 760/944-1936 ⊕ www.jcgolf.com ☰ AE, D, DC, MC, V. *Comments: Sits high on a hill overlooking the ocean. A good value.* ★★★★

FOUR SEASONS RESORT AVIARA. Facility Holes: 18. Opened: 1991. Architect: Arnold Palmer/Ed Seay. Yards: 7,007/5,007. Par: 72/72. Course Rating: 74.2/69.3. Slope: 137/127. Green Fee: $175/$215. Cart Fee: Included in green fee. Discounts: Twilight, juniors. Walking: Mandatory cart. Season: Year-round. High: June–Aug. Tee Times: Call 30 days in advance. Notes: Range (grass, mat), lodging (329). ✉ 7447 Batiquitos Dr., 92009 ☎ 760/603-6900 ☰ AE, D, DC, MC, V. *Comments: This is the definition of solitude. Each hole sits in its own private enclave, isolated from the rest. You may feel like the only person on the course.* ★★★★ ½

LA COSTA RESORT & SPA. Facility Holes: 36. Opened: 1964. Green Fee: $90/$195. Cart Fee: Included in green fee. Discounts: Guest, twilight. Walking: Walking with caddie.

Encinitas Ranch Golf Club (18)	6,523/5,235	72/72	71.2/70.3	127/118	$50/$75
Four Seasons Resort Aviara (18)	7,007/5,007	72/72	74.2/69.3	137/127	$175/$215
La Costa Resort & Spa (36)					$90/$195
North (18)	7,021/5,939	72/73	74.8/76.3	137/137	
South (18)	7,004/5,612	72/74	74.4/74.2	138/134	

Season: Year-round. Tee Times: Call golf shop. Notes: Range (grass), lodging (400). ⌧ Costa Del Mar Rd., 92009 ☎ 760/438-9111 ⊕ www.lacosta.com ▤ AE, D, DC, MC, V.

North. Holes: 18. Architect: Dick Wilson/Joe Lee. Yards: 7,021/5,939. Par: 72/73. Course Rating: 74.8/76.3. Slope: 137/137. *Comments: Play the same course as the pros do at the Mercedes Championship and World Match Play.* ★ ★ ★ ★

South. Holes: 18. Architect: Dick Wilson. Yards: 7,004/5,612. Par: 72/74. Course Rating: 74.4/74.2. Slope: 138/134. *Comments: The slightly easier of the two. Usually in better shape since it gets less play.* ★ ★ ★ ★ ¹/₂

Where to Stay

▦ **CARLSBAD INN BEACH RESORT.** Set on a wide landscaped lawn in the center of town, this inn and time-share condo complex milks some of the conventions of the picturesque: gabled rooflines and half-timbering. Rooms vary in size but all are traditionally furnished, with pencil-point beds and wing chairs; some rooms have fireplaces. The beach is a short walk away. ⌧ 3075 Carlsbad Blvd., 92008 ☎ 760/434-7020 or 800/235-3939 ⊕ 760/729-4853 ⊕ www.carlsbadinn.com ↵ 61 rooms, 1 suite ⚘ Some kitchenettes, refrigerators, cable TV, in-room VCRs, pool, exercise equipment, outdoor hot tub, laundry facilities, business services, no-smoking rooms ▤ AE, D, DC, MC, V $$$-$$$$.

▦ **FOUR SEASONS RESORT AVIARA.** This 30-acre hilltop resort overlooking Batiquitos Lagoon, a wildlife preserve, is one of the most luxurious in the San Diego area, with gleaming marble corridors, original artwork, crystal chandeliers, and enormous flower arrangements. Rooms have every possible amenity: oversize closets, private balconies or garden patios, and marble bathrooms with double vanities and deep soaking tubs. ⌧ 7100 Four Seasons Point, 92009 ☎ 760/603-6800 or 800/332-3442 ⊕ 760/603-6878 ⊕ www.fourseasons.com/aviara ↵ 285 rooms, 44 suites ⚘ 4 restaurants, room service, in-room data ports, in-room safes, minibars, cable TV with movies, 18-hole golf course, 6 tennis courts, 3 pools, health club, 2 outdoor hot tubs, massage, sauna, spa, steam room, bicycles, hiking, volleyball, shops, baby-sitting, children's programs (ages 4-12), laundry service, concierge, business services, meeting room, airport shuttle, car rental, some pets allowed (fee) ▤ AE, D, DC, MC, V $$$$.

▦ **INN AT RANCHO SANTA FE.** This genteel old resort fits in perfectly with the Spanish colonial town of Rancho Santa Fe, 15 mi south of Carlsbad. Guest rooms are in red-tiled cottages spread around the property's 20 lushly landscaped acres. Many have private patios and wood-burning fireplaces. The inn also maintains a beach house at Del

HOGAN'S RETURN

Ben Hogan won the 1948 U.S. Open at Riviera Country Club, as well as the 1947 and 1948 L.A. Opens that were held there, inspiring the golf world to nickname the course "Hogan's Alley." But it was the 1950 L.A. Open that provided the most memorable Hogan moment of all. Returning to golf after a near-fatal car accident only 12 months earlier, Hogan scraped together enough game to force a playoff with Sam Snead. He lost, but his gritty comeback touched the hearts of many, serving notice that Ben Hogan was still a force to be reckoned with.

Mar for guest use and has membership at the Rancho Santa Fe Golf Club and privileges at five other nearby courses. ✉ 5951 Linea del Cielo, Rancho Santa Fe 92067 ☎ 858/756-1131 or 800/843-4661 🖷 858/759-1604 ⊕ www.theinnatrsf.com ⇨ 73 rooms, 5 suites, 13 cottages ⟁ Dining room, room service, in-room data ports, in-room safes, some kitchens, minibars, microwaves, cable TV, 3 tennis courts, pool, exercise equipment, croquet, bar, meeting room, free parking, some pets allowed; no smoking ▭ AE, DC, MC, V $$$-$$$$.

🎇 **LA COSTA RESORT AND SPA.** This famous resort is surprisingly low-key, a collection of low-slung buildings on more than 100 tree-shaded acres. Large rooms, totally redecorated in a major renovation in 2003–2004, have a traditional look with lots of wood and gleaming marble. The resort, famed for its spa, is also the home of the Deepak Chopra Center. There are two PGA Championship golf courses and the U.S. Golf Fitness Association offers daily sports training year-round. ✉ 2100 Costa del Mar Rd., 92009 ☎ 760/438-9111 or 800/854-5000 🖷 760/931-7569 ⊕ www.lacosta.com ⇨ 397 rooms, 82 suites ⟁ Restaurant, café, room service, in-room data ports, cable TV, driving range, 2 18-hole golf courses, 21 tennis courts, pro shop, 5 pools, health club, hair salon, hot tub, massage, sauna, spa, steam room, bicycles, croquet, hiking, bar, shops, baby-sitting, children's programs (ages 5–12), laundry service, concierge, business services, meeting rooms, airport shuttle, car rental; no smoking ▭ AE, D, DC, MC, V $$$$.

🎇 **PELICAN COVE INN.** Two blocks from the beach and surrounded by palm trees, this two-story bed-and-breakfast has spacious rooms with gas fireplaces, feather beds, and private entrances. Each has a different look: yours might have a four-poster bed or a window seat. ✉ 320 Walnut Ave., 92008 ☎ 888/735-2683 🖷 760/434-7649 ⊕ - www.pelican-cove.com ⇨ 10 rooms ⟁ Cable TV; no phones in some rooms ▭ AE, MC, V ⑩ BP $-$$$.

Where to Eat

✗ **BELLEFLEUR WINERY AND RESTAURANT.** Tuscan-inspired archways and photographs of vineyards complement white tablecloths at this stylish spot with stunning views of the adjacent stretches of ranunculus and roses in Carlsbad's Flower Fields. The menu lists locally farmed Carlsbad mussels, wood-fired duck breast glazed with pomegranate molasses, and black tiger shrimp pasta. ⊠ 5610 Paseo Del Norte ☎ 760/603–1919 ⊟ AE, D, DC, MC, V $$–$$$$.

✕ **CAFE SEVILLA.** You won't lack for choice here—there's a lengthy list of tapas, plus an equally extensive dinner menu with traditional favorites such as paella, roasted leg of lamb with wine sauce and olives, and baked rabbit with rosemary and thyme. The restaurant often buzzes with music and dancing. ⊠ 3050 Pio Pico Dr. ☎ 760/730–7558 ⊟ AE, D, DC, MC, V ⊘ No lunch $$–$$$$.

✕ **NEIMAN'S.** Tables line the walls in a carousel-like manner in this round 1922 Victorian dining room. Views of downtown and the beach fill the picture windows. The menu sticks to classics like prime rib, rack of lamb, and salmon crusted with macadamias. Live music, from blues to salsa, keeps things humming. ⊠ 300 Carlsbad Village Dr. ☎ 760/729–4131 ⊟ AE, D, DC, MC, V $$–$$$$.

Essentials

Getting Here

Carlsbad is 100 mi south of Los Angeles via I-5 from downtown Los Angeles. Driving time is about two hours, but traffic congestion frequently extends that time. The coastal highway, which goes by different names between Los Angeles and San Diego, may sound appealing, but it's often a stop-and-start, traffic-clogged drive most of the way.

Visitor Information

🚩 **Carlsbad Convention and Visitors Bureau** ⊠ 400 Carlsbad Village Dr., 92008 ☎ 760/434–6093 or 800/227–5722 ⊕ www.visitcarlsbad.com.

LAS VEGAS, NV

In years past, the casino and resort managers in Vegas did everything they could to *stop* you from playing golf. After all, that meant five hours you and your buddies weren't spending on the casino floor. But finally, the developers have come to understand that if you build places like the Lake Las Vegas and Las Vegas Paiute resorts, people will come for the golf and leave some money at the casinos as well. The only barrier to golf in Las Vegas is immediately obvious as you get anywhere near the city: the natural environment. This is high desert territory, and it takes some serious cash to keep a wide swaths of fairway green. That puts green fees here on the higher end—at least $125 for the best places. On the other hand, everything else (food, entertainment, and hotel rooms) can be relatively inexpensive or downright cheap, assuming you play some blackjack or craps.

	Yards	Par	Course Rating	Slope	Green Fee
Angel Park Golf Club (36)					$65/$145
Mountain (18)	6,722/5,164	71/72	71.1/69.1	130/114	
Palm (18)	6,530/4,570	70/70	70.9/66.2	129/111	
Badlands Golf Club (27)					$50/$190
Desperado/Diablo (18)	6,926/5,221	72/72	73.8/71.0	134/132	
Desperado/Outlaw (18)	6,602/5,037	72/72	72.1/70.0	125/123	
Diablo/Outlaw (18)	6,802/5,066	72/72	72.7/70.1	129/126	
Bali Hai Golf Club (18)	7,002/5,535	71/71	73.0/71.5	130/121	$169/$325
Lake Las Vegas Resort (36)					
The Falls (18)	7,250/5,021	72/72	74.7/68.3	136/118	$165/$260
Reflection Bay (18)	7,261/5,166	72/72	74.8/70.0	138/127	$120/$260
Las Vegas Paiute Resort (54)					
Nu-Wav Kaiv Snow Mountain (18)	7,158/5,341	72/72	73.9/70.4	125/117	$60/$165
Tav-Ai Kaiv Sun Mountain (18)	7,112/5,465	72/72	73.3/71.0	130/123	$60/$165
Wolf (18)	7,604/5,910	72/72	76.3/71.4	149/130	$100/$195
Rio Secco Golf Club (18)	7,332/5,684	72/72	75.7/70.0	142/127	$125/$250
Royal Links Golf Club (18)	7,029/5,142	72/72	73.7/69.8	135/115	$160/$250
Shadow Creek Golf Club (18)	7,100/5,985	72/72	71.0/69.2	115/114	$500
Tournament Players Club at The Canyons (18)	7,063/5,039	71/71	73.0/67.0	131/109	$89/$240

The courses have some of that fantasy flavor peculiar to Vegas. If you want to go with the whole Vegas-style replica wave, for instance, you can play the best Scotland has to offer at Royal Links, a British Open tribute course. Spend enough at the Mirage and you can get on Shadow Creek, the stunning course created by Tom Fazio. In short, there's enough here to fill 24 hours and then some. If only you didn't need to sleep . . .

Courses

GolfDigest REVIEWS

ANGEL PARK GOLF CLUB. Facility Holes: 36. Architect: Arnold Palmer/Ed Seay/Bob Cupp. Green Fee: $65/$145. Cart Fee: Included in green fee. Discounts: Weekdays, twilight, juniors. Walking: Mandatory cart. Season: Year-round. Tee Times: Call 120 days in advance. Notes: Range (grass, mat). ✉ 100 S. Rampart Blvd., 89145, 5 mi from Las Vegas ☎ 702/254–4653 or 888/446–5358 ⊕ www.angelpark.com ▭ AE, D, DC, MC, V.

Mountain. Holes: 18. Opened: 1990. Yards: 6,722/5,164. Par: 71/72. Course Rating: 71.1/69.1. Slope: 130/114. *Comments: To make anything, remember that all putts break toward the Stratosphere.* ★★★ ½

Palm. Holes: 18. Opened: 1989. Yards: 6,530/4,570. Par: 70/70. Course Rating: 70.9/66.2. Slope: 129/111. *Comments: Just the right size for weekend players.* ★★★★

BADLANDS GOLF CLUB. Facility Holes: 27. Opened: 1995. Architect: Johnny Miller. Green Fee: $50/$190. Cart Fee: Included in green fee. Discounts: Weekdays, twilight. Walking: Mandatory cart. Season: Year-round. Tee Times: Call 90 days in advance. Notes: Range (grass, mat). ⊠ 9119 Alta Dr., 89128, 10 mi from Las Vegas ☎ 702/363-0754 ⊕ - www.americangolf.com ⊟ AE, D, DC, MC, V.

Desperado/Diablo. Holes: 18. Yards: 6,926/5,221. Par: 72/72. Course Rating: 73.8/71.0. Slope: 134/132.

Desperado/Outlaw. Holes: 18. Yards: 6,602/5,037. Par: 72/72. Course Rating: 72.1/70.0. Slope: 125/123.

Diablo/Outlaw. Holes: 18. Yards: 6,802/5,066. Par: 72/72. Course Rating: 72.7/70.1. Slope: 129/126.

Comments: The designer, Johnny Miller, hit it very straight—and it shows. No margin for error. ★ ★ ★ ★

BALI HAI GOLF CLUB. Facility Holes: 18. Opened: 2000. Architect: Schmit/Curly. Yards: 7,002/5,535. Par: 71/71. Course Rating: 73.0/71.5. Slope: 130/121. Green Fee: $169/$325. Cart Fee: Included in green fee. Discounts: Weekdays, twilight. Walking: Walking with caddie. Season: Year-round. Tee Times: Call 180 days in advance. Notes: Range (mat). ⊠ 5160 Las Vegas Blvd., 89119 ☎ 702/450-8000 or 888/397-2499 ⊕ www.waltersgolf. com ⊟ AE, D, DC, MC, V. *Comments: Not quite a Shadow Creek–style transformation, but close. An oasis right on the Strip. UR*

LAKE LAS VEGAS RESORT. Facility Holes: 36. Architect: Jack Nicklaus. Cart Fee: Included in green fee. Discounts: Weekdays, guest, twilight, juniors. Walking: Walking at certain times. Season: Year-round. High: Feb.–May. Tee Times: Call 14 days in advance. Notes: Range (grass), lodging (496). ⊠ 1600 Lake Las Vegas Pkwy., Henderson 89011, 17 mi from Las Vegas ☎ 702/740-4653 or 877/698-4653 ⊕ www.lakelasvegas.com ⊟ AE, D, MC, V.

The Falls. Holes: 18. Yards: 7,250/5,021. Par: 72/72. Course Rating: 74.7/68.3. Slope: 136/118. Green fee: $165/$260. *Comments: Big, muscular course with piles of forced carries and blind shots. Far too hard for the average player. UR*

Reflection Bay. Holes: 18. Opened: 1998. Yards: 7,261/5,166. Par: 72/72. Course Rating: 74.8/70.0. Slope: 138/127. Green Fee: $120/$260. *Comments: Ranked 5th in* Golf Digest*'s 2001 Best in State ranking. Infinitely more fun and playable than its sister course.* ★ ★ ★ ★ ½

LAS VEGAS PAIUTE RESORT. Facility Holes: 54. Architect: Pete Dye. Cart Fee: Included in green fee. Discounts: Weekdays, twilight. Walking: Mandatory cart. Season: Year-round. High: Sept.–June. Tee Times: Call 60 days in advance. Notes: Range (grass). ⊠ 10325 Nu-Wav Kaiv Blvd., 89124, 23 mi from Las Vegas ☎ 702/658-1400 or 800/ 711-2833 ⊕ www.lvpaiutegolf.com ⊟ AE, D, DC, MC, V.

Nu-Wav Kaiv Snow Mountain. Holes: 18. Opened: 1995. Yards: 7,158/5,341. Par: 72/ 72. Course Rating: 73.9/70.4. Slope: 125/117. Green Fee: $60/$165. *Comments: Astonishing views, just like the other two. The best course at the resort until the Wolf opened.* ★ ★ ★ ★

Tav-Ai Kaiv Sun Mountain. Holes: 18. Opened: 1997. Yards: 7,112/5,465. Par: 72/72. Course Rating: 73.3/71.0. Slope: 130/123. Green Fee: $60/$165. *Comments: Worth the 20-minute drive from the Strip.* ★ ★ ★ ★ ¹/₂

Wolf. Holes: 18. Opened: 2000. Yards: 7,604/5,910. Par: 72/72. Course Rating: 76.3/71.4. Slope: 149/130. Green Fee: $100/$195. *Comments: Finishing holes 16, 17, and 18 are among the best in Vegas. Spectacular.* ★ ★ ★ ★ ¹/₂

RIO SECCO GOLF CLUB. Facility Holes: 18. Opened: 1997. Architect: Rees Jones. Yards: 7,332/5,684. Par: 72/72. Course Rating: 75.7/70.0. Slope: 142/127. Green Fee: $125/$250. Cart Fee: Included in green fee. Discounts: Guest. Walking: Unrestricted walking. Season: Year-round. High: Mar.–June. Tee Times: Call 90 days in advance. Notes: Range (grass). ✉ 2851 Grand Hills Dr., Henderson 89052 ☎ 702/889–2400 or 888/867–3226 ⊕ www.playrio.com ⊟ AE, D, DC, MC, V. *Comments: Miss too many shots? Butch Harmon's golf school is based here.* ★ ★ ★ ★

ROYAL LINKS GOLF CLUB. Facility Holes: 18. Opened: 1999. Architect: Perry Dye. Yards: 7,029/5,142. Par: 72/72. Course Rating: 73.7/69.8. Slope: 135/115. Green Fee: $160/$250. Cart Fee: Included in green fee. Discounts: Weekdays, twilight. Walking: Unrestricted walking. Season: Year-round. Tee Times: Call golf shop. Notes: Range (grass). ✉ 5995 E. Vegas Valley Rd., 89142, 5 mi from Las Vegas ☎ 702/450–8123 or 888/427–6682 ⊕ www.waltersgolf.com ⊟ AE, D, MC, V. *Comments: I was skeptical about a British Open reproduction on an old landfill site, too—until I played it. A blast, but very expensive.* ★ ★ ★ ★

SHADOW CREEK GOLF CLUB. Facility Holes: 18. Opened: 1989. Architect: Tom Fazio/ Andy Banfield. Yards: 7,100/5,985. Par: 72/72. Course Rating: 71.0/69.2. Slope: 115/114. Green Fee: $500. Cart Fee: Included in green fee. Walking: Mandatory cart. Season: Year-round. Tee Times: Call golf shop. ✉ R-5400 Losee Rd., North Las Vegas 89030 ☎ 702/ 791–7161 or 888/778–3387 ⊕ www.shadowcreek.com ⊟ AE, D, MC, V. *Comments: You have to see this one to believe it. Fazio created something out of the Pacific Northwest (pine trees, soaring elevation changes) from a dry, flat piece of dirt. You must stay at an MGM Mirage property (MGM Grand, New York–New York, the Mirage, Bellagio, or Treasure Island) to play here. UR*

TOURNAMENT PLAYERS CLUB AT THE CANYONS. Facility Holes: 18. Opened: 1996. Architect: Bobby Weed/Raymond Floyd. Yards: 7,063/5,039. Par: 71/71. Course Rating: 73.0/67.0. Slope: 131/109. Green Fee: $89/$240. Cart Fee: Included in green fee. Discounts: Guest, twilight, juniors. Walking: Walking with caddie. Season: Year-round. High: Sept.–May. Tee Times: Call 180 days in advance. Notes: Range (grass). ✉ 9851 Canyon Run Dr., 89144, 8 mi from Las Vegas. ☎ 702/256–2000 ⊕ www.tpc.com ⊟ AE, DC, MC, V. *Comments: Like most of the other TPCs, run very well, and kept in perfect condition.* ★ ★ ★ ★

Where to Stay

▥ **GREEN VALLEY RANCH.** The intimate, Mediterranean-style lobby here opens onto 2 acres of vineyards, a striking pool with a small sand beach, and a patio. Guest rooms, with awesome views of the sparkling Strip or tranquil mountainscapes, have plenty of amenities. Of the bars and lounges, Whiskey Sky is the hottest; it has large divans strewn about the outdoor patio overlooking the pool. ⊠ 2300 Paseo Verde Pkwy., Henderson 89052 ☎ 702/617-7777 or 866/782-9487 ☐ 702/617-7885 ⊕ www.stationcasinos. com ⟿ 201 rooms ⟁ 6 restaurants, room service, in-room data ports, in-room safes, minibars, cable TV, pool, health club, hair salon, spa, 2 lounges, casino, concierge, no smoking rooms ⊟ AE, D, DC, MC, V $$-$$$$.

HYATT REGENCY LAKE LAS VEGAS RESORT. Desert surroundings notwithstanding, this luxurious resort created its own oasis: a 320-acre private lake. The hotel's style borrows from Morocco, with decorative ironwork and hand-painted Moroccan furniture in the guest rooms. In addition to the golf courses, there are plenty of practice facilities (target greens, grass hitting stations, etc.) and instructors on hand. The beach, sports options, and children's programs make this a great place to visit with kids. ⊠ 101 Montelago Blvd., Henderson 89011 ☎ 702/567-1234 ☐ 702/567-6067 ⊕ www. lakelasvegas.hyatt.com ⟿ 496 rooms, 47 suites ⟁ 5 restaurants, room service, in-room data ports, in-room safes, refrigerators, cable TV with movies and video games, 2 18-hole golf courses, putting green, 2 pools, lake, health club, spa, boating, fishing, basketball, volleyball, 2 bars, casino, children's programs (ages 3-12), concierge floor, meeting rooms, no-smoking rooms ⊟ AE, D, DC, MC, V $$$$.

JW MARRIOTT LAS VEGAS RESORT. Trade in a Strip location for proximity to the Arnold Palmer-designed Angel Park public golf club. The resort is about 10 mi from Red Rock Canyon, which makes a stunning backdrop to other nearby golf courses such as the Tournament Players Club. Guest rooms are expansive, many with marble bathrooms with whirlpool tubs; they've also got work areas and high-speed Internet access. The J. C. Woolroughan Irish Pub has a reconstructed interior straight from the Emerald Isle, with terrific food as well as carefully poured Guinness. ⊠ 221 N. Rampart Blvd., 89145 ☎ 702/869-7777 or 877/869-8777 ☐ 702/869-7771 ⊕ www.jwmarriottlv.com ⟿ 451 rooms, 77 suites ⟁ 9 restaurants, room service, in-room data ports, in-room safes, minibars, refrigerators, cable TV with movies, pool, health club, outdoor whirlpool, massage, sauna, spa, 3 bars, business services, meeting rooms, dry cleaning, concierge, no-smoking rooms ⊟ AE, D, DC, MC, V $$$-$$$$.

THE PALMS. Just minutes off the Strip, the Palms has splashed out for high-profile nightlife—eye-catching even by Vegas standards. Its lounges, clubs, and restaurants pull in a glossy, good-time crowd; locals consider the nightclub, Rain, to be one of the city's best. There's even a multiplex movie theater. Rooms are large and contemporarily swank, with duvet-topped beds and good views of the city. There are special suites for basketball players (extra-high door frames, extra-long beds) and bachelor/bachelorette parties (you can imagine). ⊠ 4321 W. Flamingo Rd., 89103 ☎ 702/942-7777 or 866/942-7777 ☐ 702/942-7001 ⊕ www.palms.com ⟿ 368 rooms, 79 suites ⟁ 7 restaurants, in-room data ports, in-room safes, minibars, cable TV, pool, health club, hair salon, spa, 3 bars, lounge, casino, cinema, baby-sitting, no-smoking rooms ⊟ AE, D, DC, MC, V $$-$$$$.

RIO ALL-SUITE HOTEL AND CASINO. The striking blue-and-red, four-tower hotel has a Brazilian theme, including the sandy beach beside the pool. The Rio stretches the definition of suite a bit, calling its spacious single-room units "studio suites"; they have extra-large sofas, sitting areas, dining tables, big bathrooms, and floor-to-ceiling windows. Staying here will net you a discounted rate at the Rio Secco golf club. ⊠ 3700 W. Flamingo Rd., 89109 ☎ 702/252-7777 or 888/746-7482 ⊟ 702/777-7611 ⊕ www. playrio.com ↪ 2,554 suites ⚒ 14 restaurants, room service, in-room safes, minibars, 5 pools, health club, hair salon, spa, lounge, casino, showroom, business services, meeting rooms, no-smoking rooms ☰ AE, D, DC, MC, V $$-$$$.

Where to Eat

✗ **BONJOUR CASUAL FRENCH.** The food at this charming country-French spot is a blend of the classic and the innovative. Among the appetizer offerings are a warm Roquefort-and-pear napoleon and onion soup gratinée; entrée choices include crusted salmon with spinach, pine nuts, and tarragon sauce, and vegetable ravioli with wild mushrooms and artichokes. A tarte Tatin is a fine finish. ⊠ 8878 S. Eastern Ave. ☎ 702/ 270-2102 ☰ AE, D, DC, MC, V ☉ Closed Mon. $$$-$$$$.

✗ **MIMI'S CAFE.** Mimi's and its interior may sound and look French, and the interior may look French, but the menu is American, and portions are huge. For starters, consider a Thai chicken wrap, Cajun popcorn shrimp, or spinach-and-artichoke dip. Entrée choices include barbecued meat loaf, penne with pine nuts and feta, and turkey breast with corn-bread dressing. And don't pass the dessert case without peeking or you might miss the warm chocolate praline bars or New Orleans bread pudding. ⊠ 1121 S. Fort Apache Rd. ☎ 702/341-0365 ☰ AE, D, MC, V $-$$.

✗ **RENOIR.** The Mirage's showcase for the contemporary Franco-Italian cuisine of Chef Alessandro Stratta lives up to its name: genuine Renoir paintings decorate the interior. Stratta's cooking is equally artful. The seasonal five-course prix-fixe menu might include Santa Barbara prawns; pancetta-wrapped veal tenderloin with lentils, arugula, and chanterelles; and braised veal cheeks with Swiss chard, black olives, and creamy polenta. ⊠ Mirage Hotel and Casino, 3400 Las Vegas Blvd. S ☎ 702/791-7111 ⚙ Reservations essential ⓜ Jacket required ☰ AE, D, DC, MC, V ☉ No lunch $$$$.

✗ **ROSEMARY'S.** Husband and wife Michael and Wendy Jordan, both skilled chefs (he honed his skills under celebrity chef Emeril Lagasse), preside here. Among signature dishes are the appetizer of veal sweetbreads and wild mushroom-garlic toast and such main courses as rosemary-coated roasted lamb and barbecued shrimp. For dessert try the chocolate beignets. ⊠ 8125 W. Sahara Ave. ☎ 702/869-2251 ⚙ Reservations essential ☰ AE, D, DC, MC, V ☉ No lunch weekends ⊠ 3700 W. Flamingo Rd. ☎ 702/ 777-2300 ☉ Closed Tues. and Wed. $$$-$$$$.

✗ **TENAYA CREEK RESTAURANT & BREWERY.** This pub's strong suit is its super customer service; it's a great place for families. You could start with crab cakes or hummus; main courses might include buffalo steak and pork chops marinated in ale. You can even take the beer theme into dessert with a "beer-a-misu," a tiramisu made with house-brewed ale. ⊠ 3101 N. Tenaya Way ☎ 702/362-7335 ☰ AE, D, DC, MC, V $-$$$.

Essentials

Getting Here

Las Vegas is approximately 300 mi northeast of Los Angeles via I-10 and I-15. Allow six hours or more for the drive. Traffic can be especially congested on holiday weekends and on Sunday.

A nonstop flight between Los Angeles and Las Vegas takes just one hour. McCarran International Airport (LAS) is Vegas's gateway. Southwest remains the dominant regional airline in terms of passenger numbers. The low-cost airline JetBlue is another good option, with flights between Vegas and Long Beach.

Visitor Information

⌗ **Las Vegas Chamber of Commerce** ✉ 3720 Howard Hughes Pkwy., 89109 ☎ 702/735-1616 🖷 702/735-2011. **Las Vegas Convention and Visitors Authority** ✉ 3150 Paradise Rd., 89109 ☎ 702/892-0711 🖷 702/892-2824 ⊕ www.lvcva.com.

OJAI

Inevitably, once the crowds find someplace special, cutting-edge travelers search for a fresh discovery. In this case, now that Santa Barbara has become one of the state's most popular tourist destinations, interest is turning to Ojai. Supporters claim that Ojai, with its charming location in the Victor Valley, its antiques stores, and small-town charm, is what Santa Barbara used to be. While the throngs haven't found Ojai yet, you can still find elite-level amenities. The Ojai Valley Inn & Spa is as posh as any in the state, and has one of the most fun resort courses you can find. Instead of a modern masterpiece from a Fazio or a Jones, the Ojai Valley Inn has preserved its circa-1920 George Thomas original, complete with turn-of-the-century quirks and challenges.

If you prefer something a little more progressive, visit La Purisima—a wonderful combination of toughness and playability. It's been a popular choice for PGA Tour qualifying tournaments because of its risk-reward holes and unpredictable wind. When it blows, La Purisima can play 15 shots harder. Also worth a visit is the Robert Muir Graves–designed Sterling Hills in nearby Camarillo.

Courses   **Golf**Digest REVIEWS

OJAI VALLEY INN & SPA. Facility Holes: 18. Opened: 1923. Architect: George Thomas/Jay Morrish. Yards: 6,235/5,225. Par: 70/71. Course Rating: 70.2/70.2. Slope: 122/

Ojai Valley Inn & Spa (18)	6,235/5,225	70/71	70.2/70.2	122/123	$103/$118
Soule Park Golf Course (18)	6,475/5,639	72/72	70.5/71.8	121/121	$27/$39
Sterling Hills Golf Club (18)	6,813/5,445	71/71	72.7/72.0	131/120	$39/$58

123. Green Fee: $103/$118. Cart Fee: $17 per person. Discounts: Guest, twilight, juniors. Walking: Unrestricted walking. Season: Year-round. Tee Times: Call 7 days in advance. Notes: Range (grass), lodging (208). ⊠ Country Club Rd., 93023 ☎ 805/646-2420 or 800/422-6524 ⊕ www.golfojai.com ⊟ AE, D, DC, MC, V. *Comments: One of the few West Coast resorts with a classic, old-school course. Great all-you-can-play deals.* ★ ★ ★ ★ ¹/₂

SOULE PARK GOLF COURSE. Facility Holes: 18. Opened: 1962. Architect: William F. Bell. Yards: 6,475/5,639. Par: 72/72. Course Rating: 70.5/71.8. Slope: 121/121. Green Fee: $27/$39. Cart Fee: $26 per cart. Discounts: Weekdays, twilight, seniors, juniors. Walking: Unrestricted walking. Season: Year-round. Tee Times: Call 7 days in advance. Notes: Range (grass). ⊠ 1033 E. Ojai Ave., 93024 ☎ 805/646-5633 ⊟ D, MC, V. *Comments: Busy Ojai muni brings plenty of challenge for the fee.* ★ ★ ★ ★

STERLING HILLS GOLF CLUB. Facility Holes: 18. Opened: 1999. Architect: Damian Pascuzzo/Robert Muir Graves. Yards: 6,813/5,445. Par: 71/71. Course Rating: 72.7/72.0. Slope: 131/120. Green Fee: $39/$58. Cart Fee: $11 per person. Discounts: Weekdays, twilight, seniors, juniors. Walking: Walking at certain times. Season: Year-round. Tee Times: Call 7 days in advance. Notes: Range (grass, mat). ⊠ 901 Sterling Hills Dr., Camarillo, 93010, 45 mi from Los Angeles ☎ 805/987-3446 ⊕ www.sterlinghillsgolf.com ⊟ AE, D, MC, V. *Comments: Affordable and challenging, Sterling is maturing nicely, with true greens and manicured fairways.* ★ ★ ★ ★

Where to Stay

🏨 **BLUE IGUANA INN & COTTAGES.** Artists run this Southwestern-style hotel; their work decorates the rooms and is for sale. The small, cozy main inn is about 2 mi west of downtown. Beds are topped with brightly colored coverlets; suites have kitchenettes. A sister property, the Emerald Iguana Inn, consists of eight more art nouveau–style cottages closer to downtown. ⊠ 11794 N. Ventura Ave. (Rte. 33), 93023 ☎ 805/646-5277 🖷 805/646-8078 ⊕ www.blueiguanainn.com ☞ 4 rooms, 7 suites, 8 cottages ᵔ Some kitchens, refrigerators, pool, hot tub, massage, some pets allowed (fee); no smoking ⊟ AE, D, DC, MC, V $-$$.

🏨 **OJAI VALLEY INN & SPA.** This outdoorsy, golf-oriented resort with a full-service spa facility is set on beautifully landscaped grounds, with hillside views in nearly all directions. Many guest rooms have fireplaces and flower-decked balconies or patios. At this writing, the resort had begun a major renovation; it includes the addition of over 300 new guest rooms and three new restaurants. During construction, the number of available guest rooms is reduced, access to the grounds is limited, and no children under

16 are allowed as guests. ⊠905 Country Club Rd., 93023 ☎805/646-5511 or 800/ 422-6524 🖶805/646-7969 ⊕ www.ojairesort.com ⟲305 rooms ♿4 restaurants, room service, in-room data ports, minibars, cable TV with movies and video games, 18-hole golf course, 8 tennis courts, 3 pools, spa, bicycles, badminton, croquet, hiking, horseback riding, 2 bars, children's programs (ages 3–12), meeting rooms, some pets allowed (fee), no-smoking rooms ▭AE, D, DC, MC, V $$$$.

Where to Eat

✗**RANCH HOUSE.** Lush foliage and streams border the redwood decks of this white-tablecloth restaurant. Menu choices run to richly flavored dishes such as pâté appetizers and New Zealand lamb medallions with guava chutney. ⊠ 102 Besant Rd., at corner of S. Lomita ☎805/646-2360 ▭AE, D, DC, MC, V ⊘ Closed Mon. No lunch $$$–$$$$.

✗**SEA FRESH.** Fresh seafood—much of it caught from the restaurant's own boat—a lively crowd, and friendly service ensure a packed dining room practically every day of the week. You can eat here for a little or a lot, depending upon your choices, which range from fish tacos and shrimp-and-chips to crab legs and steak. Popular entrées include macadamia nut-crusted halibut and a calamari and spinach salad. The family-run enterprise also includes a sushi bar and fish market. ⊠533 E. Ojai Ave. ☎805/646-7747 ▭AE, D, MC, V $–$$$$.

✗**SUZANNE'S CUISINE.** Peppered filet mignon, linguine with steamed clams, and salmon with sauerkraut in a dill beurre blanc are among the offerings here. Salads and soups star at lunchtime. ⊠502 W. Ojai Ave. ☎805/640-1961 ▭MC, V ⊘ Closed Tues. and 1st 2 wks in Jan. $$–$$$$.

Essentials

Getting Here
Ojai is about 100 mi northwest of downtown Los Angeles. Follow Hwy. 101 north to Ventura; exit at Hwy. 33, which becomes Hwy. 150. Hwy. 150 will take you into town.

Visitor Information
🛈 **Ojai Valley Chamber of Commerce** ⊠150 W. Ojai Ave., 93023 ☎805/646-8126 ⊕ www.the-ojai.org.

PALM SPRINGS

As you work your way through the twists of Hwy. 74 and over the mountain range that protects the Coachella Valley, it becomes clearer why golf is the game here. The mountains provide a stunning, 360-degree

Cimarron Golf Resort— **Long Course (18)**	6,858/5,127	71/71	72.4/69.7	123/117	$35/$75
Desert Dunes Golf Club (18)	6,876/5,359	72/72	73.8/70.7	142/122	$30/$120
Desert Falls Country Club (18)	7,077/5,344	72/72	73.7/71.7	132/124	$35/$165
Desert Princess Country Club & **Resort (27)**					$45/$125
Cielo/Vista (18)	6,815/5,403	72/72	72.9/71.9	131/124	
Lagos/Cielo (18)	6,599/5,217	72/72	72.4/70.8	126/120	
Vista/Lagos (18)	6,706/5,322	72/72	72.6/71.7	127/121	
Desert Springs: A JW Marriott **Resort & Spa (36)**					
Palms (18)	6,761/5,492	72/72	72.1/70.8	130/116	$55/$165
Valley (18)	6,627/5,262	72/72	71.5/69.6	127/110	$50/$150
Desert Willow Golf Resort (36)					$65/$165
Firecliff (18)	7,056/5,079	72/72	74.1/69.0	138/120	
Mountain View (18)	6,913/5,040	72/72	73.4/69.0	129/119	
La Quinta Resort & Club (36)					
Dunes (18)	6,747/4,997	72/72	73.1/69.1	137/125	$145
Mountain (18)	6,756/5,005	72/72	74.1/71.0	140/123	$125
PGA West Resort (54)					
Greg Norman (18)	7,156/5,281	72/72	75.1/71.0	139/122	$55/$235
Jack Nicklaus Tournament (18)	7,204/5,023	72/72	74.7/69.0	139/116	$55/$235
TPC Stadium (18)	7,266/5,092	72/72	75.9/69.0	150/124	$55/$235
Westin Mission Hills Resort (36)					$55/$145
Mission Hills, North (18)	7,062/4,907	72/72	73.4/68.0	131/118	
Pete Dye (18)	6,706/4,841	70/70	73.5/67.4	137/107	

backdrop while the flat valley invites resort developers and course designers alike. The valley even has an underground water source (Palm Springs . . . get it?) that simplifies irrigation. There are over 100 courses here, and roughly half are open to the public. You can pay anything from $20 at one of the well-loved municipal tracks to $250 at the latest resort spectacle, but around $100 is the going rate for a top-tier experience. Most of the public-access courses have affiliations with specific resorts in the constellation of towns that surrounds Palm Springs proper. Clear, dry desert weather lures in golfers by car and plane (private or otherwise) year-round. Spend a luxuriously slow-paced week here and you'll grasp why so many senior celebrities (Sinatra, Bob Hope) picked this place for retirement—it's got the triumvirate of abundant golf options, elegant dining, and snappy service. The extra-wide lanes on local roads is an added bonus.

Courses

CIMARRON GOLF RESORT—LONG COURSE. Facility Holes: 18. Opened: 2000. Architect: John Fought. Yards: 6,858/5,127. Par: 71/71. Course Rating: 72.4/69.7. Slope: 123/117. Green Fee: $35/$75. Cart Fee: Included in green fee. Discounts: Weekdays, guest, twilight, juniors. Walking: Unrestricted walking. Season: Year-round. Tee Times: Call 60 days in advance. Notes: Range (grass), lodging (80), facility also has an 18-hole par-3 course. ✉ 67-603 30th Ave., Cathedral City 92234 ☎ 760/770-6060 or 877/955-6233 ⊕ www.cimarrongolf.com ▤ AE, D, MC, V. *Comments: One of the great bargains in the area. Twice as good as its fee.* ★★★★

DESERT DUNES GOLF CLUB. Facility Holes: 18. Opened: 1989. Architect: Robert Trent Jones Jr. Yards: 6,876/5,359. Par: 72/72. Course Rating: 73.8/70.7. Slope: 142/122. Green Fee: $30/$120. Cart Fee: Included in green fee. Discounts: Weekdays, twilight. Walking: Mandatory cart. Season: Year-round. Tee Times: Call 7 days in advance. Notes: Range (grass, mat). ✉ 19300 Palm Dr., Desert Hot Springs 92240, 5 mi from Palm Springs ☎ 760/251-5367 or 888/423-8637 ⊕ www.desertdunes.com ▤ AE, MC, V. *Comments: Locals can get deep summer discounts here.* ★★★★

DESERT FALLS COUNTRY CLUB. Facility Holes: 18. Opened: 1984. Architect: Ron Fream. Yards: 7,077/5,344. Par: 72/72. Course Rating: 73.7/71.7. Slope: 132/124. Green Fee: $35/$165. Cart Fee: Included in green fee. Discounts: Twilight. Season: Year-round. High: Nov.–Apr. Tee Times: Call 3 days in advance. Notes: Range (grass). ✉ 1111 Desert Falls Pkwy., Palm Desert 92211 ☎ 760/340-4653 ⊕ www.desertfalls.com ▤ MC, V. *Comments: Mature desert grasses protect this Palm Springs mainstay. Annually picked as one of the best in the region.* ★★★★

DESERT PRINCESS COUNTRY CLUB & RESORT. Facility Holes: 27. Opened: 1984. Architect: David Rainville. Green Fee: $45/$125. Cart Fee: Included in green fee. Discounts: Weekdays, guest, twilight. Walking: Mandatory cart. Season: Nov.–Sept. High: Nov.–Mar. Tee Times: Call 2 days in advance. Notes: Range (grass). ✉ 28-555 Landau Blvd., Cathedral City 92234, 2 mi from Palm Springs ☎ 760/322-2280 or 800/637-0577 ▤ AE, MC, V.

Cielo/Vista. Holes: 18. Yards: 6,815/5,403. Par: 72/72. Course Rating: 72.9/71.9. Slope: 131/124.

Lagos/Cielo. Holes: 18. Yards: 6,599/5,217. Par: 72/72. Course Rating: 72.4/70.8. Slope: 126/120.

Vista/Lagos. Holes: 18. Yards: 6,706/5,322. Par: 72/72. Course Rating: 72.6/71.7. Slope: 127/121.

Comments: Mix and match with the three distinctly different 9s. ★★★★

DESERT SPRINGS: A JW MARRIOTT RESORT & SPA. Facility Holes: 36. Opened: 1987. Architect: Ted Robinson. Cart Fee: Included in green fee. Discounts: Weekdays, twilight, juniors. Walking: Mandatory cart. Season: Year-round. Tee Times: Call 21 days in advance. Notes: Metal spikes, range (grass), lodging (800). ✉ 74-855 Country Club Dr., Palm Desert 92260, 85 mi from Los Angeles ☎ 760/341-1756 or 800/331-3112 ▤ AE, D, DC, MC, V.

Palms. Holes: 18. Yards: 6,761/5,492. Par: 72/72. Course Rating: 72.1/70.8. Slope: 130/116. Green Fee: $55/$165. *Comments: When you see it, you'll know why the green fee is so high: check the water bill.* ★★★★

Valley. Holes: 18. Yards: 6,627/5,262. Par: 72/72. Course Rating: 71.5/69.6. Slope: 127/110. Green Fee: $50/$150. *Comments: Fun to play even from the back tees. Room to miss, and perfect lies everywhere.* ★★★★

DESERT WILLOW GOLF RESORT. Facility Holes: 36. Architect: Michael Hurdzan/Dana Fry/John Cook. Green Fee: $65/$165. Cart Fee: Included in green fee. Discounts: Weekdays, guest, twilight, seniors, juniors. Walking: Mandatory cart. Season: Year-round. High: Nov.–May. Tee Times: Call 30 days in advance. Notes: Range (grass), lodging (300). ✉ 38-995 Desert Willow Dr., Palm Desert 92260, 130 mi from Los Angeles ☎ 760/346–7060 or 800/320–3323 ⊕ www.desertwillow.com ▭ AE, D, MC, V.

Firecliff. Holes: 18. Opened: 1997. Yards: 7,056/5,079. Par: 72/72. Course Rating: 74.1/69.0. Slope: 138/120. *Comments: One of the top new courses in the area. You might catch Mike Weir practicing here.* ★★★★ ½

Mountain View. Holes: 18. Opened: 1998. Yards: 6,913/5,040. Par: 72/72. Course Rating: 73.4/69.0. Slope: 129/119. *Comments: Worthy addition to the resort property. A different feel from the Firecliff (less desert, more water) but also strong.* ★★★★ ½

LA QUINTA RESORT & CLUB. Facility Holes: 36. Architect: Pete Dye. Cart Fee: Included in green fee. Walking: Mandatory cart. Season: Year-round. Tee Times: Call golf shop. Notes: Range (grass), lodging (920). ✉ 50-200 Vista Bonita, La Quinta 92253, 15 mi from Palm Springs ☎ 760/564–7686 or 800/598–3828 ⊕ www.laquintaresort.com ▭ AE, MC, V.

Dunes. Holes: 18. Opened: 1981. Yards: 6,747/4,997. Par: 72/72. Course Rating: 73.1/69.1. Slope: 137/125. Green Fee: $145. *Comments: One of the more fun Pete Dye creations.* ★★★★

Mountain. Holes: 18. Opened: 1980. Yards: 6,756/5,005. Par: 72/72. Course Rating: 74.1/71.0. Slope: 140/123. Green Fee: $125. *Comments: Views, shot values. There's a reason the LPGA plays here.* ★★★★

PGA WEST RESORT. Facility Holes: 54. Discounts: Weekdays, twilight. Season: Year-round. High: Nov.–Apr. Tee Times: Call golf shop. Notes: Range (grass), lodging (920). ✉ 81405 Kingston Heath, La Quinta 92253, 30 mi from Palm Springs ☎ 760/564–3900 or 800/742–9378 ⊕ www.pgawest.com ▭ AE, D, MC, V.

Greg Norman. Holes: 18. Opened: 1999. Architect: Greg Norman. Yards: 7,156/5,281. Par: 72/72. Course Rating: 75.1/71.0. Slope: 139/122. Green Fee: $55/$235. Cart Fee: Included in green fee. Walking: Mandatory cart. *Comments: This is the course for the rest of us—the non-tour players in the group.* ★★★★

Jack Nicklaus Tournament. Holes: 18. Opened: 1987. Architect: Jack Nicklaus. Yards: 7,204/5,023. Par: 72/72. Course Rating: 74.7/69.0. Slope: 139/116. Green Fee: $55/$235. Cart Fee: Included in green fee. Walking: Mandatory cart. *Comments: Just as hard as the Stadium Course. Site of PGA Tour Q-School.* ★★★★ ½

TPC Stadium. Holes: 18. Opened: 1986. Architect: Pete Dye. Yards: 7,266/5,092. Par: 72/72. Course Rating: 75.9/69.0. Slope: 150/124. Green Fee: $55/$235. Cart Fee: Included in green fee. Walking: Mandatory cart. *Comments: Maintained as if the tour were here every week. Add 20 to your handicap. Get a load of the slope rating.* ★★★★ ½

WESTIN MISSION HILLS RESORT. Facility Holes: 36. Green Fee: $55/$145. Cart Fee: Included in green fee. Discounts: Weekdays, guest, twilight. Walking: Unrestricted walking. Season: Year-round. High: Nov.–May. Tee Times: Call golf shop. Notes: Range (grass), lodging (500). ✉ 71-501 Dinah Shore Dr., Rancho Mirage 92270, 5 mi from Palm Springs ☎ 760/328-3198 or 800/358-2211 ⊕ www.troongolf.com ▤ AE, D, DC, MC, V.

Mission Hills, North. Holes: 18. Opened: 1991. Architect: Gary Player. Yards: 7,062/4,907. Par: 72/72. Course Rating: 73.4/68.0. Slope: 131/118. *Comments: No houses around it to spoil the view. Player's courses are also relentlessly playable.* ★★★★

Pete Dye. Holes: 18. Opened: 1987. Architect: Pete Dye. Yards: 6,706/4,841. Par: 70/70. Course Rating: 73.5/67.4. Slope: 137/107. *Comments: Evil twin of Dye's TPC Stadium Course. Easier off the tee, but the greens are just plain nasty.* ★★★★

Where to Stay

🏨 **HYATT GRAND CHAMPIONS RESORT.** This stark white resort on 34 acres specializes in pampering. Huge suites have balconies or terraces and sunken sitting areas. Each private villa has an individual secluded garden courtyard with outdoor whirlpool tub, a living room with fireplace, a dining room, and a bedroom. The pool area is surrounded by palms and private cabanas. ✉ 44-600 Indian Wells La., 92210 ☎ 760/341-1000 or 800/552-4386 🖶 760/568-2236 ⊕ www.grandchampions.hyatt.com ⤺ 460 suites, 19 villas ♿ 2 restaurants, room service, minibars, cable TV with movies, driving range, 2 18-hole golf courses, putting green, 15 tennis courts, pro shop, 6 pools, health club, hair salon, 3 outdoor hot tubs, massage, sauna, spa, steam room, bicycles, bar, shop, children's programs (ages 3–12), dry cleaning, laundry service, business services, convention center, meeting rooms, no-smoking rooms ▤ AE, D, DC, MC, V $$$$.

🏨 **JW MARRIOTT DESERT SPRINGS RESORT & SPA.** This sprawling, convention-oriented hotel set on 450 landscaped acres has a dramatic U-shape design. The building wraps around the desert's largest private lake, which an indoor, stair-stepped waterfall flows into. Rooms have lake or mountain views, balconies, and oversize bathrooms. It's a long walk from the lobby to the rooms; if you are driving, you might want to request a room close to the parking lot. Palm Desert is roughly 8 mi southeast of Palm Springs. ✉ 74-855 Country Club Dr., Palm Desert 92260 ☎ 760/341-2211 or 800/331-3112 🖶 760/341-1872 ⊕ www.desertspringsresort.com ⤺ 833 rooms, 51 suites ♿ 11 restaurants, snack bar, minibars, cable TV with movies, driving range, 2 18-hole golf courses, putting green, 20 tennis courts, 5 pools, health club, hair salon, 4 outdoor hot tubs, spa, basketball, croquet, volleyball, 2 bars, nightclub, shop, children's programs (ages 5–12), laundry service, Internet, business services, convention center, car rental, no-smoking rooms ▤ AE, D, DC, MC, V $$$$.

🏨 **LA QUINTA RESORT AND CLUB.** The desert's oldest resort, dating to the 1920s, is a lush green oasis. Broad expanses of lawn separate the adobe casitas that house some rooms; other rooms are in newer two-story units surrounding individual swimming pools and hot tubs. Fireplaces, stocked refrigerators, and fruit-laden orange trees contribute to a discreet and sparely luxurious air. A premium is placed on privacy, which accounts for La Quinta's continuing popularity with Hollywood celebrities. You get access to the resort's pair of golf courses (Mountain and Dunes), three PGA West courses, and a Jim McLean golf school. You can even get a massage tailor-made for golfers at the spa. The resort is roughly 10 mi southeast of Palm Springs. ⊠ 49–499 Eisenhower Dr., La Quinta 92253 ☎ 760/564–4111 or 800/598–3828 ᗷ 760/564–5768 ⊕ www. laquintaresort.com ⬩ 640 rooms, 244 suites ᗷ 7 restaurants, room service, in-room data ports, refrigerators, 5 golf courses, putting green, 23 tennis courts, 42 pools, health club, hair salon, 52 outdoor hot tubs, spa, croquet, volleyball, children's programs (ages 4–16), concierge, business services, meeting room, shuttle to local golf courses, no-smoking rooms ⊟ AE, D, DC, MC, V $$$$.

🏨 WESTIN MISSION HILLS RESORT. A sprawling Moroccan-style resort on 360 acres, a few miles southeast of Palm Springs, the Westin is surrounded by fairways and putting greens. Rooms, in two-story buildings amid patios and fountains, are decorated with soft desert colors. Paths and creeks meander through the complex, and a lagoon-style swimming pool is encircled with a water slide several stories high. ⊠ 71–333 Dinah Shore Dr., Rancho Mirage 92270 ☎ 760/328–5955 or 800/335–3545 ᗷ 760/321–2607 ⊕ www.westin.com ⬩ 472 rooms, 40 suites ᗷ 2 restaurants, 3 snack bars, room service, in-room data ports, in-room safes, minibars, cable TV with movies and games, 2 18-hole golf courses, putting green, 7 tennis courts, 3 pools, health club, hair salon, 4 outdoor hot tubs, spa, steam room, croquet, shuffleboard, volleyball, bar, recreation room, children's programs (ages 4–12), convention center, no-smoking rooms ⊟ AE, D, DC, MC, V $$$$.

Where to Eat

✕ BLUE COYOTE GRILL. Diners munch on burritos, tacos, and fajitas—or more unusual items, such as Yucatán-style mahimahi or orange chicken—at this casual restaurant. Choose between several flower-decked patios and indoor dining rooms. Two busy cantinas serve tasty margaritas to a youngish crowd. ⊠ 445 N. Palm Canyon Dr. ☎ 760/327–1196 ⊟ AE, DC, MC, V $–$$$$.

✕ CUISTOT. Chef-owner Bernard Dervieux trained with French culinary star Paul Bocuse, but he's taken a more eclectic approach at his own restaurant, tucked into the back of a courtyard. Signature dishes include skillet-roasted veal chop with mushrooms and roasted garlic, fresh Maine lobster with baby asparagus, and handmade vegetable ravioli with white truffle oil. ⊠ 73–111 El Paseo, Palm Desert ☎ 760/340–1000 ᗷ Reservations essential ⊟ AE, DC, MC, V ⊗ Closed Mon. No lunch Sun. $$$$.

✕ OCEANS. This bistro tucked into the back corner of a shopping center offers a surprising selection of beautifully prepared seafood. Start with Mussels Oceans, a bowl of tender bivalves in an anisette broth. Entrées include perfectly grilled ahi tuna, blackened catfish with Cajun seasonings, and lobster ravioli with saffron cream sauce. ⊠ Canyon Plaza S, 67–555 E. Palm Canyon Dr. ☎ 760/324–1554 ᗷ Reservations essential ⊟ AE, D, DC, MC, V ⊗ No lunch weekends $$–$$$$.

✕**SHAME ON THE MOON.** Big booths, friendly service, an eclectic menu, and modest prices make this one of the most popular restaurants in the desert. Entrées include salmon napoleon stacked with Portobello mushrooms, sautéed chicken coated with hazelnuts, and Long Island duck with black figs. Portions leave you plenty to take home from this old-fashioned place. ✉ 69-950 Frank Sinatra Dr. ☎ 760/324-5515 ⌖ Reservations essential ▤ AE, MC, V ⊗ No lunch $$-$$$$.

Essentials

Getting Here

The Palm Springs area is approximately 110 mi east of Los Angeles. The most direct route is the I-10. For Palm Springs, exit at Palm Canyon Drive and go south. For Palm Desert and Rancho Mirage, exit at Monterey Avenue and drive south. For La Quinta, exit at Washington Avenue and turn south. For an alternate route from Los Angeles, take Hwy. 60 east to hook up with the I-10 near Banning. Allow two to three hours for the drive. Traffic can be very congested on Friday evenings and Sunday afternoons, especially on holiday weekends; daily traffic amplifies from January through May.

Visitor Information

🚩 **Palm Springs Desert Resorts Authority** ✉ 69-930 Rte. 111, Suite 201, Rancho Mirage 92270 ☎ 760/770-9000 or 800/417-3529, 760/770-1992 for activities hot line ⊕ www.palmspringsusa.com. **Palm Springs Visitor Information Center** ✉ 2901 N. Palm Canyon Dr., 92262 ☎ 800/347-7746 ⊕ www.palm-springs.org.

SAN DIEGO

Very few places have perfect year-round weather for golf. You need at least a sweater for Myrtle Beach in November and an IV drip to stave off dehydration in Scottsdale in August. But San Diego's weather is relentlessly perfect: somewhere between 70°F and 80°F, with low humidity and an ocean breeze. Winter? It's a little wetter and it gets dark a little earlier, but six days of sun out of seven isn't bad. The weather does have a drawback. San Diegans are very active and enjoy their golf, so a tee time at famed muni Torrey Pines is hard to get without advance preparation. If you can't get on Torrey Pines, though, there's a wealth of terrific golf in greater San Diego, from the jaw-droppingly scenic Coronado Golf Course on the bay to Singing Hills Resort's 36 quality holes. When the golf is done, make your way to the downtown Gaslamp Quarter, which is filled with upscale shops and restaurants (Chive is a cutting-edge favorite) and an eclectic collection of museums and galleries.

Course	Yards	Par	Course Rating	Slope	Green Fee
Coronado Golf Course (18)	6,590/5,742	72/72	71.5/73.7	124/126	$20
Eagle Crest Golf Club (18)	6,417/4,941	72/72	71.6/69.9	136/123	$38/$65
EastLake Country Club (18)	6,606/5,118	72/72	70.7/68.8	116/114	$18/$71
Meadows Del Mar Golf Club (18)	6,885/4,929	71/71	73.7/68.3	138/116	$70/$160
Maderas Country Club (18)	7,115/4,967	72/71	75.6/69.8	145/127	$65/$155
Pala Mesa Resort (18)	6,502/5,632	72/72	72.0/74.0	131/134\	$55/$80
Rancho Bernardo Inn Resort (18)	6,458/5,448	72/72	70.6/71.2	122/119	$85/$110
Singing Hills Resort at Sycuan (36)					$37/$45
Oak Glen (18)	6,668/5,549	72/72	71.3/71.4	122/124	
Willow Glen (18)	6,667/5,585	72/72	72.0/72.8	124/122	
Steele Canyon Golf Club (27)					$79/$109
Canyon/Meadow (18)	6,672/4,813	71/71	72.2/67.9	134/118	
Canyon/Ranch (18)	6,741/4,655	71/71	72.7/66.6	135/112	
Ranch/Meadow (18)	7,001/5,026	72/72	74.0/69.5	137/124	
Torrey Pines Golf Course (36)					
North (18)	6,874/6,122	72/74	72.1/75.4	129/134	$65/$75
South (18)	7,607/5,542	72/73	78.1/73.5	143/126	$105/$125
Vineyard at Escondido (18)	6,531/5,073	70/70	70.3/70.3	125/117	$30/$67

As for the 70 mi of beachfront that run along San Diego County's western edge, you can't miss it. Fly into San Diego's international airport and you come right down over it—almost in the sea. If you have a little extra time, take a slow drive up the Pacific Coast Hwy. to La Jolla and enjoy some hang gliding or people-watching. The pace is a little bit slower here.

Courses

Golf Digest REVIEWS

CORONADO GOLF COURSE. Facility Holes: 18. Opened: 1957. Architect: Jack Daray Sr. Yards: 6,590/5,742. Par: 72/72. Course Rating: 71.5/73.7. Slope: 124/126. Green Fee: $20. Cart Fee: $12 per person. Discounts: Twilight, juniors. Walking: Walking at certain times. Season: Year-round. Tee Times: Call 2 days in advance. Notes: Range (grass, mat). ✉ 2000 Vlia Row, Coronado 92118, 2 mi from San Diego ☎ 619/435-3121 ⊕ www. coronadoevents.com ▭ MC, V. *Comments: Sweeping water views—the ride in alone is worth the fee.* ★ ★ ★ ★

EAGLE CREST GOLF CLUB. Facility Holes: 18. Opened: 1993. Architect: David Rainville. Yards: 6,417/4,941. Par: 72/72. Course Rating: 71.6/69.9. Slope: 136/123. Green Fee: $38/$65. Cart Fee: Included in green fee. Discounts: Twilight, seniors, juniors.

Walking: Walking at certain times. Season: Year-round. Tee Times: Call 7 days in advance. Notes: Range (grass, mat). ✉ 2492 Old Ranch Rd., Escondido 92027, 20 mi from San Diego ☎ 760/737-9762 ▤ AE, D, MC, V. *Comments: Keep an eye out for the abundant wildlife: ostrich, hawks, and rattlesnakes live on the property.* ★ ★ ★ ½

EASTLAKE COUNTRY CLUB. Facility Holes: 18. Opened: 1991. Architect: Ted Robinson. Yards: 6,606/5,118. Par: 72/72. Course Rating: 70.7/68.8. Slope: 116/114. Green Fee: $18/$71. Cart Fee: Included in green fee. Discounts: Weekdays, guest, twilight, seniors, juniors. Walking: Walking at certain times. Season: Year-round. Tee Times: Call 7 days in advance. Notes: Range (grass). ✉ 2375 Clubhouse Dr., Chula Vista 91915, 15 mi from San Diego ☎ 619/482-5757 ⊕ www.geocities.com/eastlakecc/eastlake.html ▤ AE, D, MC, V. *Comments: Plenty of room to blast it from the tee.* ★ ★ ★ ½

MEADOWS DEL MAR GOLF CLUB. Facility Holes: 18. Opened: 1999. Architect: Tom Fazio. Yards: 6,885/4,929. Par: 71/71. Course Rating: 73.7/68.3. Slope: 138/116. Green Fee: $70/$160. Cart Fee: Included in green fee. Discounts: Weekdays, twilight, seniors. Walking: Mandatory cart. Season: Year-round. Tee Times: Call 60 days in advance. Notes: Range (grass, mat). ✉ 5300 Meadows Del Mar, 92130 ☎ 858/792-6200 or 877/530-0636 ⊕ www.meadowsdelmar.com ▤ AE, DC, MC, V. *Comments: One of the few Tom Fazio–designed public courses in Southern California. A great test, and finally growing in, too.* ★ ★ ★ ★

MADERAS COUNTRY CLUB. Facility Holes: 18. Opened: 1999. Architect: Damian Pascuzzo/Robert Muir Graves/Johnny Miller. Yards: 7,115/4,967. Par: 72/71. Course Rating: 75.6/69.8. Slope: 145/127. Green Fee: $65/$155. Cart Fee: Included in green fee. Discounts: Twilight, seniors, juniors. Walking: Mandatory cart. Season: Year-round. High: Jan.–Mar. Tee Times: Call 60 days in advance. Notes: Metal spikes, range (grass). ✉ 17750 Old Coach Rd., Poway 92064, 30 mi from San Diego ☎ 858/451-8100 ⊕ www.maderasgolf.com ▤ AE, MC, V. *Comments: Serves the other side of the city, opposite Torrey. Underrated, and very affordable.* ★ ★ ★ ★ ½

PALA MESA RESORT. Facility Holes: 18. Opened: 1964. Architect: Dick Rossen. Yards: 6,502/5,632. Par: 72/72. Course Rating: 72.0/74.0. Slope: 131/134. Green Fee: $55/$80. Cart Fee: Included in green fee. Discounts: Weekdays, twilight. Season: Year-round. Tee Times: Call golf shop. Notes: Range (grass, mat), lodging (133). ✉ 2001 Old Hwy. 395, Fallbrook 92028, 40 mi from San Diego ☎ 760/731-6803 or 800/722-4700 ⊕ www.palamesa.com ▤ AE, MC, V. *Comments: Mid-60s classic. Tight and fun.* ★ ★ ★ ★ ½

RANCHO BERNARDO INN RESORT. Facility Holes: 18. Opened: 1962. Architect: William F. Bell. Yards: 6,458/5,448. Par: 72/72. Course Rating: 70.6/71.2. Slope: 122/119. Green Fee: $85/$110. Cart Fee: Included in green fee. Discounts: Weekdays, guest, twilight, juniors. Walking: Walking at certain times. Season: Year-round. Tee Times: Call golf shop. Notes: Metal spikes, range (grass, mat), lodging (288). ✉ 17550 Bernardo Oaks Dr., 92128 ☎ 858/675-8470 or 800/662-6439 ⊕ www.jcresorts.com ▤ AE, D, MC, V. *Comments: Low-profile San Diego favorite has tough rough as well as variety.* ★ ★ ★ ½

SINGING HILLS RESORT AT SYCUAN. Facility Holes: 36. Opened: 1956. Architect: Ted Robinson/Dave Fleming. Green Fee: $37/$45. Cart Fee: $22 per cart. Discounts: Weekdays, twilight, juniors. Walking: Unrestricted walking. Season: Year-round. Tee Times: Call 7 days in advance. Notes: Range (grass, mat), lodging (102). ✉ 3007 Dehesa

Rd., El Cajon 92019, 17 mi from San Diego ☎ 619/442-3425 or 800/457-5568 ⊕ www. singinghills.com ▤ AE, D, MC, V.

Oak Glen. Holes: 18. Yards: 6,668/5,549. Par: 72/72. Course Rating: 71.3/71.4. Slope: 122/ 124. *Comments: Easy to get to and easy to get on. A great alternative to Torrey.* ★★★★

Willow Glen. Holes: 18. Yards: 6,667/5,585. Par: 72/72. Course Rating: 72.0/72.8. Slope: 124/122. *Comments: Carpeted with mature trees, Willow Glen calls for a variety of shots.* ★★★★

STEELE CANYON GOLF CLUB. Facility Holes: 27. Opened: 1991. Architect: Gary Player. Green Fee: $79/$109. Cart Fee: Included in green fee. Discounts: Twilight, juniors. Walking: Unrestricted walking. Season: Year-round. Tee Times: Call 60 days in advance. Notes: Range (grass, mat). ⊠ 3199 Stonefield Dr., Jamul 91935, 10 mi from San Diego ☎ 619/441-6900 ⊕ www.steelecanyon.com ▤ AE, D, MC, V.

Canyon/Meadow. Holes: 18. Yards: 6,672/4,813. Par: 71/71. Course Rating: 72.2/67.9. Slope: 134/118.

Canyon/Ranch. Holes: 18. Yards: 6,741/4,655. Par: 71/71. Course Rating: 72.7/66.6. Slope: 135/112.

Ranch/Meadow. Holes: 18. Yards: 7,001/5,026. Par: 72/72. Course Rating: 74.0/69.5. Slope: 137/124.

Comments: These 27 holes were some of Gary Player's first, and they're still some of his best work. Each of the three 9s is very distinct. ★★★★ ¹/₂

TORREY PINES GOLF COURSE. Facility Holes: 36. Opened: 1957. Architect: William F. Bell. Cart Fee: $30 per cart. Discounts: Twilight. Walking: Unrestricted walking. Season: Year-round. Tee Times: Call golf shop. Notes: Range (grass, mat). ⊠ 11480 N. Torrey Pines Rd., La Jolla 92037 ☎ 858/ 452-3226 or 800/985-4653 ⊕ www.torreypinesgolfcourse. com ▤ AE, MC, V.

> San Diego's weather is relentlessly perfect, with low humidity and an ocean breeze.

North. Holes: 18. Yards: 6,874/6,122. Par: 72/74. Course Rating: 72.1/75.4. Slope: 129/ 134. Green Fee: $65/$75. *Comments: Not nearly a good as the South, but in great shape thanks to the play it gets during early rounds of the PGA Tour's Buick Classic.* ★★★★

South. Holes: 18. Yards: 7,607/5,542. Par: 72/73. Course Rating: 78.1/73.5. Slope: 143/126. Green Fee: $105/$125. *Comments: Recent improvements have turned it into Bethpage Black-lite. It's ready for the 2006 U.S. Open.* ★★★★

VINEYARD AT ESCONDIDO. Facility Holes: 18. Opened: 1993. Architect: David Rainville. Yards: 6,531/5,073. Par: 70/70. Course Rating: 70.3/70.3. Slope: 125/117. Green Fee: $30/$67. Cart Fee: Included in green fee. Discounts: Weekdays, twilight, seniors, juniors. Walking: Walking at certain times. Season: Year-round. High: Mar.–Nov. Tee Times: Call 7 days in advance. Notes: Range (grass, mat). ⊠ 925 San Pasqual Rd., Escondido 92025, 15 mi from San Diego ☎ 760/735-9545 ⊕ www.americangolf.com ▤ AE, D, DC, MC, V. *Comments: The golf is as good as the wine made nearby.* ★★★ ¹/₂

Where to Stay

DOUBLETREE HOTEL SAN DIEGO MISSION VALLEY. Location is this chain hotel's trump card; it's in Mission Valley, San Diego's business and shopping hub. It's close to the main freeways, and a San Diego Trolley station is within walking distance. The public areas are bright and comfortable; guest rooms are spacious and well equipped. Service here is a cut above most business hotels. ⊠ 7450 Hazard Center Dr., 92108 ☎ 619/297-5466 or 800/222-8733 🖹 619/297-5499 ⊕ www.doubletree.com ⤴ 294 rooms, 6 suites ⬩ Restaurant, room service, in-room data ports, minibars, cable TV with movies, 2 tennis courts, 2 pools, gym, outdoor hot tub, sauna, 2 bars, shops, laundry facilities, laundry service, concierge, business services, meeting rooms, airport shuttle, free parking; no smoking ⊟ AE, D, DC, MC, V $$-$$$.

EMBASSY SUITES. Sleek and modern, this all-suites hotel is 15 minutes from downtown San Diego, across from the sprawling Westfield Shoppingtown UTC mall. Two-room suites, which surround a 12-story tropical atrium and central courtyard with landscaped koi ponds, include extra televisions and voice mail. ⊠ 4550 La Jolla Village Dr., La Jolla 92112 ☎ 858/453-0400 or 800/362-2779 🖹 858/453-4226 ⊕ www. embassysuites.com ⤴ 335 suites ⬩ Restaurant, in-room data ports, microwaves, refrigerators, cable TV with movies and video games, indoor pool, exercise equipment, hot tub, sauna, bar, dry cleaning, laundry facilities, business services, car rental, parking (fee), no-smoking rooms ⊟ AE, D, DC, MC, V ⧉ BP $$$.

LODGE AT TORREY PINES. Just steps from the Torrey Pines golf course, this beautiful lodge sits on a bluff between La Jolla and Del Mar, and commands a view of miles of coastline. Although the hotel was completed in 2002, it looks like a classic Greene and Greene Craftsman bungalow, with William Morris-esque upholstery and carpets. The expansive rooms have a mix of antiques and reproduction Arts and Crafts pieces. The service is excellent and the restaurant, A. R. Valentin, serves outstanding contemporary cuisine. ⊠ 11480 N. Torrey Pines Rd., La Jolla 92037 ☎ 858/453-4420 or 800/995-4507 🖹 858/453-7476 ⊕ www.lodgetorreypines.com ⤴ 175 rooms ⬩ 2 restaurants, in-room data ports, in-room safes, cable TV, 18-hole golf course, pool, gym, hot tub, massage, spa, 2 bars, Internet, meeting rooms, free parking; no smoking ⊟ AE, D, DC, MC, V $$$$.

SHERATON SAN DIEGO HOTEL & MARINA. The twin high-rises of this hotel perch on Harbor Island, a thin peninsula across from the airport. The smaller West Tower has larger rooms with separate areas suitable for business entertaining, while the East Tower has better sports facilities. Rooms throughout are decorated with plush, contemporary furnishings. Views of downtown San Diego from the upper floors of both sections are superb, but because the West Tower is closer to the water it has fine outlooks from the lower floors, too. ⊠ 1380 Harbor Island Dr., 92101 ☎ 619/291-2900 or 888/ 625-5144 🖹 619/692-2337 ⊕ www.sheraton.com ⤴ 1,045 rooms, 50 suites ⬩ 3 restaurants, room service, in-room data ports, minibars, cable TV with movies and video games, 4 tennis courts, 3 pools, wading pool, health club, 2 outdoor hot tubs, massage, sauna, beach, boating, marina, bicycles, 2 bars, shop, dry cleaning, laundry service, concierge, business services, meeting rooms, airport shuttle, parking (fee); no smoking rooms ⊟AE, D, DC, MC, V ⦿l CP $$–$$$.

🖼 **SINGING HILLS RESORT COUNTRY CLUB AT SYCUAN.** This golf resort, in eastern San Diego County, is on 425 wooded acres. Many guest rooms have views of the mountains, the Dehesa Valley, and the three 18-hole golf courses. This resort is owned by the Sycuan Indians, who operate a casino nearby; they offer shuttle service between the two properties. The resort is roughly half an hour's drive from San Diego's airport. ✉ 3007 Dehesa Rd., El Cajon 92019 ☎ 619/442–3425 or 800/457–5568 🖶 619/442–9574 ⊕ www.singinghills.com ⬳ 102 rooms ⚭ Restaurant, dining room, some microwaves, refrigerators, 2 pools, 3 18-hole golf courses, 3 putting greens, 11 tennis courts, exercise equipment, hot tub, massage, bar, laundry facilities, business services, no-smoking rooms ⊟AE, D, MC, V $–$$.

Where to Eat

✕ **INDIGO GRILL.** A showcase for chef Deborah Scott's contemporary Southwestern cuisine, Indigo Grill has a stone interior and a broad terrace, but no matter how cool either of these spaces gets, they can't moderate the chilies that heat such one-of-a-kind offerings as oven clams and jalapeño-maize pappardelle with prawns and smoked pineapple. Entrées like the wild blueberry–lacquered venison chop make a big impression, as do such desserts as a puff pastry confection dressed with pears, Stilton cheese, and balsamic vinegar. ✉ 1536 India St. ☎ 619/234–6802 ⊟AE, D, DC, MC, V ⊘ No lunch weekends $$$–$$$$.

✕ **JASMINE BISTRO.** Flavors from China, Singapore, and Thailand mingle in every lovely dish that comes from the open kitchen at this restaurant tucked into Westfield Shoppingtown. Specialties include "Crouching Tiger Hidden Dragon" (sautéed lobster tail and tiger prawns), Malay prawns and scallops, and Thai basil shrimp. You can dine inside or out, but the patio has a view of the parking lot. ✉ 315 Parkway Plaza, El Cajon ☎ 619/588–8228 ⊟AE, D, DC, MC, V $$–$$$$.

✕ **LAUREL RESTAURANT AND BAR.** Laurel has long been regarded as a premier dinner address. Polished service and contemporary design set the stage for an imaginative, expertly prepared, Mediterranean-inspired seasonal menu. Look for appetizers such as pan-roasted sweetbreads with sherry vinegar sauce, and a warm tart of Roquefort cheese and caramelized onions. Favorite main course choices include the chicken roasted in a clay pot, grilled yellowfin tuna with niçoise olive mashed potatoes, and pepper-crusted veal loin. ✉ 505 Laurel St. ☎ 619/239–2222 ⊟AE, D, DC, MC, V ⊘ No lunch $$$–$$$$.

✕ **TAPENADE.** Taking its name and its tone from southern French tables, Tapenade is unpretentious and lighthearted. Very fresh ingredients, a delicate touch with sauces, and an emphasis on seafood characterize the menu. It changes frequently, but may include a rich cassoulet, porcini-stuffed rabbit, and roasted monkfish with eggplant. ✉ 7612 Fay Ave., La Jolla ☎ 858/551–7500 ⊟AE, DC, MC, V $$$$.

Essentials

Getting Here

San Diego is 120 mi south of Los Angeles via I-5; or from LAX I-405 south and I-5 south. Allow at least 2½ hours for the journey. Expect delays due to traffic any day and any time.

Visitor Information

🛈 **San Diego Visitor & Convention Bureau** ✉ 401 B. St., Suite 1400, 92101 ☎ 619/232-3101 ⊕ www.sandiego.org.

SAN LUIS OBISPO

The climate around San Luis Obispo is ideal nearly year-round. You can play here whenever you like, and the area is one of the few coastal regions in California that doesn't feel overcrowded. Even better, the golf here is not very expensive.

Start your trip at Cypress Ridge Golf Club, with mature cypress trees, lush green fairways, and fresh ocean air. You can see the spectacular views of the Pacific from several holes of this course, whose caretakers have gone out of their way to preserve the surrounding environment. Option two is Hunter Ranch Golf Course, which is inland. Although it was only built in 1994, the course has already developed an established look, with fairways going up and down many hills.

By the way, if you happen to be traveling down from San Francisco rather than up from Los Angeles, skip boring old U.S. 101 and head down the Pacific Coast Highway instead, no matter how long it takes. From Monterey to Big Sur to Morro Bay, it's a spectacular drive with an impressive final destination.

Courses

Golf Digest REVIEWS

BLACK LAKE GOLF RESORT. Facility Holes: 27. Opened: 1964. Architect: Ted Robinson. Green Fee: $26/$61. Cart Fee: $16 per cart. Discounts: Weekdays, twilight, seniors, juniors. Walking: Unrestricted walking. Season: Year-round. High: Apr.–Sept. Tee Times: Call 14 days in advance. Notes: Metal spikes, range (grass, mat). ✉ 1490 Golf Course La., Nipomo 93444, 10 mi from Santa Maria ☎ 805/343-1214 ⊕ www.blacklake. com ⊟ AE, D, MC, V.

Canyon/Oaks. Holes: 18. Yards: 6,034/5,047. Par: 71/71. Course Rating: 69.3/70.5. Slope: 121/120.

SAN LUIS OBISPO COURSES	YARDAGE	PAR	COURSE	SLOPE	GREEN FEE
Black Lake Golf Resort (27)					$26/$61
Canyon/Oaks (18)	6,034/5,047	71/71	69.3/70.5	121/120	
Lakes/Canyon (18)	6,401/5,628	72/72	70.9/72.9	123/126	
Lakes/Oaks (18)	6,185/5,161	71/71	69.7/70.8	121/124	
Cypress Ridge Golf Club (18)	6,803/5,087	72/72	73.0/70.3	133/120	$30/$60
Dairy Creek Golf Course (18)	6,548/4,965	71/71	71.9/69.0	127/121	$13/$32
Hunter Ranch Golf Course (18)	6,741/5,639	72/72	72.2/72.8	136/132	$23/$60
Morro Bay Golf Course (18)	6,360/5,055	71/72	70.7/69.5	115/117	$20/$38

Lakes/Canyon. Holes: 18. Yards: 6,401/5,628. Par: 72/72. Course Rating: 70.9/72.9. Slope: 123/126.

Lakes/Oaks. Holes: 18. Yards: 6,185/5,161. Par: 71/71. Course Rating: 69.7/70.8. Slope: 121/124.

Comments: Narrow fairways and tall oak and eucalyptus trees. Middle-of-the-pack for this area. ★ ★ ★ ¹/₂

CYPRESS RIDGE GOLF CLUB. Facility Holes: 18. Opened: 1999. Architect: Peter Jacobsen/Jim Hardy. Yards: 6,803/5,087. Par: 72/72. Course Rating: 73.0/70.3. Slope: 133/120. Green Fee: $30/$60. Cart Fee: $15 per person. Discounts: Weekdays, twilight, juniors. Walking: Walking at certain times. Season: Year-round. Tee Times: Call 10 days in advance. Notes: Range (grass). ✉780 Cypress Ridge Pkwy., Arroyo Grande 93420, 15 mi from San Luis Obispo ☎805/474-7979 ⊕www.cypressridge.com ▤AE, D, MC, V. *Comments: Great course built by the up-and-coming design team of PGA Tour player Peter Jacobsen and architect Jim Hardy. It overlooks the Pacific Ocean—the best of the trip.* ★ ★ ★ ★ ¹/₂

DAIRY CREEK GOLF COURSE. Facility Holes: 18. Opened: 1996. Architect: John Harbottle. Yards: 6,548/4,965. Par: 71/71. Course Rating: 71.9/69.0. Slope: 127/121. Green Fee: $13/$32. Cart Fee: $22 per cart. Discounts: Weekdays, twilight, seniors, juniors. Walking: Unrestricted walking. Season: Year-round. Tee Times: Call golf shop. Notes: Range (grass). ✉2990 Dairy Creek Rd., 93405 ☎805/782-8060 ▤D, MC, V. *Comments: Basic golf, and an interesting layout with hills and few trees.* ★ ★ ★ ¹/₂

HUNTER RANCH GOLF COURSE. Facility Holes: 18. Opened: 1994. Architect: Ken Hunter Jr./Mike McGinnis. Yards: 6,741/5,639. Par: 72/72. Course Rating: 72.2/72.8. Slope: 136/132. Green Fee: $23/$60. Cart Fee: $30 per cart. Discounts: Twilight, juniors. Walking: Unrestricted walking. Season: Year-round. Tee Times: Call 7 days in advance. Notes: Range (grass). ✉4041 Hwy. 46 E, Paso Robles 93446, 25 mi from San Luis Obispo ☎805/237-7444 ⊕www.hunterranchgolf.com ▤MC, V. *Comments: Built on the gently rolling terrain of inland California, this course is almost as impressive as Cypress Ridge. The $60 weekend green fee is a bargain.* ★ ★ ★ ★

MORRO BAY GOLF COURSE. Facility Holes: 18. Opened: 1929. Architect: Russell Noyes. Yards: 6,360/5,055. Par: 71/72. Course Rating: 70.7/69.5. Slope: 115/117. Green Fee: $20/$38. Cart Fee: $22 per cart. Discounts: Twilight, seniors, juniors. Walking:

Unrestricted walking. Season: Year-round. Tee Times: Call 7 days in advance. Notes: Metal spikes, range (grass, mat). ⊠201 State Park Rd., Morro Bay 93442, 15 mi from San Luis Obispo ☎805/772-8751 ▭D, MC, V. *Comments: This course is on a hillside overlooking Morro Bay, with tree-lined fairways and wicked sloping greens that are hard to read. Robert Muir Graves redesigned the course in 1987. Good, but not great.* ★★★ ¹/₂

Where to Stay

▥ **APPLE FARM.** Decorated to the hilt with floral bedspreads and watercolors by local artists, this is the most comfortable place to stay in town. Each room in the country-style hotel has a gas fireplace; some have canopy beds and cozy window seats. There's a working gristmill in the courtyard; within the inn are a cluttered gift shop and a restaurant that serves American food. ⊠2015 Monterey St., 93401 ☎805/544-2040, 800/374-3705 in CA, 800/255-2040 outside CA 🖷805/546-9495 ⊕www.applefarm. com ⬅104 rooms ⚲Restaurant, in-room data ports, cable TV, pool, hot tub, meeting rooms; no smoking ▭AE, D, MC, V $-$$$$.

▥ **CLIFFS AT SHELL BEACH.** With a Spanish-modern exterior surrounded by manicured palm trees, this spot has everything you would expect in a beachfront resort. Many of the modern rooms have fine ocean views: be sure to request one facing the beach. Suites have huge marble bathrooms and hot tubs. ⊠2757 Shell Beach Rd., Pismo Beach 93449 ☎805/773-5000 or 800/826-7827 🖷805/773-0764 ⊕www. cliffsresort.com ⬅142 rooms, 23 suites ⚲Restaurant, pool, spa, bar, meeting room ▭AE, D, DC, MC, V $$$-$$$$.

▥ **INN AT MORRO BAY.** This beautifully situated hotel complex has romantic, contemporary-style rooms with CD players and feather beds. Many have fireplaces, private decks with spa tubs, and bay views; others look out at extensive gardens. There's an on-site wellness center with spa and massage treatments, Morro Bay Golf Course across the road, and a heron rookery nearby. (Even if you're a bird-lover, don't book a room near the nesting grounds. The morning din can be overwhelming). ⊠60 State Park Rd., Morro Bay 93442 ☎805/772-5651 or 800/321-9566 🖷805/772-4779 ⊕www.innatmorrobay.com ⬅97 rooms, 1 cottage ⚲Restaurant, room service, cable TV with movies, pool, massage, spa, mountain bikes, bar, meeting room; no smoking ▭AE, D, DC, MC, V $$$-$$$$.

▥ **LA CUESTA INN.** This adobe-style motel on the northern edge of town is known for its reasonable prices. Each cheery room has a king or queen bed, or two queens. This is a good bet for families, especially because kids 12 and under stay free. VCR and movie rentals are available. ⊠2074 Monterey St., 93401 ☎805/543-2777 or 800/543-2777 🖷805/544-0696 ⊕www.lacuestainn.com ⬅72 rooms ⚲In-room data ports, refrigerators, cable TV with movies, pool, hot tub; no smoking ▭AE, D, DC, MC, V ⦿CP $-$$.

▥ **SEA VENTURE RESORT.** Fireplaces and feather beds create a cheery mood in each room. Those with ocean views are perched over a beautiful stretch of sand. The best amenities are the private hot tubs on most balconies and a deluxe breakfast basket delivered to your room in the morning. ⊠100 Ocean View Ave., 93449 ☎805/773-4994 or 800/662-5545 🖷805/773-0924 ⊕www.seaventure.com ⬅50 rooms ⚲Restaurant, fans, in-room data ports, minibars, refrigerators, in-room VCRs, pool, hot tub, bicycles, meeting rooms; no a/c, no smoking ▭AE, D, DC, MC, V ⦿CP $$$-$$$$.

Where to Eat

✕ **BIG SKY CAFÉ.** The menu here roams the world—the Mediterranean, North Africa, and the Southwest—but many of the ingredients are local, including organic fruits and vegetables, and the chicken is hormone-free. Big Sky is a hip gathering spot for breakfast, lunch, and dinner. ✉ 1121 Broad St. ☎ 805/545-5401 ⌖ Reservations not accepted ▭ AE, MC, V $-$$.

✕ **GIUSEPPE'S.** Classic tastes of the Pugliese region in southern Italy are presented in a cheery, rustic dining room in downtown Pismo Beach. Slide into a comfortable booth to feast on breads and pizzas baked from scratch in the wood-burning oven, hearty dishes like osso buco and lamb, and homemade or imported pastas. The restaurant grows its own tomatoes, basil, peppers, and herbs. ✉ 891 Price St., Pismo Beach ☎ 805/773-2870 ⌖ Reservations not accepted ▭ AE, D, MC, V ⊘ No lunch weekends $$-$$$.

✕ **LE FANDANGO BISTRO.** Spicy Basque flavors take classic French cuisine to new heights at this intimate restaurant with an open kitchen. In the evening dine on traditional rabbit stew, escargot, foie gras, duck, seafood, and lamb dishes, or choose from eight daily specials. Casual bistro-style dishes dominate the lunch menu. ✉ 717 Higuera St. ☎ 805/544-5515 ▭ AE, D, MC, V ⊘ No lunch Sun. and Mon. $$-$$$$.

✕ **SHORE CLIFF.** With probably the best seafood and clam chowder in Pismo Beach, this restaurant also has spectacular cliff-top views. The interior is airy, with large windows that let in lots of light. ✉ 2555 Price St., Pismo Beach ☎ 805/773-4671 ▭ AE, D, DC, MC, V $$-$$$$.

✕ **SPLASH CAFÉ.** Folks line up down the block for clam chowder served in a sourdough bread bowl at this wildly popular seafood stand. You can also order fresh steamed clams, burgers, hot dogs, calamari, and more—and nearly everything on the menu is $6 or less. The cheap storefront, a favorite with locals and savvy visitors, is open daily for lunch and dinner, but closes early in the evening weekdays during low season. ✉ 197 Pomeroy St. ☎ 805/773-4653 ▭ MC, V ¢-$.

Essentials

Getting Here

Route 1 and U.S. 101 run north–south and more or less parallel along the Central Coast, with Route 1 hugging the coast and U.S. 101 remaining inland. The trip to San Luis Obispo from Los Angeles is 190 mi.

Visitor Information

🛈 **Central Coast Tourism Council** ✉ Box 14011, San Luis Obispo 93406 ☎ 805/934-2129 ⊕ www.centralcoast-tourism.com. **San Luis Obispo Chamber of Commerce** ✉ 1039 Chorro St. ☎ 805/781-2777. **San Luis Obispo County Visitors and Conference Bureau** ✉ 1037 Mill St. ☎ 805/541-8000 or 800/634-1414 ⊕ www.visitslo.com.

Alisal Ranch Golf Course (18)	6,551/5,752	72/73	72.0/74.5	133/133	$90
La Purisima Golf Course (18)	7,105/5,762	72/72	74.9/74.3	143/131	$50/$60
Rancho San Marcos Golf Club (18)	6,801/5,018	71/71	73.1/69.2	135/117	$65/$145
River Course at the Alisal (18)	6,830/5,815	72/72	73.1/73.4	126/127	$50/$60
Sandpiper Golf Course (18)	7,068/5,725	72/73	74.5/73.3	134/125	$118
Santa Barbara Golf Club (18)	6,014/5,541	70/72	69.3/71.9	126/121	$20/$38

SANTA BARBARA

When Easterners trapped in winter cold dream about California, they may think of Los Angeles or San Diego or San Francisco. That just means they haven't been to Santa Barbara yet. Spectacular beaches, the Santa Ynez mountains in the background, and low-key elegance define this area. Actually, it took the town two tries to get things the way there are now. Before a massive earthquake destroyed most of downtown in 1925, Santa Barbara was barely a blip on the cultural map. The town was rebuilt in its current harmonious style, with whitewashed adobe walls and Spanish tile roofs.

Golfers gravitate to the town for other more recent designs—those of golf courses like La Purisima, which might be the most underrated course in California. It's a Robert Muir Graves–created cyclone of shot values and risk-reward. Sandpiper Golf Course, meanwhile, has been called the "Pebble Beach of the North" for its ocean views and its layout. It's also a great walking course. There's no truth to the rumor that the locals will only let you into town after you show proof that you're going to leave, but once you visit, you may understand how that rumor got started.

Courses
GolfDigest REVIEWS

ALISAL RANCH GOLF COURSE. Facility Holes: 18. Opened: 1955. Architect: William F. Bell. Yards: 6,551/5,752. Par: 72/73. Course Rating: 72.0/74.5. Slope: 133/133. Green Fee: $90. Cart Fee: $30 per cart. Discounts: Juniors. Walking: Unrestricted walking. Season: Year-round. Tee Times: Call golf shop. Notes: Range (grass), lodging (75). ✉ 1054 Alisal Rd., Solvang 93463, 40 mi from Santa Barbara ☎ 805/688-4215 ⊕ - www.alisal.com ▤ AE, MC, V. *Comments: Plays a good bit longer than the yardage on the card. Twisting and testy.* ★ ★ ★ ½

LA PURISIMA GOLF COURSE. Facility Holes: 18. Opened: 1986. Architect: Robert Muir Graves. Yards: 7,105/5,762. Par: 72/72. Course Rating: 74.9/74.3. Slope: 143/131.

Green Fee: $50/$60. Cart Fee: $30 per cart. Discounts: Weekdays, twilight, juniors. Walking: Unrestricted walking. Season: Year-round. Tee Times: Call 30 days in advance. Notes: Range (grass). ✉ 3455 State Hwy. 246, Lompoc 93436, 40 mi from Santa Barbara ☎ 805/735-8395 ⊕ www.lapurisimagolf.com ▤ MC, V. *Comments: Deserves more publicity than it gets. One of California's best.* ★ ★ ★ ★ ½

RANCHO SAN MARCOS GOLF CLUB. Facility Holes: 18. Opened: 1998. Architect: Robert Trent Jones Jr. Yards: 6,801/5,018. Par: 71/71. Course Rating: 73.1/69.2. Slope: 135/117. Green Fee: $65/$145. Cart Fee: Included in green fee. Discounts: Weekdays, twilight, juniors. Walking: Unrestricted walking. Season: Year-round. Tee Times: Call golf shop. Notes: Range (grass). ✉ 4600 Hwy. 154, 93105, 12 mi from Santa Barbara ☎ 805/683-6334 or 877/776-1804 ⊕ www.rsm1804.com ▤ AE, MC, V. *Comments: Fast, true greens.* ★ ★ ★ ★ ½

RIVER COURSE AT THE ALISAL. Facility Holes: 18. Opened: 1992. Architect: Steve Halsey/Jack Daray. Yards: 6,830/5,815. Par: 72/72. Course Rating: 73.1/73.4. Slope: 126/127. Green Fee: $50/$60. Cart Fee: $30 per cart. Discounts: Weekdays, twilight, seniors, juniors. Walking: Unrestricted walking. Season: Year-round. Tee Times: Call 7 days in advance. Notes: Range (grass, mat). ✉ 150 Alisal Rd., Solvang 93463, 35 mi from Santa Barbara ☎ 805/688-6042 ⊕ www.rivercourse.com ▤ AE, MC, V. *Comments: Worth every penny. It's a mixture of short and tight and rolling open holes.* ★ ★ ★ ½

La Purisima might be the most underrated course in California.

SANDPIPER GOLF COURSE. Facility Holes: 18. Opened: 1972. Architect: William F. Bell. Yards: 7,068/5,725. Par: 72/73. Course Rating: 74.5/73.3. Slope: 134/125. Green Fee: $118. Cart Fee: $14 per person. Discounts: Weekdays, twilight. Walking: Unrestricted walking. Season: Year-round. High: Apr.–Nov. Tee Times: Call 7 days in advance. Notes: Range (grass). ✉ 7925 Hollister Ave., 93117, 100 mi from Los Angeles ☎ 805/968-1541 ▤ AE, MC, V. *Comments: Pebble-caliber ocean views, and the layout to back it up.* ★ ★ ★ ★

SANTA BARBARA GOLF CLUB. Facility Holes: 18. Opened: 1958. Architect: Lawrence Hughes. Yards: 6,014/5,541. Par: 70/72. Course Rating: 69.3/71.9. Slope: 126/121. Green Fee: $20/$38. Cart Fee: $24 per cart. Discounts: Weekdays, twilight, seniors, juniors. Walking: Unrestricted walking. Season: Year-round. High: Apr.–Sept. Tee Times: Call golf shop. Notes: Range (mat). ✉ 3500 McCaw Ave., 93105 ☎ 805/687-7087 ⊕ www.ci.santa-barbara.ca.us ▤ MC, V. *Comments: Santa Barbara's muni of choice—and one of California's best in that category.* ★ ★ ★

Where to Stay

🏨 **ALISAL GUEST RANCH AND RESORT.** Home to the Alisal Ranch and River golf courses, this luxury ranch has catered to outdoors-oriented families for half a century. Guests have access to 10,000 acres of oak woodlands in the Santa Ynez Valley. You can ride horses in the hills, fish or sail in the 100-acre spring-fed lake, play a round of golf, or just lounge by the pool. Simply furnished ranch-style rooms and suites have garden views, covered porches, high-beamed ceilings, and wood-burning fireplaces. ⊠ 1054 Alisal Rd., Solvang 93463 ☎ 805/688-6411 or 800/425-4725 🖷 805/688-2510 ⊕ - www.alisal.com ⇨ 36 rooms, 37 suites ⚲ Restaurant, dining room, refrigerators, 2 18-hole golf courses, 7 tennis courts, pool, outdoor hot tub, boating, fishing, bicycles, billiards, boccie, croquet, hiking, horseback riding, Ping-Pong, shuffleboard, volleyball, bar, baby-sitting, children's programs (ages 6 and up); no room TVs ▭ AE, DC, MC, V ⏏ MAP $$$$.

⚏ **FOUR SEASONS RESORT SANTA BARBARA.** The luxury of Santa Barbara's grande dame begins with location: the hotel is right on the beach and surrounded by lush, perfectly manicured gardens. Guest privileges include preferred tee times at Rancho San Marcos and Sandpiper. Rooms in the main building and surrounding cottages, renovated in 2004, now have a classic Spanish look with wrought iron and dark wood furniture, plus colorful tiles in the bathrooms. ⊠ 1260 Channel Dr., 93108 ☎ 805/969-2261 or 800/332-3442 🖷 805/565-8323 ⊕ www.fourseasons.com ⇨ 190 rooms, 17 suites ⚲ 4 restaurants, room service, fans, in-room data ports, minibars, refrigerators, cable TV with movies and games, in-room DVDs, putting green, 3 tennis courts, 2 pools, health club, 3 outdoor hot tubs, spa, beach, bicycles, croquet, piano bar, baby-sitting, children's programs (ages 5-12), concierge, Internet, business services, meeting rooms, some pets allowed; no smoking ▭ AE, D, DC, MC, V $$$$.

⚏ **SANTA YNEZ INN.** It looks like a historic B&B, but this posh, two-story, Victorian-style inn in downtown Santa Ynez was built from scratch in 2002. The owners, who also have an antiques store, furnished all the rooms with handpicked antiques. The amenities, on the other hand, are strictly up-to-date: Frette linens, DVD/CD players, and custom-made bathrobes. Most rooms have gas fireplaces and double steam showers. Rates include an evening wine and hors d'oeuvres hour as well as breakfast. Nearby golf courses include the Alisal River Course and Rancho San Marcos. ⊠ 3627 Sagunto St., Santa Ynez 93460 ☎ 805/688-5588 or 800/643-5774 🖷 805/686-4294 ⊕ www. santaynezinn.com ⇨ 14 rooms ⚲ In-room data ports, refrigerators, cable TV with movies and games, gym, outdoor hot tub, massage, sauna, library, laundry service, concierge, meeting rooms; no smoking ▭ AE, D, MC, V ⏏ BP $$$$.

Where to Eat

✕ **BROTHERS RESTAURANT AT MATTEI'S TAVERN.** In the stagecoach days, Mattei's Tavern provided hearty meals and warm beds. In early 2000, chef-owners and brothers Matt and Jeff Nichols renovated the 1886 building and transformed it into one of the best restaurants in the valley. The casual, unpretentious dining rooms reflect the history of the tavern, from red velvet wallpaper and historic photos to hostesses decked out in cowboy boots and fringe vests. The steak-house menu changes every few weeks, but often includes favorites such as foie gras with spiced apples, prime rib, and grilled veal chops and salmon. ⊠ 2350 Railway Ave., Los Olivos ☎ 805/688-4820 ⚲ Reservations essential ▭ AE, MC, V ⊘ No lunch $$-$$$$.

✕ **LA SUPER-RICA.** Praised by Julia Child, this food stand with a patio serves some of the spiciest Mexican dishes between Los Angeles and San Francisco. Fans drive for miles for the soft tacos served with spicy or mild sauces and the legendarily good beans. ⊠ 622 N. Milpas St. ☎ 805/963–4940 ▭ No credit cards ¢–$.

✕ **THE STONEHOUSE.** This restaurant in a century-old granite farmhouse balances rusticity and elegance. There's contemporary fare such as beef fillet with a Gorgonzola-mushroom-cabernet sauce, couscous-crusted salmon with creamy lentils and a pineapple curry sauce, and excellent vegetarian options. Even better than the food are the surroundings—the restaurant is part of the San Ysidro Ranch resort. Have breakfast or lunch (salads, pastas, and sandwiches) on the tree-house-like outdoor patio. At night the candlelit interior is seriously romantic. ⊠ 900 San Ysidro La., Montecito ☎ 805/969–4100 ⚝ Reservations essential ▭ AE, DC, MC, V $$$$.

✕ **TRATTORIA GRAPPOLO.** Authentic Italian fare, an open kitchen, and lively, family-style seating make this trattoria equally popular with celebrities from Hollywood and ranchers from the Santa Ynez Valley. Favorites on the extensive menu range from homemade ravioli, risottos, and seafood linguine to grilled lamb chops in red wine sauce. The noise level tends to rise in the evening, so this isn't exactly the spot for a romantic getaway. ⊠ 3687-C Sagunto St., Santa Ynez ☎ 805/688–6899 ▭ AE, MC, V ☻ No lunch Mon. $–$$$$.

Essentials

Getting Here

Santa Barbara is about 90 mi north of Los Angeles, via Hwy. 101. Hwy. 1, that scenic but heavily trafficked route, hugs the coast from Santa Monica to Ventura before merging with Hwy. 101.

Visitor Information

🄸 **Santa Barbara Conference and Visitors Bureau** ⊠ 1601 Anacapa St., 93101 ☎ 805/966–9222 or 800/549–5133 ⊕ www.santabarbaraca.com. **Santa Ynez Valley Visitors Association** ⊡ Box 1918, Santa Ynez 93460 ☎ 800/742–2843 ⊕ www.santaynezvisit.com.

AROUND
MINNEAPOLIS
& ST. PAUL

Tournament Club of Iowa

By Ron Kaspriske and Brian Boese

Golfers who bask in the year-round warmth of places like West Palm Beach, Florida, and Scottsdale, Arizona, usually stop in their golf spikes when they hear that Minnesota has more golfers per capita than any other state in the United States. You read that right: despite the fact that the golf season is only six months long, golfers arrive like dandelions in Minnesota's summer. In fact, even former governor Jesse Ventura is a self-proclaimed golf nut.

There is plenty of great golf to be found in Minneapolis and St. Paul—their metro area is the only region in the United States to play host to eight professional majors and all 17 of the United States Golf Association's National Championships. That said, rising green fees and overcrowded fairways may prompt you to venture out to some terrific golf destinations within a half-day's drive of the state capital. From the untamed wilderness in the north to the sprawling farmland due south, there's no shortage of places to play. It all depends on your taste.

The drive north to Brainerd is scenic, slicing through timber country. On arrival, you're near lakeside resorts with some of the prettiest golf courses ever carved through dense forests. Its unspoiled look should be a welcome change from the more manufactured appearance of Minneapolis golf. Brainerd is no longer a quiet, out-of-the-way destination, so be prepared for five-hour rounds of golf, some traffic, and restaurant waiting lists. But the Classic at Madden's on Gull Lake resort and the Deacon's Lodge golf course—both ranked by *Golf Digest* as among the top 10 courses in the state—are worth the wait. The northeast corner of the state, which includes Duluth and Grand Rapids, is much more tranquil.

To the south, where the phrase "amber waves of grain" comes to mind, the Iowa cities of Cedar Rapids and Des Moines offer good golf on a budget. They may not be your first choice, but don't overlook them simply because Cedar Rapids doesn't roll off the tongue like Palm Springs. In most cases here, new golf courses were once old farms: the fields provide just enough undulation to make the courses scenic, playable, and expansive. The Harvester Golf Club near Des Moines is without question one of the best public courses in the United States.

If you're looking for a little nightlife with your golf, Madison, Wisconsin, the state capital and home of UW's main campus, can be as raucous as it is scenic. And the golf is stout, too, especially the 27 holes at the House on the Rock Resort outside the city and Wisconsin's University Ridge Golf course.

Around Minneapolis

If you want your weekend trip to be close enough to let you tee up for a quick 9 before the sun goes down on Friday afternoon, head northwest along I-94 and play the linksy courses in the Sauk Centre/Alexandria area.

BRAINERD

The Brainerd Lakes region began life as a weekend getaway for Twin Cities residents who wanted a little peace and quiet near a few of the state's fabled 10,000 lakes. It has since grown into one of the top golf destinations in the Midwest, with enough diversions to keep you as busy as you want to be. If the great golf and scenery isn't enough to get you to drive the 130 mi north from Minneapolis, the service will certainly get your attention. Competition for customers is so great in this getaway destination that waiters, bellhops, and golf course attendants jump at the chance to make your day. Think of Brainerd as Branson, Missouri, with much more scenery, many fewer tourist traps, and far better golf.

> Minnesota has more golfers per capita than any other state in the U.S.

Most courses are attached to resorts like Madden's or the Grand View Lodge, which means you don't have to leave the hotel property to get a feel for the region. In many cases, a great golf course is literally just outside your cabin or room. But trust us, you'll probably want to check out some of the area's other courses as well.

Fred Boos, Grand View's general manager in the 1970s and '80s, is considered the founding father of it all. In 1990, he brought former PGA Tour player Joel Goldstrand to Brainerd to design the Pines, the first standout course in the area. Since then, more than 15 courses have been built, including such standouts as the Classic and Deacon's Lodge golf course, both ranked in the top 10 in the state by *Golf Digest*. There's plenty of reason to make Brainerd your first choice for a golf getaway.

Courses

Golf Digest REVIEWS

BREEZY POINT RESORT. Facility Holes: 36. Cart Fee: Included in green fee. Discounts: Weekdays, twilight. Walking: Unrestricted walking. Season: Apr.–Oct. High: June–Apr. Tee Times: Call golf shop. Notes: Range (grass), lodging (250). ✉9252 Breezy Point Dr., Breezy Point 56472, 20 mi from Brainerd ☎218/562-7177 or 800/950-4960 ⊕www. breezypointresort.com ▤AE, D, DC, MC, V.

Breezy Point Resort (36)					
Traditional (18)	5,192/5,127	68/72	62.9/65.5	114/111	$35/$47
Whitebirch (18)	6,730/4,711	72/71	72.2/67.3	132/114	$45/$60
Grand View Lodge Resort	63				
Deacon's Lodge (18)	6,964/4,766	72/72	73.1/68.4	134/120	$90/$98
The Pines					$78/$88
Lakes/Woods (18)	6,874/5,134	72/72	74.1/70.7	143/128	
Marsh/Lakes (18)	6,837/5,112	72/72	74.2/71.0	145/131	
Woods/Marsh (18)	6,883/5,210	72/72	74.3/71.5	145/128	
**The Preserve (18)	6,601/4,816	72/72	71.3/68.8	135/119	$50/$90
Izatys Golf & Yacht Club (36)					
Black Brook (18)	6,867/5,119	72/72	74.2/71.1	140/122	$39/$69
Sanctuary (18)	6,646/5,075	72/72	72.6/70.3	134/125	$39/$59
Legacy Courses at Cragun's (36)					$35/$99
Bobby's Legacy (18)	6,928/5,300	72/72	73.8/71.1	145/132	
Dutch Legacy (18)	6,897/5,250	72/72	73.7/71.2	145/131	
Madden's on Gull Lake (54)					
Classic (18)	7,102/4,859	72/72	75.0/69.4	143/124	$65/$105
Pine Beach East (18)	5,956/5,352	72/72	67.9/69.7	114/114	$18/$40
Pine Beach West (18)	5,070/4,478	67/67	63.7/65.2	104/103	$18/$40
Ruttger's Bay Lake Lodge (27)					
Alec's Nine (9)	2,285/2,177	34/34	30.3/30.2	95/95	$23/$24
Lakes (18)	6,626/5,052	72/72	72.5/69.3	132/125	$44/$49

Traditional. Holes: 18. Opened: 1930. Architect: Bill Fawcett. Yards: 5,192/5,127. Par: 68/72. Course Rating: 62.9/65.5. Slope: 114/111. Green Fee: $35/$47. *Comments: A short, warm-up course, it's perfect for introducing someone to the game.* ★ ★

Whitebirch. Holes: 18. Opened: 1981. Architect: Landecker & Hubbard. Yards: 6,730/4,711. Par: 72/71. Course Rating: 72.2/67.3. Slope: 132/114. Green Fee: $45/$60. *Comments: Play this course and you'll know why Breezy Point gets its name. Decent overall, although there are better layouts in the area.* ★ ★ ★ ½

GRAND VIEW LODGE RESORT. Facility Holes: 63. Cart Fee: Included in green fee. Discounts: Weekdays, twilight, juniors. Walking: Unrestricted walking. Season: Apr.–Oct. Tee Times: Call 90 days in advance. Notes: Range (grass), lodging (300). Also has a 9-hole executive course. ✉ 23521 Nokomis Ave., Nisswa 56468, 120 mi from Minneapolis ☎ 218/963-0001 or 888/437-4637 ⊕ www.grandviewlodge.com ▭ AE, D, MC, V.

Deacon's Lodge. Holes: 18. Opened: 1999. Architect: Arnold Palmer/Ed Seay. Yards: 6,964/4,766. Par: 72/72. Course Rating: 73.1/68.4. Slope: 134/120. Green Fee: $90/$98. *Comments: Ranked 9th in Minnesota by* Golf Digest. *Has a Pine Valley feel with expansive waste bunkers. May be the best public golf course in the United States to be designed by Arnold Palmer and Ed Seay.* ★ ★ ★ ★

The Pines. Opened: 1990. Architect: Joel Goldstrand. Green Fee: $78/$88. *Comments: The Lakes, Woods, and Marsh courses that make up the Pines are always in great condition. A great value.* ★ ★ ★ ★ ½

FAVORITE SON

PGA Tour standout Tom Lehman hails from Austin, Minnesota. Although he now resides in Scottsdale, Arizona, to take advantage of the year-round sunny practicing weather, he has a soft spot for the Gopher State. In addition to an impressive record that includes five career PGA Tour victories, including the 1996 British Open, Lehman is an accomplished golf course designer. One of his most respected works is the TPC of the Twin Cities, done with Arnold Palmer, which served as the second-year site of the 3M Championship, part of the Champions Tour.

Lakes/Woods. Holes: 18. Yards: 6,874/5,134. Par: 72/72. Course Rating: 74.1/70.7. Slope: 143/128.

Marsh/Lakes. Holes: 18. Yards: 6,837/5,112. Par: 72/72. Course Rating: 74.2/71.0. Slope: 145/131.

Woods/Marsh. Holes: 18. Yards: 6,883/5,210. Par: 72/72. Course Rating: 74.3/71.5. Slope: 145/128.

The Preserve. Holes: 18. Yards: 6,601/4,816. Par: 72/72. Course Rating: 71.3/68.8. Slope: 135/119. Green Fee: $50/$90. Cart Fee: Included in green fee. Walking: Unrestricted walking. *Comments: Often overlooked in favor of Deacon's Lodge and the Pines, but excellent in its own right. There are 11 downhill tee shots, so choose your clubs carefully.* ★ ★ ★ ★ ½

IZATYS GOLF & YACHT CLUB. Facility Holes: 36. Architect: John Harbottle III. Cart Fee: Included in green fee. Discounts: Weekdays, twilight. Walking: Unrestricted walking. Season: Apr.–Nov. Tee Times: Call 14 days in advance. Notes: Range (grass, mat), lodging (200). ✉ 40005 85th Ave., Onamia 56359, 90 mi from Minneapolis ☎ 320/532–3101 or 800/533–1728 ⊕ www.izatys.com ▬ AE, D, DC, MC, V.

Black Brook. Holes: 18. Opened: 1999. Yards: 6,867/5,119. Par: 72/72. Course Rating: 74.2/71.1. Slope: 140/122. Green Fee: $39/$69. *Comments: The par-3 14th, which routes along the shoreline of Lake Mille Lacs, is awesome.* ★ ★ ★ ★

Sanctuary. Holes: 18. Opened: 1998. Yards: 6,646/5,075. Par: 72/72. Course Rating: 72.6/70.3. Slope: 134/125. Green Fee: $39/$59. *Comments: Looks more like a wetlands preserve than a golf course. Fun to play, but easy to lose a ball.* ★ ★ ★ ½

LEGACY COURSES AT CRAGUN'S. Facility Holes: 36. Opened: 1999. Architect: Robert Trent Jones Jr. Green Fee: $35/$99. Cart Fee: Included in green fee. Discounts: Twilight. Walking: Unrestricted walking. Season: Apr.–Oct. Tee Times: Call 180 days in advance. Notes: Range (grass), lodging (300). ✉ 11000 Cragun's Dr., 18 mi from Brainerd, 56401 ☎ 218/825–2800 or 800/272–4867 ⊕ www.craguns.com ▬ AE, D, MC, V.

Bobby's Legacy. Holes: 18. Yards: 6,928/5,300. Par: 72/72. Course Rating: 73.8/71.1. Slope: 145/132. *Comments: Holes alongside Legacy Lake are outstanding. The slope from the back tees makes it the toughest course in the region. Try breaking 80 here.*

Dutch Legacy. Holes: 18. Yards: 6,897/5,250. Par: 72/72. Course Rating: 73.7/71.2. Slope: 145/131. *Comments: Not as secluded as Bobby's Legacy, but still a good Robert Trent Jones Jr. design.* ★ ★ ★ ½

MADDEN'S ON GULL LAKE. Facility Holes: 54. Discounts: Weekdays, seniors. Walking: Unrestricted walking. Season: Apr.–Oct. Tee Times: Call 60 days in advance. Notes: Range (grass), lodging (400). ✉ 11266 Pine Beach Peninsula, 56401 ☎ 218/829–2811 or 800/642–5363 ⊕ www.maddens.com ☰ AE, MC, V.

Classic. Holes: 18. Opened: 1997. Architect: Scott Hoffman. Yards: 7,102/4,859. Par: 72/72. Course Rating: 75.0/69.4. Slope: 143/124. Green Fee: $65/$105. Cart Fee: Included in green fee. *Comments: A great layout, fun to play, and very scenic. If you only play a couple of area courses, make sure you stop here.* ★ ★ ★ ★ ¹/₂

Pine Beach East. Holes: 18. Opened: 1926. Architect: James Delgleish. Yards: 5,956/5,352. Par: 72/72. Course Rating: 67.9/69.7. Slope: 114/114. Green Fee: $18/$40. Cart Fee: $32 per cart. *Comments: Still fun to play, but a little gimmicky (there's a par-6 hole).* ★ ★ ★ ¹/₂

Pine Beach West. Holes: 18. Opened: 1950. Architect: Paul Coates/Jim Madden. Yards: 5,070/4,478. Par: 67/67. Course Rating: 63.7/65.2. Slope: 104/103. Green Fee: $18/$40. Cart Fee: $32 per cart. *Comments: This course is great for beginners and high handicappers. Learn to hit those irons here.* ★ ★ ★

RUTTGER'S BAY LAKE LODGE. Facility Holes: 27. Architect: Joel Goldstrand. Discounts: Twilight. Walking: Unrestricted walking. Season: Apr.–Nov. Tee Times: Call golf shop. Notes: Range (grass). ✉ Rte. 2, Deerwood 56401, 15 mi from Brainerd ☎ 218/678–2885 or 800/450–4545 ☰ AE, D, MC, V.

Alec's Nine. Holes: 9. Opened: 1920. Yards: 2,285/2,177. Par: 34/34. Course Rating: 30.3/30.2. Slope: 95/95. Green Fee: $23/$24. Cart Fee: $14 per cart. *Comments: Great for a quick round or for children. Not very difficult. It's usually easy to get a tee time, since most golfers want to play the Lakes course.* UR

Lakes. Holes: 18. Opened: 1992. Yards: 6,626/5,052. Par: 72/72. Course Rating: 72.5/69.3. Slope: 132/125. Green Fee: $44/$49. Cart Fee: $31 per cart. *Comments: Holes feel a little squeezed. You may be playing into a green from another fairway. The property does, however, have an out-in-the-wilderness charm.* ★ ★ ★ ¹/₂

Where to Stay

🏨 **BREEZY POINT.** One of Minnesota's oldest resorts, Breezy Point has been in business since the 1920s. Resting on the edge of Pelican Lake, the boating options are plentiful, and tennis lessons are available. You can choose from 1- and 2-bedroom lodges, lodge apartments, and individual cabins with 3 to 10 bedrooms. ✉ 9252 Breezy Point Dr., Breezy Point 56472 ☎ 218/562–7811 or 800/432–3777 🖨 218/562–4510 ⊕ www.breezypointresort.com ⇆ 69 rooms, 132 apartments ⚐ 2 restaurants, some kitchenettes, refrigerators, cable TV, 2 18-hole golf courses, 4 tennis courts, 5 pools (2 indoor), exercise equipment, hot tubs, beach, dock, boating, cross-country skiing, ice-skating, bar, video game room, children's programs (ages 5–12), playground, business services ☰ AE, D, MC, V $-$$.

🏨 **CRAGUN'S CONFERENCE AND GOLF RESORT.** One of the largest all-season resort and conference centers in Minnesota, Cragun's has a wide assortment of rooms, suites, and cabins, many of which comes with a view of Gull Lake. The luxury rooms also include fireplaces, a sitting area with a love seat, and a compact kitchen with a microwave and refrigerator. Another highlight is the impressive spa, where you can get several massage and facial treatments. ⊠ 11000 Cragun's Dr., 56401 ☎ 218/829-3591 or 800/272-4867 🖨 218/829-9188 ⊕ www.craguns.com ⛵ 155 rooms, 21 suites, 6 apartments, 43 cabins ⟁ Restaurant, dining room, cable TV, 2 18-hole golf courses, 8 tennis courts, 2 pools, exercise equipment, hot tub, 2 beaches, boating, cross-country skiing, snowmobiling, bar, laundry facilities, business services, airport shuttle ▭ AE, D, MC, V $-$$$.

⛏ GRAND VIEW LODGE. Eight miles north of Brainerd, on Gull Lake, Grand View Lodge includes lakeside cabins and town houses, as well as charming suites. Twelve rooms are available in the historic, nationally registered Main Lodge. Cottages, on the lake or with lake views, accommodate groups of 2 on up to 20. Some include fireplaces, kitchenettes, and Jacuzzi tubs. ⊠ 23521 Nokomis Ave. S, Nisswa 56468 ☎ 218/963-2234 or 800/432-3788 🖨 218/963-2269 ⊕ www.grandviewlodge.com ⛵ 12 rooms, 17 suites, 17 town houses, 9 cabins, 60 cottages ⟁ Dining room, refrigerators, cable TV, driving range, 2 18-hole courses, 27-hole golf course, pool, hot tub, beach, boating, bar, video game room, children's programs (ages 3–12), business services, airport shuttle ▭ AE, D, MC, V $$$-$$$$.

⛏ IZATYS GOLF & YACHT CLUB. This resort on Mille Lacs Lake is as well known for its luxury as for its golf. Standard rooms include a king-size bed or two full beds. Suites come with king-size beds, a sitting room, fireplaces, a wet bar, a microwave oven, and a refrigerator. All the town houses are on the lake and come with full kitchens. ⊠ 40005 85th Ave., Onamia 56359 ☎ 800/533-1728 🖨 320/532-4910 ⊕ www.izatys.com ⛵ 28 rooms, 4 suites, 50 town houses ⟁ Restaurant, cable TV, 2 18-hole golf courses, 2 tennis courts, 2 pools (1 indoor), hot tub ▭ AE, D, MC, V $$.

⛏ MADDEN'S ON GULL LAKE. Home of the Classic and near other highly ranked courses, Madden's has rooms that border links as well as Gull Lake. The resort sprawls over 1,000 acres. ⊠ 11266 Pine Beach Peninsula, 56401 ☎ 218/829-2811 or 800/642-5363 ⊕ www.maddens.com ⛵ 287 rooms, 26 suites ⟁ 3 restaurants, some microwaves, some refrigerators, cable TV, driving range, 3 18-hole golf courses, 5 pools (3 indoor), lake, beach, dock, boating, bicycles, hiking, 2 bars, shops, video games, children's programs (ages 4–15), laundry facilities, business services, meeting rooms ▭ AE, MC, V $$-$$$.

⛏ RUTTGER'S BIRCHMONT LODGE. Five generations of the same family have owned and operated this lodge, which first opened in 1898. Some rooms face the golf course, and others face the lake. Some rooms have kitchens, fireplaces, and screened porches. ⊠ 7598 Bemidji Rd. NE, Bemidji 56601 ☎ 218/444-3463 or 888/788-8437 ⊕ www.ruttger.com ⛵ 28 rooms, 40 cottages ⟁ Dining room, in-room data ports, some kitchenettes, refrigerators, cable TV, 2 tennis courts, 2 pools (1 indoor), gym, hot tub, beach, dock, boating, cross-country skiing, bar, children's programs (ages 4–12), laundry facilities, business services, airport shuttle, some pets allowed; no a/c in some rooms ▭ AE, D, MC, V ¢-$$.

Where to Eat

✗ **BOATHOUSE EATERY.** The tall ceilings and a wood-heavy interior do indeed bring to mind a lumber baron's boathouse. The restaurant serves casual renditions of pasta, steak, and fish that include walleye and pecan-crusted catfish. Brunch is available on Sunday. ⊠ Quarterdeck Resort, 9820 Birch Bay Dr., Nisswa ☎ 218/963-2482 or 800/950-5596 ⊕ www.quarterdeckresort.com ⊟ AE, D, MC, V $-$$$.

✗ **LOST LAKE LODGE RESTAURANT.** With breads made from their flour ground in the Lost Lake Grist Mill, and beers made in Minnesota, the Lost Lake Lodge Restaurant is a showcase for distinctly homegrown cuisine. The five entrées on the menu change daily, and include favorites like French Country Chicken and top sirloin with Gorgonzola sauce. Reservations are essential between May and October. ⊠ 7965 Lost Lake Rd., Lake Shore ☎ 218/963-2681 or 800/450-2681 ⊕ www.lostlake.com ⊟ MC, V $$-$$$$.

Essentials

Getting Here

To get to Brainerd from the Twin Cities, take I-94 west 60 mi to St. Cloud. From there take Route 15 north 10 mi to U.S. 10, heading west for 30 mi. Finally, take Route 371 (the Paul Bunyan Expressway) 55 mi to Brainerd.

Visitor Information

🛈 **Brainerd/Crosslakes Area Chambers of Commerce** ⊠ 124 N. 6th St., 56401 ☎ 218/829-2838 or 800/450-2838 ⊕ www.brainerdchamber.com.

CEDAR RAPIDS, IA

Although Iowa's second city takes a backseat to Des Moines in terms of quality golf, there are still enough good courses in the area to put together a weekend golf getaway. At the top of the list is the Amana Colonies Golf Course to the southwest and Finkbine, the University of Iowa's home course, 30 minutes south of Iowa City. Golf here dates back to the 1920s. At the time, Ellis Park Municipal Golf Course had only 9 holes and was the only game in town. The course, since expanded to 18 holes, is now an outstanding classic course that you can play for less than $30. Try finding a similar value in Minneapolis.

The rolling land and tall trees around Cedar Rapids have more in common with rural areas in states like Ohio than they do with the cornfields normally associated with Iowa. Almost all the courses in the area are parkland style, harkening back to an era when fairways were routed up and back.

Amana Colonies Golf Course (18)	6,824/5,228	72/72	73.3/69.7	136/115	$32/$49
Don Gardner Golf Course (18)	6,629/5,574	72/72	69.7/70.4	111/109	$15/$17
Ellis Park Municipal Golf Course (18)	6,502/4,885	72/72	71.1/67.1	121/113	$15/$17
Finkbine Golf Course (18)	7,030/5,645	72/72	74.1/69.5	134/118	$20/$37
Hunter's Ridge Golf Club (18)	7,007/5,090	72/72	74.0/71.0	132/118	$26/$35
Pleasant Valley Golf Course (18)	6,472/5,067	72/72	71.6/68.4	127/111	$15/$25
Quail Creek Golf Course (9)	7,046/5,492	72/72	73.6/74.5	124/118	$20/$25

With typical green fees holding fast between $30 and $50, Cedar Rapids is one of the most affordable places to play in the United States. Add to that the fact that getting a room and a meal here costs less than $100, and it's a good choice for budget-conscious golfers.

Courses

Golf Digest REVIEWS

AMANA COLONIES GOLF COURSE. Facility Holes: 18. Opened: 1989. Architect: William James Spear. Yards: 6,824/5,228. Par: 72/72. Course Rating: 73.3/69.7. Slope: 136/115. Green Fee: $32/$49. Cart Fee: Included in green fee. Discounts: Weekdays, twilight, seniors, juniors. Walking: Walking at certain times. Season: Mar.–Nov. High: May–Sept. Tee Times: Call 30 days in advance. Notes: Range (grass). ✉ 451 27th Ave., Amana 52203, 20 mi from Cedar Rapids ☎ 319/622-6222 or 800/383-3636 ⊕ www.amanagolfcourse.com ▭ AE, DC, MC, V. *Comments: Hills, great views, and a GPS system that gives you accurate distances between your cart and the flagstick. This is the first pick of area courses.* ★ ★ ★ ★

DON GARDNER MEMORIAL GOLF COURSE. Facility Holes: 18. Opened: 1968. Architect: Herman Thompson. Yards: 6,629/5,574. Par: 72/72. Course Rating: 69.7/70.4. Slope: 111/109. Green Fee: $15/$17. Cart Fee: $22 per cart. Discounts: Twilight, seniors, juniors. Walking: Unrestricted walking. Season: Mar.–Dec. Tee Times: Call 10 days in advance. Notes: Range (grass). ✉ 5101 Golf Course Rd., Marion 52302, 2 mi from Cedar Rapids ☎ 319/286-5586 or 800/373-8433 ▭ MC, V. *Comments: A solid municipal golf course, but it's not as good as Ellis Park.* ★ ★ ★

ELLIS PARK MUNICIPAL GOLF COURSE. Facility Holes: 18. Opened: 1922. Architect: Lohman Golf Designs. Yards: 6,502/4,885. Par: 72/72. Course Rating: 71.1/67.1. Slope: 121/113. Green Fee: $15/$17. Cart Fee: $23 per cart. Discounts: Weekdays, twilight, seniors, juniors. Walking: Unrestricted walking. Season: Mar.–Nov. High: June–Aug. Tee Times: Call 10 days in advance. Notes: Range (grass, mat). ✉ 1401 Zika Ave. NW, 52405 ☎ 319/286-5589 ▭ D, MC, V. *Comments: A good, old muni that underwent substantial renovation in 2002. Worth your time.* ★ ★ ★

FINKBINE GOLF COURSE. Facility Holes: 18. Opened: 1955. Architect: Robert Bruce Harris. Yards: 7,030/5,645. Par: 72/72. Course Rating: 74.1/69.5. Slope: 134/118. Green Fee: $20/$37. Cart Fee: $24 per cart. Discounts: Twilight. Walking: Unrestricted walking. Season: Apr.–Nov. High: June–Aug. Tee Times: Call 7 days in advance. Notes: Range (grass). ⊠ 1362 W. Melrose Ave., Iowa City 52242, 110 mi from Des Moines ☎ 319/335-9246 ⊕ www.finkbine.com ⊟ MC, V. *Comments: University of Iowa's college course is one of the best public tracks in the state and our second choice for the area. It's done in a classic, parkland style, so get used to punching out into the fairways from behind one of the hundreds of trees that outline them.* ★ ★ ★ ★

HUNTER'S RIDGE GOLF CLUB. Facility Holes: 18. Opened: 1997. Architect: Bob Lohmann/Gordon G. Lewis. Yards: 7,007/5,090. Par: 72/72. Course Rating: 74.0/71.0. Slope: 132/118. Green Fee: $26/$35. Cart Fee: $13 per person. Discounts: Weekdays, twilight, seniors, juniors. Walking: Walking at certain times. Season: Mar.–Dec. High: May–Sept. Tee Times: Call 14 days in advance. Notes: Range (grass). ⊠ 2901 Hunter's Ridge Rd., Marion 52001 ☎ 319/377-3500 ⊕ www.huntersridgegolfcourse.com ⊟ MC, V. *Comments: Lots of water, and a windy, wide open back 9. This is our third pick for the area.* ★ ★ ★ ★

PLEASANT VALLEY GOLF COURSE. Facility Holes: 18. Opened: 1987. Architect: William James Spear. Yards: 6,472/5,067. Par: 72/72. Course Rating: 71.6/68.4. Slope: 127/111. Green Fee: $15/$25. Cart Fee: $20 per cart. Discounts: Weekdays, twilight, seniors, juniors. Walking: Unrestricted walking. Season: Apr.–Nov. Tee Times: Call 7 days in advance. Notes: Range (grass, mat). ⊠ 4390 S.E. Sand Rd., Iowa City 52240, 100 mi from Des Moines ☎ 319/337-7209 ⊕ www.pleasantvalley-ic.com ⊟ AE, D, MC, V. *Comments: One of the best in the area. Lots of water, but very well maintained.* ★ ★ ★ ★

QUAIL CREEK GOLF COURSE. Facility Holes: 9. Opened: 1969. Architect: Johnson. Yards: 7,046/5,492. Par: 72/72. Course Rating: 73.6/74.5. Slope: 124/118. Green Fee: $20/$25. Cart Fee: $23 per cart. Discounts: Weekdays. Walking: Unrestricted walking. Season: Apr.–Dec. Tee Times: Call 7 days in advance. Notes: Range (grass). ⊠ 700 Clubhouse Rd. NE, North Liberty 52317, 5 mi from Iowa City ☎ 319/626-2281 ⊟ No credit cards. *Comments: Always in good condition. The National Golf Foundation considers it one of the best 9-hole courses in the United States.* ★ ★ ★ ¹/₂

Where to Stay

🏨 **BEST WESTERN LONGBRANCH.** With over 50 restaurants and three 18-hole golf courses within 2 mi, the Best Western Longbranch is extremely convenient. The pleasantly decorated standard rooms have either one or two queen-size beds. Suites have Jacuzzi tubs and kitchenettes. ⊠ 90 Twixtown Rd. NE, 52402 ☎ 319/377-6386 or 800/528-1234 🖷 319/377-3686 ⊕ www.bestwestern.com ⤳ 106 rooms, 3 suites ♿ Restaurant, room service, in-room data ports, cable TV, some in-room VCRs, 2 bars, business services, airport shuttle, free parking ⊟ AE, D, DC, MC, V ¢–$.

🏨 **CLARION HOTEL.** The Clarion's marble-floored lobby has 16-foot ceilings, a crystal chandelier, and a large fireplace. Between the airport and downtown, it's close to several restaurants. Pleasant and spacious, the standard rooms include either two double beds or one king-size. Suites have microwaves and refrigerators. ⊠525 33rd Ave. SW, 52404 ☎319/366-8671 🖷319/362-1420 ⊕ www.clarionhotel.com ↙153 rooms, 4 suites ᕀ Restaurant, room service, in-room data ports, cable TV, indoor pool, exercise equipment, health club, hot tub, sauna, bar, business services, airport shuttle, free parking, some pets allowed, no-smoking rooms ▭AE, D, DC, MC, V $-$$.

⌗ **COLLINS PLAZA.** Each of the rooms in this hotel opens to a dramatic seven-story, tree-filled atrium, highlighted by a four-story waterfall. Refrigerators are available on request. Standard rooms are outfitted with either two double beds or a king-size bed with a sleeper sofa. Suites come with a queen-size bed, two televisions, a refrigerator, and a wet bar. ⊠1200 Collins Rd. NE, 52402 ☎319/393-6600 or 800/541-1067 🖷319/393-2308 ↙221 rooms, 85 suites ᕀ Restaurant, in-room data ports, refrigerators, cable TV, indoor pool, gym, hot tub, bar, laundry facilities, business services, airport shuttle, free parking ▭AE, D, DC, MC, V $-$$.

⌗ **CROWNE PLAZA FIVE SEASONS.** The downtown location puts the 16-story Crowne Plaza close to many restaurants and stores. Standard rooms come with either a king-size bed or two double beds. The Top of the Five rooftop restaurant has great views of the city, and the ground-level sports bar adds a casual restaurant option. ⊠350 1st Ave. NE, 52401 ☎319/363-8161 🖷319/363-3804 ⊕ www.ichotelsgroup. com ↙275 rooms, 2 suites ᕀ Restaurant, room service, in-room data ports, cable TV, indoor pool, exercise equipment, bar, business services, airport shuttle, parking (fee) ▭AE, D, DC, MC, V $-$$.

⌗ **HOLIDAY INN.** Seven miles from the famous Amana Colonies, this chain hotel is affordable, with lots of amenities. A lobby with a grandfather clock and lots of couches give it a touch of home. The spacious Holidome contains a large pool and a roomy whirlpool. Right next door is Little Amana, where there's a general store and a wine shop, which has a tasting room. ⊠2211 U Ave., Amana Colonies 52361 ☎319/668-1175 or 800/465-4329 🖷319/668-2853 ⊕ www.amanaholidayinn.com ↙155 rooms ᕀ Restaurant, room service, cable TV, indoor pool, exercise equipment, hot tub, bar, playground, laundry facilities, business services, some pets allowed ▭AE, D, DC, MC, V $-$$.

Where to Eat

✕ **BRICK HAUS RESTAURANT.** Built with native stone and wood as well as bricks, this restaurant serves pleasant family-style food. The Wiener schnitzel with spaetzle noodles is a favorite. Smoking is not allowed. ⊠728 47th Ave., Amana ☎319/622-3278 or 800/622-3471 ▭AE, MC, V $-$$$.

✕ **CEDAR BREWING COMPANY.** An assortment of sandwiches and burgers, as well as fish and steak make the Cedar Brewery Company great for a casual meal. Four kinds of beer, including the popular Golden Hawk lager, are brewed on-site, and the kitchen smokes its own chicken and ribs. The *ciabatta* garlic bread is a favorite here. There's also a Sunday brunch. ⊠500 Blairs Ferry Rd. NE ☎319/378-9090 ▭AE, D, MC, V $-$$$.

Essentials

Getting Here

To get to Cedar Rapids from the Twin Cities, take I-35W south 130 mi. Then take I-27 south 80 mi to U.S. 218. After traveling south 10 mi, get on I-380. Cedar Rapids is 50 mi to the south.

The Amana Colonies are 20 mi south of Cedar Raids. To get there take U.S. 151.

Visitor Information

🚩 **Amana Colonies Convention and Visitors Bureau** ✉ 39 38th Ave., 52203 ☎ 319/ 622-7622 or 800/579-2294 ⊕ www.amanacolonies.com. **Cedar Rapids Area Chamber of Commerce** ✉ 424 1st Ave. NE 52401 ☎ 319/398-5317 ⊕ www.cedarrapids.org. **Iowa City/Coralville Convention and Visitors Bureau** ✉ 408 1st Ave., Coralville 52241 ☎ 319/337-6592 or 800/283-6592 ⊕ www.icccvb.org.

DES MOINES, IA

The 240-mi drive down I-35 to Iowa's capital isn't terribly exciting, but trust us, you should still make the trip. The passion that Iowans have for golf is evident in the quality—and quantity—of courses in this area. There are more than a dozen tracks worth a round, and a few, most prominently the Harvester Golf Club in nearby Rhodes, may just become one of your all-time favorite places to play. *Golf Digest* ranked the Keith Foster–designed Harvester number one in the state. Apparently, whatever *Field of Dreams* implied, they aren't just building baseball diamonds in those Iowa cornfields.

Actually, the farmland in Iowa has remained largely intact. Most new golf courses, including the Harvester, are built across creeks and up and down hills, leaving the silos and tractors in the background. It's also true of Bos Landen in Pella (9th in the state) and the brand new Tournament Club of Iowa in Polk City, to the north.

Des Moines doesn't have a PGA Tour stop, but don't mistake that for a lack of enthusiasm for the sport. When the U.S. Senior Open came to Des Moines in 1999, record crowds showed up to watch, and the tournament had a complete roster of volunteers more than a year before the first ball was teed up. The only thing the area truly lacks is a choice of golf resorts. However, the Bos Landen Resort is a great place to stay if you don't mind the 35-mi drive southeast to Pella.

Course	Yards	Par	Course Rating	Slope	Green Fee
A. H. Blank Golf Course (18)	6,815/5,617	72/72	72.3/70.4	127/115	$18/$22
Bos Landen Golf Resort (18)	6,916/5,132	72/72	73.5/71.0	131/125	$30/$49
Briarwood Golf Course (18)	7,019/5,250	72/72	74.2/70.4	128/119	$22/$31
Harvester Golf Club (18)	7,340/5,115	72/72	75.6/69.4	137/120	$45/$55
Jester Park Golf Course (18)	6,801/6,062	72/73	72.9/68.4	125/109	$18/$27
Lake Panorama National Golf Course (18)	7,024/5,765	72/72	73.2/73.2	131/121	$35/$40
River Valley Golf Course (18)	6,635/5,482	72/72	71.1/67.4	121/114	$16/$39
Tournament Club of Iowa (18)	7,043/6,153	72/72	74.0/64.8	145/107	$67/$45
Veenker Memorial Golf Course (18)	6,543/5,357	72/73	71.3/70.6	124/120	$21/$27

Courses

Golf Digest REVIEWS

A. H. BLANK GOLF COURSE. Facility Holes: 18. Opened: 1971. Architect: Edward Lawrence Packard. Yards: 6,815/5,617. Par: 72/72. Course Rating: 72.3/70.4. Slope: 127/115. Green Fee: $18/$22. Cart Fee: $24 per cart. Discounts: Twilight, seniors, juniors. Walking: Unrestricted walking. Season: Year-round. High: May–Sept. Tee Times: Call golf shop. Notes: Range (grass, mat). ⌧ 808 County Line Rd., 50315 ☎ 515/285-0864 ▭ MC, V. *Comments: This solid municipal course won't dent your wallet. It's decent enough to be included as part of a trip.* ★ ★ ★

BOS LANDEN GOLF RESORT. Facility Holes: 18. Opened: 1994. Architect: Dick Phelps. Yards: 6,916/5,132. Par: 72/72. Course Rating: 73.5/71.0. Slope: 131/125. Green Fee: $30/$49. Cart Fee: Included in green fee. Discounts: Weekdays, twilight, juniors. Walking: Unrestricted walking. Season: Mar.–Oct. High: June–Sept. Tee Times: Call 21 days in advance. Notes: Range (grass), lodging (88). ⌧ 2411 Bos Landen Dr., Pella 50219, 35 mi from Des Moines ☎ 641/628-4625 or 800/916-7888 ⊕ www.boslanden.com ▭ AE, MC, V. *Comments: A strong second choice to the Harvester. Stay at the resort and make this the opening round of your Des Moines golf getaway. The layout is tight, routed through the woods and hills of this rural area. Fun but tough course.* ★ ★ ★ ½

BRIARWOOD GOLF COURSE. Facility Holes: 18. Opened: 1995. Architect: Gordon Cunningham. Yards: 7,019/5,250. Par: 72/72. Course Rating: 74.2/70.4. Slope: 128/119. Green Fee: $22/$31. Cart Fee: $12 per person. Discounts: Weekdays, twilight. Walking: Walking at certain times. Season: Mar.–Nov. Tee Times: Call golf shop. Notes: Range (grass). ⌧ 3405 N.E. Trilein Dr., Ankeny 50021, 15 mi from Des Moines ☎ 515/964-4653 ▭ MC, V. *Comments: Another four-star course. It's a pretty strong layout considering a round costs less than $50.* ★ ★ ★ ★

HARVESTER GOLF CLUB. Facility Holes: 18. Opened: 2000. Architect: Keith Foster. Yards: 7,340/5,115. Par: 72/72. Course Rating: 75.6/69.4. Slope: 137/120. Green Fee:

$45/$55. Cart Fee: $15 per person. Discounts: Twilight. Walking: Unrestricted walking. Season: Mar.–Nov. High: May–Sept. Tee Times: Call 30 days in advance. Notes: Range (grass). ⊠ 833 Foster Dr., Rhodes 50234, 25 mi from Des Moines ☎ 641/227–4653 ⊕ - www.harvestergolf.com ▤ AE, D, MC, V. *Comments: An awesome golf experience. The Harvester looks as if it has been here for 100 years. The drive from Minneapolis is worth it just to play here. The par-5 18th is one of the most memorable finishing holes in the Midwest. The scenery is so pleasant, it makes you want to be a farmer. UR*

JESTER PARK GOLF COURSE. Facility Holes: 18. Opened: 1970. Architect: Dick Phelps. Yards: 6,801/6,062. Par: 72/73. Course Rating: 72.9/68.4. Slope: 125/109. Green Fee: $18/$27. Cart Fee: $26 per cart. Discounts: Twilight, seniors, juniors. Walking: Unrestricted walking. Season: Mar.–Nov. High: May–Aug. Tee Times: Call 10 days in advance. Notes: Range (grass, mat). Also has a 9-hole par-3 course. ⊠ R.R. 1, Granger 50109, 10 mi from Des Moines ☎ 515/999–2903 ⊕ www.conservationboard.org ▤ D, MC, V. *Comments: Ho-hum. Yet another four-star Des Moines–area layout. This one doesn't get much attention, but please do check it out. It also has a fun par-3 course to settle bets once the round on the big course is over.* ★ ★ ★ ★

LAKE PANORAMA NATIONAL GOLF COURSE. Facility Holes: 18. Opened: 1970. Architect: Richard Watson. Yards: 7,024/5,765. Par: 72/72. Course Rating: 73.2/73.2. Slope: 131/121. Green Fee: $35/$40. Cart Fee: Included in green fee. Discounts: Weekdays. Walking: Walking at certain times. Season: Apr.–Nov. Tee Times: Call golf shop. Notes: Range (grass), lodging (39). ⊠ 5071 Clover Ridge Rd., Panora 50216, 45 mi from Des Moines ☎ 515/755–2024 or 800/879–1917 ▤ AE, D, MC, V. *Comments: A 45-minute drive from Des Moines but worth it—a good value.* ★ ★ ★ ½

RIVER VALLEY GOLF COURSE. Facility Holes: 18. Opened: 1995. Yards: 6,635/5,482. Par: 72/72. Course Rating: 71.1/67.4. Slope: 121/114. Green Fee: $16/$39. Discounts: Weekdays, twilight, juniors. Walking: Walking at certain times. Season: Year-round. Tee Times: Call 30 days in advance. Notes: Range (grass). ⊠ 2267 Valley View Trail, Adel 50003, 15 mi from Des Moines ☎ 515/993–4029 ⊕ www.rivervalleygolf.com ▤ AE, MC, V. *Comments: A farmland course that lacks the scenery of places like the Harvester, but is usually in decent condition. Put this on the B list.* ★ ★ ★

TOURNAMENT CLUB OF IOWA. Facility Holes: 18. Opened: 2003. Architect: Arnold Palmer Design. Yards: 7,043/6,153. Par: 72/72. Course Rating: 74.0/64.8. Slope: 145/107. Green Fee: $67/$45. Cart Fee: Included in green fee. Walking: unrestricted walking. Season: Apr.–Dec. Tee Times: Call 14 days in advance. ⊠ 1000 Tradition Dr., Polk City 50226, 15 mi north of Des Moines ☎ 515/984–9440 ⊕ www.tcofiowa.com ▤ AE, D, MC, V. *Comments: One of the area's best and newest courses. Cut through the woods north of Des Moines near Saylorville Lake. This one should be on your list. UR*

VEENKER MEMORIAL GOLF COURSE. Facility Holes: 18. Opened: 1938. Architect: Perry Maxwell. Yards: 6,543/5,357. Par: 72/73. Course Rating: 71.3/70.6. Slope: 124/120. Green Fee: $21/$27. Cart Fee: $13 per person. Discounts: Weekdays, seniors, juniors. Walking: Unrestricted walking. Season: Mar.–Nov. Tee Times: Call 7 days in advance. Notes: Range (grass). ⊠ Stange Rd., Ames 50011, 30 mi from Des Moines ☎ 515/294–6727 ⊕ www.veenkergolf.com ▤ D, MC, V. *Comments: Home course for the Iowa State University golf team.* ★ ★ ★ ★

PERRY MAXWELL

As a golf designer, Perry Maxwell (1879–1952) provided the midwest with some of its most cherished courses, including that of Veenker Memorial. A banker by trade, Maxwell got interested in golf at the age of 30. By the 1920s, he had retired from banking and began designing courses full-time. His designs at Tulsa's Southern Hills, Crystal Downs (Frankfort, Michigan, with Alister Mackenzie), and Prairie Dunes (Hutchinson, Kansas) are classic American courses. Maxwell was the first architect to use bentgrass greens, ushering in a new era of design possibilities.

Where to Stay

EMBASSY SUITES ON THE RIVER. Iowa's only all-suites hotel and conference center has a dramatic view of the Des Moines River. Each suite includes a separate living room and bedroom, with a television in each. A cooked-to-order breakfast is served daily in the tropical atrium, where there's a six-story waterfall. ⊠ 101 E. Locust St., 50219 ☎ 515/244–1700 📠 515/244–2537 ⊕ www.embassysuites.com 234 suites ♿ Restaurant, room service, microwaves, refrigerators, cable TV, some in-room VCRs, pool, exercise equipment, hot tub, bar, laundry facilities, business services, airport shuttle ☰ AE, D, DC, MC, V ⫚ BP $-$$.

FORT DES MOINES. Built in 1919, this downtown hotel has played host to some of the world's most famous celebrities and political leaders, one of the reasons it's on the National Register of Historic Places. Standard rooms have one or two queen-size beds, while suites include a separate living room, refrigerator, and wet bar. ⊠ 1000 Walnut St., 50219 ☎ 515/243–1161 or 800/532–1466 📠 515/243–4317 ⊕ www.hotelfortdesmoines.com 242 rooms, 56 suites ♿ Restaurant, in-room data ports, some refrigerators, cable TV, indoor pool, exercise equipment, hot tub, bar, business services, airport shuttle, some pets allowed ☰ AE, D, DC, MC, V $-$$.

HOLIDAY INN EXPRESS. Across from the Bos Landen Golf Resort and a quick 4-mi drive from downtown Pella and Molengracht, this hotel is a comfortable, convenient option. Rooms are typical of chain hotels, with either a king-size or two double beds in each of the standard rooms. The Holiday Inn also handles the rental of eight condos ($$$$) on the resorts. ⊠ 2508 Bos Landen Dr., Pella 50219 ☎ 641/628–4853 📠 641/628–3771 ⊕ www.hiexpress.com 88 rooms. 6 suites ♿ Indoor pool, hot tub, sauna, laundry facilities ☰ AE, D, MC, V $-$$.

HOTEL SAVERY. Listed on the National Register of Historical Places, the Georgian-style Savery was built in 1919 and served during World War II as a supplemental barracks for Wacs. Rooms are classically styled, and the suites come with kitchenettes. There's easy skyway access to downtown's shopping and entertainment, and in the hotel is a full-service day spa. ⊠ 401 Locust St., 50219 ☎ 515/244–2151 or 800/798–2151 📠 515/244–1408 ⊕ www.shanerhotels.com 224 rooms, 11 suites ♿ 2 restaurants, room service, some kitchenettes, cable TV, pool, exercise equipment, hair salon, hot tub, spa, bar, airport shuttle, some pets allowed, no-smoking rooms ☰ AE, D, MC, V $$-$$$.

ROYAL AMSTERDAM HOTEL. The Royal Amsterdam is in the heart of Molengracht, Pella's canal district, where there's an actual block-long canal. Rooms are large, and every one has a couch. Suites include microwaves, refrigerators, and Jacuzzi tubs. Some suites have great views of either the Molengracht plaza and canal, or of a 1850s-style windmill. Bos Landen is just 4 mi away. ⊠ 705 E. 1st St., Pella 50219 ☎ 641/ 620-8400 or 877/954-8400 ⊕ www.royalamsterdam.com ➪ 38 rooms, 2 suites. ⅋ Restaurant, cable TV, spa, lounge ═ AE, D, MC, V ❍ BP $$-$$$.

Where to Eat

✕ **DRAKE DINER.** This chrome-and-neon local legend appeals to the college student in all of us. The Drake is perfect for appetizers and late-night coffee, but it's also ready with juicy burgers and thick shakes when you need them. ⊠ 1111 25th St. ☎ 515/277- 1111 ═ AE, D, DC, MC, V $-$$.

✕ **SPLASH.** This sophisticated seafood restaurant has an impressive four-story atrium and 1,000 gallons worth of saltwater aquariums. The diverse menu includes some innovative touches, including swordfish based with Dijon mustard. Don't miss the garlic mashed potatoes. ⊠ 303 Locust St. ☎ 515/244-5686 ⊕ www.splash-seafood.com ═ AE, D, DC, MC, V ❍ Closed Sun. $-$$$$.

Essentials

Getting Here

Take I-35 south 230 mi to I-235. To reach Pella, take Route 163 east 40 mi.

Visitor Information

Ⓘ Greater Des Moines Convention and Visitors Bureau ⊠ 405 6th Ave., Suite 201, 50309 ☎ 515/286-4960 or 800/451-2625 ⊕ www.desmoinescvb.com. **Pella Tourism** ⊠ 518 Franklin St., 50219 ☎ 515/628-2626 ⊕ www.pella.org.

DULUTH & GRAND RAPIDS

In the "Wild North," the northeast corner of Minnesota, hunting and fishing are the most popular outdoor sports. But golfers no longer get quizzical looks when they walk into a restaurant. Land is still relatively cheap, and the woodsy, unspoiled terrain is the perfect place for golf course architects who want to build sprawling monuments to the game.

In this area south of the Canadian border and west of Lake Superior, there are several golf courses within an hour's drive of each other. The leader is

Eagle Ridge Golf Course (18)	6,772/5,220	72/72	72.2/70.0	127/117	$28/$34
Giants Ridge Golf & Ski Resort (36)					$45/$75
Legend at Giants Ridge (18)	6,930/5,084	72/72	74.3/70.3	138/124	
Quarry At Giants Ridge (18)	7,201/5,110	72/72	75.6/71.3	146/130	
Lakeview National Golf Course (18)	6,773/5,364	72/72	72.2/70.6	126/123	$12/$25
Pokegama Golf Club (18)	6,481/5,046	71/72	70.3/67.7	121/116	$28/$33
Superior National Golf Course (27)					$50/$75
Mountain/Canyon (18)	6,768/5,166	72/72	73.0/70.5	133/119	
River/Canyon (18)	6,369/4,969	72/72	71.1/69.4	127/119	
River/Mountain (18)	6,323/5,174	72/72	70.9/70.4	130/123	
Wendigo Golf Course (18)	6,532/5,151	72/72	72.0/70.0	132/127	$29/$36

Giants Ridge Golf & Ski Resort, a good place for base camp. Many of the courses are near Grand Rapids, about 80 mi northwest of Duluth, but if you have some extra time, check out Superior National. It's 90 mi in the other direction at the northeast tip of the state, and it's also worth your time.

Courses

GolfDigest REVIEWS

EAGLE RIDGE GOLF COURSE. Facility Holes: 18. Opened: 1996. Architect: Garrett Gill. Yards: 6,772/5,220. Par: 72/72. Course Rating: 72.2/70.0. Slope: 127/117. Green Fee: $28/$34. Cart Fee: $20 per person. Discounts: Weekdays, juniors. Walking: Unrestricted walking. Walkability: 4. Season: Apr.–Oct. High: Jun.–Aug. Tee Times: Call 90 days in advance. Notes: Range (grass, mat). ⊠ 1 Green Way, Coleraine 55722, 5 mi from Grand Rapids ☎ 218/245-2217 or 888/307-3245 ⊕ www.golfeagleridge.com ▤ D, MC, V. *Comments: There's a relatively harmless front 9 and a tough, tree-lined back 9 here.* ★ ★ ★ ½

GIANTS RIDGE GOLF & SKI RESORT. Facility Holes: 36. Green Fee: $45/$75. Cart Fee: Included in green fee. Discounts: Weekdays, guest, twilight, juniors. Walking: Mandatory cart. Season: May–Oct. High: June–Sept. Tee Times: Call 180 days in advance. Notes: Range (grass, mat). Lodging (140). ⊠ Box 190, County Rd. 138, Biwabik 55708 ☎ 218/865-3000 or 800/688-7669 ⊕ www.giantsridge.com ▤ AE, MC, V.

Legend at Giants Ridge. Holes: 18. Opened: 1997. Architect: Jeffrey D. Brauer/Lanny Wadkins. Yards: 6,930/5,084. Par: 72/72. Course Rating: 74.3/70.3. Slope: 138/124. *Comments: Boulders frame the fairways. The par-3 17th hole, adjacent to Sabin Lake, is spectacular.* ★ ★ ★ ★ ½

Quarry At Giants Ridge. Holes: 18. Opened: 2003. Architect: Jeffery D. Brauer. Yards: 7,201/5,110. Par: 72/72. Course Rating: 75.6/71.3. Slope: 146/130.

LAKEVIEW NATIONAL GOLF COURSE. Facility Holes: 18. Opened: 1997. Architect: Garrett Gill/William Fitzpatrick. Yards: 6,773/5,364. Par: 72/72. Course Rating: 72.2/70.6.

Slope: 126/123. Green Fee: $12/$25. Cart Fee: $24. Walking: Unrestricted walking. Season: Apr.–Oct. Tee Times: Call golf shop. ⊠ 1348 Hwy. 61, Two Harbors 55616 ☎ 218/834-2664 ⊕ www.lakeviewnationalgolf.com ⊟ AE, MC, V. *Comments: You can see Lake Superior glimmering in the distance. Note the low green fee.* UR

POKEGAMA GOLF CLUB. Facility Holes: 18. Opened: 1926. Architect: Donald Brauer. Yards: 6,481/5,046. Par: 71/72. Course Rating: 70.3/67.7. Slope: 121/116. Green Fee: $28/$33. Cart Fee: $30 per cart. Discounts: Weekdays, twilight, juniors. Walking: Unrestricted walking. Season: Apr.–Oct. High: June–Aug. Tee Times: Call 7 days in advance. Notes: Range (grass). ⊠ 3910 Golf Course Rd., Grand Rapids 55744 ☎ 218/326-3444 or 888/307-3444 ⊕ www.pokegamagolf.com ⊟ MC, V. *Comments: The 18th hole plays along a ridgeline above the lake. Very nice.* ★ ★ ★ ¹/₂

SUPERIOR NATIONAL GOLF COURSE. Facility Holes: 27. Opened: 1991. Architect: Don Herfort/Joel Goldstrand. Green Fee: $50/$75. Cart Fee: Included in green fee. Discounts: Weekdays, twilight, seniors, juniors. Walking: Mandatory cart. Season: May–Oct. High: June–Oct. Tee Times: Call golf shop. Notes: Range (grass). ⊠ Box 177, Lutsen 55612, 90 mi from Duluth ☎ 218/663-7195 or 888/616-6784 ⊕ www.superiornational. com ⊟ AE, MC, V.

Mountain/Canyon. Holes: 18. Yards: 6,768/5,166. Par: 72/72. Course Rating: 73.0/70.5. Slope: 133/119.

River/Canyon. Holes: 18. Yards: 6,369/4,969. Par: 72/72. Course Rating: 71.1/69.4. Slope: 127/119.

River/Mountain. Holes: 18. Yards: 6,323/5,174. Par: 72/72. Course Rating: 70.9/70.4. Slope: 130/123.

Comments: It's a long drive up U.S. 61 to get here, but the American Automobile Association rates it one of the best drives in the country. The course has several views of Lake Superior, and the Poplar River comes into play on several holes. You've gotta see this place. ★ ★ ★ ★ ¹/₂

WENDIGO GOLF COURSE. Facility Holes: 18. Opened: 1995. Architect: Joel Goldstrand. Yards: 6,532/5,151. Par: 72/72. Course Rating: 72.0/70.0. Slope: 132/127. Green Fee: $29/$36. Cart Fee: $26 per cart. Discounts: Twilight. Walking: Unrestricted walking. Season: Apr.–Dec. Tee Times: Call golf shop. Notes: Range (grass, mat). ⊠ 20108 Golf Crest Dr., Grand Rapids 55744, 180 mi from Minneapolis ☎ 218/327-2211 ⊕ www. grandslamgolf.com ⊟ MC, V. *Comments: This might be the toughest course in the Grand Rapids area. Has two different 4th holes to add a little variety. Needs some grooming.* ★ ★ ★ ¹/₂

Where to Stay

⌨ **COMFORT SUITES CANAL PARK.** This branch of the chain motel has direct access to Duluth's popular lake walk, which follows the shore of Lake Superior for 3 mi. Ask for a room on the north side of the hotel's east end for great views of ships entering and leaving the harbor. Rooms have either two double beds or a king-size bed. Suites with

WHERE THE GOLFING'S EASY

If you're looking for action, this is not your golf destination. Golfers accustomed to fast-paced city life will have to remind themselves to take a deep breath and relax: things sometimes move here at a glacial pace. On the other hand, there may not be a better bargain destination on the planet. Rooms are cheap, golf is cheaper, and meals come in Thanksgiving-size portions. This less-traveled area may be logging country most of the year, but between June and September, when 14–18 hours of sunlight is the norm, Paul Bunyan trades in his axe for a 2-iron.

refrigerators are available; some also have whirlpool tubs. ✉ 408 Canal Park Dr., Duluth 55802 ☎ 218/727-1378 🖷 218/727-1947 ⊕ www.comfortsuites.com ➥ 82 rooms, 6 suites △ In-room data ports, some in-room hot tubs, refrigerators, cable TV, indoor pool, 2 hot tubs, laundry facilities, business services ⊟ AE, D, DC, MC, V ⑩ CP $–$$$.

🖾 **FITGER'S INN.** Part of a complex that also includes a brewpub, a bookstore, and other shops, this former brewery made its last beer in 1972. Several of the rooms, all furnished in individual styles, have dramatic views of Lake Superior. Suites have fireplaces, wet bars, and whirlpool tubs. ✉ 600 E. Superior St., Duluth 55802 ☎ 218/722-8826 or 800/726-2982 ⊕ www.fitgers.com ➥ 62 rooms, 20 suites △ Restaurant, room service, in-room data ports, some in-room hot tubs, cable TV, exercise equipment, bar, some pets allowed, business services ⊟ AE, D, DC, MC, V $.

🖾 **LODGE AT GIANTS RIDGE GOLF & SKI RESORT.** The Lodge, which uses wood in its exterior and has a stone wall in the lobby, blends in well with its surroundings. The Legend and the Quarry courses are part of the same resort. The suites are traditionally furnished, and many come with fireplaces and Jacuzzi spas. ✉ 6373 Wynne Creek, Biwabik 55708 ☎ 218/865-7170 or 877/442-6877 🖷 218/865-7135 ⊕ www. lodgeatgiantsridge.com ➥ 92 suites △ Restaurant, some microwaves, refrigerators, cable TV, 2 18-hole golf courses, indoor pool, health club, hot tub, lounge, video game room, laundry facilities, some pets allowed (fee) ⊟ AE, DC, MC, V $–$$.

🖾 **RADISSON HOTEL DULUTH HARBORVIEW.** Six blocks from Lake Superior and Canal Park, the 15-floor circular Radisson has good views of the harbor and the city alike. Standard rooms, done in pastels, come with either two double or queen-size beds or one king-size bed. The Top of the Harbor restaurant, on the top floor, revolves. ✉ 505 W. Superior St., Duluth 55802 ☎ 218/727-8981 🖷 218/727-0162 ⊕ www. radisson.com ➥ 268 rooms, 7 suites △ Restaurant, cable TV, indoor pool, gym, hot tub, sauna, bar, video game room, business services, some pets allowed ⊟ AE, D, DC, MC, V $.

🖾 **RUTTGER'S SUGAR LAKE LODGE.** The town houses and cottages here, whether on Sugar Lake or on the golf course, generally have pine furniture and interiors. Single rooms have king-size beds, while the two- and three-bedroom town houses are outfitted with living rooms, kitchens, and fireplaces. Lodge rooms, overlooking Sugar Lake, have kitchens, living rooms, fireplaces, and Jacuzzis. ✉ Rte. 458, Grand Rapids 55744

☎ 218/327-1462 or 800/450-4555 ☎ 218/327-0454 ⊕ www.sugarlakelodge.com
☞ 85 town houses, 24 lodges, 6 cottages ♿ 2 restaurants, 18-hole golf course, pool, beach, boating, mountain bikes ═ AE, D, MC, V $-$$$$.

▦ VILLAS AT GIANTS RIDGE GOLF & SKI RESORT. Overlooking beautiful Wynne Lake, this property includes studios and suites as well as villas of up to four bedrooms. All rooms have a kitchen and whirlpool tubs, and the suites and villas come with their own fireplaces, washers, and dryers. The accommodations are in an open plan, with light-color woods used as accents. ✉ 6266 Giants Ridge Rd., Biwabik 55708 ☎ 800/843-7434 ☎ 218/865-4155 ⊕ www.villasatgiantsridge.com ☞ 32 rooms, 16 suites, 15 3- and 4-bedroom cabins ♿ In-room hot tubs, kitchens, 2 18-hole golf courses, tennis court, pool, beach, mountain bikes, basketball, horseshoes, volleyball, playground, laundry facilities ═ AE, DC, MC, V $-$$.

Where to Eat

✕ GRANDMA'S CANAL PARK. The legendary Grandma's began life as Grandma's Saloon & Grill. At this restaurant, under the Aerial Lift Bridge, you can dine on the deck and watch the big ships pass through. The big, messy double-patty bicycle burger is as good as it gets. ✉ 522 Lake Ave. S, Duluth ☎ 218/727-4192 ⊕ www.grandmasrestaurants.com ═ AE, D, DC, MC, V $-$$$.

✕ JACK'S GRILL. This resort restaurant is a good casual option for burgers, ribs, salads, and fish fry. You can dine indoors or on the deck overlooking the 18th green of the Sugarbrooke Golf Club. Otis's Restaurant, open June to August, is more formal. ✉ Ruttger's Sugar Lake Lodge, Rte. 458, Grand Rapids ☎ 218/327-1462 or 800/450-4555 ⊕ www.sugarlakelodge.com ═ AE, D, MC, V $$.

✕ NEW SCENIC CAFE. Eight miles north of Duluth, the New Scenic Cafe offers diners grand views of Lake Superior along with its fine food. The many vegetarian options, and the selection of meat and fish dishes are complemented nicely by an expansive wine and beer list. Desserts are made fresh daily. ✉ 546 North Shore Scenic Dr., Duluth ☎ 218/525-6274 ⊕ www.sceniccafe.com ═ MC, V $-$$$.

Essentials

Getting Here
To get to Duluth, take I-35 north 150 mi. Biwabik is 55 mi north near U.S. 53.

Visitor Information
🛈 City of Biwabik ✉ Box 529, Biwabik 55708 ☎ 218/865-4183 or 800/642-4154 ⊕ www.cityofbiwabik.com. **Duluth Convention and Visitors Bureau** ✉ 100 Lake Place Dr., Duluth 55802 ☎ 218/722-4011 or 800/438-5884 ⊕ www.visitduluth.com. **Grand Rapids Area Chamber of Commerce** ✉ 1 N.W. 3rd St., Grand Rapids 55744 ☎ 218/326-6619 or 800/472-6366 ⊕ www.grandmn.com.

MADISON, WI, COURSES	YARDAGE	PAR	COURSE	SLOPE	GREEN FEE
Bridges Golf Course (18)	6,888/5,322	72/72	73.0/70.4	129/119	$30/$33
Christmas Mountain Village Golf Club (27)	6,786/5,095	72/72	72.9/69.7	133/120	$35/$65
Coachman's Golf Resort (27)					$23/$26
Red/Blue (18)	6,190/4,830	71/71	69.2/68.7	115/112	
Red/White (18)	6,180/5,021	71/71	69.2/68.0	115/111	
White/Blue (18)	6,420/5,000	72/72	69.2/69.5	115/114	
Door Creek Golf Course (18)	6,475/5,189	71/71	70.5/69.7	119/111	$26/$28
House on the Rock Resort (27)					$45/$69
North Nine (9)	3,262/2,659	36/36	71.8/68.3	132/122	
Springs (18)	6,562/5,334	72/72	71.5/70.3	132/123	
Old Hickory Country Club (18)	6,721/5,372	72/73	72.8/71.4	130/125	$30/$55
Riverside Golf Course (18)	6,508/5,147	72/72	70.7/68.9	123/116	$22/$25
Trappers Turn Golf Club (27)					$48/$79
Arbor/Lake (18)	6,831/5,017	72/72	73.3/69.7	133/123	
Canyon/Arbor (18)	6,738/5,000	72/72	73.3/69.7	133/123	
Lake/Canyon (18)	6,759/5,017	72/72	72.8/69.4	133/122	
University Ridge Golf Course (18)	6,888/5,005	72/72	73.2/68.9	142/121	$36/$56
Wilderness Resort & Golf Course (18)	6,644/5,511	72/72	73.1/67.7	131/119	$65/$75

MADISON, WI

In Big Ten country, football is king. But the scenic college town of Madison and the surrounding area have quietly become a bona fide golf destination easily worth the five-hour drive from Minneapolis. Wisconsin's capital, also the home of the main branch of the University of Wisconsin, often scores high on *Money* magazine's survey of America's most livable cities. It makes you wonder if golfers helped compile the votes: Nearby are no fewer than 10 golf courses that are well worth your time.

Of the three major golf resorts in the area, our first choice is the House on the Rock, 30 mi outside of town. Sure, it has a terrible name, but the 27-hole resort has two outstanding courses. If you're not looking for an all-in-one resort, build your trip around the University Ridge Golf Course and Old Hickory Country Club. University Ridge is where the UW–Madison golf team plays; Old Hickory, 30 mi away, is a throwback to the great country clubs of the 1920s and '30s, with white powder bunkers and fairways shaped without the aid of earth-moving equipment. Golf resorts in the Wisconsin Dells are another option—they're especially appealing if your kids are with you.

Courses

BRIDGES GOLF COURSE. Facility Holes: 18. Opened: 2000. Architect: Feick Design Group. Yards: 6,888/5,322. Par: 72/72. Course Rating: 73.0/70.4. Slope: 129/119. Green Fee: $30/$33. Cart Fee: $15 per person. Discounts: Weekdays, twilight, seniors, juniors. Walking: Unrestricted walking. Season: Mar.–Dec. High: May–Sept. Tee Times: Call 7 days in advance. Notes: Range (grass, mat). ⊠ 2702 Shopko Dr., 53704 ☏ 608/244–1822 ⊕ - www.golfthebridges.com ⊟ AE, D, MC, V. *Comments: Play this decent course with a tight back 9 as a warm-up to some of area's better tracks. Lots of water.* ★ ★ ★ ¹/₂

CHRISTMAS MOUNTAIN VILLAGE GOLF CLUB. Facility Holes: 27. Opened: 1970. Architect: Art Johnson/DJ DeVictor. Yards: 6,786/5,095. Par: 72/72. Course Rating: 72.9/ 69.7. Slope: 133/120. Green Fee: $35/$65. Cart Fee: Included in green fee. Discounts: Twilight, juniors. Walking: Walking at certain times. Season: Apr.–Nov. Tee Times: Call 21 days in advance. Notes: Range (grass). ⊠ S. 944 Christmas Mountain Rd., Wisconsin Dells 53965, 40 mi from Madison ☏ 608/254–3971 ⊕ www.christmasmountainvillage. com ⊟ AE, D, MC, V. *Comments: The Pines 9-hole is almost as fun as the 18-hole Oaks course. Good solid golf destination in the Dells area.* ★ ★ ★ ★

COACHMAN'S GOLF RESORT. Facility Holes: 27. Opened: 1990. Architect: R. C. Greaves. Green Fee: $23/$26. Cart Fee: $25 per cart. Discounts: Seniors. Season: Apr.– Oct. Tee Times: Call golf shop. Notes: Metal spikes. ⊠ 984 County Hwy. A, Edgerton 53534, 15 mi from Madison ☏ 608/884–8484 ⊟ AE, D, MC, V.

Red/Blue. Holes: 18. Yards: 6,190/4,830. Par: 71/71. Course Rating: 69.2/68.7. Slope: 115/112.

Red/White. Holes: 18. Yards: 6,180/5,021. Par: 71/71. Course Rating: 69.2/68.0. Slope: 115/111.

White/Blue. Holes: 18. Yards: 6,420/5,000. Par: 72/72. Course Rating: 69.2/69.5. Slope: 115/114.

Comments: A decent course, but it's not good enough to build a golf weekend around. As far as quality of golf is concerned, the Resort should be your third choice for lodging after the House on the Rock and Wilderness Resort. ★ ★ ★

DOOR CREEK GOLF COURSE. Facility Holes: 18. Opened: 1990. Architect: Bradt Family. Yards: 6,475/5,189. Par: 71/71. Course Rating: 70.5/69.7. Slope: 119/111. Green Fee: $26/$28. Cart Fee: $12 per person. Discounts: Weekdays, seniors, juniors. Walking: Unrestricted walking. Season: Year-round. Tee Times: Call 7 days in advance. Notes: Range (grass, mat). Also has a 9-hole executive course. ⊠ 4321 Vilas, Cottage Grove 53527, 3 mi from Madison ☏ 608/839–5656 ⊟ D, MC, V. *Comments: If you're staying in Madison, this makes a decent filler course to your golf trip.* ★ ★ ★

HOUSE ON THE ROCK RESORT. Facility Holes: 27. Opened: 1971. Green Fee: $45/$69. Cart Fee: Included in green fee. Discounts: Weekdays, twilight, juniors.

Walking: Unrestricted walking. Season: Apr.–Oct. High: June–Sept. Tee Times: Call golf shop. Notes: Range (grass), lodging (80). ✉ 400 Springs Dr., Spring Green 53588, 35 mi from Madison ☎ 608/588-7000 or 800/822-7774 ⊕ www.thehouseontherock.com 🖃 AE, D, MC, V.

North Nine. Holes: 9. Architect: Roger Packard/Andy North. Yards: 3,262/2,659. Par: 36/36. Course Rating: 71.8/68.3. Slope: 132/122. ★★★★ ½

Springs. Holes: 18. Architect: Robert Trent Jones. Yards: 6,562/5,334. Par: 72/72. Course Rating: 71.5/70.3. Slope: 132/123. ★★★★ ½

Comments: You know it's a good golf destination when the 9-hole course is rated higher than the course designed by Robert Trent Jones. In truth, both are worth your time. It's the elevation that make the North Nine stand out; for the Springs course, it's the grooming. It's in great shape.

OLD HICKORY COUNTRY CLUB. Facility Holes: 18. Opened: 1920. Architect: Tom Bendelow. Yards: 6,721/5,372. Par: 72/73. Course Rating: 72.8/71.4. Slope: 130/125. Green Fee: $30/$55. Cart Fee: $15 per person. Walking: Walking at certain times. Season: Apr.–Oct. High: June–Aug. Tee Times: Call 7 days in advance. Notes: Range (grass, mat). ✉ W7596 Hwy. 33 E, Beaver Dam 53916, 30 mi from Madison ☎ 920/887-7577 ⊕ - www.oldhickorycc.com 🖃 MC, V. *Comments: Playing the 1920s era course is like taking a step back in time—but you don't have to navigate the tight fairways with hickory-shafted clubs.* ★★★★

RIVERSIDE GOLF COURSE. Facility Holes: 18. Opened: 1924. Architect: Robert Bruce Harris. Yards: 6,508/5,147. Par: 72/72. Course Rating: 70.7/68.9. Slope: 123/116. Green Fee: $22/$25. Cart Fee: $13 per person. Discounts: Weekdays, seniors, juniors. Walking: Unrestricted walking. Season: Apr.–Nov. High: May–Sept. Tee Times: Call golf shop. Notes: Range (grass). ✉ 2100 Golf Course Rd., Janesville 53545, 35 mi from Madison ☎ 608/757-3080 🖃 MC, V. *Comments: The course is old, but it still has a shotmaker's layout.* ★★★ ½

TRAPPERS TURN GOLF CLUB. Facility Holes: 27. Opened: 1991. Architect: Andy North/Roger Packard. Green Fee: $48/$79. Cart Fee: Included in green fee. Discounts: Weekdays, guest, twilight, seniors. Walking: Unrestricted walking. Season: Apr.–Nov. Tee Times: Call 30 days in advance. Notes: Range (grass). ✉ 652 Trappers Turn Dr., Wisconsin Dells 53965, 50 mi from Madison ☎ 608/253-7000 or 800/221-8876 ⊕ www.trappersturn.com 🖃 AE, D, MC, V.

Arbor/Lake. Holes: 18. Yards: 6,831/5,017. Par: 72/72. Course Rating: 73.3/69.7. Slope: 133/123.

Canyon/Arbor. Holes: 18. Yards: 6,738/5,000. Par: 72/72. Course Rating: 73.3/69.7. Slope: 133/123.

Lake/Canyon. Holes: 18. Yards: 6,759/5,017. Par: 72/72. Course Rating: 72.8/69.4. Slope: 133/122.

Comments: If you're staying in the Wisconsin Dells area, Trappers Turn is a must-play. The facility has a combination of links-style and tree-lined holes. ★★★★ ½

UNIVERSITY RIDGE GOLF COURSE. Facility Holes: 18. Opened: 1991. Architect: Robert Trent Jones Jr. Yards: 6,888/5,005. Par: 72/72. Course Rating: 73.2/68.9. Slope: 142/121. Green Fee: $36/$56. Cart Fee: $16 per person. Discounts: Twilight, juniors. Walking: Unrestricted walking. Season: Apr.–Oct. High: June–Aug. Tee Times: Call 14 days in advance. Notes: Range (grass, mat). ⊠9002 County Rd. PD, Verona 53593, 8 mi from Madison ☎608/845-7700 or 800/897-4343 ⊕www.uwbadgers.com/facilities ⊟AE, MC, V. *Comments: UW's home course. A pleasing parkland style.* ★★★★ ½

WILDERNESS RESORT & GOLF COURSE. Facility Holes: 18. Opened: 1999. Architect: Art Johnson. Yards: 6,644/5,511. Par: 72/72. Course Rating: 73.1/67.7. Slope: 131/119. Green Fee: $65/$75. Cart Fee: Included in green fee. Discounts: Weekdays, guest, twilight. Walking: Mandatory cart. Season: Apr.–Oct. High: May–Sept. Tee Times: Call 30 days in advance. Notes: Range (grass, mat), lodging (650). ⊠856 Canyon Dr., Wisconsin Dells 53965, 35 mi from Madison ☎608/253-4653 ⊕www.golfwildernesswoods.com ⊟AE, D, MC, V. *Comments: This Wisconsin Dells–area course is perfect if you're bringing the kids. While you play golf, they can play in the indoor-outdoor water park. The golf is solid, and there are also two short courses for the kids to try.* ★★★★

Where to Stay

COACHMAN'S GOLF RESORT. Twenty minutes south of Madison, Coachman's Golf Resort has many rooms decorated with a golf motif. Standard rooms include a king-size bed or two double beds; suites include fireplaces and whirlpools. Some stay-and-play packages include unlimited golf. ⊠984 County Rd. A, Edgerton 53534 ☎608/884-8484 or 800/940-8485 🖷608/884-7720 ⊕www.coachmans.com ↴61 rooms, 2 suites ♿ Restaurant, some in-room hot tubs, pool ⊟AE, D, MC, V $.

THE EDGEWATER. On the shore of Lake Mendota, this nine-story, blond-brick hotel from 1949 has wonderful views of the lake as well as downtown and the Capitol. It even has its own pier, where there's a café open from mid-April through Labor Day. ⊠666 Wisconsin Ave., 53703 ☎608/256-9071 or 800/922-5512 🖷608/256-0910 ⊕www.theedgewater.com ↴143 rooms, 12 suites ♿ Restaurant, room service, some microwaves, cable TV, massage, bar, business services, airport shuttle, free parking, some pets allowed ⊟AE, DC, MC, V $-$$$.

HOUSE ON THE ROCK INN. The House on the Rock is an amazing, kitschy architectural attraction perched on a 60-foot chimney of rock. Seven miles away is the Inn, a four-story hotel whose lobby is dominated by an enormous fireplace. Kids will want to investigate the 45-foot "submarine," which has its own waterfalls and slides. ⊠3591 S. Hwy. 23, Dodgeville 53533 ☎608/935-3711 or 888/935-3960 ⊕www. thehouseontherock.com ↴114 rooms, 7 suites ♿ In-room data ports, some microwaves, some refrigerators, cable TV, indoor-outdoor pool, health club, bar, video game room, laundry services ⊟AE, D, MC, V ⑩BP $-$$.

HOUSE ON THE ROCK RESORT. Made up of 80 two-room suites, the House on the Rock Resort is a great retreat. The suites themselves have some Frank Lloyd Wright-esque styling, and they have refrigerators, microwaves, and whirlpool tubs, as well as patios or balconies that look out on the golf course. ⊠400 Springs Dr., Spring Green

53588 ☎608/588-7000 or 800/822-7774 ⊕www.thehouseontherock.com ⟿80 suites ⟐Restaurant, cable TV, 18-hole golf course, 9-hole golf course, 2 tennis courts, indoor pool, health club, steam room, hiking, volleyball ▭AE, D, MC, V $$$-$$$$.

🏨**MADISON CONCOURSE HOTEL.** This 13-story light-brick hotel just north of Capitol Square is filled with large windows and has an elegant lobby with marble and plants. Rooms are done in a colonial style. The Governor's Club on the top three floors of the hotel has some great views to go along with its appetizers and cocktails. ✉1 W. Dayton St., 53703 ☎608/257-6000 or 800/356-8293 🖷608/257-5280 ⊕www. concoursehotel.com ⟿360 rooms ⟐2 restaurants, some in-room hot tubs, some microwaves, cable TV, pool, exercise equipment, hot tub, bar, business services, airport shuttle ▭AE, D, DC, MC, V ⦿CP $$.

🏨**MANSION HILL INN.** This 1858 Italianate mansion four blocks from the Capitol has a four-story spiral staircase and individually decorated rooms, among them the Turkish Nook (with a sultan's bed and steam shower) and the Oriental Suite (with a separate sitting room, a skylight, and double whirlpool). Breakfast is served in the rooms. ✉424 N. Pinckney St., 53703 ☎608/255-3999 or 800/798-9070 🖷608/255-2217 ⊕www.mansionhillinn.com ⟿9 rooms, 2 suites ⟐In-room data ports, some in-room hot tubs, minibars, cable TV, some in-room VCRs, business services; no kids under 12, no smoking ▭AE, MC, V ⦿CP $$-$$$$.

🏨**WILDERNESS RESORT AND GOLF COURSE.** From single rooms on up to luxury suits and five-bedroom cabins, Wilderness Resort has many good places to stay and play. Most rooms include microwaves, whirlpools, and fireplaces. There are also water parks inside and out. ✉511 E. Adams St., Wisconsin Dells 53965 ☎800/867-9453 🖷608/254-4982 ⊕www.wildernessresort.com ⟿443 rooms, 15 suites, 115 condos, 10 cabins ⟐3 restaurants, 18-hole golf course, 6-hole golf course, pool, hot tubs, health club, spa, shops, baby-sitting ▭AE, D, MC, V $-$$.

Where to Eat

✗**ESSEN HAUS.** This downtown restaurant with Bavarian charm displays some 3,000 beer steins and serves such classic fare as Wiener schnitzel and sauerbraten. ✉514 E. Wilson St. ☎608/255-4674 ▭MC, V ⊗Closed Mon. No lunch $-$$$.

✗**ISHNALA SUPPER CLUB.** Two miles south of Wisconsin Dells, this rustic log lodge overlooks Mirror Lake. The decks allow for beautiful views of the water and woods. Fresh fish and prime rib are favorites here. ✉S2011 Ishnala Rd., Lake Delton ☎608/253-1771 ⊕www.ishnala.com ⟑Reservations not accepted ▭AE, MC, V ⊗Closed Nov.–early May and Mon.–Wed. early May–Memorial Day and Labor Day–Oct. No lunch $$-$$$$.

✗**L'ÉTOILE.** Famed local chef Odessa Piper owns this French-American restaurant on Capitol Square. Recipes emphasize local ingredients and traditions: the exquisitely prepared Alaskan halibut and beef tenderloin are two fine examples. ✉25 N. Pinckney St. ☎608/251-0500 ⊕www.letoile-restaurant.com ▭D, DC, MC, V ⊗Closed Sun. No lunch $$$-$$$$.

✕ **NAU-TI-GAL.** In summer, at this nautically themed restaurant in an old tavern, you can dine 30 feet from the Yahara River, which feeds into the northern tip of Lake Mendota. Seating outdoors is on the expansive wraparound deck, and indoors at cozy tables just big enough for small groups of friends. Fresh fish is on the menu every day, but you can also feast on Key West chicken stuffed with seafood, or even a shark steak. The Wednesday- and Friday-night fish fry is a grand local tradition. ✉ 5360 Westport Rd. ☎ 608/246-3131 ☐ MC, V $$-$$$.

Essentials

Getting Here

To get to Madison, take I-94 southeast 250 mi. To go directly to the Wisconsin Dells area, take I-94 east 210 mi to Route 13 and head north.

Visitor Information

🛈 **Greater Madison Convention and Visitors Bureau** ✉ 615 E. Washington Ave., 53703 ☎ 800/373-6376 ⊕ www.visitmadison.com. **Spring Green Chamber of Commerce** ✉ Box 3, Spring Green 53588-0003 ☎ 608/588-2054 ⊕ www.springgreen. com. **Wisconsin Dells Visitors and Convention Bureau** ✉ 701 Superior St., Wisconsin Dells 53965 ☎ 800/223-3557 ⊕ www.wisdells.com.

SAUK CENTRE, ALEXANDRIA & GLENWOOD

With Brainerd and Grand Rapids to the north and golf-rich Wisconsin to the east, the area along I-94 between Minneapolis and Fargo often gets overlooked as a golf destination. But if you want to avoid the crowds that flock to Brainerd in summer, Central Minnesota has some terrific, affordable courses. Sauk Centre is less than two hours' drive from Minneapolis, leaving plenty of time to tee it up. What might be the best part of a trip here is that none of the courses cost more than $50 to play. Seven rounds here cost less than one round at Pebble Beach.

If you can only hit a few courses in this area, our picks are Lynx National, Greystone, and Minnewaska Golf Club. The relatively flat, prairie farmland is perfect for links-style courses, which is exactly what you get at Greystone and Lynx National. In addition, courses like Pezhekee National take advantage of their proximity to the many lakes in the region.

Alexandria Golf Club	6,482/5,205	72/72	71.2/69.6	128/122	$50
Geneva Golf Club (27)					$30/$34
Island/Ponds (18)	6,921/5,025	71/71	73.9/69.1	133/118	
Marsh/Island (18)	7,191/5,336	73/73	75.3/71.5	137/123	
Ponds/Marsh (18)	6,940/5,089	72/72	73.7/69.6	137/120	
Greystone Golf Club (18)	7,059/5,395	72/72	74.5/71.8	137/127	$26/$36
Lynx National Golf Club (18)	6,700/5,244	72/72	72.4/70.4	134/126	$17/$24
Minnewaska Golf Club (18)	6,457/5,398	72/73	70.7/71.7	122/123	$20/$30
Pezhekee National Golf Course (18)	6,454/5,465	72/75	70.7/67.2	124/117	

Courses

GREYSTONE GOLF CLUB. Facility Holes: 18. Opened: 2000. Architect: Tom Lehman/ Dan Hempt/Kevin Norby. Yards: 7,059/5,395. Par: 72/72. Course Rating: 74.5/71.8. Slope: 137/127. Green Fee: $26/$36. Cart Fee: $24 per cart. Discounts: Weekdays, twilight, seniors, juniors. Walking: Unrestricted walking. Season: Apr.–Oct. High: June-Aug. Tee Times: Call 21 days in advance. Notes: Range (grass). ⊠ 10548 Andrews Dr., Sauk Centre 56378, 43 mi from St. Cloud ☎ 320/351-4653 or 877/350-8849 ⊕ www.greystonegolf. com ▤ AE, D, MC, V. *Comments: Similar in presentation to Lynx National. This is a breezy course with oversize greens and bunkers. UR*

LYNX NATIONAL GOLF CLUB. Facility Holes: 18. Opened: 1999. Architect: Mike Morley. Yards: 6,700/5,244. Par: 72/72. Course Rating: 72.4/70.4. Slope: 134/126. Green Fee: $17/$24. Cart Fee: $22 per cart. Discounts: Weekdays, twilight. Walking: Unrestricted walking. Season: Apr.–Nov. High: June-Aug. Tee Times: Call 7 days in advance. Notes: Range (grass). ⊠ 40204 Primrose La., Sauk Centre 56378, 38 mi from St. Cloud ☎ 320/352-0243 or 888/637-0243 ⊕ www.lynxnationalgolf.com ▤ MC, V. *Comments: Edged by the Sauk River, this links-style course is a blast to play.*

MINNEWASKA GOLF CLUB. Facility Holes: 18. Opened: 1923. Architect: Joel Goldstrand. Yards: 6,457/5,398. Par: 72/73. Course Rating: 70.7/71.7. Slope: 122/123. Green Fee: $20/$30. Cart Fee: $28 per cart. Discounts: Weekdays, guest, twilight, seniors, juniors. Walking: Unrestricted walking. Season: Apr.–Oct. High: June and July. Tee Times: Call 7 days in advance. Notes: Range (grass, mat). ⊠ 23518 Dero Dr., Glenwood 56334, 120 mi from Minneapolis ☎ 320/634-3680 ▤ MC, V. *Comments: This shorter, older course is a great value. Rarely will you find the course so crowded that a four-hour round is not possible. An attractive, wooded layout.* ★ ★ ★ ★ ½

PEZHEKEE NATIONAL GOLF COURSE. Facility Holes: 18. Opened: 1967. Architect: Tim Murphy/Bill Peters. Yards: 6,454/5,465. Par: 72/75. Course Rating: 70.7/67.2. Slope: 124/117. Season: May–Oct. Tee Times: Call golf shop. ⊠ 2000 S. Lakeshore Dr., Glenwood 56334 ☎ 320/634-4501 or 800/356-8654 ⊕ www.petersresort.com/golf. html ▤ MC, V. *Comments: Cut through the forest near Lake Minnewaska. The course* *has no lake views, but the Peters Sunset Beach Resort is an excellent place to stay for the weekend. UR*

Where to Stay

ARROWWOOD RESORT BY CLUBHOUSE. On 450 acres on the shores of Lake Darling, the Arrowwood Resort has spacious rooms available in many types, from one-bedroom apartments with living rooms, fireplaces, and kitchenettes to two-story loft suites with a living room and a kitchenette. A 36,000-square-foot indoor water park was built here in 2003. ⊠ 2100 Arrowwood La. NW, Alexandria 56308 ☎ 320/762-1124 or 800/333-3333 🖷 320/762-0133 ⊕ www.arrowwoodresort.com ⇘ 200 rooms, 24 suites ⚫ Dining room, room service, in-room data ports, some microwaves, some refrigerators, cable TV, 18-hole golf course, putting green, 4 tennis courts, 2 pools (1 indoor), health club, hot tub, beach, boating, marina, bicycles, ice-skating, cross-country skiing, sleigh rides, snowmobiling, tobogganing, bar, video game room, children's programs (ages 5-12), playground, business services, airport shuttle, some pets allowed ⊟ AE, D, DC, MC, V $$-$$$.

> **MINNEWASKA GOLF CLUB**
>
> When it first opened, Minnewaska had just 9 holes. It wasn't until Joel Goldstrand added 9 more holes a decade later that it became the gem it is today.

CEDAR ROSE INN. Built in 1903, this Tudor Revival is on the National Register of Historic Places. A wrap-around porch and stained-glass windows distinguish the exterior. The interior is furnished with antiques and chandeliers, with polished maple floors underfoot and exposed beams overhead. A secluded 95-acre garden includes 3 mi of walking trails. The Noah P. Ward suite includes a double whirlpool bath. ⊠ 422 7th Ave., Alexandria 56308 ☎ 320/762-8430 or 888/203-5333 ⇘ 3 rooms, 2 suites ⚫ Some in-room hot tubs, bicycles ⊟ MC, V ⧀ CP $-$$.

HOLIDAY INN. One mile from downtown Alexandria, this Holiday Inn is close to golf, shopping, dining, and several lakes. The chain hotel-style rooms have either full, queen, or king-size beds. ⊠ 5637 Rte. 29 S, Alexandria 56308 ☎ 320/763-6577 🖷 320/762-2092 ⊕ www.alexandriaholidayinn.com ⇘ 149 rooms ⚫ Restaurant, room service, in-room data ports, some microwaves, some refrigerators, cable TV, indoor pool, wading pool, hot tub, sauna, basketball, volleyball, laundry facilities, business services ⊟ AE, D, MC, V $.

PALMER HOUSE HOTEL. This three-story brick home, built in 1901 in downtown Sauk Centre, claims author Sinclair Lewis as a onetime employee. Rooms and suites occupy the top two floors. A play-and-stay golf package is available with nearby Greystone Golf Club. ⊠ 500 Sinclair Lewis Ave., Sauk Centre 56378 ☎ 320/351-9100 or 866/834-9100 🖷 320/351-9104 ⊕ www.thepalmerhousehotel.com ⇘ 16 rooms, 6 suites ⚫ Restaurant, cable TV, some in-room hot tubs, bar, library, no-smoking rooms ⊟ AE, D, MC, V ⧀ CP $.

PETERS SUNSET BEACH RESORT. A few steps from the first tee of the Pezhekee National Golf Course, this resort has two-, three-, and four-bedroom cottages and town houses. Grand views of the lake are available from the dining room, which serves breakfast and dinner (included in rates). Ask about the many options for golf packages. ✉20000 S. Lakeshore Dr., Glenwood 56334 ☎320/634-4501 or 800/356-8654 🖶320/634-5606 ⊕www.petersresort.com ⤻20 cottages ♿Dining room, kitchenettes, cable TV, 18-hole golf course, putting green, 2 tennis courts, sauna, beach, boating, bicycles, business services; no phones in some rooms ▤D, MC, V ⊘Closed Nov.–mid-May ⍩MAP $$-$$$$.

Where to Eat

✕**HENNINGTON'S.** On the shores of secluded Fairy Lake, Hennington's serves everything from casual fare like burgers and ribs to upscale delights like steak Oscar (steak with crabmeat and hollandaise sauce) and tournedos (small pieces of beef tenderloin). ✉10953 County Rd. 11, Sauk Centre ☎320/352-2591 ▤AE, MC, V ¢-$$$.

✕**MAIN ST. CAFE.** Classic American cuisine and a cozy café feeling are what you find at the Main St. Cafe. The antiques used as decoration are nice, but the burgers are the real draw. ✉303 Main St., Sauk Centre ☎320/352-5396 ▤No credit cards ¢-$.

Essentials

Getting Here

To get to the area, head west on I-94 100 mi. The Route 28/U.S. 71 exit leads to Sauk Centre. The Route 29 exit, a few miles farther, takes you to Alexandria.

Visitor Information

🛈 **Alexandria Lakes Area Chamber of Commerce** ✉206 Broadway, Alexandria 56308 ☎320/763-3161 or 800/235-9441 ⊕ www.alexandriamn.org. **Glenwood Area Chamber of Commerce** ✉200 N. Franklin St., Glenwood 56334 ☎800/304-5666. **Sauk Centre Area Chamber of Commerce** ✉1220 S. Main St., Sauk Centre 56378 ☎320/352-5201 ⊕www.saukcentre.com.

AROUND
NEW YORK

Bethpage State Park Golf Courses

By Ron Kaspriske, Pam Wright, and Diane Bair

It's part geography, part society, and part apathy.

Nevertheless, the excuses don't change the fact that New York is the worst city in America for a public golfer looking for a game. Actually, that might be a little harsh. According to *Golf Digest*, it's the *second* worst. In the magazine's 2002 ranking of 314 metropolitan areas in the United States, New York finished 313th for the quality of its golf. And what was 314th? Jersey City, across the river. In fact, New York City is so golf deficient that the most popular public golf facility in the area is actually a driving range. At Chelsea Piers on Manhattan's West Side, you can pay $20 and hit 80 balls into a net. Big fun.

Once you escape from New York, the choices get much better. Far Hills, New Jersey, is worth a trip even if you don't bring the sticks. As the home of the USGA Museum and club testing center, even a rainy afternoon here can pass quickly for a true golf fan. If you're looking for mountain scenery, try the Manchester area of southwest Vermont or two old standbys for New Yorkers: the Poconos and the Catskills. The latter two have some terrific bargain golf courses for value-conscious players, and the Equinox, in Manchester, is one of the most attractive golf resorts in the United States. (If you head to Vermont in fall, be ready for big crowds and some serious price gouging to go along with the amazingly colorful leaves.)

Courses at all three destinations can resemble a roller coaster, with fairways going through as much as 100 feet of elevation changes. The views are so impressive, however, that it takes away a bit of the sting of playing poorly.

If you like the upscale qualities of Manchester, but would rather visit somewhere along the seaboard, then Newport, Rhode Island, has the best combination of good golf and great looks. It's best to travel here in the "shoulder seasons," before Memorial Day and after Labor Day.

If Newport is a little too snooty for your tastes, you may prefer the hot-dog–and–peanuts crowd in Cooperstown, New York. It's no secret that many New Yorkers would rather spend their time watching baseball than playing golf. But in Cooperstown, you can do both: the Otesaga Hotel is very close to the Baseball Hall of Fame. Our favorite time to play here is in fall, when the colonial-era village explodes with color and resembles a Norman Rockwell painting.

No matter what region you choose, most courses in the areas surrounding New York have a traditional parkland design. Tree-lined fairways, gentle hills, and the occasional pond are typical elements. One bonus to golfing on courses here is that since the majority were built before golf carts came into vogue, they are all relatively easy to walk.

Around New York

Course	Yardage	Par	Rating	Slope	Fees
Branton Woods Golf Club (18)	7,100/4,857	72/72	73.7 /73.7	131/114	$75/$100
Concord Resort & Golf Club (36)					
International (18)	6,619/5,564	71/71	72.2/73.6	127/125	$45/$55
Monster (18)	7,650/5,201	72/72	76.4/70.6	137/121	$45/$95
Grossinger Country Club (27)					
Big G (18)	7,004/5,730	71/73	73.5/72.9	133/127	$45/$85
Little G (9)	3,268/3,024	36/36	35.9/36.6	126/130	$20
Hudson Valley Resort & Spa (18)	6,351/5,300	70/70	68.4/69.4	123/145	$25/$52
Kutsher's Country Club (18)	6,843/5,676	71/71	74.1/73.1	129/128	$40/$60
Lochmor Golf Course (18)	6,550/5,129	71/71	71.0/69.4	120/116	$20/$25
Nevele Grand Resort & Country Club (27)					$35/$69
Blue/Red (18)	6,823/5,145	70/70	72.7/72.8	130/129	
Red/White (18)	6,532/4,600	70/70	71.4/71.1	128/126	
White/Blue (18)	6,573/4,600	70/70	71.8/71.1	126/126	
Tarry Brae Golf Club (18)	6,965/5,825	72/76	74.2/72.2	131/123	$23/$33
Tennanah Lake Golf (18)	6,546/5,164	72/72	72.1/70.1	128/120	$30/$51
Villa Roma Country Club (18)	6,499/5,329	71/71	70.9/70.3	124/119	$50/$65

THE CATSKILLS

The Catskill Mountains' status as a tourist destination predates the founding of the United States. Obviously, the colonists didn't bring their golf clubs to the region—it's in the past century that the area became a premier golfing destination.

Less than two hours north of New York City, the Catskills draw people with their scenery: majestic green mountain peaks surrounded by the Delaware River on its western border and the Hudson River to the east. It's New York's answer to the Poconos. Or perhaps the Poconos are Pennsylvania's answer to the Catskills? Either way, the similarities in terrain, weather, and quality of golf make them perfect complements to each other. Like the Poconos, late summer is the best time to come for golf.

The Catskills have as many solid golf courses as the Poconos, but only one stands out as a home-run destination. The Nevele Grand Resort & Country Club's 27 holes, designed by Robert Trent Jones and Tom Fazio, make for a beautiful mountain and valley course. And if you want a memorable golf experience on your way home, be sure to play Branton Woods Golf Club, east of the Catskills in the Hudson Valley. *Golf Digest* named it one of the 10 best new public courses to appear in the United States in 2003.

Courses

BRANTON WOODS GOLF CLUB. Facility Holes: 18. Opened: 2002. Yards: 7,100/4,857. Par: 72/72. Course Rating: 73.7 /73.7. Slope: 131/114. Green Fee: $75/$100. Cart Fee: Included in green fee. Tee Times: Call 7 days in advance. ✉178 Stormville Rd., Hopewell Junction 12533 ☎845/223-1600 ⊕www.brantonwoodsgolf.com ▤AE, MC, V. ★★★★

CONCORD RESORT & GOLF CLUB. Facility Holes: 36. Cart Fee: Included in green fee. Discounts: Weekdays, twilight, seniors, juniors. Walking: Unrestricted walking. Season: Apr.–Nov. High: June–Sept. Tee Times: Call 30 days in advance. Notes: Range (grass), lodging (42). ✉95 Chalet Rd., Kiamesha Lake 12751, 90 mi from New York City ☎845/ 794-4000 or 888/448-9686 ⊕www.concordresort.com ▤AE, D, DC, MC, V.

International. Holes: 18. Opened: 1950. Architect: Alfred H. Tull. Yards: 6,619/5,564. Par: 71/71. Course Rating: 72.2/73.6. Slope: 127/125. Green Fee: $45/$55. *Comments: Better for the beginning player than the Monster. Not overly decorated with trees, so errant shots stay in play.* ★★★ ½

Monster. Holes: 18. Opened: 1963. Architect: Joseph Finger. Yards: 7,650/5,201. Par: 72/ 72. Course Rating: 76.4/70.6. Slope: 137/121. Green Fee: $45/$95. *Comments: The better of the two courses at Concord, the Monster is not as toothy as it once was, but the course is plenty long. It's flat but has many water hazards.* ★★★★

GROSSINGER COUNTRY CLUB. Facility Holes: 27. Discounts: Weekdays, twilight, seniors, juniors. Walking: Unrestricted walking. Season: Apr.–Nov. High: May–Sept. Tee Times: Call 30 days in advance. Notes: Range (grass). ✉127 Grossinger Rd., Liberty 12754, 98 mi from New York City ☎914/292-9000 or 888/448-9686 ⊕www. grossingergolf.com ▤AE, MC, V.

Big G. Holes: 18. Opened: 1968. Architect: Joseph Finger/A. W. Tillinghast. Yards: 7,004/ 5,730. Par: 71/73. Course Rating: 73.5/72.9. Slope: 133/127. Green Fee: $45/$85. Cart Fee: Included in green fee. *Comments: Has a longtime reputation for being the best course in the area. Scenic parkland design is well worth your time, but it's not as good as its reputation.* ★★★★ ½

Little G (Vista) Holes: 9. Opened: 1925. Architect: A. W. Tillinghast. Yards: 3,268/ 3,024. Par: 36/36. Course Rating: 35.9/36.6. Slope: 126/130. Green Fee: $20. Cart Fee: $15 per person. *Comments: The low rate will get your attention. A better value than the Big G.* ★★★

HUDSON VALLEY RESORT & SPA. Facility Holes: 18. Opened: 1998. Architect: Lee Chen. Yards: 6,351/5,300. Par: 70/70. Course Rating: 68.4/69.4. Slope: 123/145. Green Fee: $25/$52. Cart Fee: Included in green fee. Walking: Walking at certain times. Season: Apr.–Nov. Tee Times: Call up to 30 days in advance. ✉400 Granite Rd., Kerhonkson 12446 ☎845/626-8888 or 888/948-3766 ⊕www.hudsonvalleyresort.com ▤AE, D, DC, MC, V. *Comments: A great value. UR*

KUTSHER'S COUNTRY CLUB. Facility Holes: 18. Opened: 1962. Architect: William F. Mitchell. Yards: 6,843/5,676. Par: 71/71. Course Rating: 74.1/73.1. Slope: 129/128. Green Fee: $40/$60. Cart Fee: Included in green fee. Discounts: Weekdays, guest, twilight. Walking: Mandatory cart. Season: Apr.–Nov. Tee Times: Call 7 days in advance. Notes: Range (grass, mat). ⊠ Kutsher Rd., Monticello 12701, 80 mi from New York City ☎ 845/ 794-6000 ⊕ www.kutshers.com. *Comments: This resort course is fine, but not very memorable.* ★ ★ ★ ½

LOCHMOR GOLF COURSE. Facility Holes: 18. Opened: 1958. Architect: William F. Mitchell. Yards: 6,550/5,129. Par: 71/71. Course Rating: 71.0/69.4. Slope: 120/116. Green Fee: $20/$25. Cart Fee: $15 per person. Discounts: Weekdays, twilight, seniors, juniors. Walking: Walking at certain times. Season: Apr.–Oct. High: June–Oct. Tee Times: Call 7 days in advance. Notes: Range (grass, mat). ⊠ 586 Loch Sheldrake/Hurleyville Rd., Loch Sheldrake 12779, 8 mi from Monticello ☎ 845/434-1257 ⊕ www.tarrybrae.com ⊟ MC, V. *Comments: Good value and in decent shape for a parkland municipal course. But don't lose sleep if you miss playing it.* ★ ★ ★ ½

NEVELE GRAND RESORT & COUNTRY CLUB. Facility Holes: 27. Opened: 1955. Architect: Tom Fazio/Robert Trent Jones. Green Fee: $35/$69. Cart Fee: Included in green fee. Discounts: Weekdays, guest, twilight, juniors. Walking: Walking at certain times. Season: Apr.–Nov. High: June–Sept. Tee Times: Call 30 days in advance. Notes: Range (grass, mat), lodging (750). ⊠ Rte. 209 (Nevele Rd.), Ellenville 12428, 90 mi from New York City ☎ 845/647-6000 or 800/647-6000 ⊕ www.nevele.com ⊟ AE, D, DC, MC, V.

Blue/Red. Holes: 18. Yards: 6,823/5,145. Par: 70/70. Course Rating: 72.7/72.8. Slope: 130/129.

Red/White. Holes: 18. Yards: 6,532/4,600. Par: 70/70. Course Rating: 71.4/71.1. Slope: 128/126.

White/Blue. Holes: 18. Yards: 6,573/4,600. Par: 70/70. Course Rating: 71.8/71.1. Slope: 126/126.

Comments: Fazio's work is terrific, with the holes built around a spring-fed lake, and great views of the Catskills in the distance. The White 9 has the most water holes. ★ ★ ★ ★

TARRY BRAE GOLF CLUB. Facility Holes: 18. Opened: 1962. Architect: William F. Mitchell. Yards: 6,965/5,825. Par: 72/76. Course Rating: 74.2/72.2. Slope: 131/123. Green Fee: $23/$33. Cart Fee: $15 per person. Discounts: Weekdays, twilight, juniors. Walking: Walking at certain times. Season: Apr.–Nov. Tee Times: Call 7 days in advance. Notes: Range (grass, mat). ⊠ Pleasant Valley Rd., South Fallsburg 12779, 10 mi from Monticello ☎ 845/434-2620 ⊕ www.tarrybrae.com ⊟ MC, V. *Comments: Yet another solid golf experience, but a lack of grooming hurts its overall value.* ★ ★ ★ ½

TENNANAH LAKE GOLF & TENNIS CLUB. Facility Holes: 18. Opened: 1911. Architect: Alfred H. Tull. Yards: 6,546/5,164. Par: 72/72. Course Rating: 72.1/70.1. Slope: 128/120. Green Fee: $30/$51. Cart Fee: Included in green fee. Discounts: Weekdays, twilight, seniors, juniors. Walking: Walking at certain times. Season: Apr–Oct. Tee Times: Call golf shop. Notes: Range (grass, mat), lodging (24). ⊠ 100 Belle Rd., Suite 2, Roscoe 12776, 60 mi from Middletown ☎ 607/498-5502 or 888/561-3935 ⊕ www.tennanah.

com ▭AE, D, MC, V. *Comments: A pretty mountain golf course. Tight fairways make it a challenge.* ★ ★ ★ ½

VILLA ROMA COUNTRY CLUB. Facility Holes: 18. Opened: 1987. Architect: David Postlethwaite. Yards: 6,499/5,329. Par: 71/71. Course Rating: 70.9/70.3. Slope: 124/119. Green Fee: $50/$65. Cart Fee: Included in green fee. Discounts: Weekdays, twilight, seniors, juniors. Walking: Mandatory cart. Season: Apr.–Nov. High: May–Sept. Tee Times: Call golf shop. Notes: Range (grass). ⊠356 Villa Roma Rd., Callicoon 12723, 100 mi from New York City ☎914/887–5097 or 800/727–8455 ▭AE, D, MC, V. *Comments: Good scenery on a somewhat hilly course. Typical Catskills design.* ★ ★ ★ ★

Where to Stay

📷 **BEST WESTERN MONTICELLO.** Popular with race fans, this chain hotel is across from the Monticello Raceway and gives your plenty of bang for your buck. Rooms are nondescript (think white walls, cheap art prints, and basic furnishings) but the spacious, wood-paneled lobby is inviting, as is the heated indoor pool, sauna, and hot tub. Several restaurants are within walking distance or a few minutes' drive away. There's a two-night minimum stay on weekends in July and August. ⊠16 Raceway Rd., Monticello 12701 ☎845/796–4000 🖷845/796–4000 ⊕www.bestwesternnewyork.com ⇆62 rooms ᕕ Some microwaves, some refrigerators, cable TV with movies, indoor pool, exercise equipment, hot tub, sauna, video game room, laundry service, Internet, meeting rooms, no-smoking rooms ▭AE, D, DC, MC, V ⦿CP $$.

📷 **CONCORD RESORT AND GOLF CLUB.** The basic, no-frills rooms in the golf clubhouse are very convenient for serious golfers. Guests have access to the on-site and very popular 7,650-yard Monster championship golf course and the highly rated Monster Golf Academy. The Grossinger Country Club and Concord International courses are also nearby, and the resort has plenty of packages for all three courses. Note that there are big plans in progress for a huge resort on this 1,600-acre property that will draw folks who do more than golf. ⊠219 Concord Rd., Kiamesha Lake 12751 ☎845/794–4000 or 888/448–9686 🖷845/794–6944 ⊕www.concordresort.com ⇆42 rooms ᕕ Restaurant, minibars, refrigerators, cable TV, 18-hole golf course, pro shop, meeting rooms; no smoking ▭AE, D, DC, MC, V ⦿CP $.

📷 **HUDSON VALLEY RESORT.** Twinkling chandeliers and a grand piano grace the entrance and lobby area of this modern high-rise hotel and conference center. Expect to share the place with big groups: The resort is a popular spot for weddings, as well a corporate meeting hot spot. But traveling families and serious golfers alike are attracted by the on-site amenities and conveniences, as well as the Shawangunk Mountains backdrop. Rooms are spacious, with dark wall-to-wall carpeting, wood accents, and marble bathrooms. ⊠400 Granite Rd., Kerhonkson 12446 ☎845/626–8888 or 888/948–3766 🖷845/626–2595 ⊕www.hudsonvalleyresort.com ⇆352 rooms ᕕ Restaurant, in-room data ports, cable TV, 18-hole golf course, tennis court, pro shop, 2 pools (1 indoor), health club, massage, sauna, spa, steam room, bar, lounge, children's programs (ages 3–16), business services, meeting rooms ▭AE, D, DC, MC, V $-$$$.

☷ **NEVELE GRAND RESORT & COUNTRY CLUB.** A nine-story hotel on sprawling manicured grounds in the mountains, the Nevele operates in the tradition of the famous Catskill resorts, with many sports and outdoor activities. Rooms are dressed in light woods and neutral colors with country accents. Most have views of the golf courses (there are three on site), lakes, or the surrounding mountain range. ⊠ Rte. 209 (Nevele Rd.), Ellenville 12428 ☏ 845/647–6000 or 800/647–6000 🖷 845/647–9884 ⊕ www. nevele.com ⇋ 700 rooms ⚹ Restaurant, room service, in-room data ports, cable TV, 27-hole golf course, miniature golf, 15 tennis courts, 4 pools, health club, hot tub, spa, boating, horseback riding, cross-country skiing, downhill skiing, ice-skating, sleigh rides, tobogganing, shops, children's programs (ages 3–11), business services ▭ AE, DC, MC, V ⦿I FAP $$$$.

☷ **SWAN LAKE GOLF AND TENNIS.** Asian furnishings, paintings, and accessories are scattered throughout this large, refurbished resort hotel, which overlooks Swan Lake. Rooms lack the same flourish; most are furnished like those in a small motel, with two beds, two chairs, and a small table. There are lots of things to do outside, with pools, tennis courts, and an on-site golf course. There's a two-night minimum stay on weekends in summer. ⊠ Eagle Dr., Box 450, Swan Lake 12783 ☏ 845/292–8000 or 888/254–5818 🖷 845/292–4194 ⊕ www.swanlakeresorthotelcc.com ⇋ 216 rooms, 12 suites ⚹ Restaurant, dining room, cable TV, 18-hole golf course, 2 tennis courts, pro shop, 2 pools (1 indoor), lake, fitness center, bar, recreation room, meeting rooms ▭ MC, V ⦿I FAP $$.

☷ **VILLA ROMA RESORT HOTEL.** Families have been coming to this bustling Catskills resort for generations. The blend of a casual, friendly approach and plenty of on-site activities is also a magnet for bus tour groups and corporate getaways. Rooms come in all sizes, most with walls in pastels or neutrals, and basic, cookie-cutter furnishings. There's a two-night minimum stay on summer weekends. ⊠ 356 Villa Roma Rd., Callicoon 12723 ☏ 845/887–4880 or 800/533–6767 🖷 845/887–4824 ⊕ www. villaroma.com ⇋ 182 rooms, 18 suites ⚹ 2 restaurants, dining room, in-room data ports, some refrigerators, cable TV, 18-hole golf course, pro shop, 5 pools (1 indoor), fitness center, massage, downhill skiing, bar, recreation room, children's programs (ages 3–19), meeting rooms ▭ AE, D, DC, MC, V ⦿I MAP $$$$.

Where to Eat

✕ **MANNY'S STEAKHOUSE AND SEAFOOD.** If you're yearning for a hunk of prime meat or a slab of baby back ribs, you won't go wrong at this classic steak house. Try the house specialty, a 50-ounce porterhouse steak for two, if you dare. Non-carnivores will find plenty of choices, too, from daily fresh seafood dishes, like grilled salmon, halibut, swordfish, and stuffed lobster tails. The unassuming facade hides an interior of warm woods and spacious seating. ⊠ 79 Sullivan Ave., Liberty ☏ 845/295–3170 ▭ AE, D, MC, V $$–$$$$.

✕ **PAINTER'S.** Housed in one of Cornwall-on-Hudson's historic buildings, this restaurant displays the work of local artists and is known for inventive pasta dishes, seafood, an extensive beer selection, and beer-can chicken (chicken grilled and steamed with beer on the outdoor grill). Sandwiches are also available. Sunday brunch is popular here. ⊠266 Hudson St., Cornwall-on-Hudson ☏845/534-2109 ▤AE, D, DC, MC, V $$-$$$.

✗ **PICCOLO PAESE.** Known for its homemade pasta, Piccolo Paese specializes in northern Italian cuisine. An elegant wine rack and intimate surroundings with white tablecloths and waiters decked out in tuxedoes and bow ties make this a romantic spot. Try the penne with spicy tomato cream sauce with a splash of vodka or the shrimp sautéed in champagne, cream, mushrooms, and prosciutto. ⊠5 State Rte. 52 E, Liberty ☏845/292-7210 ▤AE, D, MC, V ☉No lunch weekends $$$-$$$$.

Essentials

Getting Here
The Catskills area is an easy two-hour drive from New York City. You can reach cities and towns in the Catskills region off I-87, taking the exit for Route 17.

Visitor Information
🛈 **Ellenville Area Chamber of Commerce** ☍Box 227, Ellenville 12428 ☏845/647-4620 ⊕www.ewcoc.com. **Liberty Chamber of Commerce** ☍Box 147, Liberty 12754 ☏845/292-1878 ⊕www.libertyshops.com. **New Paltz Chamber of Commerce** ⊠257½ Main St., New Paltz 12561 ☏845/255-0243 ⊕www.newpaltzchamber.org. **Sullivan County Visitors Association** ⊠100 North St., Monticello 12701 ☏800/882-2287 ⊕www.scva.net.

COOPERSTOWN

You've undoubtedly either gone to or at least heard of Cooperstown because of the Baseball Hall of Fame. But long before bats and gloves became the town's hallmark, author James Fenimore Cooper predicted it would be a resort town. It turns out he was right.

The beautiful, Victorian-era town is a terrific golf destination. Lake Otsego provides a painting-like background for some of the area's fairways.

The best time to visit the area is in October but anytime from May to Halloween is fine. Summers can get muggy. It's about a five-hour, very scenic drive northwest from New York City. Head directly for the Otesaga Hotel, a nearly-100-year-old resort with Georgian architecture and terrific views of the lake. At the resort is the Leatherstocking Golf Course, a well-known yet often ignored gem of a golf course. It's at its prime in fall.

If things start to get a little too slow for you in Cooperstown, you may want to head an hour north to Oneida and stay and play at the Turning Stone

Canasawacta Country Club (18)	6,271/5,166	70/71	69.9/68.8	120/114	$18/$22
Cobleskill Golf Course (18)	6,133/5,212	70/73	69.2/70.1	116/118	$15/$25
Colgate University Seven Oaks Golf Club (18)	6,915/5,315	72/72	74.4/75.7	144/133	$25/$54
Leatherstocking Golf Course (18)	6,416/5,178	72/72	70.8/69.2	135/116	$80
Shenendoah Golf Club (18)	7,129/5,185	72/72	74.1/71.6	142/120	$80/$125

Casino Resort, which owns the Shenendoah Golf Club. The Rick Smith–designed course is excellent and the casino will spice up the trip. The resort also has perhaps the best par-3 9-hole course this side of Augusta National Golf Club. Another must-play is Colgate University Seven Oaks Golf Club in Hamilton, about 40 mi west of Cooperstown. The course, associated with Colgate University, is one of the best-kept secrets in New York. Designed by Robert Trent Jones, the course opened in 1957 with 9 holes and expanded to 18 in 1964.

Courses

Golf Digest REVIEWS

CANASAWACTA COUNTRY CLUB. Facility Holes: 18. Opened: 1920. Architect: Russell Bailey. Yards: 6,271/5,166. Par: 70/71. Course Rating: 69.9/68.8. Slope: 120/114. Green Fee: $18/$22. Cart Fee: $22 per cart. Discounts: Twilight, seniors, juniors. Walking: Unrestricted walking. Season: Apr.–Oct. Tee Times: Call golf shop. Notes: Range (grass). ✉ 79 S. Broad St., Norwich 13815, 37 mi from Binghamton ☎ 607/336-2685 ⊟ AE, MC, V. *Comments: Older course that's worth your time. Parkland design.* ★ ★ ★ ½

COBLESKILL GOLF COURSE. Facility Holes: 18. Opened: 1929. Yards: 6,133/5,212. Par: 70/73. Course Rating: 69.2/70.1. Slope: 116/118. Green Fee: $15/$25. Cart Fee: $14 per person. Walking: Unrestricted walking. Tee Times: Call up to 2 days in advance. ✉ Rte. 7, Cobleskill 12043 ☎ 518/234-4045 ⊕ www.nocrowds.com/enjoygolf ⊟ MC, V. *Comments: Basic, no-frills golf. Low green fee makes it worth a look.* UR

COLGATE UNIVERSITY SEVEN OAKS GOLF CLUB. Facility Holes: 18. Opened: 1957. Architect: Robert Trent Jones. Yards: 6,915/5,315. Par: 72/72. Course Rating: 74.4/75.7. Slope: 144/133. Green Fee: $25/$54. Cart Fee: $27 per cart. Discounts: Weekdays, seniors, juniors. Walking: Unrestricted walking. Season: Apr.–Oct. Tee Times: Call golf shop. Notes: Range (grass). ✉ E. Lake Rd., Hamilton 13346, 41 mi from Syracuse ☎ 315/824-1432 ⊕ sevenoaks.colgate.edu ⊟ MC, V. Comments: Fairly flat, but with an incredibly scenic parkland design. ★ ★ ★ ★ ½

LEATHERSTOCKING GOLF COURSE. Facility Holes: 18. Opened: 1909. Architect: Devereux Emmet. Yards: 6,416/5,178. Par: 72/72. Course Rating: 70.8/69.2. Slope: 135/116. Green Fee: $80. Cart Fee: $18 per person. Discounts: Twilight. Walking: Walking at certain times. Season: Apr.–Nov. Tee Times: Call 6 days in advance. Notes: Range (grass), lodging (136). ✉ 60 Lake St., 13326, 70 mi from Albany ☎ 607/547–5275 or 800/348–6200 ▬AE, MC, V. *Comments: The class of the area. Beautiful design but not as big a bargain as it used to be—rates have crept up. Plays along Lake Otsego.* ★ ★ ★ ★ ¹/₂

SHENENDOAH GOLF CLUB. Facility Holes: 18. Opened: 2000. Architect: Rick Smith. Yards: 7,129/5,185. Par: 72/72. Course Rating: 74.1/71.6. Slope: 142/120. Green Fee: $80/$125. Cart Fee: Included in green fee. Discounts: Twilight. Walking: Unrestricted walking. Season: Apr.–Nov. Tee Times: Call 2 days in advance. Notes: Range (grass), lodging (350). ✉ 5218 Patrick Rd., Verona 13478, 30 mi from Syracuse ☎ 315/361–8518 or 877/748–4653 ⊕ www.turning-stone.com ▬AE, D, MC, V. *Comments: It's 60 mi away from Cooperstown, but trust us, it's worth it. Great farmland golf course. The 9-hole par-3 course is also a blast to play.* ★ ★ ★ ★ ¹/₂

Where to Stay

▦ **INN AT COOPERSTOWN.** Built in 1874, this historic, three-story inn has Victorian woodwork and an impressive front porch. You can sit outside on the veranda and, inside, one of the sitting rooms has a fireplace with shelves full of books and cozy chairs and a sofa to sink into. Rooms are bright, tidy, and spacious. Most have wall-to-wall carpeting, warm tones, country quilts, and antique or quality reproduction furnishings. A trolley that takes you to various sites in Cooperstown stops nearby. ✉ 16 Chestnut St., 13326 ☎ 607/547–5756 ☐ 607/547–8779 ⊕ www.innatcooperstown.com ➷ 17 rooms, 1 suite ⚭ Business services, no smoking rooms; no room phones, no room TVs ▬AE, D, DC, MC, V ¶◯¶ CP $$.

▦ **ONEIDA COMMUNITY MANSION HOUSE.** This mammoth three-story brick home once belonged to the Oneida Community, a utopian religious group founded in 1848. Built in stages between 1861 and 1914, Mansion House's scale—over 200 rooms and 93,000 square feet—illustrates the needs of a society living as one family (in fact, everyone was married to everyone else). Today the building is primarily occupied by private apartments, a museum, and eight large guest rooms, which have quilts and wooden post beds. The grounds include lawns and gardens covering more than 33 acres. Tours of the house, a National Historic Landmark, are also available. ✉ 170 Kenwood Ave., Oneida 13421 ☎ 315/363–0745 ☐ 315/361–4580 ⊕ www.oneidacommunity.org ➷ 8 rooms ⚭ Some refrigerators, 18-hole golf course, library, meeting rooms, no-smoking rooms ▬MC, V ¶◯¶ CP $.

▦ **OTESAGA HOTEL.** This large Georgian Revival hotel on Lake Otsego was built in 1909. Glistening chandeliers, fine paintings, and elegant furnishings are on display throughout this gracious resort. The white columned lakeside veranda overlooks the water and is a popular spot for relaxing. Rooms are spacious, decorated in warm tones, with classic floral and striped upholsteries and dark cherry and mahogany furnishings. Some rooms overlook the south shore of Lake Otsego. ✉ 60 Lake St., 13326 ☎ 607/547–9931 or 800/348–6222 ☐ 607/547–9675 ⊕ www.otesaga.com ➷ 125 rooms, 10 suites ⚭ Restaurant, in-room data ports, cable TV, 18-hole golf course, pool, dock, business services ▬AE, D, DC, MC, V ¶◯¶ MAP $$$$.

⊞ TURNING STONE CASINO RESORT. This huge resort hotel on the grounds of the Turning Stone Casino is loaded with amenities. The guest rooms have dramatically lit marble bathrooms, contemporary furniture, and matching pink, yellow, and blue bed coverings and curtains. ⊠ 5218 Patrick Rd., Verona 13478 ☎ 800/771-7711 ⊕ www. turning-stone.com ➟ 255 rooms, 30 suites ⚐ 7 restaurants, ice cream parlor, cable TV with video games, 2 9-hole golf courses, 18-hole golf course, pool, hair salon, gym, spa, shops, business services ☰ AE, D, DC, MC, V $-$$.

Where to Eat

✕ **BLUE MINGO GRILL.** Fresh local ingredients are combined with Asian flavors to create the tasty dishes at this waterfront restaurant. You can look out at Lake Otsego from the casual indoor dining area or from porches that open off the restaurant. Specials change daily, but might include dishes like the Indian griddled corn cakes, roasted quail with grilled sweet potato, grilled salmon with red pepper marmalade, or roast duck with chipotle sauce. ⊠ W. Lake Rd. at Sam's Boatyard ☎ 607/547-7496 ☰ AE, MC, V ☾ Closed Mon. and Tues. Columbus Day–Memorial Day. No lunch Columbus Day–Memorial Day $$$-$$$$.

✕ **LAKE FRONT RESTAURANT.** Open-air dining overlooking Lake Otsego and a menu full of original seafood dishes make this a lovely dining spot. In the nautical dining room there's a full salad bar and lounge. ⊠ 10 Fair St. ☎ 607/547-8188 ☰ MC, V ☾ Closed Oct.–Apr. $$-$$$.

✕ **TURNING STONE CASINO RESORT.** With seven restaurants, including a diner, snack shop, steak house, trattoria, buffet, and an Asian eatery, you're likely to find something to match your appetite. Emerald Restaurant, open 24 hours, serves breakfast all day (and night), with burgers, steaks, fried fish, and pasta available for lunch and dinner. The Garden Buffet is open for all-you-can-eat breakfasts and dinners. There's a prime rib buffet on weekend nights. The Peach Blossom's Asian dishes include traditional Chinese and Thai touches. Try the shark's-fin soup and the sizzling and spicy seafood clay pot. The cozy Forest Grill is an informal steak house specializing in large cuts of meat, like the 24-ounce porterhouse. You can pair smaller cuts of beef with lobster or king crab legs, too. Pino Bianco has an extensive menu with loads of classic Italian dishes. For a little casual fun and comfort food, grab a booth or a seat at the counter at Crystals Diner. This 1950s-style diner, full of stainless steel and neon, serves hot dogs, burgers, grilled cheese, and tuna melts. You can wash it all down with a double chocolate milk shake. ⊠ 5218 Patrick Rd., Verona ☎ 800/771-7711 ☰ AE, D, DC, MC, V $-$$$$.

Essentials

Getting Here

Cooperstown is about 230 mi from New York City, a four-hour drive on major highways and well-traveled routes. To get here, take the New York State Thruway west to exit 21, about 165 mi; then take Route 23 west to I–88 east. Take exit 17 and follow Route 28 north to Cooperstown. Expect hordes of people in summer—and the limited in-town parking that accompanies them. If you plan to go in and out of the downtown tourist area, consider using the free perimeter parking lots and taking the trolley ($2 unlimited daily pass).

Visitor Information

🚩 **Cooperstown Chamber of Commerce** ✉ 31 Chestnut St., 13326 ☎ 607/547-9983 ⊕ www.cooperstownchamber.org.

FAR HILLS, NJ

Far Hills doesn't quite roll off the tongue like Cooperstown, but if you're a golf fan in the Northeast, the USGA headquarters here make it as worthy of a pilgrimage as baseball's own Hall of Fame.

Hominy Hill, one of the best public courses anywhere, is a short drive away from Far Hills. If it were given the attention that Bethpage or Torrey Pines got in preparation for their opens, it'd be just as grand of a test. Slightly off the main drag is Knoll Country Club outside Newark, which holds a hidden treasure—a 1928 Charles Banks layout.

Courses

Golf Digest REVIEWS

ASH BROOK GOLF COURSE. Facility Holes: 18. Opened: 1953. Architect: Alfred H. Tull/Stephen Kay. Yards: 7,040/5,661. Par: 72/72. Course Rating: 74.2/71.8. Slope: 127/ 119. Green Fee: $26/$100. Cart Fee: $26 per cart. Discounts: Weekdays, seniors, juniors. Walking: Unrestricted walking. Season: Year-round. High: Apr.–Oct. Tee Times: Call 7 days in advance. ✉ 1210 Raritan Rd., Scotch Plains 07076, 15 mi from Newark ☎ 908/ 668-8503 ▭ MC, V. *Comments: Bring plenty of balls for the dangerous 14th, a long par-4 with water in play everywhere.* ★★★ ½

FLANDERS VALLEY GOLF COURSE. Facility Holes: 36. Opened: 1963. Architect: Hal Purdy/Rees Jones. Green Fee: $40/$60. Cart Fee: $26 per cart. Discounts: Weekdays, twilight, seniors. Walking: Unrestricted walking. Season: Apr.–Dec. Tee Times: Call golf shop. ✉ Pleasant Hill Rd., Flanders 07836, 50 mi from New York City ☎ 973/584-5382 ▭ MC, V.

Red/Gold. Holes: 18. Yards: 6,770/5,540. Par: 72/72. Course Rating: 72.6/72.0. Slope: 126/123. *Comments: Both are early Rees Jones designs, with lots of elevation changes.* ★★★★

White/Blue. Holes: 18. Yards: 6,765/5,534. Par: 72/72. Course Rating: 72.7/71.6. Slope: 126/122. *Comments: Big and broad. A little more room than the Red/Gold.* ★★★★

GREEN KNOLL GOLF COURSE. Facility Holes: 18. Opened: 1960. Architect: William Gordon. Yards: 6,443/5,324. Par: 71/72. Course Rating: 70.5/71.1. Slope: 120/124. Green

Ash Brook Golf Course (18)	7,040/5,661	72/72	74.2/71.8	127/119	$26/$100
Flanders Valley Golf Course (36)					$40/$60
Red/Gold (18)	6,770/5,540	72/72	72.6/72.0	126/123	
White/Blue (18)	6,765/5,534	72/72	72.7/71.6	126/122	
Green Knoll Golf Course (18)	6,443/5,324	71/72	70.5/71.1	120/124	$15/$33
Hominy Hill Golf Course (18)	7,056/5,794	72/72	74.4/73.9	132/128	$27/$62
Knoll Country Club (36)					
East (18)	5,884/5,309	70/71	67.9	112	$22/$31
West (18)	6,735/5,840	70/74	72.2/74.4	128/128	$38/$51
Mattawang Golf Club (18)	6,800/5,469	72/75	73.1/71.8	130/123	$19/$49
Royce Brook Golf Club (36)					
East (18)	6,983/5,014	72/72	73.6/69.4	132/114	$75/$105
West (18)	7,158/5,366	72/72	74.2/70.6	134/118	$25/$65
Rutgers University Golf Course (18)	6,337/5,359	71/72	70.6/71.3	123/121	$28/$39

Fee: $15/$33. Cart Fee: $26 per cart. Discounts: Weekdays, twilight, seniors, juniors. Walking: Unrestricted walking. Season: Year-round. Tee Times: Call 7 days in advance. ✉ 587 Garretson Rd., Bridgewater 08807, 30 mi from New York City ☎ 908/722–1301 ▭ AE, D, MC, V. *Comments: Venerable county course is fun to play.* ★ ★ ★

HOMINY HILL GOLF COURSE. Facility Holes: 18. Opened: 1964. Architect: Robert Trent Jones. Yards: 7,056/5,794. Par: 72/72. Course Rating: 74.4/73.9. Slope: 132/128. Green Fee: $27/$62. Cart Fee: $33 per cart. Discounts: Weekdays, twilight, seniors, juniors. Walking: Unrestricted walking. Season: Mar.–Dec. High: Mar.–Oct. Tee Times: Call golf shop. Notes: Range (grass, mat). ✉ 92 Mercer Rd., Colts Neck 07722, 50 mi from New York City ☎ 732/462-9222 ⊕ www.monmouthcountyparks.com ▭ MC, V. *Comments: Good enough to host a U.S. Open.* ★ ★ ★ ★

KNOLL COUNTRY CLUB. Facility Holes: 36. Cart Fee: $15 per person. Discounts: Weekdays, twilight. Season: Mar.–Dec. Tee Times: Call 1 day in advance. Notes: Range (grass). ✉ Knoll and Green Bank Rds., Parsippany 07054, 16 mi from Newark ☎ 973/263-7115.

East. Holes: 18. Opened: 1963. Architect: Hal Purdy. Yards: 5,884/5,309. Par: 70/71. Course Rating: 67.9++CE: 2nd rating?++. Slope: 112++CE: 2nd slope?++. Green Fee: $22/$31. Walking: Unrestricted walking. *Comments: Too short to be dangerous.* ★ ★ ½

West. Holes: 18. Opened: 1928. Architect: Charles Banks. Yards: 6,735/5,840. Par: 70/74. Course Rating: 72.2/74.4. Slope: 128/128. Green Fee: $38/$51. Walking: Walking at certain times. *Comments: This is the one that makes it worth the trip. Some of "Steamshovel" Banks's most interesting work.* ★ ★ ★ ★

MATTAWANG GOLF CLUB. Facility Holes: 18. Opened: 1962. Architect: Mike Myles. Yards: 6,800/5,469. Par: 72/75. Course Rating: 73.1/71.8. Slope: 130/123. Green Fee:

$19/$49. Cart Fee: $17 per person. Discounts: Twilight, seniors, juniors. Walking: Walking at certain times. Season: Year-round. Tee Times: Call 9 days in advance. Notes: Range (mat). ⊠ Box 577, Belle Mead 08502, 8 mi from Princeton ☎ 908/281-0778 ⊟ AE, D, MC, V. *Comments: You almost need a microscope to find the greens.* ★ ★ ★

ROYCE BROOK GOLF CLUB. Facility Holes: 36. Opened: 1998. Architect: Steve Smyers. Tee Times: Call up to 7 days in advance. Walking: Walking at certain times. Season: Year-round. ⊠ 201 Hamilton Rd., Hillsborough 08844 ☎ 888/434-3673 ⊕ - www.roycebrook.com ⊟ AE, D, MC, V.

East. Holes: 18. Yards: 6,983/5,014. Par: 72/72. Course Rating: 73.6/69.4. Slope: 132/114. Green Fee: $75/$105. Cart Fee: Included in green fee. Discounts: Twilight. Tee Times: Call 7 days in advance. Notes: Range (grass). *Comments: It's been very popular from the day it opened.* ★ ★ ★ ★

West. Holes: 18. Yards: 7,158/5,366. Par: 72/72. Course Rating: 74.2/70.6. Slope: 134/118. Green Fee: $25/$65. Cart Fee: Included in green fee. Season: Year-round. Tee Times: Call 7 days in advance. *Comments: Oceans of sand. Natural grass range is a great feature.* UR

RUTGERS UNIVERSITY GOLF COURSE. Facility Holes: 18. Opened: 1963. Architect: Hal Purdy. Yards: 6,337/5,359. Par: 71/72. Course Rating: 70.6/71.3. Slope: 123/121. Green Fee: $28/$39. Cart Fee: $28 per cart. Discounts: Weekdays, twilight, seniors, juniors. Walking: Unrestricted walking. Season: Mar.–Dec. Tee Times: Call 5 days in advance. Notes: Range (mat). ⊠ 777 Hoes Lane W, Piscataway 08854, 3 mi from New Brunswick ☎ 732/445-2637 ⊟ MC, V. *Comments: Sporty, with slick greens.* ★ ★ ★ ★

Where to Stay

⌖ **BERNARDS INN.** This three-story mission-style inn has elegant furnishings and a helpful staff. It is characterized by elegant furnishings and a staff that is more than happy to serve your needs. Rooms resemble those in an Edwardian manor house, with imported fabrics and pastoral oil paintings. ⊠ Mine Brook and Mount Airy Rds., Bernardsville 07924 ☎ 908/766-0002 ⊟ 908/766-4604 ⊕ www.bernardsinn.com ↝ 20 rooms ↺ Restaurant, room service, in-room data ports, cable TV, business services ⊟ D, MC, V ⊙ CP $$-$$$$.

⌖ **MADISON HOTEL.** The Gilded Age lives on in this four-story Victorian inn in Morristown, surrounded by neatly manicured lawns and gardens. Inside are brocade fabrics, rich mahogany paneling, and etched glass. Some rooms have whirlpools. ⊠ 1 Convent Rd., at Madison Ave., Morristown 07960 ☎ 973/285-1800 or 800/526-0729 ⊟ 973/540-8566 ⊕ www.themadisonhotel.com ↝ 191 rooms ↺ In-room data ports, minibars, pool, gym ⊟ D, MC, V ⊙ CP $$-$$$$.

⌖ **OLDE MILL INN.** This classic American inn is in the lush rolling Somerset Hills in Basking Ridge. Rooms are decorated with a handsome simplicity, with beautifully crafted wood furnishings, sleek leather armchairs, and an appealing spaciousness. Some have whirlpools and fireplaces. ⊠ 225 U.S. 202, at N. Maple Ave., Basking Ridge 07920

GOLF HOUSE

The United States Golf Association was founded on Dec. 22, 1894, marking the formal organization of American golf. Its purpose was to establish a centralized body to write the rules of golf, conduct national championships (such as the U.S. Open), and establish a national system of handicapping. The USGA also acts as the game's historian in this country, collecting, displaying, and preserving artifacts and memorabilia at its headquarters, **Golf House** (✉ 1 Liberty Corner Rd., 07931 ☎ 908/234–2300 ⊕ www.usga.org/golfhouse).

If you visit, you'll find some of the finest golf memorabilia this side of the World Golf Hall of Fame in St. Augustine, Florida. Want to see the 1-iron Ben Hogan hit into the last green at the 1951 U.S. Open at Oakland Hills? It's here. What about the 6-iron Alan Shepard hit on the moon? In the cabinet one room over. You can also tour the facility the USGA uses to test equipment—see what sort of paces that giant new driver went through before you bought it. All told, the collection includes more than 42,000 artifacts, 20,000 books, 500,000 photographs, and thousands of hours of historic film.

☎ 908/221–1100 or 800/585–4461 🖨 908/221–1560 ⊕ www.oldemillinn.com 🛏 102 rooms ঔ Restaurant, cable TV, pub ⊟ D, MC, V $$–$$$$.

🏨 **WESTIN MORRISTOWN.** This tastefully decorated member of the Westin chain has all the amenities you expect from a national hotel. Most of the guest rooms are spacious. ✉ 2 Whippany Rd., Morristown 07960 ☎ 973/539–7300 🖨 973/984–1036 ⊕ www.westin.com 🛏 197 rooms ঔ 2 restaurants, in-room data ports, cable TV with movies, tennis courts, pool, health club, bar, meeting rooms, no-smoking rooms ⊟ D, MC, V $–$$.

Where to Eat

✕ **BERNARDS INN.** With two gracious dining rooms and a clublike bar with jazz pianists on weekends, the Bernards Inn is as traditional in its appearance as in its menu, which emphasizes classic American ingredients and dishes. The wine cellar has an abundant selection of wines to complement the dishes, which might include farmed quail, foie gras from the Hudson Valley, tenderloin of veal, and Florida black grouper. ✉ Mine Brook and Mount Airy Rds., Bernardsville ☎ 908/766–0002 ⊕ www.bernardsinn.com ⊟ AE, D, DC, MC, V ☉ Closed Sun. $$$$.

✕**LE PETIT CHATEAU.** Inside this Tudor-style cottage, the cuisine is French through and through. A few classic selections include foie gras with caramelized pears, snails in puff pastry with Brie, and a delectable Grand Marnier soufflé. ✉121 Claremont Rd., Bernardsville ☎908/766-4544 ☰AE, D, MC, V ⊙Closed Mon. $$$$.

✕**ROD'S STEAK AND SEAFOOD GRILLE.** This restaurant used to be known as Rod's 1890s Ranch House, which got its start in a log cabin. Renamed and revamped, the emphasis is on hearty, well-prepared steaks and seafood. Among the specialties are the chilled seafood tower appetizer and entrées that include Delmonico steak and North Atlantic salmon. ✉The Madison Hotel, 1 Convent Rd., at Madison Ave. ☎609/884-2555 ⊕www.themadisonhotel.com ☰AE, D, DC, MC, V ⊙Closed Mon. and Tues. No lunch $$$-$$$$.

Essentials

Getting Here
To get to Far Hills from New York, take I-78 to Exit 29. Take a right onto I-287 and take it to U.S. 202. The trip is about 40 mi.

Visitor Information
🛈**SOMERSET COUNTY CHAMBER OF COMMERCE** ✉360 Grove St., Bridgewater 08807 ☎908/725-1552 🖷908/722-7823 ⊕www.somersetcountychamber.org.

LONG ISLAND

Over Long Island's 118-mi span is a blend of New York City suburbs and wealthy beachfront communities. It also contains sprawling farmland, vineyards, and congested superhighways. Perhaps it doesn't sound like a great spot for a golf trip, but in truth, the state of public golf due east of Manhattan has gotten very good in recent years—it's a great destination. The longtime home to great private courses like Garden City, Maidstone, Shinnecock Hills, and the National Golf Links, is now also the place for plenty of quality public courses.

Places like Montauk Downs State Park Golf Course, with its low green fee, almost seem too good to be true—and Long Island National has been dubbed a poor man's Shinnecock Hills. But the real prize play of the island is Bethpage State Park and its five, count 'em, five, municipal golf courses. The Black Course played host to the 2002 U.S. Open; *Golf Digest* considers it one of the top 30 courses in America. Even better, it costs less than $80 to play.

Bethpage State Park (90)					
Black (18)	7,295/6,281	71/71	76.6/71.4	148/134	$11/$78
Blue (18)	6,684/6,213	72/72	71.7/75.0	124/129	$9/$29
Green (18)	6,267/5,903	71/71	69.5/73.0	121/126	$9/$31
Red (18)	6,756/6,198	70/70	72.2/75.1	127/130	$9/$29
Yellow (18)	6,339/5,966	71/71	70.1/72.2	121/123	$9/$29
Cherry Creek Golf Links (36)					$35/$50
The Links (18)	7,187/5,676	73/73	73.7/72.5	128/125	
The Woods (18)	6,550/5,059	71/71	70.0/69.3	128/122	
Great Rock Golf Club (18)	6,193/5,106	71/71	70.0/69.6	125/120	$40/$80
Harbor Links Golf Course (18)	6,927/5,465	72/72	73.2/71.5	128/119	$42/$102
Island's End Golf & Country Club (18)	6,639/5,039	72/72	71.4/69.6	123/117	$28/$48
Links at Shirley (36)	7,030/5,137	72/72	74.0/70.2	129/113	$65/$80
Long Island National Golf Club (18)	6,838/5,006	71/71	73.6/65.3	132/114	$59/$100
Montauk Downs State Park Golf Course (18)	6,762/5,797	72/72	73.9/75.5	139/136	$30/$36
Tallgrass Golf Club (18)	6,587/5,044	71/71	71.8/68.6	127/116	$35/$85

Golf-course topography here varies from former farmland that's now links-style courses to forests converted to parkland golf. And all it takes is five minutes in one of Bethpage Black's massive bunkers to know that sand is the primary ingredient to all Long Island courses. Just remember that if you're planning a golf trip here, you may want to avoid the congested beachgoer days between Memorial Day and Labor Day. In summer, a trip from New York City out to the eastern portion of the island to play courses like Montauk or Island's End Golf & Country Club may take longer than the round itself.

Courses

GolfDigest REVIEWS

BETHPAGE STATE PARK GOLF COURSES. Facility Holes: 90. Architect: A. W. Tillinghast. Cart Fee: $31 per cart. Discounts: Weekdays, twilight, seniors. Walking: Unrestricted walking. Season: Apr.–Nov. Tee Times: Call 7 days in advance. Notes: Range (mat). ✉ 99 Quaker Meetinghouse Rd., Farmingdale 11735, 38 mi from Manhattan ☎ 516/249-4040 ⊕ www.nysparks.state.ny.us 🖃 AE, D, MC, V.

Black. Holes: 18. Opened: 1936. Yards: 7,295/6,281. Par: 71/71. Course Rating: 76.6/71.4. Slope: 148/134. Green Fee: $11/$78. *Comments: Worth a trip all by itself. Tee times are tough to get on weekends. Don't lose the ball in the rough. Check out the slope from the back tees. Great bunkering.* ★★★★★

Blue. Holes: 18. Opened: 1935. Yards: 6,684/6,213. Par: 72/72. Course Rating: 71.7/75.0. Slope: 124/129. Green Fee: $9/$29. *Comments: The money that poured into Bethpage during and after the U.S. Open really helped improve the Blue. The front 9 will leave you black and blue.* ★★★ ½

Green. Holes: 18. Opened: 1935. Yards: 6,267/5,903. Par: 71/71. Course Rating: 69.5/ 73.0. Slope: 121/126. Green Fee: $9/$31. *Comments: Short at 6,200 yards but still a solid golf course. A good selection of holes.* ★★★ ½

Red. Holes: 18. Opened: 1935. Yards: 6,756/6,198. Par: 70/70. Course Rating: 72.2/75.1. Slope: 127/130. Green Fee: $9/$29. *Comments: Generally regarded as a decent second to the Black. First hole is a 453-yard, uphill par-4. Long and hilly.* ★★★★

Yellow. Holes: 18. Opened: 1958. Yards: 6,339/5,966. Par: 71/71. Course Rating: 70.1/ 72.2. Slope: 121/123. Green Fee: $9/$29. *Comments: Think of this as a beginner's course. Fairways are wide, and the green is relatively easy to putt.* ★★★ ½

CHERRY CREEK GOLF LINKS. Facility Holes: 36. Green Fee: $35/$50. Cart Fee: $30 per cart. Discounts: Weekdays, twilight, juniors. Walking: Walking at certain times. Season: Year-round. High: June–Sept. Tee Times: Call 14 days in advance. Notes: Range (grass). ✉ 900 Reeves Ave., Riverhead 11901 ☎ 631/369-6500 ⊕ www.cherrycreeklinks.com ▭ AE, D, MC, V.

The Links. Holes: 18. Opened: 1996. Architect: Young/Young. Yards: 7,187/5,676. Par: 73/ 73. Course Rating: 73.7/72.5. Slope: 128/125. *Comments: Wide-open fairways make you want to hit driver, but watch out for bunkers, ponds, and out-of-bounds stakes.* ★★★ ½

The Woods. Holes: 18. Opened: 2003. Architect: Charles Jurgens. Yards: 6,550/5,059. Par: 71/71. Course Rating: 70.0/69.3. Slope: 128/122. *Comments: New course has generous driving areas. Bombs away.* UR

GREAT ROCK GOLF CLUB. Facility Holes: 18. Opened: 2001. Architect: William Johnson. Yards: 6,193/5,106. Par: 71/71. Course Rating: 70.0/69.6. Slope: 125/120. Green Fee: $40/$80. Cart Fee: Included in green fee. Walking: Walking at certain times. Season: Year-round. Tee Times: Call 7 days in advance. Notes: Range (grass, mat). ✉ 141 Fairway Dr., Wading River 11792 ☎ 631/929-1200 ⊕ www.greatrockgolfclub.com ▭ AE, D, MC, V. *Comments: Dramatic elevation changes and massive rock formations. Heavily treed course.* ★★★ ½

HARBOR LINKS GOLF COURSE. Facility Holes: 18. Opened: 1998. Architect: Michael Hurdzan/Dana Fry. Yards: 6,927/5,465. Par: 72/72. Course Rating: 73.2/71.5. Slope: 128/ 119. Green Fee: $42/$102. Cart Fee: Included in green fee. Discounts: Twilight, seniors, juniors. Walking: Walking at certain times. Season: Apr.–Nov. High: May–Oct. Notes: Range (grass, mat). ✉ 1 Fairway Dr., Port Washington 11050, 25 mi from New York City ☎ 516/767-4816 or 877/342-7267 ⊕ www.harborlinks.com ▭ AE, MC, V. *Comments: Once a 300-foot-deep sand mine, it's now an environmentally friendly golf course. Neat design, three of the fairways having a choice of two fairways to play to off the tee.* ★★★ ½

ISLAND'S END GOLF & COUNTRY CLUB. Facility Holes: 18. Opened: 1961. Architect: Herbert Strong. Yards: 6,639/5,039. Par: 72/72. Course Rating: 71.4/69.6.

GOLF'S PATRON SAINT OF FORGIVENESS

Many golfers invoke the word "mulligan" practically every round they play, but who was the real Mulligan? The term is clouded in mystery, but one theory is that the term started with David Mulligan, an avid golfer who moved to New York from Canada. His problem was that he could never get off the first tee. His generous playing partners always offered him a second go at his tee ball. Mulligan later became a member at Winged Foot in Mamaroneck, and his story became part of that club's lore.

Slope: 123/117. Green Fee: $28/$48. Cart Fee: $15 per person. Discounts: Weekdays, twilight. Walking: Walking at certain times. Season: Year-round. High: June–Sept. Tee Times: Call 7 days in advance. Notes: Range (grass). ⊠ Rte. 25, Greenport 11944 ☎ 631/477-0777 ⊕ www.islandsendgolf.com ⊟ MC, V. *Comments: Way out on the north end of Long Island, this course has wondrous views of Long Island Sound. Not a links course. Many new trees have been planted.* ★ ★ ★ ★

LINKS AT SHIRLEY. Facility Holes: 36. Opened: 1999. Architect: Jeff Myers. Yards: 7,030/5,137. Par: 72/72. Course Rating: 74.0/70.2. Slope: 129/113. Green Fee: $65/$80. Cart Fee: $15 per person. Discounts: Weekdays, twilight, seniors, juniors. Walking: Walking at certain times. Season: Year-round. High: Apr.–Oct. Tee Times: Call 7 days in advance. Notes: Range (grass, mat). ⊠ 333 William Floyd Pkwy., Shirley 11967, 40 mi from New York City ☎ 631/395-7272 or 866/727-2772 ⊕ www.linksatshirley. com ⊟ AE, D, MC, V. *Comments: Pot bunkers, swerves, mounds, double greens. This course will get your attention. Pinehurst styling. Also has an 18-hole par-3 lighted course. UR*

LONG ISLAND NATIONAL GOLF CLUB. Facility Holes: 18. Opened: 1999. Architect: Robert Trent Jones Jr. Yards: 6,838/5,006. Par: 71/71. Course Rating: 73.6/65.3. Slope: 132/114. Green Fee: $59/$100. Cart Fee: Included in green fee. Discounts: Twilight. Walking: Unrestricted walking. Season: Mar.–Nov. Tee Times: Call golf shop. Notes: Range (grass). ⊠ 1793 Northville Tpke., Riverhead 11901, 60 mi from Manhattan ☎ 516/727-4653 ⊟ AE, D, MC, V. *Comments: On what was once a flat potato farm, Robert Trent Jones Jr. moved 600,000 cubic yards of solid earth and made a linksy, bumpy, beautiful golf course.* ★ ★ ★ ★

MONTAUK DOWNS STATE PARK GOLF COURSE. Facility Holes: 18. Opened: 1968. Architect: Robert Trent Jones. Yards: 6,762/5,797. Par: 72/72. Course Rating: 73.9/75.5. Slope: 139/136. Green Fee: $30/$36. Cart Fee: $15 per person. Discounts: Twilight, seniors. Walking: Unrestricted walking. Season: Year-round. High: June–Sept. Tee Times: Call 7 days in advance. Notes: Range (mat). ⊠ 50 S. Fairview Ave., Montauk 11954, 110 mi from New York City ☎ 516/668-1100 ⊟ AE, D, MC, V. *Comments: Great old links course refurbished by Robert Trent Jones. Wind plays a key role in how well you shoot.* ★ ★ ★ ★

TALLGRASS GOLF CLUB. Facility Holes: 18. Opened: 2000. Architect: Gil Hanse. Yards: 6,587/5,044. Par: 71/71. Course Rating: 71.8/68.6. Slope: 127/116. Green Fee: $35/$85.

Cart Fee: Included in green fee. Discounts: Weekdays, twilight, seniors, juniors. Walking: Walking at certain times. Season: Year-round. High: Apr.–Oct. Tee Times: Call 7 days in advance. Notes: Range (grass, mat). ⊠ 24 Cooper St., Shoreham 11786, 65 mi from New York City ☎ 631/209-9359 ▭ AE, MC, V. *Comments: Linksy design on an old sod farm. Drivable par-4s and blind shots make accuracy a must. UR*

Where to Stay

⛵ **BEACHCOMBER RESORT.** This modern motel consists of four two-story buildings overlooking the ocean and is an easy walk to the beach. All rooms are apartment-like suites with modern-style furnishings and private balconies. It's well suited for families, with an outdoor pool and tennis courts in the middle of the complex, and cooking facilities in the rooms. If you don't like kids, and the hustle and bustle that comes along with them, you won't like it here. ⊠ 727 Old Montauk Hwy., Montauk 11954 ☎ 631/668-2894 🖷 631/668-3154 ⊕ www.beachcomber-montauk.com ⛵ 88 suites ⚴ Kitchenettes, cable TV with movies, in-room VCRs, tennis court, pool, sauna, beach, laundry facilities, business services ▭ AE, D, DC, MC, V ⊗ Closed Nov.–Mar. $-$$.

⛵ **GREENPORTER HOTEL AND SPA.** This small, sleek hotel opened in 2002. Rooms are modern, with minimalistic design and furnishings, and have either queen- or king-size beds with Frette linens—the mattresses are placed on simple platforms. You can call for an in-room spa treatment or venture down the hall to a full-service spa facility. ⊠ 326 Front St., Greenport 11944 ☎ 631/477-0066 🖷 631/477-2317 ⊕ www. thegreenporter.com ⛵ 15 rooms ⚴ Restaurant, room service, in-room data ports, minibars, cable TV, pool, gym, hot tub, sauna, spa, steam room, wine bar, dry cleaning, laundry service, concierge, business services, meeting rooms, some pets allowed (fee); no kids, no smoking ▭ AE, D, MC, V $$$$.

⛵ **INN AT EAST WIND.** Opened in 2002 on 11 acres, this elaborate resort has a grand ballroom (weddings are popular here), lavish lobby, surrounding flower and water gardens, and spacious rooms. In the rooms are wall-to-wall carpeting; ornate furnishings such as hand-carved mahogany headboards, and marble bathrooms. Its closeness to many popular Long Island golf courses adds to its appeal. ⊠ 5720 Rte. 25A, Wading River 11792 ☎ 631/929-3500 🖷 631/929-4975 ⊕ www.theinnateastwind.com ⛵ 44 rooms, 6 suites ⚴ Restaurant, room service, in-room data ports, cable TV with movies, indoor pool, exercise equipment, hot tub, sauna, spa, pub, dry cleaning, laundry services, concierge, business services; no smoking ▭ AE, D, DC, MC, V $$$$.

⛵ **PANORAMIC VIEW.** This oceanfront resort hotel is on a hillside of pines and overlooks landscaped lawns, flower gardens, and 1,000 feet of private beach. Premium rooms and suites have private decks or terraces with sweeping views of sand dunes and ocean. Rooms are simply furnished with comfortable chairs and country pine and oak furniture. The large pool, overlooking the ocean, is a popular gathering spot. The resort, tucked in a residential area, is peaceful and quiet, attracting couples and families with older children. ⊠ 272 Old Montauk Hwy., Montauk 11954 ☎ 631/668-3000 🖷 631/668-7870 ⊕ www.panoramicview.com ⛵ 114 rooms, 14 suites, 3 cottages ⚴ In-room data ports, kitchenettes, refrigerators, cable TV, pool, beach, laundry facilities, business services; no kids under 10 ▭ No credit cards ⊘ Closed Nov.–Apr. $$$-$$$$.

▣ **RESIDENCE INN.** Plenty of extra on-site amenities and services make this property a step above the typical chain hotel. Rooms are of average size, with basic furnishings, but do include a desk and data ports. The hotel attracts lots of business travelers. The golf courses and tennis courts at Bethpage State Park are just ½ mi away, and the ocean is about 10 mi away. ⊠ 9 Gerhard Rd., Plainview 11803 ☏ 516/433–6200 or 800/331–3131 ᕍ 516/433–2569 ⊕ www.residenceinn.com ⤶ 170 suites ♿ Restaurant, room service, in-room data ports, some kitchenettes, cable TV, in-room VCRs, 2 pools (1 indoor), gym, hot tub, sauna, baby-sitting, laundry service, laundry facilities, concierge, business services, some pets allowed (fee) ▭ AE, MC, V ⑩ CP $$$-$$$$.

▣ **WINGATE INN.** Bright, clean, and modern, this high-rise hotel is a mid-price alternative. Standard rooms are more than 300 square feet, with a separate work area and desk. Warm tones, neutral colors, and light-wood furnishings all help make the rooms cheery. ⊠ 821 Stewart Ave., Garden City 11530 ☏ 516/705–9000 ᕍ 516/705–9100 ⊕ - www.wingateinn.com ⤶ 118 rooms, 12 suites ♿ In-room data ports, some microwaves, some refrigerators, cable TV with movies and video games, exercise equipment, dry cleaning, laundry service, concierge, Internet, business services, meeting rooms, no-smoking rooms ▭ AE, D, DC, MC, V $$.

Where to Eat

✕ **DAVE'S GRILL.** Some of the freshest seafood on Long Island is served in this tiny bistro overlooking the fishing docks of Montauk Harbor. Dishes include the cioppino, made with fresh fish, lobster, scallops, clams, shrimp, mussels, and calamari poached in a rich fish and tomato broth; the lump crab cakes with smoked bean and roasted corn salsa, or the flash-fried onion-and-potato-crusted flounder. It's popular with locals, and there's always a wait for a table. ⊠ 468 W. Lake Dr., Montauk ☏ 631/668–9190 ♿ Reservations not accepted ▭ MC, V ⊘ Closed Nov.–Apr. No lunch $$$$.

✕ **GOSMAN'S DOCK.** Built on two docks over the water, Gosman's restaurant and clam bar serves food outdoors and indoors. Tables overlook the harbor, Block Island Sound, and, beyond, the ocean. (The bar patio has the best views of the ocean.) Lobster and regional exotic seafood are on the menu along with stuffed yellowtail flounder in lobster sauce, and marinated tuna steak. ⊠ 500 W. Lake Dr., Montauk ☏ 631/668–5330 ▭ AE, MC, V ⊘ Closed mid-Oct.–mid-Apr. $$-$$$$.

✕ **PAINTERS.** More than 100 pieces of original artwork from local, national, and international artists decorate the walls of this eclectic eatery. The large 10,000-square-foot space is divided into several rooms, from a bustling bar to a quiet piano room. There's typical bar food (sandwiches, burgers, quesadillas) in addition to a more upscale menu that might include cornmeal-encrusted oysters with chipotle rémoulade, Thai mixed grill on spicy peanut noodles, or barbecue pork roast with crispy red onions. ⊠ 416 S. County Rd., Brookhaven ☏ 631/286–6264 ▭ AE, MC, V $$-$$$$.

Essentials

Getting Here

Getting here is not half the fun. Long Island, especially in summer, is jam-packed. Expect slow-moving traffic and lots of crowds. From New York City to Montauk, Long Island, is about a 125-mi, three-hour drive.

Three major highways run east–west through Long Island. Long Island Expressway (Route 495) runs from Manhattan to Riverhead. Northern State Parkway runs from Queens to Hauppauge. The Southern State Parkway (Belt Parkway) runs from Brooklyn and Queens to Oakdale. Local east–west routes include Northern Boulevard (Route 25A), Jericho Turnpike (Route 25) on the north shore and Sunrise Hwy. (Route 27) and Merrick Road/Montauk Hwy. (Route 27A) on the south shore.

Visitor Information

🚩 **Greenport-Southold Chamber of Commerce** 📫 Box 1415, Southold 11971 ☎ 631/765-3161 ⊕ www.greenportsoutholdchamber.org. **Huntington Chamber of Commerce** ✉ 151 W. Carver St., Huntington 11743 ☎ 631/423-6100 ⊕ www.huntingtonchamber.com. **Long Island Convention and Visitors Bureau** ☎ 631/951-3440 or 877/386-6654 ⊕ www.licvb.com. **Montauk Chamber of Commerce** 📫 Box 5029, Montauk 11954 ☎ 631/668-2428 ⊕ www.montaukchamber.com. **Riverhead Chamber of Commerce** ✉ 524 E. Main St., Riverhead 11901 ☎ 631/727-7600 ⊕ www.riverheadli.com/coc. **Southampton Chamber of Commerce** ✉ 76 Main St., Southampton 11968 ☎ 631/283-0402 ⊕ www.southamptonchamber.com.

MANCHESTER, VT

When you think of pumpkin patches, hayrides, and trees exploding with color, you might well be thinking about Manchester and Manchester Village, right next door. These quintessential New England villages look as if they were built specifically to showcase the changing of the seasons from summer to fall. Settled in 1764, Manchester hasn't really changed all that much in the two centuries since. It's known as the "town of taverns" because of all the colonial-era inns that are still around.

However, golfers know the area as the home of the Equinox resort and its strikingly beautiful Gleneagles Golf Course as well as the very private, equally stunning Ekwanok Country Club. You have to buddy up with a member to play Ekwanok, but all you need is a credit card over at the Equinox. Although the course has been around since 1926, it was redesigned by Rees Jones in 1992. He did a wonderful job of bringing back to life the rustic, Scottish design that Walter Travis made in 1926. With

Course	Yards	Par	Course Rating	Slope	Green Fee
Crown Point Country Club (18)	6,612/5,537	72/72	71.2/73.0	123/124	$45/$55
Gleneagles Golf Course at the Equinox (18)	6,423/5,082	71/71	71.3/65.2	129/117	$79/$125
Mount Snow Golf Club (18)	6,894/5,436	72/72	73.3/72.8	133/121	$59
Windham Golf Club (18)	6,801/4,979	72/72	72.3/68.9	129/116	$25/$72

Equinox Mountain as the backdrop, it's difficult to grow tired of the beautifully landscaped fairways.

A little more than 200 mi from New York City, in the Green Mountain National Forest of Southern Vermont, Manchester Village should be the base camp for your golf getaway. You could spend the entire trip at the Equinox, but thanks to its popularity, the area has grown into a great out-of-the-way golf destination with a handful of very good courses nearby. Other courses to visit include Windham Golf Club and Mount Snow Golf Club.

Fall is obviously the most photogenic time to visit, but watch out: when the leaves start changing color, hotel rooms fill up quickly. The Equinox charges more than $300 for a night in October, and Gleneagles's green fees are in the $125 range.

Courses

Golf Digest REVIEWS

CROWN POINT COUNTRY CLUB. Facility Holes: 18. Opened: 1953. Architect: William F. Mitchell. Yards: 6,612/5,537. Par: 72/72. Course Rating: 71.2/73.0. Slope: 123/124. Green Fee: $45/$55. Cart Fee: $17 per person. Discounts: Weekdays, twilight, seniors, juniors. Walking: Unrestricted walking. Season: Apr.–Nov. High: June–Sept. Tee Times: Call 3 days in advance. Notes: Range (grass, mat). ⊠ Weathersfield Center Rd., Springfield 05156, 40 mi from Manchester ☎ 802/885-1010 ⊕ www.crownpointcc.com ▭ D, MC, V. *Comments: This semi-mountain course has some terrific views but also some ordinary holes. A good course to round out the trip. It's not a must if you don't feel like making the drive.* ★ ★ ★

GLENEAGLES GOLF COURSE AT THE EQUINOX. Facility Holes: 18. Opened: 1926. Architect: Rees Jones/Walter Travis. Yards: 6,423/5,082. Par: 71/71. Course Rating: 71.3/65.2. Slope: 129/117. Green Fee: $79/$125. Cart Fee: Included in green fee. Discounts: Twilight. Walking: Walking at certain times. Season: May–Nov. Tee Times: Call golf shop. Notes: Lodging (183). ⊠ Historic Rte. 7A, Manchester Village 05254, 70 mi from Albany ☎ 802/362-3223 ⊕ www.equinoxresort.com ▭ AE, D, MC, V. *Comments: It's so good, it's worth driving to this course from New York and driving back in the same day. It's a parkland design at the base of a mountain and at the foot of a New England village. You'll remember this course forever.* ★ ★ ★ ★

MOUNT SNOW GOLF CLUB. Facility Holes: 18. Opened: 1969. Architect: Geoffrey Cornish. Yards: 6,894/5,436. Par: 72/72. Course Rating: 73.3/72.8. Slope: 133/121. Green Fee: $59. Cart Fee: $34 per cart. Discounts: Weekdays, twilight, seniors, juniors. Walking: Unrestricted walking. Season: May–Oct. High: July–Aug. Tee Times: Call 7 days in advance. Notes: Range (grass, mat), lodging (365). ⊠ Country Club Rd., West Dover 05356, 26 mi from Brattleboro ☎ 802/464–4254 or 800/451–4211 ⊕ www. thegolfschool.com ⊟ AE, D, MC, V. *Comments: Designed by the dean of New England golf course architecture, Mount Snow isn't always the best course, but it's fun to play and a stout 6,900 yards from the back tees.* ★ ★ ★ ½

WINDHAM GOLF CLUB. Facility Holes: 18. Yards: 6,801/4,979. Par: 72/72. Course Rating: 72.3/68.9. Slope: 129/116. Green Fee: $25/$72. Cart Fee: Included in green fee. Discounts: Weekdays, twilight, juniors. Season: Apr.–Oct. Tee Times: Call golf shop. Notes: Range (grass). ⊠ 6802 Popple Dungeon Rd., N. Windham 05143, 15 mi from Manchester ☎ 802/875–2517 ⊟ AE, MC, V. *Comments: Once a 9-holer called Tater Hill, the course now has an outstanding 18-hole configuration, with a routing through the rugged terrain of the Green Mountain National Forest.* ★ ★ ★ ½

Where to Stay

▥ **ASPEN MOTEL.** A rare find for this area, the immaculate, family-owned Aspen is set well back from the highway and moderately priced. The spacious, tastefully decorated rooms have colonial-style furnishings; a common room has a fireplace. ⊠ Rte. 7A N, 05255 ☎ 802/362–2450 ⊟ 802/362–1348 ⊕ www.thisisvermont.com/aspen ⇆ 24 rooms, 1 cottage ⚇ Some refrigerators, pool, playground; no smoking ⊟ AE, D, MC, V $.

▥ **1811 HOUSE.** At this mansion once owned by President Lincoln's granddaughter, you can experience life in an English country home without crossing the Atlantic. Three acres of lawn are given over to English formal gardens. Rooms contain period antiques; six have fireplaces and eight have four-poster beds. Bathrooms are old-fashioned but serviceable. Three rooms in the cottage have fireplaces and modern baths. ⊠ Rte. 7A, Manchester Village ⌖ Box 39, 05254 ☎ 802/362–1811 or 800/432–1811 ⊟ 802/362–2443 ⊕ www.1811house.com ⇆ 13 rooms, 1 suite ⚇ Dining room, pub, video game room, no-smoking rooms; no TV in some rooms, no kids under 16 ⊟ AE, D, MC, V ⏀ BP $$-$$$$.

▥ **THE EQUINOX.** Even before Abe Lincoln's family began summering here, this grand white-column resort was a local fixture. The spacious, sunny rooms are furnished with antiques and quality reproductions. The main hotel holds guest rooms and Presidential Suites; the Orvis Inn has one- and two-bedroom suites; and more rooms are in the Town House. The richly upholstered settees and fireplace in the Marsh Tavern make it a plush, traditional place to relax. The on-site full-service spa is an added bonus. ⊠ 3567 Main St./Rte. 7A, Manchester Village 05254 ☎ 802/362–4700 or 800/362–4747 ⊟ 802/362–1595 ⊕ www.equinoxresort.com ⇆ 163 rooms, 14 suites ⚇ 3 restaurants, 18-hole golf course, 3 tennis courts, 2 pools (1 indoor), health club, sauna, spa, steam room, fishing, mountain bikes, croquet, horseback riding, cross-country skiing, ice-skating, snowmobiling, bar, meeting rooms, no-smoking rooms ⊟ AE, D, DC, MC, V ⏀ MAP $$$$.

🏨 **INN AT ORMSBY HILL.** Once a stop on the Underground Railroad, this elegant 1774 federal-style building has guest rooms furnished with antiques and canopy or four-poster beds. Some rooms have mountain views, and all have two-person Jacuzzi tubs and fireplaces. Breakfasts are served in the conservatory. ⊠ 1842 Main St./Rte. 7A, 05255 ☎ 802/362-1163 or 800/670-2841 🖨 802/362-5176 ⊕ www.ormsbyhill.com ⇗ 10 rooms ⚕ Dining room, in-room hot tubs, library, shop; no room TVs, no kids, no smoking ➡ D, MC, V ❚❍❚ BP $$$-$$$$.

🏨 **WEST DOVER INN.** Once a stagecoach stop and a tavern, this Greek Revival inn in the center of the village has been a lodging for travelers since the mid-1800s. The interior of the structure—the wainscoting, the wide-planked wood floors, and the moldings—are all original. Antiques and hand-sewn quilts in the rooms complement these details. The inn also has two porches and a patio. ⊠ 108 Rte. 100, West Dover 05356 ☎ 802/464-5207 🖨 802/464-2173 ⊕ www.westdoverinn.com ⇗ 12 rooms, 4 suites ⚕ Dining room, cable TV; no a/c, no room phones, no kids under 8, no smoking ➡ AE, MC, V ❂ Closed mid-Apr.–Memorial Day ❚❍❚ BP $-$$.

🏨 **WILBURTON INN.** Overlooking the Battenkill Valley, this turn-of-the-20th-century Tudor mansion has 11 lovingly furnished bedrooms and suites, and richly paneled common rooms decorated with pieces from the owners' art collection. Five guest buildings are spread over the 20-acre grounds, which are also punctuated with sculpture. Eight rooms have private decks with mountain views. Note that the Wilburton is a very popular place for weddings on summer weekends. ⊠ River Rd., Manchester Village 05254 ☎ 802/362-2500 or 800/648-4944 🖨 802/362-1107 ⊕ www.wilburton.com ⇗ 30 rooms, 4 suites ⚕ Restaurant, some microwaves, some cable TV, 3 tennis courts, pool ➡ AE, MC, V ❚❍❚ BP $$-$$$$.

Where to Eat

✕ **DEERHILL INN AND RESTAURANT.** Of all the restaurants in the Mt. Snow Valley, this one between Haystack and Mt. Snow is one of the best. Overlooking the mountains, the dining room has whitewashed walls and is filled with baskets of fresh flowers. Try the portobello mushroom stuffed with crab and lobster or the chicken stuffed with pesto and sun-dried tomatoes. Other favorites include the house Wiener schnitzel and roast duckling. The menu changes every other week, and there's an extensive wine list. ⊠ Valley View Rd., West Dover ☎ 802/464-3100 or 800/993-3379 ➡ AE, MC, V ❂ Closed Wed. No lunch $$$$.

✕ **LITTLE ROOSTER CAFE.** Styled after a contemporary European café, this restaurant is popular for its creative, freshly made breakfast and lunch dishes. Don't miss the light Belgian waffles or homemade corned-beef hash, made with local organic eggs. Unique sandwiches, like the roast beef with pickled red cabbage and horseradish sauce, are popular lunch choices, as are the crab cakes. ⊠ Rte. 7A ☎ 802/362-3496 MC, V ❂ No dinner ¢-$.

✕ **THE SILO.** This unique restaurant occupies what was once a silo, hay barn, and windmill. From its walls and ceiling hang dried flowers, quilts, and Vermont antiques, complementing the rustic beauty of the building. The restaurant serves steaks, burgers, barbecued chicken and ribs, salads, homemade soups, sandwiches, and pastas. ⊠324 Rte. 100, West Dover ☎802/464-2553 ⊟AE, MC, V $-$$$$.

✕**UP FOR BREAKFAST.** A local favorite, this tiny, creative eatery specializes in fresh, natural Vermont ingredients prepared with flair. The walls are canary yellow and further decorated with parsley-green wood trim and bright art prints. The seasonal menu might include an omelet stuffed with smoked salmon, red onions, dill, cream cheese and capers; venison sausage; or cream cheese crepes topped with lingonberry hollandaise sauce. ⊠710 Main St. ☎802/362-4204 ⊟No credit cards ⊗No lunch or dinner ¢-$.

Essentials

Getting Here
Manchester is about a four-hour drive from New York City. Take Route 87 to Albany, exit 23, then follow Route 787 north to Troy/Bennington exit, Route 7 east. Route 7 turns into Vermont Route 9; follow this east to Bennington. In Bennington, take Route 7 north to exit 4, then follow Route 11/30 into Manchester. You can also follow the more scenic Route 7A from Bennington into Manchester. Expect crowds during the popular fall foliage season. Busloads of visitors cram the area.

Visitor Information
🚩 **Bennington Area Chamber of Commerce** ⊠Veterans Memorial Dr., Bennington 05201 ☎802/447-3311 or 800/229-0252 ⊕www.bennington.com. **Manchester and the Mountains Chamber of Commerce** ⊠5046 Main St., 05255 ☎802/362-2100 ⊕www.manchesterandmtns.com. **Mt. Snow Valley Chamber of Commerce** ⊠W. Main St. ⊡Box 3, Wilmington 05363 ☎802/464-8092 or 877/887-6884 ⊕www. visitvermont.com.

POCONOS, PA

The Pocono Mountain range in the northeast corner of Pennsylvania may have become famous for its ski resorts, bathtubs in the shape of champagne glasses, and headliner comedy acts like Shecky Green and Henny Youngman, but the region isn't lacking when it comes to quality golf courses, either. When you take your two-hour trip east of New York City to the region, be prepared to make a quick stop just past the Delaware River and the New Jersey/Pennsylvania border. The Shawnee Inn Golf Resort here dates back to 1906 and is the perfect kickoff to your golf trip.

After you head deeper into the Pocono Mountain region, you have many options. Favorites include the Skytop Lodge (also a great place to stay) and

Course	Yards	Par	Course Rating	Slope	Green Fee
Buck Hill Golf Club (27)					$40/$75
Red/Blue (18)	6,150/5,870	70/72	69.8/69.8	118/120	
Red/White (18)	6,300/5,620	70/72	69.4/71.0	121/124	
White/Blue (18)	6,450/5,550	72/72	72.0/71.3	132/123	
Hideaway Hills Golf Club (18)	6,933/5,047	72/72	72.7/68.4	127/116	$29/$42
Mount Airy Lodge Golf Course (18)	7,123/5,771	72/73	74.3/73.3	138/122	$45/$55
Pocono Manor Golf Resort &Spa (36)					$23/$38
East (18)	6,565/5,977	72/75	69.0/74.0	118/117	
West (18)	7,013/5,236	72/72	72.3/72.0	117/114	
Shawnee Inn Golf Resort (27)					$40/$80
Red/Blue (18)	6,800/5,650	72/74	72.2/71.4	132/121	
Red/White (18)	6,589/5,424	72/74	72.4/71.1	131/121	
White/Blue (18)	6,665/5,398	72/74	72.8/72.5	129/123	
Skytop Lodge (18)	6,656/5,789	72/72	72.0/74.8	133/127	$40/$65
Water Gap Country Club (18)	6,237/5,199	72/74	69.0/69.0	124/120	$39/$49

Hideaway Hills. Architects like Jack Nicklaus, A. W. Tillinghast, and Robert Trent Jones have all built public courses here, lending to the area's credibility as a golf destination.

Although most of the golf courses in the area have scenic overlook views and the type of terrain you may remember from summer camp, the scene does get a little monotonous. After you leave, it can be hard to recall specific holes on specific courses because it all pretty much looks the same. It looks great—but it looks the same. And although golf here never gets too expensive, it can seem a bit overpriced. Finally, there's the weather. Come here in summer, when the chilly mornings and cool evenings can help you forget about those 95° days on the streets of Manhattan.

Courses

GolfDigest REVIEWS

BUCK HILL GOLF CLUB. Facility Holes: 27. Opened: 1907. Architect: Donald Ross/ Robert White. Green Fee: $40/$75. Cart Fee: Included in green fee. Discounts: Weekdays, twilight, juniors. Walking: Mandatory cart. Season: Apr.–Oct. High: June–Aug. Tee Times: Call 7 days in advance. Notes: Metal spikes, range (grass). ⊠ Golf Dr., Buck Hill Falls 18323, 50 mi from Allentown ☎ 570/595-7730 ⊕ www.buckhillfalls.com ⊟ MC, V.

Red/Blue. Holes: 18. Yards: 6,150/5,870. Par: 70/72. Course Rating: 69.8/69.8. Slope: 118/120.

Red/White. Holes: 18. Yards: 6,300/5,620. Par: 70/72. Course Rating: 69.4/71.0. Slope: 121/124.

White/Blue. Holes: 18. Yards: 6,450/5,550. Par: 72/72. Course Rating: 72.0/71.3. Slope: 132/123.

Comments: Shorter, 27-hole course. It's OK to skip this one, even though it's hard to pass up anything designed by Donald Ross. ★ ★ ★ ½

HIDEAWAY HILLS GOLF CLUB. Facility Holes: 18. Opened: 1994. Architect: Joseph Farda. Yards: 6,933/5,047. Par: 72/72. Course Rating: 72.7/68.4. Slope: 127/116. Green Fee: $29/$42. Cart Fee: $15 per person. Discounts: Twilight. Walking: Mandatory cart. Season: Mar.–Dec. Tee Times: Call 7 days in advance. Notes: Range (grass), lodging (30). ⊠ Carney Rd., Kresgville 18333, 30 mi from Allentown ☎ 610/681-6000 ⊕ www. hideawaygolf.com ⊟ AE, D, MC, V. *Comments: One of the area's newer courses, and well worth your time. In fact, it may be the best mountain golf course in the area. Be ready for some serious elevation changes.* ★ ★ ★ ★

MOUNT AIRY LODGE GOLF COURSE. Facility Holes: 18. Opened: 1980. Architect: Hal Purdy. Yards: 7,123/5,771. Par: 72/73. Course Rating: 74.3/73.3. Slope: 138/122. Green Fee: $45/$55. Cart Fee: Included in green fee. Discounts: Weekdays, twilight. Season: Apr.–Nov. Tee Times: Call golf shop. ⊠ 42 Woodland Rd., Mount Pocono 18344, 30 mi from Scranton ☎ 570/839-8816 or 800/441-4410 ⊕ www.mountairygolfclub. com ⊟ AE, D, MC, V. *Comments: One of the Poconos' most famous resorts. The course is terrific, with mountain views.* ★ ★ ★ ★

POCONO MANOR GOLF RESORT & SPA. Facility Holes: 36. Green Fee: $23/$38. Cart Fee: $20 per person. Discounts: Weekdays, twilight. Walking: Mandatory cart. Season: Apr.–Nov. Tee Times: Call 7 days in advance. Notes: Range (grass), lodging (250). ⌂ Box 7, Pocono Manor 18349, 20 mi from Scranton ☎ 570/839-7111 or 800/233-8150 ⊟ AE, MC, V.

East. Holes: 18. Opened: 1919. Architect: Donald Ross. Yards: 6,565/5,977. Par: 72/75. Course Rating: 69.0/74.0. Slope: 118/117. *Comments: Talk about history. The course has hosted Sam Snead, Arnold Palmer, Jackie Burke, and many other famous pros. Art Wall Jr. won the Masters while serving as the golf professional here in 1959. Designed by the legendary Donald Ross.* ★ ★ ★

West. Holes: 18. Opened: 1960. Architect: George Fazio. Yards: 7,013/5,236. Par: 72/72. Course Rating: 72.3/72.0. Slope: 117/114. *Comments: Not as famous, but the course is longer and more challenging than the East.* ★ ★ ★ ½

SHAWNEE INN GOLF RESORT. Facility Holes: 27. Opened: 1906. Architect: A. W. Tillinghast/W. H. Diddel. Green Fee: $40/$80. Cart Fee: Included in green fee. Discounts: Weekdays, twilight, seniors. Walking: Walking at certain times. Season: Apr.–Dec. Tee Times: Call golf shop. Notes: Range (grass, mat). ⊠ 1 River Rd., Shawnee-on-Delaware 18356, 90 mi from New York City ☎ 570/424-4050 or 800/742-9633 ⊕ www. shawneeinn.com ⊟ AE, D, DC, MC, V.

Red/Blue. Holes: 18. Yards: 6,800/5,650. Par: 72/74. Course Rating: 72.2/71.4. Slope: 132/121.

Red/White. Holes: 18. Yards: 6,589/5,424. Par: 72/74. Course Rating: 72.4/71.1. Slope: 131/121.

White/Blue. Holes: 18. Yards: 6,665/5,398. Par: 72/74. Course Rating: 72.8/72.5. Slope: 129/123.

Comments: Great old golf course. The majority of it sits on an island in the middle of the Delaware River. Scenic and classic. ★★★★

SKYTOP LODGE. Facility Holes: 18. Opened: 1928. Architect: Robert White. Yards: 6,656/5,789. Par: 72/72. Course Rating: 72.0/74.8. Slope: 133/127. Green Fee: $40/$65. Cart Fee: $20 per person. Discounts: Guest. Walking: Walking at certain times. Season: Apr.–Dec. High: June–Sept. Tee Times: Call golf shop. Notes: Range (grass), lodging (200). ⊠ 1 Skytop, Rte. 390, Skytop 18357, 35 mi from Scranton ☎ 570/595–8910 or 800/345–7759 ⊕ www.skytop.com ⊟ AE, MC, V. *Comments: You must stay at the resort to play the course, but trust us, it's worth it. Great mountain golf course that's usually in good shape.* ★★★★ ½

WATER GAP COUNTRY CLUB. Facility Holes: 18. Opened: 1921. Architect: Robert White. Yards: 6,237/5,199. Par: 72/74. Course Rating: 69.0/69.0. Slope: 124/120. Green Fee: $39/$49. Cart Fee: Included in green fee. Discounts: Weekdays, twilight. Walking: Walking at certain times. Season: Mar.–Nov. Tee Times: Call 7 days in advance. Notes: Metal spikes, lodging (23). ⊠ Mountain Rd., Delaware Water Gap 18327, 70 mi from New York City ☎ 570/476–0300 ⊕ www.watergapcountryclub.com ⊟ AE, D, MC, V. *Comments: Great course to play as you start your trek back to New York. It's short, tight, and hilly.* ★★★

Where to Stay

▦ **CAESAR'S POCONO PALACE.** A lavish resort with many amenities, Caesar's includes unusual offerings like archery and softball fields. The hotel rooms are plush, as are the over-the-top themed fantasy suites, like the Roman Towers, which includes a fireplace, private glass-enclosed heart-shape swimming pool, sauna, steam shower for two, massage table, circular stairs leading to a bedroom loft, and whirlpool bath for two set atop a 7-foot-tall "champagne glass." Note that the standard rooms, located above the nightclub, can be noisy. ⊠ Rte. 209, Marshalls Creek 18301 ☎ 570/588–6692 or 800/233–4141 🖷 570/588–0754 ⊕ www.caesarspoconoresorts.com ↩ 189 rooms, 155 suites ♿ Dining room, room service, refrigerators, cable TV, driving range, 9-hole golf course, putting green, 2 pools (1 indoor), lake, exercise equipment, hot tub, boating, volleyball, cross-country skiing, ice-skating, snowmobiling, business services; no kids, no-smoking rooms ⊟ AE, D, DC, MC, V ¶⊙¶ MAP $$$$.

▦ **POCONO MANOR GOLF RESORT & SPA.** Built in 1902, this grand resort sits on 3,500 acres and has sweeping views of the Pocono Mountains. In the lobby are antique grandfather clocks, paintings, and a fieldstone fireplace. Rooms, spread over three buildings, have mahogany furniture and ornate rugs. You can find many unusual extras here, including trapshooting and an artificial ice rink. ☐ Box 7, Pocono Manor 18349 ☎ 570/839-7111 or 800/233-8150 ☐ 570/839-0708 ⊕ www. poconomanor.com ⇝ 257 rooms ☖ Dining room, room service, in-room data ports, driving range, 2 18-hole golf courses, putting green, tennis court, indoor-outdoor pool, exercise equipment, health club, massage, sauna, spa, bicycles, ice-skating, sleigh rides, library, children's programs (ages 3-16), business services, airport shuttle ☐ AE, DC, MC, V $$-$$$.

⊞ SHAWNEE INN. This rambling, red-roof hotel from the early 1900s sits on 2,500 acres along the banks of the Delaware River. It's a longtime favorite with families and those who love the outdoors. The expansive wraparound porch and rustic lodge-style lobby with fireplace and original maple flooring are popular hangouts, as are the outside pool areas and golf course. Rooms are basic, with neutral colors and standard furnishings, but the many activities here are likely to keep you outside. ☒ 1 River Rd., Shawnee-on-Delaware 18356 ☎ 570/421-1500 or 800/742-9633 ☐ 570/424-9168 ⊕ www.shawneeinn.com ⇝ 103 rooms ☖ Restaurant, dining room, cable TV, in-room data ports, 4 pools (1 indoor), wading pool, driving range, 27-hole golf course, miniature golf, putting green, 2 tennis courts, cross-country skiing, downhill skiing, video game room, children's programs (ages 3-16), playground, laundry facilities ☐ AE, D, DC, MC, V ⍩ BP $$-$$$.

⊞ SKYTOP LODGE. This grand mountain resort, built in 1926, overlooks Skytop Lake and West Mountain. The Dutch colonial stone manor house, a contemporary freestanding inn, and 10 cottages are surrounded by 5,500 private acres. This is a destination resort with many activities, including a championship golf course, 30 mi of hiking trails, and a full-service spa. Rooms in the main lodge are decorated in light, warm tones with country-style fabrics and furnishings. The 20 rooms in the newer inn are more spacious, with fireplaces, refrigerators, and mountain and lake views. ☒ 1 Skytop, Rte. 390, Skytop 18357 ☎ 570/595-7401 or 800/617-2389 ☐ 570/595-9618 ⊕ www. skytop.com ⇝ 145 rooms, 10 cottages ☖ 3 restaurants, picnic area, room service, some refrigerators, 18-hole golf course, miniature golf, putting green, 7 tennis courts, pro shop, 2 pools (1 indoor), lake, health club, hot tub, massage, sauna, spa, boating, fishing, mountain bikes, archery, horseshoes, bar, recreation room, playground, business services, meeting rooms, no-smoking rooms; no TV in some rooms ☐ AE, DC, D, MC, V ⍩ FAP $$$$.

⊞ STERLING INN. Gardens, nature trails, and a lakeside location make this plush, romantic inn an area favorite. Rooms and public areas are decorated with Victorian antiques and country furnishings. All rooms are individually decorated, some with fireplaces, in-room hot tubs, living areas, and private decks. The outdoor hot tub overlooking the gardens and indoor pool area are favorite hangouts. Rooms include full breakfast (buttermilk pancakes and stuffed omelets are popular) and a candlelight dinner that might include warm seafood salad, grilled New York strip steak, pan-seared tuna, and bourbon-soaked pork chops. ☒ Rte. 191, South Sterling 18460 ☎ 570/676-3311 or 800/523-8200 ☐ 570/676-9786 ⊕ www.thesterlinginn.com ⇝ 39 rooms, 27 suites, 10 cottages ☖ Dining room, some in-room hot tubs, tennis court, indoor pool, hot tub, spa, boating, fishing, hiking, sleigh rides, business services, airport shuttle; no smoking ▱ AE, D, MC, V ❌ MAP $$$-$$$$.

Where to Eat

✕ **ALASKA PETE'S ROADHOUSE GRILLE.** Brick walls, wooden interiors, mounted fish, and western antiques add to the Old West theme of this bustling restaurant in the Poconos. The menu has plenty of big-meat choices, like the 20-ounce porterhouse, 1- and 2-pound slabs of prime rib, and smaller cuts of melt-in-your-mouth filet mignon. There's also a good assortment of high-quality, fresh fish dishes, like grilled swordfish or tuna with cucumber dill sauce or halibut topped with jumbo shrimp and garlic wine sauce. For lunch and for smaller appetites, there are sandwiches, burgers, and a make-your-own salad bar. ⊠ Rte. 209, Marshalls Creek ☎ 570/839-9678 ▱ AE, D, MC, V $-$$$.

✕ **BAILEY'S STEAKHOUSE.** American and British street signs decorate the softly lit dining room here. You can choose from many cuts of prime-grade steak, including prime rib, filet mignon, center-cut sirloin, and a whopping 16-ounce T-bone. Or try hickory-smoked baby back ribs, or Crab Key Chicken—a breast of chicken sautéed in white wine and topped with crabmeat, asparagus, and béarnaise sauce. ⊠ 604 Pocono Blvd., Mount Pocono ☎ 570/839-9678 ▱ AE, D, MC, V $-$$$.

✕ **HAMPTON COURT INN.** Pictures of King Henry and etchings of scenes from British history dominate the wall space of the Hampton Court Inn, originally built as a farmhouse in 1890. The restaurant is divided into three separate dining rooms, including a flower-filled section with candlelit tables. Specials include filet mignon au poivre, roast duck Grand Marnier with cranberry sauce, and jumbo shrimp stuffed with crabmeat. Bananas Foster (sautéed caramelized bananas with rum, cognac, banana liqueur, and vanilla ice cream) is the star dessert. ⊠ Rte. 940, Mount Pocono ☎ 570/839-2119 ⟡ Reservations essential ▱ AE, DC, MC, V ⊙ Closed Tues. No lunch $$$-$$$$.

✕ **TOKYO TEAHOUSE.** This traditional Japanese restaurant is elegant and minimal, with fresh white walls, teakwood furnishings, and bamboo accents and prints. It's best known for its sushi, but the shrimp tempura, steak teriyaki, and vegetarian offerings are popular, too. ⊠ Rte. 940, Pocono Summit, ½ mi west of I-380 ☎ 570/839-8880 ▱ AE, D, DC, MC, V ⊙ Closed Tues. July and Aug. $-$$$$.

✕ **VAN GILDER'S JUBILEE.** Dubbed the "Breakfast King," this local favorite has been serving up heaping platters of eggs, pancakes, and more since 1968. It looks like a truck stop or converted motel from the outside; inside it's plain-Jane casual. Patrons feast on more than 35 breakfast offerings. All dishes come with beverage and appetizer (fresh fruit, juice, or soup) and choice of pancakes or home fries. All the usual breakfast offerings are here, as are chipped beef, corned-beef hash, and more than 11 omelets, including the Popeye, stuffed with spinach, mozzarella, and mushrooms. ⊠ Rte. 940, Pocono Pines ☎ 570/646-2377 ▱ No credit cards $.

Essentials

Getting Here

The Poconos are in the northeast corner of Pennsylvania, about a 90-minute drive from New York City. To get here, take I-80 west for about 75 mi into the Pocono region. Route 209 is a major north–south road here.

Visitor Information

🛈 **Delaware Water Gap Area Chamber of Commerce** ✆ Box 144, Delaware Water Gap 18327 ☎ 570/420-9588 🖷 570/424-6986 ⊕ www.delawarewatergap.com. **Pocono Mountains Chamber of Commerce** ✉ 556 Main St., Stroudsburg 18360 ☎ 570/421-4433 ⊕ www.poconochamber.com. **Pocono Mountains Convention and Visitors Bureau** ✉ 1004 Main St., Stroudsburg 18360 ☎ 800/762-6667 ⊕ www.800poconos.com.

AROUND
ORLANDO

Sandestin Resort

Ron Kaspriske and Gary McKecknie

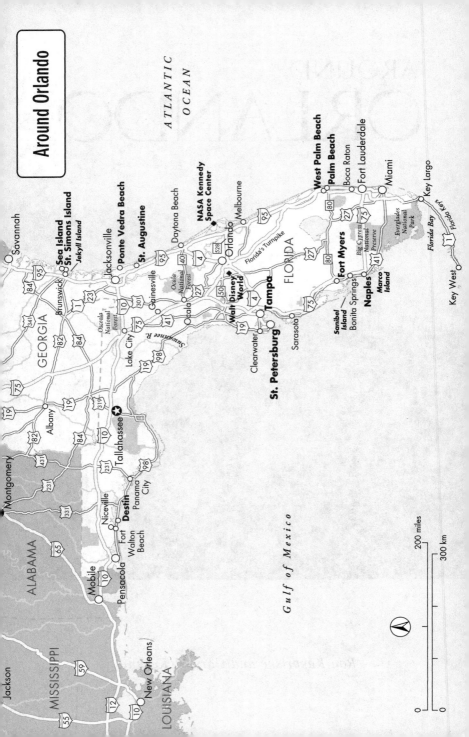

Around Orlando

If it weren't for the fact that Orlando is

landlocked, resident golfers would have a difficult time venturing out
from the citrus groves and hills of Central Florida. For golfers, Orlando is
truly one of the best destinations in the United States, rivaling the
quantity and quality of golf found in other hotbeds like Scottsdale,
Arizona, and Myrtle Beach, South Carolina. But the Atlantic Ocean to the
east and the Gulf of Mexico to the west both serve to beckon those
Orlando players. There's something about playing along the shoreline that
has been appealing to golfers ever since St. Andrews was built along the
Scottish coast some 600 years ago. The good news for Orlando residents is
that they are not alone in their appreciation for the game—at least not in
this part of the country. There are plenty of great golf destinations in
whatever direction they point their car.

When Disney traffic starts clogging I-4, head northeast to the serene
seaside golf resorts near St. Augustine, or even farther up the coast to an
even sleepier destination—the barrier islands of southeast Georgia. If you
want to head southwest, the Tampa/St. Petersburg area is your best bet for
combining good golf with great nightlife. Three hours to the south, the
Naples/Fort Myers area went from being a little-known retirement
community to a booming golf metropolis during the 1990s. If you're
looking for something a little more refined, the towns in the Palm Beaches
provide a taste of Beverly Hills in their golf courses.

And finally, if the beaches are as important as the golf, nothing beats the
remote Panhandle location of Destin. It takes some work to get here. But
trust us, it's worth it. The area is still one of the best-kept secrets, with
some gorgeous golf, and prices much more reasonable than most.

As with all of Orlando destinations, timing is everything. December
through February may be a little too chilly for golf in Destin and Sea
Island. (Even Orlando has been known to have frost delays this time of the
year.) But chances are that a sweater is all you need to play on most days.
And it rarely rains this time of the year. Conversely, June to September can
be brutally hot and thunderstorms are a daily occurrence. Speaking from
experience, a Florida thunderstorm is not be taken lightly: it's Florida's
number one weather-related killer. Then there's the humidity, even at these
coastal destinations. It's hard not to begin sweating minutes after walking
out of the pro shop. On the positive side, there are bargains to be had this
time of the year as green fees are typically slashed by 50% to 75%—
especially after 10 AM—to entice players to brave golf on a 95° day.

One thing all these destinations lack is a variety in topography. North of Orlando there are some hills, but the majority of land here is flat. A few million years ago, Florida was underwater. When the oceans receded, they left literally hundreds of lakes, aquifers, and sinkholes in the Central Florida region. When you play golf here, be prepared to donate a few balls to pond bottoms.

DESTIN

The debate among Florida's seaside towns about who has the nicest beaches always centers on places like Fort Lauderdale, Daytona Beach, Clearwater, and Naples. But none of these compare to the Panhandle town of Destin and its sugar sand. Along with being an annual stop for spring-breakers and a long-term home for ex-military men (four military bases are nearby), Destin has found a niche as an out-of-the-way golf destination. It's barely on the map, but for some golfers, that's how it ought to be. From Orlando, you've got a long drive ahead of you. It's about 400 mi or seven hours but well worth the drive. And if you must fly, take a puddle jumper from Orlando to Pensacola and backtrack 50 mi east. Some people may think of this area as the "Redneck Riviera" or "L.A.," as in "Lower Alabama," but don't think for a second that the golf is low class.

Although many new courses have been built in the area recently, we still think the Sandestin Golf and Beach Resort should be your first and only choice for lodging. The resort has 72 holes of golf, great shops and restaurants, and is right on that beautiful beach. In addition to the four strong courses at Sandestin, two new courses have opened in the last three years that are just as good—Kelly Plantation Golf Club and Camp Creek Golf Club.

You can play here year-round, but temperatures in the winter months of January and February do dip below freezing from time to time. It has even been known to snow here. But there are also days in the 60s.

Courses   Golf Digest REVIEWS

BLUEWATER BAY RESORT. Facility Holes: 36. Opened: 1981. Architect: Tom Fazio/Jerry Pate. Green Fee: $40/$54. Cart Fee: $15 per person. Discounts: Guest, twilight, juniors. Walking: Walking at certain times. Season: Year-round. Tee Times: Call 14 days in advance. Notes: Range (grass), lodging (90). ⊠2000 Bluewater Blvd., Niceville 32578, 60 mi from Pensacola ☎850/897-3241 or 800/874-2128 ⊕www.bwbresort.com ⊟AE, D, MC, V.

Bay/Magnolia. Holes: 18. Yards: 6,608/5,129. Par: 72/72. Course Rating: 72.4/70.3. Slope: 150/127.

Lake/Marsh. Holes: 18. Yards: 6,857/5,338. Par: 72/72. Course Rating: 73.9/71.9. Slope: 146/128.

Comments: Bluewater Bay is on the other side of Choctawhatchee Bay. Lots of water. ★★★

Bluewater Bay Resort (36)					$40/$54
Bay/Magnolia (18)	6,608/5,129	72/72	72.4/70.3	150/127	
Lake/Marsh (18)	6,857/5,338	72/72	73.9/71.9	146/128	
Emerald Bay Golf Course (18)	6,802/5,184	72/72	73.1/70.1	135/122	$40/$75
Indian Bayou (27)					$65/$85
Choctaw/Creek (18)	6,897/4,864	72/71	74.1/69.0	139/122	
Creek/Seminole (18)	7,047/4,938	72/71	74.7/69.1	142/124	
Seminole/Choctaw (18)	7,078/5,226	72/72	74.6/70.7	132/121	
Kelly Plantation Golf Club (18)	7,099/5,170	72/72	74.2/70.9	146/124	$60/$125
Regatta Bay Golf & Country Club (18)	6,864/5,092	72/72	73.8/70.6	149/118	$59/$114
Sandestin Resort (54)					
Baytowne At Sandestin (18)	6,890/4,862	72/72	73.4/68.5	127/114	$68/$86
Burnt Pines (18)	7,046/5,950	72/72	74.1/68.7	135/124	$88/$145
Links (18)	6,710/4,969	72/72	72.8/69.2	124/115	$68/$105
Raven (18)	6,854/5,037	71/71	73.8/70.6	137/126	$85/$135

EMERALD BAY GOLF COURSE. Facility Holes: 18. Opened: 1991. Architect: Robert Cupp Jr. Yards: 6,802/5,184. Par: 72/72. Course Rating: 73.1/70.1. Slope: 135/122. Green Fee: $40/$75. Cart Fee: $20. Discounts: Weekdays, guest, twilight, juniors. Walking: Mandatory cart. Season: Year-round. High: Mar.–Sept. Tee Times: Call golf shop. Notes: Range (grass), lodging (8). ⊠ 4781 Clubhouse Dr., 32541, 15 mi from Fort Walton Beach ☏ 850/837-5197 or 888/465-3229 ⊕ www.emeraldbaydestin.com ▭ AE, D, DC, MC, V. *Comments: Windswept, linksy design a little claustrophobic because of homes. But Bob Cupp did a good job with the property.* ★ ★ ★ ½

INDIAN BAYOU GOLF & COUNTRY CLUB. Facility Holes: 27. Opened: 1978. Architect: Earl Stone. Green Fee: $65/$85. Cart Fee: Included in green fee. Walking: Walking at certain times. Season: Year-round. Tee Times: Call golf shop. ⊠ 1 Country Club Dr. E, 32541, 30 mi from Pensacola ☏ 850/837-6191 ⊕ www.indianbayougolf.com ▭ AE, D, MC, V.

Choctaw/Creek. Holes: 18. Yards: 6,897/4,864. Par: 72/71. Course Rating: 74.1/69.0. Slope: 139/122.

Creek/Seminole Holes: 18. Yards: 7,047/4,938. Par: 72/71. Course Rating: 74.7/69.1. Slope: 142/124.

Seminole/Choctaw Holes: 18. Yards: 7,078/5,226. Par: 72/72. Course Rating: 74.6/70.7. Slope: 132/121.

Comments: Palm trees, water hazards, looks like many other older Florida courses but is in fairly good shape. Huge greens. ★ ★ ½

KELLY PLANTATION GOLF CLUB. Facility Holes: 18. Opened: 1998. Architect: Fred Couples/Gene Bates. Yards: 7,099/5,170. Par: 72/72. Course Rating: 74.2/70.9. Slope: 146/124. Green Fee: $60/$125. Cart Fee: Included in green fee. Discounts: Twilight, juniors. Walking: Unrestricted walking. Season: Year-round. High: Mar.–Aug. Tee Times: Call

30 days in advance. Notes: Range (grass). ✉ 307 Kelly Plantation Dr., 32541, 3 mi from Destin ☎ 850/650–7600 or 800/811–6757 ⊕ www.kellyplantation.com ▤ AE, D, MC, V. *Comments: Great scenery with awesome water views.* ★ ★ ★ ★ ½

REGATTA BAY GOLF & COUNTRY CLUB. Facility Holes: 18. Opened: 1998. Architect: Bob Walker. Yards: 6,864/5,092. Par: 72/72. Course Rating: 73.8/70.6. Slope: 149/118. Green Fee: $59/$114. Cart Fee: $15 per person. Discounts: Twilight, juniors. Walking: Mandatory cart. Season: Year-round. High: Apr.–Sept. Tee Times: Call 90 days in advance. Notes: Range (grass). ✉ 465 Regatta Bay Blvd., 32541 ☎ 850/337–8080 or 800/648–0123 ⊕ www.regattabay.com ▤ AE, D, MC, V. *Comments: Powder-white sand bunkers (like the sand on the beach) and marshland hazards highlight this course. The houses surrounding the property steal some of its beauty.* ★ ★ ★ ★

SANDESTIN RESORT. Facility Holes: 54. Cart Fee: Included in green fee. Discounts: Juniors. Season: Year-round. High: Feb.–May. Tee Times: Call 14 days in advance. Notes: Range (grass), lodging (740). ✉ 9300 Hwy. 98 W, 32550, 20 mi from Fort Walton Beach ☎ 850/267–6500 ⊕ www.sandestin.com ▤ AE, D, DC, MC, V.

Baytowne At Sandestin. Holes: 18. Opened: 1985. Architect: Tom Jackson. Yards: 6,890/4,862. Par: 72/72. Course Rating: 73.4/68.5. Slope: 127/114. Green Fee: $68/$86. Walking: Mandatory cart. *Comments: One of the facility's older layouts, it's still good. With the exception of a few holes, it's fairly easy to play and will give you a good break from the tougher Burnt Pines and Raven courses.* ★ ★ ★ ★ ½

Burnt Pines. Holes: 18. Opened: 1994. Architect: Rees Jones. Yards: 7,046/5,950. Par: 72/72. Course Rating: 74.1/68.7. Slope: 135/124. Green Fee: $88/$145. Walking: Unrestricted walking. *Comments: You must stay at the resort to play here. Think Pinehurst or Sea Island Golf Club. Pines, a large amount of sand, and marshland. Water comes into play on 13 holes.* ★ ★ ★ ★ ½

Links. Holes: 18. Opened: 1977. Architect: Tom Jackson. Yards: 6,710/4,969. Par: 72/72. Course Rating: 72.8/69.2. Slope: 124/115. Green Fee: $68/$105. Walking: Unrestricted walking. *Comments: This is target golf. Great views of the Choctawhatchee Bay from this shortish course.* ★ ★ ★ ★

Raven. Holes: 18. Opened: 2000. Architect: Robert Trent Jones Jr. Yards: 6,854/5,037. Par: 71/71. Course Rating: 73.8/70.6. Slope: 137/126. Green Fee: $85/$135. Walking: Unrestricted walking. *Comments: Sculpted fairways and undulating greens routed through tall pines and palmetto bushes. Those palmettos gobble up golf balls, by the way.* UR

Where to Stay

⌕ **BLUEWATER BAY GOLF & TENNIS RESORT.** This upscale resort is 12 mi north of Destin via the Mid-Bay Bridge on the shores of Choctawhatchee Bay. Popular for its 36 holes of championship golf (on courses designed by Jerry Pate and Tom Fazio), it offers vacation rentals ranging from motel rooms to villas to three-bedroom patio homes ($$$$). ✉ 1950 Bluewater Blvd., Niceville 32578 ☎ 850/897–3613 or 800/874–2128 🖶 850/897–2424 ⊕ www.bwbresort.com ⌂ 85 units ⌂ Restaurant, some kitchens, cable TV, in-room VCRs, 36-hole golf course, 19 tennis courts, pro shop, 4 pools, bar, playground, no-smoking rooms ▤AE, D, DC, MC, V $.

🖼 **HENDERSON PARK INN.** Tucked discreetly away at the end of a quiet road bordering Henderson Beach State Park, this B&B has become Destin's premier getaway for couples seeking elegance and pampering. A green mansard roof and Shaker shingle siding are reminiscent of Queen Anne–era architecture and complement the inn's Victorian-era furnishings. Each romantic room is furnished with a four-poster, canopied, or iron bed draped with fine linen. All rooms come with plush robes and refrigerators with ice makers, as well as balconies, perfect for admiring the Gulf's smashing sunsets. ✉ 2700 Scenic U.S. 98 E, 32541 ☎ 850/654–0400 or 800/336–4853 ⊕ www. hendersonparkinn.com ⇋ 35 rooms ⚅ Restaurant, in-room safes, some in-room hot tubs, microwaves, refrigerators, cable TV, pool, beach, business services, meeting rooms, no-smoking rooms; no kids ▤AE, D, MC, V ⦿ BP $$$–$$$$.

🖼 **SANDESTIN GOLF AND BEACH RESORT.** Eight miles east of Destin, this 2,400-acre resort with villas, cottages, condominiums, boat slips, an inn, and 7½ mi of beach and bay-front property caters to newlyweds, conventioneers, and families alike. The on-site Baytowne Wharf has dozens of shops and restaurants, and the Lagoon is a 7-acre family-friendly water park. All rooms have a view, either of the Gulf, Choctawhatchee Bay, a golf course, a lagoon, or a natural wildlife preserve. The four championship courses make dramatic use of the surrounding landscape: wetlands, marshes, the beach, and the bay. ✉ 9300 U.S. 98 W, Sandestin 32550 ☎ 850/267–8000 or 800/277–0800 🖨 850/267–8222 ⊕ www.sandestin.com ⇋ 175 rooms, 250 condos, 275 villas ⚅ 8 restaurants, 3 cafés, coffee shop, 2 ice cream parlors, pizzeria, tea shop, some kitchens, cable TV, some in-room VCRs, 4 18-hole golf courses, 15 tennis courts, pro shop, 11 pools, health club, beach, dock, boating, hiking, 3 bars, lounge, piano bar, pub, shops, no-smoking rooms ▤AE, D, DC, MC, V $$–$$$.

Where to Eat

✕ **ELEPHANT WALK.** Although named after an Elizabeth Taylor film, the food is the star here. Ask for a seat near the large picture windows overlooking the dunes and start with lobster spring rolls. For dinner, try either the coconut-crusted gulf prawns or the ahi tuna with a mango-wasabi glaze. Duck, pork, and steak entrées round out the menu, but stick to seafood and you won't be disappointed. The cozy Governor's Attic upstairs is the perfect spot for a sunset cocktail or an after-dinner drink. ✉ Sandestin Resort, 9300 U.S. 98, Sandestin ☎ 850/267–4800 ⚐ Reservations essential ▤AE, D, DC, MC, V $$$$.

✕ **FLAMINGO CAFÉ.** Indoors are freshly starched white linen and refined elegance; outdoors, the patio is Florida casual all the way. Either way, every seat in the house has a panoramic view of Destin's harbor, and boaters are welcome to tie up at the dock. The cuisine is a mixture of Caribbean and Florida cuisines. The chef is known for his special snapper and grouper dishes; try the delicious oven-roasted snapper fillet, layered in phyllo pastry with crabmeat and braised spinach in a cream sauce. ✉ 414 U.S. 98 E ☎ 850/837–0961 ▤AE, D, MC, V ⊗ No lunch $$$–$$$$.

✗**MARINA CAFÉ.** A harbor view, impeccable service, and sophisticated cuisine create one of the finest dining experiences on the Emerald Coast. The ocean motif is expressed in shades of aqua, green, and sand accented with marine tapestries and sea sculptures. The chef calls his cuisine contemporary Continental, with classic creole, Mediterranean, or Pacific Rim dishes. One regional specialty is the popular black pepper–crusted yellowfin tuna with braised spinach and spicy soy sauce. The menu changes daily, and the wine list is extensive. ⊠404 U.S. 98 E ☎850/837-7960 ⊕ www.marinacafe.com ⊟AE, D, DC, MC, V ⊙ No lunch $$$–$$$$.

Essentials

Getting Here

From Orlando, take the Florida Turnpike north to I-75. Follow this to I-10, which travels across the Florida Panhandle. Head west past Tallahassee to Hwy. 331, just south of DeFuniak Springs. Drive south to Hwy. 98/395, the coastal road along the Gulf of Mexico. At the end of 331, turn right (west) to Destin. The driving time is approximately seven hours, the distance 415 mi.

▨ **VISITOR INFORMATION Destin Chamber of Commerce** ⊠4484 Legendary Dr., Destin 32541 ☎850/837-6241 ⊕ www.destinchamber.com. **Emerald Coast Convention & Visitors Bureau** ⊠1540 Miracle Strip Pkwy. SE, Fort Walton Beach 32548 ☎850/651-7131 or 800/322-3319 ⊕ www.destin-fwb.com.

FORT MYERS, SANIBEL, NAPLES & MARCO ISLAND

The National Golf Foundation keeps track of the metropolitan areas with the most golf holes per capita. Although Myrtle Beach is usually at the top of the list, nothing comes close to the sheer number of golf holes found in the combined Southwest Florida cities of Naples and Fort Myers. Roughly 150 golf courses are already open for business and at least 40 more are in some stage of development. The staggering volume reflects the rapid growth of the area as well as the abundance of cheap land.

The bad news is that more than 60% of these courses are private. Some are so exclusive they are still recruiting members despite initiation fees in the $250,000 range. But rest assured that there are more than enough good public facilities to supply a lengthy golf getaway.

The topography of the region is much like the rest of South Florida: swampland, farmland, mangrove forests, palm trees, and pines. Although the area has attracted all of the game's top architects, they aren't here for the scenery. Instead, they think of Southwest Florida as a blank palette in which to create anything they want.

FORT MYERS, SANIBEL, NAPLES & MARCO ISLAND COURSES	YARDAGE	PAR	COURSE	SLOPE	GREEN FEE
Eastwood Golf Club (18)	7,176/5,393	72/72	75.3/71.9	133/120	$22/$70
Lely Resort Golf & Country Club (36)					$35/$134
Lely Flamingo Island (18)	7,171/5,377	72/72	73.9/70.6	135/126	
Lely Mustang (18)	7,217/5,197	72/72	75.2/70.5	141/120	
Miromar Lakes Beach and Golf Club (18)	7,403/5,226	72/72	76.2/69.3	145/118	$48/$135
Naples Beach Hotel & Golf Club (18)	6,488/5,142	72/72	71.7/70.0	134/121	$40/$120
Naples Grande Golf Club (18)	7,078/5,209	72/72	75.1/70.5	143/119	$70/$170
Raptor Bay Golf Club (18)	6,702/5,217	71/71	71.9/69.2	129/114	$50/$190
Rookery at Marco (18)	6.767/5,029	72/72	72.8/69.6	137/123	$40/$140
Tiburon Golf Club (36)					$58/$225
Black Course (18)	7,005/4,909	72/72	74.2/69.7	147/119	
Gold Course (18)	7,288/5,148	72/72	74.7/69.2	137/113	

You have a choice of several places to stay, but our two favorites are the Ritz-Carlton lodge at the Tiburon resort in North Naples or the Hyatt Coconut Point Resort & Spa and its Raptor Bay course. If you're looking for something a little more beach oriented, the Naples Beach Hotel & Golf Club may be a better choice.

Courses

GolfDigest REVIEWS

EASTWOOD GOLF CLUB. Facility Holes: 18. Opened: 1989. Architect: Lloyd Clifton. Yards: 7,176/5,393. Par: 72/72. Course Rating: 75.3/71.9. Slope: 133/120. Green Fee: $22/$70. Cart Fee: Included in green fee. Discounts: Weekdays, twilight, seniors, juniors. Walking: Mandatory cart. Season: Year-round. High: Dec.–Mar. Tee Times: Call golf shop. Notes: Range (grass). ⊠ 13950 Golfway Blvd., 32828, 10 mi from Orlando ☎ 407/281–4653 ⊕ www.eastwoodgolf.com ⊟ AE, D, MC, V. *Comments: This muni, one of the few area courses with no houses, has an excellent layout.* ★ ★ ★ ½

LELY RESORT GOLF & COUNTRY CLUB. Facility Holes: 36. Green Fee: $35/$134. Cart Fee: Included in green fee. Discounts: Twilight. Walking: Mandatory cart. Season: Year-round. High: Dec.–Mar. Tee Times: Call golf shop. Notes: Range (grass), lodging (100). ⊠ 8004 Lely Resort Blvd., Naples 34113, 30 mi from Fort Myers ☎ 941/793–2223 or 800/388–4653 ⊟ AE, D, DC, MC, V.

Lely Flamingo Island. Holes: 18. Opened: 1990. Architect: Robert Trent Jones. Yards: 7,171/5,377. Par: 72/72. Course Rating: 73.9/70.6. Slope: 135/126. *Comments: One of the best in the area. A lot of water—Robert Trent Jones turned boring Florida land into a fun golf course.* ★ ★ ★ ★

Lely Mustang. Holes: 18. Opened: 1997. Architect: Lee Trevino. Yards: 7,217/5,197. Par: 72/72. Course Rating: 75.2/70.5. Slope: 141/120. *Comments: A nice resort course.* ★ ★ ★ ★ ½

MIROMAR LAKES BEACH AND GOLF CLUB. Facility Holes: 18. Opened: 2001. Architect: Art Hills. Yards: 7,403/5,226. Par: 72/72. Course Rating: 76.2/69.3. Slope: 145/118. Green Fee: $48/$135. Cart Fee: Included in green fee. Discounts: Juniors. Walking: Walking at certain times. Season: Year-round. High: Oct.–Apr. Tee Times: Call 4 days in advance. Notes: Range (grass). ✉ 18520 Miromar Lakes Blvd. W, Miromar Lakes 33913, 5 mi from Fort Myers ☎ 941/482-7644 ▤ AE, MC, V. *Comments: Don't be confused: the course is nowhere near the beach. It is, however, a solid Hills design with brilliant white bunkers, sculpted fairways, and tall pines. UR*

NAPLES BEACH HOTEL & GOLF CLUB. Facility Holes: 18. Opened: 1930. Architect: Ron Garl. Yards: 6,488/5,142. Par: 72/72. Course Rating: 71.7/70.0. Slope: 134/121. Green Fee: $40/$120. Cart Fee: Included in green fee. Discounts: Twilight, juniors. Walking: Walking at certain times. Season: Year-round. High: Nov.–Apr. Tee Times: Call golf shop. Notes: Range (grass, mat), lodging (318). ✉ 851 Gulf Shore Blvd. N, Naples 34102, 25 mi from Fort Myers ☎ 239/435-2475 or 800/237-7600 ⊕ www.naplesbeachhotel.com ▤ AE, D, MC, V. *Comments: Old Ron Garl design takes you back to Florida golf of the 1950s. In great shape, but the layout in uninspiring.* ★ ★ ★ ½

NAPLES GRANDE GOLF CLUB. Facility Holes: 18. Opened: 2000. Architect: Rees Jones. Yards: 7,078/5,209. Par: 72/72. Course Rating: 75.1/70.5. Slope: 143/119. Green Fee: $70/$170. Cart Fee: Included in green fee. Discounts: Twilight. Walking: Unrestricted walking. Season: Year-round. Tee Times: Call golf shop. Notes: Range (grass). ✉ 7760 Golden Gate Pkwy., Naples 34105 ☎ 941/659-3710 ⊕ www.naplesgrande.com ▤ AE, D, MC, V. *Comments: You must stay at the Registry Resort or the Edgewater Beach Hotel to play here. Rees Jones design is well manicured and fun to play. Very upscale.* ★ ★ ★ ★ ½

RAPTOR BAY GOLF CLUB. Facility Holes: 18. Opened: 2001. Architect: Ray Floyd. Yards: 6,702/5,217. Par: 71/71. Course Rating: 71.9/69.2. Slope: 129/114. Green Fee: $50/$190. Cart Fee: Included in green fee. Discounts: Guest, twilight, juniors. Walking: Mandatory cart. Season: Year-round. High: Jan.–Apr. Tee Times: Call 7 days in advance. Notes: Range (grass), lodging (456). ✉ 23001 Coconut Point Resort Dr., Bonita Springs 34134, 10 mi from Fort Myers/Naples ☎ 941/390-4610 ▤ AE, MC, V. *Comments: This fun resort course cuts through mangroves and sand scrub. Huge bunkers and wide fairways. UR*

ROOKERY AT MARCO. Facility Holes: 18. Opened: 1991. Architect: Robert Cupp Jr. Yards: 6.767/5,029. Par: 72/72. Course Rating: 72.8/69.6. Slope: 137/123. Green Fee: $40/$140. Cart Fee: Included in green fee. Season: Year-round. Tee Times: Call up to 7 days in advance. ✉ Marco Island Marriott Resort, Fiddler's Creek, 400 S. Collier Blvd., Marco Island 34145 ☎ 239/793-6060 ⊕ www.rookeryatmarco.com ▤ AE, MC, V. *Comments: Great Arthur Hills course; you must stay at Marco Island Marriott Resort to play. UR*

TIBURON GOLF CLUB. Facility Holes: 36. Opened: 1998. Architect: Greg Norman. Green Fee: $58/$225. Cart Fee: Included in green fee. Discounts: Guest, twilight, juniors. Walking: Mandatory cart. Season: Year-round. Tee Times: Call golf shop. Notes: Range (grass), lodging (463). ✉ 2620 Tiburon Dr., Naples 34109, 12 mi from Fort Myers ☎ 239/594-2040 or 888/387-8417 ⊕ www.wcigolf.com ⊟ AE, MC, V.

Black Course. Holes: 18. Yards: 7,005/4,909. Par: 72/72. Course Rating: 74.2/69.7. Slope: 147/119. UR

Gold Course. Holes: 18. Yards: 7,288/5,148. Par: 72/72. Course Rating: 74.7/69.2. Slope: 137/113. ★ ★ ★ ★ ½

Comments: This golf course is always in great shape. Don't worry about the rough: there isn't any. Tiburon is attached to a wonderful Ritz-Carlton hotel.

Where to Stay

🏨 **HYATT COCONUT POINT RESORT & SPA.** The 18 stories that make up this luxury resort stand out sharply from the surrounding pristine estuary environment. As a guest you can take a dip in one of three swimming offerings: the lap pool, waterfall pool, or lagoon-style pool; or catch a free ferry to the hotel's private island beach and relax in the sand. Guest rooms are appointed with rich fabrics and dark woods, and balconies overlook the Gulf or the Raptor Bay golf course. Kids' programs teach about Calusa Indians and an interpretative center covers natural and prehistoric history. ✉ 5001 Coconut Rd., Bonita Springs 34134 ☎ 239/444-1234 or 800/554-9288 🖶 239/390-4277 ⊕ www.coconutpoint.hyatt.com 🛏 423 rooms, 31 suites ♿ 2 restaurants, fans, in-room data ports, in-room safes, refrigerators, cable TV, in-room VCRs, 18-hole golf course, 4 tennis courts, 3 pools, health club, hair salon, spa, beach, boating, 2 bars, video game room, shops, children's programs (ages 3–12), concierge floor, business services, no-smoking floors ⊟ AE, D, DC, MC, V $$$$.

🏨 **MARCO ISLAND MARRIOTT RESORT AND GOLF CLUB.** A circular drive and manicured grounds front this beachfront resort made up of two 11-story towers. It's delightfully beachy outside (with a special faucet you can use to wash your shelling finds). Yet the interior is elegant, with many shops and restaurants and large, plush rooms with good to exceptional water views. The hotel's golf course, a 7,180-yard, par-72 designed by Robert Cupp Jr., is 10 minutes away by tram. ✉ 400 S. Collier Blvd., Marco Island 34145 ☎ 239/394-2511 or 800/438-4373 🖶 239/642-2672 ⊕ www.marriott.com 🛏 735 rooms, 62 suites ♿ 4 restaurants, coffee shop, pizzeria, room service, in-room data ports, in-room safes, minibars, refrigerators, cable TV with movies, 18-hole golf course, miniature golf, 16 tennis courts, 3 pools, wading pool, health club, hair salon, outdoor hot tub, spa, beach, windsurfing, boating, waterskiing, fishing, bicycles, Ping-Pong, 3 bars, video game room, shops, children's programs (ages 3–12), playground, laundry facilities, laundry services, Internet, business services, meeting rooms, no-smoking rooms ⊟ AE, DC, MC, V $$$$.

🏨 **NAPLES BEACH HOTEL AND GOLF CLUB.** Family-owned and managed for more than 50 years, this beach resort is a piece of Naples history. On a prime stretch of powdery sand, it stands out for its resort course, the first one of its type in the state. Rooms, decorated in light colors, face the Gulf or the golf course, and are in six high- and mid-rise pink buildings. Some good packages make an extended stay affordable. ✉ 851 Gulf Shore Blvd. N, Naples 34102 ☎ 239/261-2222 or 800/237-7600 🖶 239/261-7380 ⊕ -

www.naplesbeachhotel.com ⌨255 rooms, 41 suites, 22 efficiencies ⌂4 restaurants, in-room data ports, in-room safes, some kitchenettes, refrigerators, cable TV, 18-hole golf course, putting green, 6 tennis courts, pro shop, pool, health club, spa, beach, 2 bars, shops, children's programs (ages 5–12), business services, meeting rooms, no-smoking rooms ▤AE, D, DC, MC, V $$$$.

🎬 **REGISTRY RESORT.** The immense, free-form family swimming pool has a 100-foot waterslide at this high-rise hotel overlooking the Gulf. The entire property rests behind the dusky, twisted mangrove forests, with 3 mi of powdery white sand a short walk or tram ride away. Rooms, each with a wet bar, are spacious and comfortable. The Naples Grande Golf Club is studded with indigenous cypress and pines; the spa offers treatments poolside or indoors. ⊠475 Seagate Dr., Naples 34103 ☎239/597-3232 ⊟239/566-7919 ⊕www.registryresort.com ⌨395 rooms, 78 suites ⌂5 restaurants, coffee shop, some in-room safes, some in-room hot tubs, some kitchenettes, some minibars, cable TV, in-room VCRs, 18-hole golf course, 15 tennis courts, 5 pools, health club, 3 outdoor hot tubs, spa, bicycles, bar, nightclub, shops, children's programs (ages 4–12), business services, convention center, meeting rooms ▤AE, DC, MC, V $$$$.

🎬 **RITZ–CARLTON GOLF RESORT.** Ardent golfers with a yen for luxury will find their dream vacation at Naples's most elegant golf resort. Ritz style prevails all the way; rooms are regal but with a touch of Florida, and all rooms have balconies with links views. ⊠2600 Tiburon Dr., Naples 34109 ☎239/593-2000 or 800/241-3333 ⊟239/593-2010 ⊕www.ritzcarlton.com ⌨257 rooms, 38 suites ⌂2 restaurants, coffee shop, in-room data ports, in-room safes, minibars, 2 18-hole golf courses, 4 tennis courts, pro shop, pool, billiards, 3 bars, concierge floors, no-smoking rooms ▤AE, D, DC, MC, V $$$$.

🎬 **SOUTH SEAS RESORT AND YACHT HARBOUR.** Like a bustling town, this polished Captiva resort packs a lot into 330 acres, but the natural world remains. Manatees and pelicans patrol the marina at the property's north end, with osprey and gulls overhead; dunes fringe a pristine 2½-mi beach; and mangroves edge the single main road. Stylish, low-rise hotel rooms, villas, and houses are all over the property but are concentrated at either end, near the marina and, to the south, near the entry gate and the small shopping complex. Where you lodge depends on the facilities, space, and location you prefer. The casual, windswept 9-hole golf course has dazzling water views. ⊠5400 Plantation Rd., Box 194, Captiva 33924 ☎239/472-5111 or 800/227-8482 ⊟239/481-4947 ⊕www.south-seas-resort.com ⌨138 units, 482 suites ⌂4 restaurants, ice cream parlor, pizzeria, snack bar, room service, kitchens, cable TV with movies, 9-hole golf course, putting green, 21 tennis courts, pro shop, 18 pools, gym, hair salon, hot tub, massage, beach, dock, windsurfing, boating, jet skiing, parasailing, waterskiing, fishing, bicycles, shuffleboard, 2 bars, shops, children's programs (ages 3–18), business center, convention center, meeting rooms, no-smoking rooms ▤AE, D, DC, MC, V $$$$.

Where to Eat

✗**BUBBLE ROOM.** Servers wear scout uniforms and funny headgear while electric trains circle overhead at this lively, kitschy favorite. The bread basket comes loaded with cheesy Bubble Bread and sweet, yeasty sticky buns. Entrées include spicy shrimp, duck, and Cornish hen; try the aged prime rib or the Eddie Fisherman (poached fresh grouper steamed in a brown paper bag). Desserts are monumental—the triple-layer red velvet cake is a favorite. Arrive early or be prepared to wait for a table. ⊠ 15001 Captiva Dr., Captiva ☎ 239/472-5558 ⊕ www.bubbleroomrestaurant.com ⌒ Reservations not accepted ⊟ AE, D, DC, MC, V $$$-$$$$.

✕ **MCT'S SHRIMPHOUSE AND TAVERN.** In this informal Sanibel landmark, the menu spotlights fresh seafood. Look for oyster and mussel appetizers and the all-you-can-eat shrimp and crab, although ribs, prime rib, and blackened chicken are also on the menu. There's always a dessert du jour, but few can resist the Sanibel mud pie, a delicious concoction heavy on the Oreos. ⊠ 1523 Periwinkle Way, Sanibel ☎ 239/472-3161 ⌒ Reservations not accepted ⊟ AE, D, MC, V $$-$$$.

✕ **OLD MARCO LODGE CRAB HOUSE.** Built in 1869, this waterfront restaurant is Marco's oldest landmark, and boats often cruise in and tie up dockside to allow their captains and crew to sit on the veranda and dine on local seafood and pasta entrées. The bowl of blue crabs in garlic butter is a specialty. ⊠ 401 Papaya St., Goodland ☎ 239/642-7227 ⊟ AE, DC, MC, V ⊘ Closed Mon. $$-$$$$.

✕ **SIGN OF THE VINE.** The menu is presented as a framed work of art at this romantic spot in an out-of-the-way cottage with a fireplace and candlelight. Roasted bourbon and peach duckling, tenderloin with cognac cream sauce, and lobster hash are signature dishes. Between courses come delightful surprises—a popover with citrus butter or grilled fruit, perhaps; after dessert, a plate of homemade fudge and sugared walnuts shows up. ⊠ 980 Solano Rd., Naples ☎ 239/261-6745 ⌒ Reservations essential ⊟ AE ⊘ Closed Mon. and some summer months; call ahead. No lunch $$$$.

✕ **SNUG HARBOR.** You can watch boats coming and going whether you sit inside or out at this casual dockside restaurant on stilts. The secret of its success is absolutely fresh seafood, which comes from the restaurant's own fishing fleet. The grouper Popeye (on spinach) is a signature dish. ⊠ 645 Old San Carlos Blvd., Fort Myers ☎ 239/463-4343 ⊕ www.snugharborrestaurant.com ⊟ AE, D, MC, V $-$$$.

Essentials

Getting Here
To get to the area from Orlando, take I-4 west 75 mi to I-75. Take I-75 100 mi south to Fort Myers.

Visitor Information
🛈 **Charlotte County Chamber of Commerce** ⊠ 2702 Tamiami Trail, Port Charlotte 33952 ☎ 239/627-2222. **Lee County Visitor and Convention Bureau** ⊠ 2180 W. 1st St., Suite 100, Fort Myers 33901 ☎ 239/338-3500 or 800/533-4753. **Marco Island Chamber of Commerce** ⊠ 1102 N. Collier Blvd., Marco Island 34145 ☎ 239/394-7549 or 800/788-6272. **Naples Chamber of Commerce** ⊠ 895 5th Ave. S, Naples 34102 ☎ 239/262-6141. **Sanibel-Captiva Chamber of Commerce** ⊠ 1159 Causeway Rd., Sanibel 33957 ☎ 239/472-1080 or 800/861-6603.

Hampton Club (18)	6,465/5,233	72/72	71.1/71.0	135/121	$68
Jekyll Island Golf Resort	63				
Great Dunes (9)	3,023/2,570	36/36	70.9/70.3	126/123	$22
Indian Mound (18)	6,469/4,964	72/72	71.3/68.8	130/118	$35
Oleander (18)	6,521/4,913	72/72	71.7/64.5	126/110	$35
Pine Lakes (18)	6,620/5,079	72/72	72.0/69.0	134/115	$45
Oak Grove Island Golf Club (18)	6,910/4,855	72/72	73.2/67.6	132/116	$6/$22
Sea Island Golf Club (54)					$125/$225
Plantation (18)	6,549/5,194	72/72	71.4/69.8	130/124	
Retreat (18)	6,760/5,273	72/72	72.2/68.9	131/121	
Seaside (18)	6,550/5,048	70/70	71.1/69.3	126/119	
Sea Palms Resort (27)					
Great Oaks/Sea Palms (18)	6,350/5,200	72/72	71.8/69.3	128/124	$35/$52
Tall Pines/Great Oaks (18)	6,658/5,350	72/72	72.1/70.9	131/120	$35/$50
Tall Pines/Sea Palms (18)	6,198/5,249	72/72	70.6/70.8	129/127	$35/$50

JEKYLL ISLAND, SEA ISLAND & ST. SIMONS ISLAND, GA

The Golden Isles of Georgia, which include St. Simons Island, Sea Island, and Jekyll Island near Brunswick, really haven't changed all that much since the days when the Rockefellers and Vanderbilts turned this into their early-20th-century playground. The service at the Cloister and Sea Island Golf Club will make you feel as if you've been transported back to the Old South, and the hospitality at places like the Jekyll Island and St. Simons Island clubs will make you wonder why more people don't know about this place. No doubt, the barrier islands of southeast Georgia have an off-the-beaten-path feel, although it's only a short ride from busy I-95 to these coastal towns. The topography here is one of tidal marshes, sea grass, tall pines, and sand scrub. The sea views are stunning, but because the land is virtually unprotected from the surf, be forewarned that gentle morning breezes can often turn into all-out gales by mid afternoon.

If you want the full treatment, try staying at the new Lodge at Sea Island Golf Club. The cottages linked to the 36-hole golf facility overlook the Atlantic Ocean and its inlets. If $400-a-night is a little too steep, try the Jekyll Island Club Hotel. It's less expensive and definitely a throwback to simpler times. Remember to bring a coat and tie when you come here. It's usually required for dinner.

FLORIDA'S DYNAMIC DUO

The names Dick Wilson and Joe Lee are very familiar to fans of Florida golf. When added together, the number of Florida courses they designed approaches 100. Wilson (1904–65) got his start in golf as a water boy during the construction of famed Merion Golf Club in his hometown of Philadelphia. It wasn't until 1945, though, that he started his own design business, based in Florida. One of his proteges was Joe Lee (1922–2003), who joined Wilson's firm after college and became a full partner in 1959. After Wilson's death, Lee carried on his mentor's tradition, designing solid, straightforward golf courses.

Courses

Golf Digest REVIEWS

HAMPTON CLUB AT HAMPTON PLANTATION. Facility Holes: 18. Opened: 1989. Architect: Joe Lee. Yards: 6,465/5,233. Par: 72/72. Course Rating: 71.1/71.0. Slope: 135/ 121. Green Fee: $79. Cart Fee: Included in green fee. Walking: Mandatory cart. Season: Year-round Tee Times: Call golf shop. ✉ 100 Tabbystone St., St. Simons Island, GA 31522, 70 mi from Jacksonville ☎912/634-0255 ⊕www.hamptonclub.com ▤AE, MC, V. *Comments: Former site of an antebellum plantation, Hampton Club is carved through marshlands. Fun to play. Owned by the King and Prince Beach and Golf Resort.* ★ ★ ★ ½

JEKYLL ISLAND GOLF RESORT. Facility Holes: 63. Cart Fee: $16 per person. Discounts: Guest, twilight, juniors. Season: Year-round. Tee Times: Call golf shop. Notes: Range (grass). ✉322 Captain Wylly Rd., Jekyll Island, GA 31527, 60 mi from Jacksonville ☎912/635-2368 or 877/453-5955 ⊕www.jekyllisland.com or www.jigolf.net ▤AE, D, MC, V.

Great Dunes. Holes: 9. Opened: 1898. Architect: Walter Travis. Yards: 3,023/2,570. Par: 36/36. Course Rating: 70.9/70.3. Slope: 126/123. Green Fee: $22. Walking: Unrestricted walking. *Comments: Designed by Walter Travis in 1928. Small greens; very cheap to play. Like going through a time warp.* ★ ★ ★

Indian Mound. Holes: 18. Opened: 1975. Architect: Joe Lee. Yards: 6,469/4,964. Par: 72/ 72. Course Rating: 71.3/68.8. Slope: 130/118. Green Fee: $35. Walking: Unrestricted walking. *Comments: Similar to Pine Lakes. If you play one, no need to play the other. Basic golf.* ★ ★ ★ ½

Oleander. Holes: 18. Opened: 1964. Architect: Dick Wilson. Yards: 6,521/4,913. Par: 72/ 72. Course Rating: 71.7/64.5. Slope: 126/110. Green Fee: $35. Walking: Unrestricted walking. *Comments: Toughest course on the property. Tall pines can't stop the wind.* ★ ★ ★ ★

Pine Lakes. Holes: 18. Opened: 1968. Architect: Dick Wilson/Joe Lee. Yards: 6,620/ 5,079. Par: 72/72. Course Rating: 72.0/69.0. Slope: 134/115. Green Fee: $45. Walking: Walking at certain times. *Comments: Tucked into the inner part of Jekyll Island. Routed through pines, ponds, and mangroves.* ★ ★ ★

OAK GROVE ISLAND GOLF CLUB. Facility Holes: 18. Opened: 1993. Architect: Mike Young. Yards: 6,910/4,855. Par: 72/72. Course Rating: 73.2/67.6. Slope: 132/116. Green Fee: $6/$22. Cart Fee: $15 per person. Discounts: Weekdays, guest, twilight, seniors, juniors. Walking: Mandatory cart. Season: Year-round. High: Feb.–Apr. Tee Times: Call 7 days in advance. Notes: Range (grass). ✉ 126 Clipper Bay, Brunswick, GA 31523, 45 mi from Jacksonville ☎ 912/280–9525 ⊕ www.oakgroveislandgolf.com ▤ AE, D, MC, V. *Comments: Built on an island between two intercoastal rivers in Brunswick. Great views of the area's wetlands. Renovated in 1997.* ★★★

SEA ISLAND GOLF CLUB. Facility Holes: 54. Green Fee: $125/$225. Cart Fee: Included in green fee. Discounts: Twilight, juniors. Walking: Walking with caddie. Season: Year-round. High: Mar.–Nov. Notes: Range (grass, mat), lodging (40). ✉ 100 Retreat Ave., St. Simons Island, GA 31522, 75 mi from Jacksonville ☎ 912/638–5118 or 800/732–4752 ⊕ www.seaisland.com ▤ AE, D, DC, MC, V.

Plantation. Holes: 18. Opened: 1998. Architect: Rees Jones. Yards: 6,549/5,194. Par: 72/72. Course Rating: 71.4/69.8. Slope: 130/124. *Comments: With views of the Atlantic Ocean on 7 holes, this course shines with Rees Jones's outstanding work.* ★★★★ ½

Retreat. Holes: 18. Opened: 2001. Architect: Davis Love III. Yards: 6,760/5,273. Par: 72/72. Course Rating: 72.2/68.9. Slope: 131/121. *Comments: Davis Love III renovated the old Joe Lee design and did a great job.* UR

Seaside. Holes: 18. Opened: 1999. Architect: Tom Fazio. Yards: 6,550/5,048. Par: 70/70. Course Rating: 71.1/69.3. Slope: 126/119. *Comments: One of the best courses in Georgia. Routed mainly around the back bay. The wind can be brutal here.* ★★★★ ½

SEA PALMS RESORT. Facility Holes: 27. Opened: 1966. Discounts: Weekdays, guest, twilight, juniors. Walking: Mandatory cart. Season: Year-round. Tee Times: Call golf shop. Notes: Range (grass, mat). ✉ 5445 Frederica Rd., St. Simons Island, GA 31522, 65 mi from Jacksonville ☎ 912/638–9041 or 800/841–6268 ▤ AE, MC, V. *Comments: These 27 holes have water in play on 17 of them. Looks, feels, and plays like a Florida course.* ★★★

Great Oaks/Sea Palms. Holes: 18. Architect: George Cobb/Tom Jackson. Yards: 6,350/5,200. Par: 72/72. Course Rating: 71.8/69.3. Slope: 128/124. Green Fee: $35/$52. Cart Fee: $18 per cart.

Tall Pines/Great Oaks. Holes: 18. Architect: George Cobb. Yards: 6,658/5,350. Par: 72/72. Course Rating: 72.1/70.9. Slope: 131/120. Green Fee: $35/$50. Cart Fee: $17 per cart.

Tall Pines/Sea Palms. Holes: 18. Architect: George Cobb. Yards: 6,198/5,249. Par: 72/72. Course Rating: 70.6/70.8. Slope: 129/127. Green Fee: $35/$50. Cart Fee: $17 per cart.

Where to Stay

🔟 **THE CLOISTER.** The Cloister undeniably lives up to its celebrity status as a grand coastal resort. You can get a spacious, comfortably appointed room or suite in the Spanish Mediterranean–style hotel—designed by Florida architect Addison Mizner—or in the property's later-built Ocean Houses, which offer 56 dramatic suites connected by lavish house parlors with fireplaces and staffed bars. The state-of-the-art spa at the Cloister is in a beautiful building all its own. You also get access to the nearby Sea Island Golf Club. ✉ Sea Island ⌖ 100 Hudson Pl., Sea Island, GA 31522 ☎ 912/638–3611 or

800/732-4752 🖶912/638-5823 ⊕ www.seaisland.com ⬏274 rooms, 32 suites ⚐4 restaurants, cable TV, golf privileges, 18 tennis courts, 2 pools, health club, spa, bicycles, bar, 2 lounges, children's programs (ages 3-11), business services, airport shuttle, no-smoking rooms ▤AE, D, DC, MC, V ⵑⵌFAP $$$$.

⛶ **JEKYLL ISLAND CLUB HOTEL.** A four-story clubhouse—with couches and a fire-place—is the focal point of this sprawling 1886 resort with wraparound verandas and Queen Anne-style towers and turrets. Guest rooms, suites, apartments, and cottages are custom-decorated with mahogany beds, armoires, and plush sofas and chairs. Two beautifully restored former "millionaires' cottages"—the Crane Cottage and the Cherokee Cottage—add 23 elegant guest rooms to this gracefully groomed compound. Note the bed-and-breakfast packages—they're a great deal. ✉ 371 Riverview Dr., Jekyll Island, GA 31527 ☎912/635-2600 or 800/535-9547 🖶912/635-2818 ⊕ www.jekyllclub.com ⬏139 rooms, 15 suites ⚐3 restaurants, room service, in-room data ports, in-room safes, cable TV, in-room VCRs, 13 tennis courts, putting green, pool, massage, beach, bicycles, croquet, bar, lounge, library, shops, baby-sitting, concierge, Internet, meeting room, no-smoking rooms ▤AE, D, DC, MC, V $$-$$$.

⛶ **KING AND PRINCE BEACH AND GOLF RESORT.** Most people who visit feel it's worth the expense to get a room with easy beach access at this cushy retreat. Guest rooms are spacious, and villas have two or three bedrooms. The villas are owned by pri-vate individuals, so the total number available for rent varies from time to time. ⌖201 Arnold Rd., St. Simons Island, GA 31522 ☎912/638-3631 or 800/342-0212 🖶912/638-7699 ⊕ www.kingandprince.com ⬏148 rooms, 10 suites, 43 villas ⚐2 restau-rants, in-room data ports, cable TV, golf privileges, 2 tennis courts, 5 pools (1 indoor), gym, 3 hot tubs, beach, boating, bicycles, bar, lounge, concierge, Internet, no-smoking rooms ▤AE, D, MC, V $$$$.

⛶ **LODGE AT SEA ISLAND GOLF CLUB.** This small but opulent lodge has assumed its place among the coast's most exclusive accommodations. Dashingly decorated rooms and suites all have water or golf-course views, and you can expect to be pampered by 24-hour butler service. You can also choose from among four stellar restaurants for din-ing. The lodge serves as the clubhouse for the Sea Island Golf Club (although this whole complex lies on St. Simons Island, so don't let the title disorient you) and encompasses a trophy room, locker rooms, and the Sea Island Golf Learning Center. ✉St. Simons Island ⌖100 Hudson Pl., Sea Island, GA 31522 ☎912/638-3611 or 866/465-3563 ⊕ - www.seaisland.com ⬏40 rooms, 2 suites ⚐4 restaurants, cable TV, in-room VCRs, 2 18-hole golf courses, tennis court, pool, health club, hot tub, bar, lounge, Internet, meet-ing room, no-smoking rooms ▤AE, D, DC, MC, V $$$$.

⛶ **SEA PALMS GOLF AND TENNIS RESORT.** Rooms have balconies overlooking the golf course, and they are large—so large they're touted as the biggest standard guest rooms in the Golden Isles. The furnishings are somewhat unimaginative, howev-er. This is a contemporary complex with fully furnished villas (suites), most with kitchens, nestled on an 800-acre site. Staying here also gains you beach club privileges. ✉5445 Frederica Rd., St. Simons Island, GA 31522 ☎912/638-3351 or 800/841-6268 🖶912/634-8029 ⊕ www.seapalms.com ⬏149 rooms, 26 suites ⚐2 restaurants, some kitchens, some microwaves, refrigerators, 27-hole golf course, 3 tennis courts, pro shop, 2 pools, wading pool, health club, outdoor hot tub, sauna, bicycles, volleyball, bar, children's programs, playground, convention center, no-smoking rooms ▭AE, DC, MC, V $$–$$$.

Where to Eat

✕**CARGO PORTSIDE GRILL.** Don't miss this superb seaside pub, a short drive across the bridge in the small city of Brunswick. The menu reads like a foodie's wish list, with succulent coastal and cross-coastal fare from many ports. All of it is creatively presented by owner-chef Alix Kanegy, formerly of Atlanta's Indigo Coastal Grill. Specials have included pasta Veracruz with grilled chicken, smoked tomatoes, poblano peppers, and caramelized onions in a chipotle cream sauce; in season, soft-shell crab is often on the menu. ✉ 1423 Newcastle St., Brunswick, GA ☎ 912/267–7330 ⊕ www.cargoportsidegrill.com ▭MC, V ⊘ Closed Sun. and Mon. $$–$$$$.

✕**COURTYARD AT CRANE.** Dine alfresco in the courtyard of Crane Cottage, part of the Jekyll Island Club Hotel, at this notable addition to the island's restaurant scene. The menu focuses on creative salads and entrées inspired by the world-famous kitchens of the Napa/Sonoma Valley wine country. You might sample the Mediterranean platter of grilled vegetables, imported olives, and fresh mozzarella with *crostini*; or a lobster-salad croissant with avocado, red onion, apple-wood-smoked bacon, tomato, and alfalfa sprouts. ✉Jekyll Island Club Hotel, 371 Riverview Dr., Jekyll Island, GA ☎912/635–2600 ▭AE, D, DC, MC, V ⊘ Closed Sun. $$$–$$$$.

✕**GRAND DINING ROOM.** The dining room of the Jekyll Island Club Hotel sparkles with silver and crystal. The cuisine reflects the elegance of the private hunting club that flourished from the late 19th century to the World War II era and which brought a fine chef and staff in from New York City's Delmonico's. Enjoy the blue-crab cakes, grilled pork with Vidalia onion, and local seafood. The restaurant has its own label pinot noir and chardonnay, made by Mountain View Vineyards. ✉Jekyll Island Club Hotel, 371 Riverview Dr., Jekyll Island, GA ☎912/635–2600 ⚠ Reservations essential ▭AE, D, DC, MC, V $$$–$$$$.

✕**SEAJAY'S WATERFRONT CAFE & PUB.** Convivial and festive, with a swamp-shack style, this tavern serves delicious—and inexpensive—seafood, including a crab chowder that locals love. This is also the home of a wildly popular shrimp-boil buffet: a Low-Country all-you-can-eat feast of local shrimp, corn on the cob, smoked sausage, and new potatoes served in a pot. ✉Jekyll Harbor Marina, 1 Harbor Rd., Jekyll Island, GA ☎912/635–3200 ⊕ www.seajays.com ▭AE, MC, V $$.

Essentials

Getting Here

From Orlando, take I–4 east to Daytona Beach and get on I–95 north. Take I–95 north past the Georgia state line. At Brunswick, follow Hwy. 17 east to the coast, where roads fork to Jekyll Island and Sea Island. The driving time is approximately four hours, the distance 220 mi.

Visitor Information

The Brunswick and the Golden Isles Visitors Center provides helpful information on all of the Golden Isles, which include Jekyll Island, Sea Island, and St. Simons Island.

🛈 **Brunswick and the Golden Isles Visitors Center** ✉ 2000 Glynn Ave., Brunswick 31520 ☎ 912/264–5337 or 800/933–2627 ⊕ www.bgivb.com.

THE PALM BEACHES

The 50-mi corridor between West Palm Beach and Port St. Lucie along I–95 in South Florida has come a long way since the 1980s. A construction boom featuring million-dollar homes, high-rise condos, and sprawling residential developments has turned this area along the Atlantic Ocean into one of the fastest-growing regions in the United States. To no one's surprise, golf is one of the main benefactors. From ultra-exclusive private clubs to resort courses to new community tracks, the area has seen its golf roster triple since 1980.

Among the golfers to call the area home are Jack Nicklaus, Greg Norman, and Nick Price as well as LPGA Tour stars like Karrie Webb and Dottie Pepper. The national headquarters for the PGA of America is here and so is the National Golf Foundation. Seminole Golf Club, a private course that used to be the winter practice facility for Ben Hogan, tops the list of exclusive clubs; Jupiter Hills and Pine Tree are also large draws: they're on *Golf Digest*'s list of the best courses in Florida. All three are on the magazine's list of America's 100 Greatest Courses.

Our pick for the area is the 54-hole PGA Golf Club in Port St. Lucie. Not only are all three courses excellent but it may have the best practice facilities anywhere, as well as new and spacious accommodations. Nothing else comes close. But if you want to spend some serious bucks, stay at one of the most famous resorts in the world—The Breakers. The golf facility is adequate, but the hotel is amazing.

One knock against the area: although the golf is plentiful, it's also monotonous. There're only so many ways you can shape flat, sandy land, so what you find here are many similar-looking, well-manicured fairways. It is true that you could spend a couple of months here and not play every worthwhile course. To keep things simple, here are just some of our favorites.

Courses   **Golf** Digest REVIEWS

BOCA RATON RESORT & CLUB. Facility Holes: 36. Green Fee: $153. Cart Fee: $17 per person. Season: Year-round. Tee Times: Call golf shop. ✉ 501 E. Camino Real, Boca Raton 33432 ☎ 561/447–3000 or 800/327–0101 ⊕ www.bocaresort.com ▤ AE, D, DC, MC, V.

Country Club. Holes: 18. Yards: 6,585/5,449. Par: 72/72. Course Rating: 72.6/72.1. Slope: 130/127. ★★★★

Boca Raton Resort & Club (36)					$153
Country Club (18)	6,585/5,449	72/72	72.6/72.1	130/127	
Resort (18)	6,253/4,503	71/71	69.3/65.5	128/112	
The Breakers (36)					$170
Breakers West (18)	6,905/5,420	71/72	69.3/70.0	135/131	
Ocean (18)	6,167/5,254	70/70	68.1/69.0	121/122	
Emerald Dunes Golf Course (18)	7,006/4,676	72/72	74.3/67.1	138/115	$80/$175
PGA Golf Club (54)					
Dye (18)	7,150/5,015	72/72	74.7/67.8	133/109	$15/$79
North (18)	7,026/4,993	72/72	73.8/68.8	133/114	$15/$79
South (18)	7,076/4,933	72/72	74.5/68.7	141/119	$26/$89
PGA National Golf Club (9)o					
Champion (18)	7,022/5,377	72/72	74.7/71.1	142/123	$109/$225
Estate (18)	6,784/4,903	72/72	73.4/68.4	131/118	$68/$130
General (18)	6,768/5,324	72/72	73.0/71.0	130/122	$68/$130
Haig (18)	6,806/5,645	72/72	73.0/72.5	130/121	$68/$130
Squire (18)	6,478/4,982	72/72	71.3/69.8	127/123	$68/$130

Resort. Holes: 18. Yards: 6,253/4,503. Par: 71/71. Course Rating: 69.3/65.5. Slope: 128/112. ★ ★ ★ ½

Comments: First opened in 1926. Tommy Armour and Sam Snead served as club pros at the course in its prime. Redesigned in 1997. Short and easy. You must stay at the resort to play either of these courses.

THE BREAKERS. Facility Holes: 36. Season: Year-round. Green Fee: $170. Cart Fee: Included in green fee. ✉ 1550 Flagler Pkwy., West Palm Beach 33411 ☎ 561/653–6320 ⊕ www.thebreakers.com ⊟ AE, D, DC, MC, V.

Breakers West. Holes: 18. Opened: 1969. Architect: Wyland Byrd. Yards: 6,905/5,420. Par: 71/72. Course Rating: 69.3/70.0. Slope: 135/131. Tee Times: Call up to 7 days in advance. Walking: Walking at certain times. UR

Ocean. Holes: 18. Opened: 2000. Architect: Brian Silva. Yards: 6,167/5,254. Par: 70/70. Course Rating: 68.1/69.0. Slope: 121/122. Tee Times: Tee Times: Call up to 30 days in advance. Walking: Walking at certain times. *Comments: Short course has an old-money, country-club feel. In great shape but not much in terms of design.* ★ ★ ½

EMERALD DUNES GOLF COURSE. Facility Holes: 18. Opened: 1990. Architect: Tom Fazio. Yards: 7,006/4,676. Par: 72/72. Course Rating: 74.3/67.1. Slope: 138/115. Green Fee: $80/$175. Cart Fee: Included in green fee. Discounts: Weekdays, twilight, juniors. Walking: Unrestricted walking. Season: Year-round. Tee Times: Call 60 days in advance. Notes: Range (grass). ✉ 2100 Emerald Dunes Dr., West Palm Beach 33411 ☎ 561/684–4653 or 888/650–4653 ⊕ www.emeralddunes.com ⊟ AE, D, DC, MC, V. *Comments: Always in great shape. Fairly flat, with a lot of water features and great bunkering.* ★ ★ ★ ★

PGA GOLF CLUB. Facility Holes: 54. Cart Fee: Included in green fee. Discounts: Twilight, juniors. Walking: Unrestricted walking. Season: Year-round. High: Jan.–Mar. Tee

Times: Call 30 days in advance. Notes: Range (grass), lodging (300). ⊠ 1916 Perfect Dr. or Port St. Lucie, 34986, 35 mi from West Palm Beach ☎ 800/800-4653 or 800/800-4653 ⊕ www.pgavillage.com ⊟ AE, D, MC, V.

Dye. Holes: 18. Opened: 1999. Architect: Pete Dye. Yards: 7,150/5,015. Par: 72/72. Course Rating: 74.7/67.8. Slope: 133/109. Green Fee: $15/$79. *Comments: Unique in design, this course has more moguls than a ski resort.* ★ ★ ★ ★ ½

North. Holes: 18. Opened: 1996. Architect: Tom Fazio. Yards: 7,026/4,993. Par: 72/72. Course Rating: 73.8/68.8. Slope: 133/114. Green Fee: $15/$79. *Comments: Tom Fazio built a fun, palm- and pine tree-covered golf course here. Great greens.* ★ ★ ★ ★ ½

South. Holes: 18. Opened: 1996. Architect: Tom Fazio. Yards: 7,076/4,933. Par: 72/72. Course Rating: 74.5/68.7. Slope: 141/119. Green Fee: $26/$89. *Comments: Easily one of Florida's best public golf courses. Feels like Pinehurst. Much harder than the North course.* ★ ★ ★ ★ ½

PGA NATIONAL GOLF CLUB. Facility Holes: 90. Cart Fee: $40 per person. Walking: Mandatory cart. Season: Year-round. High: Jan.–Apr. Tee Times: Call golf shop. Notes: Metal spikes, range (grass), lodging (300). ⊠ 1000 Ave. of the Champions, Palm Beach Gardens 33418, 15 mi from West Palm Beach ☎ 561/627-1800 or 800/633-9150 ⊟ AE, MC, V.

Champion. Holes: 18. Opened: 1981. Architect: Tom Fazio/Jack Nicklaus. Yards: 7,022/5,377. Par: 72/72. Course Rating: 74.7/71.1. Slope: 142/123. Green Fee: $109/$225. *Comments: Of the five courses here, this is the one you want to play. Site of the 1983 Ryder Cup and 1987 PGA Championship, the Champion improved drastically after its 2003 renovation.* ★ ★ ★ ★

Estate. Holes: 18. Opened: 1984. Architect: Karl Litten. Yards: 6,784/4,903. Par: 72/72. Course Rating: 73.4/68.4. Slope: 131/118. Green Fee: $68/$130. ★ ★ ★ ½

General. Holes: 18. Opened: 1984. Architect: Arnold Palmer. Yards: 6,768/5,324. Par: 72/72. Course Rating: 73.0/71.0. Slope: 130/122. Green Fee: $68/$130. ★ ★ ★ ★

Haig. Holes: 18. Opened: 1980. Architect: Tom Fazio. Yards: 6,806/5,645. Par: 72/72. Course Rating: 73.0/72.5. Slope: 130/121. Green Fee: $68/$130. ★ ★ ★ ½

Squire. Holes: 18. Opened: 1981. Architect: Tom Fazio. Yards: 6,478/4,982. Par: 72/72. Course Rating: 71.3/69.8. Slope: 127/123. Green Fee: $68/$130. ★ ★ ★ ★

Where to Stay

☷ **BOCA RATON RESORT & CLUB.** Addison Mizner built the Mediterranean-stye Cloister Inn here in 1926, and additions over time have created this sparkling, sprawling resort with a beach accessible by shuttle. There are many recreational activities here and many lodging options: traditional Cloister rooms are small, but warmly decorated; accommodations in the 27-story Tower are more spacious; Beach Club rooms are light, airy, and contemporary; golf villas are large and attractive and, naturally, near the golf course. You have access to two other courses nearby. ⊠ 501 E. Camino Real, Boca Raton

33431 ☎ 561/395-3000 or 800/327-0101 📠 561/447-5888 ⊕ www.bocaresort.com
⮫ 840 rooms, 63 suites, 60 golf villas ♢ 7 restaurants, room service, in-room safes, some kitchens, 54-hole golf course, 40 tennis courts, 5 pools, hair salon, 3 health clubs, beach, snorkeling, windsurfing, boating, marina, fishing, basketball, racquetball, 3 bars, nightclub, shops, children's programs (ages 2–17), laundry service, concierge, business services, convention center, meeting rooms ▭ AE, DC, MC, V $$$$.

▦ **THE BREAKERS.** Dating from 1896 and on the National Register of Historic Places, this opulent Italian Renaissance–style resort sprawls over 140 oceanfront acres. Cupids frolic at the main Florentine fountain, while majestic frescoes grace ceilings leading to restaurants. Jackets and ties are no longer *required* after 7 PM. A $120 million renovation included the addition of a luxury spa and beach club, golf and tennis clubhouses, and upgrades at the Ocean course, Florida's first 18-hole golf course. The Breakers West course, a 7,000-yard, par-71, contemporary-style course, is 10 mi away. ⊠ 1 S. County Rd., Palm Beach 33480 ☎ 561/655-6611 or 888/273-2537 📠 561/659-8403 ⊕ www.thebreakers.com ⮫ 569 rooms, 49 suites ♢ 5 restaurants, room service, in-room data ports, room TVs with movies and video games, 36-hole golf course, putting green, 10 tennis courts, 5 pools, health club, sauna, spa, beach, boating, croquet, shuffleboard, 4 bars, shops, baby-sitting, children's programs (ages 3–12), concierge, business services, no-smoking floors ▭ AE, D, DC, MC, V $$$$.

▦ **FOUR SEASONS RESORT PALM BEACH.** Relaxed elegance are the watchwords at this four-story resort on 6 acres with a delightful beach at the south end of town. Fanlight windows, marble, chintz, and palms make the hotel serene. Rooms are spacious, with a separate seating area and private balcony. Many have ocean views. You have access to the Atlantis Country Club, about 20 minutes away, with a Robert Simmons–designed par-72, 18-hole, 6,510-yard course. On weekends, piano music accompanies cocktails in the Living Room lounge. Jazz groups perform on some weekends in season. ⊠ 2800 S. Ocean Blvd., Palm Beach 33480 ☎ 561/582-2800 or 800/432-2335 📠 561/547-1557 ⊕ www.fourseasons.com/palmbeach ⮫ 200 rooms, 10 suites ♢ 3 restaurants, room service, in-room data ports, in-room safes, minibars, golf privileges, 3 tennis courts, pool, health club, hair salon, hot tub, sauna, spa, steam room, beach, boating, fishing, bicycles, 2 bars, shop, baby-sitting, children's programs (ages 3–12), dry cleaning, concierge, business services, meeting rooms, no-smoking rooms ▭ AE, D, DC, MC, V $$$$.

▦ **OCEAN BREEZE GOLF AND COUNTRY CLUB.** You can play the outstanding course at the adjoining Boca Teeca Country Club, otherwise available only to club members, while staying here. Rooms are in a three-story building, and most have a patio or balcony. Although the inn was built in the late 1960s, the refurbished small rooms are comfortable and contemporary. ⊠ 5800 N.W. 2nd Ave., Boca Raton 33487 ☎ 561/994-0400 📠 561/998-8279 ⮫ 46 rooms ♢ Restaurant, cable TV, 27-hole golf course, 6 tennis courts, no-smoking rooms ▭ AE, DC, MC, V $$.

▦ **OCEAN LODGE.** The price is right at this small motel: instead of being on the beach, it's across the street. Rooms are in a simple two-story building, and all have refrigerators. Eleven rooms also have small kitchenettes with a two-burner stove top. Restaurants are within walking distance. ⊠ 531 N. Ocean Blvd., Boca Raton 33432 ☎ 561/395-7772 or 800/782-9263 📠 561/395-0554 ⮫ 18 rooms ♢ Some kitchenettes, refrigerators, cable TV, pool, laundry facilities, no-smoking rooms ▤AE, DC, MC, V $-$$.

▧ **PALM BEACH HISTORIC INN.** Downtown, tucked between Town Hall and a sea-side residential block, this B&B has touches that include a deluxe Continental breakfast served in bed or in the courtyard and tea and cookies delivered to your room upon your arrival. Guest rooms tend toward the frilly, with lace, ribbons, and scalloped edges. Most are furnished with Victorian antiques and reproductions and have chiffon draped above the bed. ✉ 365 S. County Rd., Palm Beach 33480 ☎ 561/832-4009 🖷 561/832-6255 ⊕ www.palmbeachhistoricinn.com ⇋ 9 rooms, 4 suites ⎈ Refrigerators, cable TV, some in-room VCRs, library; no smoking ▤AE, D, DC, MC, V ⦿ CP $$-$$$$.

▧ **PGA NATIONAL RESORT & SPA.** The entire resort is richly detailed, from the out-standing mission-style rooms decorated in deep-tone florals to the lavish landscaping to the extensive sports facilities to the excellent dining options. Five tournament-caliber courses, three driving ranges, and six putting greens are on-site, and the combinations attract many national and international tournaments, including the PGA Seniors Championship, Ryder Cup, and PGA Championship. The spa is in a building styled after a Mediterranean fishing village, and six outdoor therapy pools, dubbed "Waters of the World," are joined by a collection of imported mineral salt pools. Flowering plants adorn golf courses and croquet courts amid a 240-acre nature preserve. Lodging options also include two-bedroom, two-bath cottages with kitchens. ✉ 400 Ave. of the Champions, Palm Beach 33418 ☎ 561/627-2000 or 800/633-9150 🖷 561/622-0261 ⊕ www.pga-resorts.com ⇋ 279 rooms, 60 suites, 80 cottages ⎈ 6 restaurants, room service, in-room data ports, in-room safes, some kitchens, minibars, cable TV, driving range, 5 18-hole golf courses, 19 tennis courts, 9 pools, lake, health club, hot tub, sauna, spa, boat-ing, croquet, bar, lounge, baby-sitting, children's programs (ages 3-12), business servic-es, meeting rooms, no-smoking rooms ▤AE, D, DC, MC, V $$$$.

Where to Eat

✕ **AREZZO.** The aroma of fresh garlic wafts outside this outstanding Tuscan grill at the PGA National Resort & Spa. Families are attracted by affordable prices (as well as the food), so romantics might be tempted to pass on by, but that would be a mistake. Dishes include chicken, veal, fish, steaks, a dozen pastas, and almost as many pizzas. An herb garden in the center of the room and upholstered banquettes lend an unusually relaxed feel to this upscale resort; you'll be equally comfortable in shorts or in jacket and tie. ✉ 400 Ave. of the Champions, Palm Beach Gardens ☎ 561/627-2000 ▤AE, MC, V ⊘ No lunch $$-$$$$.

✕ **LEOPARD SUPPER CLUB AND LOUNGE.** Black and red lacquer trim marks this elegant, intimate enclave in the Chesterfield hotel. Choose a cozy banquette by the wall or a table near the open kitchen. Daily specialties change with the season. You might start with sweet corn and crab chowder with Peruvian purple potato or a jumbo crab cake, moving on to an arugula or spinach salad followed by a prime strip steak or a glazed rack of lamb. The Leopard is superb for lunch and breakfast, too. ✉ 363 Cocoanut Row, Palm Beach ☎ 561/659-5800 ▤AE, DC, MC, V $$-$$$$.

✕**TA-BOÓ.** Table seating counts at this peach-stucco landmark, here since 1941: the best views are by the windows at the front of the bar or near the fireplace. Bloody Marys are the signature drink, and appetizers range from nachos with chili to beluga caviar. Entrées include Black Angus dry-aged beef or roast duck, along with main-course salads, pizzas, and burgers, plus desserts like apple crisp and "coconut lust" (a pielike fantasy with walnut cookie crust, coconut cream filling, and whipped cream topping). Drop in late at night in winter and you just might spot a celebrity or two. ⊠ 221 Worth Ave., Palm Beach ☎ 561/835–3500 ▭ AE, DC, MC, V $$$–$$$$.

Essentials

Getting Here

I-95 runs north–south, linking West Palm Beach with Daytona, Jacksonville, and the rest of the Atlantic coast to the north. The trip from Orlando to West Palm Beach via I-95 takes 180 mi.

Visitor Information

🗊 **Chamber of Commerce of the Palm Beaches** ⊠ 401 N. Flagler Dr., West Palm Beach 33401 ☎ 561/833–3711. **Palm Beach County Convention & Visitors Bureau** ⊠ 1555 Palm Beach Lakes Blvd., Suite 204, West Palm Beach 33401 ☎ 561/471–3995. **St. Lucie County Tourist Development Council** ⊠ 2300 Virginia Ave., Fort Pierce 34982 ☎ 561/462–1535. **Town of Palm Beach Chamber of Commerce** ⊠ 45 Cocoanut Row, Palm Beach 33480 ☎ 561/655–3282.

ST. AUGUSTINE & PONTE VEDRA BEACH

This tiny seaside community that looks out on the Atlantic Ocean southeast of Jacksonville isn't tiny anymore. When the PGA Tour headquarters moved here in the late 1970s, it sparked tremendous growth for the area—so much that A1A has become overdeveloped with strip malls, hotels, residential developments, and, of course, golf courses. If you're looking for a quiet, out-of-the-way golf trip, don't bother coming here. But if you want quality golf and enjoy all the amenities of an upscale resort town, this is your kind of place.

The best course in the area, bar none, is the Stadium course at the Tournament Players Club at Sawgrass. Home of the Players Championship on the PGA Tour, the Pete Dye course alternates between cruel and fun, with wonderful mounding, greens edged with railroad ties, oh, and let's not forget the famous island par-3 17th hole. Almost as good is the second course at Sawgrass: the Valley. But if you can only play one, do everything you can to get on the Stadium course. It ranked 67th on *Golf Digest*'s list of America's 100 Greatest Courses.

Ponte Vedra Inn & Club (36)					
Lagoon (18)	5,574/4,571	70/70	67.3/66.6	116/113	$120
Ocean (18)	6,811/4,967	72/73	73.2/69.5	138/117	$210
Royal St. Augustine Golf and Country Club (18)	6,529	71	71.9	137	$29/$46
Tournament Players Club (36)					
Stadium (18)	6,954/5,000	72/72	75.0/65.3	149/125	$115/$280
Valley (18)	6,864/5,126	72/72	72.8/68.7	130/120	$75/$135
World Golf Village (36)					
King & Bear (18)	7,279/5,119	72/72	75.2/70.1	141/123	$89/$175
Slammer & Squire (18)	6,940/5,001	72/72	73.8/69.1	135/116	$69/$150

In the last decade, the area also added another golf destination worth your time. The World Golf Village, made up of shops, restaurants, a hotel, and the World Golf Hall of Fame and museum, also has 36 holes of golf. It's roughly 25 minutes south of Ponte Vedra heading toward St. Augustine on I-95.

The first course to open there in 1998, the Slammer & Squire, is pure Florida resort golf. With the consultation of Gene Sarazen (the Squire) and Sam Snead (the Slammer), this attractive course was built through the tall pines and swampland of North Florida. Two years later, Arnold Palmer and Jack Nicklaus collaborated and designed the King & Bear. Easily the better of the two, you can see design preferences of both great players in this course.

Courses

Golf Digest REVIEWS

PONTE VEDRA INN & CLUB. Facility Holes: 36. Cart Fee: Included in green fee. Discounts: Juniors. Walking: Walking at certain times. Season: Year-round. High: Mar.–May. Tee Times: Call golf shop. Notes: Range (grass, mat), lodging (221). ⊠ 200 Ponte Vedra Blvd., Ponte Vedra Beach 32082, 20 mi from Jacksonville ☎ 904/285-1111 or 800/234-7842 ⊕ www.pvresorts.com ⊟ AE, D, DC, MC, V.

Lagoon. Holes: 18. Opened: 1978. Architect: Joe Lee. Yards: 5,574/4,571. Par: 70/70. Course Rating: 67.3/66.6. Slope: 116/113. Green Fee: $120. *Comments: Not as old as the Ocean course. More old-Florida resort golf in style. Watch out for condos.* ★ ★ ½

Ocean. Holes: 18. Opened: 1928. Architect: Herbert Strong/Bobby Weed. Yards: 6,811/4,967. Par: 72/73. Course Rating: 73.2/69.5. Slope: 138/117. Green Fee: $210. *Comments: One of the oldest courses in Florida. Has the nation's original island green at the 16th.* ★ ★ ★ ½

ROYAL ST. AUGUSTINE GOLF AND COUNTRY CLUB. Facility Holes: 18. Opened: 2001. Architect: J. Christopher Commins. Yards: 6,529. Par: 71. Course Rating: 71.9. Slope: 137. Green Fee: $29/$46. Cart Fee: Included in green fee. ⊠ 301 Royal St. Augustine Pkwy., St. Augustine 32095 ☎ 904/824-4653 ⊟ MC, V. *Comments: One exit* *south of the World Golf Village on I–95. Newest course to the area is a little crammed, but worth your time.* UR

TOURNAMENT PLAYERS CLUB AT SAWGRASS. Facility Holes: 36. Cart Fee: $31 per person. Discounts: Juniors. Walking: Walking with caddie. Season: Year-round. High: Jan.–May. Tee Times: Call golf shop. Notes: Range (grass), lodging (508). ✉ 110 TPC Blvd., Ponte Vedra Beach 32082, 15 mi from Jacksonville ☎ 904/273–3235 ⊕ www. tpcsawgrass.com ▤ AE, DC, MC, V.

Stadium. Holes: 18. Opened: 1980. Architect: Pete Dye. Yards: 6,954/5,000. Par: 72/72. Course Rating: 75.0/65.3. Slope: 149/125. Green Fee: $115/$280. *Comments: The best public-access golf course in Florida. Play it from the back tees and be prepared for a beating.* ★ ★ ★ ★ ½

Valley. Holes: 18. Opened: 1987. Architect: Pete Dye/Bobby Weed. Yards: 6,864/5,126. Par: 72/72. Course Rating: 72.8/68.7. Slope: 130/120. Green Fee: $75/$135. *Comments: Should be called the "Water course," thanks to a plethora of streams, ponds, and lakes guarding the fairways and greens. If the Stadium course wasn't next door, this course would get higher marks.* ★ ★ ★ ★

WORLD GOLF VILLAGE. Facility Holes: 36. Cart Fee: Included in green fee. Discounts: Guest, twilight, juniors. Walking: Unrestricted walking. Season: Year-round. High: Feb.– May. Tee Times: Call golf shop. Notes: Metal spikes, range (grass), lodging (600). ✉ World Golf Village, St. Augustine 32092, 5 mi from St. Augustine ☎ 904/940–6200 or 866/940–6088 ⊕ www.wgv.com ▤ AE, D, MC, V.

King & Bear. Holes: 18. Opened: 2000. Architect: Arnold Palmer/Jack Nicklaus. Yards: 7,279/5,119. Par: 72/72. Course Rating: 75.2/70.1. Slope: 141/123. Green Fee: $89/$175. *Comments: Second-best course in the area. Jack and Arnie designed a fun, scenic Florida golf experience. Bunkers are huge and greens are tricky. Enticing layout.* UR

Slammer & Squire. Holes: 18. Opened: 1998. Architect: Bobby Weed/Sam Snead/Gene Sarazen. Yards: 6,940/5,001. Par: 72/72. Course Rating: 73.8/69.1. Slope: 135/116. Green Fee: $69/$150. *Comments: Play this one only if you can also play the King & Bear. Typical of modern golf course construction in Florida. Lots of water and mounding. Complimentary range balls, and Global Positioning System in every golf cart.* ★ ★ ★ ★ ½

Where to Stay

🏨 **CASA MONICA HOTEL.** Hand-stenciled Moorish columns and arches, handcrafted chandeliers, and gilded iron tables decorate the lobby of this late-1800s Flagler-era masterpiece. A retreat for the nation's wealthiest until the Great Depression put it out of business, it has returned to its perch as St. Augustine's grande dame. The turrets, towers, and wrought-iron balconies offer a hint of what's inside. Rooms—dressed in blues, greens, and whites—include wrought-iron two- and four-poster beds and mahogany writing desks and nightstands. ✉ 95 Cordova St., 32084 ☎ 904/827–1888 or 800/648– 1888 🖷 904/827–0426 ⊕ www.casamonica.com ⤶ 138 rooms, 14 suites ♿ 2 restaurants, in-room data ports, in-room safes, some minibars, some microwaves, some refrigerators, cable TV with movies and video games, pool, gym, outdoor hot tub, bar, shop,

TOURNAMENT GOLF'S REVOLUTION

Jerry Pate's 1980 win at the inaugural Tournament Players Championship at the brand-new Sawgrass ushered in a new era of course design. The idea of a gallery-friendly golf course built specifically to host professional tournaments changed the way golf was accepted by the public and has helped give the PGA Tour the popularity it enjoys today. The TPC concept has today blossomed into more than 25 courses, although Sawgrass remains the favorite of many. The public can tee up at roughly half of the TPC courses.

dry cleaning, laundry service, concierge, Internet, business services, meeting rooms, parking (fee), no-smoking floors ⊟AE, DC, MC, V $$$-$$$$.

🏨 **GRANDE VILLAS AT WORLD GOLF VILLAGE.** Watch the action at the 17th and 18th holes from many rooms at this golfer's haven. One- and two-bedroom units are in three six-story pink-and-green buildings that overlook a golf course and lakes in World Golf Village. Rooms are painted deep shades of green or ocher and appointed with framed prints and earth-tone fabrics. All units have a separate living room, a full kitchen, a washer and dryer, and a balcony. ⊠ 100 Front 9 Dr., 32092 ☎ 904/940-2000 or 800/477-3340 🖷 904/940-2092 ⊕ www.bluegreenrentals.com ↳ 134 villas ⚑ 2 restaurants, pizzeria, in-room data ports, some kitchens, some kitchenettes, some refrigerators, cable TV, in-room VCRs, golf privileges, 2 tennis courts, pool, wading pool, health club, outdoor hot tub, basketball, volleyball, library, video game room, baby-sitting, playground, dry cleaning, laundry facilities, laundry service, concierge, Internet, business services, meeting rooms, free parking, no-smoking rooms ⊟AE, D, DC, MC, V $$$.

🏨 **THE LODGE & CLUB.** The sister property of the Ponte Vedra Inn & Club has a Mediterranean-villa inspired Spanish tile roof and a white-stucco exterior. Rooms are classy and elegant, with cozy window seats, appealing artwork, and private balconies overlooking the Atlantic; some units include a whirlpool tub and gas fireplace. The restaurants, bar, and heated pools have more ocean views. ⊠ 607 Ponte Vedra Blvd., Ponte Vedra Beach 32080 ☎ 904/273-9500 or 800/243-4304 🖷 904/273-0210 ⊕ www.pvresorts.com ↳ 32 rooms, 24 suites ⚑ 2 restaurants, fans, in-room data ports, in-room safes, some in-room hot tubs, some kitchenettes, minibars, some refrigerators, cable TV, golf privileges, 3 pools, health club, spa, beach, boating, fishing, bicycles, bar, lounge, shops, children's programs (ages 4–12), playground, laundry service, meeting rooms, no-smoking rooms ⊟AE, D, DC, MC, V $$$$.

🏨 **PONTE VEDRA INN & CLUB.** Accommodations at this 1928 landmark country-club resort are in a series of white-stucco Spanish-style buildings lining the beach; rooms are extra large and most have ocean views. The main house holds the registration area and some common spaces, including a large living room with fireplace. Part of what *Golf Digest* designated as one of the Top 75 Resorts in America, the two 18-hole courses have lagoons, undulating fairways, and greens protected by steep-faced bunkers. A prevailing sea breeze makes shots challenging. ⊠ 200 Ponte Vedra Blvd., Ponte Vedra Beach 32082 ☎ 904/285-1111 or 800/234-7842 🖷 904/285-2111 ⊕ www.pvresorts.com ↳ 180 rooms, 41 suites ⚑ 3 restaurants, snack bar, fans, in-room data ports, some kitchenettes, minibars, refrigerators, cable TV, 2 18-hole golf courses, 15 tennis courts, pro shop, 4 pools, health club, spa, beach, boating, fishing, bicycles, 2 bars, lounge, shops, children's programs (ages 4–12), laundry service, business services, meeting rooms, no-smoking rooms ⊟AE, D, DC, MC, V $$$$.

⊞ RENAISSANCE AT WORLD GOLF VILLAGE RESORT. When you want to be within walking distance of all World Golf Village has to offer, this full-service resort is an excellent choice. The 10-story building dwarfs the surrounding palm trees and overlooks a peaceful lake. Rooms and suites surround a soaring atrium, at the bottom of which is a restaurant set amid tropical foliage and cool streams. Units are oversize and are furnished in muted pastels. The hotel has an IMAX movie theater, adjoins a convention center, is adjacent to the World Golf Hall of Fame, and borders the championship golf course. ⊠ 500 S. Legacy Tr., 32092 ☎ 904/940–8000 or 800/228–9290 ⊟ 904/940–8008 ⊕ www.wgv.com ⥲ 271 rooms, 40 suites ⋄ 2 restaurants, in-room data ports, minibars, refrigerators, cable TV with movies, golf privileges, putting green, pool, health club, outdoor hot tub, sauna, beach, parasailing, fishing, billiards, bar, cinema, shops, baby-sitting, dry cleaning, laundry facilities, concierge, Internet, business services, meeting rooms, free parking, no-smoking rooms ⊟AE, D, DC, MC, V $$–$$$.

⊞ SAWGRASS MARRIOTT RESORT. The main building and lobby areas feel more like a business hotel than like a plush resort, but the grounds are beautifully manicured and the rooms are spacious and well furnished, with rich carpets and drapes, wood furniture, and roomy bathrooms. The resort is surrounded by five championship golf courses, including the famous TPC Stadium course. Also nearby are the international headquarters of the Association of Tennis Professionals (the governing body of the men's professional tennis circuit). Whether you've come to laze about or spend some time on the courts or fairways, this is truly a full-service resort. ⊠ 1000 PGA Blvd., Ponte Vedra Beach 32082 ☎ 904/285–7777 or 800/457–4653 ⊟ 904/285–0906 ⊕ www.marriotthotels.com ⥲ 508 rooms, 21 suites ⋄ 3 restaurants, room service, in-room data ports, some kitchens, minibars, cable TV with movies, golf privileges, 4 tennis courts, pro shop, 3 pools, wading pool, gym, hot tub, sauna, beach, boating, bicycles, 2 bars, lounge, shop, children's programs (ages 3–12), playground, laundry facilities, laundry service, concierge, Internet, business services, meeting rooms, some pets allowed (fee), no-smoking rooms ⊟AE, D, DC, MC, V $$$–$$$$.

Where to Eat

✕ HARRY'S SEAFOOD BAR AND GRILL. Although this casual eatery calls itself a seafood bar and grill, you might think you're on Bourbon Street when you step inside and get a whiff of the spicy cooking with a definite New Orleans flair. Red beans with rice and sausage, shrimp and crab étouffée, and jambalaya are house specialties, but the menu also includes lobster and seafood pasta, catfish Pontchartrain, and tasty desserts such as bayou brownies and bananas Foster. Dine inside or in the cool courtyard just across from Matanzas Bay. ⊠ 46 Avenida Menendez ☎ 904/824–7765 ⊟AE, MC, V $–$$$$.

✕ 95 CORDOVA. Find twists on traditional southwestern, Florida, and Asian food in the dining room of the historic Casa Monica Hotel. Appetizers include chicken-and-white bean gumbo, seafood-and-broccoli crepes, and St. Augustine shrimp cocktail. For entrées, shrimp and andouille combine with penne; apple, walnut, sausage, and rum gravy accompany pork tenderloin; and a maple-mustard-tarragon sauce dresses the blackened chicken. Save room for the St. Johns mud cake with fresh berry sauce. Other draws are a six-course tasting menu that changes weekly and an always-packed Sunday brunch. ⊠ 115 Cordova St. ☎ 904/810–6810 ⊟ AE, MC, V $$$–$$$$.

Essentials

Getting Here
St. Augustine is 100 mi north of Orlando via I–4 and I–95.

Visitor Information
🔰 **Amelia Island–Fernandina Beach Chamber of Commerce** ⊠ 102 Centre St., Amelia Island 32034 ☎ 904/261–3248 or 800/226–3542. **Daytona Convention and Visitors Bureau** ⊠ 126 E. Orange Ave., Daytona 32120 ☎ 800/854–1234 ⊕ www.daytonabeach.com. **Jacksonville and Its Beaches Convention & Visitors Bureau** ⊠ 6 E. Bay St., Suite 200, Jacksonville 32202 ☎ 904/798–9111 ⊕ www.jaxcvb.com. **St. Augustine, Ponte Vedra & The Beaches Visitors & Convention Bureau** ⊠ 10 Castillo Dr., St. Augustine 32084 ☎ 800/653–2489 ⊕ www.visitoldcity.com.

TAMPA & ST. PETERSBURG

It's hard to believe that an area as widespread as the bay cities of Tampa and St. Petersburg would be lacking in top-notch public golf courses. Especially considering all the waterfront property that can be found here. But in the past, the area's attitude toward golf was that there were so many other diversions, it wasn't a priority. That has changed in recent years, and the widespread metropolitan area has begun to catch up with the rest of the state in terms of quality golf.

If you want to hit as many of the spots on this list as you can, be prepared to do some driving. Just getting from downtown Tampa to downtown St. Petersburg takes roughly 30 minutes and none of the golf destinations listed here are close to each other. If time is a concern, be sure to stay and play at the Westin Innisbrook Golf Resort in Palm Harbor, north of St. Petersburg. The Copperhead is the signature course as it plays host to an annual event on the PGA Tour. It's one of the best public-access courses in Florida featuring hills, tight fairways, and a few ponds and lakes. The resort sank money into its other three courses in the last few years, making it a well-rounded golf destination.

If you have an extra day on your schedule while visiting this area, be sure to jump on the new 42-mi Suncoast Parkway and head north. When the highway ends, you're right at the entrance to World Woods Golf Club. If it feels like you're in the middle of nowhere, that's because you are. This wonderful public golf facility has two very good 18-hole courses, another 9-hole short course, and one of the best practice facilities anywhere. It was originally going to be a private club and then became a premium public facility. But

TAMPA & ST. PETERSBURG COURSES	YARDAGE	PAR	COURSE	SLOPE	GREEN FEE
Belleview Biltmore Resort & Golf Club (18)	6,614/5,143	71/71	70.7/72.1	118/119	$30/$40
Lake Jovita Golf & Country Club (18)	7,151/5,091	72/72	74.4/68.4	140/136	$65/$115
Saddlebrook Resort (36)					$70/$180
Palmer (18)	6,469/5,187	71/71	71.9/71.0	134/127	
Saddlebrook (18)	6,564/4,941	70/70	72.0/70.6	127/126	
Tournament Players Club of Tampa Bay (18)	6,898/5,036	71/71	73.6/69.1	135/119	$59/$145
Westin Innisbrook Golf Resort (72)					
Copperhead (18)	7,295/5,605	71/71	75.6/71.8	134/130	$100/$200
Highlands North (18)	6,515/4,955	70/70	70.5/68.4	125/118	$60/$130
Highlands South (18)	6,768/4,975	71/71	72.0/68.9	127/121	$60/$130
Island (18)	7,063/5,578	72/72	74.1/73.0	132/129	$80/$160
Westchase Golf Club (18)	6,699/5,205	72/72	72.6/70.8	131/127	$29/$69
World Woods Golf Club (36)					
Pine Barrens (18)	6,902/5,301	71/71	73.3/71.0	136/124	$40/$120
Rolling Oaks (18)	6,985/5,245	72/72	73.5/70.7	136/128	$40/$110

prices have dropped, and now it's one of the best values in golf. You can even check it out on the way home as it's about 90 minutes from Orlando.

Courses

Golf Digest REVIEWS

BELLEVIEW BILTMORE RESORT & GOLF CLUB. Facility Holes: 18. Opened: 1926. Architect: Donald Ross. Yards: 6,614/5,143. Par: 71/71. Course Rating: 70.7/72.1. Slope: 118/119. Green Fee: $30/$40. Cart Fee: Included in green fee. Walking: Mandatory cart. Season: Year-round. Tee Times: Call up to 4 days in advance. ✉ 1501 Indian Rocks Rd., Belleair 33756, 1 mi from Clearwater ☎ 727/581-5498 ⊕ www.belleviewbiltmore.com ▤ AE, D, MC, V. *Comments: Old Donald Ross course is never in great shape but is still a worthwhile round because of the architect.* ★ ★

LAKE JOVITA GOLF & COUNTRY CLUB. Facility Holes: 18. Opened: 1999. Architect: Kurt Sandness/Tom Lehman. Yards: 7,151/5,091. Par: 72/72. Course Rating: 74.4/68.4. Slope: 140/136. Green Fee: $65/$115. Cart Fee: Included in green fee. Walking: Unrestricted walking. Season: Year-round. Tee Times: Call golf shop. Notes: Range (grass). ✉ 12900 Lake Jovita Blvd., Dade City 33525, 20 mi from Tampa ☎ 352/588-9200 or 877/481-2652 ⊕ www.lakejovita.com ▤ AE, MC, V. *Comments: Well north of Tampa, this is one of the top 20 courses in Florida.* ★ ★ ★ ★ ½

SADDLEBROOK RESORT. Facility Holes: 36. Green Fee: $70/$180. Cart Fee: Included in green fee. Discounts: Guest. Walking: Mandatory cart. Season: Year-round. Tee Times: Call golf shop. Notes: Range (grass). ✉ 5700 Saddlebrook Way, Wesley Chapel 33543, 20 mi from Tampa ☎ 813/973-1111 or 800/729-8383 ⊕ www.saddlebrookresort.com ▤ AE, D, MC, V.

Palmer. Holes: 18. Opened: 1986. Architect: Arnold Palmer/Ed Seay. Yards: 6,469/5,187. Par: 71/71. Course Rating: 71.9/71.0. Slope: 134/127. *Comments: Punishing if you're not hitting the ball straight. A little expensive but always in good shape.* ★ ★ ★ ★

Saddlebrook. Holes: 18. Opened: 1976. Architect: Dean Refram. Yards: 6,564/4,941. Par: 70/70. Course Rating: 72.0/70.6. Slope: 127/126. *Comments: Not as tight as the Palmer. Good resort course routed through hotel property.* ★ ★ ★ ★

TOURNAMENT PLAYERS CLUB OF TAMPA BAY. Facility Holes: 18. Opened: 1991. Architect: Bobby Weed/Chi Chi Rodriguez. Yards: 6,898/5,036. Par: 71/71. Course Rating: 73.6/69.1. Slope: 135/119. Green Fee: $59/$145. Cart Fee: Included in green fee. Discounts: Weekdays, twilight, juniors. Walking: Walking with caddie. Season: Year-round. High: Jan.–Mar. Tee Times: Call 60 days in advance. Notes: Range (grass). ✉ 5300 W. Lutz Lake Fern Rd., Lutz 33558, 15 mi from Tampa ☎ 813/949-0090 ⊕ www.tpc.com ▤ AE, DC, MC, V. *Comments: A little pricey in winter for the quality of golf. But still solid. Home of the Champion Tour's Verizon Classic.* ★ ★ ★ ★ ¹/₂

WESTCHASE GOLF CLUB. Facility Holes: 18. Opened: 1992. Architect: Clifton/Ezell/ Clifton. Yards: 6,699/5,205. Par: 72/72. Course Rating: 72.6/70.8. Slope: 131/127. Green Fee: $29/$69. Cart Fee: Included in green fee. Discounts: Weekdays, twilight, juniors. Walking: Mandatory cart. Season: Year-round. High: Jan.–Apr. Tee Times: Call 3 days in advance. Notes: Range (grass). ✉ 11602 Westchase Dr., Tampa 33626 ☎ 813/854-2331 ⊕ www.westchasegc.com ▤ AE, MC, V. *Comments: A housing-development course routed through dense forests of pines, palms, and mangroves north of Tampa. Tight fairways.* ★ ★ ★ ¹/₂

WESTIN INNISBROOK GOLF RESORT. Facility Holes: 72. Cart Fee: Included in green fee. Discounts: Guest, twilight, juniors. Walking: Mandatory cart. Season: Year-round. Tee Times: Call golf shop. Notes: Metal spikes, range (grass), lodging (600). ✉ 36750 Hwy. 19 N, Palm Harbor 34684, 25 mi from Tampa ☎ 727/942-2000 ⊕ www.westin-innisbrook.com ▤ AE, D, MC, V.

Copperhead. Holes: 18. Opened: 1972. Architect: Edward Lawrence Packard/Roger Packard. Yards: 7,295/5,605. Par: 71/71. Course Rating: 75.6/71.8. Slope: 134/130. Green Fee: $100/$200. *Comments: Fantastic Florida course. Very difficult—hilly for Central Florida. Use that 3-wood to stay in play.* ★ ★ ★ ★ ¹/₂

Highlands North. Holes: 18. Opened: 1971. Architect: Lawrence Packard. Yards: 6,515/ 4,955. Par: 70/70. Course Rating: 70.5/68.4. Slope: 125/118. Green Fee: $60/$130. *Comments: A little short and tight, so hit irons off the tees. Water comes into play on many holes.* ★ ★ ★

Highlands South. Holes: 18. Opened: 1997. Architect: Edward Lawrence Packard. Yards: 6,768/4,975. Par: 71/71. Course Rating: 72.0/68.9. Slope: 127/121. Green Fee: $60/$130. *Comments: Pinehurst feel. Fun to play and not as punishing as Copperhead and Island courses.* ★ ★ ★ ¹/₂

Island. Holes: 18. Opened: 1970. Architect: Edward Lawrence Packard. Yards: 7,063/ 5,578. Par: 72/72. Course Rating: 74.1/73.0. Slope: 132/129. Green Fee: $80/$160. *Comments: A strong second to Copperhead thanks to some upgrading. Watch out for the water.* ★ ★ ★ ★ ¹/₂

WORLD WOODS GOLF CLUB. Facility Holes: 36. Opened: 1993. Architect: Tom Fazio. Cart Fee: Included in green fee. Discounts: Weekdays, twilight, juniors. Walking: Unrestricted walking. Season: Year-round. High: Jan.–Mar. Tee Times: Call 30 days in advance. Notes: Range (grass). Facility also has a 9-hole par-3 course and 4 practice holes. ⊠ 17590 Ponce de Leon Blvd., Brooksville 34614, 60 mi from Tampa ☎ 352/796–5500 ⊕ www.worldwoods.com ⊟ AE, D, DC, MC, V.

Pine Barrens. Holes: 18. Yards: 6,902/5,301. Par: 71/71. Course Rating: 73.3/71.0. Slope: 136/124. Green Fee: $40/$120. *Comments: Inspired by Pine Valley, Golf Digest's number one golf course in America. Massive sand waste areas and decent elevation changes. Visually striking—and tough.* ★ ★ ★ ★ ★

Rolling Oaks. Holes: 18. Yards: 6,985/5,245. Par: 72/72. Course Rating: 73.5/70.7. Slope: 136/128. Green Fee: $40/$110. *Comments: White-powder bunkers and rolling terrain will remind you of country-club designs in the Northeast and Midwest. A very good course.* ★ ★ ★ ★ ¹/₂

Where to Stay

⚏ **DON CESAR BEACH RESORT.** Once a favorite of Scott and Zelda Fitzgerald, this sprawling beachfront "Pink Palace" has long been a Gulf Coast landmark because of its remarkable architecture. Steeped in early-1900s elegance, the hotel claims a rich history, complete with a resident ghost. The restaurant, Maritana Grille, specializes in Florida seafood and is lined with huge saltwater fish tanks. The more casual Don CeSar Beach House, less than a half mile from the main building, has one-bedroom suites and a great little beach bar. ⊠ 3400 Gulf Blvd., St. Pete Beach 33706 ☎ 727/360–1881 🖷 813/367–3609 ⊕ www.doncesar.com ⇆ 277 rooms, 50 suites at resort; 63 rooms at Beach House ⌂ 3 restaurants, ice cream parlor, room service, in-room data ports, some kitchens, golf privileges, 2 pools, gym, hair salon, 2 spas, beach, boating, jet skiing, parasailing, 3 bars, shops, baby-sitting, children's programs (ages 4–12), dry cleaning, laundry facilities, laundry service, concierge, business services, meeting room, airport shuttle, no-smoking rooms ⊟ AE, DC, MC, V $$$$.

⚏ **RENAISSANCE VINOY RESORT.** Rooms in the original 1925 hotel building, listed on the National Register of Historic Places, have more character than others at the property, but all of the spacious units are comfortable and stylish. They come with three phones, two TVs, and bathrobes. A tiny beach adjoins the property. Transportation is provided to ocean beaches 20 minutes away. Other offerings include a big marina and tours that include downtown museums. The location makes the hotel a good base for walking to downtown museums or the Pier and the BayWalk entertainment complexes. ⊠ 501 5th Ave. NE, St. Petersburg 33701 ☎ 727/894–1000 🖷 727/822–2785 ⊕ www.renaissancehotels.com ⇆ 360 rooms ⌂ 5 restaurants, room service, in-room data ports, minibars, 18-hole golf course, 14 tennis courts, 2 pools, health club, hair salon, outdoor hot tub, massage, dock, boating, marina, croquet, 2 bars, lobby lounge, shop, baby-sitting, laundry facilities, laundry service, concierge, business services, car rental, no-smoking rooms ⊟ AE, DC, MC, V $$$$.

⚏ **SADDLEBROOK RESORT TAMPA.** This is arguably one of Florida's premier resorts of its type, largely because it has so many things in one spot. The heavily wooded grounds sprawl over 480 acres just 15 mi north of Tampa. Varied accommodations include many one- and two-bedroom, two-bath suites with kitchens. ⊠ 5700 Saddlebrook Way, Wesley Chapel 33543 ☎ 813/973-1111 or 800/729-8383 ᕱ 813/773-4504 ⊕ www.saddlebrookresort.com ↘ 790 units ⌂ 4 restaurants, room service, in-room data ports, some kitchens, some minibars, cable TV, some in-room VCRs, driving range, 2 18-hole golf courses, 45 tennis courts, pro shop, pool, wading pool, health club, sauna, spa, fishing, bicycles, 2 bars, concierge, business services, convention center, meeting rooms, no-smoking rooms ⊟ AE, D, DC, MC, V ⭘︎ MAP $$$$.

TRADEWINDS RESORT. Most rooms have a view of the beach at this large but intimate 18-acre gulf-front property. Choose from parlor rooms; one-, two-, and three-bedroom suites; and penthouses in four buildings. The resort has some of the showmanship of an Orlando hotel, with a huge man-made lagoon inside the complex, complete with boats on its labyrinthine waterways. ⊠ 5500 Gulf Blvd., St. Pete Beach 33706 ☎ 727/363-2212 or 800/237-0707 ᕱ 727/562-1214 ⊕ www.tradewindsresort.com ↘ 744 rooms, 303 suites (Island Grand: 585 rooms, 200 suites; Sandpiper: 159 rooms, 103 suites) ⌂ 11 restaurants, ice cream parlor, pizzeria, in-room data ports, in-room safes, some kitchenettes, some minibars, refrigerators, cable TV, some in-room VCRs, 4 tennis courts, 4 pools, health club, spa, jet skiing, parasailing, 4 lounges, children's programs (ages 4-12), laundry facilities, laundry service, Internet, business services, meeting rooms, no-smoking rooms ⊟ AE, D, DC, MC, V $$$$.

WESTIN INNISBROOK RESORT. Seventy-two holes of championship golf, including the famed Copperhead and Island courses, are minutes from this sprawling, 600-acre resort. Grounds are beautifully maintained, and guest suites are in 28 two-story lodges tucked in the trees between golf courses. Some of the roomy units have balconies or patios. Once fairly remote, the Innisbrook has built in enough restaurant and lounge choices to make it self-contained, though today the area around it offers plenty of competition. The children's program is excellent. ⊠ 36750 U.S. 19 N, Palm Harbor 34684 ☎ 727/942-2000 ᕱ 727/942-5576 ⊕ www.westin-innisbrook.com ↘ 1,000 rooms, 700 suites ⌂ 4 restaurants, in-room data ports, in-room safes, some kitchenettes, minibars, cable TV with movies, driving range, 4 18-hole golf courses, miniature golf, putting green, 13 tennis courts, 6 pools, health club, spa, racquetball, 5 bars, nightclub, baby-sitting, children's programs (ages 3-12), playground, dry cleaning, laundry service, concierge, business services, meeting rooms, airport shuttle, car rental, no-smoking rooms ⊟ AE, DC, MC, V $$$$.

Where to Eat

✕ **BERN'S STEAK HOUSE.** Fine mahogany paneling and ornate chandeliers define the elegance at legendary Bern's. Chef-owner Bern Lexer ages his own beef, grows his own organic vegetables, roasts his own coffee, and maintains his own saltwater fish tanks. The wine list includes some 7,000 selections (with 1,800 dessert wines), ranging from $10 to $10,000 a bottle. Dinners are served in several small rooms filled with gaudy—or quaint, depending on your taste—memorabilia. After dinner, head upstairs to intimate, glass-enclosed rooms for dessert. ⊠ 1208 S. Howard Ave., Tampa ☎ 813/251-2421 ⊕ www.bernssteakhouse.com ⊟ AE, DC, MC, V ⊘ No lunch $$$-$$$$.

✕ **COLUMBIA.** A fixture since 1905, this magnificent structure occupies a city block and has spacious dining rooms and a sunny atrium. Before Ybor City became trendy, Columbia carried the neighborhood on its shoulders, drawing people whose families had eaten here for generations. They still come. The paella is possibly the best in Florida and the Columbia 1905 salad—with ham, olives, cheese, and garlic—is legendary. There's flamenco dancing nightly, and you can buy and smoke hand-rolled cigars in the bar. A shop across the street sells the restaurant's hand-painted tiles. Columbia has six additional locations in Florida. ⊠ 2117 E. 7th Ave., Tampa ☎ 813/248-4961 ⊕ www. columbiarestaurant.com ⊟ AE, DC, MC, V $$–$$$$.

✕ **MARCHAND'S GRILL.** Once the Pompeii Room in the former Vinoy Hotel, opened in 1925, this wonderful eatery has frescoed ceilings and a spectacular view of Tampa Bay and the nearby boat docks. The food is impressive as well. The imaginative menu includes farfalle with Portobello mushrooms, Asiago cheese, and sun-dried tomato pesto; prosciutto-wrapped prawns with porcini mushroom fettuccine; and grilled swordfish with a tropical fruit salsa. The wine list is extensive. There is live music Tuesday through Saturday nights. ⊠ Renaissance Vinoy Resort, 501 5th Ave. NE, St. Petersburg ☎ 727/894-1000 ⊟ AE, DC, MC, V $$$–$$$$.

✕ **MISE EN PLACE.** Owners Marty and Marianne Blitz have become local celebrities thanks to a menu replete with Floribbean dishes, including creative takes on swordfish and grouper. Other entrées include roast duck and the occasional venison. Marty's forte is combining seemingly incompatible ingredients to make a masterpiece. Try the shrimp, manchego cheese, and chorizo grits with Puerto Rican red-bean salsa. The Blitzes operate 442, the ultracool jazz club next door, which serves appetizers from the Mise en Place kitchen. ⊠ 442 W. Kennedy Blvd. ☎ 813/254-5373 ⊕ www.miseonline.com ⊟ AE, D, DC, MC, V ⊙ Closed Sun. $$–$$$$.

Essentials

Getting Here

Coming from Orlando, you're likely to drive west into Tampa on I-4. It's an hour drive—add another 30 minutes to get to St. Petersburg.

Visitor Information

🛈 **Greater Tampa Chamber of Commerce** ⬠ Box 420, Tampa 33601 ☎ 813/228-7777, 813/223-1111 Ext. 44 visitor information department ⊕ www.tampachamber.com. **St. Petersburg Area Chamber of Commerce** ⊠ 100 2nd Ave. N, St. Petersburg 33701 ☎ 727/821-4069 ⊕ www.stpete.com. **St. Petersburg/Clearwater Area Convention & Visitors Bureau** ⊠ 14450 46th St. N, Suite 108, St. Petersburg 33762 ☎ 727/464-7200 ⊕ www. floridasbeach.com. **Tampa Bay Beaches Chamber of Commerce** ⊠ 6990 Gulf Blvd., St. Pete Beach 33706 ☎ 727/360-6957 or 800/944-1847 ⊕ www.tampabaybeaches.com. **Tampa Bay Convention and Visitors Bureau** ⊠ 111 Madison St., Suite 1010, Tampa 33601-0519 ☎ 813/223-1111 or 800/826-8358 ⊕ www.visittampabay.com.

AROUND
PHILADELPHIA

Country Club of Hershey

By Matthew Rudy and Laura Knowles Callanan

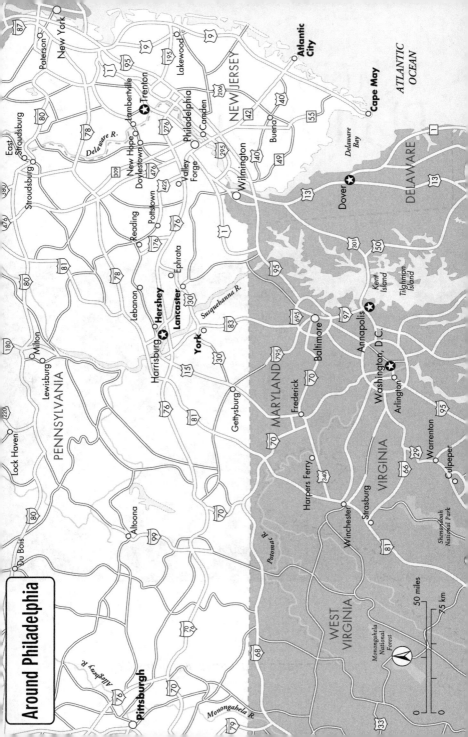

Around Philadelphia

Organized golf came to America in 1864, when the original five private clubs met to form the United States Golf Association. Just two years later, Philadelphia's golf association was created, its founding members the Aronomink Golf Club, Philadelphia Cricket Club, and Philadelphia Country Club. From the 1907 U.S. Open at Philadelphia Cricket Club to the Senior PGA and U.S. Women's Amateur championships at Aronomink and Philadelphia Country Club in 2003, Philadelphia has had a long and rich golf tradition. Bobby Jones finished the original Grand Slam at Merion in 1930, winning the U.S. Amateur to go with his U.S. Open, British Open, and British Amateur titles. Byron Nelson, Ben Hogan, and Lee Trevino all won U.S. Opens on Philadelphia courses.

So it is only fitting that you can drive 20 mi in any direction from the city, from the Main Line west of town to the Atlantic City corridor, and find wonderful golf courses. New daily-fee courses are springing up in Bucks County, north of the city, and in southern New Jersey, just across the river.

Other good options are a little farther afield. Atlantic City is a one-hour shot east on the Black Horse Pike. Sure there are gambling and shows here, but more important for present company, there's also a piece of golf history. The Seaview Marriott Resort's Bay course is a treasure, with funky Donald Ross–designed greens and windblown approaches. Make your way south from Atlantic City for some equally good golf. Cape May National, on New Jersey's southern tip, is a spectacular test carved into a nature preserve.

Destinations west and north of Philly don't have the benefit of Atlantic frontage, but they make up for it with mature trees and rolling landscapes. The Country Club of Hershey gained fame in the 1940s as Ben Hogan's home course. Now, you can visit the chocolate factory in the morning and play a round there in the afternoon—as long as you stay at a Hershey resort.

ATLANTIC CITY, NJ

Despite the casinos, nobody ever confuses Atlantic City with Las Vegas, but when it comes to golf, that's not necessarily a bad thing. Water constraints and the desert landscape limit possible course designs in Nevada, but the rolling, sandy soil around Atlantic City is perfect for golf courses. Sure, you won't find any Celine Dion command performances on the fading Atlantic

Blue Heron Pines Golf Club (36)					$51/$126
East (18)	7,300/5,500	71/71	74.8/69.0	135/120	
West (18)	6,777/5,053	72/72	72.9/69.2	132/119	
Buena Vista Country Club (18)	6,869/5,651	72/72	71.8/72.6	127/124	$27/$35
Eagle Ridge Golf Course (18)	6,607/4,792	71/71	72.4/68.3	132/125	$37/$57
Harbor Pines Golf Club (18)	6,827/5,099	72/72	73.0/68.8	134/118	$54/$120
Lakewood Country Club (18)	6,566/5,135	72/72	71.7/65.9	133/116	$27/$32
Mays Landing Country Club (18)	6,662/5,432	72/71	71.8/69.7	123/114	$20/$70
Ocean County Golf Course at Atlantis. (18)	6,848/5,579	72/72	73.6/71.8	134/124	$15/$42
Pine Barrens Golf Club (18)	7,118/5,209	72/72	74.2/70.2	132/120	$57/$115
Seaview Marriott Resort & Spa (36)					$49/$129
Bay (18)	6,247/5,017	71/71	70.7/68.4	122/114	
Pines (18)	6,731/5,276	71/71	71.7/69.8	128/119	

City boardwalk, but spend a weekend at the Seaview Marriott Resort to play its Donald Ross masterpiece, and you won't miss the desert heat.

There may be a glitz deficit at Atlantic City, but you do get more for your money, whether you're gambling, having dinner, or staying at a hotel room. Atlantic City's larger casinos are player-friendly, with blackjack and craps games with lower limits than their Vegas counterparts. The boardwalk casinos all have their signature restaurants, but to get a more "authentic" Atlantic City feel, head a couple of blocks inland and try the White House Sub Shop. You won't find anything like this in Vegas.

Another thing you won't find there is the kind of high-quality, bargain-rate golf that surrounds Atlantic City on three sides. Developers made great use of the terrain in the Pine Barrens between Atlantic City and Philadelphia, and they've also been quick to capitalize on the marketing potential of having one of the world's greatest courses, the private Pine Valley, next door. Blue Heron Pines and Pine Barrens are both perfect examples of their work.

Courses

GolfDigest REVIEWS

BLUE HERON PINES GOLF CLUB. Facility Holes: 36. Green Fee: $51/$126. Cart Fee: Included in green fee. Discounts: Weekdays, twilight, juniors. Walking: Unrestricted walking. Season: Year-round. Tee Times: Call 10 days in advance. Notes: Range (grass, mat). ✉ 550 W. Country Club Dr., Cologne, Galloway Township 08213, 16 mi from

REMEMBERING TILLIE

Philadelphia native A. W. Tillinghast (1874–1942) is remembered these days as a master architect from golf's golden age. His designs are praised, studied, and emulated by today's architects. Among his best-known courses are those at Philadelphia Cricket Club (1922), San Francisco Golf Club (1915), Baltusrol (1922), Winged Foot (1923), and Bethpage (1936). Some say that Tillinghast coined the term "birdie" at a Philadelphia club (Atlantic City Country Club's Ab Smith claims the same honor, however, saying a fellow member hit a "bird of a shot.")

Atlantic City ☎ 609/965-1800 or 888/478-2746 ⊕ www.blueheronpines.com ▤ AE, D, DC, MC, V.

East. Holes: 18. Opened: 2000. Architect: Steve Smyers. Yards: 7,300/5,500. Par: 71/71. Course Rating: 74.8/69.0. Slope: 135/120. *Comments: A 7,300-yard monster from the back. Great test.* ★★★★

West. Holes: 18. Opened: 1993. Architect: Stephen Kay. Yards: 6,777/5,053. Par: 72/72. Course Rating: 72.9/69.2. Slope: 132/119. *Comments: The first 3 holes are average, but be patient. The rest make up for it.* ★★★★

BUENA VISTA COUNTRY CLUB. Facility Holes: 18. Opened: 1957. Architect: William Gordon & Son. Yards: 6,869/5,651. Par: 72/72. Course Rating: 71.8/72.6. Slope: 127/124. Green Fee: $27/$35. Cart Fee: $28 per cart. Discounts: Weekdays, twilight. Walking: Walking at certain times. Season: Year-round. Tee Times: Call golf shop. Notes: Range (grass). ✉ Box 307, Rte. 40 & Country Club La., Buena, NJ 08310, 25 mi from Philadelphia ☎ 856/697-3733 ⊕ www.allforeclub.com ▤ MC, V. *Comments: An easy 30-minute drive from Philadelphia. Great warm-up course for your trip into Atlantic City.* ★★★ ½

EAGLE RIDGE GOLF COURSE. Facility Holes: 18. Opened: 1999. Architect: Brian Ault. Yards: 6,607/4,792. Par: 71/71. Course Rating: 72.4/68.3. Slope: 132/125. Green Fee: $37/$57. Cart Fee: $16 per person. Discounts: Weekdays, twilight, seniors, juniors. Walking: Walking at certain times. Season: Year-round. Tee Times: Call golf shop. Notes: Range (grass, mat). ✉ 2 August Blvd., Lakewood 08701, 60 mi from New York City ☎ 732/901-4900 ⊕ www.eagleridgegolf.com ▤ AE, MC, V. *Comments: Don't be fooled by the card—plays longer and harder than its actual yards.* ★★★★

HARBOR PINES GOLF CLUB. Facility Holes: 18. Opened: 1996. Architect: Stephen Kay. Yards: 6,827/5,099. Par: 72/72. Course Rating: 73.0/68.8. Slope: 134/118. Green Fee: $54/$120. Cart Fee: Included in green fee. Discounts: Weekdays, twilight, juniors. Walking: Walking at certain times. Season: Year-round. High: Apr.–Sept. Tee Times: Call 7 days in advance. Notes: Range (grass, mat). ✉ 500 St. Andrews Dr., Egg Harbor Township 08234, 2 mi from Somers Point ☎ 609/927-0006 ⊕ www.harborpines.com ▤ AE, D, MC, V. *Comments: Follows the Stephen Kay mold—room to hit it, beautiful conditioning.* ★★★ ½

LAKEWOOD COUNTRY CLUB. Facility Holes: 18. Opened: 1902. Architect: Willie Dunn Jr. Yards: 6,566/5,135. Par: 72/72. Course Rating: 71.7/65.9. Slope: 133/116. Green

Fee: $27/$32. Cart Fee: $30 per cart. Walking: Walking at certain times. Season: Year-round. Tee Times: Call golf shop. ✉ 145 Country Club Dr., Lakewood 08701, 40 mi from New York City ☎ 732/364–8899 ⊕ www.lakewoodcountryclub-nj.com ▤ AE, MC, V. *Comments: A classic, with recent modifications.* ★ ★ ½

MAYS LANDING COUNTRY CLUB. Facility Holes: 18. Opened: 1962. Architect: Hal Purdy. Yards: 6,662/5,432. Par: 72/71. Course Rating: 71.8/69.7. Slope: 123/114. Green Fee: $20/$70. Cart Fee: $16 per person. Discounts: Weekdays, twilight. Walking: Walking at certain times. Season: Year-round. Tee Times: Call 7 days in advance. Notes: Range (grass). ✉ 1855 Cates Rd., Mays Landing 08330, 10 mi from Atlantic City ☎ 609/641–4411 ⊕ www.mayslandinggolf.com ▤ AE, D, DC, MC, V. *Comments: Renovations have turned this into one of the area's better courses.* ★ ★ ★

OCEAN COUNTY GOLF COURSE AT ATLANTIS. Facility Holes: 18. Opened: 1961. Architect: George Fazio. Yards: 6,848/5,579. Par: 72/72. Course Rating: 73.6/71.8. Slope: 134/124. Green Fee: $15/$42. Cart Fee: $24 per person. Discounts: Twilight, seniors, juniors. Walking: Walking at certain times. Season: Year-round. Tee Times: Call 8 days in advance. Notes: Range (mat). ✉ Country Club Blvd., Tuckerton 08087, 30 mi from Atlantic City ☎ 609/296–2444 ▤ MC, V. *Comments: Great conditions, even in winter. By the "original" Fazio.* ★ ★ ★ ½

PINE BARRENS GOLF CLUB. Facility Holes: 18. Opened: 1999. Architect: Eric Bergstol. Yards: 7,118/5,209. Par: 72/72. Course Rating: 74.2/70.2. Slope: 132/120. Green Fee: $57/$115. Cart Fee: Included in green fee. Discounts: Twilight. Walking: Unrestricted walking. Season: Year-round. High: May–Sept. Tee Times: Call golf shop. Notes: Range (grass). ✉ 540 S. Hope Chapel Rd., Jackson 08527, 65 mi from Newark ☎ 732/408–1151 or 877/746–3227 ⊕ www.pinebarrensgolf.com ▤ AE, MC, V. *Comments: Feels like you're in North Carolina. Take a camera for some of the views on the back 9.* ★ ★ ★ ★

SEAVIEW MARRIOTT RESORT & SPA. Facility Holes: 36. Green Fee: $49/$129. Cart Fee: Included in green fee. Discounts: Weekdays, twilight, juniors. Walking: Walking at certain times. Season: Year-round. High: May–Nov. Tee Times: Call 30 days in advance. Notes: Range (grass, mat), lodging (300). ✉ 401 S. New York Rd., Galloway 08205, 10 mi from Atlantic City ☎ 609/748–7680 or 800/932–8000 ⊕ www.seaviewgolf.com ▤ AE, D, DC, MC, V.

Bay. Holes: 18. Opened: 1914. Architect: Donald Ross. Yards: 6,247/5,017. Par: 71/71. Course Rating: 70.7/68.4. Slope: 122/114. *Comments: Site of the LPGA ShopRite Classic. Nice ocean views, with a nasty set of green.* ★ ★ ★ ★

Pines. Holes: 18. Opened: 1929. Architect: Toomey/Flynn/Gordon. Yards: 6,731/5,276. Par: 71/71. Course Rating: 71.7/69.8. Slope: 128/119. *Comments: Feels like a straitjacket compared to the open Bay course.* ★ ★ ★ ★

Where to Stay

🏨 **BALLY'S ATLANTIC CITY.** The main building here, once the 1860 Dennis Hotel, has a traditional interior. The Claridge Tower rooms are contemporary, bright, and airy, and the Bally's Tower rooms have art deco touches. The hotel's multitiered complex of mosa-

A LEGEND OF THE GAME

Willie Anderson is a name known to many golf aficionados. He moved to America from Scotland as a teenager, and had won the U.S. Open four times, including the three consecutive championships in 1903–05. In 1910 he moved to Philadelphia to take a job as head professional at the Philadelphia Cricket Club–he wanted an edge for the Open, which was being held at the club that year. To his chagrin, Anderson didn't win, finishing 11th. He died that fall at the age of 32 and is buried in a cemetery near the club in Chestnut Hill.

ic-tile whirlpools and an atrium pool with water-aerobics classes lead to an outdoor pool with an outstanding view of the Atlantic Ocean. ⊠ Boardwalk at Park Pl., 08401 ☎ 609/340-2000 or 800/225-5977 🖷 609/340-4713 ⊕ www.ballysac.com ⤶ 1,753 rooms, 100 suites ⚅ 21 restaurants, room service, some refrigerators, cable TV, golf privileges, 2 pools (1 indoor), health club, hair salon, hot tub, sauna, spa, steam room, bar, casino, dry cleaning, laundry service, business services, meeting rooms, parking (fee), no-smoking rooms ⊟ AE, D, DC, MC, V $$–$$$$.

🏨 **BORGATA HOTEL CASINO & SPA.** This hotel has raised the city's bar on style and class. Floor-to-ceiling windows and tasteful furnishings are in the standard rooms, which are large and have a spacious bathroom with a shower that's big enough for two. Suites all have entertainment centers, wet bars, and bathrooms with deep tubs and two separate vanity sets. The spa here is the biggest in Atlantic City, and the restaurants include one owned by Susanna Foo, a famed Philly restaurateur, and an outpost of New York City's Old Homestead steak house. ⊠ 1 Borgata Way, 08401 ☎ 609/317-1000 or 866/692-6742 🖷 609/317-1100 ⊕ www.theborgata.com ⤶ 2,002 rooms, 402 suites ⚅ 11 restaurants, room service, in-room data ports, some minibars, cable TV, pool, gym, hair salon, hot tub, spa, 2 bars, casino, comedy club, concert hall, nightclub, theater, shops, dry cleaning, laundry service, concierge, meeting rooms, parking (fee), no-smoking rooms ⊟ AE, D, MC, V ⍾ EP $$$$.

🏨 **CAESARS ATLANTIC CITY HOTEL/CASINO.** The Roman statues help make this massive boardwalk hotel stand out even more than it otherwise would. In addition to the many guest rooms, the interior also holds 24 casinos, 3,595 slot machines, and a theater seating 1,100. Rooms are luxurious, and many have breathtaking ocean views. ⊠ 2100 Pacific Ave., 08401 ☎ 609/348-4411 or 800/443-0104 🖷 609/347-8089 ⊕ - www.caesars.com ⤶ 1,138 rooms, 186 suites ⚅ 11 restaurants, room service, in-room data ports, cable TV, golf privileges, pool, health club, hair salon, hot tub, spa, steam room, 4 bars, piano bar, casino, concert hall, shops, dry cleaning, laundry service, concierge, concierge floor, business services, meeting rooms, parking (fee), no-smoking rooms ⊟ AE, D, DC, MC, V $$–$$$$.

🏨 **SEAVIEW MARRIOTT RESORT & SPA.** The 670-acre Seaview feels refreshingly spacious, with gardens, perfectly manicured lawns, and a certain elegance. It got its start in 1914 as the Seaview Country Club and still offers such refined diversions as golf and tennis. The rooms are a classic blend of traditional fabrics and period furniture. The spa is an Elizabeth Arden Red Door facility. ⊠ 401 S. New York Rd., Galloway Township

08205 ☎ 609/652-1800 ⊕ www.seaviewgolf.com ⇔ 260 rooms, 37 suites ♿ 2 restaurants, room service, in-room data ports, minibars, cable TV with movies and video games, 2 18-hole golf courses, 6 tennis courts, pro shop, 2 pools (1 indoor), health club, sauna, spa, steam room, lobby lounge, recreation room, business services, meeting rooms, no-smoking rooms ▭ AE, D, DC, MC, V ⦿ EP $$$$.

▦ **TRUMP PLAZA HOTEL AND CASINO.** Visible from anywhere in town, this white tower is the first hotel you see as you leave the expressway and enter Atlantic City. It's close to trains and buses and right on the boardwalk. The modern guest rooms have lots of mirrors, and suites have jet tubs. One side of the hotel overlooks the ocean; the other overlooks the city. ⊠ Mississippi Ave. and Boardwalk, 08401 ☎ 609/441-6000 or 800/ 677-7378 🖷 609/441-2603 ⊕ www.trumpplaza.com ⇔ 904 rooms, 142 suites ♿ 12 restaurants, room service, in-room data ports, some in-room hot tubs, some refrigerators, cable TV with movies, 2 tennis courts, pool, gym, hair salon, hot tub, massage, shuffleboard, 3 bars, casino, shops, dry cleaning, laundry service, business services, meeting rooms, parking (fee), no-smoking rooms ▭ AE, D, DC, MC, V ⦿ EP $$$-$$$$.

▦ **TRUMP TAJ MAHAL CASINO RESORT.** The extravagantly decorated, over-the-top Taj has rooms overlooking the ocean or the city, and suites with master bedrooms, living rooms, dining areas, and hot tubs. ⊠ 1000 Boardwalk, 08401 ☎ 609/449-1000 or 800/825-8786 🖷 609/449-6818 ⊕ www.trumptaj.com ⇔ 980 rooms, 224 suites ♿ 7 restaurants, coffee shop, pizzeria, room service, some in-room hot tubs, some minibars, some refrigerators, cable TV, indoor pool, gym, hair salon, hot tub, massage, steam room, bicycles, 3 bars, lounge, casino, concert hall, nightclub, showroom, shops, dry cleaning, laundry service, concierge floor, business services, convention center, parking (fee), no-smoking rooms ▭ AE, D, DC, MC, V ⦿ EP $$$$.

Where to Eat

✕ **ANGELONI'S.** In the traditionally Italian Ducktown section of Atlantic City, this restaurant serves family-style beef, veal, and seafood dishes. Angeloni's *braciole* (rolled veal stuffed with sausage and cheese) is popular. The Italian restaurant's wine list is extensive. ⊠ 2400 Arctic Ave. ☎ 609/344-7875 ▭ AE, D, DC, MC, V $$-$$$$.

✕ **ANGELO'S FAIRMOUNT TAVERN.** Locals flock to this unassuming Ducktown favorite, decorated with New York Yankees and other sports memorabilia. Open since 1935, the restaurant is known for Italian standards as well as steaks and seafood. ⊠ 2300 Fairmount Ave. ☎ 609/344-2439 ▭ AE, D, MC, V ⊘ No lunch weekends $-$$$$.

✕ **DOCK'S OYSTER HOUSE.** Owned and operated by the Dougherty family since 1897, the city's oldest restaurant serves seafood amid wood and stained glass engraved with nautical scenes. Try the pan-seared ahi tuna and fresh soft-shell crab. ⊠ 2405 Atlantic Ave. ☎ 609/345-0092 ▭ AE, DC, MC, V ⊘ Closed Dec. and Jan. No lunch Mon. $$-$$$$.

✕ **IRISH PUB AND INN.** Live Irish music is performed nightly at this informal spot, which serves pub fare such as corned-beef sandwiches, turkey dinners, and beef stew. The $1.95 lunch special is one of the city's great bargains. The bar is open 24 hours, and you can order dinner until 7:30 AM. ⊠ 164 St. James Pl. ☎609/344-9063 ▭No credit cards ¢-$.

✗ **SCANNICCHIO'S.** One of Atlantic City's most popular eateries, this intimate, candlelit, classic Italian restaurant has eight fish specials daily and an extensive pasta menu. Filet mignon stuffed with crab, shrimp, and scallops is one of the most requested dishes, and the homemade cannoli is a must for dessert. Reservations are essential on weekends. ⊠ 119 S. California Ave. ☎609/348-6378 ▭AE, MC, V ⊙No lunch $$-$$$$.

✗ **WHITE HOUSE SUB SHOP.** When you're hungry for a great New Jersey–style sub, this is the place to go. This casual shop claims to have made more than 17 million of the sandwiches since 1946. Be sure to check out the many celebrity photos on the walls. ⊠ 2301 Arctic Ave., at Mississippi Ave. ☎ 609/345-1564 or 609/345-8599 ⌂ Reservations not accepted ▭No credit cards ¢-$.

Essentials

Getting Here
Atlantic City is a straight shot from Philadelphia. Take the Atlantic City Expressway east. The trip takes about an hour.

Visitor Information
🔋 **Atlantic City Convention Center & Visitors Authority** ⊠ 2314 Pacific Ave., 08401 ☎800/262-7395 ⊕ www.atlanticcitynj.com.

CAPE MAY, NJ

When you consider Cape May's location at the tip of a 30-mi peninsula stretching into the Atlantic Ocean, it's a wonder the area doesn't have more golf courses than it does. Luckily, the few courses that *are* here make it worth a trip. Cape May National, delicately sculpted out of a 500-acre wildlife preserve, and Sand Barrens, showing off its Pine Valley roots proudly, deserve to be on any mid-Atlantic golf itinerary.

Any nongolfers in your party are also likely to be happy with a trip to Cape May. The town is very protective of its status as the nation's oldest seaside resort, and rows of perfectly preserved Victorians line its miles of coastline. The town also serves as the launch point for many pleasure-boating and deep-sea-fishing activities. You can park your own boat, or you can drive in and rent one for the day. And whether or not you catch anything yourself, the many good restaurants in town are good at satisfying seafood cravings.

Avalon Golf Club (18)	6,325/4,924	71/72	70.3/70.7	122/122	$29/$87
Cape May National Golf Club (18)	6,905/4,711	71/71	72.9/68.8	136/115	$35/$85
Sand Barrens Golf Club (27)					$42/$125
North/West (18)	7,092/4,951	72/72	73.2/67.9	135/119	
South/North (18)	6,969/4,946	72/72	72.7/68.0	133/120	
South/West (18)	6,895/4,971	72/72	71.7/68.3	130/119	

Courses

Golf Digest REVIEWS

AVALON GOLF CLUB. Facility Holes: 18. Opened: 1971. Architect: Bob Hendricks. Yards: 6,325/4,924. Par: 71/72. Course Rating: 70.3/70.7. Slope: 122/122. Green Fee: $29/$87. Cart Fee: Included in green fee. Discounts: Weekdays, twilight, juniors. Walking: Walking at certain times. Season: Year-round. High: May–Oct. Tee Times: Call 14 days in advance. Notes: Range (mat). ⊠ 1510 Rte. 9 N, Cape May Court House 08210, 30 mi from Atlantic City ☎ 609/465-4653 or 800/643-4766 ⊕ www.avalongolfclub.net ▤ D, MC, V. *Comments: Convenient to town.* ★ ★ ★

CAPE MAY NATIONAL GOLF CLUB. Facility Holes: 18. Opened: 1991. Architect: Karl Litten/Robert Mullock. Yards: 6,905/4,711. Par: 71/71. Course Rating: 72.9/68.8. Slope: 136/115. Green Fee: $35/$85. Cart Fee: Included in green fee. Discounts: Weekdays, twilight, juniors. Walking: Unrestricted walking. Season: Year-round. High: May–Oct. Tee Times: Call golf shop. Notes: Range (grass, mat). ⊠ Rte. 9 and Florence Ave., 08204, 35 mi from Atlantic City ☎ 609/884-1563 or 800/227-3874 ⊕ www.cmngc.com ▤ MC, V. *Comments: Isolated location keeps this one underrated.* ★ ★ ★ ½

SAND BARRENS GOLF CLUB. Facility Holes: 27. Opened: 1997. Architect: Michael Hurdzan/Dana Fry. Green Fee: $42/$125. Cart Fee: Included in green fee. Discounts: Weekdays, twilight, juniors. Walking: Unrestricted walking. Season: Year-round. High: June–Sept. Tee Times: Call 10 days in advance. Notes: Range (grass). ⊠ 1765 Rte. 9 N, Swainton 08210, 60 mi from Philadelphia ☎ 609/465-3555 or 800/465-3122 ⊕ www. sandbarrensgolf.com ▤ D, MC, V.

North/West. Holes: 18. Yards: 7,092/4,951. Par: 72/72. Course Rating: 73.2/67.9. Slope: 135/119.

South/North. Holes: 18. Yards: 6,969/4,946. Par: 72/72. Course Rating: 72.7/68.0. Slope: 133/120.

South/West. Holes: 18. Yards: 6,895/4,971. Par: 72/72. Course Rating: 71.7/68.3. Slope: 130/119.

Comments: Twenty-seven holes of Pine Valley-esqe waste areas and punishment for wayward shots. ★ ★ ★ ★

Where to Stay

THE ABBEY. This Gothic Revival–style bed-and-breakfast in the heart of the historic district is whimsical and a bit offbeat. Painted in deep shades of green, the main house of the inn is meant to look like an abbey, which it never was. The common rooms and guest rooms are abundantly decorated with Victorian antiques. ⊠ 34 Gurney St., 08204 ☎ 609/884–4506 🖶 609/884–2379 ⊕ www.abbeybedandbreakfast.com ⤶ 14 rooms ↺ Refrigerators, library; no room phones, no kids under 12, no smoking ⊟ D, MC, V ⊘ Closed Jan.–early Mar. ⏀CP $–$$$$.

CONGRESS HALL. Restored and reopened in 2002, Congress Hall dates back to 1816, when it was one of Cape May's most elegant hotels. The rooms are painted in refreshing seaside colors, with white furniture and crisp linens. The ballroom has classic black-and-white-checked floors and black bentwood chairs. The restaurant here, the Blue Pig, is done in homey checks and subdued reds (not blue). ⊠ 251 Beach Dr., 08204 ☎ 609/884–8421 🖶 609/884–6094 ⊕ www.congresshall.com ⤶ 106 rooms ↺ Restaurant, cable TV, pool, gym, spa, shops, meeting rooms ⊟ MC, V $–$$$$.

MAINSTAY INN. Perfectly groomed and handsomely elegant, the main house of the Mainstay is painted in warm yellow, with deep green trim. There's also a smaller cottage next door and another building across the street. Two blocks from the historic district, the B&B is furnished in a Victorian style that's not too frilly, with period antiques and furnishings. Across the street, the luxury suites are more contemporary, with hot tubs, kitchens, and fireplaces. Everyone here gets beach passes. Best of all, the breakfasts and afternoon teas are excellent, with creations like strawberry-stuffed French toast and baked eggs in pastry. ⊠ 635 Columbia Ave., 08204 ☎ 609/884–8690 ⊕ www.mainstayinn.com ⤶ 9 rooms, 7 suites ↺ No smoking ⊟ No credit cards ⏀BP $$$–$$$$.

VIRGINIA HOTEL. More contemporary than many of the Victorian hotels in Cape May, the rooms of the Virginia are decorated in soft shades of green and beige, accented with touches like fringed lamp shades and potted palms. All rooms have down comforters, and some have private porches overlooking historic Jackson Street. The restaurant serves excellent seafood dishes and the bar is a good place to relax. Summertime rates include beach passes, chairs, and towels. ⊠ 25 Jackson St., 08204 ☎ 609/884–5700 or 800/732–4236 🖶 609/884–1236 ⊕ www.virginiahotel.com ⤶ 24 rooms ↺ Restaurant, room service, in-room data ports, some in-room hot tubs, cable TV, in-room VCRs, bar, business services ⊟ AE, D, DC, MC, V ⏀CP $$–$$$$.

Where to Eat

✕ 410 BANK STREET. Housed in this 1850s summer cottage is one of southern New Jersey's top restaurants. Most people eat outside in season, either on the partially covered patio or on the front porch. It's known for mesquite-grilled fish and steaks and home-smoked meats. Try smoked prime rib, barbecued jumbo shrimp, blackened striped bass, and fresh Maine lobster tails. ⊠ 410 Bank St. ☎ 609/884–2127 ⊟ AE, D, DC, MC, V ⏀BYOB ⊘ Closed Nov.–Apr. No lunch $$$$.

✕ **MAD BATTER.** Housed in a lovely old building, this restaurant is known for fresh seafood and desserts. Try classic crab *mappatello*—a pastry puff filled with fresh crabmeat, spinach, and ricotta cheese, baked and served with a roasted red pepper and white wine cream sauce—the Jackson Street crab cakes, or the orange almond French toast. The dining room has purple walls, a green ceiling, Victorian lamps, and art that changes monthly. Mad Batter also serves breakfast. You can dine outside on the front porch or the garden terrace. ⊠ 19 Jackson St. ☎ 609/884–5970 ▭ AE, D, DC, MC, V ⏐⏐ BYOB ☾ Closed Jan. $$–$$$$.

✕ **MERION INN.** This turn-of-the-20th-century dining room has been serving since 1885, and its beautiful mahogany bar is the oldest in Cape May. Try the crab imperial, stuffed lobster tail, steaks, or the daily seafood special. ⊠ 106 Decatur St. ☎ 609/884–8363 ▭ AE, D, DC, MC, V ☾ Closed Jan.–Mar. $$–$$$$.

Essentials

Getting Here
To get to Cape May from Philly, take the Atlantic City Expressway east to the Garden State Parkway south. This takes you directly into Cape May. It's a trip of roughly 90 mi.

Visitor Information
🖪 **CAPE MAY COUNTY CHAMBER OF COMMERCE** ⊠ 13 Crest Haven Rd., Cape May Court House 08210 ☎ 609/465–7181 🖶 609/465–5017 ⊕ www.capemaycountychamber.com. **CHAMBER OF COMMERCE OF GREATER CAPE MAY** ⊠ Box 556, Cape May 08204 ☎ 609/884–5508 🖶 609/884–2054 ⊕ www.capemaycountychamber.com. **MID-ATLANTIC CENTER FOR THE ARTS** ⊠ 1048 Washington St., 08204 ☎ 609/884–5404 ⊕ www.capemaymac.org.

HERSHEY

If you love chocolate, it doesn't even matter if there's golf in Hershey, does it? Luckily, you can tour the factory and play memorable golf on the same trip to this company town, just outside Harrisburg.

Staying at the Hotel Hershey is a good choice, since you get access to a wonderful collection of courses along with your room. The best is the West course, a 1930s gem best known for being Ben Hogan's home course, but even the short course behind the hotel is a blast. Work your way through the front 9 on the West Course and you pass not only the Hershey factory, but Milton Hershey's mansion, on a hill overlooking the company grounds. You can even smell chocolate in the air.

Country Club of Hershey (54)					
East (18)	7,061/5,645	71/71	73.6/71.6	128/127	$60/$80
Parkview Golf Course (18)	6,332/4,979	71/72	69.9/69.6	121/107	$65
West (18)	6,860/5,908	73/76	73.1/74.7	131/127	$75/$95
Dauphin Highlands Golf Course (18)	7,035/5,327	72/72	73.4/70.1	125/114	$23/$38
Penn National Golf Club & Inn (36)					$20/$52
Founders (18)	6,958/5,367	72/72	73.2/71.4	129/123	
Iron Forge (18)	7,009/5,246	72/72	73.8/70.3	133/120	
Royal Oaks Golf Club (18)	6,486/4,695	71/71	71.4/66.9	121/109	$18/$49

If you can tear yourself away, make the drive to Penn National. The Founders and Iron Forge courses there are a modern counterpoint to the classic Hershey designs.

Courses

COUNTRY CLUB OF HERSHEY. Facility Holes: 54. Cart Fee: Included in green fee. Discounts: Weekdays, twilight, seniors, juniors. Season: Mar.–Dec. Tee Times: Call golf shop. Notes: Range (grass), lodging. Holes: 18. ⌧ 600 W. Derry Rd., 17033, 12 mi from Harrisburg ☎ 717/534–3450 ⊕ www.golfhershey.com ▤ AE, D, MC, V.

East. Holes: 18. Opened: 1970. Architect: George Fazio. Yards: 7,061/5,645. Par: 71/71. Course Rating: 73.6/71.6. Slope: 128/127. Green Fee: $60/$80. Walking: Mandatory cart. *Comments: Doesn't have the history of the West, but definitely has the challenge.* ★ ★ ★ ★

Parkview Golf Course. Holes: 18. Opened: 1927. Architect: Maurice McCarthy. Yards: 6,332/4,979. Par: 71/72. Course Rating: 69.9/69.6. Slope: 121/107. Green Fee: $65. Walking: Walking at certain times. *Comments: Similar vintage and similar traits to the West. Shorter.* ★ ★ ★ ½

West. Holes: 18. Opened: 1930. Architect: Maurice McCarthy. Yards: 6,860/5,908. Par: 73/76. Course Rating: 73.1/74.7. Slope: 131/127. Green Fee: $75/$95. Walking: Mandatory cart. *Comments: One of Pennsylvania's greats. Walk in Hogan's footsteps.* ★ ★ ★ ★

DAUPHIN HIGHLANDS GOLF COURSE. Facility Holes: 18. Opened: 1995. Architect: Bill Love. Yards: 7,035/5,327. Par: 72/72. Course Rating: 73.4/70.1. Slope: 125/114. Green Fee: $23/$38. Cart Fee: $12 per person. Discounts: Weekdays, twilight, seniors, juniors. Walking: Unrestricted walking. Season: Year-round. High: Apr.–Nov. Tee Times: Call 6 days in advance. Notes: Range (grass, mat). ⌧ 650 S. Harrisburg St., Harrisburg 17113 ☎ 717/986–1984 ▤ MC, V. *Comments: Coming into its own as it matures.* ★ ★ ★ ★

PENN NATIONAL GOLF CLUB & INN. Facility Holes: 36. Green Fee: $20/$52. Cart Fee: $16 per person. Discounts: Weekdays, twilight, seniors, juniors. Walking: Unrestricted walking. Season: Year-round. High: Apr.–Oct. Tee Times: Call 30 days in advance. Notes: Range (grass), lodging (36). ⌧ 3720 Clubhouse Dr., Fayetteville 17222,

39 mi from Harrisburg ☎717/352-3000 or 800/221-7366 ⊕ www.penngolf.com ▭AE, D, MC, V.

Founders. Holes: 18. Opened: 1968. Architect: Edmund B. Ault. Yards: 6,958/5,367. Par: 72/72. Course Rating: 73.2/71.4. Slope: 129/123. *Comments: Off the beaten path, but worth a drive. Parkland style.* ★★★★

Iron Forge. Holes: 18. Opened: 1996. Architect: Bill Love. Yards: 7,009/5,246. Par: 72/72. Course Rating: 73.8/70.3. Slope: 133/120. *Comments: A links-style delight.* ★★★★

ROYAL OAKS GOLF CLUB. Facility Holes: 18. Opened: 1992. Architect: Ron Forse. Yards: 6,486/4,695. Par: 71/71. Course Rating: 71.4/66.9. Slope: 121/109. Green Fee: $18/$49. Cart Fee: Included in green fee. Discounts: Weekdays, twilight, seniors, juniors. Walking: Walking at certain times. Season: Year-round. Tee Times: Call 7 days in advance. Notes: Range (grass). ✉ 3350 W. Oak St., Lebanon 17042, 15 mi from Hershey ☎717/274-2212 ▭AE, MC, V. *Comments: Great value, and an easy drive from the Hershey attractions.* ★★★★

Where to Stay

⚅ **ADDEY'S.** A 1920s brick farmhouse on a hill overlooking the Hershey valley, this inn has 12 rooms, each of which is designed after a different month of the year. Hersheypark and the famous Zeigler's Antique Mall are both close by, as are a large playground, tennis courts, a softball field, and a track. ✉ 150 E. Governor Rd., U.S. 322 E, 17033 ☎717/533-2591 ⊕ www.go2pa.com/addeys_inn ⇌ 12 rooms ♿ Picnic area, cable TV, playground; no smoking ▭AE, D, MC, V ⏏CP $-$$$.

⚅ **HERSHEY LODGE & CONVENTION CENTER.** This bustling, expansive modern resort is for business travelers and vacationers, with two casual restaurants, as well as a more formal dining room. The hotel hosts groups of up to 1,300 in its Chocolate Ballroom, and it can be hectic during conventions. The best rooms are in the Guest Tower, so put in a request for one of these. ✉ W. Chocolate Ave. and University Dr., 17033 ☎717/533-3311 or 800/533-3131 ⊕ www.800hershey.com/accommodations/lodge ⇌ 637 rooms, 28 suites ♿ 3 restaurants, coffee shop, room service, miniature golf, 2 tennis courts, 3 pools (1 indoor), gym, basketball, 2 lounges, recreation room, baby-sitting, laundry service, concierge, convention center ▭AE, D, DC, MC, V $$-$$$.

⚅ **HOTEL HERSHEY.** The grande dame of Hershey, this gracious Mediterranean villa-style hotel is a sophisticated resort with plenty of options for recreation, starting with the golf course that surrounds the hotel. The hotel abounds in elegant touches, from the mosaic-tile lobby to rooms with maple armoires, paintings from local artists, and tile baths. The spa's treatments here include a chocolate bean polish, a cocoa butter scrub, a chocolate fondue wrap, and whipped cocoa bath. Carriage rides, a ropes course, and nature trails are all on the property. ✉ 400 Hotel Rd., 17033 ☎717/533-2171 or 800/533-3131 ⊕ www.hersheypa.com ⇌ 234 rooms, 20 suites ♿ 3 restaurants, coffee shop, room service, 2 18-hole golf courses, 1 9-hole golf course, 3 tennis courts, 2 pools (1 indoor), gym, sauna, spa, bicycles, basketball, lounge, baby-sitting, laundry service, concierge, business services, meeting rooms ▭AE, D, DC, MC, V $$$$.

HERSHEYPARK

Touted as "the Sweetest Place on Earth," this amusement park (☎ 717/534–3090 ⊕ www.hersheypa.com) has more than 100 landscaped acres, with 60 rides, five theaters, and a zoo dedicated to animals from North America. Begun in 1907, it's prized as one of America's cleanest and greenest theme parks. Among its historical rides are the Comet, a 1946-vintage wooden roller coaster, and a carousel built in 1919 with 66 hand-carved wooden horses.

SPINNER'S INN. If you want something homier than the resort and chain hotels, then this two-level farmhouse brick inn 1 mi from Hersheypark might be a good choice. The interior of this peaceful getaway is done in a country style. ⊠ 845 E. Chocolate Ave., 17033 ☎ 717/533-9157 ☎ 717/534-1189 ⊕ www.spinnersinn.com ◄ 52 rooms (4 with shower only) ⚑ Restaurant, picnic area, room service, some microwaves, some refrigerators, cable TV, pool, bar, video game room, business services, free parking ⊟ AE, D, DC, MC, V ⎸⎸ CP $-$$.

Where to Eat

✕ **CATHERINE'S AT SPINNER'S INN.** This candlelit restaurant has fine china and linen-covered tables, with portraits of the Hershey founders on the wall. Try the beef medallions stuffed with crabmeat and pesto, followed with tiramisu for dessert. ⊠ Spinner's Inn, 845 E. Chocolate Ave. ☎ 717/533-9157 ⊟ AE, D, DC, MC, V ☉ Closed Sun. and Mon. No lunch $$$-$$$$.

✕ **CHOCOLATE TOWN CAFE.** If you're looking for a casual spot to grab a bite to eat, along with some choco-mania, consider Chocolate Town. On the menu are tasty half-pound burgers, chicken tenders, and the thickest milk shakes around (chocolate is the specialty, of course). The restaurant, painted in bright colors with Hershey's characters on the walls, is popular with families. ⊠ 800 Park Blvd. ☎ 717/533-2917 ⊟ AE, D, MC $-$$.

✕ **CIRCULAR DINING ROOM.** What might be Hershey's most spectacular place to eat is on the first floor of the Hotel Hershey. The circular glassed-in dining room overlooks formal gardens and ponds. The Continental entrées include fillet of salmon, grilled filet mignon, roast leg of lamb, and (naturally) chocolate-related entrées, such as cocoa-dusted scallops. Chocolate-lovers will find the chocolate dessert buffet hard to resist. Selections include such options as chocolate cream pie, crème caramel, chocolate-dipped strawberries, and white-chocolate cheesecake. ⊠ 400 Hotel Rd. ☎ 717/533-2171 ⚑ Jacket required ⊟ AE, D, DC, MC, V $$$$.

✕ **HERSHEY PANTRY.** Inside a building from the 1930s, this family restaurant is about a mile from Hershey. Awnings line the interior and exterior of the restaurant. You can eat outdoors on the enclosed porch. The breakfasts served here are well regarded, with the stuffed French toast especially popular. ⊠ 801 E. Chocolate Ave. ☎ 717/533-7505 ⊟ No credit cards ☉ Closed Sun. $$.

✕ **ISAAC'S.** Off Hwy. 422 and about a mile from downtown, Isaac's has an interior with exposed ceilings, aquariums, and paintings of wildlife. Sandwiches are the attraction here, with folks coming in for piled-high creations named after birds, like the Scarlet Ibis with turkey, melted cheese, lettuce, and tomato on French bread, or the Jamaican Tody with grilled Caribbean jerk chicken breast, pineapple, and ranch dressing on pumpernickel. Isaac's also has pita pizzas, pretzel sandwiches, salads, and good soups. ✉ 1201 W. Chocolate Ave. ☎ 717/533-9665 ▭ AE, D, MC, V $.

Essentials

Getting Here
Hershey is 100 mi from Philadelphia. To get here take the Schuylkill Expressway (I-76) west to the Pennsylvania Turnpike. Take exit 266 and turn left onto 72 North and take it to 322 West. Follow 322 into Hershey.

Visitor Information
🗗 **HARRISBURG–HERSHEY–CARLISLE TOURISM AND CONVENTION BUREAU**
✉ 25 N. Front St., Suite 100, Harrisburg 17101 ☎ 717/231-7788 or 800/995-0969.

LANCASTER & YORK

First of all, they don't have horse-drawn golf carts in Lancaster. Although influence the Amish and the Pennsylvania Dutch have on the area is considerable, that would be taking things a bit too far.

That said, more than 5 million people come to greater Lancaster each year to immerse themselves in Amish culture, crafts, and food. Amish families still ride in horse-drawn carriages on their way to the Central Market in Lancaster, which has been in business since the 1770s. Craft stores selling baskets and furniture dot the roadsides, and believe it or not, there's even a Dutch Wonderland Family Amusement Park.

Both Lancaster and nearby York have plenty for the weekend golfer as well. Springwood Golf Club in York is a terrific test, and worth a trip on its own, as is the Bridges Golf Club. Pilgrim's Oak, built on the site of an old dairy farm, is the latest on the scene. Its collection of tiny greens will challenge your short game. And if the children in your group don't have the attention span for a full 18 holes, Greater Lancaster might have the densest concentration of miniature golf courses in the world. Just pick your theme.

Bridges Golf Club (18)	6,713/5,104	72/72	72.5/70.1	133/117	$26/$41
Foxchase Golf Club (18)	6,796/4,690	72/72	72.7/66.9	124/116	$14/$45
Hawk Valley Golf Club (18)	6,628/5,661	72/72	70.3/70.2	132/119	$22/$30
Honey Run Golf & Country Club (18)	6,797/5,948	72/72	72.4/74.0	123/125	$20/$32
Pilgrim's Oak Golf Course (18)	6,766/5,064	72/71	73.4/70.7	138/129	$20/$45
Springwood Golf Club (18)	6,826/5,075	72/72	73.4/69.7	131/113	$35/$65
Tanglewood Manor Golf Club & Learning Center (18)	6,457/5,321	72/74	70.7/70.0	118/118	$18/$32

Courses

Golf Digest REVIEWS

BRIDGES GOLF CLUB. Facility Holes: 18. Opened: 1995. Architect: Altland Brothers. Yards: 6,713/5,104. Par: 72/72. Course Rating: 72.5/70.1. Slope: 133/117. Green Fee: $26/$41. Cart Fee: $14 per person. Discounts: Weekdays, twilight, seniors, juniors. Walking: Walking at certain times. Season: Year-round. High: Mar.–Nov. Tee Times: Call golf shop. Notes: Range (grass, mat), lodging (12). ✉ 6729 York Rd., Abbottstown 17301, 35 mi from Harrisburg ☎ 717/624-9551 ⊕ www.bridgesgc.com ▭ AE, MC, V. *Comments: You can stay on the grounds in one of the club's 13 rooms.* ★ ★ ★ ★

FOXCHASE GOLF CLUB. Facility Holes: 18. Opened: 1991. Architect: John Thompson. Yards: 6,796/4,690. Par: 72/72. Course Rating: 72.7/66.9. Slope: 124/116. Green Fee: $14/$45. Cart Fee: Included in green fee. Discounts: Weekdays, twilight, seniors, juniors. Walking: Unrestricted walking. Season: Year-round. Tee Times: Call 90 days in advance. Notes: Range (grass, mat). ✉ 300 Stevens Rd., Stevens 17578, 50 mi from Philadelphia ☎ 717/336-3673 ⊕ www.foxchasegolf.com ▭ D, MC, V. *Comments: They're serious about golf here. Rangers get you moving, and no alcohol is served.* ★ ★ ★ ¹/₂

HAWK VALLEY GOLF CLUB. Facility Holes: 18. Opened: 1971. Architect: William Gordon. Yards: 6,628/5,661. Par: 72/72. Course Rating: 70.3/70.2. Slope: 132/119. Green Fee: $22/$30. Cart Fee: $14 per person. Discounts: Twilight, seniors, juniors. Walking: Walking at certain times. Season: Year-round. Tee Times: Call golf shop. Notes: Range (mat). ✉ 1309 Crestview Dr., Denver 17517 ☎ 800/522-4295 ⊕ www.golfthehawk. com ▭ AE, D, MC, V. *Comments: Some of the quickest public course greens you'll find.* ★ ★ ★ ¹/₂

HONEY RUN GOLF & COUNTRY CLUB. Facility Holes: 18. Opened: 1971. Architect: Edmund B. Ault. Yards: 6,797/5,948. Par: 72/72. Course Rating: 72.4/74.0. Slope: 123/125. Green Fee: $20/$32. Cart Fee: $13 per person. Discounts: Weekdays, twilight, seniors, juniors. Walking: Walking at certain times. Season: Year-round. Tee Times: Call golf shop. Notes: Metal spikes, range (grass). ✉ 3131 S. Salem Church Rd., York 17404 ☎ 717/792-9771 or 800/475-4657 ▭ MC, V. *Comments: Straightforward, solid course.* ★ ★ ★ ¹/₂

PILGRIM'S OAK GOLF COURSE. Facility Holes: 18. Opened: 1996. Architect: Michael Hurdzan. Yards: 6,766/5,064. Par: 72/71. Course Rating: 73.4/70.7. Slope: 138/129. Green Fee: $20/$45. Cart Fee: $12 per person. Discounts: Weekdays, twilight, seniors, juniors. Walking: Unrestricted walking. Season: Year-round. Tee Times: Call golf shop. Notes: Range (grass). ✉ 1107 Pilgrim's Pathway, Peach Bottom 17563, 24 mi from Lancaster ☎ 717/548-3011 ⊕ www.pilgrimsoak.com ☰ AE, D, MC, V. *Comments: No. 3 is a brutal, all-carry 200-yard par-3.* ★★★★

SPRINGWOOD GOLF CLUB. Facility Holes: 18. Opened: 1998. Architect: Tom Clark/Dan Schlegel. Yards: 6,826/5,075. Par: 72/72. Course Rating: 73.4/69.7. Slope: 131/113. Green Fee: $35/$65. Cart Fee: Included in green fee. Discounts: Weekdays, twilight, seniors, juniors. Walking: Walking at certain times. Season: Year-round. High: Apr.–Oct. Tee Times: Call 7 days in advance. Notes: Range (grass, mat). ✉ 601 Chestnut Hill Rd., York 17402 ☎ 717/747-9663 ☰ AE, D, DC, MC, V. *Comments: New management has turned this into one of southeastern Penn's best.* ★★★★

TANGLEWOOD MANOR GOLF CLUB & LEARNING CENTER. Facility Holes: 18. Opened: 1969. Architect: Chester Ruby. Yards: 6,457/5,321. Par: 72/74. Course Rating: 70.7/70.0. Slope: 118/118. Green Fee: $18/$32. Cart Fee: $13 per person. Discounts: Weekdays, twilight, seniors, juniors. Walking: Walking at certain times. Season: Mar.–Dec. High: May–Oct. Tee Times: Call 14 days in advance. Notes: Range (grass, mat). ✉ 653 Scotland Rd., Quarryville 17566, 10 mi from Lancaster ☎ 717/786-2500 ⊕-www.twgolf.com ☰ D, MC, V. *Comments: Golf isn't enough? They've got minigolf and batting cages, too.* ★★★

Where to Stay

▥ BEST WESTERN EDEN RESORT INN. Attractive grounds and spacious rooms with cherrywood colonial furnishings make a stay here pleasant. The inn has a tropical indoor pool and a whirlpool under a retractable roof; you can request a poolside room. If you're spending a few days in the area, consider one of the extended-stay suites. ✉ 222 Eden Rd., U.S. 30 and Rte. 272, Lancaster 17601 ☎ 717/569-6444 or 800/528-1234 ☐ 717/569-4208 ⊕ www.edenresort.com ✍ 276 rooms, 40 suites ⚭ 2 restaurants, room service, in-room data ports, in-room safes, refrigerators, tennis court, 2 pools (1 indoor), gym, sauna, lounge ☰ AE, D, DC, MC, V ⧖ CP $$-$$$.

▥ GENERAL SUTTER INN. Built in 1764, the oldest continuously run inn in Pennsylvania was named after the man who founded Sacramento in 1839, 10 years before the discovery of gold on his California property started the gold rush. He later retired to Lititz. His namesake, full of Victorian furnishings, is within easy walking distance of the historic district. ✉ 14 E. Main St., corner of Rtes. 501 and 772, Lititz 17543 ☎ 717/626-2115 ☐ 717/626-0992 ⊕ www.generalsutterinn.com ✍ 16 rooms, 3 suites ⚭ Restaurant, café, bar, no-smoking rooms ☰ AE, D, MC, V $.

▥ INNS OF ADAMSTOWN. These two elegant Victorian inns are less than a half block from each other. The Adamstown and the Amethyst inns both have spacious rooms with handmade quilts, fresh flowers, and lace curtains. A number of the rooms have whirlpools, fireplaces, and steam showers. Set high on a hill, the Amethyst is painted with deep eggplant, green, and five other colors. There's even an Old English sheep-dog to greet you. A hearty Continental breakfast is served each morning in the Adamstown Inn's dining room. ⊠ 62 W. Main St., Adamstown 17522 ☎ 717/484-0800 or 800/594-4808 ⊕ www.adamstown.com ✍ 8 rooms ⟋ Dining room, some in-room hot tubs ▤ AE, MC, V ⦿ CP $-$$.

▦ **KING'S COTTAGE.** An elegant 1913 Spanish mission–revival mansion on the National Register of Historic Places is now a B&B. The blend of decorative and architec-tural elements encompasses Chippendale-style furniture in the dining room and an art deco fireplace and stained-glass windows. Several rooms have whirlpools and fireplaces, including the first-floor bedroom chamber. An outdoor goldfish pond and a patio with seating are pleasant in warmer weather. The price includes full breakfast and afternoon tea; a small kitchen is available for those staying here. ⊠ 1049 E. King St., Lancaster 17602 ☎ 717/397-1017 or 800/747-8717 ⊟ 717/397-3447 ⊕ www.kingscottagebb. com ✍ 7 rooms, 1 cottage ⟋ Dining room, in-room data ports, library, free parking; no smoking ▤ D, MC, V ⦿ BP $$-$$$$.

▦ **SWISS WOODS.** Innkeepers Werner and Debrah Mosimann designed this chalet while they were still living in Werner's native Switzerland. On the edge of the woods overlooking a lake, it's an airy building with light pine and contemporary country fur-nishings. Extensive flower gardens surround the house. Each room has its own patio or balcony, and goose-down comforters are on all the beds. ⊠ 500 Blantz Rd., Lititz 17543 ☎ 717/627-3358 or 800/594-8018 ⊟ 717/627-3483 ⊕ www.swisswoods.com ✍ 6 rooms, 1 suite ⟋ Boating, fishing, hiking ▤ AE, D, MC, V ⦿ BP $$-$$$.

Where to Eat

✗ **CARR'S RESTAURANT.** Owner Tim Carr and chef Kathy Walls have created a sim-ple and appealing restaurant with the look of a French café. Fresh meats, vegetables, fruit, and fowl are all featured. A signature dish is the shrimp-and-basil ravioli in Provençale sauce. ⊠ Market and Grant Sts. across from Central Market, Lancaster ☎ 717/299-7090 ▤ AE, D, DC, MC, V ⊘ Closed Mon. $$$$.

✗ **LANCASTER DISPENSING CO.** Fajitas, salads, sandwiches, and pizzas with pita crusts are served until midnight in this boisterous Victorian pub, which has a vast selec-tion of imported beers. There's live music on weekends. ⊠ 33-35 N. Market St., Lancaster ☎ 717/299-4602 ▤ AE, D, MC, V $-$$.

✗ **LILY'S ON MAIN.** Chef and manager Steve Brown's food draws on regional American dishes for its inspiration. Favorite dishes include raspberry chicken with Brie and almonds, and horseradish-crusted Atlantic salmon. You can also dine on lighter fare, such as a panini sandwich or Lily's special salad with fresh greens and vegetables. The food is served on tables draped with crisp white linens and topped with a single lily. The gorgeous view overlooking town is another reason to dine here. ⊠ Brossman Business Complex, 124 E. Main St., Ephrata ☎ 717/738-2711 ▤ AE, D, DC, MC, V $$-$$$$.

✗ **MILLER'S SMORGASBORD.** The lavish spread here has a good selection of Pennsylvania Dutch foods. The breakfast buffet (served daily June through October and on weekends November through May) is sensational, with omelets, pancakes, eggs cooked to order, fresh fruits, pastries, bacon, sausage, and potatoes. ⊠ 2811 Lincoln Hwy. E (U.S. 30), Ronks ☎ 717/687-6621 ☰ AE, D, MC, V $.

✕ **SILK CITY DINER.** At this classic diner with chrome fixtures, checkerboard floors, and a jukebox of old-time hits, the big helpings and consistent quality keep the parking lot full. The large menu includes baked meat loaf, grilled chicken, country-fried steak, and club sandwiches. The many desserts, all made on the premises, include chocolate chip cheesecake and éclairs. ⊠ 1640 N. Reading Rd. (Rte. 272), Stevens ☎ 717/335-3833 ☰ AE, DC, MC, V ¢-$$.

Essentials

Getting Here
From Philadelphia take the Schuylkill Expressway (I-76) west to the Pennsylvania Turnpike. Lancaster County sights are accessible from Exits 20, 21, and 22. Another option is to follow U.S. 30 west from Philadelphia, but be prepared for major highway construction on Route 30 in Lancaster. It's about 65 mi to Pennsylvania Dutch Country.

Visitor Information
🚺 **Pennsylvania Dutch Convention & Visitors Bureau** ⊠ 501 Greenfield Rd., Lancaster 17601 ☎ 717/299-8901 or 800/723-8824 ⊕ www.padutchcountry.com.

PITTSBURGH

If you haven't been to Pittsburgh for a while, then you haven't been to Pittsburgh. Revitalized by downtown investment, Steel Town is starting to shine as it did during the boom times of the 1950s, albeit with a lot less smoke pouring out of the stacks.

Because it's in the foothills of the Allegheny Mountains, Pittsburgh has many different kinds of terrain, making it very suitable for golf courses. There are some great ones surrounding the city. For a complete golf-lodging-and-spa experience, Nemacolin Woods is tough to beat, and its Mystic Rock course is one of the most highly regarded resort courses in the country. For those interested in something a bit more low key, Chestnut Ridge Golf Club has 36 holes that rival anything else in Pennsylvania. Don't forget to visit the nearby town of Latrobe for a Rolling Rock beer, and a look at Arnold Palmer's childhood home. He still spends half the year there.

PITTSBURGH COURSES	YARDAGE	PAR	COURSE	SLOPE	GREEN FEE
Cedarbrook Golf Course (36)					$22/$32
Gold (18)	6,710/5,138	72/72	72.4/70.2	135/121	
Red (18)	6,154/4,577	71/71	68.3/65.3	120/111	
Chestnut Ridge Golf Club (36)					
Chestnut Ridge (18)	6,321/5,130	72/72	70.7/70.2	129/119	$28/$33
Tom's Run (18)	6,812/5,363	72/72	73.0/71.0	135/126	$45/$50
Nemacolin Woodlands Resort & Spa (36)					
The Links (18)	6,643/4,835	71/71	73.0/67.3	131/115	$55/$84
Mystic Rock (18)	7,329/4,804	72/72	76.4/68.1	147/123	$130/$150
Oakmont East Golf Course (18)	5,750	72	65.5	113	$18/$21
Olde Stonewall Golf Club (18)	6,944/5,051	70/70	73.2/69.7	140/123	$80/$135
Stoughton Acres Golf Club (18)	6,081/5,012	71/72	67.3/68.5	114/116	$10/$11
Quicksilver Golf Club (18)	7,120/5,067	72/74	75.7/68.6	145/115	$40/$65

Courses

Golf Digest REVIEWS

CEDARBROOK GOLF COURSE. Facility Holes: 36. Opened: 1986. Architect: Michael Hurdzan. Green Fee: $22/$32. Cart Fee: $13 per person. Discounts: Weekdays, twilight, seniors, juniors. Walking: Unrestricted walking. Season: Year-round. Tee Times: Call 7 days in advance. Notes: Range (grass). ✉ 215 Rte. 981, Belle Vernon 15012, 25 mi from Pittsburgh ☎ 724/929-8300 ▭ AE, D, MC, V.

Gold. Holes: 18. Yards: 6,710/5,138. Par: 72/72. Course Rating: 72.4/70.2. Slope: 135/121. *Comments: A solid golf experience.* ★★★★

Red. Holes: 18. Yards: 6,154/4,577. Par: 71/71. Course Rating: 68.3/65.3. Slope: 120/111. *Comments: Shorter and easier than the Gold.* ★★★★

CHESTNUT RIDGE GOLF CLUB. Facility Holes: 36. Cart Fee: $10 per person. Discounts: Weekdays, twilight. Walking: Unrestricted walking. Season: Mar.–Dec. High: May–Oct. Tee Times: Call 7 days in advance. Notes: Metal spikes, range (grass). ✉ 1762 Old William Penn Hwy., Blairsville 15717, 35 mi from Pittsburgh ☎ 724/459-7188 ▭ AE, MC, V.

Chestnut Ridge. Holes: 18. Opened: 1964. Architect: Harrison/Garbin. Yards: 6,321/5,130. Par: 72/72. Course Rating: 70.7/70.2. Slope: 129/119. Green Fee: $28/$33. *Comments: A pleasant course to walk.* ★★★★

Tom's Run. Holes: 18. Opened: 1993. Architect: Bill Love/Brian Ault/Clark. Yards: 6,812/5,363. Par: 72/72. Course Rating: 73.0/71.0. Slope: 135/126. Green Fee: $45/$50. *Comments: Might be the best public course in western Pennsylvania.* ★★★★ ½

NEMACOLIN WOODLANDS RESORT & SPA. Facility Holes: 36. Cart Fee: Included in green fee. Discounts: Guest, twilight. Walking: Mandatory cart. Season: Apr.–Oct. High: May–Aug. Tee Times: Call 30 days in advance. Notes: Range (grass, mat). ✉ 1001

LaFayette Dr., Farmington 15437, 75 mi from Pittsburgh ☎724/329–6111 or 800/422–2736 ⊕www.nemacolin.com ⊟AE, D, DC, MC, V.

The Links. Holes: 18. Opened: 1987. Architect: Willard Rockwell. Yards: 6,643/4,835. Par: 71/71. Course Rating: 73.0/67.3. Slope: 131/115. Green Fee: $55/$84. *Comments: Highlighted by a scenic back 9.* ★★★¹/₂

Mystic Rock. Holes: 18. Opened: 1995. Architect: Pete Dye. Yards: 7,329/4,804. Par: 72/72. Course Rating: 76.4/68.1. Slope: 147/123. Green Fee: $130/$150. *Comments: Ranked 4th in Golf Digest's 1995 Best New Resort Courses. Top-ranking Dye design.* ★★★★¹/₂

OAKMONT EAST GOLF COURSE. Facility Holes: 18. Opened: 1938. Architect: Emil Loeffler/John McGlynn. Yards: 5,750. Par: 72. Course Rating: 65.5. Slope: 113. Green Fee: $18/$21. Cart Fee: $12 per person. Walking: Unrestricted walking. Season: Year-round Tee Times: Call golf shop. ⊠Rte. 909 at Hulton Rd., Oakmont 15139, 15 mi from Pittsburgh ☎412/828–5335 ⊟MC, V. UR

OLDE STONEWALL GOLF CLUB. Facility Holes: 18. Opened: 1999. Architect: Michael Hurdzan/Dana Fry. Yards: 6,944/5,051. Par: 70/70. Course Rating: 73.2/69.7. Slope: 140/123. Green Fee: $80/$135. Cart Fee: Included in green fee. Walking: Unrestricted walking. Season: Apr.–Nov. Tee Times: Call 14 days in advance. Notes: Range (grass). ⊠1495 Mercer Rd., Ellwood City 16117, 30 mi from Pittsburgh ☎724/752–4653 ⊕www.oldestonewall.com ⊟AE, D, DC, MC, V. *Comments: Worth a trip just for the scenery.* ★★★★¹/₂

QUICKSILVER GOLF CLUB. Facility Holes: 18. Opened: 1990. Architect: Don Nagode/Arnold Palmer. Yards: 7,120/5,067. Par: 72/74. Course Rating: 75.7/68.6. Slope: 145/115. Green Fee: $40/$65. Cart Fee: Included in green fee. Discounts: Twilight, seniors, juniors. Walking: Walking at certain times. Season: Mar.–Dec. Tee Times: Call 6 days in advance. Notes: Metal spikes, range (grass). ⊠2000 Quicksilver Rd., Midway 15060, 18 mi from Pittsburgh ☎724/796–1594 ⊕www.quicksilvergolf.com ⊟AE, D, DC, MC, V. *Comments: Designed by local hero Arnold Palmer, it's a popular place.* ★★★★

STOUGHTON ACRES GOLF CLUB. Facility Holes: 18. Opened: 1964. Architect: Van Smith. Yards: 6,081/5,012. Par: 71/72. Course Rating: 67.3/68.5. Slope: 114/116. Green Fee: $10/$11. Cart Fee: $16 per cart. Walking: Unrestricted walking. Season: Apr.–Dec. Tee Times: Call golf shop. Notes: Metal spikes. ⊠904 Sunset Dr., Butler 16001, 40 mi from Pittsburgh. *Comments: Might be the best golf for your money in Pennsylvania.* ★★★★

Where to Stay

🏨 **INN AT OAKMONT.** On top of a hill above the town of Oakmont stands this small B&B, where each room has a golf motif. The Oakmont East Golf Course is across the street, and Pittsburgh itself is 15 mi away. ⊠300 Rte. 909, Verona 15147 ☎412/828–

0410 🏠 412/828-1358 ⊕ www.pittsburghbnb.com/oakmont.html ⤵8 rooms (1 with shower only) ♿ Some in-room hot tubs, business services; no kids under 6, no smoking ☰AE, D, MC, V ❍❙BP $$.

🎬 **NEMACOLIN WOODLANDS RESORT & SPA.** This large complex, once a game reserve, includes the Chateau LaFayette, a traditional European-style hotel; the Lodge, done in an English Tudor style; and Falling Rock, whose design is a homage to Frank Lloyd Wright. In addition the large spa and golf facilities here, Nemacolin also has an adventure center with facilities for off-road driving, paintball, and fly fishing. ✉ 1001 LaFayette Dr., Farmington 15437 ☎ 724/329-8555 or 800/422-2736 🖨 724/329-6947 ⊕ www.nemacolin.com ⤵ 190 rooms, 31 suites, 66 town houses ♿ 8 restaurants, tea, shop, in-room data ports, in-room safes, minibars, cable TV, 2 18-hole golf courses, miniature golf, 4 tennis courts, spa, fishing, mountain bikes, hiking, horseback riding, 3 bars, pub, shops, children's programs (4–18) ☰AE, D, MC, V $$$.

🎬 **OMNI WILLIAM PENN.** Pittsburgh's grand hotel has a stately lobby with a coffered ceiling, ornate moldings, and crystal chandeliers. Most of the guest rooms are light and airy, and spacious enough to hold a couch and a wing chair. ✉ 530 William Penn Pl., Mellon Sq., 15219 ☎ 412/281-7100 🖨 412/553-5252 ⊕ www.omnihotels.com ⤵ 596 rooms ♿ 2 restaurants, health club ☰AE, D, DC, MC, V $$–$$$.

Where to Eat

✕**ASAGIO.** Italian and French cuisines are united at this trendy restaurant, with selections such as puff pastry with artichokes and mushrooms in Madeira cream sauce, and asparagus ravioli with tomato basil sauce. Entrées might include veal normande with apples, mushrooms, and walnuts in calvados sauce, and crab cakes in an orange sauce. ✉ Oxford Centre, 301 Grant St. ☎ 412/392-0225 ☰AE, D, DC, MC, V $$$–$$$$.

✕**CASBAH.** The eclectic menu, influenced by the cuisines of southern France, Italy, Greece, Turkey, and Tunisia, includes dishes such as grilled quail with red-grape relish and saffron basmati rice, or salmon steamed in grape leaves with a lemon–pine nut vinaigrette. More than 40 wines are available by the glass. ✉ 229 S. Highland Ave. ☎ 412/661-5656 ☰AE, D, DC, MC, V $$$–$$$$.

✕**CHEESE CELLAR.** Inside the former freight house that's now a mall, the Cheese Cellar overlooks the Monongahela River. Dishes are fun and casual, such as beer-and-cheese flounder, grilled swordfish, and several kinds of fondue. ✉ Station Square Mall, 25 Freight House Shops ☎ 412/471-3355 🖨 412/281-0549 ⊕ www.selectrestaurants.com ♿ Reservations not accepted ☰AE, D, DC, MC, V $–$$$.

✕**MONTEREY BAY FISH GROTTO.** This restaurant on top of Mt. Washington has more than 20 kinds of fish—sautéed, char-grilled, blackened, and other preparations—and an unrivaled view of the downtown skyline. Pastas and meat dishes round out the menu. ✉ 1411 Grandview Ave. ☎ 412/481-4414 ☰AE, D, DC, MC, V $$$–$$$$.

Essentials

Getting Here

To reach Pittsburgh from Philadelphia, take the Pennsylvania Turnpike (I–76) west 300 mi. The Turnpike merges with I–70 roughly 125 mi from Pittsburgh.

Visitor Information

🛈 **GREATER PITTSBURGH CONVENTION AND VISITORS BUREAU, INC.** ✉ Regional Enterprise Tower, 425 6th Ave., 15219 ☎ 412/281–7711 or 800/366–0093 🖷 412/644–5512 ⊕ www.pittsburgh-cvb.org.

AROUND
SAN FRANCISCO

Sonoma Golf Club

By Ron Kaspriske and John Vlahides

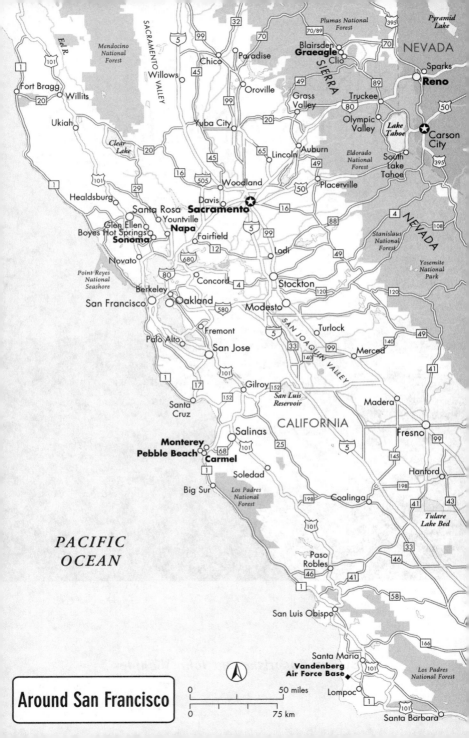

Around San Francisco

When golfers think of San Francisco, they

generally think of it as a point of departure for golf trips to places like the Monterey Peninsula or Lake Tahoe. It's tough to argue with that. Residents of the "City by the Bay" know they don't have to leave town to play quality golf, but who wouldn't want to head north to the Napa and Sonoma valleys or down to the coast to Pebble Beach, golf's hallowed ground?

The Monterey Peninsula is the most popular golf getaway for Bay Area residents, and rightly so. Not only is Pebble Beach Golf Links consistently rated among the top five golf courses in America by *Golf Digest*, but the region also has several other spectacular seaside tracks, including Spyglass Hill and Links at Spanish Bay.

If you're looking for the road less traveled, and if $200-plus green fees ($380 in the case of Pebble) aren't for you, then you may want to venture east of San Francisco to Sacramento, or north of the Lake Tahoe region to Graeagle and Truckee. The many quality golf courses in these destinations cost less than half as much as the courses along Monterey's famous 17-Mile Drive.

Of the golf destinations in this chapter, the sleeper of the group is San Luis Obispo. It has never been known as a good place for a golf trip, and that's why we like it—there are plenty of good-but-not-great courses in the area that aren't nearly as expensive or crowded as other destinations.

Aside from the plethora of great golf courses, another advantage in leaving San Francisco is getting away from the somewhat frustrating microclimate of cool weather and fog. Keep in mind that you don't have to travel too far away from the city to find a more suitable weather pattern. In Napa and Sacramento, for instance, summers are at least 20°–30° warmer than they are in San Francisco. And Lake Tahoe is spectacular in late summer and early fall. Pebble Beach is a year-round destination, but there's a much better chance of a sunny day in October than in January.

If you want a place to take your family and they don't golf themselves, then Lake Tahoe is your best bet: boating, bike riding, and hiking are all easy to find there. Napa and Sonoma, with their scores of wineries, have plenty to offer to keep the (over-21) nongolfer busy as well.

Dragon at Gold Mountain (18)	7,077/4,611	72/72	74.2/66.6	147/128	$79/$139
Golf Club at Whitehawk Ranch (18)	6,928/4,816	71/71	72.4/65.4	130/122	$75/$135
Graeagle Meadows Golf Course (18)	6,725/5,589	72/72	72.1/71.0	129/127	$20/$55
Plumas Pines Golf Resort (18)	6,504/5,240	72/72	71.3/69.9	132/125	$65/$80

GRAEAGLE

Some golfers discover the Graeagle area by accident. Instead of heading south on State Hwy. 89 down to Lake Tahoe, they go north, toward the fertile valley town of Graeagle. In this region are some of the best golf courses in California.

When this was lumber country, the trees in the Sierra Nevada Mountain range and the Tahoe National Forest provided the wood. Now they also provide scenery for the golf courses that have been built here. The Whitehawk course is a good choice: it's routed through towering pines and five lakes and streams in a meadow bordered by the mountain range.

The Graeagle courses are all different, but they have one thing in common: solitude. There can't be many places more peaceful than Graeagle. Despite its size, there are also plenty of places to stay, including cabins at Whitehawk Ranch. However, remember that you're basically in the middle of nowhere. You're not going to find your favorite chain restaurant and if you want nightlife, you may be better off staying in Lake Tahoe or Reno, a little more than an hour away.

Courses
Golf Digest REVIEWS

DRAGON AT GOLD MOUNTAIN. Facility Holes: 18. Opened: 2000. Architect: Robin Nelson. Yards: 7,077/4,611. Par: 72/72. Course Rating: 74.2/66.6. Slope: 147/128. Green Fee: $79/$139. Cart Fee: Included in green fee. Walking: Unrestricted walking. Season: Late Apr.–mid-Nov. High: Late May–mid-Oct. Tee Times: Call up to a year in advance. ✉ 3887 County Rd. A15, Clio 96106 ☎ 530/832–4887 ⊕ www.dragongolf.com ⊟ AE, D, MC, V. *Comments: The scenery is awesome, the clubhouse wonderful, and the grooming impeccable. With that said, the course is way too gimmicky and way too hard. That slope from the back tees will get your attention. Play here, but don't bother using the scorecard.* UR

GOLF CLUB AT WHITEHAWK RANCH. Facility Holes: 18. Opened: 1996. Architect: Dick Bailey. Yards: 6,928/4,816. Par: 71/71. Course Rating: 72.4/65.4. Slope: 130/122.

Green Fee: $75/$135. Cart Fee: Included in green fee. Discounts: Weekdays, twilight, juniors. Walking: Unrestricted walking. Season: May–Nov. High: June–Oct. Tee Times: Call 180 days in advance. Notes: Range (grass), lodging (14). ⌨ 768 Whitehawk Dr., Clio 96106, 60 mi from Reno, NV ☎ 530/836-0394 or 800/332-4295 ⊕ www.golfwhitehawk. com ☰ AE, MC, V. *Comments: If more people knew where this course was, it might be in the top 25 in the state. But let's keep this rustic course in a valley to ourselves. It's a great deal of fun to play.* ★★★★ ½

GRAEAGLE MEADOWS GOLF COURSE. Facility Holes: 18. Opened: 1967. Architect: Ellis Van Gorder. Yards: 6,725/5,589. Par: 72/72. Course Rating: 72.1/71.0. Slope: 129/127. Green Fee: $20/$55. Cart Fee: $15 per person. Discounts: Weekdays, twilight. Walking: Unrestricted walking. Season: Apr.–Nov. High: June–Sept. Tee Times: Call 180 days in advance. Notes: Metal spikes, range (grass). ⌨ Hwy. 89, Graeagle 96103, 58 mi from Reno, NV ☎ 530/836-2323 ⊕ www.playgraeagle.com ☰ D, MC, V. *Comments: A river and two lakes help shape this valley course. The tall pines act as sentries.* ★★★ ½

PLUMAS PINES GOLF RESORT. Facility Holes: 18. Opened: 1980. Architect: Homer Flint. Yards: 6,504/5,240. Par: 72/72. Course Rating: 71.3/69.9. Slope: 132/125. Green Fee: $65/$80. Cart Fee: Included in green fee. Discounts: Weekdays, twilight. Walking: Unrestricted walking. Season: May–Nov. Tee Times: Call golf shop. Notes: Range (grass, mat). ⌨ 402 Poplar Valley Rd., Blairsden 96103, 63 mi from Reno, NV ☎ 530/836-1420 ⊕ - www.plumaspinesgolf.com ☰ AE, D, DC, MC, V. *Comments: Tight fairways, but a beautiful course that's very scoreable. It was carved out of Plumas National Forest.* ★★★ ½

> Graeagle courses are all different, but they have one thing in common: solitude.

Where to Stay

⊞ FEATHER RIVER INN. Giant rough-hewn sugar-pine beams support the vast main lodge of the Feather River Inn, a rambling early-20th-century vacation resort. There's nothing slick or pretentious about the place, and it retains its original charm—though it could use an infusion of cash. Rooms in the comfortable lodge include breakfast and have more amenities than the outlying rustic cabins. From the lodge's sweeping veranda, you can watch golfers playing the inn's 9-hole golf course. ⌂ Box 67, Graeagle 96103 ☎ 530/836-2623 or 888/324-6400 🖶 530/836-0927 ⊕ www.featherriverinn.com ⮒ 24 lodge rooms, 2 suites, 35 cabin rooms ♿ Restaurant, fans, some in-room data ports, some refrigerators, cable TV in some rooms, 9-hole golf course, putting green, tennis court, pro shop, pool, fishing, badminton, basketball, horseshoes, Ping-Pong, volleyball, bar, playground, meeting rooms, some pets allowed (fee); no a/c in some rooms, no phones in some rooms, no TV in some rooms, no smoking ☰ AE, D, MC, V ⏍ BP ⊘ Closed mid-Nov.–Mar. ¢–$$.

⊞ GRAEAGLE VACATION RENTALS. Because of limited traditional lodging in the Graeagle area, you may wish to opt for a golf-course home rental at Graeagle, Plumas Pines, or Whitehawk. All of the two-, three-, and four-bedroom condos, cabins, and custom homes come with outdoor decks and barbecues. The longer you stay, the better the rate. ⌂ Box 307, Graeagle 96103 ☎ 530/836-2500 or 800/836-0269 🖷 530/836-2025 ⊕ www.graeagleproperties.com ⇋ 32 units ⌂ Cable TV, kitchens; no a/c in some units, no smoking ▤ MC, V $$-$$$$.

🏠 **LODGE AT WHITEHAWK RANCH.** Underneath towering pines, the modern, attractive, and spacious one- and two-bedroom peaked-roof cabins at the edge of Whitehawk golf course have comfortable furnishings that include country quilts and big pinewood bed frames. Several cabins overlook a fly-fishing pond. Rates include full breakfast and afternoon wine-and-cheese service. ✉ 985 Whitehawk Dr., Box 175, Clio 96106 ☎ 530/836-4985 or 877/945-6343 🖷 530/836-4990 ⊕ www. lodgeatwhitehawk.com ⇋ 12 cabins ⌂ Restaurant, cable TV, in-room VCRs, refrigerators, tennis, pool, outdoor hot tub, fishing, bicycles, hiking; no smoking ▤ AE, D, MC, V ⍟ BP ⊘ Closed mid-Oct.-mid-Apr. $$$-$$$$.

🏠 **NAKOMA RESORT AND SPA.** You can stay on the 10th fairway of Dragon by renting one of the resort's ultra-deluxe villas. Each comes with fireplace, surround-sound stereos with DVD players, high-end linens, custom furnishings, and Jacuzzi tubs. You also get privileges at the spa and golf club. ⌂ Bear Run Rd., Graeagle 96103 ☎ 530/832-6304 or 877/418-0880 🖷 530/832-4894 ⊕ www.nakomaresort.com ⇋ 7 villas ⌂ Restaurant, fans, in-room data ports, in-room fax, in-room safes, in-room hot tubs, kitchenettes, cable TV, driving range, 18-hole golf course, golf privileges, putting green, 2 tennis courts, pro shop, indoor lap pool, pool, gym, hair salon, hot tub, massage, sauna, spa, steam room, hiking, bar, concierge, Internet, meeting rooms, airport shuttle; no smoking ▤ AE, D, MC, V $$$$.

🏠 **RIVER PINES RESORT AND RENTALS.** If you want to save money on lodging, River Pines has standard-issue motel rooms, and housekeeping cottages equipped with linens and basic kitchen supplies. Kids love the big swimming pool. River Pines also rents golf course homes—some on the fairway—at Whitehawk and Plumas Pines. ✉ Hwy. 89, Blairsden ⌂ Box 249, Clio 96106 ☎ 530/836-2552 or 800/696-2551 🖷 530/836-1556 ⊕ www.riverpines.com ⇋ 45 motel rooms, 18 housekeeping cottages, 40 vacation homes ⌂ Restaurant, snack bar, fans, kitchens, cable TV in some rooms, pool, outdoor hot tub, Ping-Pong, shuffleboard, bar, no-smoking rooms; no a/c in some rooms, no phones in some rooms ▤ AE, D, MC, V $.

Where to Eat

✕ **GRIZZLY GRILL.** Just off Hwy. 89 in Blairsden, the convivial Grizzly Grill has a very capable chef-owner who can cook dishes to please just about anyone, from pasta to pot roast. Since the room has hardwood floors and walls, it can get noisy, but the food is good and the staff friendly. ✉ 250 Bonta St., Blairsden ☎ 530/836-1300 ⌂ Reservations essential ▤ MC, V ⊘ Call for winter hrs $$$-$$$$.

✕ **LONGBOARDS BAR AND GRILL.** After golfing at Plumas Pines, stay for dinner in the clubhouse, at the resort's very fine restaurant. The contemporary Italian menu includes several preparations of risotto and pasta, as well as roasted and grilled seafood and steaks. On summer weekends, Longboards serves brunch; on Saturday nights, live bands perform in the bar. ⊠402 Poplar Valley Rd., Graeagle ☎530/836-1111 ⚛Reservations essential ⊟AE, D, MC, V ⊘No brunch Mon.-Thurs. $$$-$$$$.

✕**NAKOMA.** One of the most visually dramatic dining rooms in the Sierra Nevada, Nakoma was built in 2000 after a 1923 design by Frank Lloyd Wright. The restaurant specializes in updated American classics, such as lamb shanks served with garlic mashed potatoes, trout coated with almonds, and filet mignon wrapped in bacon. But come for the room, not the food. If you're planning to golf at Dragon, make it a point to stop by. ⊠Hwy. A15, Graeagle ☎530/832-6304 ⚛Reservations essential ⊟AE, D, MC, V ⊘Closed 1 month in winter, usually Jan. or Feb. $$-$$$$.

✕**RESTAURANT AT WHITEHAWK RANCH.** Book a table by the window inside the high-ceilinged dining room, or sit outside on the veranda overlooking the mountains and golf course, and dine on excellent preparations of European-inspired California cuisine. This is one of the area's best white-tablecloth restaurants. ⊠985 Whitehawk Dr., Graeagle ☎530/836-4985 ⚛Reservations essential ⊟AE, MC, V ⊘Closed Tues. July and Aug.; Mon. and Tues. Apr.-June, Sept., and Oct.; Nov.-Mar. No lunch $$$$.

Essentials

Getting Here

To reach Graeagle, take I-80 north roughly 200 mi to Truckee (⇨ see the Reno section for some of its area courses). Then take Hwy. 89 north for approximately 45 mi. This drive takes about an hour. In spring or fall, be prepared for surprise snowstorms: if you don't have four-wheel drive, carry chains. Contact Caltrans for highway information. It gets cold at night in the mountains. Carry extra clothing and food in case you break down. In a highway emergency, dial 911 or contact the California Highway Patrol.

🚩 **California Highway Patrol** ☎530/587-3510. **Caltrans Highway Information Line** ☎916/445-7623, 800/427-7623 California and Reno/Lake Tahoe areas only ⊕www. dot.ca.gov.

Visitor Information

🚩 **Eastern Plumas Chamber of Commerce** ⊠8889 Hwy. 89, Box 1043, Blairsden 96103, ☎530/831-1811 or 800/995-6057 ⊕ www.easternplumaschamber.com.

MONTEREY PENINSULA

If you haven't yet been to Monterey, Carmel, the "17-Mile Drive"along the peninsula, or the Pebble Beach Golf Links, then prepare for two things: some of the most beautiful topography in the world and some serious prices. A room at the Inn at Spanish Bay goes for around $500. A round at Pebble Beach is a whopping $380. Even a drive on those 17 mi costs $8.

Bayonet/Black Horse Golf Courses (36)					$72/$97
Bayonet Course (18)	7,094/5,763	72/74	75.1/73.7	139/134	
Black Horse Course (18)	7,009/5,648	72/72	74.4/72.5	135/129	
Carmel Valley Ranch Golf Club (18)	6,234/4,337	70/70	70.5/64.7	134/112	$155/$175
Del Monte Golf Course (18)	6,339/5,526	72/74	71.3/71.1	122/118	$95
Golf Club at Quail Lodge (18)	6,449/5,488	72/72	71.4/72.0	128/127	$125/$195
Links at Spanish Bay (18)	6,820/5,309	72/72	74.8/70.6	146/129	$105/$215
Pacific Grove Municipal Golf Links (18)	5,732/5,305	70/72	67.5/70.5	117/114	$32/$38
Pebble Beach Golf Links (18)	6,737/5,198	72/72	73.8/71.9	142/130	$380
Poppy Hills Golf Course (18)	6,835/5,403	72/72	74.6/72.1	144/131	$50/$160
Rancho Canada Golf Club (36)					
East (18)	6,109/5,267	71/72	69.8/69.4	122/114	$35/$65
West (18)	6,357/5,576	71/72	71.4/71.9	125/118	$45/$80
Spyglass Hill Golf Course (18)	6,855/5,642	72/74	75.3/73.7	148/133	$145/$265

But all that said, if you love golf, you have to make the pilgrimage to the Monterey Peninsula.

Save your pennies, call way in advance, and book a round at the Pebble Beach Golf Links, which has been played by just about every famous golfer who ever lived, not to mention presidents, princes, and other notables. The legendary course was ranked No. 1 in the country (public or private) in *Golf Digest*'s 2001 rankings of America's 100 Greatest Courses. It's fallen a few notches since, but it remains a must-play.

Right next door is another top-100 gem: Cypress Point. This ultra-private club does not allow nonmembers to play, but there's no law keeping you from stopping and getting a look. Both courses overlook Carmel Bay, as does yet another top-100 course: Spyglass Hill Golf Course. This public course is one of the four owned by the Pebble Beach Company. The firm's other two, Poppy Hills and the Links at Spanish Bay, are also very good. Although the Lodge at Pebble Beach is an experience unto itself, we like staying at Spanish Bay better, at least for a night.

It might be tempting to spend all your time at Pebble, but there are other courses in the area worth a visit. The Bayonet and Black Horse golf courses, on the property once occupied by Fort Ord in Seaside, are excellent. And if you want to save some bucks, Pacific Grove Municipal Golf Links may be the cheapest seaside course in the United States.

Just about the only thing wrong with this area is the fickle weather. Sun one day, high winds the next. Clouds and rain are as common as golf balls landing in the surf. But come anyway. You just might feel compelled to.

Courses   **Golf**Digest REVIEWS

BAYONET/BLACK HORSE GOLF COURSES. Facility Holes: 36. Green Fee: $72/$97. Cart Fee: $18 per cart. Discounts: Weekdays, twilight, seniors, juniors. Walking: Walking at certain times. Season: Year-round. Tee Times: Call golf shop. Notes: Metal spikes, range (grass, mat). ⊠ Fort Ord, 1 McClure Way, Seaside 93955, 8 mi from Monterey ☎ 831/899-7271 ▤ AE, MC, V.

Bayonet Course. Holes: 18. Opened: 1954. Architect: General Bob McClure. Yards: 7,094/5,763. Par: 72/74. Course Rating: 75.1/73.7. Slope: 139/134. ★ ★ ★ ★

Black Horse Course. Holes: 18. Opened: 1963. Architect: General Karnes/General McClure. Yards: 7,009/5,648. Par: 72/72. Course Rating: 74.4/72.5. Slope: 135/129. ★ ★ ★ ★

Comments: At Fort Ord's impressive facility, the courses were actually designed by the base's generals. Plays through cypress and pine tree forests, with the occasional peek at the ocean.

ALONG THE WAY

If you're traveling to either Monterey or San Luis Obispo, consider stopping along the way at either Ritz-Carlton's Half Moon Bay resort or at Stanford's great 18-hole track, where Tiger honed his game.

CARMEL VALLEY RANCH GOLF CLUB. Facility Holes: 18. Opened: 1981. Architect: Pete Dye. Yards: 6,234/4,337. Par: 70/70. Course Rating: 70.5/64.7. Slope: 134/112. Green Fee: $155/$175. Cart Fee: Included in green fee. Discounts: Twilight, juniors. Walking: Walking at certain times. Season: Year-round. Tee Times: Call 30 days in advance. Notes: Range (grass), lodging (144). ⊠ 1 Old Ranch Rd., Carmel 93923, 6 mi from Carmel by the Sea ☎ 831/626-2510 or 800/422-7635 ⊕ www.cvrgolf.com ▤ AE, D, MC, V. *Comments: Above-average resort golf. You must stay at the resort to play.* ★ ★ ★ ★

DEL MONTE GOLF COURSE. Facility Holes: 18. Opened: 1897. Architect: Charles Maud. Yards: 6,339/5,526. Par: 72/74. Course Rating: 71.3/71.1. Slope: 122/118. Green Fee: $95. Cart Fee: $20 per person. Discounts: Twilight, juniors. Walking: Unrestricted walking. Season: Year-round. Tee Times: Call 60 days in advance. Notes: Metal spikes. ⊠ 1300 Sylvan Rd., Monterey 93940, 60 mi from San Jose ☎ 831/373-2700 ⊕ www.delmontegolf.com ▤ AE, D, MC, V. *Comments: Close to Pebble. Narrow, meandering, tree-lined layout has undergone several alterations. Short course with tiny greens, but very well manicured.* ★ ★ ★ ★

GOLF CLUB AT QUAIL LODGE. Facility Holes: 18. Opened: 1964. Architect: Robert Muir Graves. Yards: 6,449/5,488. Par: 72/72. Course Rating: 71.4/72.0. Slope: 128/127. Green Fee: $125/$195. Cart Fee: Included in green fee. Walking: Unrestricted walking.

Season: Year-round. High: Apr.–Oct. Tee Times: Call golf shop. ✉ 8205 Valley Greens Dr., Carmel 93923 ☎ 831/624-2888 or 888/828-8787 ⊕ www.quaillodge.com ▤ AE, D, MC, V. *Comments: Carmel Valley course is attractive, but lacks the eye candy of the courses on the water. Still, it's solid.* UR

LINKS AT SPANISH BAY. Facility Holes: 18. Opened: 1987. Architect: Robert Trent Jones Jr./Tom Watson/Sandy Tatum. Yards: 6,820/5,309. Par: 72/72. Course Rating: 74.8/ 70.6. Slope: 146/129. Green Fee: $105/$215. Cart Fee: $25 per cart. Discounts: Twilight. Walking: Unrestricted walking. Season: Year-round. Tee Times: Call 60 days in advance. Notes: Lodging (270). ✉ 2700 17-Mile Dr., Pebble Beach 93953, 2 mi from Monterey ☎ 831/647-7495 or 800/654-9300 ⊕ www.pebblebeach.com ▤ AE, D, MC, V. *Comments: Holes along the water are brutally hard but gorgeous. The holes on the back side of the resort are easy and boring.* ★ ★ ★ ★ ½

PACIFIC GROVE MUNICIPAL GOLF LINKS. Facility Holes: 18. Opened: 1932. Architect: Jack Neville/Chandler Egan. Yards: 5,732/5,305. Par: 70/72. Course Rating: 67.5/70.5. Slope: 117/114. Green Fee: $32/$38. Cart Fee: $28 per cart. Discounts: Twilight, juniors. Walking: Unrestricted walking. Season: Year-round. Tee Times: Call 7 days in advance. Notes: Range (grass, mat). ✉ 77 Asilomar Blvd., Pacific Grove 93950, 2 mi from Monterey ☎ 831/648-5775 ⊕ www.ci.pacific-grove.ca.us ▤ MC, V. *Comments: The poor man's Pebble Beach. Hard to believe a muni was built along the Pacific Ocean. Pay $38, sink a birdie, and see a whale. Top that.* ★ ★ ★ ★

PEBBLE BEACH GOLF LINKS. Facility Holes: 18. Opened: 1919. Architect: Jack Neville/Douglas Grant. Yards: 6,737/5,198. Par: 72/72. Course Rating: 73.8/71.9. Slope: 142/130. Green Fee: $380. Cart Fee: $25 per person. Walking: Unrestricted walking. Season: Year-round. Tee Times: Call golf shop. Notes: Metal spikes, range (grass, mat). ✉ 1700 17-Mile Dr., Pebble Beach 93953, 115 mi from San Francisco ☎ 831/624-3811 or 800/654-9300 ⊕ www.pebblebeach.com ▤ AE, D, DC, MC, V. *Comments: A once-in-a-lifetime experience, but you'll want seconds for sure. The first few holes are not memorable, but the rest is.* ★ ★ ★ ★ ★

POPPY HILLS GOLF COURSE. Facility Holes: 18. Opened: 1986. Architect: Robert Trent Jones Jr. Yards: 6,835/5,403. Par: 72/72. Course Rating: 74.6/72.1. Slope: 144/131. Green Fee: $50/$160. Cart Fee: $30 per cart. Discounts: Juniors. Walking: Unrestricted walking. Season: Year-round. Tee Times: Call 30 days in advance. Notes: Range (grass). ✉ 3200 Lopez Rd., Pebble Beach 93953, 60 mi from San Jose ☎ 831/625-2154 ⊕ www. poppyhillsgolf.com ▤ AE, MC, V. *Comments: Often overlooked by the other seaside gems at Pebble Beach, Poppy is a terrific rustic design. Hilly and tree-lined.* ★ ★ ★ ★ ½

RANCHO CANADA GOLF CLUB. Facility Holes: 36. Opened: 1970. Architect: Robert Dean Putman. Cart Fee: $34 per cart. Discounts: Twilight, juniors. Walking: Unrestricted walking. Season: Year-round. High: Aug.–Oct. Tee Times: Call golf shop. Notes: Range (grass, mat). ✉ 4860 Carmel Valley Rd., Carmel 93923, 8 mi from Monterey ☎ 831/624-0111 or 800/536-9459 ⊕ www.ranchocanada.com ▤ AE, DC, MC, V.

East. Holes: 18. Yards: 6,109/5,267. Par: 71/72. Course Rating: 69.8/69.4. Slope: 122/114. Green Fee: $35/$65. ★ ★ ★ ½

West. Holes: 18. Yards: 6,357/5,576. Par: 71/72. Course Rating: 71.4/71.9. Slope: 125/118. Green Fee: $45/$80. ★ ★ ★ ½

GRAY WHALES

From mid-November to early May, the Gray Whales make their annual journey from their feeding grounds in Alaska to the warm breeding lagoons in Baja California and back again. Although they pass off the shores of Canada, Washington, and Oregon, most of the best viewing locations are along the California coast. Spouts and the occasional tail flap can be seen from the shoreline, but whale watch tours get you far more up close and personal. Tours are offered in several locations from San Francisco to Monterey: contact San Francisco Bay Whale Watching (www.sfbaywhalewatching.com) for more information.

Comments: This Carmel Valley facility is very good. Like Quail Lodge and Carmel Valley Ranch, only come here after you've seen the courses along 17-Mile Drive.

SPYGLASS HILL GOLF COURSE. Facility Holes: 18. Opened: 1966. Architect: Robert Trent Jones. Yards: 6,855/5,642. Par: 72/74. Course Rating: 75.3/73.7. Slope: 148/133. Green Fee: $145/$265. Cart Fee: $25 per person. Discounts: Guest, twilight. Walking: Unrestricted walking. Season: Year-round. High: Apr.–Nov. Tee Times: Call golf shop. Notes: Metal spikes, range (grass, mat). ⊠ Spyglass Hill Rd. and Stevenson Dr., Pebble Beach 93953, 60 mi from San Jose ☎ 831/625-8563 or 800/654-9300 ▤ AE, D, DC, MC, V. *Comments: This expensive course is a strong second to Pebble. The holes along the water are awesome.* ★ ★ ★ ¹⁄₂

Where to Stay

▥ **BERNARDUS LODGE.** The first-rate spa and the outstanding restaurant are the focus at this luxury resort, where services are geared to those who love good wine and food. Spacious guest rooms have vaulted ceilings, feather beds, fireplaces, patios, double-size bathtubs, and complimentary wine and snacks. You can have lunch poolside or in the bar; dinner is in the Marinus restaurant. The hotel's car and driver can drop you off at Quail Lodge for golf. ⊠ 415 Carmel Valley Rd., Carmel Valley 93924 ☎ 831/659-3131 or 888/648-9463 🖶 831/659-3529 ⊕ www.bernardus.com ◁ 57 rooms ⚭ 2 restaurants, room service, in-room data ports, minibars, refrigerators, cable TV with movies, some in-room VCRs, tennis court, pool, gym, hair salon, hot tub, sauna, spa, steam room, croquet, hiking, lawn bowling, bar, lobby lounge, laundry service, concierge, Internet, meeting room; no smoking ▤ AE, D, DC, MC, V $$$$.

▥ **CARMEL VALLEY LODGE.** One of the few moderately priced lodgings in Carmel Valley, this small inn has rooms surrounding a garden patio and separate one- and two-bedroom cottages with fireplaces and full kitchens. ⊠ 8 Ford Rd., at Carmel Valley Rd., 93924 ☎ 831/659-2261 or 800/641-4646 🖶 831/659-4558 ⊕ www.valleylodge.com ◁ 19 rooms, 4 suites, 8 cottages ⚭ Kitchenettes, refrigerators, cable TV, in-room VCRs, pool, exercise equipment, hot tub, sauna, horseshoes, Ping-Pong, Internet, some pets allowed (fee), no-smoking rooms ▤ AE, MC, V ⓄⓁ CP $$$.

▥ **CARMEL VALLEY RANCH RESORT.** This all-suites resort, well off Carmel Valley Road on a 400-acre estate overlooking the valley, is typical of contemporary California architecture. Standard amenities include wood-burning fireplaces and watercolors by local artists. Rooms have cathedral ceilings, fully stocked wet bars, and large decks. If you're staying here, the green fee at the resort's 18-hole golf course is $155, including cart; special golf packages can reduce this rate considerably. ✉1 Old Ranch Rd., 93923 ☎831/625–9500 or 800/422–7635 ⊟831/624–2858 ⊕www.wyndham.com ⇌144 suites ⟁2 restaurants, in-room data ports, in-room safes, some in-room hot tubs, mini-bars, some microwaves, refrigerators, cable TV with movies and video games, some in-room VCRs, 18-hole golf course, 13 tennis courts, 2 pools, 2 hot tubs, 2 saunas, steam room, 2 bars, laundry service, concierge, Internet, business services, meeting rooms; no smoking ⊟AE, D, DC, MC, V $$$$.

CASA PALMERO. This exclusive spa resort captures the essence of a Mediterranean villa. Rooms are decorated with sumptuous fabrics and fine art, and each has a wood-burning fireplace and heated floor. Some also have a private outdoor patio with an in-ground Jacuzzi. Complimentary cocktail service is offered each evening in the main hall and library. The spa is very up-to-date, and by staying here you have use of all facilities at the Lodge at Pebble Beach and the Inn at Spanish Bay. ✉1518 Cypress Dr., Pebble Beach 93953 ☎831/622–6650 or 800/654–9300 ⊟831/622–6655 ⊕www. pebblebeach.com ⇌21 rooms, 3 suites ⟁Room service, in-room data ports, some in-room hot tubs, minibars, refrigerators, cable TV with movies and video games, in-room VCRs, golf privileges, pool, health club, spa, bicycles, billiards, lounge, library, laundry service, concierge, meeting rooms; no a/c, no smoking ⊟AE, D, DC, MC, V $$$$.

INN AT SPANISH BAY. This resort sprawls across a breathtaking stretch of shore-line. Under the same management as the Lodge at Pebble Beach—where you have priv-ileges—this inn is slightly more casual, and its 600-square-foot rooms are no less luxu-rious. Peppoli's restaurant ($–$$$), which serves Tuscan cuisine, overlooks the coast and the golf links. Try Roy's Restaurant ($–$$$) for more casual and innovative Euro-Asian fare. ✉2700 17-Mile Dr., Pebble Beach 93953 ☎831/647–7500 or 800/654–9300 ⊟831/644–7960 ⊕www.pebblebeach.com ⇌252 rooms, 17 suites ⟁3 restaurants, room service, in-room data ports, minibars, refrigerators, cable TV with movies and video games, in-room VCRs, 18-hole golf course, 8 tennis courts, pro shop, pool, fitness class-es, health club, sauna, steam room, beach, bicycles, hiking, bar, lobby lounge, laundry service, concierge, Internet, business services, meeting rooms; no smoking ⊟AE, D, DC, MC, V $$$$.

LODGE AT PEBBLE BEACH. Luxurious rooms with fireplaces and wonderful views set the tone at this resort, built in 1919. The golf course, tennis club, and equestrian cen-ter are highly regarded; you also have privileges at the Inn at Spanish Bay. Overlooking the 18th green, Club XIX restaurant ($$$$) is an intimate, clubby dining room serving French food. ✉1700 17-Mile Dr., Pebble Beach 93953 ☎831/624–3811 or 800/654–9300 ⊟831/644–7960 ⊕www.pebblebeach.com ⇌142 rooms, 19 suites ⟁3 restau-rants, coffee shop, in-room data ports, some in-room hot tubs, minibars, refrigerators, cable TV with movies and video games, in-room VCRs, 18-hole golf course, 12 tennis courts, pro shop, pool, gym, health club, sauna, spa, beach, bicycles, horseback riding, 2 bars, lobby lounge, laundry service, concierge, Internet, business services, meeting rooms, some pets allowed; no a/c, no smoking ⊟AE, D, DC, MC, V $$$$.

ALISTER'S PLAYGROUNDS

Alister Mackenzie (1870–1934) may be the most renowned of the classic architects of golf. Born in Scotland, he came to the United States at the age of 48,
having turned his attention to golf courses after a career as a physician and military strategist. In fact, his theory of bunkering on golf courses derived from his
studies of military bunkering in the Boer War. Although he designed courses
throughout the United States, his Northern California designs, including
Cypress Point in Pebble Beach and Pasatiempo in Santa Cruz, are favorites.
Dr. Mackenzie lived in a home on the sixth fairway of Pasatiempo until his death.

QUAIL LODGE. At this resort on the grounds of a private country club you have
access to an 850-acre wildlife preserve frequented by deer and migratory fowl. Modern
rooms with European styling are clustered in several low-rise buildings. Each room has
a private deck or patio overlooking the golf course, gardens, or lake. The Covey at Quail
Lodge ($$–$$$$; jacket recommended) serves Continental cuisine in a romantic lake-
side dining room. ⊠ 8205 Valley Greens Dr., Carmel Valley 93923 ☎ 831/624–1581 or
800/538–9516 🖷 831/624–3726 ⊕ www.quaillodge.com ⟋ 83 rooms, 14 suites ௸ 2
restaurants, room service, some fans, in-room data ports, some in-room faxes, some in-
room safes, some in-room hot tubs, minibars, refrigerators, cable TV with movies and
video games, 18-hole golf course, putting green, 4 tennis courts, pro shop, 2 pools, gym,
hot tub, sauna, spa, steam room, bicycles, croquet, hiking, 2 bars, baby-sitting, laundry
service, concierge, Internet, business services, meeting rooms, some pets allowed (fee),
no-smoking rooms; no a/c in some rooms ☱ AE, DC, MC, V $$$$.

Where to Eat

✕ **CAFÉ RUSTICA.** Italian-inspired country cooking is the focus at this lively road-
house. Specialties include roasted meats, pastas, and pizzas from the wood-fired oven.
Because of the tile floors, it can get noisy inside; opt for a table outside for a quieter
meal. ⊠ 10 Delfino Pl., Carmel Valley ☎ 831/659–4444 ௸ Reservations essential
☱ MC, V ⊘ Closed Wed. $–$$$.

✕ **ROBERT'S BISTRO.** The menu at chef-owner Robert Kincaid's French bistro stress-
es seasonal ingredients. Dried sage and lavender hanging from exposed ceiling beams,
painted floors, and ocher-washed walls bring to mind an old farmhouse in Provence.
Cassoulet, made with white beans, duck confit, rabbit sausage, and garlic prawns, is
always on the stove. Leave room for dessert, particularly the soufflé with lemon and
orange zest, or the chocolate "bag" with chocolate shake, a wonderful invention.
⊠ Crossroads Center, 217 Crossroads Blvd., Carmel ☎ 831/624–9626 ௸ Reservations
essential ☱ AE, D, DC, MC, V ⊘ Closed Mon. No lunch $$$–$$$$.

✕ **STOKES RESTAURANT & BAR.** Inside an 1833 adobe, Stokes seamlessly balances
innovative cooking and traditional design. Looking to Provence, northern Italy, and
Catalan Spain for inspiration, the kitchen here turns out imaginative pasta, seafood, and
vegetarian dishes that change seasonally. Dishes have included slow-roasted duck

breast on squash-chestnut risotto and rustic pasta tubes with fennel sausage and Manila clams. ⊠500 Hartnell St., Monterey ☎831/373-1110 ⚘Reservations essential ▤AE, D, DC, MC, V ⊘No lunch Sun. $$-$$$$.

✕**WAGON WHEEL COFFEE SHOP.** Grab a seat at the counter or wait for a table at this local hangout decorated with wood-beam ceilings, hanging wagon wheels, cowboy hats, and lassos. Then chow down on substantial breakfasts of *huevos rancheros,* Italian sausage and eggs, or trout and eggs; this is also a place for biscuits and gravy. For lunch choose among a dozen types of burgers and other sandwiches. ⊠Valley Hill Center, Carmel Valley Rd. next to Quail Lodge, Carmel Valley ☎831/624-8878 ▤No credit cards ⊘No dinner ¢-$.

Essentials

Getting Here

Two-lane Route 1 runs north–south along the coast, linking the towns of Santa Cruz, Monterey, and Carmel. The drive south from San Francisco to Monterey can be made comfortably in three hours or less. The most scenic way is to follow Route 1 down the coast past flower, pumpkin, and artichoke fields and the seaside communities of Pacifica, Half Moon Bay, and Santa Cruz. Unless you drive on sunny weekends when locals are heading for the beach, the two-lane coast highway may take no longer than the freeway.

A sometimes faster route is I-280 south from San Francisco to Route 17, north of San Jose. Route 17 crosses the forested Santa Cruz Mountains between San Jose and Santa Cruz, where it intersects with Route 1. The traffic can crawl to a standstill, however, heading into Santa Cruz. Another option is to follow U.S. 101 south through San Jose to Prunedale and then take Route 156 west to Route 1 south into Monterey.

From Los Angeles the drive to Monterey can be made in five to six hours by heading north on U.S. 101 to Salinas and then west on Route 68. The spectacular but slow alternative is to take U.S. 101 to San Luis Obispo and then follow the hairpin turns of Route 1 up the coast. Allow about three extra hours if you take this route.

Visitor Information

🚹 **Monterey County Convention & Visitors Bureau** ☎800/555-9283 ⊕www. gomonterey.org. **Monterey Peninsula Visitors and Convention Bureau** ⊠380 Alvarado St., Monterey 93942 ☎831/649-1770 ⊕www.monterey.com.

NAPA-SONOMA

It's no secret that vineyards heavily outnumber golf courses in Napa, about an hour north of San Francisco via U.S. 101. Over 400 wineries are here, compared to a dozen noteworthy public golf courses. Actually, the two kinds of institutions make an impressive pairing. For many golfers, it's hard to top

			COURSE	SLOPE	
Chardonnay Golf Club (36)					
Club Shakespeare **(18)**	7,001/5,448	72/72	74.5/70.9	137/125	$110/$130
Vineyards **(18)**	6,811/5,200	72/72	73.7/70.1	133/126	$55/$95
Links at Bodega Harbour (18)	6,253/4,757	70/69	71.4/70.1	127/120	$40/$80
Napa Golf Course (18)	6,704/5,690	72/73	72.7/72.8	131/126	$19/$41
Rooster Run Golf Club (18)	7,001/5,139	72/72	73.9/69.1	128/117	$32/$51
Silverado Country Club & Resort (36)					
North **(18)**	6,900/5,847	72/72	73.1/73.1	134/128	$70/$150
South **(18)**	6,685/5,672	72/72	72.1/72.7	131/127	$70/$150
Sonoma Golf Club (18)	7,087/5,511	72/72	74.1/71.8	132/125	$110/$150

playing 18 holes and then sipping on a cabernet or puffing on a Cohiba. The Napa area is a great place to be.

At the top of our golf picks is the Sonoma Golf Club, which once hosted the Charles Schwab Cup Championship, the final event on the Champions Tour. No less an authority than Sam Snead called the course's design the best he'd ever seen. Tied for a close second are the two courses each at the Silverado Country Club and the Chardonnay Golf Club.

If you can hit all five of those courses in one trip, there's really no need to hit anything else except your pillow, right before the lights go out. But there are other options. To help spice up the trip, a good first stop on the journey is Rooster Run Golf Club, in Petaluma. Opened in 1998, the former farmland was reshaped to give it gentle slopes. From there, you can take your pick of where to play next, but try to save enough time for the Links at Bodega Harbour, 30 mi west of Napa on the coast. Not many people know about this course, but it's awesome.

Courses

GolfDigest REVIEWS

CHARDONNAY GOLF CLUB. Facility Holes: 36. Architect: Johnny Miller/Jack Barry. Cart Fee: Included in green fee. Discounts: Weekdays, twilight. Walking: Mandatory cart. Season: Year-round. Tee Times: Call 30 days in advance. Notes: Metal spikes, range (grass). ✉2555 Jameson Canyon Rd. (Hwy. 12), Napa 94558, 38 mi from San Francisco ☎707/257-1900 or 800/788-0136 ⊕www.chardonnaygolfclub.com ▭AE, D, DC, MC, V.

Club Shakespeare. Holes: 18. Opened: 1992. Yards: 7,001/5,448. Par: 72/72. Course Rating: 74.5/70.9. Slope: 137/125. Green Fee: $110/$130. *Comments: Back 9 is the gem here. Pretty.* ★ ★ ★ ★

Vineyards. Holes: 18. Opened: 1987. Yards: 6,811/5,200. Par: 72/72. Course Rating: 73.7/70.1. Slope: 133/126. Green Fee: $55/$95. *Comments: The course runs through a 340-acre vineyard of merlot and chardonnay.* ★★★★

LINKS AT BODEGA HARBOUR. Facility Holes: 18. Opened: 1976. Architect: Robert Trent Jones Jr. Yards: 6,253/4,757. Par: 70/69. Course Rating: 71.4/70.1. Slope: 127/120. Green Fee: $40/$80. Cart Fee: Included in green fee. Discounts: Weekdays, guest, twilight, seniors, juniors. Walking: Walking at certain times. Season: Year-round. Tee Times: Call 90 days in advance. Notes: Metal spikes, range (mat). ✉ 21301 Heron Dr., Bodega Bay 94923, 20 mi from Santa Rosa ☎ 707/875-3538 ⊕ www.bodegaharbourgolf.com ⊟ AE, MC, V. *Comments: If you have time, play this amazing ocean-side links course. A hidden gem.* ★★★★

NAPA GOLF COURSE AT KENNEDY PARK. Facility Holes: 18. Opened: 1968. Architect: Jack Fleming/Bob Baldock. Yards: 6,704/5,690. Par: 72/73. Course Rating: 72.7/72.8. Slope: 131/126. Green Fee: $19/$41. Cart Fee: $12 per person. Discounts: Weekdays, twilight, seniors, juniors. Walking: Unrestricted walking. Season: Year-round. High: Apr.–Nov. Tee Times: Call 14 days in advance. Notes: Metal spikes, range (mat). ✉ 2295 Streblow Dr., Napa 94558, 45 mi from San Francisco ☎ 707/255-4333 ⊕ www. playnapa.com ⊟ AE, MC, V. *Comments: A good parkland golf course, and a great value.* ★★★ ¹/₂

ROOSTER RUN GOLF CLUB. Facility Holes: 18. Opened: 1998. Architect: Fred Bliss. Yards: 7,001/5,139. Par: 72/72. Course Rating: 73.9/69.1. Slope: 128/117. Green Fee: $32/$51. Cart Fee: $12 per person. Discounts: Twilight, seniors, juniors. Walking: Unrestricted walking. Season: Year-round. Tee Times: Call 7 days in advance. Notes: Range (grass). ✉ 2301 E. Washington St., Petaluma 94954, 30 mi from San Francisco ☎ 707/778-1211 ⊟ MC, V. *Comments: A large amount of earth was moved to create this hilly course, where five lakes border the fairways. A good value.* ★★★ ¹/₂

SILVERADO COUNTRY CLUB & RESORT. Facility Holes: 36. Opened: 1955. Architect: Robert Trent Jones Jr. Season: Year-round. Tee Times: Call up to 2 days in advance. ✉ 1600 Atlas Peak Rd., Napa 94558 ☎ 707/257-0200 or 800/362-4727 ⊕ www. silveradoresort.com ⊟ AE, D, MC, V.

North. Holes: 18. Yards: 6,900/5,847. Par: 72/72. Course Rating: 73.1/73.1. Slope: 134/128. Green Fee: $70/$150. Cart Fee: Included in green fee. Walking: Unrestricted walking. *Comments: Tree-lined pastures, hills, and vineyards off in the distance. Very pretty.* ★★★★

South. Holes: 18. Yards: 6,685/5,672. Par: 72/72. Course Rating: 72.1/72.7. Slope: 131/127. Green Fee: $70/$150. Cart Fee: Included in green fee. Walking: Unrestricted walking. *Comments: Also very beautiful. Large, fast greens. Like the North, it's great for walking.* ★★★★

SONOMA GOLF CLUB. Facility Holes: 18. Opened: 1928. Architect: Sam Whiting/Willie Watson. Yards: 7,087/5,511. Par: 72/72. Course Rating: 74.1/71.8. Slope: 132/125. Green Fee: $110/$150. Cart Fee: $15 per person. Discounts: Weekdays. Walking: Unrestricted walking. Walkability: 2. Season: Year-round. High: Apr.–Oct. Tee Times: Call 14 days in advance. Notes: Range (grass, mat). ✉ 17700 Arnold Dr., Sonoma 95476, 45 mi from

San Francisco ☎ 707/996-0300 ⊕ www.sonomagolfclub.com ☰ AE, MC, V. *Comments: In a valley with streams, trees, and well-groomed fairways that add to its beauty. You must be a guest of the Fairmont Sonoma Mission Inn & Spa to play.* ★ ★ ★ ½

Where to Stay

🏨 **AUBERGE DU SOLEIL.** Rooms at this elegant hotel have terraces, from which you can take in views of the stunning property and its steep slopes, planted with olive trees. Guest rooms are done in cool tile and soothing earth tones, with a nod to the spare side of Southwestern style, and the bathrooms are grand. The Auberge du Soleil restaurant ($$$$) serves New French cuisine and has an impressive wine list. It's not near the courses, but it's worth the drive. ⊠ 180 Rutherford Hill Rd., off Silverado Trail north of Rte. 128, 94573 ☎ 707/963-1211 or 800/348-5406 🖶 707/963-8764 ⊕ www. aubergedusoleil.com ⬎ 18 rooms, 32 suites ⚑ 2 restaurants, in-room data ports, kitchenettes, refrigerators, cable TV, in-room VCRs, 3 tennis courts, pool, gym, hot tub, massage, sauna, spa, bar, concierge, business services, meeting rooms ☰ AE, D, DC, MC, V $$$$.

NAPA WEATHER

Weather in the Napa Valley is variable, but it's generally warmer than in San Francisco. Your day may start in a jacket and end in shorts.

🏨 **CHATEAU HOTEL.** Despite the name, this is a fairly simple motel that makes only the barest nod to France. The clean, relatively inexpensive rooms, a good location at the southern end of the Napa Valley, and an adjacent restaurant all make up for its lack of charm. The 9-hole Yountville Golf Course is also near. ⊠ 4195 Solano Ave. (west of Rte. 29, exit at Trower Ave.), 94558 ☎ 707/253-9300, 800/253-6272 in CA 🖶 707/253-0906 ⊕ www.napavalleychateauhotel.com ⬎ 109 rooms, 6 suites ⚑ Some refrigerators, cable TV, pool, hot tub ☰ AE, D, DC, MC, V ⦿CP $$-$$$.

🏨 **FAIRMONT SONOMA MISSION INN & SPA.** California mission-style architecture combines with the elegance of a European luxury spa at this beautifully landscaped property. Everything is on a grand scale, from the Olympic-size pool to the spa facilities, where warm mineral water is pumped up from wells. Thirty suites in a secluded, tree-shaded area have verandas or patios, whirlpools, and fireplaces. The resort is affiliated with the Sonoma Golf Club. ⊠ 18140 Rte. 12, Box 1447, 2 mi north of Sonoma at Boyes Blvd., Boyes Hot Springs 95476 ☎ 707/938-9000 or 800/862-4945 🖶 707/938-4250 ⊕ www.sonomamissioninn.com ⬎ 168 rooms, 60 suites ⚑ 2 restaurants, room service, in-room data ports, in-room safes, minibars, refrigerators, cable TV, 2 pools, 18-hole golf course, pro shop, fitness classes, gym, hair salon, hot tub, spa, bicycles, hiking, 2 bars, shops, baby-sitting, dry cleaning, laundry service, concierge, business services, meeting rooms; no smoking ☰ AE, DC, MC, V $$$$.

🏨 **MEADOWOOD RESORT.** At the end of a semiprivate road, this 256-acre resort has accommodations in a rambling country lodge and several bungalows. You need never leave the luxurious confines of the resort, where you can engage in golf, tennis, hiking, fitness classes, and other sporty activities as well a good number of spa treatments. The elegant dining room, open at dinner only, specializes in California Wine Country cooking. Seating is also available outdoors on a terrace overlooking the golf course. The Grill, a less formal, less expensive restaurant, serves pizzas and spa food. ⊠ 900 Meadowood La., 94574 ☎ 707/963-3646 or 800/458-8080 🖨 707/963-5863 ⊕ www.meadowood. com ⟷ 40 rooms, 45 suites ⟷ 2 restaurants, room service, in-room data ports, refrigerators, cable TV, 9-hole golf course, 7 tennis courts, 2 pools, health club, hot tub, massage, sauna, spa, steam room, croquet, bar, concierge, business services, meeting rooms; no smoking ⊟ AE, D, DC, MC, V $$$$.

🖼 **SILVERADO COUNTRY CLUB & RESORT.** This luxurious if somewhat staid 1,200-acre property in the hills east of Napa has cottages, kitchen apartments, and one- to three-bedroom condominiums, many with fireplaces. It's a place for serious sports enthusiasts and anyone who enjoys the conveniences of a full-scale resort. There are also two restaurants of note on the grounds. The elegant Vintner's Court has California-Pacific Rim cuisine ($$$-$$$$), and Royal Oak ($$$-$$$$) serves steak and seafood nightly. ⊠ 1600 Atlas Peak Rd., 6 mi east of Napa via Rte. 121, 94558 ☎ 707/257-0200 or 800/532-0500 🖨 707/257-2867 ⊕ www.silveradoresort.com ⟷ 277 condo units ⟷ 3 restaurants, bar, kitchenettes, 2 18-hole golf courses, 23 tennis courts, 9 pools, bicycles ⊟ AE, D, DC, MC, V $$$-$$$$.

Where to Eat

✕ **BISTRO DON GIOVANNI.** The views of the valley from the covered patio are extraordinary, and the wine list is as local as the menu is eclectic. Don't miss the individual pizzas, the handmade pastas, or the focaccia sandwiches encasing grilled vegetables. Wood-roasted whole fish is a specialty and a standout. The terra-cotta tile floors and high ceilings give the place a Mediterranean sheen. ⊠ 4110 St. Helena Hwy. (Rte. 29), Napa ☎ 707/224-3300 ⊟ AE, D, DC, MC, V $$-$$$.

✕ **FRENCH LAUNDRY.** An old stone building houses the most acclaimed restaurant in Napa Valley—and, indeed, one of the most highly regarded in the country. The prix-fixe menus ($110-$135), one of which is vegetarian, include five or nine courses and usually have two or three additional surprises, such as a tiny cone filled with salmon tartare. A full three hours will likely pass before you reach dessert. Reservations are hard won and not accepted more than two months in advance (call two months ahead to the day). Didn't get a reservation? Try stopping by on the day you'd like to dine in case there's a cancellation. ⊠ 6640 Washington St., Yountville ☎ 707/944-2380 ⟷ Reservations essential ⊟ AE, MC, V ⊙ Closed 1st 2 wks in Jan. No lunch Mon.-Thurs. $$$$.

✕ **MUSTARDS GRILL.** Mustards attracts a capacity crowd almost every night. Grilled fish, steak, local fresh produce, and an impressive wine list are the trademarks of this boisterous bistro with a black-and-white marble floor and upbeat artwork. The thin, crisp, golden onion rings are addictive. ⊠ 7399 St. Helena Hwy. (Rte. 29), 1 mi north of Yountville ☎ 707/944-2424 ⟷ Reservations essential ⊟ D, DC, MC, V $$-$$$$.

Essentials

Getting Here

Although traffic on the two-lane country roads can be heavy, the best way to get around the sprawling Wine Country is by car.

From San Francisco, cross the Golden Gate Bridge, and then go north on U.S. 101, east on Route 37, and north and east on Route 121. For Sonoma, head north at Route 12; for Napa, turn left (to the northwest) when Route 121 runs into Route 29.

From Berkeley and other East Bay towns—or if there's a major backup on the Golden Gate Bridge—take I-80 north to Route 37 west to Route 29 north, which will take you directly up the middle of the Napa Valley. To reach Sonoma County, take Route 121 west off Route 29 south of the city of Napa. From points north of the Wine Country, take U.S. 101 south to Geyserville and take Route 128 southeast to Calistoga and Route 29. Most Sonoma County wine regions are clearly marked and accessible off U.S. 101; to reach the Sonoma Valley, take Route 12 east from Santa Rosa.

Visitor Information

7 **Napa Valley Conference and Visitors Bureau** ⊠ 1310 Napa Town Center, Napa 94559 ☏ 707/226-7459 ⊕ www.napavalley.com. **Sonoma County Tourism Program** ⊠ 520 Mendocino Ave., Suite 210, Santa Rosa 95401 ☏ 707/565-5383 or 800/576-6662 ⊕ www.sonomacounty.com. **Sonoma Valley Visitors Bureau** ⊠ 453 1st St. E, Sonoma 95476 ☏ 707/996-1090 ⊕ www.sonomavalley.com.

RENO, NV & LAKE TAHOE

Even though they're linked by geography and by gambling, it seems a little strange that Reno and Lake Tahoe are always mentioned in the same breath. Not only is the topography dramatically different between the two areas, but so is the golfing experience. Reno is a desert town with manufactured green golf courses and cheesy casinos. Lake Tahoe is a mountain-lake resort town with rustic, tree-lined parkland courses and not-as-cheesy casinos.

Before you even get to Reno, consider making a stop at Truckee, near where Hwy. 89 intersects with I-80. The mountainous layout of Truckee's Coyote Moon Golf Course is stunning, with great views. The track is 7,177 yards, but since you're teeing up at 5,000 feet above sea level, it plays short. After the round you can either head north to Graeagle (⇨ see above) or continue on to Reno.

The first "must" on your list should be the Edgewood Tahoe Golf Course, at an elevation of 6,200 feet at the south shore of Lake Tahoe. This gorgeous

RENO, NV & LAKE TAHOE COURSES	YARDAGE	PAR	COURSE	SLOPE	GREEN FEE
Coyote Moon Golf Course (18)	7,177/5,022	72/72	74.1/68.4	138/127	$140/$155
D'Andrea Golf and Country Club (18)	6,849/5,162	71/71	72.2/69.2	133/123	$25/$85
Edgewood Tahoe Golf Course (18)	7,470/5,547	72/72	75.7/71.3	139/136	$150/$200
Golf Club at Genoa Lakes (18)	7,263/5,008	72/72	73.5/67.6	134/117	$55/$110
Lake Ridge Golf Course (18)	6,714/5,159	71/71	71.8/64.0	130/121	$45/$95
Northstar-at-Tahoe Resort (18)	6,897/5,470	72/72	72.4/71.2	137/134	$65/$105
Red Hawk Golf Club (18)	7,127/5,115	72/72	72.9/69.2	137/125	$50/$95
Resort at Squaw Creek (18)	6,931/5,097	71/71	72.9/68.9	143/127	$85/$120
Rosewood Lakes Golf Course (18)	6,693/5,073	72/72	70.7/67.8	125/118	$14/$36
Sierra Nevada Golf Ranch (18)	7,358/5,129	72/72	75.3/69.5	137/119	$70/$90
Wolf Run Golf Club (18)	6,936/5,294	71/71	72.1/69.7	130/128	$35/$65

course hosts the Celebrity Golf Championship each year, and also hosted the 1985 U.S. Senior Open. (Remember to always use one club less than you would at sea level: balls travel farther through the lighter air at this elevation.) Other area courses worth visiting include the Northstar-at-Tahoe Resort Golf Course and the Resort at Squaw Creek, which played host to the 1960 Winter Olympics. Both are also good places to stay.

If you stay in Reno, you're likely to stay at a casino and play such interesting courses as Red Hawk Golf Club and Rosewood Lakes. But our favorite is D'Andrea Golf and Country Club in Sparks. The course winds through rocky terrain that brings to mind the courses in Las Vegas or Scottsdale.

If you have time, you may also want to travel to the Carson City area, south of Reno and east of Lake Tahoe. Here there are two great courses, the Sierra Nevada Golf Ranch and the Golf Club at Genoa Lakes.

Courses

Golf Digest REVIEWS

COYOTE MOON GOLF COURSE. Facility Holes: 18. Opened: 2000. Architect: Brad Bell. Yards: 7,177/5,022. Par: 72/72. Course Rating: 74.1/68.4. Slope: 138/127. Green Fee: $140/$155. Cart Fee: Included in green fee. Discounts: Twilight. Walking: Unrestricted walking. Season: May–Oct. High: July–Sept. Tee Times: Call 30 days in advance. ✉ 10685 Northwoods Blvd., Truckee 96161, 35 mi from Reno, NV ☎ 530/587-0886 ⊕ www. coyotemoongolf.com ▤ AE, MC, V. *Comments: A real mountain golf course that's in ter-*

rific shape. Only downer is the quirky finishing hole. Otherwise, this is as good as public golf gets. UR

D'ANDREA GOLF AND COUNTRY CLUB. Facility Holes: 18. Opened: 2000. Architect: Keith Foster. Yards: 6,849/5,162. Par: 71/71. Course Rating: 72.2/69.2. Slope: 133/123. Green Fee: $25/$85. Cart Fee: Included in green fee. Discounts: Weekdays, twilight, juniors. Walking: Mandatory cart. Season: Year-round. Tee Times: Call 14 days in advance. Notes: Range (grass, mat). ⊠ 2900 S. D'Andrea Pkwy., Sparks 89434, 10 mi from Reno ☎ 775/331-6363 ⊟ AE, MC, V. *Comments: Get ready for some desert target golf. It's 450 feet above the Reno/Sparks valley floor.* UR

EDGEWOOD TAHOE GOLF COURSE. Facility Holes: 18. Opened: 1968. Architect: George Fazio/Tom Fazio. Yards: 7,470/5,547. Par: 72/72. Course Rating: 75.7/71.3. Slope: 139/136. Green Fee: $150/$200. Cart Fee: Included in green fee. Walking: Unrestricted walking. Season: May-Oct. Tee Times: Call 90 days in advance. Notes: Range (grass). ⊠ 180 Lake Pkwy., Stateline 89449, 50 mi from Reno ☎ 775/588-3566 ⊕ www. edgewood-tahoe.com ⊟ AE, MC, V. *Comments: One of the best public courses in the United States. The par-3 17th hole plays right along the shore of Lake Tahoe. A memorable golf experience.* ★★★★ ½

GOLF CLUB AT GENOA LAKES. Facility Holes: 18. Opened: 1993. Architect: John Harbottle/Peter Jacobsen. Yards: 7,263/5,008. Par: 72/72. Course Rating: 73.5/67.6. Slope: 134/117. Green Fee: $55/$110. Cart Fee: Included in green fee. Discounts: Weekdays, twilight, juniors. Walking: Unrestricted walking. Season: Year-round. Tee Times: Call 30 days in advance. Notes: Range (grass). ⊠ 1 Genoa Lakes Dr., Genoa 89411, 15 mi from South Lake Tahoe ☎ 775/782-4653 ⊕ www.genoalakes.com ⊟ AE, D, MC, V. *Comments: Set against the slopes of the Sierra Nevada and bordered by numerous lakes and the Carson River. A great visual experience.* ★★★★

LAKE RIDGE GOLF COURSE. Facility Holes: 18. Opened: 1969. Architect: Robert Trent Jones. Yards: 6,714/5,159. Par: 71/71. Course Rating: 71.8/64.0. Slope: 130/121. Green Fee: $45/$95. Cart Fee: Included in green fee. Walking: Walking at certain times. Season: Mar.-Dec. High: Apr.-Oct. Tee Times: Call up to 7 days in advance. ⊠ 1200 Razorback Rd., Reno 89509 ☎ 775/825-2200 ⊕ www.lakeridgegolf.com ⊟ AE, MC, V. *Comments: Older, country-club design within Reno's city limits. Fun, but not memorable.* ★★★ ½

NORTHSTAR-AT-TAHOE RESORT GOLF COURSE. Facility Holes: 18. Opened: 1975. Architect: Robert Muir Graves. Yards: 6,897/5,470. Par: 72/72. Course Rating: 72.4/71.2. Slope: 137/134. Green Fee: $65/$105. Cart Fee: Included in green fee. Discounts: Weekdays, guest, twilight, seniors, juniors. Walking: Unrestricted walking. Season: May-Nov. High: June-Sept. Tee Times: Call 45 days in advance. Notes: Range (mat), lodging (257). ⊠ 168 Basque Dr., Truckee 96160, 40 mi from Reno ☎ 530/562-2490 or 800/ 466-6784 ⊕ www.skinorthstar.com ⊟ AE, D, MC, V. *Comments: Great mountain-golf experience. The views of nearby Mt. Pluto are spectacular.* ★★★★

RED HAWK GOLF CLUB. Facility Holes: 18. Opened: 1997. Architect: Robert Trent Jones Jr. Yards: 7,127/5,115. Par: 72/72. Course Rating: 72.9/69.2. Slope: 137/125. Green Fee: $50/$95. Cart Fee: Included in green fee. Discounts: Weekdays, twilight, juniors. Walking: Unrestricted walking. Walkability: 3. Season: Year-round. High: May.-Nov. Tee Times: Call 6 days in advance. Notes: Range (grass). ⊠ 6600 N. Wingfield Pkwy., Sparks

89436, 12 miles from Reno ☎ 775/626-6000 ⊕ www.wingfieldsprings.com ▤ AE, MC, V. *Comments: Fun to play, with wide fairways and potential birdies on every hole. Very flat.* ★★★★

RESORT AT SQUAW CREEK. Facility Holes: 18. Opened: 1992. Architect: Robert Trent Jones Jr. Yards: 6,931/5,097. Par: 71/71. Course Rating: 72.9/68.9. Slope: 143/127. Green Fee: $85/$120. Cart Fee: Included in green fee. Discounts: Weekdays, guest, twilight, juniors. Walking: Unrestricted walking. Season: May–Oct. Tee Times: Call 90 days in advance. Notes: Range (mat), lodging (403). ⊠ 400 Squaw Creek Rd., Olympic Valley 96146, 45 mi from Reno ☎ 530/581-6637 or 800/327-3353 ⊕ www.squawcreek.com ▤ AE, D, DC, MC, V. *Comments: An excellent, fun resort course, but it's tough to compete with Edgewood for beauty.* ★★★ ½

ROSEWOOD LAKES GOLF COURSE. Facility Holes: 18. Opened: 1991. Architect: Bradford Benz. Yards: 6,693/5,073. Par: 72/72. Course Rating: 70.7/67.8. Slope: 125/118. Green Fee: $14/$36. Cart Fee: $24 per cart. Discounts: Twilight, juniors. Walking: Unrestricted walking. Season: Year-round. High: May–Sept. Tee Times: Call 7 days in advance. Notes: Metal spikes, range (grass). ⊠ 6800 Pembroke Dr., Reno 89502 ☎ 775/857-2892 ⊕ www.rose-woodlakes.com ▤ MC, V. *Comments: Very affordable Reno course. Flat, high-desert design with many water hazards.* ★★★

SIERRA NEVADA GOLF RANCH. Facility Holes: 18. Opened: 1998. Architect: Johnny Miller/John Harbottle. Yards: 7,358/5,129. Par: 72/72. Course Rating: 75.3/69.5. Slope: 137/119. Green Fee: $70/$90. Cart Fee: Included in green fee. Discounts: Weekdays, twilight, juniors. Walking: Unrestricted walking. Season: Year-round. High: May–Sept. Tee Times: Call golf shop. Notes: Range (grass). ⊠ 2901 Jacks Valley Rd., Genoa 89411, 6 mi from Carson City ☎ 775/782-7700 or 888/452-4653 ⊕ www.sierranevadagolfranch. com ▤ AE, MC, V. *Comments: The championship design is routed over western sage. Dramatic elevation changes and great mountain views.* ★★★★ ½

WOLF RUN GOLF CLUB. Facility Holes: 18. Opened: 1998. Architect: John Fleming/Steve van Meter/Lou Eiguren. Yards: 6,936/5,294. Par: 71/71. Course Rating: 72.1/69.7. Slope: 130/128. Green Fee: $35/$65. Cart Fee: Included in green fee. Discounts: Weekdays, twilight, seniors, juniors. Walking: Unrestricted walking. Season: Year-round. High: May–Oct. Tee Times: Call 14 days in advance. Notes: Range (grass, mat). ⊠ 1400 Wolf Run Rd., Reno 89511 ☎ 775/851-3301 ▤ AE, D, MC, V. *Comments: Home of the University of Nevada's golf program, Wolf Run's definitely worth playing.* ★★★★

Where to Stay

▦ **BEST WESTERN STATION HOUSE INN.** It's a short walk to the beach or the casinos from this modern, very-well-kept two-story motel off the main drag, near the state line. The beds and the furniture are very comfortable, and the entire property is immaculate. ⊠ 901 Park Ave., South Lake Tahoe 96150 ☎ 530/542-1101 or 800/822-5953 🖷 530/542-1714 ⊕ www.stationhouseinn.com ⇌ 100 rooms, 2 suites ⚖ Restaurant, pool, hot tub ▤ AE, D, DC, MC, V ▯◈ BP $-$$$$.

▦ **BLACK BEAR INN BED AND BREAKFAST.** South Lake Tahoe's best and most luxurious inn resembles one of the great old lodges of the Adirondacks, its living room complete with rough-hewn timber beams, plank floors, knotty-pine cathedral ceiling, hand-knotted Persian rugs, and even an elk's head over the giant river-rock fireplace. The five inn rooms and three cabins are furnished with 19th-century American antiques, fine art, and fireplaces; cabins also have kitchenettes. Never intrusive, the affable innkeepers provide a sumptuous breakfast in the morning and wine and cheese in the afternoon. ⊠ 1202 Ski Run Blvd., South Lake Tahoe 96150 ☎ 530/544–4451 or 877/232–7466 ⊕ - www.tahoeblackbear.com ⟷ 5 rooms, 3 cabins ⌂ Dining room, in-room data ports, some in-room hot tubs, some kitchenettes, cable TV with movies, in-room VCRs, outdoor hot tub, ski storage, lounge; no kids under 16, no smoking ☰ MC, V ⓘ BP $$$$.

EMBASSY SUITES. This opulent all-suites hotel, decorated like a Sierra lodge, has fountains and waterwheels splashing in the nine-story atrium, where complimentary breakfasts and evening cocktails are served daily. Glass elevators rise to the guest suites, which each have a living room, dining area, and separate bedroom. ⊠ 4130 Lake Tahoe Blvd., South Lake Tahoe 96150 ☎ 530/544–5400 or 800/362–2779 ☐ 530/544–4900 ⊕ www.embassysuites.com ⟷ 400 suites ⌂ 4 restaurants, microwaves, cable TV with movies, indoor pool, gym, hot tub, sauna, nightclub, meeting rooms ☰ AE, D, DC, MC, V ⓘ BP $$$–$$$$.

PLUMPJACK SQUAW VALLEY INN. If style and luxury are a must, PlumpJack should be your first choice. The inn building originally housed visiting dignitaries at the 1960 Olympics. Every guest room comes equipped with down comforters, luxurious linens, and hooded terry robes to wear on your way to the outdoor hot tubs. The bar is a happening afternoon destination, and the restaurant is superb. It may not have an on-site spa or fitness center, but the service—personable and attentive—can't be beat. Not all of the rooms have bathtubs, so request one when you book if this is important to you. ⊠ 1920 Squaw Valley Rd., 96146 ☎ 530/583–1576 or 800/323–7666 ☐ 530/583–1734 ⊕ www.plumpjack.com ⟷ 56 rooms, 5 suites ⌂ Restaurant, some in-room hot tubs, minibars, cable TV, in-room VCRs, 2 outdoor hot tubs, massage, bar, shop, dry cleaning, laundry service, concierge, meeting rooms, free parking ☰ AE, MC, V ⓘ BP $$$–$$$$.

RESORT AT SQUAW CREEK. Designed during the Reagan era, the glass-and-concrete buildings at this vast, 650-acre resort-within-a-resort are more typical of Scottsdale than the Sierra. The resort's extensive facilities make it great for large groups and families with kids. Some units have fireplaces and full kitchens, and all have original art, custom furnishings, and good views. The Glissandi restaurant ($$$$) serves excellent contemporary California cuisine in a dramatic glass-walled room. ⊠ 400 Squaw Creek Rd., Olympic Valley 96146 ☎ 530/583–6300 or 800/327–3353 ☐ 530/ 581–5407 ⊕ www.squawcreek.com ⟷ 203 rooms, 200 suites ⌂ 3 restaurants, coffee shop, some kitchens, minibars, cable TV with movies and video games, 18-hole golf course, 2 tennis courts, 3 pools, health club, hair salon, 4 hot tubs, sauna, spa, sports bar, shops, children's programs, dry cleaning, laundry service, concierge, Internet, business services, meeting rooms, free parking ☰ AE, D, DC, MC, V $$$$.

SIENA HOTEL SPA CASINO. Reno's most luxurious hotel also has beautiful rooms and very comfortable beds, which are made up with Egyptian cotton sheets and down comforters. At check-in, you won't have to navigate past miles of slot machines to find the front desk, since the casino is in a self-contained room off the elegant lobby. Lexie's ($$$–$$$$) serves organic steaks and fresh seafood in a sleek dining room overlooking the river. ⊠ 1 S. Lake St., 89501 ☎ 775/337-6260 or 877/743-6233 🖷 775/321-5870 ⊕ www.sienareno.com 🖘 193 rooms, 21 suites ⚴ Restaurant, coffee shop, room service, in-room data ports, minibars, refrigerators, cable TV, pool, health club, spa, lounge, wine bar, casino, dry cleaning, laundry service, concierge, Internet, business center, meeting rooms, airport shuttle 🚍 AE, D, DC, MC, V ¢-$$.

Where to Eat

✗ **BEAUJOLAIS BISTRO.** Modern adaptations of classic French dishes are served in a comfortable, airy dining room with exposed brick walls and parquet floor. Everything here is French—the waiters, the wine, and even the music—with warm and friendly service. On the menu, expect beef burgundy, roast duck, seafood sausage, and steak. ⊠ 130 West St., Reno ☎ 775/323-2227 ⚴ Reservations essential 🚍 AE, D, MC, V $$-$$$.

✗ **EDGEWOOD TAHOE.** South Lake Tahoe's only high-end waterfront restaurant not only has sweeping views and delicious European-inspired cooking, it's also right inside the dramatic, peaked-roof clubhouse at Edgewood. Book an early table and watch the sun set. ⊠ 100 Lake Pkwy. at U.S. 50, Stateline ☎ 775/588-2787 ⚴ Reservations essential 🚍 AE, D, MC, V ⊗ No lunch $$$-$$$$.

✗ **FOURTH ST. GRILL.** Deliciously simple, perfectly prepared, contemporary cooking bursts with flavor at this charming bistro, where the chef-owner uses organic produce and meats when possible. The casual white-tablecloth dining room, with its sponge-painted walls, is comfortable and inviting. ⊠ 3065 W. 4th St., Reno ☎ 775/323-3200 ⚴ Reservations essential 🚍 AE, D, DC, MC, V ⊗ Closed Mon. and Tues. No lunch $$$-$$$$.

✗ **LULOU'S.** Modern art adorns the exposed brick walls of the small dining room at Reno's most innovative restaurant. Drawing influences from Europe and Asia, the chef has imported contemporary urban cooking to the area near the Great Basin Desert. The menu changes frequently, but expect to see everything from foie gras and duck confit to pot stickers and chicken curry. ⊠ 1470 S. Virginia St., Reno ☎ 775/329-9979 ⚴ Reservations essential 🚍 AE, D, DC, MC, V ⊗ Closed Sun. and Mon. No lunch $$$-$$$$.

✗ **PLUMPJACK.** PlumpJack serves exquisite contemporary haute cuisine in a luxurious, beautifully lighted dining room, where there's little to distract from the food and wine. On the menu, expect seafood, and lots of meat, including game. Most dishes are served with reductions of natural juices to maximize the food's flavors. If you have dietary restrictions, the chef can make something special—and delicious—for you. The wine list is exceptional for its variety and surprisingly low prices. ⊠ 1920 Squaw Valley Rd., Olympic Valley ☎ 530/583-1576 or 800/323-7666 ⚴ Reservations essential 🚍 AE, MC, V $$$-$$$$.

✗ **WILD GOOSE.** The food is as sublime as the view at Wild Goose. You can site on buttery-soft leather banquettes at polished mahogany tables and dine on exquisite contemporary French-California cuisine, like poached crab and artichoke hearts, roasted lobster and chanterelles, or a deliciously simple sirloin steak and french fries. Sliding glass doors line the casually elegant 100-seat dining room, opening up to a lakeside deck for outdoor dining. ⊠ 7320 N. Lake Blvd., Tahoe Vista ☎ 530/546-3640 ⚮ Reservations essential ▤ AE, MC, V ⊘ Closed Mon. $$$-$$$$.

Essentials

Getting Here

Lake Tahoe is 198 mi northeast of San Francisco, a drive of less than 4 hours in good weather. The heaviest traffic is on Friday afternoon, with an equally heavy amount heading back to San Francisco on Sunday afternoon. The major route is I-80, which cuts through Truckee, about 14 mi north of the lake, and 30 mi west of Reno. From Truckee Hwy. 89 and Hwy. 267 reach the west and north shores, respectively. U.S. 50 is the more direct route to the south shore from the west, taking about 2½ hours from Sacramento. From Reno you can get to the north shore by heading west on Hwy. 431 for 35 mi. For the south shore, head south on U.S. 395 through Carson City, and then turn west on U.S. 50 (50 mi total).

The scenic 72-mi highway around the lake is marked Hwy. 89 on the southwest and west shores, Hwy. 28 on the north and northeast shores, and U.S. 50 on the east and southeast. Sections of Hwy. 89 sometimes close due to snow in winter, spring, and fall, making it impossible to complete the circular drive. I-80, U.S. 50, and U.S. 395 are all-weather highways, but there may be delays as snow is cleared during major storms. Carry tire chains from October through May.

🚗 **California Highway Patrol** ☎ 530/587-3510. **Caltrans Highway Information Line** ☎ 916/445-7623, 800/427-7623 California and Reno/Lake Tahoe areas only ⊕ www. dot.ca.gov. **Nevada Department of Transportation Road Information** ☎ 877/687-6237. **Nevada Highway Patrol** ☎ 775/687-5300.

Visitor Information

🚗 **Lake Tahoe Visitors Authority** ⊠ 1156 Ski Run Blvd., South Lake Tahoe 96150 ☎ 530/544-5050 or 800/288-2463 ⊕ www.virtualtahoe.com. **North Lake Tahoe Resort Association** ✉ Box 5578, Tahoe City 96145 ☎ 530/583-3494 or 800/824-6348 🖨 530/581-4081 ⊕ www.tahoefun.org. **Reno-Sparks Convention and Visitors Authority** ⊠ 4590 S. Virginia St., Reno 89502 ☎ 775/827-7600 or 800/367-7366 ⊕ www.renolaketahoe.com.

SACRAMENTO

Like most of inland California, Sacramento is an afterthought for most golfers. Sure, it's the state capital, but folks aren't exactly flocking here to tee up. That may be a mistake. In fact, Sacramento may be the best cost-conscious golf destination in the state. Many public courses in the area

Ancil Hoffman Golf Course (18)	6,794/5,954	72/73	72.5/73.4	123/123	$20/$25
Cherry Island Golf Course (18)	6,562/5,163	72/72	71.9/70.0	129/117	$19/$23
Haggin Oaks Golf Course (36) Alister Mackenzie (18)	6,991/5,452	72/72	72.7/70.5	125/117	$10/$51
Lincoln Hills Club (18)	6,985/6,001	72/72	73.2/73.2	127/125	$42/$60
Mather Golf Course (18)	6,721/5,976	72/74	71.3/72.4	125/121	$23/$29
Ridge Golf Club (18)	6,734/5,855	71/71	72.3/70.7	142/128	$35/$55
Twelve Bridges Golf Club (18)	7,150/5,310	72/72	74.6/71.0	139/123	$30/$70
Whitney Oaks Golf Club (18)	6,793/4,983	71/71	74.2/70.9	138/127	$49/$69
Wildhawk Golf Club (18)	6,695/4,847	72/72	71.2/67.2	124/109	$31/$41

charge less than $50 for a round, and the standout courses of the area, including Twelve Bridges Golf Club, cost only around $70 to play.

In addition to Twelve Bridges, the best area courses are the Lincoln Hills Club and Ridge Golf Club. Lincoln Hills has scenic water features, broad fairways, and some of the area's noticeable elevation changes. Views of the distant hills provide a backdrop for your play. Ridge, within a few miles of Twelve Bridges, was designed by noted architect Robert Trent Jones Jr.

Speaking of architects, Sacramento even has a course designed by Alister Mackenzie—the same Mackenzie who designed Augusta National and Cypress Point, two of the four best courses in the United States. But although Haggin Oaks is no Cypress Point, it has been completely refurbished in the past few years. Ten of the holes are considered new.

Although San Francisco is only 90 mi to the east via I-80, Sacramento is dry and warm for most of the year. You can play here when the links are cold and wet by the bay.

Courses

Golf Digest REVIEWS

ANCIL HOFFMAN GOLF COURSE. Facility Holes: 18. Opened: 1965. Architect: William F. Bell. Yards: 6,794/5,954. Par: 72/73. Course Rating: 72.5/73.4. Slope: 123/123. Green Fee: $20/$25. Cart Fee: $22 per cart. Discounts: Twilight, seniors, juniors. Walking: Unrestricted walking. Season: Year-round. Tee Times: Call 7 days in advance. Notes: Metal spikes, range (grass, mat). ✉ 6700 Tarshes Dr., Carmichael 95608, 12 mi from

Sacramento ☎916/575-4653 ▤MC, V. *Comments: Rolling terrain on a tree-lined, classic course. This is a low-cost muni.* ★★★ ½

CHERRY ISLAND GOLF COURSE. Facility Holes: 18. Opened: 1990. Architect: Robert Muir Graves. Yards: 6,562/5,163. Par: 72/72. Course Rating: 71.9/70.0. Slope: 129/117. Green Fee: $19/$23. Cart Fee: $22 per cart. Discounts: Twilight, seniors, juniors. Walking: Unrestricted walking. Season: Year-round. Tee Times: Call golf shop. Notes: Metal spikes, range (grass, mat). ✉2360 Elverta Rd., Elverta 95626, 10 mi from Sacramento ☎916/ 991-7293. *Comments: Owned by Sacramento County. If you like target golf, this is your place. Quirky design.* ★★★

HAGGIN OAKS GOLF COURSE. Facility Holes: 36. Discounts: Weekdays, twilight, seniors, juniors. Walking: Unrestricted walking. Season: Year-round. High: Apr.–Oct. Tee Times: Call 7 days in advance. Notes: Range (mat). ✉3645 Fulton Ave., 95821 ☎916/ 575-2525 ⊕ www.mortongolf.biz ▤AE, D, MC, V.

Alister Mackenzie. Holes: 18. Opened: 1932. Architect: Alister Mackenzie. Yards: 6,991/5,452. Par: 72/72. Course Rating: 72.7/70.5. Slope: 125/117. Green Fee: $10/$51. Cart Fee: Included in green fee. *Comments: Built when the legendary architect was making his rounds through Northern California, designing courses like Cypress Point and Pasatiempo. This parkland-style golf course was completely refurbished a few years ago.* ★★★ ½

LINCOLN HILLS CLUB. Facility Holes: 18. Opened: 1999. Architect: Casper/Nash & Associates. Yards: 6,985/6,001. Par: 72/72. Course Rating: 73.2/73.2. Slope: 127/125. Green Fee: $42/$60. Cart Fee: Included in green fee. Season: Year-round. Tee Times: Call up to 10 days in advance. ✉ 1005 Sun City La., Lincoln 95648 ☎916/434-7454 or 916/ 434-7450 ⊕ www.lincolnhillsclubgolf.com ▤AE, MC, V. *Comments: The waterfalls are a little corny, but all the same it's a very scenic high-desert course.* UR

MATHER GOLF COURSE. Facility Holes: 18. Opened: 1963. Architect: Jack Fleming. Yards: 6,721/5,976. Par: 72/74. Course Rating: 71.3/72.4. Slope: 125/121. Green Fee: $23/$29. Cart Fee: $13 per cart. Discounts: Weekdays, twilight, seniors, juniors. Walking: Unrestricted walking. Season: Year-round. Tee Times: Call 7 days in advance. Notes: Metal spikes, range (grass). ✉4103 Eagles Nest Rd., Mather 95655, 7 mi from Sacramento ☎916/364-4354 ⊕ www.courseco.com ▤MC, V. *Comments: Older parkland-style course. Nothing special, but not bad.* ★★★

RIDGE GOLF CLUB. Facility Holes: 18. Opened: 1999. Architect: Robert Trent Jones Jr. Yards: 6,734/5,855. Par: 71/71. Course Rating: 72.3/70.7. Slope: 142/128. Green Fee: $35/$55. Cart Fee: $14 per person. Discounts: Twilight. Walking: Unrestricted walking. Season: Year-round. Tee Times: Call 7 days in advance. Notes: Range (grass, mat). ✉ 2020 Golf Course Rd., Auburn 95602, 25 mi from Sacramento ☎530/888-7888 ⊕ - www.ridgegc.com ▤AE, MC, V. *Comments: The surprise of the trip. Northwest of the city in Auburn, the Ridge is an excellent design combining parkland golf course styling with rustic touches. Very scenic and very tough.* ★★★★

TWELVE BRIDGES GOLF CLUB. Facility Holes: 18. Opened: 1996. Architect: Dick Phelps. Yards: 7,150/5,310. Par: 72/72. Course Rating: 74.6/71.0. Slope: 139/123. Green Fee: $30/$70. Cart Fee: Included in green fee. Discounts: Twilight, juniors. Walking:

Unrestricted walking. Season: Year-round. High: Mar.–Oct. Tee Times: Call 30 days in advance. Notes: Range (grass). ⊠ 3075 Twelve Bridges Dr., Lincoln 95648, 25 mi from Sacramento ☎ 916/645-7200 or 888/893-5832 ⊕ www.twelvebridgesofgolf.com ⊟ AE, MC, V. *Comments: Amid tall oak trees and large granite outcroppings. The LPGA plays here.* ★ ★ ★ ★ ½

WHITNEY OAKS GOLF CLUB. Facility Holes: 18. Opened: 1997. Architect: Johnny Miller. Yards: 6,793/4,983. Par: 71/71. Course Rating: 74.2/70.9. Slope: 138/127. Green Fee: $49/$69. Cart Fee: Included in green fee. Discounts: Weekdays, twilight, seniors, juniors. Walking: Unrestricted walking. Season: Year-round. Tee Times: Call 7 days in advance. Notes: Range (grass). ⊠ 2305 Clubhouse Dr., Rocklin 95765, 30 mi from Sacramento ☎ 916/632-8333 ⊕ www.whitneyoaksgolf.com ⊟ AE, MC, V. *Comments: A well-manicured, modern-looking course. Sometimes you feel as if you have to play like the architect to survive it, though. Interesting design.* ★ ★ ★ ★

WILDHAWK GOLF CLUB. Facility Holes: 18. Opened: 1997. Architect: J. Michael Poellot/Mark Hollinger. Yards: 6,695/4,847. Par: 72/72. Course Rating: 71.2/67.2. Slope: 124/109. Green Fee: $31/$41. Cart Fee: $8 per person. Discounts: Twilight, seniors, juniors. Walking: Unrestricted walking. Season: Year-round. Tee Times: Call 7 days in advance. Notes: Range (grass, mat). ⊠ 7713 Vineyard Rd., 95829 ☎ 916/688-4653 ⊕ - www.wildhawkgolf.com ⊟ AE, MC, V. *Comments: High-desert feel with a touch of Scottish links. Bring your driver, because the fairways are generous.* ★ ★ ★ ½

Where to Stay

🏨 **AMBER HOUSE BED & BREAKFAST INN.** This B&B near the capitol takes up three separate houses. The first, called the Poet's Refuge, is craftsman-style, with five bedrooms named for famous writers. The 1913 Mediterranean-style Artist's Retreat has a French impressionist motif. The third, an 1897 Dutch Colonial-revival home named Musician's Manor, has gardens sometimes used for weddings. Baths are tiled in Italian marble; some have skylights and two-person spa tubs. The Emily Dickenson Room's double-sided fireplace warms both the bathroom and bedroom. ⊠ 1315 22nd St., 95816 ☎ 916/444-8085 or 800/755-6526 🖶 916/552-6529 ⊕ www.amberhouse.com 🛏 13 rooms ♿ In-room data ports, some in-room hot tubs, cable TV, in-room VCRs, concierge, no-smoking rooms ⊟ AE, D, DC, MC, V ¶⊙¶ BP $$-$$$$.

🏨 **BEST WESTERN SUTTER HOUSE.** Many of the pleasant, modern rooms in this downtown hotel open onto a courtyard surrounding a pool. Along with the breakfast, the covered parking helps make Sutter House a bargain among downtown's pricey options. ⊠ 1100 H St., 95814 ☎ 916/441-1314 or 800/830-1314 🖶 916/441-5961 ⊕ - www.thesutterhouse.com 🛏 97 rooms, 1 suite ♿ Restaurant, cable TV, pool, lounge, laundry service, free parking, no-smoking floor ⊟ AE, D, DC, MC, V ¶⊙¶ CP $.

🏨 **POWERS MANSION INN.** If you're planning on golfing at Twelve Bridges or the Ridge, stay in Auburn rather than Sacramento. This inn hints at the lavish lifestyle enjoyed by some during the gold rush. Two light-filled parlors have gleaming oak floors, Asian antiques, and ornate Victorian chairs and settees. A second-floor maze of narrow corridors leads to the guest rooms, which have brass and pencil-post beds. The honeymoon suite has a fireplace and a heart-shape hot tub. ⊠ 164 Cleveland Ave., Auburn 95603 ☎ 530/885-1166 🖷 530/885-1386 ⊕ www.vfr.net/~powerinn ⤲ 10 rooms, 3 suites ⚿ In-room hot tubs, meeting rooms, free parking ⊟ AE, MC, V ⑩ BP $$-$$$.

Where to Eat

✕ **BIBA.** Owner Biba Caggiano is the author of several Italian cookbooks and the star of a national cooking show. The capitol crowd flocks here for homemade ravioli, osso buco, grilled pork loin, and veal and rabbit specials. Make reservations for Friday and Saturday. ⊠ 2801 Capitol Ave. ☎ 916/455-2422 ⊟ AE, DC, MC, V ⊗ Closed Sun. No lunch Sat. $$$-$$$$.

✕ **CHADWICK'S.** At Twelve Bridges Golf Club, the breakfast and lunch restaurant in the clubhouse serves sandwiches and salads. The attractive dining room has an exposed-beam peaked ceiling and a big river-rock fireplace. ⊠ 3070 Twelve Bridges Dr., Lincoln ☎ 916/645-6700 ⊟ AE, D, MC, V ⊗ No dinner $-$$.

✕ **THE FIREHOUSE.** The rich, well-presented meals here include dishes such as seared foie gras and pan-roasted elk with a blueberry-and-chestnut chutney. Consistently rated by local publications as among the city's top 10 restaurants, the very formal Firehouse has courtyard seating as well as a full bar and courtyard seating. ⊠ 1112 2nd St. ☎ 916/442-4772 ⊟ AE, MC, V ⊗ Closed Sun. No lunch Sat. $$$-$$$$.

✕ **LATITUDES.** The menu at this 1870 Victorian includes monthly specials from diverse geographical regions. The seafood, chicken, beef, and turkey entrées are prepared with such accompaniments as Mexican spices, curries, cheeses, or teriyaki sauce. Vegetarians and vegans have several inventive choices, too. Sunday brunch is deservedly popular. ⊠ 130 Maple St., Auburn ☎ 530/885-9535 ⊟ AE, D, MC, V ⊗ Closed Mon. and Tues. $$-$$$$.

✕ **LE BILIG FRENCH CAFÉ.** Simple and elegant cuisine is the goal of the chefs at this country-French café on the outskirts of Auburn. Escargots, coq au vin, and quiche are standard offerings; specials might include salmon in parchment paper. ⊠ 11750 Atwood Rd., off Hwy. 49 near the Bel Air Mall, Auburn ☎ 530/888-1491 ⊟ MC, V ⊗ Closed Mon. and Tues. No lunch $$-$$$$.

Essentials

Getting Here

Sacramento lies at the junction of I-5 and I-80, about 90 mi northeast of San Francisco. I-80 continues northeast through the so-called Gold Country, north of Lake Tahoe, and eventually through Reno, which lies about 136 mi (3 hours or so) from Sacramento.

From Sacramento I-80 heads 30 mi northeast to Auburn; Route 50 goes east 40 mi to Placerville; and Hwy. 16 angles southeast 45 mi to Plymouth. Hwy. 49 is an excellent two-lane road that winds and climbs through the foothills and valleys, linking the principal Gold Country towns, if you want to make a loop from Auburn.

Visitor Information

✴ Auburn Chamber of Commerce ✉ 601 Lincoln Way, Auburn 95603 ☎ 530/885-5616 ⊕ www.auburnchamber.net.

Sacramento Convention and Visitors Bureau ✉ 1303 J St., Suite 600, 95814 ☎ 916/264-7777 ⊕ www.sacramentocvb.org.

AROUND
SEATTLE

Coeur d'Alene Resort Golf Course

By Ron Kaspriske and Shelley Arenas

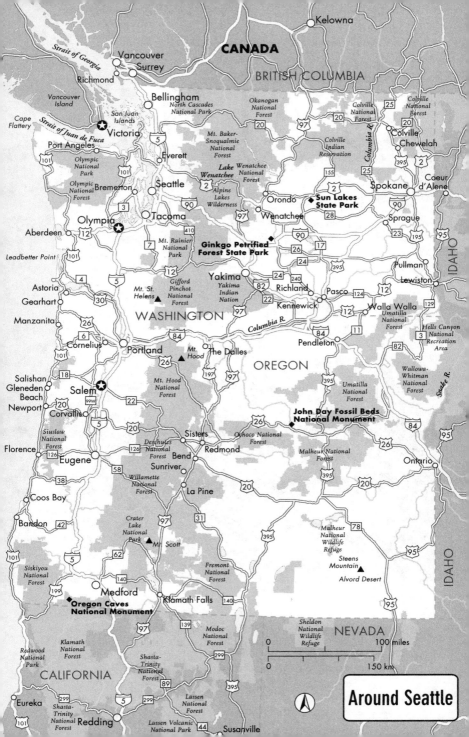

Around Seattle

Maybe it's the 3 feet of rain the city gets each year.

Maybe it's the Pacific Northwest's relative isolation from the rest of the country. Or maybe it's because Seattle is best known for grunge bands and $4 cups of highly roasted coffee. Whatever the reason, the Pacific Northwest is often ignored as a golf destination. But what Seattle residents know is that if you're willing to do some driving, it's tough to compete with the quality of golf in this region. Sure, Bend, Oregon, and Vancouver, BC, have already gained a good reputation for top-rated courses. Now Oregon's coast, Portland, and Spokane are also getting noticed as solid options for a weekend golf trip.

The choices here range from the linksy, seaside-style courses along the Oregon Coast to the parkland designs around Portland and the Richland/Kennewick area, to the rustic, tree-lined fairways in Spokane and Vancouver. Where you go depends on what you're looking for. Although it's a far cry from Myrtle Beach, Bend is the closest thing the Pacific Northwest has to a pure golf destination, and the Sunriver Resort there leads the list of places to stay and play.

With the addition of the Bandon Dunes and Pacific Dunes golf courses, which stand at the top of 100-foot cliffs overlooking the Pacific Ocean, Coastal Oregon has gained a reputation as Scotland West. In fact, if you're looking for a one-stop, stay-and-play golf destination, the 36 holes at Bandon Dunes may be the best golf experience of your life. One caveat, however: if you don't like to play in windy conditions, you may not enjoy the courses here.

Portland and Vancouver give golfers the opportunity to add nightlife to their golf getaway. Spokane, clear on the other side of the state, has the bonus of being 30 mi from Idaho's Coeur d'Alene Resort, which *Golf Digest* consistently ranks among the top 50 golf resorts in the United States. Richland/Kennewick, probably the least glamorous of the choices in this chapter, is a closer and cheaper choice, with many courses in the $50-or-less green fee range.

Seattle, and the rest of the Pacific Northwest, gets a bad rap for its cool, drizzly climate, but monthly rainfall totals in summer are typically less than an inch. And when you consider the temperature rarely gets over 90° at any of the destinations covered here, summer months can bring ideal golf weather. The seasons are all nearly identical, lasting from April to October, with the Richland/Kennewick courses playable the longest.

Aspen Lakes Golf Club (18)	7,302/5,594	72/72	75.4/71.7	135/125	$40/$56
Black Butte Ranch (36)					$32/$65
Big Meadow (18)	6,850/5,678	72/72	71.3/70.4	125/124	
Glaze Meadow (18)	6,574/5,616	72/72	71.5/72.1	128/120	
Eagle Crest Resort (54)					
Mid Iron (18)	4,160/2,982	63/63	60.3/56.5	100/91	$40
Resort (18)	6,927/4,792	72/72	73.0/66.2	131/115	$55
Ridge (18)	6,927/4,792	72/72	73.0/66.1	131/115	$65
Lost Tracks Golf Club (18)	7,003/5,287	72/73	72.7/71.1	131/128	$35/$60
Quail Run Golf Course (9)	7,024/5,414	72/72	73.4/71.0	135/128	$40
River's Edge Golf Resort (18)	6,683/5,381	72/73	72.0/71.2	134/136	$29/$52
Sunriver Lodge & Resort (54)					
Crosswater Club (18)	7,683/5,359	72/72	76.9/69.8	153/125	$95/$175
Meadows (18)	7,012/5,304	71/71	72.8/69.8	128/127	$55/$125
Woodlands (18)	6,880/5,446	72/72	73.0/70.3	131/118	$55/$125
Widgi Creek Golf Club (18)	6,903/5,070	72/72	71.9/67.4	134/119	$29/$80

BEND, OR

Given that there's no large city for at least 100 mi and no major body of water within a four-hour drive, Bend seems like one of the most unlikely places you would ever find a golf destination. All the same, *Golf Digest* ranked the area as one of the top 25 golf destinations in the world.

You read that right. The epicenter of golf in the Pacific Northwest is a small city in the middle of Oregon that sits in a valley at 3,600 feet, with Mt. Bachelor and the Paulina Mountain range. Thanks to the Lava Butte Cinder Cone, formed by volcano cinders, some area courses even have hardened lava incorporated into their designs. Because the area is protected by mountains, the average annual temperature is 52°.

It's a 320-mi haul to get from Seattle to Bend, but this is a small price to pay for the quality of golf offered here. Of the 20-odd courses in the area, all but a few are open to the public. At the top of our list of places to visit is the Sunriver Resort, ranked the 19th-best resort in the nation by *Golf Digest*. The Crosswater Club has what is easily the area's best course. It once played host to a Shell's Wonderful World of Golf match. The Crosswater is also a great place to park your clubs while visiting the area, but there are at least two other resorts worthy of a night's stay, including the Black Butte Ranch, which offers an even more quiet stay than Sunriver.

Courses   **Golf**Digest REVIEWS

ASPEN LAKES GOLF CLUB. Facility Holes: 18. Opened: 2000. Architect: William Overdorf. Yards: 7,302/5,594. Par: 72/72. Course Rating: 75.4/71.7. Slope: 135/125. Green Fee: $40/$56. Cart Fee: $14 per person. Discounts: Twilight, juniors. Walking: Unrestricted walking. Season: Mar.–Dec. High: May–Sept. Tee Times: Call golf shop. Notes: Range (grass). ✉ 16900 Aspen Lakes Dr., Sister 97759, 20 mi from Bend ☎ 541/ 549-4653 ▭ AE, D, MC, V. *Comments: Residential community course with interesting reddish-brown bunkers made from ground lava. UR*

BLACK BUTTE RANCH. Facility Holes: 36. Green Fee: $32/$65. Cart Fee: $30 per cart. Discounts: Weekdays, twilight, juniors. Walking: Unrestricted walking. Season: Mar.–Oct. Tee Times: Call golf shop. Notes: Range (grass). ✉ Hwy. 20, Black Butte Ranch 97759, 29 mi from Bend ☎ 541/595-1500 or 800/399-2322 ⊕ www.blackbutteranch.com ▭ AE, D, MC, V.

Big Meadow. Holes: 18. Opened: 1971. Architect: Robert Muir Graves. Yards: 6,850/ 5,678. Par: 72/72. Course Rating: 71.3/70.4. Slope: 125/124. *Comments: Not as good as Glaze Meadow, but the parkland layout has gorgeous scenery and is always in good shape.* ★★★★

Glaze Meadow. Holes: 18. Opened: 1982. Architect: Gene (Bunny) Mason. Yards: 6,574/ 5,616. Par: 72/72. Course Rating: 71.5/72.1. Slope: 128/120. *Comments: Tight, long course. Bunkering is exceptional, but it's the view of the Three Sisters Peaks you'll remember.* ★★★★

EAGLE CREST RESORT. Facility Holes: 54. Cart Fee: $25 per cart. Discounts: Twilight, juniors. Walking: Unrestricted walking. Season: Mar.–Nov. High: June–Sept. Tee Times: Call golf shop. Notes: Range (grass), lodging (150). ✉ 1522 Cline Falls Rd., Redmond 97756, 18 mi from Bend ☎ 541/923-4653 or 877/818-0286 ⊕ www.eagle-crest.com ▭ AE, D, MC, V.

Mid Iron. Holes: 18. Opened: 2001. Architect: John Thronson. Yards: 4,160/2,982. Par: 63/63. Course Rating: 60.3/56.5. Slope: 100/91. Green Fee: $40. *Comments: Nine par-3s and 9 par-4s. Leave the driver at home. A lot of fun. UR*

Resort. Holes: 18. Opened: 1985. Architect: Gene "Bunny" Mason. Yards: 6,927/4,792. Par: 72/72. Course Rating: 73.0/66.2. Slope: 131/115. Green Fee: $55. *Comments: Not as resort-friendly as the Ridge, but the wide-open fairways are great for long hitters.* ★★★★

Ridge. Holes: 18. Opened: 1993. Architect: John Thronson. Yards: 6,927/4,792. Par: 72/ 72. Course Rating: 73.0/66.1. Slope: 131/115. Green Fee: $65. *Comments: Friendly, resort-style course. Lava rock comes as a surprise—you're not in Hawaii, after all. Make sure you look at it, but don't play through it.* ★★★★

LOST TRACKS GOLF CLUB. Facility Holes: 18. Opened: 1996. Architect: Brian Whitcomb. Yards: 7,003/5,287. Par: 72/73. Course Rating: 72.7/71.1. Slope: 131/128.

Green Fee: $35/$60. Cart Fee: $15 per person. Discounts: Guest, twilight, seniors, juniors. Walking: Unrestricted walking. Season: Year-round. Tee Times: Call 14 days in advance. Notes: Range (grass). ✉ 60205 Sunset View Dr., 97702 ☎ 541/385-1818 ⊟ AE, D, MC, V. *Comments: Second-best course in the area behind Crosswater. Short, with many doglegs. Number 16 is terrific—you walk through an old railroad car to get to the par-3 green.* ★ ★ ★ ★

QUAIL RUN GOLF COURSE. Facility Holes: 9. Opened: 1991. Architect: Jim Ramey. Yards: 7,024/5,414. Par: 72/72. Course Rating: 73.4/71.0. Slope: 135/128. Green Fee: $40. Cart Fee: $13 per person. Discounts: Twilight, juniors. Walking: Unrestricted walking. Season: Mar.–Nov. Tee Times: Call 180 days in advance. Notes: Range (grass). ✉ 16725 Northridge Dr., La Pine 97739, 10 mi from Sunriver ☎ 541/536-1303 or 800/895-4653 ⊕ www.oregongolf.com ⊟ MC, V. *Comments: The best 9-holer in the region.* ★ ★ ★ ★

RIVER'S EDGE GOLF RESORT. Facility Holes: 18. Opened: 1988. Architect: Robert Muir Graves. Yards: 6,683/5,381. Par: 72/73. Course Rating: 72.0/71.2. Slope: 134/136. Green Fee: $29/$52. Cart Fee: $14 per person. Discounts: Weekdays, guest, twilight, seniors, juniors. Walking: Unrestricted walking. Season: Year-round. High: June–Aug. Tee Times: Call golf shop. Notes: Range (grass, mat), lodging (200). ✉ 400 N.W. Pro Shop Dr., 97701 ☎ 541/389-2828 ⊕ www.riverhouse.com ⊟ MC, V. *Comments: Built on steep hills, so be prepared to get some funky lies. On a clear day, you can see Washington and Idaho from the 16th tee.* ★ ★ ★ ★

SUNRIVER LODGE & RESORT. Facility Holes: 54. Cart Fee: Included in green fee. Discounts: Guest, twilight, juniors. Walking: Unrestricted walking. Season: Apr.–Oct. Tee Times: Call golf shop. Notes: Range (grass), lodging (200). ✉ 17600 Canoe Camp Dr., Sunriver 97707, 12 mi from Bend ☎ 541/593-4402 or 800/547-3922 ⊟ AE, D, DC, MC, V.

Crosswater Club. Holes: 18. Opened: 1995. Architect: Bob Cupp/John Fought. Yards: 7,683/5,359. Par: 72/72. Course Rating: 76.9/69.8. Slope: 153/125. Green Fee: $95/$175. *Comments: Thankfully, you don't have to play from the back tees. Set in a valley, the course puts a high premium on accuracy. You must be a guest at the resort to play.* ★ ★ ★ ★ ½

Meadows. Holes: 18. Opened: 1999. Architect: John Fought. Yards: 7,012/5,304. Par: 71/71. Course Rating: 72.8/69.8. Slope: 128/127. Green Fee: $55/$125. *Comments: The oldest course at Sunriver, it was remodeled to include wider fairways and striking bunkers.* ★ ★ ★ ★

Woodlands. Holes: 18. Opened: 1981. Architect: Robert Trent Jones Jr. Yards: 6,880/5,446. Par: 72/72. Course Rating: 73.0/70.3. Slope: 131/118. Green Fee: $55/$125. *Comments: Homes come into play on many holes, which is a downer. Still, it's very scenic.* ★ ★ ★ ★

WIDGI CREEK GOLF CLUB. Facility Holes: 18. Opened: 1991. Architect: Robert Muir Graves. Yards: 6,903/5,070. Par: 72/72. Course Rating: 71.9/67.4. Slope: 134/119. Green Fee: $29/$80. Cart Fee: $28 per person. Discounts: Weekdays, twilight, juniors. Walking: Unrestricted walking. Season: Mar.–Nov. Tee Times: Call 30 days in advance. Notes: Range (grass), lodging (6). ✉ 18707 S.W. Century Dr., 97702, 160 mi from Portland ☎ 541/382-4449 ⊕ www.widgi.com ⊟ D, MC, V. *Comments: Yes, the creek does come into play. Course looks easier than it is.* ★ ★ ★ ★

Where to Stay

BLACK BUTTE RANCH. Near the town of Sisters, this resort has an abundance of recreational activities on its 1,830 wooded acres. All rentals are privately owned and individually decorated by owners. The condo units and homes have wood-burning fireplaces and kitchens, and many units look onto the golf course. ⊠ 13653 Hawkes Beard, Black Butte Ranch 97759 ☎ 541/595-6211 or 800/452-7455 ᕭ 541/595-2077 ⊕ - www.blackbutte.com ᐧ 120 rooms ᐧ 2 restaurants, snack bar, some kitchens, some microwaves, cable TV, in-room VCRs, driving range, 2 18-hole golf courses, putting green, tennis courts, 4 pools, wading pool, exercise equipment, bicycles, Ping-Pong, cross-country skiing, downhill skiing, bar, video game room, children's programs (ages 3–12), playground, business services ⊟ AE, D, DC, MC, V $–$$$$.

EAGLE CREST RESORT. Eagle Crest is 5 mi west of Redmond, above the canyon of the Deschutes River. In this high desert area, the grounds are covered with juniper and sagebrush. Lodging choices include condos, chalets, hotel rooms, and vacation homes. The hotel rooms are in a single building on the landscaped grounds, and some of the suites have gas fireplaces. The 1,700-acre resort has 10 mi of bike trails, a 2-mi hiking trail, and a river for fishing. ⊠ 1522 Cline Falls Rd., Redmond 97756 ☎ 541/923-2453 or 800/682-4786 ᕭ 541/923-1720 ⊕ www.eagle-crest.com ᐧ 100 rooms, 38 suites, 300 town houses, 4 vacation homes ᐧ Restaurant, 2 cafés, picnic area, some kitchenettes, some microwaves, driving range, 3 18-hole golf courses, putting green, tennis court, 2 pools (1 indoor), wading pool, gym, hair salon, hot tubs, bicycles, racquetball, cross-country skiing, downhill skiing, children's programs, playground, laundry facilities, business services, airport shuttle, some pets allowed ⊟ AE, D, MC, V $–$$$$.

INN OF THE SEVENTH MOUNTAIN. This resort, surrounded by ponderosa pines in the Deschutes National Forest, is on the banks of the Deschutes River, so white-water rafting and fishing are right at your doorstep in summer. The property's recreational facilities include a 65-foot waterslide, canoeing, and an outdoor ice-skating rink. Five golf courses are within 15 minutes. Accommodations include standard bedrooms with a queen-size bed, deluxe bedrooms with an additional Murphy bed and private deck, and studios with fireplaces and full kitchens. There are also suites and lofts with extra amenities. ⊠ 18575 S.W. Century Dr., 97702 ☎ 800/452-6810 ᕭ 541/382-3517 ⊕ - www.7thmtn.com ᐧ 300 rooms ᐧ 2 restaurants, grocery, 4 tennis courts, 2 pools, hot tub, fishing, horseback riding, ice-skating, bar, children's programs, meeting rooms, no-smoking rooms ⊟ AE, D, DC, MC, V $–$$.

THE RIVERHOUSE. A cut or two above what you'd expect given the reasonable rates, this hotel, within earshot of the rushing Deschutes River, contains large rooms with contemporary oak furniture. Those with river views cost an extra $20. The hotel is part of a 300-acre resort that also includes River's Edge course, and packages are available. ⊠ 3075 N. Hwy. 97, 97701 ☎ 541/389-3111 or 800/547-3928 ᕭ 541/389-0870 ⊕ www.riverhouse.com ᐧ 220 units ᐧ 3 restaurants, room service, 18-hole golf course, 2 tennis courts, 2 pools, gym, hot tub, sauna, bar, laundry facilities, business services ⊟ AE, D, DC, MC, V ⋈ CP $.

SUNRIVER RESORT. This former army base within a pine-scented desert landscape is convenient to many outdoor activities. It's a self-contained community, with stores, restaurants, contemporary houses, condominiums, and even a private airstrip. You can choose from condos, hotel rooms, or houses; shops can rent you many kinds of outdoors paraphernalia. ✆ Box 3609, Sunriver 97707 ✛ (west of U.S. 97, 15 mi south of Bend) ☎ 541/593-1000 or 800/547-3922 🖷 541/593-5458 ⊕ www.sunriver-resort.com ☛ 510 units ♨ 6 restaurants, 3 18-hole golf courses, 28 tennis courts, 2 pools, hot tub, sauna, boating, fishing, bicycles, horseback riding, no-smoking rooms ☰AE, D, DC, MC, V $$-$$$$.

Where to Eat

✕ **COHO GRILL.** Innovative Pacific Northwest dishes, geared to the season, are the hallmarks of this well-respected restaurant. Asparagus, fresh fish, and Cascade morels are on the spring menu; come fall expect Oregon crab and fruits from the Hood River valley; and in winter American classics like pot roast and braised lamb shanks. ✉ 61535 Fargo La. ☎ 541/388-3909 ☰AE, MC, V $-$$$.

✕ **DESCHUTES BREWERY & PUBLIC HOUSE.** Try the admirable Black Butte Porter at this brewpub, which serves upscale Pacific Northwest cuisine. Hearty dishes such as burgers, a house-cured pastrami Reuben, a smoked-salmon sandwich, and chicken enchiladas dominate the menu. Vegetarians can go for the smoked vegetable sandwich or the black bean chili. Dinner specials change daily (check the blackboard). Portions are large. ✉ 1044 N.W. Bond St. ☎ 541/382-9242 ⌕ Reservations not accepted ☰MC, V $-$$.

✕ **GIUSEPPE'S RISTORANTE.** This downtown restaurant is known for its southern Italian dishes, especially its homemade pastas, and hearty seafood and beef entrées. There's a separate menu for "Goomba's Bar." ✉ 932 N.W. Bond St. ☎ 541/389-8899 ⊕ www.giuseppesofbend.com ☰AE, DC, MC, V ⊙ Closed Mon. No lunch $-$$$.

✕ **PINE TAVERN.** Opened in 1936, this is Bend's oldest restaurant. The 200-year-old, 100-foot-tall ponderosa pines growing inside are the centerpiece of the dining room, which overlooks the Deschutes River. All the produce is locally grown at the Pine, which is known for seafood and steak. Seating on the patio looks out onto a pond and a beautifully landscaped area. Smoking is not allowed. ✉ 967 N.W. Brooks, 97701 ☎ 541/382-5581 ☰AE, D, DC, MC, V ⊙ No lunch Sun. $$-$$$$.

Essentials

Getting Here

The 325-mi drive to Bend from Seattle takes about seven hours. Go south on I-5 150 mi to I-205 and proceed about 15 mi to I-84 east. Follow signs to U.S. 26 east and take it 100 mi. Turn onto U.S. 97 south. Bend is 40 mi ahead.

Horizon and United Express fly to Bend. A direct flight from Seattle takes about 1 hour and 15 minutes.

🛪 **Bend-Redmond Municipal Airport** ☎ 541/548-6059.

Visitor Information

📋 **Central Oregon Visitors Association** ✉ 63085 N. Hwy. 97, Suite 104, 97701 ☎ 541/389-8799 or 800/800-8334 ⊕ www.covisitors.com.

COASTAL OREGON

For the past few years, like mail being delivered by the Pony Express, news has spread to serious golfers across the nation about an amazing 36-hole golf resort on the Oregon coast that rivals anything ever built—including Pebble Beach. That may sound like folklore, but Bandon Dunes is the real thing. The Bandon Dunes and Pacific Dunes courses are so good, they are almost worth a drive from New York City, let alone the eight-hour drive from Seattle.

There is an airport just north of the resort in Coos Bay if you can't sit in a car that long, but the trip doesn't have to be done in one chunk. Instead, Coastal Oregon, along the incredibly scenic U.S. Hwy. 101, has several great golf courses to play along the way to Bandon. Pacific Dunes debuted on *Golf Digest*'s list of America's 100 Greatest Courses at number 47, but you're unlikely to be disappointed in any of the beachside golf courses in Oregon.

Don't forget, this is links golf. Windswept fairways and tall, wispy grasses are the norm. We suggest that you start in the northwest corner of the state near Astoria and work your way down U.S. Hwy. 101, hitting Gearhart, Manzanita, Salishan, Ocean Dunes, and Sandpines Golf Links before arriving at the wonderful resort at Bandon Dunes. Think of its two courses as part of a grand finale.

Courses

Golf Digest REVIEWS

BANDON DUNES GOLF RESORT. Facility Holes: 36. Green Fee: $50/$200. Cart Fee: Included in green fee. Discounts: Weekdays. Walking: Walking with caddie. Season: Year-round. High: June–Oct. Tee Times: Call 365 days in advance. Notes: Range (grass), lodging (150). ✉ 57744 Round Lake Dr., Bandon 97411, 16 mi from Coos Bay ☎ 541/347-4380 or 888/345-6008 ⊕ www.bandondunesgolf.com ⊟ AE, D, MC, V.

Bandon Dunes. Holes: 18. Opened: 1999. Architect: David McLay Kidd. Yards: 6,844/5,178. Par: 72/72. Course Rating: 74.2/72.1. Slope: 138/127. *Comments: A very strong second to Pacific, the first course at Bandon Dunes (ranked 62nd on Golf Digest's list of America's 100 Greatest Courses) doesn't have as many seaside holes, but it's still a modern classic.* ★★★★★

					$50/$200
Bandon Dunes Golf Resort (36)					
Bandon Dunes (18)	6,844/5,178	72/72	74.2/72.1	138/127	
Pacific Dunes (18)	6,557/5,107	71/71	72.9/71.1	133/131	
Gearhart Golf Links (18)	6,218/5,353	72/74	71.0/73.1	133/137	$35/$45
Ocean Dunes Golf Links (18)	6,018/5,044	71/73	70.0/73.8	124/129	$28/$35
Salishan Lodge & Golf Resort (18)	6,453/5,389	72/72	72.3/72.3	132/128	$35/$75
Sandpines Golf Links (18)	7,252/5,346	72/72	76.3/72.7	131/129	$35/$59

Pacific Dunes. Holes: 18. Opened: 2001. Architect: Tom Doak. Yards: 6,557/5,107. Par: 71/71. Course Rating: 72.9/71.1. Slope: 133/131. *Comments: If you play this gorgeous, cliff-side ocean links, you may just think it's the best golf course you've ever seen.* UR

GEARHART GOLF LINKS. Facility Holes: 18. Opened: 1892. Yards: 6,218/5,353. Par: 72/74. Course Rating: 71.0/73.1. Slope: 133/137. Green Fee: $35/$45. Cart Fee: $25 per cart. Discounts: Twilight, juniors. Walking: Unrestricted walking. Season: Year-round. Tee Times: Call golf shop. Notes: Metal spikes, range (grass), lodging (100). ✉ N. Mason St., Gearhart 97138, 90 mi from Portland ☎ 503/738-3538 ⊕ www.gearhartgolflinks.com ▭ MC, V. *Comments: First established as 9 holes in 1892, Gearhart is now a strong 18 with only three par-3s and three par-5s. Great pot bunkering. A real links course.* ★ ★ ★ ½

OCEAN DUNES GOLF LINKS. Facility Holes: 18. Opened: 1963. Architect: William Robinson. Yards: 6,018/5,044. Par: 71/73. Course Rating: 70.0/73.8. Slope: 124/129. Green Fee: $28/$35. Cart Fee: $26 per cart. Discounts: Twilight, seniors, juniors. Walking: Unrestricted walking. Season: Year-round. Tee Times: Call golf shop. Notes: Metal spikes, range (grass, mat). ✉ 3345 Munsel Lake Rd., Florence 97439, 60 mi from Eugene ☎ 541/997-3232 or 800/468-4833 ▭ MC, V. *Comments: A mile inland from the coast, tucked in a field of brilliant white sand dunes. Several new holes have double greens like St. Andrews.* ★ ★ ★ ½

SALISHAN LODGE & GOLF RESORT. Facility Holes: 18. Opened: 1965. Architect: Fred Federspiel. Yards: 6,453/5,389. Par: 72/72. Course Rating: 72.3/72.3. Slope: 132/128. Green Fee: $35/$75. Cart Fee: $30 per cart. Discounts: Twilight, juniors. Walking: Unrestricted walking. Season: Year-round. High: June-Oct. Tee Times: Call golf shop. Notes: Range (mat), lodging (205). ✉ 7760 U.S. Hwy. 101 N, Gleneden Beach 97388, 58 mi from Salem ☎ 541/764-3632 or 800/452-2300 ⊕ www.salishan.com ▭ AE, D, DC, MC, V. *Comments: Homes take up most of the good seaside property, so 12 holes are more mountainous than linksy. The 11th through 16th are built on sand dunes.* ★ ★ ★ ★

SANDPINES GOLF LINKS. Facility Holes: 18. Opened: 1993. Architect: Rees Jones. Yards: 7,252/5,346. Par: 72/72. Course Rating: 76.3/72.7. Slope: 131/129. Green Fee: $35/$59. Cart Fee: $26 per cart. Discounts: Twilight, juniors. Walking: Unrestricted walk- ing. Season: Year-round. High: July-Sept. Tee Times: Call golf shop. Notes: Metal spikes, range (grass, mat). ⊠ 1201 35th St., Florence 97439, 60 mi from Eugene ☎ 541/997–1940 or 800/917–4653 ⊕ www.sandpines.com ▤ AE, D, MC, V. *Comments: The third-best links course on the coast. Huge fairways and greens help keep the ball in play when the wind is howling. A few holes are cut through shore pines.* ★ ★ ★ ★ ½

Where to Stay

☷ **BANDON DUNES GOLF RESORT.** Stay here if you want to fully immerse yourself in the game of golf. Rooms in the Lodge overlook the course, the dunes, and beyond to the Pacific; others in the Lily Pond and Chrome Lake buildings look out onto a pond or lake. Before hitting the course, you can perfect your shots at the 32-acre practice center, which includes a 1-acre putting green and a practice bunker area. The Gallery restaurant is open for breakfast, lunch, and dinner; the Pacific Dunes Grill in the clubhouse is open for breakfast and lunch. ⊠ 57744 Round Lake Dr., Bandon 97411 ☎ 541/347–4380 or 888/345–6008 ⊕ www.bandondunes.com ↜ 65 rooms, 4 suites ♨ 2 restaurants, 2 18-hole golf courses, putting green, gym, hot tub, massage, sauna, spa, 2 lounges, library ▤ AE, D, DC, MC, V $$–$$$$.

☷ **BEST WESTERN INN AT FACE ROCK.** This modern resort hotel, landscaped with flowers and greenery, is across the road from Bandon's great walking beach. The rooms are spacious, and each suite has a fireplace and an ocean view. Seven of the suites also have large hot tubs. ⊠ 3225 Beach Loop Rd., Bandon 97411 ☎ 541/347–9441 or 800/638–3092 🖷 541/347–2532 ⊕ www.facerock.net ↜ 54 guest rooms, 20 suites ♨ Restaurant, 9-hole golf course, hot tub, bar, laundry facilities ▤ AE, D, DC, MC, V $.

☷ **HALLMARK RESORT.** Large suites with fireplaces and great views make this triple-decker oceanfront resort a good choice for families or couples looking for a romantic splurge. The rooms, all with oak-tile baths, have soothing color schemes. The least expensive units do not have views. ⊠ 1400 S. Hemlock, Cannon Beach 97110 ☎ 503/436–1566 or 888/448–4449 🖷 503/436–0324 ⊕ www.hallmarkinns.com ↜ 142 rooms and suites ♨ Some kitchenettes, refrigerators, some in-room hot tubs, 2 pools (1 indoor), wading pool, exercise equipment, 3 hot tubs, laundry facilities, Internet, business services, airport shuttle, some pets allowed (fee), no smoking rooms ▤ AE, D, DC, MC, V $$$–$$$$.

☷ **INN AT MANZANITA.** This 1987 Scandinavian complex for four buildings, filled with light-color woods, beams, and glass, is half a block from the beach. Shore pines on the property make the upper-floor patios feel like tree houses. All rooms have decks, and two have skylights. A nearby café serves breakfast, and several restaurants are within walking distance. In winter, the inn is a great place for storm-watching. There's a minimum stay of two days on weekends. ⊠ 67 Laneda Ave., Manzanita 97130 ☎ 503/368–6754 🖷 503/368–5941 ⊕ www.innatmanzanita.com ↜ 13 rooms ♨ Refrigerators, in-room hot tubs; no a/c in some rooms, no TV in some rooms, no children, no smoking ▤ MC, V $$.

☷ **SALISHAN LODGE AND GOLF RESORT.** The most famous resort on the Oregon coast is high above placid Siletz Bay. This expensive collection of guest rooms, vacation homes, condominiums, restaurants, golf fairways, tennis courts, and covered walkways blends into a forest preserve; if not for the signs, you'd scarcely be able to find it. Beginning with the soothing rooms covered in silvered cedar, Salishan embodies a uniquely Oregonian elegance. Each of the quiet rooms has a wood-burning fireplace, a balcony, and original works by Northwest artists. ☒ 7760 U.S. Hwy. 101 N, Salishan 97388 ☎ 541/764-3600 or 800/452-2300 ☐ 541/764-3681 ⊕ www.salishan.com ⇨ 205 rooms ⚑ 2 restaurants, room service, in-room data ports, minibars, driving range, 18-hole golf course, putting green, 4 tennis courts, indoor pool, gym, hair salon, massage, sauna, beach, billiards, hiking, bar, library, piano, baby-sitting, playground, dry cleaning, laundry service, concierge, no-smoking rooms ═ AE, D, DC, MC, V $$$-$$$$.

Where to Eat

✗ **BANDON BOATWORKS.** A local favorite, this romantic jetty-side eatery serves seafood, steaks, and prime rib with a view of the Coquille River harbor and lighthouse. Try the panfried oysters flamed with brandy and anisette or the quick-sautéed seafood combination, which is heavy on shrimp and scallops. ☒ 275 Lincoln Ave. SW, Bandon ☎ 541/347-2111 ═ AE, D, MC, V $-$$$.

✗ **BLUE HERON BISTRO.** Subtle preparations of local seafood, chicken, and pasta are served up at this busy bistro, which also has some innovative soups and desserts available, as well as a large selection of imported beers. The skylighted tile-floor dining room is decorated with natural wood and blue linen, and there's dining outside on the patio. ☒ 100 W. Commercial Ave., Coos Bay ☎ 541/267-3933 ═ AE, D, MC, V ⊙ Closed Sun. Sept.–June $$.

✗ **CHEZ JEANETTE.** This country-French cottage, is among the shore pines between U.S. Hwy. 101 and the ocean. A fireplace, antiques, and tables set with linen and crystal enhance the tranquility. Try the carpetbagger steak, a thick fillet stuffed with tiny local oysters and wrapped in bacon. The rest of the menu puts a Parisian spin on local products from the sea, sky, and pasture. ☒ 7150 Old Hwy. 101, Gleneden Beach, (turn west from U.S. 101 at the Salishan entrance, then turn south and go ¼ mi) ☎ 541/764-3434 ⚑ Reservations essential ═ AE, D, MC, V ⊙ Closed Sun. and Mon. Labor Day–June. No lunch $$-$$$$.

✗ **DINING ROOM AT SALISHAN.** The Salishan resort's main dining room, a multi-level expanse of hushed waiters, hillside ocean views, and snow-white linen, serves Pacific Northwest cuisine. House specialties include fresh local fish, game, beef, and lamb. The wine cellar holds more than 10,000 bottles. ☒ 7760 U.S. Hwy. 101 N, Salishan ☎ 541/764-2371 ⚑ Reservations essential ᝫ Jacket and tie ═ AE, D, DC, MC, V ⊙ No lunch $$-$$$$.

✗ **LORD BENNETT'S.** His lordship has a lot going for him: a location atop a cliff, modern decor, sunsets visible through picture windows overlooking Face Rock Beach, and musical performers on weekends. The rich dishes include prawns sautéed with sherry and garlic and steaks topped with shiitake mushrooms. A Sunday brunch is served. ☒ 1695 Beach Loop Rd., Bandon ☎ 541/347-3663 ═ AE, D, MC, V $$-$$$.

Essentials

Getting Here

The most direct route from Seattle to Bandon is to take I-5 south to Hwy. 42 then go east to U.S. Hwy. 101 and south to Bandon. It will take about eight hours to drive the 415 mi. For a more scenic route, with stops along the way en route to Bandon, take I-5 only to Portland then go west on U.S. 26 to the Cannon Beach area, then south on coastal U.S. Hwy. 101.

Visitor Information

7 Astoria-Warrenton Area Chamber of Commerce ⊠ 143 U.S. Hwy. 101 S, Astoria 97103 ☎ 503/861-1031 or 800/875-6807. **Bay Area Chamber of Commerce** ⊠ 50 E. Central St., Coos Bay 97420 ☎ 541/269-0215 or 800/824-8486 ⊕ www. oregonsbayareachamber.com. **Cannon Beach Chamber of Commerce** ⊠ 2nd and Spruce Sts., 97110 ☎ 503/436-0910 ⊕ www.cannonbeach.org.**Lincoln City Visitors Center** ⊠ 801 U.S. Hwy. 101 SW, Suite 1, 97367 ☎ 541/994-8378 or 800/452-2151 ⊕ www.oregoncoast.org.

PORTLAND, OR

Before we talk about golf, a little-known fact about Portland: 30% of the world's hops are grown in the area. And since it's safe to say that beer and golf go together like hot dogs and baseball, that should be enough information to tempt any golfer to visit Oregon's largest city.

But it just so happens that the golf is good, too. There are more than 40 courses in the Portland area and there was a time in the 1980s when the Pacific Northwest city had more golf holes per capita than anywhere else in the United States. A construction boom during the 1990s brought a handful of great courses on line, including Pumpkin Ridge Golf Club, the area's best 36-hole facility, and the Oregon Golf Association Members Course at Tukwila. If you prefer, there are still plenty of classic designs to play, including Forest Hills (1927) and Eastmoreland (1918).

Portland's Pumpkin Ridge Golf Club was the site of Tiger Woods's infamous 1996 duel with Steve Scott in the U.S. Amateur and also played host to the dramatic play-off won by Hilary Lunke at the 2003 U.S. Women's Open. The Ghost Creek course is open to the public, but the higher-rated Witch Hollow course is for members only. You may not be welcome there, so try the formerly private Persimmon Country Club in Gresham. One of 20 courses in

Eastmoreland Golf Course (18)	6,529/5,646	72/74	71.7/71.4	123/117	$19/$29
Forest Hills Golf Course (18)	6,173/5,673	72/74	69.7/72.1	126/123	$30
Heron Lakes Golf Course (36) Great Blue Course (18) Greenback Course (18)	6,902/5,258 6,608/5,240	72/72 72/72	73.3/71.0 71.6/69.5	135/123 123/115	$25/$39 $19/$29
Langdon Farms Golf Club (18)	6,950/5,249	71/71	73.3/69.4	125/114	$49/$84
Oregon Golf Association Members Course at Tukwila (18)	6,650/5,498	72/72	71.7/71.8	131/129	$51
Persimmon Country Club (18)	6,678/4,852	72/72	71.2/66.1	125/112	$40/$65
Pumpkin Ridge Golf Club (18)	6,839/5,206	71/71	73.8/70.4	139/125	$30/$120
Reserve Vineyards & Golf Club (36) North (18) South (18)	6,852/5,198 7,172/5,189	72/72 72/72	72.6/69.6 74.3/70.1	132/115 134/121	$45/$90 $45/$79

the area designed by architect Gene "Bunny" Mason, Persimmon has spectacular views of Mt. Hood, Mt. Adams, and Mt. St. Helens.

Courses

GolfDigest REVIEWS

EASTMORELAND GOLF COURSE. Facility Holes: 18. Opened: 1918. Architect: H. Chandler Egan. Yards: 6,529/5,646. Par: 72/74. Course Rating: 71.7/71.4. Slope: 123/117. Green Fee: $19/$29. Cart Fee: $26 per cart. Discounts: Weekdays, seniors, juniors. Walking: Unrestricted walking. Season: Year-round. High: May–Sept. Tee Times: Call 6 days in advance. Notes: Range (mat). ✉ 2425 S.E. Bybee Blvd., 97202 ☎ 503/775-2900 ⊕ www.eastmorelandgolfcourse.com ▤ MC, V. *Comments: Looks like an arboretum. The late Walter Hagen once called the 13th hole one of the best he had ever played. Egan also designed Pebble Beach.* ★ ★ ★ ½

FOREST HILLS GOLF COURSE. Facility Holes: 18. Opened: 1927. Architect: Don Bell. Yards: 6,173/5,673. Par: 72/74. Course Rating: 69.7/72.1. Slope: 126/123. Green Fee: $30. Cart Fee: $20 per cart. Season: Year-round Tee Times: Tee Times: Call 6 days in advance. ✉ 36260 S.W. Tongue La., Cornelius 97113 ☎ 503/357-3347 ⊕ www.golfforesthills. com ▤ AE, MC, V. *Comments: First 9 built in 1927, second in 1950. Greens are elevated. Huge fir trees frame many holes, and fruit and nut orchards are nearby.* ★ ★ ½

HERON LAKES GOLF COURSE. Facility Holes: 36. Architect: Robert Trent Jones Jr. Cart Fee: $26 per cart. Discounts: Weekdays, twilight, seniors, juniors. Walking: Unrestricted walking. Season: Year-round. Tee Times: Call golf shop. Notes: Metal spikes, range (grass). ✉ 3500 N. Victory Blvd., 97217 ☎ 503/289-1818 ▤ AE, D, MC, V.

Great Blue Course. Holes: 18. Opened: 1992. Yards: 6,902/5,258. Par: 72/72. Course Rating: 73.3/71.0. Slope: 135/123. Green Fee: $25/$39. *Comments: Robert Trent Jones Jr.*

BUNNY MASON

Few outside the Pacific Northwest are likely to have heard of Gene "Bunny" Mason, but this 1981 inductee into the Pacific Northwest PGA Section Hall of Fame had a national impact on golf. Mason gained prominence as a merchandiser, teacher, and golf shop operator during his tenures at Salem Golf Club, Columbia Edgewater Country Club, and Black Butte Ranch. He was also very active in the PGA of America, founding the PGA Education Program and Business Schools. But, Mason is also one of the Pacific Northwest's most prolific course architects, with more than 20 layouts bearing his signature.

created a brutally challenging links-style course designed over and around wetlands, with views of Mt. Hood. Has hosted the U.S. Amateur Public Links Championship. ★ ★ ★ ★

Greenback Course. Holes: 18. Opened: 1970. Yards: 6,608/5,240. Par: 72/72. Course Rating: 71.6/69.5. Slope: 123/115. Green Fee: $19/$29. *Comments: Another Trent Jones Jr. design, with elevated greens. It has some forced carries but is not overly difficult.* ★ ★ ★ ½

LANGDON FARMS GOLF CLUB. Facility Holes: 18. Opened: 1995. Architect: John Fought/Bob Cupp. Yards: 6,950/5,249. Par: 71/71. Course Rating: 73.3/69.4. Slope: 125/114. Green Fee: $49/$84. Cart Fee: Included in green fee. Discounts: Weekdays, twilight, juniors. Walking: Unrestricted walking. Season: Year-round. Tee Times: Call golf shop. Notes: Range (grass, mat). ⊠ 24377 N.E. Airport Rd., Aurora 97002, 15 mi from Portland ☎ 503/678-4653 ⊕ www.langdonfarms.com ▤ AE, D, MC, V. *Comments: Farm-theme layout south of city. Carved through the Willamette Valley, with recessed fairways framed by man-made mounds.* ★ ★ ★ ★

OREGON GOLF ASSOCIATION MEMBERS COURSE AT TUKWILA. Facility Holes: 18. Opened: 1996. Architect: William Robinson. Yards: 6,650/5,498. Par: 72/72. Course Rating: 71.7/71.8. Slope: 131/129. Green Fee: $51. Cart Fee: $25 per cart. Discounts: Twilight, juniors. Walking: Unrestricted walking. Season: Year-round. High: Apr.–Nov. Tee Times: Call 5 days in advance. Notes: Range (grass, mat). ⊠ 2850 Hazelnut Dr., Woodburn 97071 ☎ 503/981-6105 ▤ D, MC, V. *Comments: A terrific course with a variety of looks. The front 9 plays through a forest of hazelnut trees. The greens are fast.* ★ ★ ★ ★ ½

PERSIMMON COUNTRY CLUB. Facility Holes: 18. Opened: 1993. Architect: Gene "Bunny" Mason. Yards: 6,678/4,852. Par: 72/72. Course Rating: 71.2/66.1. Slope: 125/112. Green Fee: $40/$65. Cart Fee: Included in green fee. Discounts: Twilight, juniors. Walking: Unrestricted walking. Season: Year-round. Tee Times: Call golf shop. Notes: Metal spikes, range (grass, mat). ⊠ 500 S.E. Butler Rd., Gresham 97080, 25 mi from Portland ☎ 503/661-1800 ⊕ www.persimmoncc.com ▤ AE, MC, V. *Comments: Hilly, tough, and gorgeous. Your golf score will pay the price for the scenery, but you probably won't mind.* ★ ★ ★ ★

PUMPKIN RIDGE GOLF CLUB. Facility Holes: 18. Opened: 1992. Architect: Bob Cupp. Yards: 6,839/5,206. Par: 71/71. Course Rating: 73.8/70.4. Slope: 139/125. Green Fee: $30/$120. Cart Fee: $18 per person. Discounts: Weekdays, twilight, juniors. Walking: Unrestricted walking. Season: Year-round. Tee Times: Call golf shop. Notes: Range (grass, mat). ⊠ 12930 Old Pumpkin Ridge Rd., North Plains 97133, 20 mi from Portland ☎ 503/647-9977 or 888/594-4653 ⊕ www.pumpkinridge.com ⊟ AE, D, DC, MC, V. *Comments: The public course here, Ghost Creek, is an awesome trip through the woods northwest of Portland. One of the most expensive courses in the area, but well worth it.* ★ ★ ★ ★ ¹/₂

RESERVE VINEYARDS & GOLF CLUB. Facility Holes: 36. Cart Fee: $20 per cart. Discounts: Weekdays, twilight, juniors. Walking: Unrestricted walking. Season: Year-round. Tee Times: Call 14 days in advance. Notes: Range (grass). ⊠ 4805 S.W. 229th Ave., Aloha 97007, 20 mi from Portland ☎ 503/649-8191 ⊕ www.reservegolf.com ⊟ AE, D, MC, V.

North. Holes: 18. Opened: 1998. Architect: Bob Cupp. Yards: 6,852/5,198. Par: 72/72. Course Rating: 72.6/69.6. Slope: 132/115. Green Fee: $45/$90. *Comments: Open and linksy, but sly, with plenty of hazards thanks to two creeks that come into play.* ★ ★ ★ ★

South. Holes: 18. Opened: 1997. Architect: John Fought. Yards: 7,172/5,189. Par: 72/72. Course Rating: 74.3/70.1. Slope: 134/121. Green Fee: $45/$79. *Comments: If the 100 bunkers don't get you, the many water hazards will. Built on the edge of Oregon wine country.* ★ ★ ★ ★ ¹/₂

Where to Stay

⊞ **BENSON HOTEL.** Portland's grandest hotel was built in 1912. The hand-carved Russian Circassian walnut paneling and the Italian marble staircase are among the note-worthy touches in the public areas. In the guest rooms expect to find small crystal chandeliers, inlaid mahogany doors, and the original ceilings. Extra touches include fully stocked private bars, bathrobes, and nightly turndown service. ⊠ 309 S.W. Broadway, 97205 ☎ 503/228-2000 or 888/523-6766 ⊟ 503/226-4603 ⊕ www.bensonhotel.com ↩ 286 rooms ⚐ 2 restaurants, coffee shop, room service, in-room data ports, minibars, gym, bar, laundry service, concierge, business services, meeting rooms, airport shuttle, parking (fee) ⊟ AE, D, DC, MC, V $$$$.

⊞ **DOUBLETREE HOTEL JANTZEN BEACH.** The four-story Doubletree, on the Columbia River, has larger-than-average guest rooms, many with balconies and good views of the river and Vancouver, on the other side. Public areas glitter with brass and bright lights that accentuate the greenery and the burgundy, green, and rose color scheme. The menu at Maxi's Seafood Restaurant highlights local ingredients. ⊠ 909 N. Hayden Island Dr., Jantzen Beach, 97217, (east of I-5's Jantzen Beach exit) ☎ 503/283-4466 or 800/222-8733 ⊟ 503/283-4743 ⊕ www.doubletree.com ↩ 320 rooms ⚐ Restaurants, coffee shop, room service, in-room data ports, tennis court, indoor pool, gym, hot tub, bar, dry cleaning, laundry facilities, concierge, business services, meeting room, airport shuttle, free parking, no-smoking rooms ⊟ AE, D, DC, MC, V $$.

⊞ **EMBASSY SUITES.** The grand lobby welcomes you to this property, inside what was once the Multnomah Hotel (1912). The spacious suites have large windows, sofa beds, and wet bars. There's also a basement-level pool and exercise area. A complimentary van will take you anywhere within a 2-mi radius. A full breakfast, cooked to order, and happy-hour cocktails are included in the room rate. The riverfront and MAX light

GOLF'S ROCK STAR

Portland native Peter Jacobsen is one of today's most colorful players. After attending the University of Oregon, he spent more than 28 years on the PGA Tour and now the Champions Tour. His zest for life shows in the color commentary he gives on the occasional TV broadcast. His former rock band, Jake Trout and the Flounders, assembled with other golf stars, used to perform hilarious parodies of favorite rock songs at many Tour stops, where such "real" musicians as Stephen Stills, Graham Nash, Glenn Frey, and Darius Rucker (of Hootie & the Blowfish) often joined in.

rail are within walking distance. ⊠ 319 S.W. Pine St., 97204 ☎ 503/279–9000 or 800/362–2779 🖷 503/497–9051 ⊕ www.embassysuites.com ⤴ 276 suites ⚘ Restaurant, in-room data ports, refrigerators, indoor pool, gym, hot tub, spa, steam room, bar, babysitting, laundry service, concierge, business services, meeting room, valet parking ☰ AE, D, DC, MC, V ⊙ BP $$$.

⊡ **FIFTH AVENUE SUITES HOTEL.** This hotel is on the site of the former 1912 Lipman Wolfe Department Store. A tall vestibule with a marble mosaic floor leads to the art-filled lobby, where you can gather by the fireplace for the Continental breakfast or for an early-evening glass of wine. Curtained sliding doors divide the 10-story property's 550-square-foot suites. Upholstered chairs, fringed ottomans, and other appointments in the sitting areas may make you feel right at home (or wish you had one like this). The large bathrooms are stocked with many amenities. ⊠ 506 S.W. Washington St., 97205 ☎ 503/222–0001 or 800/711–2971 🖷 503/222–0004 ⊕ www.5thavenuesuites.com ⤴ 221 suites ⚘ Restaurant, room service, in-room data ports, minibars, health club, massage, bar, dry cleaning, laundry service, business services, meeting rooms, parking (fee), no-smoking floor ☰ AE, D, DC, MC, V ⊙ CP $$$.

⊡ **GOVERNOR HOTEL.** With its mahogany walls and mural of Pacific Northwest Indians fishing, the clubby lobby sets the overall tone for the Governor, done in a sort of 1920s arts-and-crafts style. Painted in soothing earth tones, the tastefully appointed guest rooms have large windows, honor bars, and bathrobes. Some have whirlpool tubs, fireplaces, and balconies. Jake's Grill is off the lobby, the streetcar runs right out front, and the hotel is one block from the town's light-rail system. ⊠ 611 S.W. 10th Ave., 97205 ☎ 503/224–3400 or 800/554–3456 🖷 503/241–2122 ⊕ www.govhotel.com ⤴ 68 rooms, 32 suites ⚘ Restaurant, room service, in-room data ports, minibars, indoor pool, fitness classes, gym, health club, sauna, steam room, bar, dry cleaning, laundry service, concierge, business services, meeting rooms, parking (fee), no-smoking rooms ☰ AE, D, DC, MC, V $$$.

⊡ **HOTEL VINTAGE PLAZA.** This landmark takes its theme from the area's vineyards. You can fall asleep counting stars when staying on the top floor, where skylights and wall-to-wall conservatory-style windows set the rooms there apart. Hospitality suites have extra-large rooms with a full living area, and the deluxe rooms have a bar. All are appointed in warm colors and have cherrywood furnishings; some rooms have hot tubs. Complimentary wine is served in the evening, and an extensive collection of Oregon vintages is in the tasting room. Two-story town-house suites are named after local wineries. ✉ 422 S.W. Broadway, Downtown, 97205 ☎ 503/228-1212 or 800/263-2305 🖨 503/228-3598 ⊕ www.vintageplaza.com 🛏 107 rooms, 21 suites ⚐ Restaurant, room service, in-room data ports, minibars, gym, piano bar, concierge, business services, meeting room, parking (fee) ⊟ AE, D, DC, MC, V $$$.

Where to Eat

✗ **BRIDGEPORT BREWPUB & RESTAURANT.** The specialty here is thick, hand-thrown pizza with sourdough crust, served inside a cool, ivy-covered, industrial building. The boisterous crowds wash down the pizza with frothing pints of Bridgeport's English-style ale, brewed on the premises at Oregon's oldest microbrewery. Handmade focaccia, sandwiches, and salads are also on the menu. In summer the flower-festooned loading dock becomes a beer garden. ✉ 1313 N.W. Marshall St., Pearl District ☎ 503/241-7179 ⊟ MC, V ¢-$.

✗ **CAPRIAL'S.** Caprial Pence serves Mediterranean-inspired creations at her bustling bistro, where there's an open kitchen and full bar. The dinner menu, which changes monthly, is limited to four or five choices—typical entrées include pan-roasted salmon as well as smoked and grilled pork loin chop. The wine "wall" (you pick the bottle) has more than 200 varieties. ✉ 7015 S.E. Milwaukie Ave. ☎ 503/236-6457 ⊟ MC, V ⊗ Closed Sun. and Mon. $$$-$$$$.

✗ **JAKE'S FAMOUS CRAWFISH.** Diners have been eating fresh Pacific Northwest seafood in this warren of wood-paneled dining rooms since 1892. The back bar came around Cape Horn during the 1880s, and the chandeliers hanging from the high ceilings are from 1881. The restaurant gained a national reputation in 1920 when crawfish was added to the menu. Year-round the white-coated waiters take your order from a long sheet of daily seafood specials, but from May to September, crawfish season, you can sample the crustaceans in pie, cooked creole style, or in a Cajun-style stew over rice. ✉ 401 S.W. 12th Ave. ☎ 503/226-1419 ⊟ AE, D, DC, MC, V ⊗ No lunch weekends $-$$$$.

✗ **RED STAR TAVERN & ROAST HOUSE.** Cooked in a wood-burning oven, smoker, rotisserie, or grill, the cuisine at Red Star can best be described as American comfort food inspired by the bounty of the Pacific Northwest. Spit-roasted chicken, maple-fired baby back ribs with a brown-ale glaze, charred salmon, and crayfish étouffée are some of the better entrées. The wine list includes regional and international vintages, and 12 local microbrews are on tap. The spacious restaurant feels like a lodge, with tufted leather booths, murals, and copper accents. It's adjacent to the Fifth Avenue Suites Hotel. ✉ 503 S.W. Alder St., Downtown ☎ 503/222-0005 ⊟ AE, D, DC, MC, V $-$$$$.

✗ **SAUCEBOX.** At this restaurant and nightspot near the big downtown hotels, the dishes make use of several Asian cuisines, from Korean baby back ribs and Vietnamese salad rolls to Thai green curry and Indonesian roasted Javanese salmon. Inside the long, narrow space, the tables are spaced close together and draped with white cloths. The bar draws a sophisticated crowd and serves specialty cocktails; a bar menu is available in the late afternoon. ✉ 214 S.W. Broadway, Downtown ☎ 503/241-3393 ⊟ AE, MC, V ⊗ Closed Sun. and Mon. No lunch $-$$.

Essentials

Getting Here

Portland is about a three-hour drive south from Seattle on I-5.

Visitor Information

⑦ Portland/Oregon Information Center ✉ Pioneer Courthouse Sq., 701 S.W. 6th Ave.,
Downtown, 97204 ☎ 503/275-8355 or 877/678-5263 ⊕ www.pova.com.

RICHLAND, KENNEWICK & PASCO

When other golf resorts are closing up shop for winter, you can bet that
some of the courses around the "Tri-Cities" will still be open. Even though
sweaters and jackets are the norm until late summer, the temperature rarely
dips below freezing here.

Fewer than four hours from Seattle on I-82, these river towns can provide a
more affordable golf vacation than Vancouver, Portland, or Spokane can.
The area doesn't have a large number of quality golf courses, but there are
still a few gems, including Canyon Lakes and Horn Rapids Golf Club. The
best part is the price. Golf fees rarely get above $50 in this area. It's also true
that the area sorely lacks a golf resort, but it wouldn't fit into the budget
quality of this trip, anyway.

Some area courses were built through hilly terrain (like Canyon Lakes), but
the Columbia River valley, east of the Cascade Mountain range, is fairly flat,
allowing big hitters to air out their drivers. There's also something to be said
for playing courses that are routed through the middle of a wine-producing
region, as the Columbia Point Golf Course is.

On your way down to Kennewick, you may also want to stop about an hour
northwest of town to play Apple Tree Golf Course, in Yakima. This valley
course has a lot of water, including a pond that surrounds the apple-shape
17th green.

Courses

Golf Digest REVIEWS

APPLE TREE GOLF COURSE. Facility Holes: 18. Opened: 1992. Architect: John Steidel/
Apple Tree Partnership. Yards: 6,892/5,428. Par: 72/72. Course Rating: 73.3/72.0. Slope:

PASCO COURSES	YARDAGE	PAR	COURSE	SLOPE	GREEN FEE
Apple Tree Golf Course (18)	6,892/5,428	72/72	73.3/72.0	129/124	$28/$55
Canyon Lakes Golf Course (18)	7,026/5,533	72/72	73.8/72.3	129/128	$28/$38
Columbia Park Golf Course (18)	2,682/2,682	55/55	n/a	n/a	$19/$25
Columbia Point Golf Course (18)	6,571/4,692	72/72	70.0/65.9	121/107	$25/$32
Sun Willows Golf Course (18)	6,740/5,640	72/72	72.0/71.0	117/119	$13/$28
Tri-City Country Club (18)	4,855/4,300	65/65	62.2/65.2	108/115	$30/$40

129/124. Green Fee: $28/$55. Cart Fee: $25 per cart. Discounts: Weekdays, twilight, seniors, juniors. Walking: Unrestricted walking. Season: Year-round. High: Apr.–Oct. Tee Times: Call 30 days in advance. Notes: Range (grass). ✉ 8804 Occidental Ave., Yakima 98903, 170 mi from Seattle ☎ 509/966-5877 ⊕ www.appletreegolf.com ▤ MC, V. *Comments: Fun but flat. The island green shaped like an apple makes it a little gimmicky, but this is a strong golf course with a lot of water.* ★ ★ ★ ★

CANYON LAKES GOLF COURSE. Facility Holes: 18. Opened: 1981. Architect: John Steidel. Yards: 7,026/5,533. Par: 72/72. Course Rating: 73.8/72.3. Slope: 129/128. Green Fee: $28/$38. Cart Fee: $13 per person. Discounts: Weekdays, guest, twilight, juniors. Walking: Unrestricted walking. Season: Year-round. Tee Times: Call 7 days in advance. Notes: Range (grass), lodging (87). ✉ 3700 Canyon Lakes Dr., Kennewick 99337 ☎ 509/ 582-3736 ▤ AE, D, MC, V. *Comments: The best of the area's courses by far, with a low green fee. Massive greens and more undulation than on the rest of the area courses combined.* ★ ★ ★ ★

COLUMBIA PARK GOLF COURSE. Facility Holes: 18. Opened: 1948. Yards: 2,682/ 2,682. Par: 55/55. Green Fee: $19/$25. Season: Year-round. Tee Times: Call golf shop. ✉ Columbia Park, 7422 W. Clearwater, Kennewick 99336 ☎ 509/586-2800 ▤ AE, MC, V. *Comments: Don't confuse this executive, par-55 course with Columbia Point. This muni plays alongside the Columbia River and is perfect for beginners. UR*

COLUMBIA POINT GOLF COURSE. Facility Holes: 18. Opened: 1997. Architect: Jim Engh. Yards: 6,571/4,692. Par: 72/72. Course Rating: 70.0/65.9. Slope: 121/107. Green Fee: $25/$32. Cart Fee: $12 per person. Discounts: Weekdays, twilight, seniors, juniors. Walking: Unrestricted walking. Season: Year-round. Tee Times: Call 10 days in advance. Notes: Range (grass). ✉ 225 Columbia Point Dr., Richland 99352 ☎ 509/946-0710 ⊕ - www.cybergolf.com/columbiapoint ▤ AE, MC, V. *Comments: Good valley course rolling through an area near the region's wine vineyards. Throw in some palm trees and you'd think you were playing a Florida course. Well, except for the mountains.* ★ ★ ★ ½

SUN WILLOWS GOLF COURSE. Facility Holes: 18. Opened: 1959. Architect: A. Vernon Macan. Yards: 6,740/5,640. Par: 72/72. Course Rating: 72.0/71.0. Slope: 117/119. Green Fee: $13/$28. Cart Fee: $12 per cart. Walking: Unrestricted walking. Season: Year-round. Tee Times: Call golf shop. ✉ 2535 N. 20th Ave., Pasco 99301 ☎ 509/545-3440 ⊕ www.

sunwillowsgolfcourse.com ▭AE, MC, V. *Comments: Decent parkland-style course, but it shouldn't be anything more than a throw-in on your itinerary.* UR

TRI-CITY COUNTRY CLUB. Facility Holes: 18. Opened: 1938. Architect: Bert Lesley. Yards: 4,855/4,300. Par: 65/65. Course Rating: 62.2/65.2. Slope: 108/115. Green Fee: $30/$40. Cart Fee: $25 per cart. Discounts: Twilight, juniors. Walking: Unrestricted walking. Season: Year-round. Tee Times: Call 2 days in advance. ⊠314 N. Underwood, Kennewick 99336, 120 mi from Spokane ☎509/783-6014 ⊕ www.tccountryclub.com ▭AE, D, MC, V. *Comments: A short course in great condition, but a little expensive. Work on your iron play here.* ★★★

Where to Stay

RED LION HOTEL RICHLAND HANFORD HOUSE. One of three Red Lion Hotels in the Tri-Cities area, Richland's Red Lion Hotel overlooks the Columbia River and is near many major businesses and government facilities. The hotel borders a greenbelt park on the river and has easy access to levee trails that run along the edge of the Columbia. The hotel has a private boat dock and offers poolside food and drink service. Ask for a room with a river view. ⊠802 George Washington Way, Richland 99352 ☎509/946-7611 🖷509/943-8564 ⊕www.redlion.com ↵149 rooms ⌂ Restaurant, room service, in-room data ports, pool, gym, outdoor hot tub, bar, laundry service, business services, airport shuttle, free parking, some pets allowed ▭AE, D, DC, MC, V $.

ROYAL HOTEL. Many rooms overlook a tropical garden courtyard at the Royal, which provides some frills along with fairly inexpensive rates. It's three blocks from the Columbia River and 2 mi from Hwy. 182. There's a Japanese-American restaurant and lounge here, as well as a cantina by the pool. Golf packages with the Horn Rapids Golf Course are available. ⊠1515 George Washington Way, Richland 99352 ☎509/946-4121 or 800/635-3980 🖷509/946-2222 ⊕www.towerinn.net ↵190 rooms, 5 suites ⌂Restaurant, refrigerators, cable TV, pool, wading pool, hot tub, lounge, laundry facilities, business services, convention center, airport shuttle ▭AE, D, DC, MC, V ⏍CP $-$$.

SILVER CLOUD INN. This comfortable business travelers' and family hotel is across the street from the Columbia Center Shopping Mall and a short drive to three golf courses and two wineries. The straightforward rooms are outfitted with irons, ironing boards, and coffeemakers. ⊠7901 W. Quinault Ave., 99336 ☎509/735-6100 or 800/205-6938 🖷509/735-3084 ⊕www.silvercloud.com ↵110 rooms, 15 suites ⌂In-room data ports, refrigerators, cable TV with movies and video games, 2 pools (1 indoor), gym, hot tub, laundry facilities, business services, no smoking rooms ▭AE, D, DC, MC, V ⏍CP $.

Where to Eat

✕**CEDAR'S RESTAURANT.** On the edge of the Columbia River, this restaurant offers beautiful views as well as a 200-foot dock for boaters to tie up at when coming to dinner. The menu includes top quality steaks, pasta, poultry, and fresh salmon. There's also an extensive wine list, with bottles from many local wineries. ⊠355 Clover Island Dr., Kennewick ☎509/582-2143 ▭AE, D, DC, MC, V $$-$$$$.

✕**MONTEROSSO'S RESTAURANT.** Inside a refurbished railroad dining car, this small, charming Italian restaurant is fun for families, but also suitable for a romantic meal. It is known for its cheese tortellini in a creamy pesto sauce as well as its manicotti and its chicken dishes. Try the tiramisu and cheesecake. ✉ 1026 Lee Blvd., Richland ☎ 509/946-4525 ▭ AE, D, MC, V $$-$$$$.

✕**O'CALLAHAN'S RESTAURANT AND LOUNGE.** This restaurant, part of the Shilo Inn Rivershore, has a lounge with a view of the Columbia River. When it's warm, you can dine on the deck overlooking the water. On the menu are fresh seafood daily, aged hand-cut beef, pastas, and salads. Some popular items are the country-fried steak and the southern fried catfish. O'Callahan's also serves breakfast. ✉ 50 Comstock St., Richland ☎ 509/946-9006 ▭ AE, D, DC, MC, V $-$$$.

✕**RATTLESNAKE MOUNTAIN BREWING COMPANY.** The spacious deck of this pub and restaurant has wonderful views of the Columbia River. Serving chicken, steak, pasta, and shrimp dishes, the eatery is famous for its buffalo wings and its seven home-brewed beers. ✉ 2696 N. Columbia Center Blvd., Richland ☎ 509/783-5661 ▭ AE, D, DC, MC, V $-$$$.

✕**SUNDANCE GRILL.** Table candles and live piano music make this restaurant a romantic place for dinner. The riverfront location makes for good views of the Columbia River from the patio. On the dinner menu are prime beef, pasta, and fresh seafood; sandwiches, salads, and pasta dishes are served for lunch. The wine list here is impressive. ✉ 450 Columbia Point Dr., Richland ☎ 509/942-7120 ▭ AE, D, MC, V $$-$$$$.

Essentials

Getting Here

The Tri-Cities are about a 3¹/₂-hour drive from Seattle. Take I-90 east 110 mi to Ellensburg, then take I-82 southeast 100 mi to the Tri-Cities.

Visitor Information

🛈 **TRI-CITIES VISITOR AND CONVENTION BUREAU** ✉ 6951 W. Grandridge Blvd., Kennewick 99302 ☎ 800/254-5824 ⊕ www.visittri-cities.com.

SPOKANE

You may think twice about wanting to make the five-hour drive on I-90 from Seattle to the eastern edge of Washington, but it's well worth the trip. Spokane has several good golf courses ranging in style from parkland to links to desert. There's even a full-blown resort in the area. The only thing Spokane lacks is warm weather year-round. The temperatures from November through February may be a little too cold for golf.

Chewelah Golf & Country Club (18)	6,645/5,393	72/72	72.2/66.1	126/114	$12/$22
Coeur d'Alene Resort Golf Course (18)	6,802/5,490	71/71	69.9/70.3	121/118	$100/$185
The Creek at Qualchan (18)	6,599/5,538	72/72	71.6/72.3	127/126	$16/$21
Desert Canyon Golf Resort (18)	7,293/4,939	72/74	74.0/67.2	134/106	$39/$89
Downriver Golf Club (18)	6,130/5,592	71/73	68.8/70.9	115/114	$19/$21
Esmeralda Golf Course (18)	6,249/5,594	70/72	68.7/72.7	114/112	$21
Indian Canyon Golf Course (18)	6,255/5,943	72/72	69.8/70.2	121/125	$23
Liberty Lake Golf Club (18)	6,373/5,801	70/74	69.8/75.7	121/134	$17/$23
Meadowwood Golf Course (18)	6,846/5,880	72/72	72.1/73.5	126/114	$12/$22

The best two courses in the immediate Spokane area are Meadowwood Golf Course in Liberty Lake and Indian Canyon Golf Course. Indian Canyon is one of four municipal courses run by the city. They're all cheap and fairly good.

Although you may be tempted to stay in Spokane, consider driving 30 mi into Idaho and staying at the Coeur d'Alene Resort instead. Home of the infamous floating green that can be reached only by boat, this resort has excellent service, and the scenery along Lake Coeur d'Alene is breathtaking. The golf course is ranked number one in the state by *Golf Digest*.

On your way either to or from Seattle, you may want to break up the trip by staying a night at the Desert Canyon Golf Resort, 180 mi west of Spokane, near U.S. Hwy. 2 at the base of the Wenatchee National Forest. This exceptional resort's course sits on a high bluff overlooking the Columbia River.

Courses

Golf Digest REVIEWS

CHEWELAH GOLF & COUNTRY CLUB. Facility Holes: 18. Opened: 1976. Architect: Keith Hellstrom/Jim Kraus. Yards: 6,645/5,393. Par: 72/72. Course Rating: 72.2/66.1. Slope: 126/114. Green Fee: $12/$22. Cart Fee: $24 per cart. Discounts: Seniors, juniors. Walking: Walking at certain times. Season: Apr.–Nov. High: July–Sept. Tee Times: Call 21 days in advance. Notes: Range (mat). ✉ 2537 Sand Canyon Rd., Chewelah 99109, 40 mi from Spokane ☎ 509/935-6807 ⊕ www.ch-ewlahgolf.com ▭ AE, MC, V. *Comments: Deep in the woods north of Spokane, Chewelah feels like a campground.* ★ ★ ★

COEUR D'ALENE RESORT GOLF COURSE. Facility Holes: 18. Opened: 1991. Architect: Scott Miller. Yards: 6,802/5,490. Par: 71/71. Course Rating: 69.9/70.3. Slope:

121/118. Green Fee: $100/$185. Cart Fee: Included in green fee. Walking: Walking with caddie. Season: Apr.–Oct. High: June–Sept. Tee Times: Call golf shop. Notes: Range (grass), lodging (338). ✉ 900 Floating Green Dr., Coeur d'Alene, ID 83814, 32 mi from Spokane ☎ 208/667–4653 or 800/688–5253 ⊕ www.cdaresort.com ▤ AE, D, MC, V. *Comments: It's hard to get tired of playing this golf course. Beautiful views of blue lakes and mountains, and immaculate fairways. One of the best in the Pacific Northwest.* ★ ★ ★ ★ ¹/₂

THE CREEK AT QUALCHAN GOLF COURSE. Facility Holes: 18. Opened: 1993. Architect: William Robinson. Yards: 6,599/5,538. Par: 72/72. Course Rating: 71.6/72.3. Slope: 127/126. Green Fee: $16/$21. Cart Fee: $25 per cart. Discounts: Seniors, juniors. Walking: Unrestricted walking. Season: Mar.–Nov. High: June–Sept. Tee Times: Call golf shop. Notes: Metal spikes, range (grass). ✉ 301 E. Meadowlane Rd., 99224 ☎ 509/448–9317 ▤ MC, V. *Comments: Newest of the city's municipal golf courses. Terrific layout considering the low green fee.* ★ ★ ★ ★

DESERT CANYON GOLF RESORT. Facility Holes: 18. Opened: 1993. Architect: Jack Frei. Yards: 7,293/4,939. Par: 72/74. Course Rating: 74.0/67.2. Slope: 134/106. Green Fee: $39/$89. Cart Fee: Included in green fee. Discounts: Weekdays, twilight, seniors, juniors. Walking: Mandatory cart. Season: Mar.–Nov. Tee Times: Call golf shop. Notes: Range (grass), lodging (10). ✉ 1201 Desert Canyon Blvd., Orondo 98843, 25 mi from Wenatchee ☎ 509/784–1111 or 800/258–4173 ⊕ www.desertcanyon.com ▤ AE, MC, V. *Comments: Three hours west of Spokane, with stunning views.* ★ ★ ★ ★ ¹/₂

DOWNRIVER GOLF CLUB. Facility Holes: 18. Opened: 1916. Architect: Local Citizens Committee. Yards: 6,130/5,592. Par: 71/73. Course Rating: 68.8/70.9. Slope: 115/114. Green Fee: $19/$21. Cart Fee: $25 per cart. Walking: Unrestricted walking. Season: Mar.–Nov. High: June–Sept. Tee Times: Call golf shop. Notes: Range (mat). ✉ 3225 N. Columbia Circle, 99205 ☎ 509/327–5269 ▤ MC, V. *Comments: Mature trees and classic layout. This old course is still fun to play and easy on your scorecard. One of the city's four muni courses.* ★ ★ ★ ¹/₂

ESMERALDA GOLF COURSE. Facility Holes: 18. Opened: 1956. Architect: Francis James. Yards: 6,249/5,594. Par: 70/72. Course Rating: 68.7/72.7. Slope: 114/112. Green Fee: $21. Cart Fee: $24 per cart. Discounts: Twilight, seniors, juniors. Walking: Unrestricted walking. Season: Mar.–Nov. High: Apr.–Aug. Tee Times: Call golf shop. Notes: Metal spikes, range (grass, mat). ✉ 3933 E. Courtland, 99217 ☎ 509/487–6291 ⊕ www.spokaneparks.org ▤ MC, V. *Comments: Another Spokane muni. This one is flat and tree-lined but still good.* ★ ★ ★

INDIAN CANYON GOLF COURSE. Facility Holes: 18. Opened: 1935. Architect: H. Chandler Egan. Yards: 6,255/5,943. Par: 72/72. Course Rating: 69.8/70.2. Slope: 121/125. Green Fee: $23. Cart Fee: $23 per cart. Discounts: Twilight, juniors. Walking: Unrestricted walking. Season: Apr.–Oct. Tee Times: Call golf shop. Notes: Metal spikes, range (grass, mat). ✉ W. 4304 West Dr., 99204 ☎ 509/747–5353 ▤ MC, V. *Comments: Quality, tree-lined golf course. Condition is not always perfect, but the rate will leave a smile on your face.* ★ ★ ★ ★

LIBERTY LAKE GOLF CLUB. Facility Holes: 18. Opened: 1959. Architect: Curly Houston. Yards: 6,373/5,801. Par: 70/74. Course Rating: 69.8/75.7. Slope: 121/134. Green Fee: $17/$23. Cart Fee: $26 per cart. Discounts: Twilight, seniors, juniors. Walking: Unrestricted walking. Season: Year-round. Tee Times: Call 7 days in advance. Notes: Metal spikes, range (grass, mat). ⊠ E. 24403 Sprague, Liberty Lake 99019, 20 mi from Spokane ☎ 509/255-6233 ▭ D, MC, V. *Comments: Since Liberty Lake is close to Meadowwood, the two would be perfect for a 36-hole doubleheader.* ★ ★ ★ ¹/₂

MEADOWWOOD GOLF COURSE. Facility Holes: 18. Opened: 1988. Architect: Robert Muir Graves. Yards: 6,846/5,880. Par: 72/72. Course Rating: 72.1/73.5. Slope: 126/114. Green Fee: $12/$22. Cart Fee: $25 per cart. Discounts: Twilight, seniors, juniors. Walking: Walking at certain times. Season: Mar.–Nov. Tee Times: Call golf shop. Notes: Metal spikes, range (mat). ⊠ E. 24501 Valley Way, Liberty Lake 99019, 12 mi from Spokane ☎ 509/255-9539 ⊕ www.meadowwoodgolf.com ▭ D, MC, V. *Comments: Run by Spokane County Parks Dept. Fairly wide open, but very pretty and in decent condition.* ★ ★ ★ ¹/₂

Where to Stay

🍽 **COEUR D'ALENE RESORT.** The plush rooms at this lakeside high-rise resort have either fireplaces or balconies with terrific views of the water. The lower-priced rooms are in a standard motel style. The top-of-the-line restaurant, Beverly's, is known for its fine Northwest cuisine, superb wine cellar, and incomparable views. ⊠ 2nd and Front Sts., Coeur d'Alene, ID 83814 ☎ 208/765-4000 or 800/688-5253 ♻ 208/667-2707 ⊕ www. cdaresort.com ⇱ 336 rooms ⟁ 4 restaurants, minibars, cable TV with video games and movies, 18-hole golf course, putting green, pro shop, pool, gym, spa, Internet, business services, meeting rooms, no-smoking rooms ▭ AE, D, DC, MC, V $$-$$$$.

🍽 **DAVENPORT HOTEL.** Spokane's oldest hotel reopened in 2002 after being shuttered for more than 15 years. The rooms are elegant because of hand-carved mahogany furniture and fine Irish linens. They're up-to-date, too, with high-speed Internet access and 27-inch flat-screen TVs. Although the rooms' sleeping areas are not huge, the marble bathrooms, with big soaking tubs and separate showers, are spacious and inviting. The Palm Court Restaurant is open for three meals daily; the Peacock Lounge has light fare and a cigar room. On the lobby level there are also an espresso bar, a candy shop, a flower shop, and an art gallery. ⊠ 10 S. Post St., 99201 ☎ 509/455-8888 or 800/899-1482 ♻ 509/624-4455 ⊕ www.davenporthotel.com ⇱ 260 rooms, 24 suites ⟁ Restaurant, indoor pool, hot tub, spa, lounge, shops, concierge, business services, convention center, some pets allowed (fee); no smoking ▭ AE, D, DC, MC, V $$$.

🍽 **DESERT CANYON GOLF RESORT.** Town-house condominium units, with kitchens and satellite TV, overlook the course here. The resort's Oasis Mesquite Grill continues the desert theme with southwestern cuisine and furnishings. If you ever happen to tire of the links, there are other outdoor sports to sample here. The resort is equidistant from Seattle and Spokane, between Wenatchee and Lake Chelan and off U.S. Hwy 97. ⊠ 1201 Desert Canyon Blvd., Orondo 98843 ☎ 509/784-1111 or 800/

258-4173 ⌂ 509/784-2701 ⊕ www.desertcanyon.com ⇥ 22 lodge rooms, 10 condos ⅃ Restaurant, kitchens, cable TV, 18-hole golf course, tennis courts, hiking, lounge ▭ AE, D, DC, MC, V $$-$$$$.

⊞ DOUBLETREE HOTEL SPOKANE CITY CENTER. This chain hotel is convenient to Riverfront Park, RiverPark Square shopping, and downtown cultural facilities. Standard furnishings and amenities are in the comfortable rooms, as are some extras, like irons and ironing boards, coffeemakers, and Doubletree's signature warm chocolate chip cookies upon arrival. ⊠ 322 N. Spokane Falls Ct., 99201 ☎ 509/455-9600 or 800/222-8733 ⌂ 509/455-6285 ⊕ www.doubletree.com ⇥ 375 rooms ⅃ 2 restaurants, room service, in-room data ports, minibars, cable TV with video games and pay movies, indoor pool, gym, sauna, lounge, laundry service, concierge, business services, meeting rooms, car rental, no-smoking rooms ▭ AE, D, DC, MC, V $-$$.

⊞ RED LION HOTEL AT THE PARK. Modern rooms with all the standard amenities are what you find at the Red Lion, which has the additional asset of a location adjacent to Riverfront Park and very near the downtown shopping district. All floors in the main building open onto an atrium lobby; more guest rooms are in two newer wings. Rooms have coffeemakers, hair dryers, and feather beds. In summer, you can cool off with the outdoor swimming lagoon's waterfalls and waterslide. ⊠ 303 W. North River Dr., 99201 ☎ 509/326-8000 or 800/733-5406 ⌂ 509/325-7329 ⊕ www.redlion.com ⇥ 400 rooms ⅃ 3 restaurants, room service, in-room data ports, minibars, cable TV with video games and movies, 2 pools (1 indoor), hot tub, sauna, 2 lounges, concierge, convention center, airport shuttle, no-smoking rooms ▭ AE, D, DC, MC, V $-$$$.

⊞ RESIDENCE INN. East of Spokane, right off I-90, the Residence Inn is convenient to Coeur d'Alene, and just 5 mi from Meadowwood and Liberty Lake golf courses. It's also right across from the Spokane Valley Mall, numerous restaurants, and a Krispy Kreme shop. Walk a mile north to get to Sullivan Park on the Spokane River, a stop on the city's 37-mi Centennial Trail. The spacious suites include full kitchens, and some have fireplaces and separate bedrooms. Besides the complimentary hot breakfast every morning, you can also fill up on complimentary snacks and beverages during the evening hospitality hour—as well as at the weekly barbecues. ⊠ 15915 E. Indiana Ave., 99207 ☎ 509/892-9300 ⌂ 509/892-9400 ⊕ www.residenceinn.com ⇥ 84 suites ⅃ In-room data ports, kitchens, tennis court, pool, hot tub, laundry facilities, Internet, business services, concierge, some pets allowed (fee), no-smoking rooms ▭ AE, D, DC, MC, V ⅧI BP $.

Where to Eat

✕ CLINKERDAGGER'S. A former flour mill, with great views of the Spokane River, houses "Clink's," a Spokane institution since 1974. The interior has exposed brick walls and handsome oak floors and trim. The seafood, steaks, and prime rib are excellent, and you won't have to pick just one: you can mix and match from entrées to make your own combinations. ⊠ 621 W. Mallon Ave. ☎ 509/328-5965 ▭ AE, D, DC, MC, V ☉ No lunch Sun. $$-$$$$.

✕ **ELK PUBLIC HOUSE.** This eatery is in the relaxed Browne's Addition neighborhood, west of downtown. On the upscale pub menu are such dishes as lamb sandwiches, pastas, salads, and many vegetarian dishes, together with 18 microbrews, mostly from the Northwest. A copper bar stands along one wall, in front of a mirror, giving the interior a saloonlike appearance. ⊠ 1931 W. Pacific Ave. ☎ 509/363–1973 ⚑ Reservation not accepted ☰ MC, V ¢–$.

✕ **LUNA.** On offer here are inventive approaches to classics—pork chops, salmon, lamb, and game hen dishes all have pride of place, and the menu highlights fresh ingredients grown in the restaurant's own garden. Sunday brunch has such treats as scrambled egg salad with field greens and smoked bacon, and French toast with caramelized bananas. A terrace is open in summer. Luna's wine list has more than 500 vintages. ⊠ 5620 S. Perry St. ☎ 509/448–2383 ☰ AE, DC, MC, V $–$$$$.

✕ **MIZUNA RESTAURANT AND WINE BAR.** Fresh flowers adorn the redbrick walls, adding color to this downtown vegetarian. Local produce is the inspiration for the scrumptious fare, which may include Moroccan portobello "steak," white cheddar and apple salad, and ahi served with wilted spinach and sun-dried tomato vinaigrette. (If you don't eat fish, you can have the dish with tofu or wheat gluten instead.) At the wine bar you can sample bottles by the "taste" (2 ounces) or glass. You might wish to inquire about the five-course winemakers' dinner, which occurs several times per year. ⊠ 214 N. Howard St. ☎ 509/747–2004 ⊕ www.mizuna.com ☰ AE, D, MC, V ⊙ No lunch weekends, no dinner Sun. and Mon. $$–$$$.

✕ **ROCK CITY GRILL.** Upbeat and close to Riverfront Park, the Grill prepares excellent pastas and pizzas baked in wood-fired ovens. Expect some kidding around from the outgoing, friendly staff, who keep the free refills coming for soft drinks and lemonade. Save room for such desserts as tiramisu for two and the Snickers pie. You can get validated parking at Spokane's City Ramp or Parkade. ⊠ 505 W. Riverside Ave. ☎ 509/455–4400 ⊟ 509/459–6790 ☰ AE, D, DC, MC, V $–$$$.

✕ **STEAM PLANT GRILL.** Inside a 1916 steam plant in operation for over 70 years, this restaurant has several distinct dining rooms. You can eat inside a boiler, inside a hot-water tank, or on a balcony overlooking the entire complex. The menu options are equally broad; there is a coconut curry salad, a halibut fish taco, steak, and lamb chops. The most popular dish is the fish-and-chips, fried in a batter made from locally brewed beer. ⊠ 159 S. Lincoln ☎ 509/777–3900 ☰ AE, D, MC, V $–$$$.

Essentials

Getting Here
To drive from Seattle to Spokane, take I–90 east. The 280-mi drive takes about five hours.

Visitor Information
🛈 **Spokane Area Visitors Information** ⊠ 801 W. Riverside, Suite 301, 99201 ☎ 509/624–1341 ⊕ www.visitspokane.com.

Furry Creek Golf & Country Club (18)	6,025/4,749	72/71	69.1/68.8	122/119	$70/$100
Mayfair Lakes Golf & Country Club (18)	6,641/5,277	71/72	71.3/71.3	123/126	$45/$85
Meadow Gardens Golf Course (18)	7,041/5,519	72/72	73.1/71.3	126/116	$35/$65
Morgan Creek Golf Course (18)	6,961/5,223	72/73	73.2/69.4	133/120	$55/$95
Northview Golf & Country Club (36)					
Canal (18)	7,101/5,314	72/72	73.2/70.1	130/108	$45/$75
Ridge (18)	6,900/5,231	72/72	72.6/70.1	135/123	$50/$95
The Redwoods (18)	6,516/5,452	71/71	72.3/71.3	131/123	$15/$65
Swan-E-Set Bay Resort & Country Club (18)	7,000/5,632	72/72	73.8/71.5	130/120	$40/$85
University Golf Club (18)	6,584/5,653	72/72	71.0/70.9	122/114	$50/$65
Westwood Plateau Golf & Country Club (18)	6,770/5,014	72/72	71.9/68.2	136/123	$99/$159

VANCOUVER, BC

Because it's where the mountains meet the sea, some people consider Vancouver the prettiest city in the world. The area is the ultimate locale on which golf course architects can build. Granted, for at least six months out of the year, only the heartiest of golfers are on the links—unless they're riding snowmobiles. But from May to October, there are few places on the planet that are more beautiful to play.

There are many high-quality golf courses in the area and the prices are cut-rate, especially considering the current exchange rate of the Canadian dollar.

The only three-figure green fee in town is Westwood Plateau, but make sure you save up to play this course, on a promontory north of the city. On a clear morning, you can see Mt. Baker. If you want to see the beautiful skyline of Vancouver, however, you have to find a way to sneak on the ultra-exclusive Capilano Golf & Country Club. Furry Creek Golf & Country Club, another must-play for your list, has views so gorgeous that they might help you forget how bad you're playing.

Courses

FURRY CREEK GOLF & COUNTRY CLUB. Facility Holes: 18. Opened: 1993. Architect: Robert Muir Graves. Yards: 6,025/4,749. Par: 72/71. Course Rating: 69.1/68.8. Slope: 122/119. Green Fee: $70/$100. Cart Fee: Included in green fee. Discounts: Weekdays, twilight, seniors, juniors. Walking: Mandatory cart. Season: Mar.–Oct. High: June–Sept. Tee Times: Call 10 days in advance. Notes: Metal spikes, range (grass). ⊠ 150 Country Club Rd., Furry Creek, V0N 3Z2, 12 mi (19 km) from Lions Bay ☎ 604/896–2216 or 888/922–9462 ⊕ www.golfbc.com ⊟ AE, MC, V. *Comments: Perhaps the most scenic course in all of British Columbia. Plays along the Howe Sound at the edge of Mt. Seymour. Don't miss this course.* ★ ★ ★ ★

MAYFAIR LAKES GOLF & COUNTRY CLUB. Facility Holes: 18. Opened: 1989. Architect: Les Furber. Yards: 6,641/5,277. Par: 71/72. Course Rating: 71.3/71.3. Slope: 123/126. Green Fee: $45/$85. Cart Fee: $30 per cart. Discounts: Weekdays, twilight, seniors, juniors. Walking: Unrestricted walking. Season: Year-round. High: May–Oct. Tee Times: Call 5 days in advance. Notes: Range (grass, mat). ⊠ 5460 No. 7 Rd., Richmond, V6V 1R7, 7 mi (11 km) from Vancouver ☎ 604/276–0505 or 800/446–5322 ⊕ www.golfbc. com ⊟ AE, MC, V. *Comments: Flat, valley course with water on 10 holes. A little pricey for what you get.* ★ ★ ★

MEADOW GARDENS GOLF COURSE. Facility Holes: 18. Opened: 1994. Architect: Les Furber/Jim Eremko. Yards: 7,041/5,519. Par: 72/72. Course Rating: 73.1/71.3. Slope: 126/116. Green Fee: $35/$65. Cart Fee: $28 per cart. Discounts: Weekdays, twilight, seniors, juniors. Walking: Unrestricted walking. Season: Year-round. High: May–Sept. Tee Times: Call 7 days in advance. Notes: Range (grass, mat). ⊠ 19675 Meadow Gardens Way, Pitt Meadows, V3Y 1Z2, 25 mi (40 km) from Vancouver ☎ 604/465–5474 or 800/667–6758 ⊕ www.meadowgardens.com ⊟ AE, DC, MC, V. *Comments: Valley course with great views. Fun to play.* ★ ★ ★ ½

MORGAN CREEK GOLF COURSE. Facility Holes: 18. Opened: 1995. Architect: Thomas McBroom. Yards: 6,961/5,223. Par: 72/73. Course Rating: 73.2/69.4. Slope: 133/120. Green Fee: $55/$95. Cart Fee: $34 per cart. Discounts: Weekdays, twilight, seniors, juniors. Walking: Unrestricted walking. Season: Year-round. High: May–Oct. Tee Times: Call golf shop. Notes: Range (grass). ⊠ 3500 Morgan Creek Way, Surrey, V3S 0J7, 35 mi (56 km) from Vancouver ☎ 604/531–4653 or 800/513–6555 ⊕ www.morgancreekgolf. com ⊟ AE, DC, MC, V. *Comments: Solid parkland-style course south of town.* ★ ★ ★ ½

NORTHVIEW GOLF & COUNTRY CLUB. Facility Holes: 36. Architect: Arnold Palmer. Cart Fee: $32 per cart. Discounts: Weekdays, twilight, seniors, juniors. Walking: Unrestricted walking. Season: Year-round. Tee Times: Call golf shop. Notes: Range (grass, mat). ⊠ 6857 168th St., Surrey, V3S 8E7, 18 mi (29 km) from Vancouver ☎ 604/576–4653 or 888/574–2211 ⊕ www.northviewgolf.com ⊟ AE, DC, MC, V.

Canal. Holes: 18. Opened: 1995. Yards: 7,101/5,314. Par: 72/72. Course Rating: 73.2/70.1. Slope: 130/108. Green Fee: $45/$75. ★ ★ ★ ½

Ridge. Holes: 18. Opened: 1994. Yards: 6,900/5,231. Par: 72/72. Course Rating: 72.6/ 70.1. Slope: 135/123. Green Fee: $50/$95. ★★★★

Comments: Site of the PGA Tour's Greater Vancouver Open. Flat, wide open, and treeless but fun to play. Watch out for the water.

THE REDWOODS. Facility Holes: 18. Opened: 1994. Architect: Ted Locke. Yards: 6,516/ 5,452. Par: 71/71. Course Rating: 72.3/71.3. Slope: 131/123. Green Fee: $15/$65. Cart Fee: $28 per cart. Discounts: Weekdays, twilight, seniors, juniors. Walking: Unrestricted walking. Season: Year-round. Tee Times: Call 365 days in advance. Notes: Metal spikes, range (mat). ✉ 22011 88th Ave., Langley, V1M 2M3, 25 mi (40 km) from Vancouver ☎ 604/ 882-5132 or 877/882-5130 ⊕ www.redwoods-golf.com ⊟ AE, MC, V. *Comments: Heavily treed, with great elevation changes. Winds through a forest.* ★★★ ¹/₂

SWAN-E-SET BAY RESORT & COUNTRY CLUB. Facility Holes: 18. Opened: 1993. Architect: Lee Trevino. Yards: 7,000/5,632. Par: 72/72. Course Rating: 73.8/71.5. Slope: 130/120. Green Fee: $40/$85. Cart Fee: $25 per cart. Discounts: Weekdays, twilight, juniors. Walking: Unrestricted walking. Season: Year-round. Tee Times: Call 7 days in advance. Notes: Range (grass, mat). ✉ 16651 Rannie Rd., Pitt Meadows, V3Y 1Z1, 27 mi (43 km) from Vancouver ☎ 604/465-3888 or 800/235-8188 ⊕ www. swaneset.com ⊟ AE, DC, MC, V. *Comments: This flat course is right on the Pitt River.* ★★★

THE GOLF HOUSE MUSEUM

Vancouver's golf history is still being written, but its past is on display at the British Columbia Golf House Museum, near the 17th tee of the University Golf Club course.

UNIVERSITY GOLF CLUB. Facility Holes: 18. Opened: 1929. Architect: Davey Black. Yards: 6,584/5,653. Par: 72/ 72. Course Rating: 71.0/70.9. Slope: 122/114. Green Fee: $50/$65. Cart Fee: $32 per cart. Discounts: Twilight, seniors. Walking: Unrestricted walking. Season: Year-round. High: Mar.–Oct. Tee Times: Call 7 days in advance. Notes: Metal spikes, range (mat). ✉ 5185 University Blvd., V6T 1X5 ☎ 604/224-1818 ⊕ www.universitygolf.com ⊟ AE, MC, V. *Comments: Parkland-style course with more trees than you can handle.* ★★★ ¹/₂

WESTWOOD PLATEAU GOLF & COUNTRY CLUB. Facility Holes: 18. Opened: 1995. Architect: Michael Hurdzan. Yards: 6,770/5,014. Par: 72/72. Course Rating: 71.9/68.2. Slope: 136/123. Green Fee: $99/$159. Cart Fee: Included in green fee. Discounts: Weekdays, juniors. Walking: Mandatory cart. Season: Apr.–Oct. Tee Times: Call 90 days in advance. Notes: Range (grass, mat). ✉ 3251 Plateau Blvd., Coquitlam, V3E 3B8, 30 mi (48 km) from Vancouver ☎ 604/552-0777 or 800/580-0785 ⊕ www. westwoodplateaugolf.bc.ca ⊟ AE, DC, MC, V. *Comments: Awesome mountain course, but a little pricey. Flat in some areas, but great elevation changes in others. Easily the best course in the area.* ★★★★ ¹/₂

Where to Stay

⛨ **FAIRMONT WATERFRONT.** An underground walkway leads from this striking 23-story glass hotel to Vancouver's Convention and Exhibition Centre and cruise-ship terminal. Views from the lobby and from 60% of the guest rooms are of Burrard Inlet,

Stanley Park, and the North Shore Mountains. Other rooms look onto the city skyline and a terraced herb garden. The spacious rooms have big picture windows and are furnished with blond-wood furniture and contemporary Canadian artwork. Large corner rooms have the best views. Rooms on the Entrée Gold floor have extra amenities, including in-room safes, a private lounge, and a concierge. ⊠ 900 Canada Place Way, Downtown, V6C 3L5 ☎ 604/691-1991 🖷 604/691-1828 ⊕ www.fairmont.com 🛏 489 rooms, 29 suites ⚐ Restaurant, room service, in-room data ports, some in-room safes, minibars, cable TV with movies and video games, pool, gym, hot tub, massage, steam room, lobby lounge, shops, baby-sitting, dry cleaning, laundry service, concierge, concierge floor, Internet, business services, meeting rooms, parking (fee), some pets allowed (fee), no-smoking floors ⊟ AE, D, DC, MC, V $$$-$$$$.

▥ LORD STANLEY SUITES ON THE PARK. These small, attractive, fully equipped suites are right of the edge of Stanley Park. Each has an office nook, a sitting room, and one or two bedrooms. Each suite overlooking busy Georgia Street has an enclosed sun-room; those backing onto quieter Alberni Street have balconies. You're also close to many restaurants on Denman Street, a block away. ⊠ 1889 Alberni St., West End V6G 3G7 ☎ 604/688-9299 or 888/767-7829 🖷 604/688-9297 ⊕ www.lordstanley.com 🛏 100 suites ⚐ In-room data ports, cable TV, in-room VCRs, gym, sauna, dry cleaning, laundry service, meeting rooms, parking (fee), no-smoking floors ⊟ AE, DC, MC, V ⑩ CP $$-$$$.

▥ METROPOLITAN HOTEL. Warm up for your golf game in the heart of the city at the hotel's outdoor putting green—a feature that's unique among Vancouver's down-town hotels. The spacious rooms are decorated in muted colors; public areas highlight Asian art, including two lions guarding the entrance and a striking antique gold-leaf temple carving in the lobby. Standard room amenities include down comforters, bathrobes, marble bathrooms with soaking tubs and separate showers, Internet access, and newspapers; business-class rooms come with printers, fax machines, and cordless phones. Service is consistently gracious. Catch glimpses of the hotel's restaurant, Diva at the Met, through an etched-glass wall in the lobby. ⊠ 645 Howe St., Downtown, V6C 2Y9 ☎ 604/687-1122 or 800/667-2300 🖷 604/689-7044 ⊕ www.metropolitan.com 🛏 179 rooms, 18 suites ⚐ Restaurant, in-room data ports, some in-room faxes, in-room safes, minibars, cable TV with movies and video games, indoor pool, gym, hot tub, sauna (women only), steam room (men only), racquetball, squash, bar, concierge, Internet, business services, meeting rooms, parking (fee), some pets allowed, no-smok-ing floors ⊟ AE, D, DC, MC, V $$$-$$$$.

▥ SUTTON PLACE. Closer to an exclusive European guest house than a large modern hotel, Sutton Place has guest rooms furnished with rich, dark woods, and the service is gracious and attentive. The hotel's Fleuri restaurant is known for its Continental cuisine, Sunday brunch, afternoon tea, and weekend-evening "chocoholic" bar. The full European health spa (also open to nonguests) offers a massage using river stones as well as wraps, facials, manicures, and reflexology. ⊠ 845 Burrard St., Downtown, V6Z 2K6 ☎ 604/682-5511 or 800/961-7555 🖷 604/682-5513 ⊕ www.suttonplace.com 🛏 350 rooms, 47 suites ⚐ Restaurant, room service, some in-room safes, minibars, cable TV with movies and video games, indoor pool, health club, sauna (women only), spa, steam room (men only), lounge, piano bar, shop, baby-sitting, children's programs (ages 0–12), dry cleaning, laundry service, concierge, Internet, business services, meeting rooms, parking (fee), some pets allowed (fee), no-smoking rooms ▤AE, D, DC, MC, V $$$-$$$$.

📺 **WESTIN GRAND VANCOUVER.** With its minimalist approach to furnishings and its cherrywood and marble lobby, the Westin Grand, shaped like a grand piano, is one of Vancouver's more stylish hotels. Most of the compact studios and one-bedroom suites have floor-to-ceiling windows with skyline views, and all units have fully equipped kitchenettes with microwaves and dishwashers tucked into armoires. Corner suites are larger and have small balconies. Office suites come with a combination fax-photocopier-printer; all rooms have high-speed Internet access. The hotel is close to the main sports-and-entertainment district and to the fashionable restaurants of Yaletown. ✉433 Robson St., Downtown, V6B 6L9 ☎604/602-1999 or 888/680-9393 🖨604/647-2502 ⊕www.westingrandvancouver.com ⟿23 rooms, 184 suites ⟁Restaurant, room service, in-room data ports, in-room safes, minibars, cable TV with movies and video games, some in-room VCRs, pool, gym, outdoor hot tub, sauna, steam room, bar, nightclub, shop, baby-sitting, children's programs (ages 0–12), dry cleaning, laundry service, concierge, business services, meeting rooms, parking (fee), no-smoking floors ▤AE, D, DC, MC, V $$-$$$$.

Where to Eat

✗ **BRIX.** The greenery-draped courtyard is a romantic summer dining spot. The interior of the former warehouse, built in 1912, is fashionably comfortable, with vaulted ceilings, exposed brick, and local art exhibits. The seasonally changing fare, dubbed "progressive Pacific Northwest," presents creative treatments of local ingredients, many with Asian touches. Try the Wild B.C. caribou with a panko crust or the Saltspring Island lamb stuffed with morel and wild mushrooms. An equally creative lunch menu, tapas, and more than 60 wines by the glass are available all day. ✉1138 Homer St. ☎604/915-9463 ⊕www.brixvancouver.com ▤AE, MC, V ⊘Closed Sun. No lunch Sat. $$-$$$.

✗ **C RESTAURANT.** Dishes such as lobster-and-crab-stuffed roasted turbot and octopus-bacon-wrapped scallops have established C as Vancouver's most innovative seafood restaurant. An eight-course tasting menu highlights regional seafood, such as wild salmon, sablefish, and tanner crab. Both the chic, ultramodern interior and the waterside patio overlook the yacht and sailboat traffic on False Creek. ✉2-1600 Howe St., Downtown ☎604/681-1164 ▤AE, DC, MC, V ⊘No lunch weekends or Oct.–Apr. $$$-$$$$.

✗ **DIVA AT THE MET.** At this multitiered restaurant in the Metropolitan Hotel, the presentation of the innovative contemporary cuisine is as appealing as the art deco interior. The menu changes seasonally, but top creations from the open kitchen have included wild sockeye salmon with crab and leek gratin, and organic cinnamon-smoked Fraser Valley duck breast. The after-theater crowd heads here for late-evening snacks, desserts, and rich handmade chocolates. The creative breakfasts and weekend brunches are popular options. ✉645 Howe St., Downtown ☎604/602-7788 ▤AE, D, DC, MC, V $$$-$$$$.

✗ **EARL'S.** This local chain is a favorite among Vancouverites looking for a lively place to go with a group. Big rooms, cozy booths, upbeat music, chipper service, and consistently good burgers, soups, sandwiches, pastas, steaks, and vegetarian options keep people coming back. Food and drink are served all day until midnight, and the Robson Street location has a big outdoor deck away from traffic. Reservations are accepted only for parties of eight or more. ⊠1185 Robson St., Downtown ☎604/669-0020 ☰AE, MC, V $-$$.

✕**INCENDIO.** The hand-flipped thin-crust pizzas, with toppings that include Asiago cheese, prosciutto, roasted garlic, and sun-dried tomatoes, and the mix-and-match pastas and sauces (try the hot smoked-duck sausage, artichoke, and tomato combination, or the mango-basil-butter sauce) draw crowds to this Gastown eatery. The room, in a circa-1900 building, with exposed brick, local artwork, and big curved windows, has plenty of atmosphere. Incendio West has a similar menu in a more modern room. ⊠ 103 Columbia St., Gastown ☎604/688-8694 ⊠Incendio West, 2118 Burrard St., Kitsilano ☎604/736-2220 ☰AE, MC, V ⊘No lunch weekends in Gastown; no lunch Sun. in Kitsilano $.

✕**LILIGET FEAST HOUSE.** This intimate room looks like the interior of a longhouse, with wooden walkways across pebble floors, contemporary First Nations art on the walls, and cedar-plank tables with tatami-style benches. Liliget is one of the few places in the world serving the original Northwest Coast First Nations cuisine. A feast platter lets you try most of the fare, which includes bannock bread, baked sweet potato with hazelnuts, alder-grilled salmon, buffalo smokies (small sausages), venison strips, oysters, mussels, and steamed fern shoots. ⊠1724 Davie St., West End ☎604/681-7044 ☰AE, DC, MC, V ⊘Closed Mon. and Tues. Dec.–Feb. No lunch $$-$$$$.

✕**ZIN.** Curved lines, plush banquettes, and an eye-popping color scheme of plum, raspberry, and tangerine make for a mod and trippy room. The menu is global, sampling cuisines from around the world (mainly the tropics), but doesn't mess with fusion. Each dish, whether it's Mediterranean lamb chops, Jamaican jerk tuna, or Indonesian noodles, is true to its roots. Zin has kick-start breakfasts, too, including smoked salmon frittata and French toast with melted Brie. ⊠1277 Robson St., West End ☎604/408-1700 ⊕www.zin-restaurant.com ☰AE, D, DC, MC, V ⊘Closed Mon. No dinner Sun. Oct.–Apr. $$-$$$.

Essentials

Getting Here
I-5 becomes Hwy. 99 at the U.S.–Canada border. Vancouver is a three-hour drive (226 km [140 mi]) from Seattle.

Visitor Information
🛈 **Granville Island Information Centre** ⊠1398 Cartwright St., Granville Island ☎604/666-5784 ⊕www.granvilleisland.com. **Hello B.C.** ☎800/435-5622 ⊕www.hellobc.com. **Vancouver Tourist Info Centre** ⊠200 Burrard St., Downtown ☎604/683-2000 ⊕www.tourismvancouver.com.

AROUND
WASHINGTON, D.C.

Hawk Lake Golf Club

By Ron Kaspriske and CiCi Williamson

The great thing about living so close to so many politicians is that when they're not kissing babies or belting out another filibuster on the Capitol floor, they're likely to be playing golf. Area residents benefit by having more green space, whether given over to golf courses or to something else, than any major city in the United States. Of course, you're not likely find Ted Kennedy or Dick Cheney at one of the area's public tracks. Instead, they'll be at the country clubs in and around Washington, such as Congressional Country Club and the Robert Trent Jones Golf Club.

But when you consider the golf options here, missing out on a few tee times in the private sector is no great loss. Take our advice, pack the car, and head to one of the many golf destinations within a few hours' drive of the nation's capital. If you want to hit the beach for coastal marshland or links-style courses, Virginia Beach and Ocean City are excellent choices. If you're looking to play in the shadows of the Blue Ridge Mountains, then head to White Sulphur Springs or Hot Springs. If you're a history buff, the farmland courses around Gettysburg, and the densely wooded tracks near Williamsburg, give you a chance to experience some history along with your golf. Richmond, meanwhile, has traditional parkland-style courses as well as more modern designs, built in recent years to help the city establish itself as a golf destination.

None of D.C.'s top golf getaways are within an hour's drive, but the farthest away, White Sulphur Springs, is only four hours by car. The impressive resort here, the Greenbrier, even has an Amtrak train stop for those trying to avoid the heavy traffic getting out of D.C. The Homestead, within 40 mi of the Greenbrier, gives the area the perfect one-two punch. Of the six destinations covered in this chapter, the two resorts are our picks for the best places to spend a long weekend.

The Greenbrier and the Homestead represent golf's tonier side, but Ocean City has them beat for selection, with more than enough quality choices for a long weekend. The sleeper pick of the spots mentioned in this chapter is Gettysburg, where many courses have green fees under $50.

Generally, the golf season is the same whether you're in the Blue Ridge Mountains or at the Virginia Coast. You can count on decent golf weather from April to October with March and November still being tolerable—particularly in Virginia Beach. In mid-August, however, there are few places on the planet more humid than the Mid-Atlantic states. Williamsburg leads the list of hot, sticky summertime stops: the mountain-region courses on the other side of the state and the courses along the coast do offer cooler reprieves.

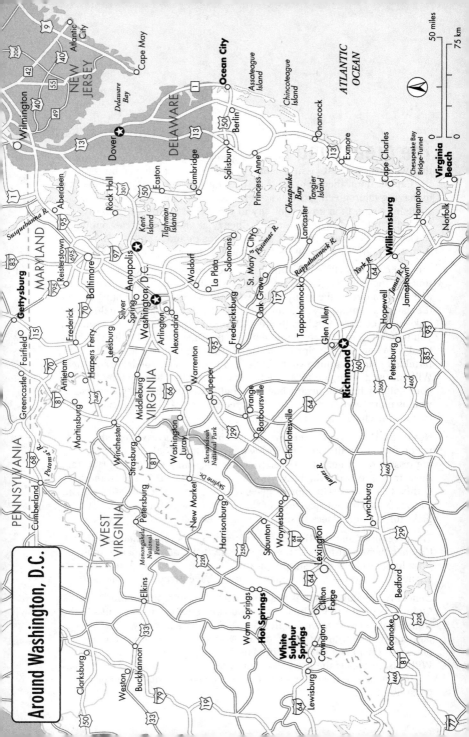

Around Washington, D.C.

GETTYSBURG, PA. COURSES	YARDAGE	PAR	COURSE	SLOPE	GREEN FEE
Briarwood Golf Club (36)					
East (18)	6,608/5,193	72/72	71.2/69.2	122/114	$23/$31
West (18)	6,400/4,820	70/70	71.2/69.2	122/114	$23/$31
The Bridges Golf Club (18)	6,713/5,104	72/72	72.5/70.1	133/117	$26/$41
Carroll Valley Golf Resort (36)					
Carroll Valley (18)	6,663/5,004	71/72	72.3/68.8	128/116	$17/$39
Mountain View (18)	6,382/5,004	71/70	71.2/68.4	128/118	$13/$32
Greencastle Greens Golf Club (18)	6,908/5,315	72/74	72.6/70.3	129/124	$25/$40
Hawk Lake Golf Club (18)	6,611/5,116	72/72	72.6/70.5	124/123	$25/$52
Heritage Hills Golf Resort (18)	6,628/5,147	71/72	70.8/69.9	122/111	$34/$42
Links at Gettysburg (18)	7,031/4,861	72/72	73.9/68.8	128/116	$50/$80

GETTYSBURG, PA

Tourists have long visited the southern Pennsylvania town of Gettysburg to contemplate its place in American history. Golfers can also appreciate the area for its terrain. Framed by nearby mountain ranges and giant hardwood trees, the area is perfect for golf. When the leaves turn, the surroundings can even be awe-inspiring.

If you are interested in a stay-and-play package, consider Fairfield's Carroll Valley Resort, which has two 18-hole courses. If you do stay or at another resort, make sure you head back to town to play the Links at Gettysburg. This great course is set among hills, streams, and hardwood forests and plays through magnificent red-rock formations. The Bridges Golf Club, east of town, is another must-play.

Courses

Golf Digest REVIEWS

BRIARWOOD GOLF CLUB. Facility Holes: 36. Season: Year-round. Tee Times: Call up to 180 days in advance. ⊠ 4775 W. Market St., York 17404 ☎ 717/792-9776 ▤ MC, V.

East. Holes: 18. Opened: 1955. Architect: Charles Klingensmith. Yards: 6,608/5,193. Par: 72/72. Course Rating: 71.2/69.2. Slope: 122/114. Green Fee: $23/$31. Cart Fee: $13 per person. Walking: Unrestricted walking. ★ ★ ★ ½

West. Holes: 18. Opened: 1990. Architect: Altland Brothers. Yards: 6,400/4,820. Par: 70/70. Course Rating: 71.2/69.2. Slope: 122/114. Green Fee: $23/$31. Cart Fee: $13 per person. Walking: Unrestricted walking. ★ ★ ★ ½

Comments: The East course is worth your time, but don't bother with the West.

THE BRIDGES GOLF CLUB. Facility Holes: 18. Opened: 1995. Architect: Altland Brothers. Yards: 6,713/5,104. Par: 72/72. Course Rating: 72.5/70.1. Slope: 133/117. Green Fee: $26/$41. Cart Fee: $14 per person. Discounts: Weekdays,twilight, seniors, juniors. Walking: Walking at certain times. Season: Year-round. High: Mar.–Nov. Tee Times: Call golf shop. Notes: Range (grass, mat), lodging (12). ⊠ 6729 York Rd., Abbottstown 17301, 35 mi from Harrisburg ☎ 717/624–9551 ⊕ www.bridgesgc.com ⊟ AE, MC, V. *Comments: Course gets its name from 10 cart bridges that allow you to navigate wetlands and dense woodlands around the course. Not suitable for walking.* ★★★★

CARROLL VALLEY GOLF RESORT. Facility Holes: 36. Architect: Ed Ault. Season: Mar.–Nov. Tee Times: Call golf shop. ⊠ 121 Sanders Rd., Fairfield 17320 ☎ 717/642–8252 or 800/548–8504 ⊕ www.carrollvalley.com ⊟ AE, D, MC, V.

Carroll Valley. Holes: 18. Opened: 1965. Yards: 6,663/5,004. Par: 71/72. Course Rating: 72.3/68.8. Slope: 128/116. Green Fee: $17/$39. Cart Fee: $15 per person. Walking: Walking at certain times. *Comments: Tom's Creek borders 3 greens.* ★★★★

GETTYSBURG OPTIONS

Be sure to check out the Hershey section of the Philadelphia chapter, which lists Penn National and other facilities that are reasonably close to Gettysburg.

Mountain View. Holes: 18. Opened: 1979. Yards: 6,382/5,004. Par: 71/70. Course Rating: 71.2/68.4. Slope: 128/118. Green Fee: $13/$32. Cart Fee: $14 per person. Walking: Unrestricted walking. *Comments: Front 9 is wide open, but back 9 is tight and woody.* ★★★★

GREENCASTLE GREENS GOLF CLUB. Facility Holes: 18. Opened: 1991. Architect: Robert Elder. Yards: 6,908/5,315. Par: 72/74. Course Rating: 72.6/70.3. Slope: 129/124. Green Fee: $25/$40. Cart Fee: Included in green fee. Walking: Walking at certain times. Season: Apr.–Nov. Tee Times: Call up to 7 days in advance. ⊠ 2000 Castlegreen Dr., Greencastle 17225 ☎ 717/597–1188 ⊟ AE, MC, V. *Comments: Memorable island green surrounded by two rock waterfalls. Otherwise, course is solid but not spectacular.* ★★★ ½

HAWK LAKE GOLF CLUB. Facility Holes: 18. Opened: 2001. Architect: James Ganley. Yards: 6,611/5,116. Par: 72/72. Course Rating: 72.6/70.5. Slope: 124/123. Green Fee: $25/$52. Cart Fee: Included in green fee. Walking: Walking at certain times. Season: Year-round. Tee Times: Call up to 7 days in advance. ⊠ 1605 Loucks Rd., York 17404 ☎ 717/764–2224 ⊕ www.gothamgolf.com ⊟ AE, MC, V. *Comments: One of newest courses in the area, with great views of the York. Was the old Yorktowne Golf Club before renovations.* ★★★★

HERITAGE HILLS GOLF RESORT. Facility Holes: 18. Opened: 1989. Architect: Russell Roberts. Yards: 6,628/5,147. Par: 71/72. Course Rating: 70.8/69.9. Slope: 122/111. Green Fee: $34/$42. Cart Fee: $20 per person. Walking: Walking at certain times. Season: Year-round. Tee Times: Call up to 14 days in advance. ⊠ 2700 Mt. Rose Ave., York 17402 ☎ 717/755–4653 or 800/942–2444 ⊕ www.hhgr.com ⊟ AE, D, MC, V. *Comments: York course is very busy. Third option for lodging.* ★★★ ½

LINKS AT GETTYSBURG. Facility Holes: 18. Opened: 1999. Architect: Lindsay Ervin/Steve Klein. Yards: 7,031/4,861. Par: 72/72. Course Rating: 73.9/68.8. Slope: 128/116. Green Fee: $50/$80. Cart Fee: Included in green fee. Discounts: Twilight, seniors, juniors.

Walking: Unrestricted walking. Season: Year-round. High: May–Oct. Tee Times: Call 7 days in advance. Notes: Range (grass, mat). ✉ 601 Mason-Dixon Rd., 17325, 40 mi from Baltimore ☎ 717/359-8000 ⊕ www.thelinksatgettysburg.com ⊟ AE, MC, V. *Comments: Thirty-five-foot-high rock cliffs, stone walls, platform tee boxes, and lots of water.* ★ ★ ★ ★

Where to Stay

⊞ BALADERRY INN. On 4 acres with a gazebo, this brick Federal home was built in 1812 and served as a field hospital during the Civil War. You can stay in the original home or in a newer addition. The rooms, given floral names like Primrose and Garden, are bright and airy; some have private patios and fireplaces. ✉ 40 Hospital Rd., 17325 ☎ 717/337-1342 ⊕ www.baladerryinn.com ⤷ 9 rooms ⚹ Tennis court; no room TVs, no kids under 12, no smoking ⊟ AE, D, DC, MC, V ⵏⵔ BP $$-$$$.

⊞ BEST WESTERN GETTYSBURG HOTEL. The hotel is a pre–Civil War structure in the heart of the downtown historic district; prominent guests have included Carl Sandburg, Henry Ford, and General Ulysses S. Grant. Rooms are furnished in a traditional style, and suites have fireplaces and whirlpool baths. Ask about the cannonball from the battle that is still embedded in the brick wall across the street. ✉ 1 Lincoln Sq., 17325 ☎ 717/337-2000 ⎙ 717/337-2075 ⊕ www.gettysburg-hotel.com ⤷ 83 rooms, 23 suites ⚹ Restaurant, room service, in-room data ports, in-room hot tubs, microwaves, refrigerators, cable TV, pool, hot tub, bar, laundry service, business services, free parking, no-smoking rooms ⊟ AE, D, DC, MC, V $-$$.

⊞ BRAFFERTON. The original stone town house, a half block from Lincoln Square, was built in 1786, the brick addition in 1815. The town house once served as a chapel. Some suites have their own entrance and exposed-brick walls. ✉ 44 York St., 17325 ☎ 717/337-3423 ⎙ 717/334-8185 ⊕ www.brafferton.com ⤷ 9 rooms, 4 suites ⚹ No room phones, no TV in some rooms, no smoking ⊟ AE, D, MC, V ⵏⵔ BP $-$$$.

⊞ BRICKHOUSE INN BED AND BREAKFAST. The guest rooms, named for states that fought in Gettysburg, are furnished with antiques and reproductions and come with ceiling fans and pastel or off-white walls. The wood floors are all original. There are two formal parlors in the main 1898 brick Victorian house; two guest rooms are in a separate house next door. ✉ 452 Baltimore St., 17325 ☎ 717/338-9337 or 800/864-3464 ⎙ 717/338-9265 ⊕ www.brickhouseinn.com ⤷ 7 rooms ⚹ Free parking; no smoking ⊟ AE, D, MC, V ⵏⵔ BP $-$$.

⊞ FARNSWORTH HOUSE INN. This inn is an early-19th-century Federal brick house that Confederate sharpshooters occupied during the Battle of Gettysburg. You can take a tour of the house and cellar, rumored to be haunted. Each Victorian guest room is lushly decorated with period sewing machines, Victrolas, and antique clothing; some have claw-foot bathtubs. An art gallery and bookstore are on the premises. ✉ 401 Baltimore St., 17325 ☎ 717/334-8838 ⎙ 717/334-5862 ⊕ www.farnsworthhousedining.com ⤷ 11 rooms ⚹ Restaurant, library, shops, business services; no room phones ⊟ AE, D, MC, V ⵏⵔ CP $$.

HERR TAVERN AND PUBLICK HOUSE. Antiques set the scene in this antebellum tavern and inn 1 mi from the town square. All rooms have fireplaces, and some have Jacuzzis. Sitting on the front porch, you can see a pond with a water garden. ☒ 900 Chambersburg Rd., 17325 ☎ 717/334-4332 or 800/362-9849 ⎙ 717/334-3332 ⊕ - www.herrtavern.com ↩ 18 rooms ⏶ Restaurant, some in-room hot tubs, some microwaves, some refrigerators, cable TV; no kids under 12, no smoking ⊟ D, MC, V ⦶ CP $-$$$.

JAMES GETTYS HOTEL. Just off the town square, this four-story all-suites hotel was established in 1804—the main staircase is original. The individually decorated rooms are in a country style. When you've had enough sightseeing, you can relax with full English afternoon tea at the neighboring Thistlefields tearoom. ☒ 27 Chambersburg St., 17325 ☎ 717/337-1334 ⎙ 717/334-2103 ⊕ www.jamesgettyshotel.com ↩ 11 suites ⏶ Restaurant, kitchenettes, microwaves, refrigerators, cable TV, laundry service, business services; no smoking ⊟ AE, D, MC, V ⦶ CP $$.

Where to Eat

✕ BLUE PARROT BISTRO. Here's a great place to take a group of friends with dissimilar eating tastes. White linen tablecloths cover each table, but the food ranges from pita pizza and creative homemade soups and salads to eggs Benedict, fried rice with vegetables, and porterhouse steaks. As the name suggests, parrot decorations fill a main dining room and a smaller side room. Both rooms have bars, and there's also a pool table. ☒ 35 Chambersburg St. ☎ 717/337-3937 ⊟ AE, D, DC, MC, V $-$$$$.

✕ DUNLAP'S RESTAURANT AND BAKERY. This casual family restaurant is owned by a couple who fell in love with the town and bought the restaurant after visiting their son at Gettysburg College. You can get burgers, sandwiches, salads, and American classics like chicken and dumplings. Be sure to save room for a piece of cake or pie. ☒ 90 Buford Ave. ☎ 717/334-4816 ⊕ www.dunlapsrestaurant.com ⊟ D, MC, V ¢-$.

✕ FARNSWORTH HOUSE INN. You can eat like a fortunate Civil War soldier here: wild game pie, peanut soup, pumpkin fritters, and spoon bread are all served in the antiques-filled dining room. The historic home, riddled by bullets during the war, has an attic full of war memorabilia that you can examine. ☒ 401 Baltimore St. ☎ 717/334-8838 ⊕ - www.farnsworthhousedining.com ⏶ Reservations essential ⊟ AE, D, MC, V $-$$.

✕ GETTYSBREW RESTAURANT AND BREWERY. Inside a building used as a field hospital by the Confederates during the Civil War, Gettysbrew has a patio overlooking the surrounding farmland. Standouts include beer-cheese soup, sandwiches on focaccia bread, buffets with 10 cold salads and six hot entrées, and handcrafted root beer and sodas. ☒ 248 Hunterstown Rd. ☎ 717/337-1001 ⊟ D, MC, V ⊘ No lunch weekdays $-$$.

✕ GINGERBREAD MAN. Brass fixtures, exposed brick walls, and Civil War photographs and prints make up the interior of the Gingerbread Man. Chili, New York deli-style sandwiches, hearty salads, and other classics are the offerings here, where there's also an extensive kids' menu. ☒ 217 Steinwehr Ave. ☎ 717/334-1100 ⊕ www.thegingerbreadman.net ⊟ AE, D, DC, MC, V $-$$$.

✕**HERR TAVERN AND PUBLICK HOUSE.** Built in 1815, this tavern, the first Confederate hospital, survived a direct hit from artillery during the Battle of Gettysburg. You can eat in the dining room, with a view of the battlefield, or on the porch. Choose from cream of crab soup, prime rib, and chicken stuffed with crabmeat and Mornay sauce. Dessert offerings include cheesecake, pecan pie, or apple dumplings. ✉900 Chambersburg Rd. ☎717/334-4332 ▭D, MC, V ⊙No lunch Sun. $$-$$$$.

✕**HISTORIC CASHTOWN INN.** The menu at Cashtown includes such choices as steaks, seafood, pecan-crusted chicken, and crab cakes. The restaurant is in an old building with a walk-up porch, 8 mi west of downtown Gettysburg. ✉1325 Old Rte. 30, Cashtown ☎717/334-9722 or 800/367-1797 ⊕www.cashtowninn.com ▭AE, D, MC, V ⊙Closed Mon. No lunch Sun. $-$$.

✕**LINCOLN DINER.** Locals flock to this 24-hour diner for its American classics as well as cakes, pies, and pastries. You can get breakfast at any time. ✉32 Carlisle St. ☎717/334-3900 ▭No credit cards ¢-$.

✕**PUB & RESTAURANT.** A casual, friendly downtown restaurant with an extensive menu ranging from Tex-Mex to pitas to burgers. Try the chicken marsala, broiled scallops, or sausage jambalaya. There's also an impressive selection of beer. ✉20-22 Lincoln Sq. ☎717/334-7100 ⊕www.the-pub.com ▭AE, MC, V $-$$$.

Essentials

Getting Here
To get to Gettysburg, take I-270 north to U.S. 15 north, near Frederick. It's a trip of roughly 80 mi.

Visitor Information
🛈 **Gettysburg Convention and Visitors Bureau** ✉89 Steinwehr Ave. ☎717/334-2100 ⊕www.gettysburg.com. **Gettysburg National Military Park Visitor Center** ✉97 Taneytown Rd. ☎717/334-1124 ⊕www.nps.gov/gett.

HOT SPRINGS, VA & WHITE SULPHUR SPRINGS, WV

No matter how stressful the drive, no matter how bad the week, no matter how many problems you left back at the job, the minute you arrive at either the Homestead in Hot Springs, Virginia, or the Greenbrier in White Sulphur Springs, West Virginia, the stress seems to wither away in the mountain breeze. The philosophy of the two grande ole dames of American resort golf

	Yards	Par	Rating	Slope	Fee
The Greenbrier (54)					$100/$325
Greenbrier (18)	6,675/5,095	72/72	73.1/70.3	135/120	
Meadows (18)	6,807/5,001	71/71	73.7/68.0	130/111	
Old White Course (18)	6,652/5,179	70/70	72.2/69.7	130/119	
Homestead Resort (54)					
Cascades (18)	6,679/4,967	70/70	73.0/70.3	137/124	$100/$165
Lower Cascades (18)	6,752/4,710	72/70	72.6/66.2	134/110	$45/$103
Old (18)	6,211/4,852	72/72	69.7/67.7	120/116	$45/$103

is simply this: your worries will not make the trip. The scenery is breathtaking, and the service is impeccable.

The resorts are just 40 mi from each other on either side of the Virginia/West Virginia border, about four hours from D.C. Between the two of them, there's enough great golf to keep you busy for a long weekend, and probably much longer.

The Greenbrier gets the nod on service. In 2002 *Golf Digest* selected it as the third-best golf resort in the United States. The late Sam Snead spent most of his time at the Greenbriar: up until his death in 2001, it wasn't uncommon to bump into him on the driving range. The Greenbrier course, one of three on the property, is the only public course to play host to a Ryder Cup and a Solheim Cup.

The Homestead, which ranked 8th in the *Golf Digest* ranking, is mountain golf, pure and simple. It, too, has three courses: its Cascades, designed by William Flynn in 1923, is the best course on either resort.

Courses

Golf Digest REVIEWS

THE GREENBRIER. Facility Holes: 54. Green Fee: $100/$325. Cart Fee: Included in green fee. Discounts: Guest, juniors. Walking: Walking at certain times. Season: Apr.–Oct. Tee Times: Call golf shop. Notes: Range (grass, mat), lodging (803). ⊠ 300 W. Main St., White Sulphur Springs 24986, 250 mi from Washington ☎ 304/536-7862 or 800/624-6070 ⊕ www.greenbrier.com ⊟ AE, D, DC, MC, V.

Greenbrier. Holes: 18. Opened: 1924. Architect: Seth Raynor/Jack Nicklaus. Yards: 6,675/5,095. Par: 72/72. Course Rating: 73.1/70.3. Slope: 135/120. *Comments: Ranked 2nd in West Virginia by* Golf Digest. *Very tough playing along valley at the base of the Blue Ridge Mountains. This impeccable course offers great variety.* ★ ★ ★ ★

Meadows. Holes: 18. Opened: 1999. Architect: Bob Cupp. Yards: 6,807/5,001. Par: 71/71. Course Rating: 73.7/68.0. Slope: 130/111. *Comments: Weakest of the three courses at the Greenbrier, but still excellent.* ★ ★ ★ ★ ½

WHITE HOUSE GOLF

Golf has been the sport of choice for sitting presidents since Dwight D. Eisenhower. Ike wasn't a great golfer, but his passion for the game is legendary. Trees from Augusta, Georgia, to Honolulu are named after him, poking a bit of fun at his propensity for getting in and behind them. Eisenhower is not the only president whose golf skills linger on: Bob Hope once remarked that President Gerald Ford didn't decide which course he was going to play until after he had teed off. President Bill Clinton, a voracious golfer, was known for playing a good game, but also for sometimes questionable scoring habits.

Old White Course. Holes: 18. Opened: 1913. Architect: C. B. Macdonald/Seth Raynor. Yards: 6,652/5,179. Par: 70/70. Course Rating: 72.2/69.7. Slope: 130/119. *Comments: Ranked 3rd in West Virginia. A classic design.* ★★★★

HOMESTEAD RESORT. Facility Holes: 54. Cart Fee: Included in green fee. Discounts: Guest, twilight, juniors. Walking: Unrestricted walking. Season: Apr.–Nov. Tee Times: Call golf shop. Notes: Metal spikes, range (grass, mat), lodging (500). ⊠ U.S. 220 (Main St.), Hot Springs 24445, 65 mi from Roanoke ☎ 540/839-7994 or 800/838-1766 ⊕ www.thehomestead.com ⊟ AE, D, DC, MC, V.

Cascades. Holes: 18. Opened: 1923. Architect: William Flynn. Yards: 6,679/4,967. Par: 70/70. Course Rating: 73.0/70.3. Slope: 137/124. Green Fee: $100/$165. *Comments: Incredibly scenic, hilly course. Greens are ultrafast. One of the best mountain courses anywhere. Ranked No. 1 in Virginia by* Golf Digest. ★★★★★

Lower Cascades. Holes: 18. Opened: 1962. Architect: Robert Trent Jones. Yards: 6,752/4,710. Par: 72/70. Course Rating: 72.6/66.2. Slope: 134/110. Green Fee: $45/$103. *Comments: Wonderful old course that plays through streams and valleys. A notch below the Cascades.* ★★★★

Old. Holes: 18. Opened: 1892. Architect: Donald Ross. Yards: 6,211/4,852. Par: 72/72. Course Rating: 69.7/67.7. Slope: 120/116. Green Fee: $45/$103. *Comments: If you love Donald Ross designs and the bowl-shape greens he's known for, you'll appreciate one of the oldest courses in the United States.* ★★★★

Where to Stay

🏨 **GENERAL LEWIS COUNTRY INN.** The brick building is furnished with 19th-century pieces and antiques collected in the area. Every room has china, glass, prints, and other memorabilia; you can be sure the bed you sleep in is at least a century old. Lewisburg historical sites are three blocks away. ⊠ 301 E. Washington St., Lewisburg, WV 24901 ☎ 800/628-4454 ⊕ www.generallewisinn.com ⟲ 24 rooms, 2 suites ⚹ Restaurant, dining room, room service, cable TV, bar; no pets, no smoking ⊟ AE, D, MC, V $-$$.

🏨 **THE GREENBRIER.** Built in 1760 and surrounded by 6,500 acres, this resort's elegant main building has a grand style amid rustic surroundings. Enter between massive six-story white columns and walk through a colorfully carpeted lobby area with nine spacious chandeliered chambers. Every guest room is different and decorated in pastel prints. There is a tea and concert each afternoon in the lobby, and live music with dinner in the dining room. ✉300 W. Main St., White Sulphur Springs 24986 ☎304/536–1110 or 800/624–6070 ⊞304/536–7854 ⊕www.greenbrier.com ⬩443 rooms, 32 suites, 67 cottages, 4 estate houses ♿4 restaurants, dining room, room service, in-room data ports, some refrigerators, cable TV, driving range, 3 18-hole golf courses, 2 putting greens, 20 tennis courts, pro shop, 2 pools (1 indoor), wading pool, gym, hot tub, spa, boating, fishing, bicycles, bowling, croquet, hiking, ice-skating, sleigh rides, bar, theater, shops, Internet, meeting rooms, airport shuttle ⊟AE, D, DC, MC, V ¶⊙¶MAP $$$–$$$$.

🏨 **THE HOMESTEAD.** Host to a prestigious clientele since 1766, the Homestead has evolved from a country spa to a 15,000-acre resort and conference facility. From the glorious columns of the entry hall to the stunning views of the Allegheny Mountains, magnificence constantly surrounds those who stay here. Rooms in the sprawling redbrick building, built in 1891, have Georgian-style furnishings; some have fireplaces. An orchestra plays nightly in the formal dining room (dinner is included in the room rate), where Continental cuisine and regional specialties are served during six-course extravaganzas. ✉U.S. 220, Hot Springs 24445 ☎540/839–1766 or 800/838–1766 ⊞540/839–7670 ⊕www.thehomestead.com ⬩429 rooms, 77 suites ♿6 restaurants, cable TV with movies and video games, 3 18-hole golf courses, 8 tennis courts, 2 pools (1 indoor), spa, bicycles, bowling, horseback riding, downhill skiing, ice-skating, cinema, video game room, Internet, meeting rooms, airport shuttle ⊟AE, D, DC, MC, V ¶⊙¶MAP $$–$$$$.

🏨 **INN AT GRISTMILL SQUARE.** Occupying five restored buildings at the same site as the Waterwheel Restaurant, the rooms inside this state historical landmark are done in a colonial-Virginia style. Four units are in the original miller's house; others occupy the former blacksmith's shop, hardware store, gristmill, and cottage. Some rooms have fireplaces and patios. ✉Gristmill Sq., Warm Springs, VA 24484 ☎540/839–2231 ⊞540/839–5770 ⊕www.gristmillsquare.com ⬩12 rooms, 5 suites, 1 apartment ♿Restaurant, cable TV, 3 tennis courts, pool, sauna, bar, meeting rooms ⊟D, MC, V ¶⊙¶BP $–$$.

🏨 **LILLIAN'S ANTIQUE SHOP AND BED & BREAKFAST** Just a block from the Greenbrier, this 1905 Queen Anne–style cottage is filled with antiques, all of them for sale. One guest room is in the servant's outbuilding. The three-course breakfast is served in the dining room. ✉204 W. Main St., White Sulphur Springs 24986 ☎877/536–1048 ⊕www.lilliansbedandbreakfast.com ⬩4 rooms ♿Dining room, cable TV; no pets, no smoking ⊟AE, MC, V ¶⊙¶BP $.

🏨 **MILTON HALL.** This 1874 Gothic brick house, built as a country house by English nobility, is on 44 acres that are close to the George Washington National Forest. The spacious rooms have Victorian furnishings and large beds. Box lunches can be ordered in advance. ✉207 Thorny La., Covington VA 24426, (I–64 [exit 10] at Callaghan) ☎540/965–0196 or 877/764–5866 ⊕www.milton-hall.com ⬩6 rooms ♿Cable TV with movies, hiking; no smoking, no kids under 8 ⊟AE, MC, V ¶⊙¶BP $–$$.

🏨 **ROSELOE MOTEL.** At the opposite extreme from the Homestead in terms of cost and of level of fanciness, this brick-front, family-owned 1950s motel is between Warm Springs and Hot Springs. Four of the inexpensive and well-maintained rooms have full kitchens, and two have kitchenettes. The others have refrigerators. It's very popular with leaf watchers and deer hunters in fall, so book early. ⊠ Rte. 1, Box 590, Hot Springs 24445 ☎ 540/839-5373 ◄┚ 14 rooms ᗒ Some kitchenettes, some refrigerators, cable TV, some pets allowed ⊟ AE, D, MC, V ¢.

Where to Eat

✕ **COUNTRY CAFE.** A dining room with blue-checked tablecloths on the tables hints at the down-home cooking available here. Crafts and antiques line the walls, and a cast-iron stove sits in the corner. The Friday-night special is steamed shrimp, Saturday is prime rib night, and steaks and fried chicken are available every night. ⊠ U.S. 220, Hot Springs ☎ 540/839-2111 ⊟ MC, V ☺ Closed Mon. $$-$$$$.

✕ **HOMESTEAD DINING ROOM.** The Dining Room serves Continental cuisine under the direction of the resort's executive chef for 37 years, Albert Schnarwyler. The traditional menu, which also includes regional specialties such as Virginia smoked trout and Maryland soft-shell crab—are complemented with distinctive wines selected from the exquisitely designed Wine Room. Jacket and tie are required in the evening. Meals at the Dining Room are included in rates if you're staying at the Homestead, but the bill can easily top $100 if you're not. An orchestra performs nightly and a bountiful breakfast buffet is served daily. ⊠ The Homestead, U.S. 220, Hot Springs ☎ 540/839-1766 or 800/838-1766 ⊟ AE, D, DC, MC, V $$$$.

✕ **SAM SNEAD'S TAVERN.** Across the street from the main Homestead property, this is a casual choice for when you're looking for good food without dressing up. A creek runs under the old bank building that houses the tavern. The fare includes fresh trout and smoked ribs. The tavern's namesake frequented the tavern until his death in 2002. As you might expect from a place named for a golfing legend, the sports bar that's also here displays a great deal of PGA memorabilia. ⊠ U.S. 220, Hot Springs ☎ 540/839-7666 ⊟ AE, MC, V $-$$$$.

✕ **WATERWHEEL RESTAURANT.** Part of a complex of five historic buildings, this restaurant is in a gristmill from 1700. A walk-in wine cellar, set among the gears of the original waterwheel, has 100 wine selections; you can step right in and choose a bottle for yourself. The dining area is decorated with Currier & Ives and Audubon prints. Menu favorites include fresh smoked trout and breast of chicken stuffed with wild rice, sausage, apples, and pecans. Desserts include such Old Virginny favorites as deep-dish apple pie, flavored with bourbon. Sunday brunch is both hearty and a good deal. ⊠ Gristmill Sq., Warm Springs, VA ☎ 540/839-2231 ⊟ D, MC, V ☺ Closed Tues. Nov.–May $$-$$$$.

Essentials

Getting Here

Unless you have a private jet, the best way to reach the Greenbrier and the Homestead is by car. It's about a four-hour drive to either resort from Washington. The drive to the

Greenbrier is almost entirely on interstate highways (you can even see the resort from a rest stop overlook on I-64). To get to the Greenbrier, take I-66 west to I-81, travel south to I-64 at Lexington (I-64 and I-81 share the same route between Staunton and Lexington), then go west on I-64, crossing into West Virginia. Take exit 181, White Sulphur Springs. From there, the Greenbrier entrance is only 2 mi away on U.S. 60, which heads through the heart of the village.

One way to get to the Homestead is to take I-64 to Covington and then head 16 mi north on U.S. 220. For an alternate route that's shorter but also makes less use of interstates, first take I-66 west to I-81. Head south to exit 240, toward Bridgewater, and then take Route 257 west to Route 42 heading south. From Route 42 take Route 39 west to U.S. 220. Following Route 39 west from Lexington will take you through the dramatic Maury River gorge at Goshen Pass. The sight is worth a side trip, even if it's not directly on your route.

The drive to either resort is very scenic in good weather, but it can be hazardous in poor conditions. The winding, rugged roads, at much higher elevations that those in and near Washington, may be covered with ice and snow when temperatures are still well above freezing farther east. Fog, rain, and wind are other mountain hazards to look out for.

An Amtrak station is directly across from the Greenbrier's main gate in White Sulphur Springs. The Homestead is served by a station at Clifton Forge, 25 mi south. Neither station is staffed.

🚆 TRAIN LINE AND STATIONS Amtrak ☎800/872-7245 ⊕ www.amtrak.com. **Clifton Forge** ✉400 S. Ridgeway St. **White Sulphur Springs** ✉315 W. Main St.

Visitor Information
🚆 **Bath County Chamber of Commerce** ✉U.S. 220, Box 718, Hot Springs 24445 ☎540/839-5409 or 800/628-8092 ⊕ www.bathcountyva.org. **White Sulphur Springs Convention and Visitors Bureau** ✉34 W. Main St., White Sulphur Springs 24986 ☎304/536-3590 or 800/284-9440.

OCEAN CITY, MD

One day, we'll probably realize that the golden era for golf course construction was in the 1990s. Destinations like Scottsdale, Arizona, Naples, Florida, and Myrtle Beach, South Carolina, saw a record number of courses built in the previous decade. On a smaller scale, the seaside town of Ocean City enjoyed a similar boom. For 50 years, it was known as a great getaway for sport fishermen, beachgoers, and anyone who was in the mood for great soft-shell crab. Now it may also be a better, closer option for golfers along the Northeast Corridor who used to travel to Myrtle Beach.

There's no great golf resort in this area, so it's best to stay at one of the many ocean-side hotels. Many travel operators, also taking a cue from Myrtle

Bay Club (36)					$25/$75
East (18)	7,004/5,231	72/72	74.6/67.4	134/115	
West (18)	6,958/5,609	72/72	73.1/71.3	126/118	
Eagle's Landing Golf Course (18)	7,003/4,896	72/72	73.6/67.9	126/112	$24/$49
Links at Lighthouse Sound Golf Club (18)	7,031/4,553	72/72	73.3/67.1	144/107	$89/$145
Ocean City Golf & Yacht Club (36)					
Newport Bay (18)	6,526/5,396	72/72	71.7/71.3	121/119	$35/$97
Seaside (18)	6,520/5,848	73/75	70.9/73.1	115/119	$25/$79
River Run Golf Club (18)	6,705/5,002	71/71	70.4/73.1	128/117	$40/$105
Rum Pointe Seaside Golf Links (18)	7,001/5,276	72/72	72.6/70.3	122/120	$30/$109

Beach, have set up great stay-and-play packages for golfers. And wherever you intend to stay, remember to bring an appetite. Ocean City is the Middle Atlantic's hub for fresh seafood.

Ocean City lacks a course built along the ocean, but plenty have bay-side views and a linksy feel. At the top of your list should be the Links at Lighthouse Sound, which was ranked 6th in the state by *Golf Digest* magazine. Built in 2000, the course was built on marshland. It comes with good views of the sound it was named for, as well as the condos and hotels on the other side in Ocean City proper.

Courses

BAY CLUB. Facility Holes: 36. Green Fee: $25/$75. Cart Fee: Included in green fee. Discounts: Weekdays, twilight, seniors, juniors. Walking: Unrestricted walking. Season: Year-round. Tee Times: Call 365 days in advance. Notes: Range (grass). ⌧ 9122 Libertytown Rd., Berlin 21811, 7 mi from Ocean City ☎ 800/229-2582 or 800/229-2582 ⊕ www.thebayclub.com ▤ AE, MC, V.

East. Holes: 18. Opened: 1999. Architect: Charles Priestley. Yards: 7,004/5,231. Par: 72/72. Course Rating: 74.6/67.4. Slope: 134/115. *Comments: Tall pines outline the fairways. Fairways are zoysia grass. Nice.* ★ ★ ★ ½

West. Holes: 18. Opened: 1989. Architect: Russell Roberts. Yards: 6,958/5,609. Par: 72/72. Course Rating: 73.1/71.3. Slope: 126/118. *Comments: Slightly better than the East, though both courses are solid. No. 14 has an island green.* ★ ★ ★ ½

EAGLE'S LANDING GOLF COURSE. Facility Holes: 18. Opened: 1991. Architect: Michael Hurdzan. Yards: 7,003/4,896. Par: 72/72. Course Rating: 73.6/67.9. Slope: 126/112. Green Fee: $24/$49. Cart Fee: $20 per person. Discounts: Weekdays, twilight, juniors. Walking: Unrestricted walking. Season: Year-round. High: Apr.–Oct. Tee Times: Call 365 days in advance. ✉ 12367 Eagle's Nest Rd., Berlin 21811, 3 mi from Ocean City ☎ 410/213-7277 or 800/283-3846 ⊕ www.eagleslandinggolf.com ▤ AE, D, MC, V. *Comments: Routed through salt marshes, with great scenery, though not as attractive as the Links at Lighthouse Sound.* ★★★★

LINKS AT LIGHTHOUSE SOUND GOLF CLUB. Facility Holes: 18. Opened: 2000. Architect: Arthur Hills. Yards: 7,031/4,553. Par: 72/72. Course Rating: 73.3/67.1. Slope: 144/107. Green Fee: $89/$145. Cart Fee: Included in green fee. Discounts: Twilight. Walking: Unrestricted walking. Season: Year-round. High: Mar.–Oct. Tee Times: Call 365 days in advance. Notes: Range (grass). ✉ 12723 St. Martin's Neck Rd., Bishopville 21813, 2 mi from Ocean City ☎ 410/352-5767 or 888/554-4557 ⊕ www.lighthousesound.com ▤ AE, D, MC, V. *Comments: The class of Ocean City. Arthur Hills designed a beautiful wetlands-style course. The bridge system for the carts means walking is not the best option.* ★★★★ ½

OCEAN CITY GOLF & YACHT CLUB. Facility Holes: 36. Cart Fee: Included in green fee. Discounts: Weekdays, twilight, juniors. Walking: Walking at certain times. Season: Year-round. High: Apr.–Oct. Tee Times: Call golf shop. Notes: Range (grass, mat). ✉ 11401 Country Club Dr., Berlin 21811, 5 mi from Ocean City ☎ 410/641-1779 or 800/ 442-3570 ▤ MC, V.

Newport Bay. Holes: 18. Opened: 1998. Architect: Russell Roberts/Lester George. Yards: 6,526/5,396. Par: 72/72. Course Rating: 71.7/71.3. Slope: 121/119. Green Fee: $35/$97. *Comments: Holes play along the water. Tough, but great scenery. Second-best course in the area after the Links at Lighthouse Sound.* ★★★★

Seaside. Holes: 18. Opened: 1959. Architect: William Gordon/David Gordon/Russell Roberts. Yards: 6,520/5,848. Par: 73/75. Course Rating: 70.9/73.1. Slope: 115/119. Green Fee: $25/$79. *Comments: Easier than Newport Bay. Play this one first to get your game together.* ★★★ ½

RIVER RUN GOLF CLUB. Facility Holes: 18. Opened: 1991. Architect: Gary Player. Yards: 6,705/5,002. Par: 71/71. Course Rating: 70.4/73.1. Slope: 128/117. Green Fee: $40/$105. Cart Fee: Included in green fee. Discounts: Weekdays, twilight, seniors, juniors. Walking: Walking at certain times. Season: Year-round. Tee Times: Call 180 days in advance. Notes: Range (grass). ✉ 11605 Masters La., Berlin 21811 ☎ 410/641-7200 or 800/733-7786 ⊕ www.riverrungolf.com ▤ AE, D, MC, V. *Comments: Front 9 is open, long, and windswept. Back 9 slithers through mature pine forests.* ★★★★

RUM POINTE SEASIDE GOLF LINKS. Facility Holes: 18. Opened: 1997. Architect: Pete Dye/P. B. Dye. Yards: 7,001/5,276. Par: 72/72. Course Rating: 72.6/70.3. Slope: 122/ 120. Green Fee: $30/$109. Cart Fee: Included in green fee. Discounts: Weekdays, twilight, juniors. Walking: Unrestricted walking. Season: Year-round. Tee Times: Call 365 days in advance. Notes: Range (grass). ✉ 7000 Rum Pointe La., Berlin 21811, 7 mi from Ocean City ☎ 410/629-1414 or 888/809-4653 ⊕ www.rumpointe.com ▤ AE, D, MC, V. *Comments: Excellent Pete Dye/P. B. Dye course with holes adjacent to the bay, including the spectacular Numbers 9 and 18.* ★★★★

Where to Stay

ATLANTIC HOTEL. You can trace the history of this resort town by looking at the pictures from the 1920s and 1930s that hang in the lobby of this hotel, the oldest in town. Family-owned and -operated, the three-story, H-shape frame hotel is a replacement of the original Victorian hotel that burned in 1922. Rooms are as plainly furnished and decorated as they were originally, but now with modern comforts. This is ocean-side vacationing as it was in a calmer era. The annual fourth of July fireworks are ignited from the beach just steps from the hotel, making the block-long sundeck a popular spot. ⊠ Boardwalk and Wicomico St., 21843 ☎ 410/289-9111 or 800/328-5268 🖶 410/289-2221 ⊕ www.atlantichotelocmd.com ➷ 80 rooms ♿ Cable TV, beach ⊟ AE, D, MC, V ⊘ Closed Oct.–Apr. $$.

COMMANDER HOTEL. Built where the original 1930 Ocean City mainstay once stood, the current Commander opened in 1998. Family-owned and -operated since its inception, the hotel is owned by the fourth generation of the Lynch family. All rooms have private balconies with ocean views. Rooms have carpeting and tile and are decorated in a blue-and-white motif that employs photos of the original hotel. ⊠ 14th St. at the boardwalk, 21842 ☎ 410/289-6166 or 888/289-6166 ⊕ www.commanderhotel. com ➷ 109 suites ♿ Restaurant, microwaves, refrigerators, 2 pools (1 indoor), lounge, free parking ⊟ MC, V ⊘ Closed Dec.–Feb. and weekdays in Mar. and Nov. $$$–$$$$.

THE EDGE. Each of the rooms at this boutique hotel is uniquely furnished to evoke such locales as Bali or the Caribbean, the French Riviera or southern Italy, a safari or even the *Orient Express*. The Island Monkey Room is filled with simian statuettes and pictures. From queen- and king-size feather beds to gas fireplaces, amenities here are special. Windows that take up the entire west-facing room walls allow for panoramic views at sunset. ⊠ 56th St. at the bay, 21842 ☎ 410/524-5400 or 888/371-5400 🖶 410/524-3928 ⊕ www.fagers.com ➷ 12 suites ♿ In-room hot tubs, minibars, refrigerators ⊟ AE, D, DC, MC, V ⍣CP $$$$.

HOTEL MONTE CARLO. This small hotel is in the pulsing heart of southern Ocean City. One highlight: the spectacular ocean and bay views from the pool or from the roof deck's hot tub. The compact rooms, which all have balconies, are basic, with simple furnishings. The hotel is very family-friendly, with a small shaded indoor pool and cribs available at no extra charge. A two-minute walk will get you to the beach or the boardwalk. ⊠ 216 N. Baltimore Ave., 21842 ☎ 410/289-7101 or 877/375-6537 🖶 410/289-4464 ⊕ www.montecarlo-2000.com ➷ 70 rooms ♿ Microwaves, refrigerators, indoor pool, hot tub, free parking ⊟ AE, D, MC, V $$$–$$$$.

LIGHTHOUSE CLUB HOTEL. Built to resemble a Chesapeake Bay "screw-pile" lighthouse, this elegant hotel is just blocks from the busy Coastal Hwy. Its airy, contemporary suites have high ceilings and views of sand dunes that slope to the Assawoman Bay. Rooms are furnished with white-cushioned rattan furniture and have marble bathrooms with two-person hot tubs. Sliding glass doors lead to private decks with steamer chairs. It all makes for a luxurious and uncommonly quiet hotel. ⊠ 56th St. at the bay, 21842 ☎ 410/524-5400 or 888/371-5400 🖶 410/524-3928 ⊕ www.fagers.com ➷ 23 suites ♿ In-room hot tubs, minibars, refrigerators ⊟ AE, D, DC, MC, V ⍣CP $$$$.

☎ **PHILLIPS BEACH PLAZA.** This oceanfront hotel is near everything you're likely to seek in Ocean City—restaurants, shops, the beach, and the boardwalk. Victorian-style furnishings add to its retro charm; it's one of the older hotels on the Golden Mile. The rooms with queen beds have classic four-poster beds. Some rooms have spectacular ocean views, and you can also watch the boardwalk crowds from your window. It's a great location if you want to be in the middle of the action. ⊠ 13th St. at the board-walk, 21842 ☎ 410/289-9121 or 800/492-5834 🖶 410/289-3041 ⊕ www. phillipsbeachplaza.com ⇆ 96 units ⚫ Restaurant, some kitchenettes, cable TV, beach, bar, business services ☰ AE, D, DC, MC, V ⊗ Closed Jan., Feb., and weekdays in Mar. $$.

Where to Eat

✕ **BAGELS N' BUNS.** In season, this popular bagel shop is open until 4 AM on week-days and all night on weekends. The fresh bagels baked throughout the day are served with numerous spreads that include pineapple and mandarin orange. The typical deli fare includes corned beef, pastrami, and Reuben sandwiches. Omelets, burgers, and gyros are served all day, and kosher meats are available. ⊠ 7111 Coastal Hwy. ☎ 410/ 723-2253 ☰ No credit cards ¢–$.

✕ **CAPTAIN'S GALLEY.** The claim to fame of this harborside restaurant is its crab cakes, the best in town. Locals pack the many dining rooms, but the open-air deck is the most popular place in summer. On the menu are favorites such as the crab imperial sandwiches and a plethora of dock-fresh fish. ⊠ West Ocean City Harbor, 12817 S. Harbor Rd., West Ocean City ☎ 410/213-2525 ☰ AE, D, DC, MC, V $$–$$$$.

✕ **CRAB ALLEY.** Sitting at the edge of the harbor in West Ocean City, where commer-cial fisherman dock nightly, Crab Alley is a local favorite for fresh seafood, especially steamed blue crabs. Clams, served steamed on the half shell, or "casino" style with cheese, bread crumbs, and bacon, are also favorites, and so is the in-house smoked fish. The typically Maryland soups available here include clam chowder and Maryland crab. The seafood market, open May through September, serves fresh seafood takeout and prepared favorites such as cream of crab soup. ⊠ 9703 Golf Course Rd., West Ocean City ☎ 410/213-7800 ☰ D, MC, V ⊗ Closed mid. Nov.–Dec. $–$$$$.

✕ **DUMSER'S DRIVE-IN.** Making ice cream since 1939, Dumser's whips up such fla-vors as strawberry, peanut butter fudge, and butter pecan daily. Don't leave without try-ing an ice cream soda or a thick milk shake made with hand-dipped ice cream. If you want something a bit more substantial at this 1950s-style diner, go for the subs, burg-ers, and fries. There's another branch at 123rd Street and Coastal Hwy. ⊠ 49th St. and Coastal Hwy. ☎ 410/524-1588 ☰ MC, V ¢–$.

✕ **FAGER'S ISLAND.** This swanky bay-side restaurant gives you white-linen treatment along with large windows perfect for viewing sunsets and the wetlands. White stucco walls and white columns contrast with red tile floors and brass chandeliers. Entrées include lobster, prime rib, crab cakes, and salmon. There's an outside deck for more infor-mal dining and a raw bar with lighter fare. In summer, Tchaikovsky's *1812 Overture* is played every evening, with the tumultuous finale timed to coincide with the setting of the sun. ⊠ 60th St. at the bay ☎ 410/524-5500 ☰ AE, D, DC, MC, V $$$–$$$$.

Essentials

Getting Here

To reach Ocean City from Washington, D.C., travel east on U.S. 50/301 and cross the 4½-mi Chesapeake Bay Bridge ($2.50 toll, eastbound only) northeast of Annapolis. Soon after U.S. 301 breaks off to head north, but U.S. 50 continues on directly to Ocean City. The drive from Washington takes approximately three hours, but if you're heading there for a weekend, plan to leave the city late Friday evening or before sunrise on Saturday morning to avoid massive backups at the Bay Bridge and beyond.

Visitor Information

🚺 **Ocean City Dept. of Tourism and Visitor Information Center** ✉ 4001 Coastal Hwy., at 41st St., 21842 ☎ 410/289-8181 or 800/626-2326 ⊕ www.ococean.com.

RICHMOND, VA

The greater area in and around Richmond, which includes Petersburg and the suburbs to the southwest and northwest of town, has what many have come to expect of Virginia—terrain that alternates between dense woods and rolling farmland.

For the longest time, private golf was king in the Richmond area. It has some terrific, nationally known private courses, including two (Jefferson Lakeside and Westhampton) designed by Donald Ross. But in the past five years, some of the state's best courses have been public ones within a 45-minute drive of downtown Richmond. At the top of the list is Independence Golf Club, the only Tom Fazio daily-fee course in the state. The gorgeous property also includes a Virginia State Golf Association museum, with one of the best junior golf programs in the nation. Speaking of junior golfers, there's also a First Tee center in Chesterfield with great practice facilities.

If you're a golf course aficionado, then take note that the 100-year-old Belmont Golf Course was designed by none other than A. W. Tillinghast. Belmont is a terrific throwback to classic golf courses and is a must-play at its very affordable green fee. (By the way, don't bother with Jordan Point Golf Club in Hopewell or Lee Park Golf Course in Petersburg.)

The only downside to a trip to Richmond is that there are no golf resorts in the area. If you're coming here, start checking for hotels outside the city on the west side of town.

Course	Yards	Par	Course Rating	Slope	Green Fee
Belmont Golf Course (18)	6,350/5,418	71/73	70.6/72.6	126/130	$19/$22
First Tee Chesterfield (18)	4,608/3,382	66/64	61.7/58.3	61.7/58.3	$20/$28
Highlands Golfers' Club (18)	6,711/5,019	72/72	72.1/68.7	133/120	$21/$56
Hunting Hawk Golf Club (18)	6,832/5,164	71/72	73.3/69.7	137/120	$15/$45
Independence Golf Club (18)	7,127/5,022	72/72	74.2/64.0	137/112	$35/$78
River's Bend Golf Club (18)	6,671/4,932	71/71	71.9/68.7	132/119	$19/$39
Royal Virginia Golf Club (18)	7,125/5,426	72/71	73.4/74.7	131/132	$35/$45
Sycamore Creek Golf Course (18)	6,256/4,431	70/70	70.0/64.6	126/111	$35/$45

Courses

BELMONT GOLF COURSE. Facility Holes: 18. Opened: 1916. Architect: A. W. Tillinghast. Yards: 6,350/5,418. Par: 71/73. Course Rating: 70.6/72.6. Slope: 126/130. Green Fee: $19/$22. Cart Fee: $12 per person. Discounts: Weekdays, seniors, juniors. Walking: Unrestricted walking. Season: Year-round. Tee Times: Call 7 days in advance. ✉ 1600 Hilliard Rd., 23228 ☎ 804/501-4653 ⊕ www.belmontgolfcourse.com ▤ MC, V. *Comments: Tillinghast courses are always worth your time. Great to see how courses were designed before the age of modern earth-moving equipment.* ★★★

FIRST TEE CHESTERFIELD. Facility Holes: 18. Opened: 2000. Yards: 4,608/3,382. Par: 66/64. Course Rating: 61.7/58.3. Slope: 104/93. Green Fee: $20/$28. Cart Fee: $9 per person. Walking: Unrestricted walking. Season: Year-round. Tee Times: Call golf shop. ✉ Iron Bridge Park, 6736 Hunting Creek Dr., 23237 ☎ 804/275-8050 ⊕ www.firstteechesterfield.com ▤ MC, V. *Comments: It's not only for kids, but be sure to bring one with you.* UR

HIGHLANDS GOLFERS' CLUB. Facility Holes: 18. Opened: 1995. Architect: Steve Smyers. Yards: 6,711/5,019. Par: 72/72. Course Rating: 72.1/68.7. Slope: 133/120. Green Fee: $21/$56. Cart Fee: Included in green fee. Discounts: Twilight, seniors, juniors. Walking: Mandatory cart. Season: Year-round. Tee Times: Call 7 days in advance. Notes: Range (grass). ✉ 8136 Highland Glen Dr., Chesterfield 23838, 15 mi from Richmond ☎ 804/796-4800 ⊕ www.golfmatrix.com ▤ AE, MC, V. *Comments: Good variety of holes. Hills, hardwood trees, and typical Virginia golf terrain.* ★★★ ½

HUNTING HAWK GOLF CLUB. Facility Holes: 18. Opened: 2000. Architect: W. R. Love. Yards: 6,832/5,164. Par: 71/72. Course Rating: 73.3/69.7. Slope: 137/120. Green Fee: $15/$45. Cart Fee: $14 per person. Discounts: Seniors, juniors. Walking: Walking at certain times. Season: Year-round. High: Apr.–Oct. Tee Times: Call 7 days in advance. Notes: Range (grass). ✉ 15201 Ashland Rd., Glen Allen 23059, 12 mi from Richmond ☎ 804/749-1900 ⊕ www.huntinghawkgolf.com ▤ AE, MC, V. *Comments: When it opened, Golf Digest named it one of the best new affordable courses in the country.* UR

VENTURI'S CONGRESSIONAL MARCH

Ken Venturi, longtime CBS golf analyst, was a prominent PGA Tour professional during the late 1950s and early 1960s. He had a successful amateur career prior to turning professional, highlighted by a second place finish at the 1956 Masters tournament. After suffering minor injuries in an car accident in 1961, however, his career slumped. In 1964, Venturi's career blossomed again, reaching its zenith with a stirring victory at that year's U.S. Open at Congressional Country Club, after nearly collapsing in the scorching heat during the 36-hole final round. His win earned him the Sportsman of the Year award.

INDEPENDENCE GOLF CLUB. Facility Holes: 18. Opened: 2001. Architect: Tom Fazio. Yards: 7,127/5,022. Par: 72/72. Course Rating: 74.2/64.0. Slope: 137/112. Green Fee: $35/$78. Cart Fee: Included in green fee. Discounts: Weekdays, twilight, seniors, juniors. Walking: Unrestricted walking. Season: Year-round. Tee Times: Call 14 days in advance. Notes: Range (grass, mat). ✉ 600 Founders Bridge Blvd., Midlothian 23113, 15 mi from Richmond ☎ 804/594-0261 or 866/463-2582 ⊕ www.independencegolfclub.com ▤ AE, D, DC, MC, V. *Comments: Make this the first course you visit. Great woodsy layout in terrific condition. And it's cheaper than the usual three-digit Fazio green fee.* ★★★★ ¹/₂

RIVER'S BEND GOLF CLUB. Facility Holes: 18. Opened: 1990. Architect: Steve Smyers. Yards: 6,671/4,932. Par: 71/71. Course Rating: 71.9/68.7. Slope: 132/119. Green Fee: $19/$39. Cart Fee: $15 per person. Discounts: Weekdays, twilight, seniors, juniors. Walking: Unrestricted walking. Season: Year-round. High: Apr.–Oct. Tee Times: Call 7 days in advance. Notes: Range (grass). ✉ 11700 Hogans Alley, Chester 23836, 10 mi from Richmond ☎ 804/530-1000 or 800/354-2363 ⊕ www.riversbendgolf.com ▤ AE, D, MC, V. *Comments: Greens are terrific. Long par-4s make it challenging. Great views along James River make it one of the first courses you should play.* ★★★ ¹/₂

ROYAL VIRGINIA GOLF CLUB. Facility Holes: 18. Opened: 1993. Architect: Algie Pulley. Yards: 7,125/5,426. Par: 72/71. Course Rating: 73.4/74.7. Slope: 131/132. Green Fee: $35/$45. Cart Fee: Included in green fee. Discounts: Weekdays, twilight, seniors, juniors. Walking: Mandatory cart. Season: Year-round. Tee Times: Call 7 days in advance. Notes: Range (grass). ✉ 3016 Royal Virginia Pkwy., Louisa 23093, 31 mi from Charlottesville ☎ 804/457-2041 ⊕ www.commonwealthgolftrail.com ▤ MC, V. *Comments: Between Richmond and Charlottesville. The course is hilly and challenging.* ★★★

SYCAMORE CREEK GOLF COURSE. Facility Holes: 18. Opened: 1992. Architect: Michael Hurdzan. Yards: 6,256/4,431. Par: 70/70. Course Rating: 70.0/64.6. Slope: 126/111. Green Fee: $35/$45. Cart Fee: Included in green fee. Discounts: Weekdays, twilight, seniors, juniors. Walking: Walking at certain times. Season: Year-round. Tee Times: Call 7 days in advance. Notes: Range (grass). ✉ 1991 Manakin Rd., Manakin Sabot 23103, 15 mi from Richmond ☎ 804/784-3544 ⊕ www.sycamorecreekgc.com ▤ AE, MC, V. *Comments: Hurdzan, one of the most unheralded but extremely talented architects working today, designed this hidden gem northwest of Richmond. Definitely worth your time.* ★★★

Where to Stay

BERKELEY HOTEL. Built in 1995 to blend in with the rest of Richmond's buildings, this handsome, European-style hotel combines intimacy with the services of a much larger property—and it's just two blocks from the Capitol. Passes to the Capital Club health club are free. ⊠ 1200 E. Cary St., 23219 ☎ 804/780-1300 ⊟ 804/343-1885 ⊕ - www.berkeleyhotel.com ⇌ 54 rooms, 1 suite ⌂ Restaurant, in-room data ports, gym, lobby lounge, dry cleaning, laundry service, concierge, meeting rooms, no-smoking rooms ⊟ AE, D, DC, MC, V $$-$$$.

COMFORT INN EXECUTIVE CENTER. On the northwest side of Richmond, this three-building redbrick motel is near the University of Richmond and convenient to I-95 and I-64. From the street the motel appears attractive but deceptively small; you see only the first of three buildings. The others stretch away from the street in a sort of private cul-de-sac. Thirty rooms have whirlpool bathtubs. ⊠ 7201 W. Broad St., 23294 ☎ 804/672-1108 ⊟ 804/755-1625 ⊕ www.comfortinn.com ⇌ 123 rooms ⌂ Pool, gym, lobby lounge, laundry facilities ⊟ AE, D, DC, MC, V ⋈ CP $.

COMMONWEALTH PARK SUITES HOTEL. Rub elbows with the senators and representatives who make this their home when the state legislature is in session. The original brick structure was established in 1846 as a saloon that offered rooms for its drunk clientele. It burned during the Civil War battle for Richmond and was rebuilt around 1896 as a 10-story hotel. Across the street from the Capitol and its magnolia-filled park, the hotel could be somewhere in Europe; still, its reproduction 18th-century mahogany furniture, museum prints, and brass chandeliers confirm that you are in a southern state. A deluxe Continental breakfast is included weekdays. ⊠ 901 Bank St., 23219 ☎ 804/343-7300 or 888/343-7301 ⊟ 804/343-1025 ⊕ www.commonwealthparksuites.com ⇌ 59 suites ⌂ In-room data ports, minibars, dry cleaning, laundry service, meeting rooms, no-smoking rooms ⊟ AE, D, DC, MC, V $$$.

LINDEN ROW INN. Edgar Allan Poe played in the garden that became the beautiful brick courtyards within this row of 1840s Greek Revival town houses. The main building is furnished in antiques and period reproductions; the carriage-house garden quarters are decorated in an old-English style and have homemade quilts. Afternoons end with a wine-and-cheese reception in the beautiful parlor. Also complimentary are transportation to nearby historic attractions and passes to the YMCA's health club. The inn's dining room, open for breakfast, lunch, and dinner, is in the former stables. ⊠ 101 N. 1st St., at Franklin St., 23219 ☎ 804/783-7000 or 800/348-7424 ⊟ 804/648-7504 ⊕ www.lindenrowinn.com ⇌ 60 rooms, 10 suites ⌂ Restaurant, in-room data ports, dry cleaning, laundry service, no-smoking rooms ⊟ AE, D, DC, MC, V ⋈ CP $-$$$.

OMNI RICHMOND. This luxury hotel is close to many small restaurants and shops. The impressive coral marble lobby has a mural of old Richmond along the river. The rooms are furnished in a contemporary style, with honey and peach tones. You may even want to bring binoculars to enjoy the spectacular view from the upper floors, particularly from rooms facing the James River. Guest privileges at the Capital Club health club are available for a day fee. ⊠ 100 S. 12th St., 23219 ☎ 804/344-7000 🖷 804/648-6704 ⊕ www.omnihotels.com ⇌ 361 rooms, 12 suites �⎮ 2 restaurants, room service, in-room data ports, indoor-outdoor pool, gym, sauna, bar, meeting rooms, parking (fee) ⊟ AE, D, DC, MC, V $-$$$.

Where to Eat

✗ **AMICI RISTORANTE.** Game dishes such as pheasant ravioli, stuffed quail, buffalo with Gorgonzola, and ostrich appear regularly on the menu along with osso buco and other northern Italian dishes. In the cozy first floor of this restaurant in the Carytown neighborhood, the walls around the booths are adorned with flowered tapestries and oil paintings of Italy. The more formal second floor has white walls trimmed with stenciled grapes and vines. ⊠ 3343 W. Cary St. ☎ 804/353-4700 ⊟ AE, MC, V $$$$.

✗ **EUROPA.** At this Mediterranean café and tapas bar, there are plenty of enticing main dishes, but many diners opt to make a meal from the extensive list of tapas priced in the single digits: Spanish meats and cheeses, lamb meatballs, codfish fritters, and stewed squid. Housed in a former warehouse just a few blocks from the Capitol, the lively restaurant has a quarry-tile floor and original brick walls. If you like paella, there are three versions to choose from: La Valencia (the traditional meats, fish, and shellfish); La Marinera (fish and shellfish); or La Barcelonesa (chicken, chorizo, and lamb). ⊠ 1409 E. Cary St. ☎ 804/643-0911 ⊕ www.europarichmond.com ⊟ AE, MC, V ⊙ Closed Sun. $$-$$$$.

✗ **JOE'S INN.** Spaghetti is the specialty here—especially the Greek version, with feta and provolone cheese baked on top—and sandwiches (around $5) are distinguished for their generous proportions. It's mostly locals here, but they make newcomers feel right at home. Brunch is served on Sunday. ⊠ 205 N. Shields Ave. ☎ 804/355-2282 ⊟ AE, MC, V $-$$.

✗ **LEMAIRE.** The formal rooms of the grandest restaurant in Richmond have an elegant glass conservatory highlighted with ornamental iron and a copper roof. Named for the maître d' Jefferson employed while president, Lemaire serves a seasonal menu with a French accent as well as a deep Virginia drawl. Local Virginia specialties and produce appear throughout: mainstays include peanut soup, smoked local trout, roasted boneless rack of Virginia lamb, and Chesapeake crab cakes. Breakfast is also available here. ⊠ Jefferson Hotel, 101 W. Franklin St., at Adams St. ☎ 804/788-8000 ⊕ www.jefferson-hotel.com ⊟ AE, D, DC, MC, V $$$$.

✗ **TOBACCO COMPANY.** A tobacco warehouse built in the 1860s houses this popular spot. Prime rib (with seconds on the house), fresh seafood, and daily specials are good choices here. Perennials include chicken Chesapeake (with crabmeat) and veal marsala. The Atrium bar has live music nightly. ⊠ 1201 E. Cary St. ☎ 804/782-9431 ⊕ www.thetobaccocompany.com ⊟ AE, D, MC, V $$-$$$$.

Essentials

Getting Here

Richmond is at the intersection of I-95 and I-64, which run north–south and east–west, respectively. From downtown Washington, take the 14th Street bridge (I-395 south), which becomes I-95 south, and drive about 100 mi. This major north–south artery of the East Coast is always jammed with traffic leaving Washington during the evening rush hour from 4 PM to 7 PM, and on Saturday morning when travelers are heading out of town for the weekend. Try to avoid driving during these times.

Amtrak trains operate between Washington's Union Station and Richmond daily. The train station is north of town. A one-way ticket costs $21–$26.

🚩 **TRAIN LINE Amtrak** ☎ 800/872–7245.

🚩 **TRAIN STATION Richmond station** ✉ 7519 Staples Mill Rd. ☎ 804/553–2903.

Visitor Information

🚩 **Richmond Region Visitor Center** ✉ 405 N. 3rd St., 23219 ☎ 804/783–7450 ⊕ - www.richmondva.org. **Virginia Tourism Corporation** ✉ 901 E. Byrd St. ☎ 800/932–5827 ⊕ www.richmondva.org ✉ Bell Tower at Capitol Sq., 9th and Franklin Sts. ☎ 804/648–3146 ✉ information by mail ✉ 403 N. 3rd St., 23219.

VIRGINIA BEACH, VA

Not everyone travels to a beach community with a novel in one hand and Coppertone in the other. Myrtle Beach learned in the 1950s that golfers love beachside towns as much as anyone. Now, finally, Virginia Beach has caught on, too.

A few hours southeast of Washington past Norfolk, Virginia Beach has a colorful history that includes witch trials, Revolutionary War battles, and Blackbeard. There's enough to see and do when the round is done to keep you busy, but the golf has gotten so good here that you may not want to do anything else.

Of all the new courses that have opened, the links-style Arnold Palmer's Bay Creek should be at the top of your list. It has 4 holes along the shore of Chesapeake Bay. Another relatively new course is the Tournament Players Club of Virginia Beach. Designed by Pete Dye, it plays host to the Nationwide Tour's Virginia Beach Open.

Although the new courses are generating a lot of buzz, many of the established courses are also worth your time, including Hell's Point, a Rees

Course	Yards	Par	Course Rating	Slope	Green Fee
Bay Creek Golf Club (18)	7,024/5,229	72/72	75.2/69.8	142/119	$35/$75
Bide-A-Wee Golf Club (18)	7,069/5,518	72/74	72.2/66.4	121/113	$25/$35
Cahoon Plantation	45				$49/$59
Saltire/Tricolour (18)	7,076/5,226	72/72	73.5/68.7	116/112	
Union Jack/Saltire (18)	6,676/5,193	72/72	71.2/68.7	118/112	
Union Jack/Tricolour (18)	7,180/5,257	72/72	73.3/68.9	121/112	
Cypress Point Country Club (18)	6,680/5,440	72/72	71.5/70.8	124/114	$33/$55
Hell's Point Golf Club (18)	6,966/5,003	72/72	73.3/71.2	130/116	$35/$67
Heron Ridge Golf Club (18)	7,017/5,011	72/72	73.9/68.5	131/111	$34/$59
Honey Bee Golf Club (18)	6,075/4,929	70/70	69.6/67.0	123/104	$25/$45
Signature at West Neck (18)	7,010/5,012	72/72	73.8/68.5	135/117	$39/$73
Sleepy Hole Golf Course (18)	6,813/5,121	72/72	72.6/64.8	124/108	$31/$38
Stumpy Lake Golf Club (18)	6,800/5,200	72/72	71.8/67.1	121/97	$19/$28
Suffolk Golf Course (18)	6,340/5,561	72/72	70.3/71.1	121/112	$11/$19
TPC of Virginia Beach (18)	7,432/5,314	72/72	75.8/70.1	142/114	$68/$118

Jones design, and the renovated Bide-A-Wee Golf Club in Portsmouth. City Park, Red Wing Lake, and Kempsville Greens are the cheaper municipal courses in the area, but consider them only when funds start to dwindle.

Because Virginia Beach is an area of water sports and water activities in addition to golf, the most crowded time to visit is summer. If your vacation schedule is flexible, it's best to visit on the shoulder seasons of spring or fall. Even in winter, the weather tends to be temperate, and although ocean water will be too cold for swimming, it's fine weather for playing golf.

Courses

GolfDigest REVIEWS

BAY CREEK GOLF CLUB. Facility Holes: 18. Opened: 2001. Architect: Arnold Palmer. Yards: 7,024/5,229. Par: 72/72. Course Rating: 75.2/69.8. Slope: 142/119. Green Fee: $35/$75. Cart Fee: Included in green fee. Discounts: Guest, twilight, seniors, juniors. Walking: Walking at certain times. Season: Year-round. High: Apr.–Oct. Tee Times: Call 8 days in advance. Notes: Range (grass). ✉ 1 Clubhouse Way, Cape Charles 23310, 35 mi from Norfolk ☎ 757/331-9000 ⊕ www.baycreekgolfclub.com ▤ AE, MC, V. *Comments: One of Arnold Palmer design group's best efforts. This newest course in the area is spectacular.* ★ ★ ★ ★ ½

BIDE-A-WEE GOLF CLUB. Facility Holes: 18. Opened: 1999. Architect: Curtis Strange/ Tom Clark. Yards: 7,069/5,518. Par: 72/74. Course Rating: 72.2/66.4. Slope: 121/113. Green Fee: $25/$35. Cart Fee: $10 per person. Discounts: Weekdays, twilight, seniors, juniors. Walking: Walking at certain times. Season: Year-round. Tee Times: Call 7 days in advance. Notes: Range (grass, mat). ⊠1 Bide-A-Wee Dr., Portsmouth 23701 ☎757/ 393-8600 ⊟AE, D, MC, V. *Comments: Curtis Strange took a dumpy old course and made it into a must-play for the area—it's 20 mi west of Virginia Beach.* ★★★★

CAHOON PLANTATION. Facility Holes: 45. Opened: 1999. Architect: Tom Clark. Green Fee: $49/$59. Cart Fee: Included in green fee. Discounts: Weekdays, twilight, seniors, juniors. Walking: Mandatory cart. Season: Year-round. High: May–Sept. Tee Times: Call golf shop. Notes: Range (grass, mat). ⊠1501 Cedar Rd., Chesapeake 23322, 15 mi from Norfolk ☎757/436-2775 ⊕www.cahoonplantation.com ⊟AE, MC, V.

Saltire/Tricolour. Holes: 18. Yards: 7,076/5,226. Par: 72/72. Course Rating: 73.5/68.7. Slope: 116/112.

Union Jack/Saltire. Holes: 18. Yards: 6,676/5,193. Par: 72/72. Course Rating: 71.2/68.7. Slope: 118/112.

Union Jack/Tricolour. Holes: 18. Yards: 7,180/5,257. Par: 72/72. Course Rating: 73.3/ 68.9. Slope: 121/112.

Comments: Relatively new 27-hole facility. Fun, links-style course inspired by British Isles golf. ★★★★

CYPRESS POINT COUNTRY CLUB. Facility Holes: 18. Opened: 1987. Architect: Tom Clark/Brian Ault. Yards: 6,680/5,440. Par: 72/72. Course Rating: 71.5/70.8. Slope: 124/114. Green Fee: $33/$55. Cart Fee: Included in green fee. Walking: Walking at certain times. Season: Year-round. High: Apr.–Oct. Tee Times: Call golf shop. Notes: Range (grass). ⊠5340 Club Head Rd., 23455 ☎757/490-8822 ⊕www.cypresspointcc.com ⊟AE, MC, V. *Comments: One of the best bargains in the area. Bent-grass greens are usually in great shape, and long hitters will love the wide fairways.* ★★★ ½

HELL'S POINT GOLF CLUB. Facility Holes: 18. Opened: 1982. Architect: Rees Jones. Yards: 6,966/5,003. Par: 72/72. Course Rating: 73.3/71.2. Slope: 130/116. Green Fee: $35/$67. Cart Fee: Included in green fee. Discounts: Weekdays, guest, twilight, seniors, juniors. Walking: Mandatory cart. Season: Year-round. Tee Times: Call golf shop. Notes: Range (grass, mat). ⊠2700 Atwoodtown Rd., 23456, 15 mi from Norfolk ☎757/721- 3400 or 888/821-3401 ⊕www.hellspoint.com ⊟AE, MC, V. *Comments: Water, woods, big greens, a great layout. Rees Jones isn't one of the best architects in the game for nothing. Definitely play here.* ★★★★

HERON RIDGE GOLF CLUB. Facility Holes: 18. Opened: 1999. Architect: Fred Couples/ Gene Bates. Yards: 7,017/5,011. Par: 72/72. Course Rating: 73.9/68.5. Slope: 131/111. Green Fee: $34/$59. Cart Fee: Included in green fee. Discounts: Weekdays, twilight, seniors, juniors. Walking: Mandatory cart. Season: Year-round. Tee Times: Call golf shop. Notes: Range (grass). ⊠2973 Heron Ridge Dr., 23456 ☎757/426-3800 ⊕www. heronridge.com ⊟AE, MC, V. *Comments: Built on old farmland, so be ready for some serious wind. Solid course.* ★★★★

HONEY BEE GOLF CLUB. Facility Holes: 18. Opened: 1988. Architect: Rees Jones. Yards: 6,075/4,929. Par: 70/70. Course Rating: 69.6/67.0. Slope: 123/104. Green Fee: $25/$45. Cart Fee: Included in green fee. Discounts: Weekdays, twilight, seniors, juniors. Walking: Walking at certain times. Season: Year-round. Tee Times: Call 7 days in advance. Notes: Range (grass). ⊠ 2500 S. Independence Blvd., 23456 ☎ 757/471-2768 ⊟ AE, MC, V. *Comments: Don't let the name fool you. Rees Jones designed as good a short course (6,075 yards) as you can find anywhere. Great for beginners.* ★ ★ ★ ½

SIGNATURE AT WEST NECK. Facility Holes: 18. Opened: 2002. Architect: Arnold Palmer. Yards: 7,010/5,012. Par: 72/72. Course Rating: 73.8/68.5. Slope: 135/117. Green Fee: $39/$73. Cart Fee: Included in green fee. Discounts: Twilight, seniors, juniors. Walking: Walking at certain times. Season: Year-round. High: Apr.–Oct. Tee Times: Call 8 days in advance. Notes: Range (grass). ⊠ 3100 Arnold Palmer Dr., 23456, 12 mi from Norfolk ☎ 757/721-2900 ⊕ www.signaturewestneck.com ⊟ AE, MC, V. *Comments: Second-best Arnold Palmer course in the area, but still very good. Lakes, wetlands, tall pines, and white-powder bunkers frame the course beautifully. UR*

SLEEPY HOLE GOLF COURSE. Facility Holes: 18. Opened: 1972. Architect: Russell Breeden. Yards: 6,813/5,121. Par: 72/72. Course Rating: 72.6/64.8. Slope: 124/108. Green Fee: $31/$38. Cart Fee: $16 per cart. Discounts: Weekdays, twilight, seniors, juniors. Walking: Unrestricted walking. Season: Year-round. Tee Times: Call golf shop. Notes: Range (grass, mat). ⊠ 4700 Sleepy Hole Rd., Suffolk 23435, 12 mi from Norfolk ☎ 757/538-4100 ⊟ AE, MC, V. *Comments: Thirty-year-old course is tight. A great bargain.* ★ ★ ★ ½

STUMPY LAKE GOLF CLUB. Facility Holes: 18. Opened: 1944. Architect: Robert Trent Jones. Yards: 6,800/5,200. Par: 72/72. Course Rating: 71.8/67.1. Slope: 121/97. Green Fee: $19/$28. Cart Fee: $11 per person. Discounts: Weekdays, twilight, seniors, juniors. Walking: Walking at certain times. Season: Year-round. Tee Times: Call 7 days in advance. Notes: Range (grass, mat). ⊠ 4797 E. Indian River Rd., 23456 ☎ 757/467-6119 ⊟ AE, MC, V. *Comments: Robert Trent Jones designed it, so it gets some nostalgia points. But don't put it at the top of your lineup.* ★ ★ ★

SUFFOLK GOLF COURSE. Facility Holes: 18. Opened: 1950. Architect: Dick Wilson. Yards: 6,340/5,561. Par: 72/72. Course Rating: 70.3/71.1. Slope: 121/112. Green Fee: $11/$19. Cart Fee: $10 per person. Discounts: Weekdays, seniors, juniors. Walking: Walking at certain times. Season: Year-round. High: Apr.–Nov. Tee Times: Call golf shop. Notes: Range (mat). ⊠ 1227 Holland Rd., Suffolk 23434 ☎ 757/539-6298 ⊟ AE, D, V. *Comments: Great old Dick Wilson (of Doral Blue Monster fame) design. Doglegs galore!* ★ ★ ★

TPC OF VIRGINIA BEACH. Facility Holes: 18. Opened: 1999. Architect: Pete Dye/Curtis Strange. Yards: 7,432/5,314. Par: 72/72. Course Rating: 75.8/70.1. Slope: 142/114. Green Fee: $68/$118. Cart Fee: Included in green fee. Walking: Mandatory cart. Season: Year-round. Tee Times: Call golf shop. Notes: Range (grass). ⊠ 2500 Tournament Dr., 23456, 15 mi from Norfolk ☎ 757/563-9440 or 877/484-3872 ⊕ www.playatpc.com ⊟ AE, MC, V. *Comments: One of the weaker Tournament Players Club courses, but still very, very good public golf. Bring your driver: it's 7,432 yards. The trees are so tall, don't bother trying to go over them.* ★ ★ ★ ★

Where to Stay

⊞ BEST WESTERN OCEANFRONT. The small, neat lobby of this seven-story chain hotel opens onto the boardwalk and beach. All rooms have an ocean view and are decorated with tropical floral spreads and beach paintings. Coffeemakers and hair dryers are included with your room. ⊠ 1101 Atlantic Ave., 23451 ☎ 757/422–5000 or 800/ 631–5000 🖷 757/425–2356 ⊕ www.bestwestern.com ⇋ 96 rooms, 14 suites ♿ Restaurant, pool, bar, laundry facilities, no-smoking rooms ▤AE, D, MC, V $$–$$$$.

⊞ CAVALIER HOTELS. In the quieter north end of town, this 18-acre resort complex combines the original Cavalier Hotel of 1927, a seven-story redbrick building on a hill, with an oceanfront high-rise built across the street in 1973. The clientele is about evenly divided between conventioneers and families. F. Scott and Zelda Fitzgerald stayed regularly in the older section (it has since been lavishly refurbished). If you stay on the hilltop, you can see the water—and get to it easily by shuttle van or a short walk. The newer building overlooks 600 feet of private beach. There is a fee for tennis, but the other athletic facilities are free. ⊠ Atlantic Ave. and 42nd St., 23451 ☎ 757/425–8555 or 888/ 746–2327 🖷 757/425–0629 ⊕ www.cavalierhotel.com ⇋ 400 rooms ♿ 5 restaurants, in-room data ports, putting green, 4 tennis courts, 2 pools (1 indoor), wading pool, gym, beach, croquet, volleyball, baby-sitting, playground, no-smoking rooms ▤AE, D, DC, MC, V $$–$$$$.

⊞ CLARION HOTEL TOWN CENTER VIRGINIA BEACH. This sparkling-white, modern hotel is well situated for business and pleasure, midway between Norfolk and the beach. The skylighted lobby overlooks a glassed-in indoor pool. Rooms have a sitting area with sofa and desk; there are floral spreads and moss-color carpeting, with prints of flowers on the wall. Every room has a hair dryer, iron, ironing board, and coffeemaker. Coffee in the lobby is complimentary. ⊠ 4453 Bonney Rd., 23462 ☎ 757/473–1700 or 800/847– 5202 🖷 757/552–0477 ⊕ www.clarionhotels.com ⇋ 149 rooms ♿ Restaurant, in-room data ports, refrigerators, indoor pool, gym, hot tub, lobby lounge, dry cleaning, laundry service, meeting rooms, no-smoking rooms ▤AE, D, DC, MC, V ¢–$.

⊞ PICKETT'S HARBOR BED & BREAKFAST. All rooms and the porch overlook Chesapeake Bay from this bed-and-breakfast, which is on farmland granted the owner's family in the 1600s. The "backyard" is 27 acres of private beach, allowing for bird-watching, running, and biking as well as beachcombing. The full country breakfast includes seasonal fruits, Virginia ham, quiches, casseroles, homemade breads, and jams. Pickett's Harbor is 4 mi north of the Chesapeake Bay Bridge Tunnel. ⊠ 28288 Nottingham Ridge La., Cape Charles 23310 ☎ 757/331–2212 ⊕ www.pickettsharbor.com ⇋ 6 rooms, 3 with bath ♿ Beach, bicycles, some pets allowed (fee); no room phones, no room TVs, no smoking ▤No credit cards. ⍟ BP $–$$.

⊞ WILSON–LEE HOUSE. A businessman built this turn-of-the-20th-century home. Guest rooms are whimsically decorated with a mélange of periods and styles, a clawfoot tub in one bathroom, a hot tub in another. The elaborate breakfast is served seasonally on the screened, wraparound porch. Golfing packages for play at the Bay Creek Golf Club are available. ⊠ 403 Tazewell Ave., Cape Charles 23310 ☎ 757/331–1954 ⊕ - www.wilsonleehouse.com ⇋ 6 rooms. ♿ Golf privileges, boating, fishing, bicycles; no room phones, no room TVs, no smoking ▤MC, V ⍟ BP $$–$$$.

Where to Eat

✕**CROAKER'S.** A great local favorite, Croaker's isn't a restaurant that many people passing through the area know about. Far from the crowds, it's at the north end of Shore Drive. Along with melt-in-your-mouth crab cakes, Croaker's serves a mean Oysters William (oysters with white wine, butter, and shallots). Another surprise is the excellent steaks, which are cut to order. ✉ 3629 Shore Dr. ☎ 757/363-2490 ⊟ AE, D, DC, MC, V ⊘ No lunch $$-$$$$.

✕**HAVANNA'S.** As the name hints, this upbeat bistro is all about Cuban-inspired cuisine. The cedar furnishings and low-hanging lights over the long tables make this local favorite look sophisticated. With dishes such as grilled flank steak *mojo* (marinated with bitter-orange juice, garlic, and spices), saffron-infused bouillabaisse, and *picadillo* (spicy ground beef), this tony place leaves you craving a cigar and a cocktail. Luckily, there's a fine line of cigars as well as an assortment of margaritas. ✉ 1423 N. Great Neck Rd. ☎ 757/496-3333 ⊟ AE, D, MC, V $$-$$$$.

✕**THE LIGHTHOUSE.** Many of the oilcloth-covered tables in these six nautically themed dining rooms overlook the ocean or the inlet. The floors are red clay tile; the walls have dark-wood paneling. But the main attraction here is the seafood. If you can't decide whether you want Maine lobster, chicken, shrimp, or crab cakes, try the mixed grill, where you can mix and match any two items. ✉ 1st St. and Atlantic Ave. ☎ 757/428-7974 ⊟ AE, D, DC, MC, V $$-$$$$.

Essentials

Getting Here

I-664 creates a circular beltway through the Hampton Roads area. I-664 connects Newport News and Norfolk, via Suffolk. I-64 runs northwest through Norfolk to intersect with I-664 in Hampton and I-95 at Richmond. U.S. 58 and what was once I-44 is now just an extension of I-264 (part of I-64).

Visitor Information

🛈 **Virginia Beach Visitor Information Center** ✉ 2100 Parks Ave., 23451 ☎ 757/437-4888 ⊕ www.vbfun.com.

WILLIAMSBURG, VA

When the earliest settlers from Scotland and England braved the Atlantic Ocean with their children and pets to reach Virginia, they also brought their golf equipment—seriously. "Goff clubs, balls, etc." and similar statements can be found on colonial ships' cargo manifests. In fact, the last British colonial

Course	Yardage	Par	Rating	Slope	Price
Colonial Golf Course (18)	6,885/4,568	72/72	73.2/66.3	133/109	$40/$85
Ford's Colony Country Club (54)					
Blackheath (18)	6,621/4,605	71/71	71.8/70.5	133/119	
Blue Heron (18)	6,769/5,424	71/71	72.3/72.3	124/109	$40/$90
Marsh Hawk (18)	6,738/5,579	72/72	72.3/72.3	124/124	$40/$90
Golden Horseshoe Golf Club (36)					
Gold (18)	6,817/5,168	71/71	73.8/69.8	144/126	$40/$150
Green (18)	7,120/5,348	72/72	75.1/70.5	138/120	$30/$100
Kingsmill Resort & Club (54)					
Plantation (18)	6,543/4,880	72/72	71.3/67.9	119/116	$55/$105
River (18)	6,837/4,646	71/71	73.3/65.3	137/116	$65/$145
Woods (18)	6,784/5,140	72/72	72.7/68.7	131/120	$60/$105
Kiskiack Golf Club (18)	6,775/4,902	72/71	72.5/67.8	134/112	$25/$75
Tradition Golf Club (54)					
Tradition Golf Club at Crossings (18)	6,657/5,625	72/72	70.7/73.2	126/128	$23/$48
Tradition Golf Club at Royal New Kent (18)	7,291/5,231	72/72	76.5/72.0	147/130	$40/$85
Tradition Golf Club at Stonehouse (18)	6,963/5,013	71/71	75.0/69.1	140/121	$49/$84
Williamsburg National Golf Club (18)	6,950/5,200	72/72	72.9/69.7	130/127	$33/$53

governor, John Murray, the Earl of Dunmore, reportedly enjoyed practicing the game at the Governor's Palace during the 1770s.

If you follow in the footsteps of some of America's earliest settlers, you may find that little has changed in terms of the importance golf holds in the Williamsburg area. The densely wooded region is a hub for some terrific golf courses and some of the game's most well-known players, including two-time U.S. Open champion Curtis Strange. There might be only two major negatives to the area: the competition with nongolfing tourists for seats and beds in restaurants and hotels, and summers can be brutally hot and humid.

Although there are dozens of golf courses in the area, the standbys are the courses at the Kingsmill Resort & Club and the nearby Golden Horseshoe Golf Club. The Golden Horseshoe's Gold course is ranked 8th in the state by *Golf Digest*. The River course at Kingsmill, which used to play host to the PGA Tour's Michelob Championship, is now the site for the LPGA's Michelob Light Open.

Although you may want to stay at Kingsmill, be sure to play the Tradition Golf Club at Royal New Kent and the Tradition Golf Club at Stonehouse.

These spectacular courses, both built by the aptly named Traditional Golf Properties Group in 1996, get *Golf Digest* rankings of 6th and 9th, respectively, in Virginia.

Courses

COLONIAL GOLF COURSE. Facility Holes: 18. Opened: 1995. Architect: Lester George. Yards: 6,885/4,568. Par: 72/72. Course Rating: 73.2/66.3. Slope: 133/109. Green Fee: $40/$85. Cart Fee: Included in green fee. Discounts: Guest, twilight, juniors. Walking: Unrestricted walking. Season: Year-round. Tee Times: Call golf shop. Notes: Range (grass, mat). ⊠ 8285 Diascund Rd., Lanexa 23089, 12 mi from Williamsburg ☎ 757/566-1600 or 800/566-6660 ⊕ www.golfcolonial.com ▤ AE, D, MC, V. *Comments: Quiet, secluded course is often overlooked. But trust us, you'll love it.* ★ ★ ★ ★

FORD'S COLONY COUNTRY CLUB. Facility Holes: 54. Cart Fee: Included in green fee. Discounts: Weekdays, guest, twilight, juniors. Walking: Mandatory cart. Season: Year-round. High: Apr.–Oct. Tee Times: Call up to 7 days in advance. Notes: Range (grass, mat). ⊠ 240 Ford's Colony Dr., 23188 ☎ 757/258-4130 or 800/334-6033 ⊕ www.fordscolony.com ▤ AE, MC, V.

Blackheath. Holes: 18. Opened: 1999. Architect: Dan Maples. Yards: 6,621/4,605. Par: 71/71. Course Rating: 71.8/70.5. Slope: 133/119. Green Fee: $40/$90. *Comments: Water comes into play on 13 holes. Routed through dense trees but has a lowland feel.* ★ ★ ★ ★

Blue Heron. Holes: 18. Opened: 1987. Architect: Dan Maples. Yards: 6,769/5,424. Par: 71/71. Course Rating: 72.3/72.3. Slope: 124/109. Green Fee: $40/$90. *Comments: Housing development golf. Similar in style to Blackheath. Worth your time.* ★ ★ ★ ★

Marsh Hawk. Holes: 18. Opened: 1985. Architect: Dan Maples. Yards: 6,738/5,579. Par: 72/72. Course Rating: 72.3/72.3. Slope: 124/124. Green Fee: $40/$90. *Comments: Water only comes into play on 9 holes but seems like it's always there when you don't want it. Tough, target golf course.* ★ ★ ★ ★ ½

GOLDEN HORSESHOE GOLF CLUB. Facility Holes: 36. Cart Fee: Included in green fee. Discounts: Weekdays, guest, twilight, juniors. Walking: Unrestricted walking. Season: Year-round. Tee Times: Call 30 days in advance. Notes: Metal spikes, range (grass, mat). ⊠ 401 S. England St., 23185, 45 mi from Richmond ☎ 757/220-7696 or 800/447-8679 ⊕ www.colonialwilliamsburg.com ▤ AE, D, DC, MC, V.

Gold. Holes: 18. Opened: 1963. Architect: Robert Trent Jones. Yards: 6,817/5,168. Par: 71/71. Course Rating: 73.8/69.8. Slope: 144/126. Green Fee: $40/$150. *Comments: Scenery, conditioning, and pace of play is commendable for a busy resort course. Don't miss it.* ★ ★ ★ ★ ★

Green. Holes: 18. Opened: 1991. Architect: Rees Jones. Yards: 7,120/5,348. Par: 72/72. Course Rating: 75.1/70.5. Slope: 138/120. Green Fee: $30/$100. *Comments: Rees Jones course complements his dad's Gold course. Rolling terrain and panoramic views make it another solid choice.* ★ ★ ★ ★ ½

KINGSMILL RESORT & CLUB. Facility Holes: 54. Cart Fee: Included in green fee. Discounts: Guest, twilight. Walking: Mandatory cart. Season: Year-round. Tee Times: Call 30 days in advance. Notes: Metal spikes, range (grass, mat), lodging (400). ⊠ 1010 Kingsmill Rd., 23185, 50 mi from Norfolk ☎ 757/253-3906 or 800/832-5665 ⊕ www. kingsmill.com ⊟ AE, D, MC, V.

Plantation. Holes: 18. Opened: 1986. Architect: Arnold Palmer/Ed Seay. Yards: 6,543/ 4,880. Par: 72/72. Course Rating: 71.3/67.9. Slope: 119/116. Green Fee: $55/$105. *Comments: After getting beat up at the River course, this is where you come to feel good about your game again.* ★ ★ ★ ★ ¹/₂

River. Holes: 18. Opened: 1975. Architect: Pete Dye. Yards: 6,837/4,646. Par: 71/71. Course Rating: 73.3/65.3. Slope: 137/116. Green Fee: $65/$145. *Comments: Best of the three here. Routing along the James River gives this difficult course some beautiful views.* ★ ★ ★ ★ ¹/₂

Woods. Holes: 18. Opened: 1995. Architect: Tom Clark/Curtis Strange. Yards: 6,784/ 5,140. Par: 72/72. Course Rating: 72.7/68.7. Slope: 131/120. Green Fee: $60/$105. *Comments: Designed by local resident and two-time U.S. Open champ Curtis Strange. Parkland course feels isolated from the rest of the resort. Very peaceful.* ★ ★ ★ ★ ¹/₂

KISKIACK GOLF CLUB. Facility Holes: 18. Opened: 1997. Architect: John LaFoy/Vinny Giles. Yards: 6,775/4,902. Par: 72/71. Course Rating: 72.5/67.8. Slope: 134/112. Green Fee: $25/$75. Cart Fee: Included in green fee. Discounts: Twilight, seniors, juniors. Walking: Mandatory cart. Season: Year-round. Tee Times: Call 30 days in advance. Notes: Range (grass, mat). ⊠ 8104 Club Dr., 23188, 45 mi from Richmond ☎ 757/566-2200 or 800/989-4728 ⊟ AE, D, DC, MC, V. *Comments: Another quality course in Williamsburg. Great greens.* ★ ★ ★ ★

TRADITION GOLF CLUB. Facility Holes: 54. Discounts: Weekdays, guest, twilight, juniors. Season: Year-round. High: Apr.–Oct. Tee Times: Call 120 days in advance. Notes: Range (grass). ⊠ 800 Virginia Center Pkwy., Glen Allen 23059, 10 mi from Williamsburg ☎ 804/261-0000 ⊕ www.traditionalclubs.com ⊟ AE, D, MC, V.

Tradition Golf Club at Crossings. Holes: 18. Opened: 1979. Architect: Joe Lee. Yards: 6,657/5,625. Par: 72/72. Course Rating: 70.7/73.2. Slope: 126/128. Green Fee: $23/$48. Cart Fee: $14 per person. Walking: Unrestricted walking. *Comments: Nothing extravagant, just good, solid parkland-style golf course.* ★ ★ ★

Tradition Golf Club at Royal New Kent. Holes: 18. Opened: 1996. Architect: Mike Strantz. Yards: 7,291/5,231. Par: 72/72. Course Rating: 76.5/72.0. Slope: 147/130. Green Fee: $40/$85. Cart Fee: $20 per person. Walking: Unrestricted walking. *Comments: Set upon the low hills between Diascund Creek and the Chickahominy River. Very scenic, great design. May be the best course of the trip.* ★ ★ ★ ★ ¹/₂

Tradition Golf Club at Stonehouse. Holes: 18. Opened: 1996. Architect: Mike Strantz. Yards: 6,963/5,013. Par: 71/71. Course Rating: 75.0/69.1. Slope: 140/121. Green Fee: $49/$84. Cart Fee: Included in green fee. Walking: Walking at certain times. *Comments: Stonehouse is laid over wild, tumbling hills near the York River in the Tidewater Region. Bring enough balls for the ravine holes.* ★ ★ ★ ★

WILLIAMSBURG NATIONAL GOLF CLUB. Facility Holes: 18. Opened: 1995. Architect: Jim Lipe. Yards: 6,950/5,200. Par: 72/72. Course Rating: 72.9/69.7. Slope: 130/ 127. Green Fee: $33/$53. Cart Fee: $20 per person. Discounts: Weekdays, twilight. Walking: Walking at certain times. Season: Year-round. Tee Times: Call golf shop. Notes: Range (grass). ✉ 3700 Centerville Rd., 23188, 40 mi from Richmond ☎ 757/258–9642 or 800/826–5732 ⊕ www.wngc.com 🟰 AE, MC, V. *Comments: Decent course for the money, but should be a consideration only if other Williamsburg courses are booked.* ★ ★ ★ ¹/₂

Where to Stay

🏨 **GOVERNOR SPOTTSWOOD MOTEL.** This one-story redbrick motel has been extended gradually, section by section, since the 1950s. Furnishings reflect the influence of Colonial Williamsburg. In classic motel style, each room faces its parking space. There's lawn space and a sunken garden area for the swimming pool. Seven cottages sleep four to seven people, and 14 rooms have kitchens. It's a good value for the location. ✉ 1508 Richmond Rd., 23185 ☎ 757/229–6444 or 800/368–1244 🖷 757/253–2410 ⊕ www.govspottswood.com 🛏 78 rooms, 7 cottages ↻ Picnic area, pool, playground 🟰 AE, DC, MC, V ¢.

🏨 **KINGSMILL RESORT.** This manicured, 3,000-acre resort on the James River has almost everything you might want, including even a marina and boat ramp. The largest golf resort in Virginia, this is where the Michelob Ultra Open on the LPGA Tour is held each year. You can play year-round on the three championship courses; a fourth course—par-3, and 9 holes, is free if you stay here. The brands of beer served at the property's Moody's Tavern are a clue to the acreage's owner: they're all Anheuser-Busch products. Accommodations include beautifully decorated guest rooms and one- to three-bedroom suites with fully equipped kitchens and washers and dryers. The menu at the expensive Bray Dining Room includes inventive dishes that employ seafood, game birds, and steak. A free shuttle bus travels several times daily to and from Williamsburg, Busch Gardens (also owned by Anheuser-Busch), and Water Country USA. ✉ 1010 Kingsmill Rd., 23185 ☎ 757/253–1703 or 800/832–5665 🖷 757/253–8246 ⊕ www.kingsmill.com 🛏 235 rooms, 175 suites ↻ 5 restaurants, in-room data ports, 3 18-hole golf courses, 9-hole golf course, putting green, 15 tennis courts, 2 pools (1 indoor), wading pool, health club, sauna, spa, steam room, beach, boating, fishing, billiards, bar, baby-sitting, dry cleaning, laundry service, concierge, business services, meeting rooms 🟰 AE, D, DC, MC, V $$$.

🏨 **QUALITY INN LORD PAGET.** Tall white columns front this modern motel, which has a 2¹/₂-acre lake and lovely gardens. Eight rooms are accessed via stairs off the spacious lobby, which has Oriental carpets; others have parking at the front door. Some rooms have canopy beds. Refrigerators and microwaves are available for a fee. ✉ 901 Capitol Landing Rd., 23185 ☎ 757/229–4444 or 800/537–2438 🛏 94 rooms ↻ Coffee shop, putting green, pool, dock, fishing, laundry service, no-smoking rooms 🟰 AE, D, DC, MC, V 🍽 CP ¢–$.

🏨 **WAR HILL INN.** This inn was designed by a Colonial Williamsburg architect to resemble a period structure: the two-story redbrick building at the center has two wood-frame wings. Inside are antiques and reproductions, and rooms are painted in authentic colors. The inn is part of a 32-acre operating cattle farm 4 mi from the Colonial Williamsburg information center. If you want some extra privacy, choose one of the cottages or the first-floor suite—other rooms open onto a common hallway. ✉ 4560 Long Hill Rd., 23188 ☎ 757/565-0248 or 800/743-0248 ⊕ www.warhillinn.com ⇔ 3 rooms, 1 suite, 2 cottages ⚒ Cable TV ⊟ MC, V ⏹ BP $–$$.

☷ **WILLIAMSBURG INN.** The rooms in this 1937 grand hotel are beautifully and individually furnished with reproductions and antiques in the English Regency style. Genteel service and tradition reign. Rooms come with such perks as complimentary morning coffee and afternoon tea, a free daily newspaper, turndown service, and bathrobes. The Providence Wings, adjacent to the inn, overlook the tennis courts, a private pond, and a wooded area, and the inn's Golden Horseshoe Golf Club is a few steps away. The 25 Colonial Houses share the facilities of the Inn and the Williamsburg Lodge. ✉ 136 E. Francis St., Box 1776, 23187 ☎ 757/229-1000 or 800/447-8679 ☟ 757/220-7096 ⊕ - www.colonialwilliamsburg.com ⇔ 62 rooms, 14 suites ⚒ Restaurant, room service, in-room VCRs, 2 18-hole golf courses, 9-hole golf course, 8 tennis courts, 2 pools (1 indoor), gym, spa, croquet, hiking, lawn bowling, lounge, piano, children's programs (ages 5–12), dry cleaning, laundry service, concierge, meeting rooms, no-smoking rooms ⊟ AE, D, DC, MC, V $$$$.

☷ **WILLIAMSBURG LODGE.** Larger and less formal than the Williamsburg Inn across the street, the furnishings are just as interesting. Reproductions from the adjacent Abby Aldrich Rockefeller Folk Art Museum accent the rooms, which are getting a bit worn. The paneled lobby, where there's a fireplace, is cozy. The expansive health club is shared by those staying at the Williamsburg Inn and Colonial Houses. Every room has a hair dryer, iron, and ironing board; some rooms have coffeemakers. Nightly entertainment includes music or plays (free with special passes) in the lobby lounge. ✉ 310 S. England St., 23187 ☎ 757/229-1000 or 800/447-8679 ☟ 757/220-7799 ⊕ www. colonialwilliamsburg.com ⇔ 264 rooms, 2 suites ⚒ 2 restaurants, 2 18-hole golf courses, 9-hole golf course, 2 pools (1 indoor), health club, sauna, bicycles, lobby lounge, dry cleaning, laundry facilities, laundry service, concierge, business services, meeting rooms, no-smoking rooms ⊟ AE, D, DC, MC, V $$–$$$.

☷ **WOODLANDS HOTEL AND SUITES.** An official Colonial Williamsburg property next to the visitor center, the Woodland is on the edge of a 40-acre pine forest. Furnishings are traditional, with quilted bedspreads and printed wallpaper. It's a good lodging choice for families. ✉ 102 Visitor Center Dr., 23185 ☎ 757/229-1000 or 800/447-8679 ☟ 757/565-8797 ⊕ www.colonialwilliamsburg.com ⇔ 204 rooms, 96 suites ⚒ Restaurant, pool, horseshoes, Ping-Pong, lobby lounge, playground ⊟ AE, D, DC, MC, V ⏹ CP $–$$.

Where to Eat

✕ **ABERDEEN BARN.** Saws, pitchforks, oxen yokes, and the like hang on the barn walls, but the wood tables are lacquered, and the napkins are linen. Specialties include slow-roasted prime rib of beef; baby-back Danish pork ribs barbecued with a sauce of peach preserves and Southern Comfort; and shrimp Dijon. An ample but not esoteric wine list is dominated by California vintages (there are Virginia selections, too). ✉ 1601 Richmond Rd. ☎ 757/229-6661 ▤ AE, D, MC, V ⊘ No lunch $$-$$$$.

✘ **BERRET'S RESTAURANT AND RAW BAR.** In Merchants Square, this upscale but casual restaurant opens its pleasant outdoor patio in temperate weather. Entrées and appetizers make use of fresh Chesapeake Bay seafood. It's usually a sure bet to try any of the nightly specials of fresh fish, which often include perfectly prepared tuna. The she-crab soup, a house favorite, is made with crabmeat, cream, crab roe, and a hint of sherry. ✉ 199 Boundary St. ☎ 757/253-1847 ▤ AE, D, DC, MC, V ⊘ Closed Mon. Jan. and early Feb. $$$-$$$$.

✘ **COLLEGE DELLY.** The white-brick eatery with forest-green canvas awnings is fairly dark and scruffy inside. Walls are hung with college pictures and memorabilia. Booths and tables are in the William and Mary colors of green and gold. Deli sandwiches, pasta, stromboli, and Greek dishes are prepared with fresh ingredients, and there is a wide selection of beers on tap. The Delly delivers dinner orders free to nearby hotels. ✉ 336 Richmond Rd. ☎ 757/229-6627 ▤ MC, V $-$$.

✘ **REGENCY ROOM.** This restaurant in the Williamsburg Inn is known for its elegance, attentive service, and fine cuisine. Amid crystal chandeliers, Asian silk-screen prints, and full silver service, you can have chateaubriand carved table-side, as well as lobster bisque and rich ice cream desserts. It may almost seem as if you're treated like royalty. A jacket and tie are required at dinner and Sunday brunch. ✉ Williamsburg Inn, 136 E. Francis St. ☎ 757/229-1000 ⌘ Reservations essential ▤ AE, D, DC, MC, V $$$-$$$$.

✘ **SAL'S RESTAURANT BY VICTOR.** Locals love this family Italian restaurant and pizzeria. Victor Minichiello and his staff cook in a wood-fired oven and serve up pasta, fish, chicken, and veal dinners as well as subs and pizzas. The restaurant delivers free to nearby hotels. ✉ 1242 Richmond Rd. ☎ 757/220-2641 ▤ AE, D, MC, V $-$$.

✘ **THE TRELLIS.** With vaulted ceilings and hardwood floors, the Trellis is an airy and pleasant place for romantic dinners. The imaginative lunch and dinner menus change with the seasons. A dazzling wine list complements such tasty dishes as homemade bisque, wild boar, and soft-shell crabs. The seafood entrées are particularly good, and many patrons wouldn't leave without ordering the rich Death by Chocolate, the restaurant's signature dessert. ✉ Merchants Sq. ☎ 757/229-8610 ▤ AE, MC, V $$-$$$$.

✘ **WHALING COMPANY.** Fresh seafood is the drawing card at this large wooden building, which wouldn't look out of place on a New England shore. Despite its out-of-town look, the restaurant has an authenticity sometimes hard to find in touristy towns. Locals come for the fresh scallops, fish, and other tasty morsels from the sea. Steaks are available, but no poultry or other meats are served. The restaurant is off U.S. 60 west just after the Route 199 interchange. ✉ 494 McLaws Circle ☎ 757/229-0275 ▤ AE, DC, MC, V ⊘ No lunch $$-$$$.

Essentials

If your schedule is flexible, it's best to avoid visiting this hugely popular tourism area during the height of summertime crowds, when the temperature is frequently in the

90s. Spring and fall have better weather and fewer people; from January to the end of March and from mid-September through November the crowds are thinnest.

Getting Here

A nonstop trip from Washington to Williamsburg via I-95 and I-64 takes about 3 to 3½ hours. If you have more time, consider taking the I-295 Richmond Bypass off I-95 and exit at Route 5, designated a Virginia Byway and one of the loveliest roads in the state. The two-lane road runs between stands of pecan, hickory, cherry, and feathery cedar trees.

Visitor Information

🚩 Colonial Williamsburg Visitor Center ✉ Box 1776, 23187 ☎ 800/246-2099. Williamsburg Area Convention and Visitors Bureau ✉ 421 N. Boundary St., Box 3585, 23187 ☎ 757/253-0192 or 800/368-6511 ⊕ www.visitwilliamsburg.com.

INDEX